CHURCH AND STATE
IN THE
UNITED STATES

Revised one-volume Edition

CHURCH
AND
STATE
IN THE
UNITED
STATES

by

ANSON PHELPS STOKES

(1874-1958)

and

LEO PFEFFER

Harper & Row, Publishers

New York, Evanston, and London

FIRST EDITION

F–O

LIBRARY OF CONGRESS CATALOG CARD NUMBER: 64-14382

CONTENTS

Part One
THE FOUNDATIONS OF AMERICAN CHURCH-STATE
SEPARATION AND RELIGIOUS FREEDOM

Part Two
THE ESTABLISHMENT AND ADJUSTMENT OF CHURCHES INDEPENDENT OF THE STATE

Part Three

MODERN AND CONTEMPORARY PROBLEMS
AND THEIR SOLUTION

PREFACE

The publication in 1950 of Canon Anson Phelps Stokes's *Church and State in the United States* marked a milestone in the history of Church-State relations in this country. The work not only was an account of that history but since 1950 has played a significant role in shaping it. More attention has been paid to the subject of Church-State relations by the American people during the past decade and a half than in all the preceding years since the founding of our republic, and during this period no work was cited more often or deemed more authoritative by courts, legislators, teachers, and writers than Canon Stokes's book.

I was therefore highly gratified when the executors of Canon Stokes's Estate and Harper & Row requested me to bring the original work up to date so as to include an account of the momentous events in Church-State relations during the fifteen years since Canon Stokes wrote it. Practical consideration dictated that the three volumes be compressed into one.

In discharging my responsibility I have sought to maintain the basic viewpoints, structure, organization, and style of the original. Whenever possible, I have used Canon Stokes's words rather than my own, except of course in the post-1950 materials. As the concluding chapter, I have included, but with slight modification, the section of the original work entitled "The General Conclusions." I find myself in substantial agreement with these conclusions, although I might differ in respect to some of the non-essential details.

The necessary condensation was in large measure effected by summarizing much source material quoted in full in the original. For the specialist and the student engaged in a specific research project, the convenient availability of this source material in the three-volume work is invaluable. However, for the general reader or the university student for whom this one-volume book is intended, brief summaries of these source materials should be adequate.

The bibliography in the original work has been brought up to date by inclusion of a large number of works published since 1950. To keep the list within manageable limits, some of the works contained in the original bibliography have been omitted. These have in the main been works containing only small portions relevant to the subject of this book, such as encyclopedias, general histories, and biographies of persons whose activities only partially or tangentially affected Church-State relations.

Because the decisions of the United States Supreme Court in the area of Church-State relationships play so major a role, I have added a chapter summarizing these decisions in language understandable to the non-lawyer. Most of these decisions are also discussed under the appropriate topics in the main text, with the result that there is some duplication. I have sought to keep this to a minimum, but to the extent that it is still present, I deem it justified by the convenience of having in one chapter brief summaries of all the Supreme Court decisions on Church and State.

For her invaluable assistance in all aspects of the preparation of this book and especially in the preparation of the index, I acknowledge my indebtedness and express my appreciation to my wife.

LEO PFEFFER

New York
January, 1964

Part One

THE FOUNDATIONS OF AMERICAN CHURCH-STATE SEPARATION AND RELIGIOUS FREEDOM

Chapter 1

THE BACKGROUND OF AMERICAN RELIGIOUS FREEDOM AND CHURCH-STATE RELATIONS

The Threefold Colonial Tradition

The ultimate roots of American Church-State separation and religious freedom are, of course, to be found in the history of the Old World.[1] Major Old-World influences include the Decalogue, which provided the basis of the moral law of Israel and in a later simplified form of Christianity; the Greek city-states, and especially Athens, which must be mentioned among the historic precursors of American democracy; the philosophers who lived in and inspired the lives of these city-states; the teachings of Christianity; the Roman Empire and its religions; the Catholic Church and its doctrines and practices; and the Renaissance and the Reformation which it made possible. Of the two greatest leaders of the Reformation, Martin Luther and John Calvin, the latter had the deeper influence on political organization and religious thought in the United States. It was his views that largely molded the thinking of the Congregationalists of New England and the Scotch Presbyterians, together with the closely related Dutch Reformed Church, of the middle states, and even of the Anglicans in the South.

A vital role was played too by the Anabaptists and other despised and persecuted Christian sects originating in Central Europe in the second quarter of the sixteenth century. By upholding their right to religious freedom based on Biblical and Reformation teachings, they paved the way, through the Baptists, Quakers, and others, for our American religious freedom. Among the strongest promoters of religious freedom were the Socinians of the sixteenth century, later to be called Unitarians. But of the religious groups it was the Independents or Separatists who made the greatest contribution to civil liberty, education, and democratic polity in the United States.

Various provisions of the English constitution—some embodied in statutes, others in unwritten laws and customs—had direct impact on the development of the ideas of liberty in the American frame of government. Among these should be mentioned the Magna Charta, the Bill of Rights of 1689, and the Acts of Toleration of 1689 and 1693.

3

The thinking of Thomas Jefferson and other founders of the American republic was greatly influenced too by a group of seventeenth- and eighteenth-century philosophers on the European continent and in England: Charles Louis Montesquieu, a believer in a written constitution, whose *L'esprit des lois* appeared in 1748 with its comparative study of the ideas of a republic, a monarchy, and a despotism; Jean Jacques Rousseau, whose *Contrat social*, with its theory of popular sovereignty and the need of full citizenship for the complete development of manhood, appeared in 1762; and François Marie de Voltaire, who strongly opposed any State Church with exclusive rights and privileges and pleaded for full religious freedom.

However, it was the Englishman John Locke who of all modern philosophers carried the most weight among statesmen such as Thomas Jefferson and James Madison, who in turn laid the framework of our civil and religious liberties.[2] He taught that the magistrate had no authority to rule over souls; that religion must depend on inward conviction, not on external compulsion; and that the rights of conscience in matters of personal religious faith must be treated with respect. He believed in government by consent and maintained that liberty, life, and property or "estate" were inalienable rights, inherent in or natural to every individual, and thus antedated government.[3]

These, then, were some of the major intellectual and spiritual Old World forces, religious and non-religious, that helped shape American concepts of democracy, religious freedom, and Church-State relationships. But the more immediate influences must be sought in the New World and particularly in the threefold colonial tradition in what was to become the United States.

Although Church-State conditions in colonial times varied with the type of colony, in general the colonies largely reflected the spirit of the home government at the time, as far as toleration was concerned. More specifically, the relation between Church and State, and the resulting degree of religious freedom, developed along three independent though parallel lines: in Puritan New England, in Anglican Virginia and some other Southern colonies, and in the proprietary middle and Southern colonies.

The Pilgrims of Plymouth and the Puritans of Massachusetts Bay had all been originally Puritans—men who wished to purify the Church of England. After about two generations of separate existence in New England, the Puritans, who had always been non-conformists but had also become Separatists as far as the Church of England was concerned, again absorbed their more liberal-minded Separatist brethren of Plymouth. This occurred in 1692 when Plymouth and Massachusetts were united under a new charter. Before that, however, although they were almost all Calvinists, there were distinct differences among the members of the two groups.

In Plymouth, which was definitely more liberal and less theocratic than Massachusetts Bay, the seal of effective authority was in the rank and file of yeomen rather than, as in Massachusetts Bay, in the magistrates and ministers. The Pilgrims repudiated the Church of England but recognized their allegiance to the king, while the Puritans, desiring to build a State without a king, rejected the royal authority as much as they dared but recognized their fealty to the English Church in all things spiritual.[4] The Pilgrims differed most from the Puritans in their more democratic spirit, as may be seen from the Mayflower Compact of 1620, with its acceptance of the principle of majority rule.[5] Because of the inability of the Plymouth colonists to secure a charter from the home government, this Compact virtually served them as their constitution.

The democratic spirit prevailing at Plymouth is indicated by the fact that in the early years legislation was shared by all freemen, although later it was vested in an elected governor and General Court. Not to accept election when first chosen to office was a serious, punishable offense.

However, it was not Plymouth but Massachusetts Bay, with Boston as the principal port of entry into New England, that became the colony destined to develop Puritanism in its most influential form and to place its mark on the United States more than any colony other than Virginia (which led in the making of political constitutions). Here religion, of an intolerant Calvinistic type, and government were to be closely associated in accordance with English tradition; a Puritan State Church, especially closely related to town government, gradually developed from non-conformity to take the place of the old Anglican State Church to which the Puritans had been accustomed in England. The Church was a carefully selected group of communicants who emphasized their prerogatives and would brook no serious dissent from their duly adopted tenets. They expected the State to support public worship and suppress heresy.[6] They did not wish it to interfere in strictly religious questions but recognized that in matters of Church government and ecclesiastical affairs State and Church should work together.

In New England, the (Congregational) meetinghouse, the nucleus of every township, was used both for governmental purposes and for religious worship. Furthermore, municipal and certain parochial duties were frequently performed by the same officials. In some cases the minutes of the two organizations were kept in the same book, the facts and votes of both groups being included. Yet, even in Puritan New England, a fairly clear distinction was maintained between the functions of Church and State. For example, the elder was not considered eligible for the civil magistracy nor the magistrate for the office of elder. The two functions were considered separate.

During most of the colonial period Congregationalism was the Established

Church in New England, outside of Rhode Island.[7] It received all taxes for the support of religion, although, under certain conditions in the later period, the individual taxpayer might designate that his taxes be assigned to another publicly recognized religious group.[8]

It was only as the early settlers died off and with the decrease of emphasis on church membership—based on religious experience, the usual test of suffrage among the freemen—that the voting privilege was extended and that both Church and State became more democratic. Before that time there was a close connection between the two "powers" in New England, especially in Massachusetts. When Anne Hutchinson was put out of the church in Boston the action was taken first by the church and subsequently by the magistrate; when the first council or synod was held in New England, it was attended not only by twenty-three ministers from Massachusetts and two from Connecticut, but by the body of the magistrates, and its expenses were met out of the general colonial treasury. The governor and his assistants in Massachusetts Bay were frequently referred to as "the nursing fathers of the churches," for they concerned themselves with diverse matters involving congregational life, doctrine, and policy and played a major part in determining certain church matters, such as where new arrivals among the clergy should be assigned. They even called synods of the church and ordered ministers to formulate a confession of faith and a form of discipline.

The influence of the clergy in New England was undoubtedly very large. The ministers, however, generally refrained from accepting important political office and had to bow to the civil authorities in many Church matters. They were content so long as the State was administered by sympathetic members of their Church but bitterly opposed the entire separation of Congregationalism from the State in its two great strongholds, Massachusetts and Connecticut. In the early days, especially in Massachusetts Bay, Quakers, Baptists, and other dissenting groups were outrageously treated, but no more so than in England at the same time.

In Connecticut, the general Church-State setup was about the same as in Massachusetts. The fact is that outside of Rhode Island, where two groups of Independents—Baptists and Quakers—were powerful, and where Roger Williams and John Clarke proved great leaders in behalf of entire separation of Church and State, very little was accomplished in the way of religious freedom as distinct from toleration until the period of the American Revolution.

As Puritanism dominated New England, so Anglicanism dominated Virginia and the other Southern colonies. It was at Jamestown in Virginia that the Anglican-Protestant tradition was legally recognized when the first representative body of legislators to meet in North America, assembling in 1619 in their place of worship, established the authority of the Church of England and took measures for its support. In a word, the Anglican Church became a State Church in Virginia, much as the Puritan Church was somewhat later established in Massachusetts, but with this difference: in Virginia the State controlled the Church; in Massachusetts the Church tended to control the State. In Virginia in the seventeenth century the governor, within his limited sphere, executed the ecclesiastical prerogatives of the crown and, in the absence of a resident bishop, assumed a quasi-episcopal direction of the clergy. His instructions and colonial statutes recognized the exclusive claims of the Church of England. This condition lasted until the Revolutionary period. Even then the leaders of the state favored the government's retaining a definite relationship to religion and education, which would mean in most communities that the Episcopal Church would continue to be responsible for the latter.[9]

In general the Southern colonies had an official tie-up with the Anglican Church much as most of the New England colonies had with the Congregational churches. However, the seat of authority for Anglicanism was in England, for Puritanism in New England. New England's official religion was mainly master of its own destinies; in the South official religion was not. So in the colonial period the Northern clergy developed more leadership and more influence on State policy than did their Southern colleagues. Furthermore, the clergy in the Southern colonies, being by church tradition dependent on Episcopal supervision but having none except that of the distant Bishop of London, were frequently disloyal to their trust as spiritual and moral leaders, thereby helping to bring about disestablishment in Virginia about half a century before it took place in Connecticut and Massachusetts.

The proprietary middle and Southern provinces—New York (including originally New Jersey and Delaware), the Carolinas, Pennsylvania, and Maryland—provided more of a melting pot of religious and national groups than any other part of America and consequently were generally ahead of other sections in developing religious freedom. Moreover, we find here a semifeudal association of government with land ownership, where the proprietors' prosperity depended upon the steady flow of immigration.[10] In these colonies or provinces, consequently, a practical type of liberalism prevailed in welcoming newcomers of various types, although Quakers dominated in Pennsylvania; Roman Catholics, followed by Anglicans, in Maryland; and Presbyterians and Quakers, following Anglicans, in New Jersey. The Dutch Reformed and Anglicans sought mastery in New York, where, in spite of alternating Dutch and English rule, there was more tolerance than in New England.[11]

An early example was the attitude of the town of Flushing, Long Island, many of whose freemen, incensed by Governor Peter Stuyvesant's banning of the Quakers in 1657 in spite of the provisions of their town charter of 1645 guaranteeing "the right to have and enjoy liberty of conscience," drew up the "Flushing Remonstrance." In this they proclaimed that they would welcome not only members of this sect but any "sons of Adam who came in love among us," and would not "condemn, punish, banish, prosecute or lay violent hands upon anyone, in whatever name, form or title he might appear." We are, therefore, not surprised to find that in the middle of the eighteenth century the spirit of toleration had so developed—howbeit largely for prudential rather than for ideological or idealistic reasons—that the advertisement regarding the opening of King's (Columbia) College in New York in 1754 read, "there is no intention to impose on the scholars the peculiar tenets of any particular sect of Christians, but to inculcate upon their tender minds, the great Principles of Christianity and Morality, in which true Christians of each Denomination are generally agreed." [12] Similar ideals prevailed at about the same time at the leading institution of learning in another one of the middle colonies—what is now the University of Pennsylvania.

Conditions in New Jersey were not dissimilar to those in New York, with which it was generally associated, sharing the alternating Dutch and English supremacy. In 1677 "West Jersey" came under William Penn's control, and his "Concessions and Agreements of the Proprietors, Freeholders and Inhabitants" assured religious toleration, a relatively large portion of which continued after the provinces were transferred to the crown of England.

Penn's efforts for religious freedom in Pennsylvania were particularly notable. Indeed, only here, in Delaware—which was originally part of the province—and in Rhode Island do we find "free colonies" with substantial liberty of conscience even for non-Christians and without any established Church. Even in Pennsylvania, however, religious tests, in spite of the absence of an establishment, were of a rather narrow Protestant type.[13] But for its day the attitude was relatively liberal, owing mainly to Penn's "Frame of Government" of 1683, which welcomed to full rights all citizens "who profess to believe in Jesus Christ."

As early as 1700, the General Assembly of Delaware enacted a law granting full liberty of conscience to any person professing belief in Almighty God.[14] In Carolina considerable liberty of conscience was promised to all Protestant dissenters who emigrated to the colony, and in Maryland a special act tolerating all Trinitarian Christians was passed by the Assembly in 1649.

In respect to the proprietary colonies it may be said that in general not only did the proprietors, eager to advance the economic prosperity of territories under their control by securing more settlers, let down theological and ecclesiastical bars but the Quaker influence centering in Pennsylvania stood in the main for freedom. Furthermore, in the period from 1660 to 1775 when the proprietary colonies were being developed with such enthusiasm, the colonial population was being increased by over two million people—an increase largely due to this new type of land-grant colony. The new settlers were generally attracted by the religious freedom offered and were determined to continue and develop it.[15]

The Colonial Advocates of Religious Freedom

In the century and a half between the earliest permanent settlement of what is now the United States and the Revolution seven persons stand out as worthy of consideration for their contributions to religious liberty: Anne Hutchinson, Congregationalist; Thomas Hooker, Congregationalist; Cecil Calvert (Lord Baltimore), Roman Catholic; Roger Williams, Independent, Baptist, Seeker; John Clarke, Baptist; William Penn, Quaker; and Samuel Davies, Presbyterian.

ANNE HUTCHINSON [16]

Although the controversy around Anne Hutchinson appears to be primarily a theological dispute, she deserves to be included as an example of early independence in courageously upholding views opposed by the State as well as by the Church of her time, and because she made an important contribution to the cause of freedom. Indeed, the so-called Antinomian controversy, of which she was the leading figure, reflects more accurately than any other incident the fundamental character of Church-State relations in Massachusetts, which remained almost unchanged until after the Revolution.

Nominally, the basis of the trial of Anne Hutchinson by the General Court of Massachusetts in 1638 was that she stubbornly persisted in teaching the heretical and immoral doctrine of Antinomianism, which denied the need of good works and held that a believer whose heart was right toward God was fulfilling the law irrespective of his conduct. She advocated a "covenant of grace"—a religious belief based upon the individual's direct intuition of God's grace and love—as opposed to the preaching of a "covenant of works"—a religion based upon obedience to the laws of Church and State. Yet, it is probable that equally and perhaps more important as a cause of her condemnation was her own character and spirit. She was a woman of exceptional force and independence, tending to egotism, who inherited a tendency to a more liberal outlook than was customary in New England. She had an able mind, strong convictions, and a fearless disposition. She was fond of disputation but also had a mystical side to her nature, laying much emphasis on the "indwelling" of the Holy Spirit. At the close of her trial one of the accusers summarized the complaint against her by stating that "you have stepped out of your place, you have rather been a Husband than a Wife, a preacher than a Hearer, a Magistrate than a subject and so you have thought to carry all Things in Church and Commonwealth as you would."

The trial before the General Court ended in a verdict of guilty against her and her brother-in-law, the Reverend John Wheelwright, "and other erroneous and seditious persons" for disturbance of the public peace. She was ordered banished, and after a Church trial for breach of ecclesiastical discipline which culminated in a sentence of excommunication, she fled with her family to Rhode Island. Later she went to New York, where she and most of her children were murdered by the Indians in 1642.

THOMAS HOOKER

Hooker had fled England because of persecution on the part of Archbishop Laud for non-conformity. He arrived in New England in 1633. After three years as pastor of a church in Massachusetts he migrated, together with his congregation, to Connecticut, where he founded the town of Hartford. In 1662 Hartford and the New Haven colony, less advanced in matters of religious freedom, united, receiving a charter under which Congregationalism became the established ecclesiastical system. However, in 1727 the Church of England was authorized to organize, and two years later so too were the Baptists and Quakers.

Although Hooker worked for a free Church in a free State, he unquestionably believed in an intimate relation between the two. But the fact that he had a tolerant mind, without any of the persecuting spirit of some of the Massachusetts Puritans, and that his "Fundamental Orders" of 1639 contained pronounced democratic principles resulted in the end in his contributing considerably to the cause of religious freedom. The Orders provided that government should be by the consent of the governed, with rulers responsible to the will of the electorate, and that civil privilege was not necessarily related under them to church membership except in the case of the governor, who was to be a member of "some approved congregation." This was a great gain; it established a principle which implied, at least, that loyalty to the state did not entail loyalty to the Established Church. There was no special religious test necessarily required for the franchise, citizenship being a political matter although determined by church membership. Indeed, in 1708 the colony of Connecticut gave dissenters, under certain regulations, permission to have separate churches, still bound though they were to pay the tax for the support of the established Congregational ministry.[17]

Parrington, in *Main Currents in American Thought*, has well summed up Hooker's contribution to political thought:

. . . Three creative ideas seem to have determined his thinking: the compact theory of the state, the doctrine of popular sovereignty, and the conception of the state as a public-service corporation, strictly responsible to the will of the majority—ideas that Roger Williams elaborated in detail and during many years of service reduced to a working system in the commonwealth of Rhode Island. That Hooker should have grasped so firmly the essentials of the new democratic theory will surprise no one who is acquainted with the political speculations of English Independency. . . .[18]

CECIL CALVERT, LORD BALTIMORE

This founder and proprietary of Maryland, son of George Calvert, first Baron Baltimore and originator of the Maryland project, was by charter "Absolute Lord of Maryland and Avalon" and consequently head of the Church as well as of the State.[19]

The charter contemplated a definitely Christian State but was silent on the issue of denominationalism, referring merely to "God's holy and true Christian religion." [20] This attitude was motivated partly by a Christian spirit unusually broad for the period and partly by the demands of the situation, as the population of the colony already included a large number of Protestants, and the groups from which further immigration could be mainly expected were of the same religious persuasion. It is consequently quite probable that the king, whose government at the time was opposed both to Puritans and to Roman Catholics, would not have given a charter under any narrower conditions. But this circumstance should not detract unduly from the recognition due Lord Baltimore for his tolerant attitude. Clearly, in his feudal character as "Lord Proprietor" it was within Calvert's jurisdiction to administer ecclesiastical as well as State affairs in what was virtually a palatinate. The fact that he took up this work in a broad spirit was greatly to his credit.[21]

The instructions which Cecil Calvert issued in 1683 to his brother, Leonard Calvert, deputy governor of the province of Maryland, and his commissioners directed them to "be very careful to preserve unity and peace" and to "suffer no scandal or offense to be given to any of the Protestants, whereby any just complaint may hereafter be made by them in Virginia or in England." [22] He obviously wanted to provide an asylum for persecuted Roman Catholics and also to attract Protestant colonists.

In 1636 Calvert prescribed a liberal oath to be taken by Maryland governors under which they bound themselves not to "trouble, molest or discountenance any person professing to believe in Jesus Christ, for or in respect to religion," and to punish any who molest any person believing in Jesus Christ.[23]

The Maryland colonial Assembly issued "An Act concerning Religion," generally referred to as the Toleration Act, in 1649. It provided toleration for all "professing to believe in Jesus Christ" who did not deny his divinity or the doctrine of the Trinity. The act is sometimes extravagantly referred to as the first decree granting complete religious liberty to emanate from an assembly,[24] but this is claiming too much. It is, however, significant in itself and because it came from a public assembly of sixteen members of whom at least half, and probably a slight majority, were Roman Catholics.[25] The act did not provide for Jews, who continued to suffer discriminations in the state until 1828, or for the various groups with Unitarian tendencies, but it made the position of Roman Catholic, Episcopalian, and Presbyterian equally favorable.

Specifically the act provided, first, that any person "who shall from henceforth blaspheme God, . . . or shall deny our Saviour Jesus Christ to be the son of God, or shall deny the holy Trinity the father, son and holy Ghost, or the Godhead of any of the said Three persons of the Trinity or the Unity of the Godhead . . . shall be punished with death and confiscation or forfeiture of all his or her lands." It then stated that no person within the province who professed belief in Jesus Christ "shall henceforth be in any ways troubled, molested or discountenanced for or in respect to his or her religion nor in the free exercise thereof, nor any way compelled to the belief or exercise of any other religion against his or her consent." Finally, the act provided for a fine, or, on inability to pay the fine, public whipping and imprisonment for calling any person a "heretic, Schismatic, Idolator, Puritan, Independent, Presbyterian, Popish priest, Jesuit, Jesuited papist, Lutheran, Calvinist, Anabaptist, Brownist, Antinomian, Barrowist, Roundhead, Separatist, or any other name in a reproachful manner relating to matter of religion." [26]

It is difficult to determine accurately the motives of the act. They were complex. The desire to prevent dissatisfaction on the part of the Protestant element in the population—due especially to the considerable Puritan migration from Virginia about 1648—and to attract more Protestant settlers; the determination to prevent the Jesuits from gaining control; the need of saving the proprietor's authority in the province; fear that events in England might compromise the Catholics' liberty in Maryland; and Calvert's own generosity of outlook—all these were factors. It is to his credit that the act was passed not only with his support but on his urging. Also to be remembered is the fact that this action was taken by a deliberative Assembly divided as to religious affiliation between Protestants and Catholics, whereas in Rhode Island, whose Assembly had taken somewhat similar action two years earlier, the background was entirely Protestant and more democratic.

The subsequent history of religious freedom and Church-State separation in Maryland shows many variations, but in general, during Maryland's first century under Catholic control more respect had been shown for religious freedom than in the Protestant period. Following the English Revolution of 1688 a royal government was set up and the Church of England established, and in 1715 the proprietary, the fifth Lord Baltimore, who had become a Protestant, was restored. But Catholics did not fare as well under the Protestant regime as Protestants had under the more tolerant rule of the Catholic Calverts.

Cecil Calvert should be gratefully remembered for the Act of Toleration of 1649, which gave Maryland a more liberal policy in matters of religion than any other colony in America at the time, excepting only Rhode Island and Pennsylvania. Calvert also, with the support of the Assembly, subjected testamentary affairs and the recording of marriages to the civil authority, thereby making a notable departure from precedent in the interest of Church-State separation,[27] and provided for the principle of voluntary parochial support.[28] He never visited his proprietary province, so his inclusion in this list of leaders in the cause of American religious freedom might be questioned; but as he planned to settle in America and was prevented only by the exigencies of the home situation affecting his colony, and as he governed Maryland through his resident deputies with much wisdom and toleration for forty-three years, his place seems deserved.

ROGER WILLIAMS

Roger Williams arrived in Massachusetts in 1630. Although at first kindly received,[29] within five years he had alienated the leaders of the Church and was banished for having "broached and divulged divers new and dangerous opinions against the authority of the magistrates." [30]

Williams had been suspected by the colonial authorities on many grounds, such as what John Cotton referred to as his "violent and tumultuous" disposition; his condemnation of the Puritan State-Church system; his conscientious objection to certain oaths by which the Massachusetts oligarchy was attempting to bind discontented elements to submission; his statement that the civil authorities had no power to enforce the religious injunctions of the Ten Commandments; and his upholding of the property rights of Indians in opposition to English claims. He had found in Massachusetts freedom from the rule of ecclesiastical superiors in the person of bishops, to which he had specially objected in England, but not what was to him the other most important part of "soul liberty," freedom from interference by the civil authority.

Banished from Massachusetts Bay in the winter of 1635-36 because of these and other views, including his sympathy with the accused Antinomian leaders, he became the founder, in Providence, Rhode Island, of what has generally been considered the first Baptist Church in America. After a few months in this denomination Williams became a Seeker, one who was skeptical of the special divine claims of all Churches and creeds but accepted the fundamentals of Christianity.[31] He took the ground that the State had no jurisdiction over the consciences of men, who must have "soul liberty." He wanted a colony which would shelter all "distressed in conscience." His toleration included even "popish and Jewish consciences," so that as a result of his efforts Providence became a refuge for victims of religious persecution. It was an evidence of his tolerant spirit that he considered the Indians his brothers, in whose welfare he was always deeply interested.

The Bloudy Tenent of Persecution for cause of Conscience, which was in many ways Williams' most important contribution of a literary character, appeared in the same year (1644) as Milton's great plea for freedom of conscience, the *Areopagitica*, and was followed three years later by Jeremy Taylor's *Liberty of Prophesying. The Bloudy Tenent* was but an enlargement of Williams' view that "God requireth not an uniformity of Religion." It was prepared by its author with a synopsis or résumé of the argument of the book. It is not too much to say that the lapse of three centuries since its writing has increased rather than decreased its significance. It stands out as representing an epoch-marking milestone in the history of the separation of Church and State and of religious freedom.

The following extracts from the synopsis present vividly the scope and substance of the book.

First, That the blood of so many hundred thousand soules of *Protestants* and *Papists*, spilt in the *Wars of present and former Ages*, for their respective *Consciences*, is not *required nor accepted by Jesus Christ the Prince of Peace.*

. . . . .

Fourthly, *The Doctrine of persecution* for cause of *Conscience,* is proved guilty of all the *blood* of the *Soules* crying for *vengeance* under the Altar.

Fifthly, All *Civill States* with their *Officers of justice* in their respective *constitutions and administrations* are proved *essentially Civill,* and therefore not *Judges, Governours or Defendours* of the Spirituall or Christian State and Worship.

Sixthly, It is the will and command of *God,* that (since the coming of his Sonne the *Lord Jesus*) *a permission* of the most *Paganish, Jewish,* Turkish, or Antichristian consciences and worships, bee granted to all men in all *Nations* and *Countries*: and they are onely to bee *fought* against with that *Sword* which is only (*in Soule matters*) *able to conquer,* to wit, the *Sword of Gods Spirit,* the *Word of God.*

. . . . .

Eighthly, *God* requireth not an *uniformity of Religion* to be *inacted* and *inforced* in any *civill State*; which inforced *uniformity* (sooner or later) is the greatest occasion of *civill Warre, ravishing of conscience, persecution of Christ*

Jesus in his servants, and of the *hypocrisie and destruction of millions of souls.*

. . . . .

Tenthly, An inforced *uniformity of Religion* throughout a *Nation or civill* State, confounds the *Civill and Religious*, denies the principles of Christianity and civility, and that *Jesus Christ* is come in the Flesh.[32]

Williams was not content with expressing these views as to the importance of toleration. He was willing to work to put them into practice. In the same year in which the *Bloudy Tenent* appeared he went far toward realizing its ideal by securing a charter for the united "Providence Plantations in Narragansett Bay in New England," in which only civil government was recognized. Three years later (1647) a civil code was drawn up under his leadership granting complete liberty of conscience.

In 1654, only a few months after his election to be the chief official of the town of Providence, certain difficulties arose which led Williams to write his famous "ship" letter on religious freedom. In this he said,

There goes many a ship to sea, with many hundred souls in one ship, whose weal and woe is common, and is a true picture of a commonwealth, or a human combination or society. It hath fallen out sometimes, that both papists and protestants, Jews and Turks, may be embarked in one ship; upon which supposal I affirm, that all the liberty of conscience, that ever I pleaded for, turns upon these two hinges—that none of the papists, protestants, Jews, or Turks, be forced to come to the ship's prayers or worship, nor compelled from their own particular prayers or worship, if they practice any. I further add, that I never denied, that notwithstanding this liberty, the commander of this ship ought to command the ship's course, yea, and also command that justice, peace and sobriety, be kept and practiced, both among the seamen and all the passengers. If any of the seamen refuse to perform their services, or passengers to pay their freight; if any refuse to help, in person or purse, towards the common charges or defence; if any refuse to obey the common laws and orders of the ship, concerning their common peace of preservation; if any shall mutiny and rise up against their commanders and officers; if any should preach or write that there ought to be no commanders or officers, because all are equal in Christ, therefore no masters nor officers, no laws nor orders, nor corrections nor punishments;—I say, I never denied, but in such cases, whatever is pretended, the commander or commanders may judge, resist, compel and punish such transgressors, according to their deserts and merits.[33]

This letter merits the most careful study, for it sets forth in clarity and brevity the three basic principles upon which a religious pluralistic society can best survive and flourish according to the assumptions of the great American experiment of religious liberty and the separation of Church and State: (1) There is a difference between the sacred (the ship's prayer and worship) and the secular (command of the ship's course and enforcement of justice, peace, and sobriety). (2) Compulsion may be exercised by officials of the State (the ship's captain) in the area of the secular but not of the sacred. (3) Where the safety and security of the commonwealth are concerned, religious conscience is not a valid excuse for refusal to obey the lawful commands of the State.

These three principles were later to become the First Amendment declaration against laws respecting any establishment of religion or prohibiting the free exercise thereof and the basis of the decisions of the United States Supreme Court interpreting that amendment.

Williams' theory of the Church was that of a voluntary association of people for a specific object, much like the medieval theory of the corporation. Its internal affairs were no concern of the government so long as its members kept the peace and performed their obligations to the community at large.[34]

Williams substituted the compact theory for the divine-right theory of the State. He believed that the civil government had to do only with civil affairs, and that it rested on the consent of the people. It must not mix in church matters, for any attempt by the State to force uniformity of religion causes civil wars, the "ravishing of conscience," and many other ills. The right of religious liberty was to him fundamental. It had never been surrendered to the State. It was not the gift of government but something which the people retained when they formed their government.

The monumental contribution made by Roger Williams to the cause of democracy, not only in the United States but throughout the world, was summarized by Professor Georg Jellinek of the University of Heidelberg in 1901:

The idea of legally establishing inalienable, inherent and sacred rights of the individual is not of political but religious origin. What has been held to be a work of the Revolution was in reality a fruit of the Reformation and its struggles. Its first apostle was not Lafayette but Roger Williams, who, driven by powerful and deep religious enthusiasm, went into the wilderness in order to found a government of religious liberty, and his name is uttered by Americans even today with the deepest respect.[35]

JOHN CLARKE

This early liberal-minded Baptist physician and preacher has not received as much credit as he deserves, primarily because he was overshadowed by his great friend and co-worker, Roger Williams. Nevertheless, few men of his day had such advanced views regarding religious freedom. Born in England, he emigrated to Boston in 1637. Though he sympathized deeply with the Puritan movement, he was so distressed at the theological intolerance in the Massachusetts colony, as evidenced by the edicts of banishment against Anne

Hutchinson and others, that he proposed to some friends—largely among the liberal elements in the Boston church who had been influenced by Mistress Hutchinson—that they settle in some new jurisdiction where they could enjoy religious freedom.[36]

First stopping at Providence, they went on and bought from the Indians the island of Aquidneck, later known as Rhode Island. There they founded the town of Newport, which in 1640 was united with Portsmouth and adopted "a Democracie or Popular Government." The General Court of the combined town declared that "none be accounted a Delinquent for Doctrine." In 1647 the combined town joined with Providence and other towns to form what later became the state of Rhode Island. The laws of the united colony, probably drafted by Clarke, stated that "the Forme of Government Established . . . is Democraticall; that is to say, a Government Held by ye Free and Voluntarie Consent of all or the Greater Parte of the Free Inhabitants." Further, otherwise than "what is herein forbidden, all men may walk as their consciences persuade them, everyone in the name of his God."

In 1651 Clarke went to England with Roger Williams to promote the interests of Rhode Island. While abroad he published a remarkable little book entitled *Ill Newes from New England: or a Narrative of New Englands Persecution.* This pamphlet is one of the ablest defenses of religious liberty which early New England produced. It starts with an account of the persecutions that Clarke had himself experienced at the hands of the established order. He refers to being among those "who together for liberty of their consciences, and worship of their God, as their hearts were persuaded, long since fled from the persecuting hands of the Lordly Bishops" only to find intolerance and persecution of another type.[37]

After an account of his persecutions, due mainly to his preaching without the necessary licenses and his denying the lawfulness of infant baptism, the author gives quotations from the intolerant laws of Massachusetts. He is specially concerned about the one which calls for the banishment of those who oppose the baptizing of infants.[38] But the most interesting part of the book is the closing section, which considers the arguments for religious liberty. The author lays special emphasis on the fact that "no servant of Christ Jesus hath any liberty, much less authority, from his Lord, to smite his Fellow-servant,"[39] and that Christ taught his disciples "to be meek, and lowly and gentle, yea, kind and curteous to all. . . ."[40] He sees clearly that any attempt to force worship "is the ready way to make dissemblers and hypocrites before God."[41] "This outward forcing of men in matters of conscience towards God to believe as others believe, and to practise and worship as others do, cannot stand with the Peace, Liberty, Prosperity, and safety of a Place, Commonwealth, or nation." [42] All in all the appeal is a powerful one.

In one of his addresses to the king (Charles II), probably written in 1662, he referred to the Rhode Island colony as desiring "to be permitted to hold forth in a lively experiment that a flourishing civil state may stand, yea, and best be maintained, and that among English spirits, with a full liberty of religious concernments." [43] This was a theory based on experience, for by 1658 both Quakers and Jews had been received kindly in his own settlement of Newport.

As a result of his efforts in England Clarke obtained from the king in 1663 a charter whose provisions were of exceptional liberality as far as differences of religion were concerned. It provided that "noe person within the sayd colonie, at any time hereafter, shall bee in any wise molested, punished, disquieted, or called in question, for any differences in opinions in matters of religion . . . but that all and everye person and persons may . . . freelye and fullye have and enjoy his and theire own judgments and consciences in matters of religious concernments . . . they behaving themselves peaceably and quietly, and not using this libertie to lycentiousnesse and profanesse, nor to the civill injurye or outward disturbance of others. . . ." [44]

It was Roger Williams who best summarized Clarke's life and career in his statement that Clarke's "grand motive" was to give "a just liberty to all men's spirits in spiritual matters." [45]

WILLIAM PENN

As early as 1676 in his *Concessions* or proposed constitution for his colony in America, Penn provided for a large measure of religious freedom. He wanted to establish "a free colony for all mankind that will come hither." This idea was incorporated in the "Frame of Government" published at the end of April, 1682, and supplemented by a bill of rights appended the next month. These were substantially in force throughout the colonial period. Penn provided that "All persons who profess to believe in Jesus Christ the Saviour of the World, shall be capable to serve this government in any capacity, both legislatively and executively." [46] This was broad enough, it will be noticed, to permit Catholics as well as Protestants of all denominations to hold office, and there was nothing in this or later documents to prevent non-Christians, if they would obey the laws, from entering the colony. The plan generally followed in Pennsylvania was that embodied in Penn's Charter of Privileges, granted in 1701, which guaranteed freedom of worship to all who believed in "One Almighty God" and the right to hold office to all who believed in Jesus Christ.[47]

All of Penn's charters and grants of privilege show the same tolerant point of view. Probably most important from this standpoint was "The Great Law" or "The Body of Laws," adopted by the province of Pennsylvania at an assembly held in December, 1682. It provided

That no person, now or at any time hereafter, Living in this Province, who shall confess and acknowledge one Almighty God to be the Creator, Upholder and Ruler of the World, And who professes, him or herself Obliged in Conscience to Live peaceably and quietly under the civil government, shall in any case be molested or prejudiced for his, or her Conscientious persuasion or practice. Nor shall hee or shee at any time be compelled to frequent or Maintain anie religious worship, place or Ministry whatever, Contrary to his, or her mind, but shall freely and fully enjoy his, or her, Christian Liberty in that respect, without any Interruption or reflection. And if any person shall abuse or deride any other, for his, or her different persuasion and practice in matters of religion, such person shall be lookt upon as a Disturber of the peace, and be punished accordingly.[48]

Because of his practical philanthropy and sense of responsibility, his common sense, and his toleration Penn has been frequently called "the first American." Certain it is that as a Christian statesman he was well ahead of his time and highly influential with Thomas Jefferson and others of the founding fathers.

SAMUEL DAVIES

Davies, who in 1747 was sent from Delaware to Hanover County, Virginia, is one of the little-recognized heroes in securing American religious freedom. He was the forerunner of Thomas Jefferson in advocating the complete separation of Church and State and helped to lay the foundations for Jefferson's immortal work. In fact, this service is even more noteworthy than his work as president of Princeton, where he succeeded Jonathan Edwards for a short period.[49]

To understand the historical significance of the work of Davies and of the Hanover Presbytery, in which he played the leading part, it is necessary to remember that Virginia was settled and governed mainly by Cavaliers and their sympathizers, Anglicans who had little regard for the rights of dissenters. The Church of England was established by law, and no other religious body had been allowed to erect church buildings in the towns, whereas the parish churches of the Established Church were erected at public expense. In spite of the fact that the Presbyterian ministers were, as a general rule, the most educated and best qualified for effective pastoral work in the colony, they and the Baptists, who were equally earnest but less educated, had to pay taxes to support the Episcopal Church, too many of whose incumbents were virtually political appointees with few spiritual qualifications. Furthermore, most of the Episcopal ministers, being educated abroad and members of the established English Church, were intensely loyal to the crown, while Presbyterians were largely educated in this country and were devoted to the cause of liberty.[50]

Davies' ministrations in Hanover County were interfered with by the governor and council, undoubtedly at the instigation of the Episcopal clergy. In 1748 he carried the matter of the rights of dissenters under the Act of Toleration of 1689 before Peyton Randolph, the king's attorney in Virginia, and later before influential individuals and groups in England. Finally he secured action which implied that the Act of Toleration did indeed extend to the colony.

As a result of Davies' various efforts the Presbyterians' whole status was improved. Moreover, he and his associates of the Hanover Presbytery, supported by the Baptists and Quakers and a small sprinkling of liberal Episcopal laymen, had the courage to demand religious freedom as a natural right, not being satisfied to obtain a measure of "toleration."[51] They did not oppose the religious doctrines of the Episcopal Church. They felt, however, that these doctrines were not being "faithfully preached" and that freedom was at stake because the parishes had no final say in the selection of their own ministers. Their vestries could only recommend a clergyman, the government having the right to put him in actual possession of a parish.[52]

The final result in behalf of toleration in Virginia was not attained until after Samuel Davies' death; but it was the Presbytery of Hanover, which he established in 1755, and which, as its first moderator, he had inspired with his ideals, that carried the struggle through to a successful end. In 1773 this presbytery appointed a commission to lay the whole matter of church privileges and rights before the Virginia Assembly, following it up by similar actions in subsequent years, until final success was secured in 1785.

While Davies could probably not be called a champion of religious liberty in the sense of demanding complete freedom of worship for all—he did not commit himself on that question—he nevertheless fought vigorously for the religious rights of those to whom he ministered; and what he gained for them he gained for all dissenters in Virginia. For that reason he merits prominent mention in this listing of the great colonial advocates of religious freedom.

Major Colonial Influences Encouraging Religious Freedom

Having reviewed briefly some of the most notable advocates of religious freedom during the colonial period and their major contributions to this cause and to Church-State separation, we may appropriately consider some of the major factors in colonial life that encouraged the development of religious freedom. Most prominent were the colonists' migrations and the resulting divergent religious sects, the small percentage of Church members in the colonies, the colonists' experience with and without establishments, the effects of the Great Awakening, Freemasonry, and foreign trade.

THE COLONISTS' MIGRATIONS AND RESULTING DIVERGENT SECTS

There were undoubtedly many factors which encouraged early American settlement. Some modern historians have emphasized the economic note, that is, the colonists' desire for improving financial conditions, and especially for securing land of their own. Others have been impressed with the struggle for national ascendance in America because of its effect on the balance of power in Europe, especially the curbing of Catholic Spain and France—a movement encouraged by the British government. Still others call attention to the desire of large groups of middle-class people to get away from conservative restraints and to improve their social status by leaving countries where class lines were still fairly rigid. The reasons for making the long journey were indeed many and varied. Some Europeans yielded to their love of change and adventure, generally because a new world meant to them a new economic opportunity (available good land in the old countries was scarce); some hoped to escape political oppression, including some of the burdens of supporting reactionary governments in the old lands, with heavy taxes, military service, and other obligations.

These and other factors, social, economic, political, all played their part. Yet the fact remains that the religious factor, at one time so exclusively emphasized and so exaggerated as to produce a reaction, is beginning again to receive due attention: One of the prime causes for early migration to America, and especially to New England, was the desire for religious freedom.

This does not mean that there were many among the colonists who held convictions as to the rightness of religious freedom per se, but rather that they wished to escape from what they believed to be ecclesiastical tyranny, as far as the treatment of their own sect or denomination was concerned. Members of various Protestant groups wished to avoid persecution or hampering regulations for themselves; yet they might be found to turn around on arrival in America and persecute their old enemies or opponents, whether these were Roman Catholics, Anglicans, or adherents of some dominantly Calvinist body. There were also group migrations based on common religious bonds where some non-conformists, such as the Mennonites, came over in communities so as to have freedom to develop their own religious and social convictions. Religious freedom in America had its roots three hundred years ago in the desire of tens of thousands of settlers to free themselves and the religious group to which they belonged from State interference with their development. This factor also played an important part in twentieth-century immigration, especially on the part of the Jews of Eastern Europe and the people of Ireland, cases in which economic, religious, and political elements were all combined.

The founders of the American colonies were, relatively speaking, largely political liberals and religious non-conformists, at least insofar as dissatisfaction with European conditions was concerned.[53] This was true not only of the early English immigration but even more so of the West European migration which followed in 1660 and included so many German sectaries with Ana-baptist backgrounds—Mennonites, Moravians, Quakers, and so on. Different colonies also had their distinctive religious and ecclesiastical flavor due to the dominant point of view, such as that of the Puritans in Massachusetts or of the Anglicans in Virginia; but there were probably more different religious backgrounds than have been generally recognized. Hence the existence of elements in the colonies which in time would oppose the historic union of Church and State and advocate religious freedom. There were a few such liberals even in Massachusetts; but most of the very pronounced ones migrated to Rhode Island, where they had entire freedom of conscience, or to some of the middle colonies, such as Pennsylvania, where they had it in large measure.

Calvinism, with the "infallible" Bible which the colonists carried with them, was too firmly entrenched, especially in New England, for liberalism to show itself prominently in the field of theology. But the Calvinists were separated by three thousand miles of sea from the center of government, and communication was irregular and slow. It was inevitable that they would break away from the conservative traditions of government to which they had been accustomed, and from whose extremes they had fled, to try something new, although they would not depart from Calvin's principle of some partnership between Church and State. The simple character of colonial life in most sections outside of the few large towns and the plantation South added its influence, as did the democratic ideal of brotherhood in the New Testament.[54]

The fact that immigration to the United States in the colonial period and the period when our government was being formed was mainly English was of great importance from the standpoint of religious freedom; for although England retained a State Church she increasingly, after the Revolution of 1688 and the issuance the following year of the Act of Toleration, practiced a considerable measure of toleration. When we compare the conditions in England, for instance, with those in the Latin countries of Europe up to the time of the French Revolution, we can see how much more freedom came to America as a result of our Anglo-Saxon tradition than would have come had our tradition been dominantly Latin.

The factor of experience of European persecution must also be taken into account as a stimulus to religious freedom in this country. People who have suffered for their views naturally want freedom to express them, and the large majority of pre-Revolutionary settlers in America—except in some parts of the South—had been members of reluctantly tolerated or actively persecuted groups abroad. A full list of these persecutions would be a large one, but for our purpose the important thing to remember is that the persecuted groups became to a large extent the leaders in behalf of religious freedom in the new land.

The variety of sects with differing European backgrounds that colonized America was a potent factor in bringing about religious freedom. The perpetual conflict among the sects was in the long run conducive to liberty. Some of the fathers of the Republic, such as Jefferson and Madison, realized this. Indeed, the idea goes back at least to Voltaire, who put the matter extremely and bluntly but with much truth in his *Lettres sur les Anglais*: 'If there were one religion in England, its despotism would be terrible; if there were only two, they would destroy each other; but there are thirty, and therefore they live in peace and happiness."[55] Voltaire tells us that he based this conclusion, not on the natural tolerance of the English people, but on a study of the intolerance of various groups, including Anglicans and Scotch Presbyterians.

SMALL PERCENTAGE OF CHURCH MEMBERS IN THE COLONIES

The Church leaders in the colonies, especially in early New England, took their religion so seriously that we are inclined to overestimate the Church devotion of the majority of the population. Even in the earliest days, a majority of the colonists, in spite of the religious objectives stated by their leaders, were probably actuated mainly by economic considerations. Earnest ministers and laymen gave a religious note to the early settlements. However, after the first generation with its heroic qualities died off, the impulse for converting the Indians waned, and ecclesiastical rigidity and arid theological controversy dried up the sources of religious vitality, the number of active church members was almost everywhere very small. A leading authority has estimated that at the close of the colonial period New England, the best-churched section of the thirteen colonies, had no more than one church member to every eight persons in the total population.[56] Another authority, writing of a slightly earlier period in New England—the end of the seventeenth century and the beginning of the eighteenth—does not think that over one out of twenty or twenty-five New Englanders belonged to the churches. In comparison with these figures, the *Yearbook of American Churches* for 1962 reported a total church membership in the United States of close to 115 million persons, or some 63.6 per cent of the nation's estimated population.[57]

These typical facts and figures are sufficient to show that non-church members at the time our state and national constitutions were being formed were in a large majority, and that it was quite natural for them to oppose any organic connection between Church and State.

EXPERIENCE WITH AND WITHOUT ESTABLISHMENTS

∨   Nothing had a larger effect on the framers of our Constitution and Bill of Rights than colonial experience as well as experience during the Revolutionary period, when the states were being formed. Most of the features of Church-State separation and of religious freedom can be traced back in the colonial period to the achievements of Roger Williams in Rhode Island and of William Penn in Pennsylvania, and in the state period to the achievements of Virginia and New York in securing virtually complete religious freedom and entire separation between Church and State. Furthermore, those colonies which had an Established Church, although that Church had much support from its adherents, had developed a strong opposition party, made up in the South of nonconformists, as far as Anglicanism was concerned, and in the North of non-conformists who opposed the special privileges of the Congregational establishment. It was clear to the great majority in the Constitutional Convention of 1787 not only that the Federal government must have no Church connection but that such connection would gradually disappear in the various states, although the new government could not go too far or too fast in definitely aiding this movement.

Any impartial person who knew the conditions in an American colony with an Established Church well knew the difficulties. He might wish to maintain his Church in his own colony in spite of these, but when it came to legislating for the nation starting under a new republican form of government he could not but see the need of a change. In such states as Massachusetts with its entrenched Congregationalism there had been an increasingly persistent and bitter struggle. The "outs" were constantly agitating publicly and petitioning the legislatures to give up tithes and other forms of taxes for the support of the establishment, and to grant the people entire freedom before the law for their work. Indeed, in a good many cases that had come before the courts, individuals—often on conscientious grounds—had declined to support the Established Church, and the dissenters were steadily increasing their demands. If such was the condition in a relatively homogeneous state, what would it be in the nation at large if an establishment of religion were attempted? It was quite obvious that, with all the extreme dissenting German sects in Pennsylvania, the Dutch Reformed and Presbyterians in New York, the Roman Catholics in Maryland, the Episcopalians in Virginia, the Quakers in Rhode Island, the Jews in a few cities like New York, Charleston, and Newport, and the vigorous Baptists expanding along the Appalachian frontier and stirring up trouble for establishments everywhere, a national State Church was out of the question.

Four of the original thirteen colonies had secured and experienced religious freedom with entire separation of Church and State and found that it actually worked well. The object lesson of Rhode Island's experiment in New England and the success of Pennsylvania, with its closely related Delaware, in the middle states, of Maryland's early efforts under Cecil Calvert, and of Virginia's recent victory in the South were bound to make the framers of the Constitution appreciate the importance of religious freedom and guard against any Federal Church for the United States. The founding fathers sensed full well that any other solution would be inconsistent with the principles of independence and democracy.

EFFECTS OF THE GREAT AWAKENING

One very definite evangelical movement aided the cause of religious freedom just prior to the formation of the Union. This was the Great Awakening in the middle of the eighteenth century. Its origin was due to two major factors: the middle colonies revival, which had its roots in German Pietism, and the New England "awakening." The efforts of the leaders of the middle colonial revival did much both for vital religion and for democracy, especially on the frontier, and in some places, such as Virginia, contributed to overthrowing the domination of the State Church. This result was due partly to accessions to non-conformist strength and partly to the breaking up of the old parish system with its one recognized minister and church with responsibility for nearly all in the community.[58]

The New England movement had its beginnings in 1734, a few years after the onset of the revival in the middle colonies, but it was probably even more influential and was identified with the name of Jonathan Edwards, the greatest of the Puritans. A theologian and a mystic, Edwards cared little about political matters. Yet he contributed mightily—even though indirectly, being far from a liberal in theology—to the cause of religious freedom. He preached the importance of individual conversion; he insisted that the Church and the State were very different and that the Church should be exalted as a spiritual and not a political institution; he effectively proclaimed that each individual is answerable to God alone; and his strict theological and ecclesiastical views alienated the more liberal, who considered a moral life more important than Calvinistic orthodoxy and so tended to leave established Congregationalism for other religious groups more sympathetic with their point of view. Edwards, perhaps far beyond all men of his time, smote the staggering blow which made ecclesiastical establishments impossible to America, although it is unlikely that he meant to do anything of the kind.[59]

The Great Awakening profoundly moved all Protestant groups and prepared the soil for change. It affected the Anglicans by reactions from without rather than direct internal influence, in that the extremes of the revival led many to seek the more restrained and orderly worship of the Episcopal Church. It put new life in those dissenting churches in New England, especially the Baptists, and the Methodist group then included among the Episcopalians, upon which the cause of religious liberty so much depended. In these churches the Awakening was considered a protest against the deadness of what was virtually State religion, corresponding in this respect to Pietism in Germany and Methodism in England.[60] The stricter new standards strengthened the moral and religious tone of the established Congregational Church, which had been weakened by compromise, and girded it for new crusades. The Great Awakening was, on the whole, a severe blow to the cause of Church establishments.

The movement against slavery; the development of a humanitarian interest in many other causes; the bringing of men together in a common movement from different colonies and from different Protestant groups; the encouraging of democratic ideals; the providing of religion on the frontier; the founding of educational institutions such as Princeton College; and the strengthening of the Presbyterian, Baptist, Congregational, and other Churches, which contributed so much popular support to the cause of the American Revolution —these are among the direct and indirect historical influences of the Great Awakening on American civil and religious life.

As this movement had its effective beginnings in New England and has been largely discussed by New England authors, its influence on the South and West has not always been adequately realized. It was, however, demonstrably a mighty force in other distant colonies. For instance, in Virginia it gave great stimulus through the Baptist and Presbyterian churches to the cause of civil and religious liberty. It aided these movements by pressure from below, opposing all monarchical forms of State and Church control and encouraging mightily the democratic movement.[61]

FREEMASONRY √

A large number of the leaders of the movement that resulted in the American

Revolution and in the establishment of the American Constitution were Freemasons. These included James Otis, Benjamin Franklin, George Washington (who took his oath of office as president upon his Masonic Bible), as well as fourteen signers of the Declaration of Independence and many who were active in the Constitutional Convention.[62] There were, however, some conspicuous exceptions: John Adams, Patrick Henry, and Thomas Jefferson. Possibly the secret aspects of Freemasonry made them feel that it was inadvisable to identify themselves with the movement.

Although the matter has been little referred to by American historians other than Masonic writers, it seems clear that the Masonic lodges, which had been active for a generation prior to the Revolution, influenced not only the impulse toward the new republic but also the cause of religious toleration, and in several ways.

They brought together, through correspondence, visitation, conventions, encampments, and various other meetings, the Anglicans of the South, the Congregationalists of New England, the Presbyterians of the middle colonies, the Baptists, and other groups.

They established military lodges in the Revolutionary army which encouraged the same broadening of friendships and contacts.

They asserted their belief in "the great Architect of the universe" and yet took the ground that they would not identify themselves as an organization with any denomination.

They helped to develop a deep interest in the general cause of social welfare, with loyalty to both the moral and the spiritual ideals of the Bible and the Crusades, emphasis on self-government, and respect for differences of religious convictions and for honest craftsmanship in any occupation.

They encouraged a friendly attitude toward the Jews, for whose ancient standards of personal and public righteousness and for whose temple ceremonies, symbols, and mystic rites they had a profound respect. The Scottish Rite today includes many representative Jews in its membership.

They showed a sympathetic interest in the Negro, granting a warrant for the first colored lodge, in Boston, in 1784, and the first state grand lodge, in Massachusetts, in 1808.[63]

They emphasized the idea which is at the basis of the Declaration of Independence: that the universe and all men in it are of divine origin, and that natural law demands the treatment of all men fairly in accordance with their origin and destiny.

They were naturally antagonistic to the Church-State idea, laying supreme emphasis on the individual's freedom of conscience.

They tended to emphasize national rather than purely local or international organization.

FOREIGN TRADE

Foreign trade involves contact with other nationals and with other religions. People cannot deal effectively with other racial groups if they are intolerant. There must be some capacity for give-and-take, and some breadth of sympathy. Consequently, we have reason to believe that the development of commerce with the American colonies, especially by the British and Dutch in the seventeenth and eighteenth centuries, had some effect on the growth of a spirit of toleration at home and abroad. For instance, those responsible for drafting colonial charters increasingly saw the need of attracting settlers of different religious beliefs. This is why the proprietary colonies, which were developed largely for commercial purposes, showed on the whole a larger amount of toleration than other colonies. Merchant proprietors with much land for sale in America, as was the case in New Jersey, New York, Georgia, Maryland, and the Carolinas, found it a matter of necessity to insure a measure of toleration.

There is evidence that the agency in England most interested in promoting commerce with the colonies believed that toleration was important. This factor was probably even more prominent with the Dutch, as they had large trading interests with the New World in the seventeenth and eighteenth centuries. Antwerp in the time of Charles V, and Amsterdam then and somewhat later were among the trade centers of Europe, and they were also places where religious differences were most respected. Indeed, the port and business metropolis of Amsterdam and the university town of Leyden, only twenty-five miles away, were in the forefront of the movement for greater religious freedom. The Dutch, who came to the American colonies to trade and to settle, carried with them religious toleration, and their record in New Amsterdam (New York), except under Stuyvesant, was on the whole a good one for the time.

A recent study has shown that in the sixteenth and seventeenth centuries Anglican, Puritan, and Roman Catholic clergymen in England did much to promote the trading and colonial ventures that laid the foundations of the later British Empire. Among those who preached trade expansion were not only Protestants identified with discovery but also such Catholic divines as Nicholas Farrar and John Donne. By persuading ministers of different denominations to support their trading ventures, these and other men, although their purposes may not have been altogether beyond reproach, helped to attract settlers of different churches, and these laid the foundations for later toleration.[64]

There is another way in which the commercial and industrial progress of the colonies advanced toleration. Trade tended to distract colonies from their absorbing preoccupation with and exclusiveness in the matter of religion and encouraged their thinking relatively less of the Church and more of the State and of commerce. The colonists began, in turn, to see the enormous advantage commerce would derive from liberty.[65] By way of illustration: The two greatest commercial powers of the seventeenth century, England and Holland, were those that showed the largest measure of religious tolerance in their colonial laws. The laws were still very inadequate, but in comparison with their greatest rival, Spain, these two countries were progressive, and their history indicates clearly that foreign trade during the colonial period constituted one or the major influences encouraging religious freedom.

Chapter 2

FACTORS FOR RELIGIOUS FREEDOM IN THE REVOLUTIONARY AND EARLY NATIONAL PERIODS

The Effect of Political Independence and Democracy

The achievement of political independence and the establishment of a democratic form of government in this country were major factors in promoting religious freedom and in securing the legal separation of Church and State. The Protestant churches no longer looked to Europe for authority, and in due time all American churches except the Roman Catholic became entirely autonomous. It was inevitable that they should adopt forms of government that were largely democratic in character. Even the Roman Catholic Church, sometimes unwillingly, was obliged by circumstances to place some responsibility on the laity, although not in matters strictly ecclesiastical. The doctrine embedded in the Declaration of Independence and in other American charters of liberty laid emphasis not only on the worth of the individual but on the individual's right to determine his own views and to act in accordance with the dictates of conscience.

It is true that the ideas of religious freedom developed by Roger Williams and other American thinkers stimulated ideas of political freedom, but it is equally true that when political freedom was achieved it tended to encourage religious freedom still more. Democracy in matters political could not justify any exclusive Church-State connection in this country. All religious groups that observed the law must be treated alike. They could be impartially encouraged by the State, but the State must have nothing to do with their administration. The forces tending to the legal separation of ecclesiastical and political functions in all activities of government were beginning to be overwhelming.

Independence released all the churches from many bonds and gave them new opportunities. Their policies were no longer controlled by the State, either through subsidies, through hampering restrictions, or—except in rare cases— by unequal laws. Now they had to make their own decisions and support their own work. They were all to be treated alike, without fear or favor, as long as they observed the laws and showed sympathy with our form of government. Free men could now have free institutions of their own making in the field of religion.

The Effect of the Quebec Act (1774)

The act of Parliament supplementing and correcting the Treaty of Paris of 1763, which ended the Seven Years' War and ceded Canada, with about sixty thousand French Canadians, to Great Britain, is the most significant official declaration involving religious toleration covering a large area of the continent prior to American independence. Roman Catholics were granted the free exercise of their religion and much the same rights, including the collection of tithes, which they had enjoyed under the French when Canada (including most of our present Northwest) was almost entirely a Catholic country. Indeed, "the religion of the Church of Rome" was given such favorable treatment as to cause many intolerant outbursts and a good deal of resentment among Puritans and Anglicans in the thirteen colonies, who feared the effect on their own Protestant traditions.

The act was interpreted in Protestant America as an "establishment" of the Roman Catholic religion in Canada, and Alexander Hamilton, in opposing it, made much of this attitude. In British government circles and among Catholics in the United States it was generally defended rather as an act of toleration and freedom. The wording shows that it was probably intended to be both, but in reality it was not completely either. The Roman Catholics could continue to get their old tithes, and this fact was emphasized, but the government was also authorized, though this was secondary, to apply government funds "towards the encouragement of the Protestant religion." [1]

The attitude of that leader among American Revolutionary patriots, Samuel Adams, may be taken as characteristic. In an address to the Mohawk Indians, he said,

Brothers,—They have made a law to establish the religion of the Pope in Canada, which lies so near you. We much fear some of your children may be induced, instead of worshipping the only true God, to pay his dues to images made with their own hands.[2]

There were many protests. The most important early one is found in the Suffolk County resolutions of September, 1774, which contain some of the anti-Catholic sentiments to appear a month later in the "Address to the People of Great Britain" and the "Petition to the King." [3] It read,

That the late act of parliament for establishing the Roman Catholic Religion and the French laws in that extensive country, now called Canada, is dangerous in an extreme degree to the Protestant religion and to the civil rights and liberties of all Americans; and, therefore, as men and Protestant Christians, we are indispensably obliged to take all proper measures for our security.[4]

The most significant protests, however, were those drawn up by the Continental Congress, which began its sessions in Philadelphia in September, 1774. In October it adopted resolutions asserting the rights of the colonies and enumerating the acts of Parliament which were considered "infringements and violations of the foregoing rights." Among these was the act passed

. . . for establishing the Roman Catholic Religion in the province of Quebec, abolishing the equitable system of English laws, and erecting a tyranny there, to the great danger, from so total a dissimilarity of Religion, law, and government of the neighboring British colonies, by the assistance of whose blood and treasure the said country was conquered from France.[5]

The "Address to the People of Great Britain" adopted by the Congress on October 26 referred to many grievances, among them the following:

That we think the Legislature of Great-Britain is not authorized by the constitution to establish a religion, fraught with sanguinary and impious tenets, or, to erect an arbitrary form of government, in any quarter of the globe. These rights, we, as well as you, deem sacred. And yet sacred as they are, they have, with many others been repeatedly and flagrantly violated. . . .[6]

This matter was again referred to in a petition of Congress "To the King's most excellent majesty" adopted in October. Various alleged illegal acts of the British government are mentioned, including.

. . . a fourth for extending the limits of Quebec, abolishing the English and restoring the French laws, whereby great numbers of British freemen are subjected to the latter, and establishing an absolute government and the Roman Catholic religion throughout those vast regions, that border on the westerly and northerly boundaries of the free protestant English settlements. . . .[7]

Although the Quebec Act was bitterly opposed by the inhabitants of the thirteen colonies at the time of its promulgation, as they feared that Quebec's "popish slaves" would be used to overthrow the ideas of civil and religious liberty which were growing apace in most of the colonies, later it was without doubt a factor in determining the liberal policy regarding religion which marked the great Ordinance of 1787 for the government of the Northwest. The Quebec Act is considered today to have been on the whole a wise and farsighted one on the part of a dominantly Protestant nation in dealing with the large Roman Catholic population of an important province.

One aspect of the controversy around the Quebec Act is of particular significance in this study of Church-State relations. Seventeen years after the act, the people of the United States were to adopt the First Amendment to their Constitution, with its provision that "Congress shall make no law respecting an establishment of religion." The meaning of the word "establishment" has been the subject of considerable debate.[8] The Quebec Act did not seek to displace the Anglican Church as the paramount church of Canada but merely granted Roman Catholicism certain benefits such as freedom of religion and the right to collect tithes from Catholics. Yet the widespread opposition to it among the colonies that were shortly to become the United States was based on the claim that thereby the Roman Catholic Church was "established." It seems quite clear that during the last quarter of the eighteenth century the term "establish" had a far broader meaning than merely according monopolistic or even preferential treatment to one church or sect over others, and encompassed a tax for religion even though it was collected only from persons adhering to that religion.

The Effect of French Thought

The direct political influence of France on the form of our government was probably not as great as was previously thought. A study of the chronology is revealing. It was only on June 17, 1789, that the Third Estate declared itself a National Assembly; on July 14 of that year that the Bastille was destroyed; and in the following month that the Declaration of the Rights of Man and of Citizen was adopted; whereas the Constitutional Convention in this country met and drafted our Constitution in the summer of 1787; its formal ratification was announced by Congress on September 13, 1788; and the Bill of Rights received Senate approval on September 25, 1789. Indeed, it was the bill of rights of the various American states that mainly influenced the French Declaration.

And yet the French influences were considerable. France supplied cumulative evidence in the last half of the eighteenth century of the dangers of absolute monarchy and of the union of Church and State, and of the need to place the electorate on a broader basis and to fit government to play a more socially progressive part in a new age. Furthermore, at least three French writers had a strong impact on early American political thought: Montesquieu, Rousseau, and Condorcet.

French philosophic skepticism had a great effect in weakening the orthodox churches and in efforts to form a creedless "national religion" here. This movement goes back to Benjamin Franklin, who had reacted against orthodoxy not only in theology but in many other fields, and who consequently formed a bridge between the liberalism brewing in French philosophical and religious thought and the thinking of the new republic. When the seniors in Yale College debated in 1785 "Whether Infidels and Libertines in Morals ought to be admitted into Civil Magistracy," they doubtless had in mind both France and the questions of religious liberty being discussed in the new states.[9]

The Illuminati of New England, who were believed to have some connection with Masonry, formed a group much influenced by French philosophy. Among them were some ministers of religion interested in liberal thought and in breaking the bond between Congregationalism and the State. The Columbian Illuminati of New York, sometimes known as the Clintonian Faction, were closely related to the New England Illuminati. So was the Society of Ancient Druids, formed by a group of apostate Masons. Perhaps the most characteristic manifestation of the Illuminati was the holding of a meeting in New York in 1804 to promote the building of a "Temple of Nature." Its advocates stated: "While so many altars are raised to advance the cause of superstition, it will be a pity indeed if one cannot be reared in honor of the true and living God, and to promote the exalted cause of a pure and incorruptible morality!"[10]

All these movements of freethinkers were closely related to French Deism, which had some popular support in the early days of the republic because of its repudiation of all forms of Calvinistic election and its belief in the equality of all men. It tended to strengthen the rationalistic as distinct from the evangelistic wing of Protestantism.

Jefferson and Franklin had done much to make the liberal French point of view regarding religion and government known in this country, but perhaps the three men most identified in the public mind with its more radical aspects were Thomas Paine, author of *The Age of Reason*, Ethan Allen, who wrote the *Compendious System of Natural Religion*, and Elihu Palmer. Palmer was violently anti-clerical and an ardent Republican who tried without success to make Deism the popular religion. He was a leader in founding the Deistical Society of the State of New York, which advocated a return to the laws of nature.[11]

Deism as a skeptical attitude of mind rather than as a creed was prominent at several institutions of learning through the first decade of the nineteenth century—that is, until there came a realization of the extreme consequences of the lack of vital religion resulting from the French Revolution, and until the Great Revival (1797-1805), a constructive movement in the interest of religion and democracy in spite of its emotional excesses, had exerted its profound influence.

The Effect of Soldiers' and Chaplains' Experience in the Revolutionary Army

The soldiers who served in the Revolutionary Army broadened their outlook with reference to both their own denomination and their political allegiance. They came in contact with men of different religious bodies from different parts of the country and gained respect for them. They increasingly felt that they were fighting not for their colony only but for the united colonies which were to form a new nation. Massachusetts Congregationalists, Rhode Island Baptists, New York Episcopalians and Dutch Reformed, New Jersey Presbyterians, Pennsylvania members of many small Protestant sects with a continental background, Maryland Roman Catholics, and a scattering of Jews from the seaboard cities, to give a few examples, met in the same camps and acquired a new idea of the need and possibility of religious tolerance. Such an intermingling of men of different religious faiths and backgrounds had not taken place before in America except in a few of the larger cities, and in three or four small colleges that had broken away, at least in actual practice, from rather narrow local and denominational antecedents. Furthermore, soldiers visiting sections of the emerging independent nation could not fail to be impressed by what they saw of the contributions to social life of such differing groups as Quakers, Lutherans, Congregationalists, and Anglicans.

The contribution of the chaplains to these results was important. Detached from their own local church, they developed a sense of responsibility for all the men in their regiment and rendered a large service. Whatever may be the other effects of serving as a chaplain, there can be no doubt that it tends to broaden a man's outlook and to break down narrow denominationalism. In some states, such as Virginia, action was early taken opening the regimental chaplaincies, which had been established in 1758 at the request of Colonel George Washington, not only to members of the Establishment but to other religious bodies, a movement taken largely at the instigation of the Baptists.[12]

As far as a continental or Federal, as distinct from the colonial, system of chaplains is concerned, the legal origin of the corps of chaplains is found in the resolutions of the Continental Congress in July, 1775, providing that their pay be twenty dollars a month, the same as then provided for captains.[13] The following year chaplains were specifically authorized by General Washington, who was emphatic in his belief that religion and public worship were essential to morale both in civil and in military life.[14]

The Practical Needs of the Situation

The actual situation in the states at the beginning of the national period made further guarantees of religious freedom essential. It is estimated that from 1776 to 1820 nearly 250,000 immigrants came to the United States.[15] This influx, although small in comparison with the movement that set in after the War of 1812, was nonetheless highly significant from our standpoint, especially as it included a considerable number of Roman Catholics, some Jews, and representatives of many other religious groups from nearly all parts of Europe. The realization grew that the United States, partly because it was a new country with vast resources, partly because of its democratic form of government, and partly because of hard conditions of life in certain European areas, would attract constantly increasing numbers of immigrants, and that they were needed for the development of the country. In view of the increasingly variegated character of its population, the nation must have religious freedom.

Turning from without to within, we find the situation equally significant. It was manifestly impossible under existing conditions to have a Federal Congregational Church, even should some extremists in New England want it, or a Federal Episcopal Church, even if some Southern Episcopalians had thought it desirable. The only way Congregationalists, Presbyterians, Baptists, and Episcopalians, the four largest colonial groups, in the order named, as well as Mennonites, Quakers, Dutch Reformed, Roman Catholics, Jews, Methodists, Lutherans, and others, could unite in forming a Federal government was on the basis of religious freedom.

It will be seen then, that, leaving out of account for the moment the influence of the theories of European and American philosophers and various historical factors, the actual, practical necessities of the situation at the end of the eighteenth century in the United States could not be met by a State Church or even by mere toleration on the part of the dominant Protestants of other religious groups. Complete religious freedom, as long as it did not involve acts contrary to the safety of the State or public morals, was clearly indicated as the only possible solution. The mere fact that new religious denominations could be established at will without government approval would of itself prevent much criticism by those dissatisfied with existing conditions and would tend to create a spirit of good will.

The Influence of the Churches During and Immediately After the Revolution

At the beginning of the American Revolution nine out of the thirteen colonies had an Established Church. During its course some progress was made in the direction of separation and religious freedom by the newly organized states. At its close, when the Constitutional Convention was meeting in Philadelphia in 1787, all the New England states except Rhode Island retained what was virtually established Congregationalism; Maryland and South Carolina continued their Church of England connection, which had just been given up by Virginia, North Carolina, and Georgia; Rhode Island, Pennsylvania, and Delaware had never had any Established Church; and New York and New Jersey retained only vestiges of their former connection with the Episcopal and Dutch Reformed Churches.[16]

When we consider the matter of religious tests,[17] which was the only religious matter definitely dealt with at the Federal Constitutional Convention, we find them as a qualification for office held over from colonial times by many of the original thirteen states. Maryland and Massachusetts required a belief "in the Christian religion." [18] Georgia, New Hampshire, New Jersey, and North Carolina had Protestant tests. The most theological was in Delaware, where the requirement adopted in 1776 included "faith in God the Father, and in Jesus Christ, His only Son, and in the Holy Ghost, One God, blessed forever more." Some of the states had further requirements as to belief in the inspiration of the Bible, and one, Pennsylvania, demanded the belief that God was "the rewarder of the good and the punisher of the wicked."

As to the general attitude toward religion and religious freedom which prevailed in this country in its formative years, there is evidence to the effect that in spite of much indifference toward regular attendance at public worship both were held in high regard and indeed considered indispensable for the rising republic. However, the trend of developments in the church situation at the time the government was formed can be understood only as we have a clear picture of the attitude of the churches toward the colonial cause during the preceding Revolutionary period.

With the exception of the Anglicans, who had taken an oath of allegiance to the king, the major religious bodies supported the colonial cause.[19] Among the Protestants, three groups of ministers were specially active in backing the Revolution: the Congregationalists of New England,[20] the Presbyterians of the middle colonies,[21] and the Baptists generally.[22] Although the Episcopal clergy (including the Methodists who were still under Episcopal aegis) generally opposed it,[23] the laity, especially in Virginia and South Carolina, included some of the most influential patriots. The Lutherans have a strong tradition of Church and State separation and have in the past been inclined to leave political matters severely alone. During the American Revolution, the Lutheran churches on the whole seem to have preserved their traditional attitude of aloofness from civil strife. There were exceptions, however, particularly among the Muhlenberg family, who ardently supported the Revolution.[24]

Although the Roman Catholic clergy as such took little active part in promoting the patriotic cause, Catholics were sympathetic to it. There were practically no Tories among them. This fact is the more remarkable in view of the anti-Catholic feeling which had always been latent and which had been lashed into a good deal of a fury by the Quebec Act.[25]

At the beginning of the Revolution Jews in the United States were counted by the hundreds, rather than by many thousands. Their total did not reach ten thousand until well after its close, but about one hundred men served in the American army or navy. On the whole they had been well treated in their principal settlements, Newport, Rhode Island, New York City, Philadelphia, and Charleston, South Carolina; therefore most of their leaders decided to support the colonies, realizing that the cause of American democracy and of religious freedom went hand in hand.[26]

The New Faith in Humanity

The idea of progress, which had become so dominant toward the close of the eighteenth century, should be added to the factors contributing to the development of complete religious freedom in the United States. This idea was due largely to the Enlightenment, which assumed not only the worth and potentiality of man but his right to do his own thinking; it held out a glorious future for humanity if it would only work intelligently toward its goal. In fact, as has often been pointed out, the Enlightenment really constituted a new religious faith, with human progress as its goal. A movement for the enfranchisement of the human spirit and the attainment of great new social ends for the world was in the air.

Paine's writings gave recognition to these ideas and introduced them to the public at large, as did, to a more limited group, those of Joel Barlow, especially his *Columbiad* (1807). This took the ground that human nature and human institutions had an amazing opportunity for fresh, untrammeled development in America, if the effort were only made with sufficient earnestness and intelligence. Barlow saw in his vision of democracy in the new land "the last ascending steps of the creating God." [27]

Faith in progress was enormously stimulated by the fact that the United States was a virgin continent as far as Western civilization was concerned. Here were vast areas which none but the Indians had ever known. The mere size of the continent, its plains, mountains, lakes and rivers, forests, waterfalls, minerals, fertile lands—what we call today natural resources—all gave a sense of latent power and made the settlers feel that they had an opportunity to do creative work of a new character. This was strengthened by the inherited conviction of Puritans that New England was a New Canaan and that here they might work out their religious ideals. The citizens of the emerging United States were virtually all Christians. They differed much in matters of Church membership and loyalty, in theological belief, and even, especially in the middle colonies, in national background, but they were one in their realization that God was their Father and they were His children, that there was in all of them a spark of the divine life which made them capable of great things if they would live worthy of their birthright.

And so, through a combination of the ideas of the Enlightenment and the ideals of the Christian religion, together with the fact of the unspoiled land that lay around them, and the absence of most of the hampering bonds of an old civilization, they could start out on a new experiment in community living. One of its major features would be a fair field and no special favor for any religious body, with the old causes of jealousy due to favoritism removed and with an opportunity for religious groups to dwell together in peace with much mutual sympathy and cooperation.

The Statesmen and Religious Leaders Interested in Religious Freedom

No list of the more important factors which produced the American system of Church-State separation—one of the distinctive contributions of America to the idea of government—would be complete without some reference to the extraordinary group of statesmen in America in the last third of the eighteenth century, and especially from 1775 to 1790. These men, and a few farsighted ministers of religion who supported them, were convinced that the emerging Federal government should have no connection with any Church and that religious freedom should prevail. There were a dozen or more such men whose ability and vision it would be hard to match in one country in any other time in history. Several of them, notably Jefferson, Madison, Mason, and Pinckney, knew the history of political philosophy and government in different parts of the world. They had liberal ideas of freedom of conscience and its demands based on the theory of the natural rights of men. It is no exaggeration to say that their contribution in bringing about the separation of Church and State, first in Virginia, then in the United States, with its resulting religious freedom, was epoch making.

In contrast with the leaders of the same cause in the colonial period, the majority of the new group were not from New England; about half were from the South—five out of thirteen from the one state of Virginia. The Episcopal Church, which was not represented in the earlier group, now comes to the front with its laymen—Baptist ministers taking second place.

The new names are thirteen in number, beginning with Benjamin Franklin, who may be considered a link with the colonial leaders treated in the previous chapter. They are Benjamin Franklin, nominal Episcopalian with Presbyterian background, Deist in belief; John Witherspoon, Presbyterian; George Mason, Episcopalian; Isaac Backus, Baptist; George Washington, Episcopalian; Patrick Henry, Episcopalian, with Presbyterian affiliations; Samuel Livermore, Episcopalian; Thomas Paine, Deist; John Carroll, Roman Catholic; Thomas Jefferson, nominal Episcopalian, Deist in belief; James Madison, Episcopalian; Charles Pinckney, Episcopalian; John Leland, Baptist.

BENJAMIN FRANKLIN

Franklin is broadly known for his services as a discoverer and inventor, especially of the lightning rod; for his philanthropic efforts in promoting hospitals, libraries, and schools of learning, especially the University of Pennsylvania; for his scientific leadership in many fields, culminating in his establishing the American Philosophical Association; for his distinguished work as author, editor, and printer; for his career as diplomat and statesman; for his ethical maxims; and for his outstanding work as a citizen of Philadelphia. But his contribution to the American ideal of religious toleration has seldom been emphasized. He was not influential, in the sense that Madison and Jefferson were, in bringing about the constitutional separation of Church and State in the United States. His attitude was a factor of importance in the struggle, however, and, though he wrote relatively little on the subject, he was known to be a supporter of religion, an opponent of an Established Church, and a believer in religious freedom.[28]

His lack of dogmatism and ecclesiasticism, along with his faith in God and his righteous conduct, led to his becoming very active in Freemasonry, a movement which did much to bring about religious toleration in this country, especially among different Protestant groups and between Protestants and Jews. Closely related was his interest in forming, in 1728, the Philadelphia club known as the Junto, suggested by Mather's *Essays to Do Good*. In an address before it he broached his ideal of having different religious exponents work together to advance human welfare.

His *Parable Against Persecution*, first published in 1764, is a classic. It was an adaptation by Franklin of an ancient Persian story. He had it printed and incorporated in his copy of the Bible and frequently read it to his friends, who were discomfited by not recognizing the insertion of what purported to be the fifty-first chapter of the Book of Genesis. In the parable Abraham rebukes a stranger for not worshiping "the most high God" in the accepted Hebrew manner. He later repents when God asks, "Couldst not thou, that art thyself a sinner, bear with him one night?" Abraham replies, "Lo, I have sinned, forgive me, I pray thee." As a result, God changes His threatened affliction of his descendants into a blessing. The brief chapter—only fifteen verses—well deserves reading.[29]

Franklin's views of the importance of the independence of Church and State are characteristically expressed in a letter written in 1780: "When a religion is good, I conceive that it will support itself; and, when it cannot support itself, and God does not take care to support it, so that its professors are obliged to call for the help of the civil power, it is a sign, I apprehend, of its being a bad one. . . ."[30]

JOHN WITHERSPOON

This patriot-educator-theologian did much by his temper of mind and work to encourage the cause of freedom and to adjust his great Church to conditions in a democracy. Before coming to America, Witherspoon had rendered yeoman service in Scotland in defending the right of the people to choose their own ministers and in opposing the theory of a State Church. He came to this country in 1768 to accept the presidency of the College of New Jersey and from his Princeton home soon identified himself with the patriot cause, serving in the Continental Congress and effectively urging there the cause of independence.[31]

Witherspoon was forever preaching that mere toleration was not enough, for that implied superiority and condescension; the only proper principle for a republic was complete liberty to worship how one chose or not at all. He believed that every church should be supported by its own members or funds without help from the taxing power of the State. His pupils, among whom James Madison was conspicuous, were always to be found on the side of religious liberty.[32]

A remarkable letter written by Witherspoon opposed a constitutional provision in Georgia for the exclusion of clergymen from certain public offices.[33] It was contrary to his idea of religious freedom that a citizen, merely because he happened to be a clergyman, should be prevented from public service if he conscientiously felt that this was his duty. Even more, his theory of the separation of Church and State led him to think, such a regulation involving the clergy as such was a matter that should be the result of public opinion acting through an ecclesiastical assembly, not a political one.

GEORGE MASON

This liberal churchman and publicist, one of the outstanding figures in the story of religious freedom in America, wrote the Declaration of Rights of Virginia and most of the state constitution. The former was of particular significance since it formed the basis on which the other states and the Federal government itself took action to guarantee religious freedom. It was drawn upon by Thomas Jefferson for the first part of the Declaration of Independence and was later the foundation of the Federal Bill of Rights. The clause regarding religious liberty, as originally drafted by Mason, reads,

That religion, or the duty which we owe to our Creator, and the manner of discharging it, can be directed only by reason and conviction, not by force or violence; and, therefore, that all men should enjoy the fullest toleration in the exercise of religion, according to the dictates of conscience, unpunished and unrestrained by the magistrate, unless, under color of religion, any man disturb the peace, the happiness, or the safety of society. And that it is the mutual duty of all to practise Christian forbearance, love, and charity towards each other.[34]

James Madison objected to the word "toleration," as implying a system in which "the free exercise of religion was permissive, instead of an unquestioned natural right." [35] Madison's intention, as he tells us, was "to substitute for the idea expressed by the term 'toleration' an absolute and equal right in all to the exercise of religion according to the dictates of conscience."[36] He also objected to the clause giving the courts power to punish one who disturbed the peace in the practice of his religion, proposing as a substitute,

That religion, or the duty we owe to our Creator, and the manner of discharging it, being under the direction of reason or conviction only, not of violence or compulsion, all men are equally entitled to the full and free exercise of it, according to the dictates of conscience, and, therefore, that no men or class of men ought, on account of religion, to be invested with peculiar emoluments or privileges, nor subjected to any penalties or disabilities unless under color of religion, the preservation of equal liberty and the existence of the state be manifestly endangered.[37]

This clause was further modified by the committee of the whole and, as finally adopted by the Convention in June, 1776, included the first and last portions of Mason's original draft verbatim and the middle section somewhat altered:

That religion, or the duty which we owe to our Creator, and the manner of discharging it, can be directed only by reason and conviction, not by force or violence, and therefore all men are equally entitled to the free exercise of religion, according to the dictates of conscience; and that it is the mutual duty of all to practise Christian forbearance, love, and charity towards each other.[38]

When the Virginia Assembly first met under the state constitution, it took steps to put into definite law the provisions of the Virginia Declaration of Rights regarding religious liberty. George Mason very naturally was chosen as chairman of the committee appointed to prepare a suitable act. This was the second law adopted by the Virginia legislature under its constitution, indicating the priority that the people accorded to religious freedom. It contained six provisions, as follows: (1) Every act of Parliament penalizing opinion in matters of religion, requiring attendance or non-attendance at church, or prescribing any mode of worship is declared void. (2) All dissenters, of whatever denomination, are to be wholly free and exempt from any tax for the maintenance of the church established by law. (3) The vestries are permitted to levy assessments on all, including dissenters, to pay for salaries of ministers for services which had already been rendered, and also to be able to continue to take care of the poor of the parish as in the past. (4) The lands and personal property which had already been given over to the Established Church were to be retained by them. (5) Because of the great variety of opinion as to the propriety of a general assessment for religion or whether every religious society should be left exclusively to voluntary contributions for the support of its ministers and teachers, and because an agreement at that time could not be achieved, the question is left open for future determination. (6) However, since exemption of dissenters would impose an unbearable burden upon the non-dissenting parishioners if they were required to maintain the ministers on the basis of the salaries fixed by Parliament, the act of Parliament is temporarily suspended.[39]

Mason, a frequent and effective speaker in the Federal Constitutional Convention of Philadelphia, did not sign the Constitution because of what he believed to be certain defects. These were, notably, the recognition given by the Constitution to slavery, which he considered "diabolical in itself and disgraceful to mankind," and the omission of a bill of rights. It took more than two generations for the first error to be corrected, but the second was promptly remedied in the first group of amendments proposed by Congress in 1789.

ISAAC BACKUS

Isaac Backus, though little known even to the intelligent public today, was one of the small band of fearless, farsighted men living in the Revolutionary period to whom we owe our religious freedom. Indeed, he is considered by some to be the greatest advocate of the cause in the country since Roger

Williams. Profoundly influenced by the preaching of Whitefield in the Great Awakening, he early showed his lifelong opposition to all ideas of Church-State connection by refusing to pay a tax of five pounds toward the support of the Massachusetts standing order, Congregationalism. In 1770 he wrote *A Seasonable Plea for Liberty of Conscience*, and the following year *A Letter to a Gentleman in the Massachusetts General Assembly Concerning Taxes to Support Religious Worship*. He became increasingly interested in the cause of freeing the Church from all forms of State or civil control. From 1772 on, he served as the agent of the Warren Association in Massachusetts to deal with relations with the state and to present clearly the grievances of Baptists. In 1773 he published *An Appeal to the Public for Religious Liberty*, opposing the blending of civil and ecclesiastical authority in his state. He followed this by *The Exact Limits between Civil and Ecclesiastical Government, True Policy requires Equal Religious Liberty, A Door opened for Christian Liberty*, and other works.[40] These all contributed effectively to the cause of religious freedom through their advocacy of entire separation of Church and State.

As representative of the Warren Association, an influential group of New England Baptists, he pleaded the cause of the Baptists from pulpit and platform.[41] He fought strongly against any form of establishment, and especially taxes to support the Established Church. In 1774 he wrote a strong letter to the Massachusetts Assembly protesting the Baptist grievances in the state and saying that they were much more serious than the three-penny tax on tea, which anyone could avoid by abstaining from tea drinking.[42] It was an application of the taxation-without-representation plea which he often used in the field of church support. In the same year John Adams, a defender of the Massachusetts Congregationalist establishment, stated of the Congregationalists that "we might as well expect a change in the solar system, as to expect they would give up their establishment." [43]

Undaunted, Backus continued the battle. In 1776 the Warren Association, acting under his stimulus, presented to the Massachusetts Assembly a resolution on the subject of religious freedom in which it stated,

That the Representatives in former Assemblies, as well as the present, were elected by virtue only of civil and worldly qualifications, is a truth so evident, that we presume it need not be proved to this Assembly; and for a civil Legislature to impose religious taxes, is, we conceive, a power which their constituents never had to give; and is therefore going entirely out of their jurisdiction.[44]

In 1787 he journeyed to Philadelphia to present his views before the Constitutional Convention. Representing the New England Baptists, he urged that provision be made for liberty of conscience and for protection against taxation demands of a State Church. Chosen a delegate to the Massachusetts convention called in 1788 to consider ratifying the Federal Constitution, he ardently defended the provision in the Constitution barring religious tests for public office.

Nothing is more evident, both in reason, and in the holy scriptures, than that religion is ever a matter between God and individuals; and therefore no men or man can impose any religious test, without invading the essential prerogatives of our Lord Jesus Christ. Ministers first assumed this power under the Christian name; and then Constantine approved of the practice, when he adopted the profession of Christianity, as an engine of state policy. And let the history of all nations be searched, from that day to this, and it will appear that the imposing of religious tests hath been the greatest engine of tyranny in the world.[45]

GEORGE WASHINGTON

Washington's major contribution to the cause of religious freedom came after the establishment of our government, and he should be considered a supporter of this movement rather than one who played an important part in initiating it prior to the adoption of our constitutional guarantees. Indeed, in an earlier time he had favored the assessment plan in Virginia by which the state would make contributions to the various Christian denominations, although he gave up his support when he found that the plan was becoming a cause of friction and acrimonious debate.[46]

His primary interests in religion as far as the nation was concerned were twofold: that the citizens should recognize its importance and that in the interest of harmony all religions should be treated alike by the State. He manifested these convictions by his own life, involving loyal attachment to the Episcopal Church in which he had been brought up, a tolerant spirit in all matters that had to do with religion and the churches, and a strict observance in all his public relations of the religious freedom and Church-State guarantees of the Constitution.

PATRICK HENRY

Patrick Henry did not speak as frequently of religious liberty as he did of civil liberty, yet he made substantial contributions to the former cause, seeing clearly that the two types of liberty were closely related. He was definitely opposed both to any Church's having an exclusive State position and to the British government's interfering in any way in Virginia's affairs involving religion. This attitude first came prominently to the fore in 1763, when, in the Parson's case,[47] he represented a Virginia vestry outraged by the union of the Episcopal clergy with the king in council in trying to thwart the will of the people in the matter of commuting the payment of salaries to the clergy in a way authorized by the Assembly. His advocacy of this somewhat complicated case began his deep interest both in weakening the strangle hold of the Episcopal clergy and in freeing Virginia's religious life from any link with the British crown.

Henry was particularly interested in securing freedom for Baptists and Presbyterians. He was brought up in the Episcopal Church, but his mother had come from a Presbyterian home, and Henry frequently attended Presbyterian services. He was much drawn to the preaching of the Reverend Samuel Davies, whose views on religious liberty undoubtedly influenced him, since he attended Davies' church from his eleventh to his twenty-second year.[48] In several cases Henry paid the fines of ministers imprisoned for conscience's sake and defended them in the courts. It was he who, petitioned by the Baptists, secured permission from the Virginia convention in August, 1775, for their ministers and those of other dissenting groups to preach to the troops.[49] He had about him no element of denominational narrowness and was clear in his opposition to a State Church. On the other hand, he differed from many of the liberal men of his time in favoring the proposed general assessment "for the support of the Christian religion" in Virginia which Madison and Mason fortunately prevented in 1785. This seems to have been his one serious lapse as an advocate of religious freedom. It should be remembered, however, that the proposal did not discriminate among Christian groups; further, Washington's letter indicating that in theory he had no strong objection to it shows that, if it passed, Jews and other non-Christians were to be allowed to obtain "proper relief." [50]

Henry favored adoption of the clause in the Virginia Bill of Rights, drafted by George Mason, to secure religious freedom.[51] He strongly opposed adoption of the Federal Constitution in absence of a bill of rights guaranteeing civil and religious freedom. He refused to be satisfied by the assurances of the proponents of the Constitution that by reason and logic no such express guarantee was needed. "This sacred right," he said, "ought not to depend on constructive, logical reasoning." [52] He prepared a resolution, consisting of a declaration of rights, and announced that if this or a similar declaration were adopted he would approve ratification of the Constitution, but not otherwise. Ultimately, a declaration substantially the same as that proposed by Henry was adopted by the Virginia convention.

SAMUEL LIVERMORE

Probably no other name included in this list of men who contributed to the cause of religious freedom is so little known to the public as that of Livermore. Yet Livermore provided the original proposal which was made the basis of

Congressional debate on religious freedom guarantees, referred to in the records of Congress as "Livermore's motion." He also supplied the main ideas and some of the wording of the First Amendment to the Federal Bill of Rights and promoted religious freedom in other ways.

Livermore first came to national attention in 1781 as a delegate to Congress, empowered to act for New Hampshire in the matter of the boundary dispute with Vermont. He became chief justice of the state in 1784, though he had little legal learning or knowledge of the details of law or of legal procedure. He again represented New Hampshire in Congress in 1785, 1789 and 1791.

An assembly or convention was held in Exeter, New Hampshire, in February, 1788, to decide whether the state should ratify the proposed Federal Constitution. As eight states had already voted in its favor and one more was needed, the session was crucial. Livermore served as chairman of the committee on amendments, proposing a dozen. His motion prevailed to the effect "That in case the Constitution be adopted, that the amendments reported by the committee be recommended to Congress." [53] Of these the eleventh was the highly important one: "Congress shall make no laws touching religion or to infringe the rights of Conscience." [54] After the reading of the report by Judge Livermore and its consideration by the convention we are told that it "was received and accepted." [55] This means that Judge Livermore, who seems to have been the most influential man both in the committee on amendments and in the assembly itself, was mainly responsible for putting his state squarely on record in favor of religious freedom.

Judge Livermore's most important contribution was, however, to come later. He was a member of Congress when it proposed various amendments to the Constitution and, undoubtedly recalling the action of the state of New Hampshire in committing itself to the cause of religious freedom, he made an effective fight for this principle.[56] When religious-freedom guarantees were under discussion, a matter in which James Madison had long been specially interested, the latter proposed that the amendment might read "no national religion shall be established by law, nor shall the rights of conscience be infringed." This bears some resemblance to a proposal by Charles Pinckney at the Constitutional Convention of 1787.

There follow in the journal of Congress two significant entries: "Mr. Livermore was not satisfied with that amendment; but he did not wish them to dwell long on the subject. He thought it would be better if it was altered, and made to read in this manner, that Congress shall make no laws touching religion, or infringing the rights of conscience." This, it will be noticed, is in its first half a more inclusive prohibition than that proposed by Madison, and it had an important influence on the ultimate wording of the First Amendment.

Livermore wished to prevent not only a national Church but also the adoption of any Federal laws touching religion. Some remarks by Mr. Gerry followed, criticizing Mr. Madison's proposal, principally because he considered the government a federal rather than a national one. Then comes this epoch-making entry: "Mr. Madison withdrew his motion, but observed that the words 'no national religion shall be established by law,' did not imply that the government was a national one; the question was then taken on Mr. Livermore's motion, and passed in the affirmative, thirty-one for, and twenty against it." [57] And so the general form which the religious-freedom guarantee later took in our Federal Bill of Rights was largely due to Samuel Livermore.

Madison, by his "Remonstrance" to the Virginia legislature in 1785, and Jefferson, by his "Bill for Establishing Religious Freedom" in Virginia, 1786, were the spiritual fathers of the First Amendment guaranteeing religious freedom, and Madison was responsible for bringing the matter effectively before the first session of Congress. Many minds played their part in the Congressional and committee discussions, but it was Livermore's proposal which, according to the official records, formed the actual basis of the final action.

THOMAS PAINE

Thomas Paine vigorously attacked what he believed to be the errors in the Bible and in commonly accepted forms of Christianity, and advocated Deism. He favored liberty and opposed all forms of religious oppression, but his contribution to the cause of religious freedom as distinct from civil freedom was indirect. It came mainly from his passionate desire to set men free from the inherited tyrannies of orthodox views of political absolutism and ecclesiastical religion. As a result the established churches were weakened and independence of thought was encouraged.

Perhaps Paine's clearest expression of his views on religious freedom and the relationship of Church and State were made in the year 1776. At that time, in his *Epistle to the Quakers* (he was himself of Quaker stock and a believer in a Divine Being, although out of sympathy with the idea of revealed religion) he stated that "To God, and not to man, are all men accountable on the score of religion." It was "of the utmost danger to society to make . . . [religion] a party in political disputes. . . ." [58] In the same year, in his great and enormously influential pamphlet *Common Sense,* Paine epitomized his views on the relation of religion and government in the sentence "As to religion, I hold it to be the indispensable duty of government to protect all conscientious professors thereof, and I know of no other business which government hath to do therewith." [59] It is both interesting and significant to note that this dual concept—government must protect religious liberty but otherwise not concern itself with religion—was fifteen years later to be incorporated in the Bill of Rights in the words "Congress shall make no law respecting an establishment of religion or prohibiting the free exercise thereof."

To Paine freedom of worship was a matter of right rather than of toleration. In the *Rights of Man,* published in London in 1791, largely as an answer to Burke's critical *Reflections on the French Revolution,* he wrote,

> The French Constitution hath abolished or renounced *Toleration* and *Intolerance* also, and hath established UNIVERSAL RIGHT OF CONSCIENCE.

> Toleration is not the *opposite* of Intolerance, but is the *counterfeit* of it. Both are despotisms. The one assumes to itself the right of withholding Liberty of Conscience, and the other of granting it. The one is the Pope armed with fire and faggot, and the other is the Pope selling or granting indulgence. The former is Church and State, and the latter is Church and traffic.[60]

Like so many others of his time, he was convinced that all religions are noble in their origin and purpose but become corrupted by association with government. In the same reply to Burke, who criticized the French National Assembly for refusing to unite Church and State, Paine said,

> All religions are in their nature kind and benign, and united with principles of morality. They could not have made proselytes at first by professing anything that was vicious, cruel, persecuting, or immoral. Like everything else, they had their beginning; and they proceeded by persuasion, exhortation, and example. How then is it that they lose their native mildness and become morose and intolerant?

> It proceeds from the connection which Mr. Burke recommends. By engendering the Church with the State, a sort of mule-animal, capable only of destroying, and not of breeding up, is produced, called *the Church established by Law.* It is a stranger, even from its birth, to any parent mother, on whom it is begotten, and whom in time it kicks out and destroys. . . .

> Persecution is not an original feature in any *religion*; but it is always the strongly-marked feature of all law-religions, or religions established by law. Take away the law-establishment, and every religion re-assumes its original benignity. In America, a Catholic priest is a good citizen, a good character, and a good neighbour; an Episcopalian minister is of the same description: and this proceeds independently of the men, from there being no law-establishment in America.[61]

Paine also shared the view widespread in America that union of Church and State was detrimental not only to religion but to the temporal State as well. He pointed out further in the pamphlet that

> If also we view this matter in a temporal sense, we shall see the ill-effects it has had on the prosperity of nations. The union of Church and State has impoverished Spain. The revoking the edict of Nantes drove the silk manufacture from that

country into England; and Church and State are now driving the cotton manufacture from England to America and France.[62]

For a long time Paine, notwithstanding his great contributions to the Revolutionary cause, was held low in American public opinion. Theodore Roosevelt's unfair description of him as a "filthy little atheist" represented all too accurately the public estimate.[63] However, the general standing of Paine both as a man and as a patriot has greatly improved in recent years, as evidenced by his election to the Hall of Fame in 1945. His devotion to such liberal causes as political freedom, human equality, free universal education, women's emancipation, abolition of slavery, world federation, and, although he said relatively less about it, separation of Church and State, was undoubted. In this last respect—separation of Church and State—he faithfully reflected the temper of the times in the United States, even though in the other respects he was scores of years if not more ahead of his generation.[64]

JOHN CARROLL

Some readers may question the inclusion of Archbishop Carroll among the "leaders interested in religious freedom." With the inherited tradition of the Roman Catholic Church, whose members conscientiously believe that they are the only true Church of Christ, it has not always been easy for them to advocate complete religious freedom, especially in Catholic countries. Many doubted whether they could identify themselves consistently with a movement for such freedom in the United States. Although Archbishop Carroll's specific utterances on the subject are not many, it seems right and proper that he should be included because, as the leading Catholic priest in the colonies, he was a sincere patriot believing in the Revolutionary cause. He was also a stanch supporter of the Constitution with its religious-freedom guarantees; an advocate of an American-selected hierarchy; a promoter of a Church adjusted to the needs of a democratic nation with a Protestant background by having in local affairs considerable independence of Rome, except in matters doctrinal and ecclesiastical. Finally, he was a man so tolerant that he almost never allowed criticisms of other religious bodies to pass his lips.

As a Catholic priest Carroll took the leading part in the organization of his Church in this country after the Revolution. He advocated taking away the immediate control of the American Church from London and making it independent except for its spiritual reliance on the Holy See. He was appointed prefect apostolic in 1784, being named "head of the missions in the provinces of the new Republic of the United States of North America." [65] He was a leader in the founding of Georgetown University. At a meeting of the General

Chapter of the Clergy in 1786 he urged the appointment of a bishop to be chosen by the American clergy and to be accountable directly to Rome, stating that "the representatives of the Clergy of the United States are the only proper persons to chuse the same." [66] This plea was consented to "for this time only;" [67] and in 1788 he was nominated by an assembly of twenty-six priests, all but two of whom voted for him. Carroll was consequently named by the Holy See in 1789 and was consecrated the following year in England.

In the letter to Cardinal Antonelli accepting the appointment of the position of prefect apostolic, written in February, 1786, Father Carroll calls attention to the plan adopted by the Episcopal Church to elect their own bishops and suggests that some such plan be allowed the American clergy by the Catholic Church, without their renouncing the divine authority of the Holy See. American tradition and public opinion, he thought, made some concessions of this character advisable, especially in view of the sixth of the Articles of Confederation drafted by the Continental Congress and ratified by all the states in 1781. This provided that "no one who holds any office under the United States, shall be allowed to receive any gift, office or title of any kind whatsoever from any king, prince or foreign government." Carroll was of the opinion that this prohibition extended only to those appointed to public office in the republic, but added, "it will perhaps be wrested by our opponents to apply also to ecclesiastical offices." [68]

Carroll's consecration as the first American bishop of the Roman Catholic Church was the occasion of an act highly significant of his tolerance. He was chosen to this office in 1789 but not consecrated until the following year. The delay was due partly to the confused conditions of the time, partly to the difficulties of communication, and partly to Carroll's desire to have the objectionable medieval phrase *exterminare haereticos* omitted from the enumeration of the bishop's duties in his oath of consecration. That he succeeded in accomplishing his aim was highly important for the whole future of the Church in America, for, although the clause originally seems to have meant merely to drive heretics beyond the borders of the bishop's jurisdiction, it was nonetheless objectionable in itself and sure to be misunderstood and to prejudice the Catholic cause among Americans.[69]

Carroll's views on religious freedom in the United States were summarized in a letter he wrote in 1787 answering a magazine article criticizing the Catholic faith, in which he said,

Thanks to genuine spirit and Christianity, the United States have banished intolerance from their system of government, and many of them have done the justice to every denomination of Christians, which ought to be done to them in all, of placing them on the same footing of citizenship, and conferring an equal right of participation in national privileges. Freedom and independence, acquired by the united efforts, and cemented with the mingled blood of Protestant and Catholic fellow-citizens, should be equally enjoyed by all. . . .[70]

THOMAS JEFFERSON

Roger Williams is the only person in our history who can dispute the claim of the author of the "Bill for Establishing Religious Freedom" to primacy in influence in the cause of religious liberty and Church-State separation. The sources of Jefferson's views on religious liberty included, in addition to his own independent thinking on the actual needs of the American situation, many factors such as the study of European political history and theory from the days of Greece on, the Bible, John Locke, the French philosophers, and the Presbyterians and Baptists of Virginia.

Jefferson's bill to incorporate in legislation the religious freedom guaranteed by the Virginia convention of 1776 was originally prepared in the following year, presented to the Assembly in 1779, and passed in December, 1785, being duly signed and declared law a month later.[71] The adoption of his proposal was of epoch-making significance at home and abroad, as Virginia is believed to have been the first state in the world to provide by self-imposed statute for complete religious freedom and equality. Jefferson, who was interested in religious liberty from the political more than from the religious standpoint, deserves full credit for this legislation, but it would not have been possible without the effective work along similar lines of James Madison, George Mason, and others.

At the time this and other legislation aiming at securing religious freedom and the complete separation of Church and State were under consideration, Jefferson wrote his *Notes on Virginia* (1782). In this book he gives a careful statement of his conviction that the State has no authority whatever over religious views unless and until these result in acts which endanger the commonwealth. He adds that several different churches are better than one, as a variety of religious opinions is in the interest of progress and freedom. After expressing amazement that people who have lavished their lives and fortunes for the establishment of "civil freedom" are willing to continue in "religious slavery"—and here he had the Virginia Episcopal Church-State bond especially in mind—he says,

The error seems not sufficiently eradicated, that the operations of the mind, as well as the acts of the body, are subject to the coercion of the laws. But our rulers can have no authority over such natural rights, only as we have submitted to them. The rights of conscience we never submitted, we could not submit. We are answerable for them to our God. The legitimate powers of government extend to such acts only as are injurious to others. But it does me no injury for my neighbor to say there are twenty gods, or no God.

. . . It is error alone which needs the support of government. Truth can stand by itself. Subject opinion to coercion: whom will you make your inquisitors? Fallible men; men governed by bad passions, by private as well as public reasons. And why subject it to coercion? To produce uniformity. But is uniformity of opinion desirable? No more than of face and stature. Introduce the bed of Procrustes then, and as there is danger that the large men may best the small, make us all of a size, by lopping the former and stretching the latter. Difference of opinion is advantageous to religion. The several sects perform the office of a *censor morum*.[72]

Early in his administration as president of the United States he had another opportunity to express his views on Church-State relations. Replying on January 1, 1802, to an address from a committee of the Danbury Baptist Association, of Connecticut, he wrote,

Believing with you that religion is a matter which lies solely between man and his God, that he owes account to none other for his faith or his worship, that the legislative powers of government reach actions only, and not opinions, I contemplate with sovereign reverence that act of the whole American people which declared that their legislature should "make no law respecting an establishment of religion, or prohibiting the free exercise thereof," thus building a wall of separation between Church and State. Adhering to this expression of the supreme will of the nation in behalf of the rights of conscience, I shall see with sincere satisfaction the progress of those sentiments which tend to restore to man all his natural rights, convinced he has no natural right in opposition to his social duties.[73]

His general conviction on the subject of religious freedom was clearly brought out in his second inaugural as president. He doubtless had in mind particularly his well-known objection to presidential Thanksgiving Day proclamations:

In matters of religion, I have considered that its free exercise is placed by the constitution independent of the powers of the general government. I have therefore undertaken, on no occasion, to prescribe the religious exercises suited to it; but have left them, as the constitution found them, under the direction and discipline of state or church authorities acknowledged by the several religious societies.[74]

In a letter to Albert Gallatin written in 1817 he spoke approvingly of a contemporary vote of the Pennsylvania legislature. This body rejected by a great majority, a proposition to make the belief in God a necessary qualification for office, although assuredly there was not a single atheist in it.[75]

Jefferson's devotion to the cause of religious liberty is best shown by the fact that in the epitaph he wrote for himself he listed his authorship of the

Virginia Statute for Religious Freedom as one of the three accomplishments he was most proud of, the others being his authorship of the Declaration of Independence and his founding of the University of Virginia.

That Jefferson, in spite of his strong opposition both to an Established Church and to all narrow sectarianism, had a deep respect for religion,[76] is shown by his plan for the University of Virginia. He said that "The proof of the being of a God, the Creator, Preserver, and Supreme Ruler of the Universe, the author of all the relations of morality, and the laws and obligations which these infer, will be in the province of the professor of ethics." [77] He secured works on the evidences of Christianity for the library, and in planning the buildings of the university he provided in the rotunda for a special room "for religious worship." [78] He gave his support to a proposal to invite the four major religious denominations of the state to establish independent theological schools in the immediate neighborhood of the university, with the idea that their clerical professors would be invited from time to time to preach there.[79] This project did not materialize, but the details of the plan, set forth in a letter sent in 1822, are of great interest:

In our annual report to the legislature, after stating the constitutional reasons against a public establishment of any religious instruction, we suggested the expedience of encouraging the different religious sects to establish, each for itself, a professorship of its own tenets, on the confines of the University, so near as that its students may attend lectures there, and have the free use of the library; and every other accommodation we can give them; *preserving, however, their independence of us* and each other. This fills a chasm objected to in ours as a defect in an institution professing to give instruction in all useful sciences. I think the invitation will be accepted by some sects from candid intentions and by others out of jealousy and rivalship. And by bringing the sects together, we shall soften their asperities, liberalize and neutralize their prejudices, and make the general religion a religion of peace, reason and morality.[80]

The board of visitors of the university in 1824, referring to this proposal, adopted a resolution indicating that if it were carried out, "the students of the University will be free, and expected to attend religious worship at the establishment of their respective sects, in the morning, and in time to meet their school in the University at its stated hour." [81] There was, however, to be no compulsion.[82]

Jefferson did not wish the Federal government to be tied up in any official way with Christianity. His argument against considering America a Christian nation is contained in a letter dated June 5, 1823, in which he specially denied that "Christianity is a part of the Common Law." [83] Yet, despite his vigorous and uncompromising opposition to any connection between Church and State,

Jefferson was a deeply religious if unorthodox person. He believed that civil liberties in the last analysis were dependent on religion, on belief in God. "Can the liberties of a nation," he said, "be thought secure, when we have removed their only firm basis, a conviction in the minds of the people that these liberties are the gifts of God?"[84] His emphasis in the Declaration of Independence on natural law, which recognized that man as man had inalienable rights, was based on the conviction that God was man's creator and that as a child of God he enjoyed certain capacities and privileges which human law could not take away from him. The "natural rights" of man have frequently been advocated by men who were far from orthodox, such as Thomas Jefferson and Thomas Paine, but they have almost always recognized their divine origin.

JAMES MADISON

As a student at Princeton, Madison came under the broad influence of President Witherspoon, a strong advocate of the tolerant attitude in things ecclesiastical. His studies, and his membership in the Whig society, led him to a deep interest in political and constitutional problems, and to the conviction that a successful republic must lay emphasis on the preservation of freedom under law even more than on equality. He carried this emphasis on liberty into the religious as well as the political sphere. His strong anti-federalism made him the collaborator of Jefferson in many matters, including that of religious freedom.

As a young man he had an experience which profoundly influenced him. He stood outside the jail in Orange, Virginia, and heard an imprisoned Baptist minister preach from the window—the only pulpit legally available to him. He did not believe that "toleration" was sufficient. "The right of every man is to liberty—not toleration," he said. Because of this criticism, and the resulting discussion, the original draft of the Virginia Bill of Rights of 1776, which used the word "toleration," was modified to read "all men are equally entitled to the free exercise of religion, according to the dictates of conscience."[85]

Madison was the author of the widely circulated and highly influential "Memorial and Remonstrance" of 1785 against the proposal of the House of Delegates of Virginia to provide, through assessments, for teachers of the Christian religion. This Memorial is one of the most important and eloquent documents in the history of the achievement of religious liberty and the separation of Church and State in the United States. We are therefore setting it forth here in full.

To the Honorable the General Assembly of the State of Virginia

We, the subscribers, citizens of the said commonwealth, having taken into serious consideration a bill printed by order of the last session of the general assembly, entitled "A bill for establishing a provision for teachers of the Christian religion," and conceiving that the same, if finally armed with the sanctions of a law, will be a dangerous abuse of power, are bound, as faithful members of a free state, to remonstrate against the said bill—

1. Because we hold it for a "fundamental and undeniable truth," that religion, or the duty which we owe to our creator, and the manner of discharging it, can be directed only by reason and conviction, not by force or violence. The religion, then, of every man, must be left to the conviction and conscience of every man; and it is the right of every man to exercise it as these may dictate. This right is, in its nature, an unalienable right. It is unalienable, because the opinions of men, depending only on the evidence contemplated in their own minds, cannot follow the dictates of other men; it is unalienable, also, because what is here a right towards men, is a duty towards the creator. It is the duty of every man to render the creator such homage, and *such only*, as he believes to be acceptable to him; this duty is precedent, both in order of time and degree of obligation, to the claims of civil society. Before any man can be considered as a member of civil society, he must be considered as a subject of the governor of the universe; and if a member of civil society, who enters into any subordinate association, must always do it with a reservation of his duty to the general authority, much more must every man who becomes a member of any particular civil society do it *with the saving his allegiance to the universal sovereign.* We maintain, therefore, that in matters of religion no man's right is abridged by the institution of civil society; and that religion is wholly exempt from its cognizance. True it is, that no other rule exists, by which any question which may divide society can be ultimately determined, but the will of the majority; but it is also true, that the majority may trespass on the rights of the minority.

2. Because, if religion be exempt from the authority of the society at large, still less can it be subject to that of the legislative body. The latter are but the creatures and vicegerents of the former. Their jurisdiction is both derivative and limited. It is limited with regard to the coordinate departments; more necessarily is it limited with regard to the constituents. The preservation of a free government requires not merely that the metes and bounds which separate each department of power be universally maintained; but more especially, that neither of them be suffered to overleap the great barrier which defends the rights of the people. The rulers who are guilty of such an encroachment, exceed the commission from which they derive their authority, and are tyrants. The people who submit to it are governed by laws made neither by themselves, nor by an authority derived from them, and are slaves.

3. Because it is proper to take alarm at the first experiment on our liberties. We hold this prudent jealousy to be the first duty of citizens, and one of the noblest characteristics of the late revolution. The freemen of America did not wait till usurped power had strengthened itself by exercise, and entangled the question in precedents. They saw all the consequences by denying the principle. We revere this lesson too much soon to forget it. Who does not see that the same authority which can establish Christianity, in exclusion of all other religions, may establish, with

the same ease, any particular sect of Christians, in exclusion of all other sects? That the same authority that can call for each citizen to contribute three pence only of his property for the support of only one establishment, may force him to conform to any one establishment, in all cases whatsoever?

4. Because the bill violates that equality which ought to be the basis of every law, and which is more indispensable in proportion as the validity or expediency of any law is more liable to be impeached. If "all men by nature are equally free and independent," all men are to be considered as entering into society on equal conditions, as relinquishing no more, and, therefore, retaining no less, one than another, of their rights. Above all, they are to be considered as retaining an "equal right to the free exercise of religion, according to the dictates of conscience." While we assert for ourselves a freedom to embrace, to profess, and to observe, the religion which we believe to be of divine origin, we cannot deny an equal freedom to those whose minds have not yet yielded to the evidence which has convinced us. If this freedom be abused, it is an offense against God, *not against man*: to God, therefore, *not to man*, must an account of it be rendered. As the bill violates equality by subjecting some to peculiar burdens, so it violates the same principle by granting to others peculiar exemptions. Are the Quakers and Menonists the only sects who think compulsive support of their religions unnecessary and unwarrantable? Can their piety alone be entrusted with the care of public worship? Ought their religions to be endowed, above all others, with extraordinary privileges, by which proselytes may be enticed from all others? We think too favorably of the justice and good sense of these denominations to believe that they either covet preeminence over their fellow citizens, or that they will be seduced by them from the common opposition to the measure.

5. Because the bill implies, either that the civil magistrate is a competent judge of truth, or that he may employ religion as an engine of civil policy. The first is an arrogant pretension, falsified by the contradictory opinions of rulers in all ages, and throughout the world: the second is an unhallowed perversion of the means of salvation.

6. Because the establishment proposed by the bill is not requisite for the support of the Christian religion. To say that it is, is a contradiction to the Christian religion itself; for every page of it disavows a dependence on the powers of this world: it is a contradiction to fact; for it is known that this religion both existed and flourished, not only without the support of human laws, but in spite of every opposition from them; and not only during the period of miraculous aid, but long after it had been left to its own evidence, and the ordinary care of Providence. Nay, it is a contradiction in terms; for a religion not invented by human policy must have pre-existed and been supported before it was established by human policy. It is, moreover, to weaken in those who profess this religion a pious confidence in its innate excellence, and the patronage of its author; and to foster in those who still reject it, a suspicion that its friends are too conscious of its fallacies to trust it to its own merits.

7. Because experience witnesseth that ecclesiastical establishments, instead of

maintaining the purity and efficacy of religion, have had a contrary operation. During almost fifteen centuries has the legal establishment of Christianity been on trial. What have been its fruits? More or less, in all places, pride and indolence in the clergy; ignorance and servility in the laity; in both, superstition, bigotry, and persecution. Enquire of the teachers of Christianity for the ages in which it appeared in its greatest lustre; those of every sect point to the ages prior to its incorporation with civil policy. Propose a restoration of this primitive state, in which its teachers depended on the voluntary rewards of their flocks; many of them predict its downfall. On which side ought their testimony to have the greatest weight, when for, or when against, their interest?

8. Because the establishment in question is not necessary for the support of civil government. If it be urged as necessary for the support of civil government only as it is a means of supporting religion, and if it be not necessary for the latter purpose, it cannot be necessary for the former. If religion be not within the cognizance of civil government, how can its legal establishment be said to be necessary to civil government? What influences, in fact, have ecclesiastical establishments had on civil society? In some instances they have been seen to erect a spiritual tyranny on the ruins of civil authority; in many instances they have been seen upholding the thrones of political tyranny; in no instance have they been seen the guardians of the liberties of the people. Rulers who wished to subvert the public liberty may have found an established clergy convenient auxiliaries. A just government, instituted to secure and perpetuate it, needs them not. Such a government will be best supported by protecting every citizen in the enjoyment of his religion with the same equal hand that protects his person and property; by neither invading the equal rights of any sect, nor suffering any sect to invade those of another.

9. Because the proposed establishment is a departure from that generous policy which, offering an asylum to the persecuted and oppressed of every nation and religion, promised a lustre to our country, and an accession to the number of its citizens. What a melancholy mark is the bill, of sudden degeneracy. Instead of holding forth an asylum to the persecuted, it is itself a signal of persecution. It degrades from the equal rank of citizens all those whose opinions in religion do not bend to those of the legislative authority. Distant as it may be, in its present form, from the inquisition, it differs only in degree. The one is the *first* step, the other the *last*, in the *career of intolerance.* The magnanimous sufferer under this cruel scourge in foreign regions, must view the bill as a beacon on our coast, warning him to seek some other haven, where liberty and philanthropy, in their due extent, may offer a more certain repose from his troubles.

10. Because it will have a like tendency to banish our citizens. The allurements presented by other situations are every day thinning their numbers. To superadd a fresh motive to emigration, by revoking the liberty which they now enjoy, would be the same species of folly which has dishonored and depopulated flourishing kingdoms.

11. Because it will destroy the moderation and harmony which the forbearance of our laws to intermeddle with religion has produced among its several sects. Tor-

rents of blood have been spilt in the world in vain attempts of the secular arm to extinguish religious discord, by proscribing all differences in religious opinions. Time, at length, has revealed the true remedy. Every relaxation of narrow and rigorous policy, wherever it has been tried, has been found to assuage the disease. The American theatre has exhibited proofs, that equal and complete liberty, if it does not wholly eradicate it, sufficiently destroys its malignant influence on the health and prosperity of the state. If, with the salutary effects of this system under our own eyes, we begin to contract the bounds of religious freedom, we know no name that will too severely reproach our folly. At least, let warning be taken at the first fruits of the threatened innovation. The very appearance of the bill has transformed that "Christian forbearance, love, and charity," which of late mutually prevailed, into animosities and jealousies, which may not soon be appeased. What mischiefs may not be dreaded, should this enemy to the public quiet be armed with the force of a law!

12. Because the policy of the bill is adverse to the diffusion of the light of Christianity. The first wish of those who enjoy this precious gift ought to be, that it may be imparted to the whole race of mankind. Compare the number of those who have as yet received it, with the number still remaining under the dominion of false religions, and how small is the former! Does the policy of the bill tend to lessen the disproportion? No: it at once discourages those who are strangers to the light of revelation from coming into the region of it: countenances, by example, the nations who continue in darkness, in shutting out those who might convey it to them. Instead of levelling, as far as possible, every obstacle to the victorious progress of truth, the bill, with an ignoble and unchristian timidity, would circumscribe it with a wall of defence against the encroachments of error.

13. Because attempts to enforce by legal sanctions acts obnoxious to so great a proportion of citizens, tend to enervate the laws in general, and to slacken the bands of society. If it be difficult to execute any law which is not generally deemed necessary or salutary, what must be the case where it is deemed invalid and dangerous? And what may be the effect of so striking an example of impotency in the government on its general authority?

14. Because a measure of such general magnitude and delicacy ought not to be imposed, without the clearest evidence that it is called for by a majority of citizens: and no satisfactory method is yet proposed, by which the voice of the majority in this case may be determined, or its influence secured. "The people of the respective counties are, indeed, requested to signify their opinion, respecting the adoption of the bill, to the next sessions of assembly;" but the representation must be made equal before the voice either of the representatives or the counties will be that of the people. Our hope is, that neither of the former will, after due consideration, espouse the dangerous principle of the bill. Should the event disappoint us, it will still leave us in full confidence that a fair appeal to the latter will reverse the sentence against our liberties.

15. Because, finally, "the equal right of every citizen to the free exercise of his religion, according to the dictates of conscience," is held by the same tenure with

all our other rights. If we recur to its origin, it is equally the gift of nature; if we weigh its importance, it cannot be less dear to us; if we consult the "declaration of those rights which pertain to the good people of Virginia, as the basis and foundation of government," it is enumerated with equal solemnity, or, rather, studied emphasis.

Either, then, we must say that the will of the legislature is the only measure of their authority, and that, in the plenitude of this authority, they may sweep away all our fundamental rights; or, that they are bound to leave this particular right untouched and sacred: either we must say that they may control the freedom of the press, may abolish the trial by jury, may swallow up the executive and judiciary powers of the state; nay, that they may despoil us of our right of suffrage, and erect themselves into an independent and hereditary assembly: or, we must say, that they have no authority to enact into law the bill under consideration. We, the subscribers, say, that the general assembly of this commonwealth have no such authority; and that no effort may be omitted, on our part, against so dangerous an usurpation, we oppose to it in this remonstrance—earnestly praying, as we are in duty bound, that the SUPREME LAWGIVER OF THE UNIVERSE, by illuminating those to whom it is addressed, may, on the one hand, turn their councils from every act which affronts his holy prerogative, or violates the trust committed to them; and, on the other, guide them into every measure that may be worthy of his blessing, may redound to their own praise, and may establish more firmly the liberties of the people, and the prosperity and happiness of the commonwealth.

A few later examples of Madison's effective interest in Church-State separation and religious freedom may be given. In 1785 he was among those who opposed the decision of a committee of Congress to recommend setting aside one section of each township in the Western territories for the support of religion. He rejoiced when he heard a report that the plan would be abandoned, writing,

How a regulation so unjust in itself, so foreign to the authority of Congress, so hurtful to the sale of public land, and smelling so strongly of an antiquated bigotry, could have received the countenance of a committee is truly a matter of astonishment.[87]

Madison's interest in preserving the separation between Church and State led to his having some misgivings regarding Federal Thanksgiving Day proclamations.[88] He had also some doubts as to the advisability of including reference to ministers of religion in the first Federal census of 1790 because of his strong belief in the entire separation of Church and State.[89] The case of chaplaincies to be supported from public funds seemed to him more serious and he opposed their appointment:

If Religion consist in voluntary acts of individuals, singly or voluntarily associated, and if it be proper that public functionaries, as well as their constituents, should discharge their religious duties, let them, like their constituents, do so at their own expense. How small a contribution from each member of Congress would suffice for the purpose! How just would it be in its principle! How noble in its exemplary sacrifice to the genius of the Constitution; and the divine right of conscience! Why should the expense of a religious worship for the Legislature, be paid by the public, more than that for the Executive or Judiciary branches of the Government? . . .[90]

Similarly, he opposed the incorporation by the Federal government of religious institutions, believing that such action would tend to break down the "wall of separation" between Church and State. He sent special messages to Congress vetoing proposals for incorporating the Episcopal Church in Georgetown near Washington, and also for setting apart land in Mississippi territory for a Baptist congregation.[91]

He logically extended his religious-freedom views to exclude the teaching of religion in public institutions. Writing in 1823 to Edward Everett of Massachusetts, he said,

The difficulty of reconciling the Christian mind to the absence of a religious tuition from a university established by law, and at the common expense, is probably less with us than with you. The settled opinion here is that religion is essentially distinct from civil government, and exempt from its cognizance; that a connection between them is injurious to both.[92]

He believed it was best for the country to have a large number of religious sects and was fond of quoting Voltaire's aphorism, quoted in Chapter 1, regarding the happiness and peace of the English people because of the multiplicity of religions. "In a free government," added Madison, "the security for civil rights must be the same as that for religious rights; it consists in the one case in the multiplicity of interests and in the other in the multiplicity of sects." [93]

Among leaders in America Roger Williams and William Penn were path makers in darker days, and Jefferson may have had more intuitive flashes of genius in dealing with the subject; but for logical and consistent development of the constitutional ideal of religious freedom Madison still ranks in many ways as supreme among our statesmen.

CHARLES PINCKNEY

Although Pinckney is principally known as the author of the "Pinckney Plan" for a system of government for the United States, the records of the Federal Constitutional Convention of 1787 show clearly (1) that he wished to secure freedom from religious tests for office and that he was the proposer of the only clause on the subject of religion finally incorporated in the original Constitution of the United States, namely, that "no religious test shall ever be required as a qualification to any office or public trust under [the authority of] the United States"; (2) that he wished to satisfy the religious scruples of Quakers and some other groups, and so secured the ratification by the Convention of the substitution of an alternative "affirmation" for an "oath" to support the Constitution by all members of Congress and state legislatures and by all executives and judicial officers both of the United States and of the several states; (3) that he wished to guarantee religious freedom in the Federal Constitution by providing that "The legislature of the United States shall pass no law on the subject of religion"—a proposal which, though referred to the committee on detail, was apparently dropped, as we do not hear of it again until it appears in slightly revised form in the First Amendment to the Bill of Rights of two years later; and (4) that he united with James Madison in proposing that Congress should be specifically empowered to establish a university "in which no preference or distinction should be allowed on account of religion."

Pinckney has received but slight recognition for his services to the cause of religious freedom. He showed more interest in the subject at the Constitutional Convention than any member other than James Madison and fully deserves a place among the American heroes of religious liberty.[94]

JOHN LELAND

One of the most effective leaders in the cause of religious freedom during the constitutional period was the Reverend John Leland, a Congregationalist by upbringing and a Baptist by profession. His contributions were mainly divided between Massachusetts, his native state, and Virginia, where he spent much of his life. After his first removal to Virginia in 1775 he frequently appeared before the Virginia Assembly as a spokesman in behalf of religious freedom. He was chairman of the general committee of the Baptists of the state, which took such an active part in the Virginia struggle against an Established Church, and he prepared the strong letter addressed to President Washington on their behalf with reference to the new government. He was specially concerned with disestablishing the Episcopal Church, being instrumental in the repeal of the incorporation act and in working to have the Church's glebe lands returned to the state. The Baptists played a large part in securing religious freedom and the abolition of the State Church in Virginia, and Leland was their most effective advocate.

His second great contribution was in helping to bring about the overthrow of the Established Church in Connecticut and Massachusetts, and to guarantee complete religious freedom in these states. (In 1791 he returned to Massachusetts to spend there most of the remaining years of his life.)[95]

In 1794, although then a Massachusetts resident, he addressed a crowd of angry Baptists from the steps of the Connecticut state capitol, urging them to work for freedom of conscience and complete separation of Church and State.[96] In 1806 he urged that Connecticut call a constitutional convention in the interest of disestablishing the Congregational Church and securing complete religious freedom—not finally achieved until over a decade later. He advised his followers to throw support to the Republican party in spite of the Deists in its midst, as only in this way could the Congregationalist-Federalist grip on Connecticut be broken.

In 1820, in his *Short Essays on Government*, he proposed an amendment to the constitution of Massachusetts to separate Church and State. Leland was one of the foremost early defenders in the United States of complete religious freedom. He had contempt for mere toleration.

> Government [he said] should protect every man in thinking and speaking freely, and see that one does not abuse another. The liberty I contend for is more than toleration. The very idea of toleration is despicable; it supposes that some have a pre-eminence above the rest to grant indulgence; whereas all should be equally free, Jews, Turks, Pagans and Christians. Test Oaths and established creeds should be avoided as the worst of evils.[97]

Our study of the work of the twenty heroes of religious freedom in the two periods of the colonies and the formation of our government shows clearly that most of the founders of our Federal government believed that religious freedom was ultimately desirable throughout the country. Some of them, as we have seen—such as Madison and Jefferson—were outspoken advocates of it, and it is approved or implied in the writings of Franklin and others; but a majority felt that it was best to make haste slowly. So the Constitution guaranteed freedom only as far as the Federal government was concerned, not wishing to jeopardize its passage by unduly antagonizing the believers in Puritan establishments in New England or in Anglican establishments in the South. The action of Virginia in providing for complete religious freedom in 1785, followed by some other states, probably convinced them that the final result for all the states was inevitable.

Chapter 3
STATE BATTLES FOR RELIGIOUS FREEDOM

*Priority of States over Federal Government
in the Battle for Religious Freedom*

To understand Church-State relations in this country historically and con-temporaneously we must remember that a large measure of religious toleration, and in some cases complete religious freedom, had been won by some of the thirteen original states before the adoption of the Federal Constitution and its Bill of Rights. The fact that the movement for separation of Church and State was already well under way in the newly formed states which had succeeded to the responsibilities of the old colonies was one of the reasons that the Constitutional Convention in Philadelphia in 1787 did not go farther in the matter. Indeed, the state-making process had been going on for over a decade. The Virginia Bill of Rights was adopted in June, 1776, three weeks before the Declaration of Independence, which it profoundly influenced.

The other bills of rights prior to the adoption of the Constitution in 1789 were those of Pennsylvania, Maryland, North Carolina, Delaware, Vermont, Massachusetts, and New Hampshire. Religious liberty was also specifically safe-guarded in the constitution of New York, accepted in 1777. These American states, in adopting their bills of rights, built on the foundations of colonial rights and privileges. Consequently there was not in some fields, such as free-dom of the press, as much of a change as might have appeared. But it was a great step forward to have all these rights, with religious liberty and freedom of speech included, specifically recognized by these states in fundamental writ-ten constitutions adopted freely by the duly chosen representatives of the people.

An important fact is that these rights are a guarantee of freedom to indi-viduals and to minority groups as well as of protection against arbitrary acts of government. The individual is not the possessor of rights through favor of the State; but because of his own nature as man he has inalienable and inde-feasible rights.[1] Such fundamentals as religious liberty, the right of assembly, and liberty of the press are not specifically referred to in the English statutes but are rather protected by the general principles of law.[2]

The religious freedom secured under the state and Federal constitutions can be understood only as we realize the earlier victories in three colonies. These were, in order:

Maryland, which granted toleration to all Trinitarian Christians in 1649, through the efforts of the proprietor, Cecil Calvert, second Lord Baltimore, a Roman Catholic. The character and significance of the act are described in the first chapter, where Cecil Calvert is dealt with as a leader in the cause of religious freedom. Unfortunately, and not as the fault of the original proprietary, this toleration was short-lived.

Rhode Island, whose charter, secured from King Charles II in 1663, provided for complete religious freedom. This stipulation was due mainly to the efforts of the Reverend John Clarke, leader of the liberal colony of Aquidneck. He was a co-worker of Roger Williams, the most advanced and effective advocate of religious freedom in colonial times. The provisions of the charter are given in the sketch of Clarke.

Pennsylvania, whose "Frame of Government," granted by William Penn in 1683, provided that all who believed in "One Almighty God" should be protected and all who believed "in Jesus Christ the Saviour of the World" were capable of holding civil office. Penn's efforts for religious freedom have also been described in the first chapter. They had marked influence on Delaware, too, which for most of the colonial period was under Pennsylvania's jurisdiction.

The Epoch-Making Struggle and the Earliest Victory—Virginia [3]

The struggle which took place in Virginia in its last days as a colony and in its early days as a state calls for special attention, for it influenced the American theories of Church-State separation and religious freedom more than any other historical factor. Indeed, it is doubtful that any other legislative body ever had so significant a debate on the subject. Those who took the leading part in it—Thomas Jefferson, James Madison, George Mason, and Patrick Henry—were all powerful advocates of civil liberty and (with some lapses on the part of Patrick Henry) such profound believers in religious liberty that we have already included sketches of their contributions to the cause. Virginia was now to take the place of leadership in the cause of religious freedom held in the middle of the seventeenth century by Rhode Island. Here again the Baptists, now supported by Presbyterians and other dissenters as well as by a remarkable group of political philosophers, were to play a leading part, but this time against the entrenched Episcopalians instead of the New England Puritans.

We are here concerned primarily with the great Bill for Establishing Religious Freedom of 1786 and the events of the previous decade. To understand the results we must remember that the Virginia colony was in its inception mainly a mercantile venture; that from 1662 on, for about a century, its General Assembly required ministers to present evidence of ordination by an English bishop, and the governor and council were empowered to silence the teaching or preaching of all other persons; that the Episcopal Church had been long and exclusively established in Virginia and was heavily endowed with land; that the leading statesmen, especially in the tidewater region, had been identified with it; that it was both class-conscious and spiritually inactive; that its ministers were mostly latitudinarian in tendency, lacking in seriousness of purpose, unsympathetic with the zeal of the Methodists, whom they denounced for their "fanaticism" and "enthusiasm," and opposed to giving up their exclusive public prerogatives; and that the Presbyterians and Baptists, who had been coming in large numbers into the Shenandoah Valley and adjoining regions and had a vital religious message to give to the people, were greatly hampered in their work by restrictive laws.

The beginnings of effective organized Church opposition to the ecclesiastical situation go back to the discussion of the payment of clerical salaries. These stipends were fixed by law in pounds of tobacco, a staple much used as a currency in certain parts of the South. Owing to the deficient crops in 1755 and 1758, the price of tobacco had risen, and payments in it in fixed pounds of tobacco often involved special hardships on vestries. The Virginia Assembly, to relieve the situation, made debts payable at the rate of twopence to a pound of tobacco—much less than the market price, which was six cents a pound. This law affected all creditors and all officers of the government, but especially the clergy, who were seldom large planters and who consequently received no compensating benefit by the rise in tobacco prices.[4]

The clergy resisted the commutation, believing it contrary to statutes enacted for their protection, and induced the Board of Trade to persuade the British government to invalidate the act. They further tried to force their parishioners to pay them the difference between the legal rate and the market price. This controversy became known as the Parson's case, because a parson in Hanover County, the Reverend James Maury, sued for the payment of back salary, which had been paid at the new rate and in paper money. In the Parson's case Patrick Henry came to the front in 1763 by resisting, on behalf of the vestry, the enforcement of the British government's decision. He claimed that, by vetoing the Virginia law, the king was guilty of tyranny. His eloquence resulted in the jury's giving the parson only one penny as damages. The effort of the clergy, for personal purposes and in opposition to the wishes of the people, to thwart the will of their own Assembly made them very unpopular. On the whole, the Parson's case injured the prestige of both the establishment and its ministers, encouraged the dissenters, and marked the beginning of the effective co-operation between the Baptists and the Presbyterians in the attempt to overthrow the establishment and secure the independence of Church and State.[5]

The Baptists had been the first to enter the fray. The earliest petition to the House of Burgesses of Virginia regarding religious freedom came from them. Among other things they prayed for relief from "the hardships they suffer from the prohibition to their ministers to preach in meeting-houses not particularly mentioned in their licenses." [6] In 1772 they began their long series of strong memorials to the Assembly for "Liberty of Conscience." They declined to accept any act of mere toleration but wanted absolute freedom in religious matters and the abolition of the Church establishment.[7]

In 1775 the Baptist General Association demanded that their ministers share in the right to preach to the troops.[8] In the same year, with the co-operation of the Hanover Presbytery, the Association successfully opposed as inadequate a proposed toleration law,[9] particularly for its refusal to permit public worship except during the daytime.[10]

When the new republican legislature of Virginia met in 1776 it was greeted by a number of petitions from the Baptists calling for religious freedom and an end to the establishment.[11] They protested the law under which only ministers of the established Episcopal Church could legally solemnize marriages, and it was not until the end of 1780 that non-Episcopal clergymen were authorized to perform the ceremony.[12] But by far the greatest contribution made by the Baptists to the cause of separation of Church and State in Virginia was their opposition to the General Assessment Bill for the support of teachers of the Christian religion.[13] Not content with the defeat of the bill in 1785,[14] they demanded further that the legislature repeal the act which incorporated the Protestant Episcopal Church. They asserted that the Declaration of Rights prohibited the regulation of ecclesiastical affairs by the legislature, and that the latter consequently had no right to adopt any regulations for the Episcopal Church.[15] With the help of other groups they were successful in securing the repeal of the Incorporation Act, but the glebe lands were still left in the hands of the Episcopal clergy, in spite of the feeling of a majority of the Baptists that they should be considered public property.[16]

Second only to the Baptists among the religious groups in contributing to the successful struggle for religious freedom and the separation of Church and State in Virginia were the Presbyterians. As early as 1776 the Hanover Presbytery submitted to the Virginia legislature a memorial which, in calling for the end of all establishments, not only greatly influenced the course of disestablishment in Virginia but also set forth concisely and eloquently the philosophy upon which the Constitution of the United States was later to be based. The memorial said in part,

We would also humbly represent that the only proper objects of civil government are the happiness and protection of men in their present state of existence, the security of the life, liberty, and the property of the citizens, and to restrain the vicious and to encourage the virtuous, by wholesome laws equally extending to every individual; but that the duty which we owe to our Creator, and the manner of discharging it, can only be directed by reason or conviction, and is nowhere cognizable but at the tribunal of the Universal Judge.[17]

The Baptists and the Presbyterians were not the only religious bodies which helped to secure religious freedom in Virginia, although they were by far the most active and the most influential. In October, 1776, the Lutherans united with them in asking the legislature to be relieved from further support of the Establishment. The Methodists, who, however, became a church body distinct from the Episcopalians only near the end of 1784, also helped, though they feared that the abolition of the Establishment might have some undesirable consequences.

The contributions of the religious groups in the Virginia struggle for Church-State separation, monumental as they were, would probably not have been successful without the equally monumental contributions of an extraordinary number of able political thinkers and statesmen found in Virginia in the second half of the eighteenth century. Many of them had been influenced by John Milton, Algernon Sidney, the friend and adviser of Penn, and especially John Locke, whose *Two Treatises on Government* appeared in 1690. Among them were three whose contribution to religious liberty was so notable that they have been dealt with independently. They were, in the order of their effective appearance on the political scene as protagonists of the cause, George Mason, Thomas Jefferson, and James Madison. These statesmen, and to some extent Thomas Paine, had all developed, more or less independently, convictions as to the importance of disestablishment and of the fundamental equality of all churches under the law; but they were greatly stimulated to intelligent and vigorous action by the Presbyterian and Baptist groups already mentioned. The dissenting ministers provided the facts of the serious difficulties and handicaps under which they were laboring and helped to create a strong public opinion demanding a change; the statesmen gave classic expression to the logical reasons for religious freedom and put into admirable legal form the constitutional provisions and statutes needed to make it effective.

This combination of religious and political leaders caused the introduction and passage in the Virginia legislature of the Declaration of Rights, three weeks before the adoption of the Declaration of Independence. It was mainly the work of George Mason,[18] although at one stage Madison proposed an amendment which would have prevented a general assessment for religion and thus would have brought the Establishment to a close a decade earlier than was actually the case. But this was too radical a doctrine for the time and was therefore passed over.[19]

The next step was the adoption, in December, 1776, of an act repealing the laws making it an offense to hold particular religious opinions and removing penalties against those who did not attend the services of the Established Church or who worshiped elsewhere.[20] This act exempted dissenters from contributing to the support of the Church but left the latter in possession of the wealth it had acquired by taxation.[21]

In 1779 the legislature finally discontinued the payment of salaries to Episcopal clergymen,[22] and the next year it broadened the powers of dissenting ministers to solemnize marriages.[23] However, the final victory for religious freedom and Church-State separation came with the defeat of the General Assessment Bill and the enactment of the Bill for Establishing Religious Freedom.

The leader of the move for a general assessment was Patrick Henry.[24] In November, 1784, he succeeded in getting the legislature to adopt a resolution "That the people of this Commonwealth, according to their respective abilities, ought to pay a moderate tax or contribution annually, for the support of the Christian religion, or of some Christian church, denomination or communion of Christians, or of some form of Christian worship." [25] Madison, however, by an effective speech, secured postponement of the third and final reading.[26] The effect of postponing action until the next session was to afford the opponents of the measure an opportunity to distribute widely Madison's historic Memorial and Remonstrance, which has been set forth in full earlier in this book where Madison is described as a hero of religious freedom. This document, together with similar memorials from the Baptists and Presbyterians, as well as other factors, resulted in the final defeat of the assessment plan in October, 1785.[27]

Madison quickly followed up his victory in defeating the Assessment Bill by calling for a vote on Jefferson's Bill for Establishing Religious Freedom, which had been introduced in the legislature in 1779 and had been laid over from session to session. This Bill is so important a document in the history of man's struggle for religious liberty that we are setting it forth here in full.

Well aware that Almighty God hath created the mind free; that all attempts to influence it by temporal punishments or burdens, or by civil incapacitations, tend only to beget habits of hypocrisy and meanness, and are a departure from the plan of the Holy Author of our religion, who being Lord both of body and mind, yet chose not to propagate it by coercions on either, as was in his Almighty power to do; that the impious presumption of legislators and rulers, civil as well as ecclesiastical, who, being themselves but fallible and uninspired men have assumed dominion over the faith of others, setting up their own opinions and modes of thinking as the only true and infallible, and as such endeavoring to impose them on others, hath established and maintained false religions over the greatest part of the world, and through all time; that to compel a man to furnish contributions of money for the propagation of opinions which he disbelieves, is sinful and tyrannical; that even the forcing him to support this or that teacher of his own religious persuasion, is depriving him of the comfortable liberty of giving his contributions to the particular pastor whose morals he would make his pattern, and whose power he feels most persuasive to righteousness, and is withdrawing from the ministry those temporal rewards, which proceeding from an approbation of their personal conduct, are an additional incitement to earnest and unremitting labors for the instruction of mankind; that our civil rights have no dependence on our religious opinions, more than our opinions in physics or geometry; that, therefore, the proscribing any citizen as unworthy the public confidence by laying upon him an incapacity of being called to the offices of trust and emolument, unless he profess or renounce this or that religious opinion, is depriving him injuriously of those privileges and advantages to whcih in common with his fellow citizens he has a natural right; that it tends also to corrupt the principles of that very religion it is meant to encourage, by bribing, with a monopoly of worldly honors and emoluments, those who will externally profess and conform to it; that though indeed these are criminal who do not withstand such temptation, yet neither are those innocent who lay the bait in their way; that to suffer the civil magistrate to intrude his powers into the field of opinion and to restrain the profession or propagation of principles, on the supposition of their ill tendency, is a dangerous fallacy, which at once destroys all religious liberty, because he being of course judge of that tendency, will make his opinions the rule of judgment, and approve or condemn the sentiments of others only as they shall square with or differ from his own; that it is time enough for the rightful purposes of civil government, for its officers to interfere when principles break out into overt acts against peace and good order; and finally, that truth is great and will prevail if left to herself, that she is the proper and sufficient antagonist to error, and has nothing to fear from the conflict, unless by human interposition disarmed of her natural weapons, free argument and debate, errors ceasing to be dangerous when it is permitted freely to contradict them.

Be it therefore enacted by the General Assembly. That no man shall be compelled to frequent or support any religious worship, place or ministry whatsoever, nor shall be enforced, restrained, molested, or burthened in his body or goods, nor shall otherwise suffer on account of his religious opinions or belief; but that all men shall be free to profess, and by argument to maintain, their opinions in matters of religion, and that the same shall in nowise diminish, enlarge, or affect their civil capacities.

And though we well know this Assembly, elected by the people for the ordinary purposes of legislation only, have no power to restrain the acts of succeeding assemblies, constituted with the powers equal to our own, and that therefore to declare this act irrevocable, would be of no effect in law, yet we are free to declare, and do declare, that the rights hereby asserted are of the natural rights of mankind, and that if any act shall be hereafter passed to repeal the present or to narrow its operation, such act will be an infringement of natural right.[29]

Jefferson, in his *Autobiography*, notes that

Where the preamble declares that coercion is a departure from the plan of the holy author of our religion, an amendment was proposed, by inserting the word Jesus Christ, so that it should read a departure from the plan of Jesus Christ, the holy author of our religion. The insertion was rejected by a great majority, in proof that they meant to comprehend, within the mantle of its protection, the Jew and the Gentile, the Christian and Mahometan, the Hindoo, and infidel of every denomination.[30]

The bill was adopted by the legislature and became law upon the governor's approval in January, 1786.[31] The final step in the disestablishment process took place in 1802 when the Virginia Assembly ordered that the vacant glebes of the Episcopal parishes, and those that would become vacant on the death of the incumbent, should be sold by the overseers of the poor, who were to use the receipts, after paying parish debts, for the support of the poor or for any other non-religious purpose which a majority of the voters might decide.[32]

And so Virginia won religious freedom for herself, and indirectly for the whole country, because of the influence of her action on other states and on the Federal government. Her victory was due primarily to the efforts of five men—the Reverend Samuel Davies, George Mason, Thomas Jefferson, James Madison, and the Reverend John Leland—whose names should always be held in high honor.

The Victory in North Carolina

During most of the colonial period Carolina retained an Anglican Church establishment, although non-Anglicans were in a majority, especially in the section which by 1712 had become North Carolina.

In 1711 the Assembly had for the first time put Protestant dissenters on the same basis as they were in England; that is, they were granted "indulgences" as tolerated groups, in keeping with the Toleration Act of 1689.[33] But from 1730 to 1773 the home and colonial governments of North Carolina enforced the objectionable Schism Act, which excluded dissenters from virtually all offices of power, dignity, or profit, even preventing them from holding positions in schools, academies, and seminaries. During most of this period dissenters in North Carolina were on the same footing as those in England.

It was not until after North Carolina became independent of Great Britain in 1776 that non-Anglican ministers were authorized to solemnize marriages.[34]

Indeed, aside from one or two favors granted to Presbyterians and Quakers, dissenters received no official recognition until independence. There seem to have been no cases in which they were elected to the council or to the governorship. They were not persecuted by being put in jail, but they had to pay tithes, suffered under muster laws, and had to undergo the disabilities of the Marriage and Schism acts. But the Vestry Act of 1768, which attempted to perpetuate an endowed Church at the expense of other denominations, expired by limitation in 1773. The Establishment was now dead, and discussions were soon in the air regarding a constitution providing for religious freedom.

The constitution adopted in 1776, by the so-called Halifax Congress, for the new state of North Carolina reflected the strong influence of the Scotch-Irish Presbyterians, who were numerous in the state. It began with a Declaration of Rights, one section of which stated "That all men have a natural and unalienable right to worship Almighty God according to the dictates of their own consciences." [35]

Other sections disqualified on the one hand clergymen of any denomination from serving in the legislature and on the other non-Protestants from holding any political office in the state. The most significant section, however, declared,

That there shall be no establishment of any one religious church or denomination in this State, in preference to any other; neither shall any person, on any pretence whatsoever, be compelled to attend any place of worship contrary to his own faith or judgment, nor be obliged to pay, for the purchase of any glebe, or the building of any house of worship, or for the maintenance of any minister or ministry, contrary to what he believes right, or has voluntarily and personally engaged to perform; but all persons shall be at liberty to exercise their own mode of worship:—*Provided*, That nothing herein contained shall be construed to exempt preachers of treasonable or seditious discourses, from legal trial and punishment.[36]

In 1835 the disqualification of clergymen from service in the legislature was removed, and at the same time eligibility for political office was extended to all Christians.[37] Not until 1868 was the constitution changed to disqualify from public office only persons "who deny the being of Almighty God," [38] thus removing all Jewish disabilities.

New York

The New York constitutional convention of 1777 was, next to that of Virginia, the most important in its declarations regarding religious freedom. The committee which drafted the provisions included originally the phrase that "free toleration be forever allowed," but before adoption by the convention it was changed, in conformity with the broader Virginia idea, to "free exercise and enjoyment of religious profession and worship."

In the discussion John Jay proposed an amendment which would have excepted "the professors of the religion of the Church of Rome" and would have required all Roman Catholics seeking to own land in the state or enjoy other civil rights to "solemnly swear that they verily believe in their consciences that no pope, priest, or foreign authority on earth has power to absolve the subjects of this State from their allegiance to the same." [39] The convention defeated this amendment by a vote of 19 to 10 but did insert a statement that it was the duty of the government "not only to expel civil tyranny, but also to guard against that spiritual aggression and intolerance wherewith the bigotry and ambition of weak and wicked priests and princes have scourged mankind." [40]

The constitution of 1777 excluded from office all ministers of the gospel, as they are "by their profession, dedicated to the service of God and the care of souls, and ought not to be diverted from the great duties of their function." [41] It also abrogated all parts of the common and statute law of England and of colonial statutes and acts which "may be construed to establish or maintain any particular denomination of Christians or their ministers." [42] This action was necessary because the Episcopalians, though a minority group in the state, were still nominally "established" in four counties, being especially strong in Westchester.

The Episcopal Church, however, still retained some special privileges, so in 1784 the legislature repealed all acts granting it "certain emoluments and privileges." It also required that all persons naturalized by the state should take an oath to abjure all foreign allegiance and subjection in all matters "ecclesiastical as well as civil"—a restriction aimed at the Roman Catholics—which remained on the statute books for over two decades. In 1806 the test oath was abolished to permit Francis Cooper to take his seat in the Assembly, the first member of the Roman Catholic Church to have this privilege. [43]

Later constitutions of the state contained the usual guarantees of religious freedom in satisfactory form. [44]

Connecticut

The Church-State struggle in Connecticut is one of the most dramatic and interesting in the American national period. The state inherited from the colony an Established Church. As a result, though the persecution of previous days had passed, a writer, boldly attacking the system just before the outbreak of the Revolution, stated that "the ecclesiastical Laws of this Colony deny Liberty of Conscience." [45]

The "Standing Order," that is, the established Congregational ministry, continued a dominant power in Connecticut for more than a generation after independence. It controlled the Governor's Council or upper house, for no one was chosen to this important body, which virtually controlled public policy, who was not a Congregationalist. Its members were generally nominated after consultation with the leaders of the clergy, and they were almost invariably known for their strong support of the ecclesiastical status quo. They were men of character, ability, and public spirit, but opposed to yielding the inherited prerogatives of an Established Church. The General Assembly—the lower house of the legislature—was more liberal, but with the Council entrenched in power it could accomplish relatively little. The Reverend Timothy Dwight, who was president of Yale College from 1795 to 1817, was frequently referred to as the Connecticut pope, and under him almost every Congregational minister of the state took his place in the maintenance of the Church-State situation. Since the Congregational ministers controlled the schools and their teaching, preached all the election day sermons before the legislature, and had enormous social prestige, it was hard to bring about any reform against their will.[46]

To this entrenched Federalist-Congregational group [47] Jefferson was "the man of sin." The Connecticut clergy were drawn up solidly to prevent his election in 1800; and by 1803 all dissenters, except for some Episcopalians, were members of the new Jeffersonian Republican (now Democratic) party.[48] The battle was consequently a religious-political one, with those who wished to maintain the State Church mostly on one side and those opposed to it almost entirely on the other. Connecticut's established ministers also became politicians in large numbers and as such continued to be active supporters of Congregational privilege. The Republicans all over the country became interested in the Connecticut battle, even outside papers aligned with Jeffersonian Democracy joining the fray to such an extent that they helped give the new party an anti-clerical reputation, though not necessarily an anti-religious one.[49]

It may be said that dissent began in Connecticut with the conversion to Episcopacy in 1722 of Rector Timothy Cutler of Yale and two of his tutors, followed by the opening of the first Connecticut Anglican Church in Stratford with the Reverend Samuel Johnson, one of these tutors, as its pastor two years later. The established Congregational Church later lost many adherents to the Baptists and the Methodists, so that probably at the time of the Revolution the dissenters in Connecticut constituted about a third of the population of the state. The Baptists were the most active in demanding religious freedom. From 1802 to 1818, when Church and State were finally separated, they petitioned the legislature every year on the subject, but the Council was so conservative that it never even considered any of the petitions until 1815. The Baptists threw themselves heart and soul into the Jeffersonian Republican party movement, their elders frequently offering prayers at Republican gatherings. The efforts of the Baptists and Methodists were aided by the fact that the orthodox Congregational churches had become quite weak, being influenced by Deistic and other forms of radical philosophic thought, due largely to European contacts. This was at a time when the more outgiving dissenting churches, with a vital evangelical message, were increasing their influence by demanding the extension of the suffrage, more representation in the actual government of the state, the abolition of the tax for the support of Congregationalism, and the entire separation of Church and State.

The struggle of the liberal religious forces in Connecticut against the Standing Order was greatly aided by the growing interest in the cause of the Revolution. In 1770 the legislature granted conscientious dissenters permission to worship in edifices and congregations of their own choice and exempted the estates of their ministers from taxation. But the old requirement to which the non-conformists in the state specially objected—that the laity pay taxes to the established Congregational Church—remained in force.[50] The most important forward step in the decade after the transformation of the colony into a state was taken in 1784, when the Toleration Act was adopted.[51] The act removed all disabilities save that of "certificates," the certificate plan providing that those who were not orthodox Congregationalists and who wished to be exempt from the tax for the Established Church were allowed to pay their tax to their own body, provided they were regular attendants at another church.[52]

Thus dissent inserted an opening wedge, but Congregationalists continued to receive special favors,[53] and it was not until 1818 that the final victory for religious freedom was achieved in Connecticut. In that year a new constitution was adopted, stating "That the exercise and enjoyment of religious profession and worship without discrimination, shall forever be free to all persons in this State; provided that the right hereby declared and established shall not be construed as to excuse acts of licentiousness or to justify practices inconsistent with the peace and safety of the State." [54]

The next section provided that "no preference shall be given by law to any Christian sect or mode of worship." [55] This meant that, although all religious forms consistent with morality and order were given protection, Christianity was virtually recognized as the state's belief.

The article regarding religion in the constitution, as drafted by a subcommittee of Jeffersonian Republicans, was adopted in the following form:

It being the right and duty of all men to worship the Supreme Being, the Great Creator and Preserver of the universe, in the mode most consistent with the dictates of their consciences; no person shall be compelled to join or support, nor by law be classed with, or associated to any congregation, church or religious association. . . . And each and every society or denomination of Christians in this State, shall have and enjoy the same and equal powers, rights and privileges; and shall have power and authority to support and maintain the Ministers or Teachers of their respective denominations, and to build and repair houses for public worship, by a tax on the members of their respective societies only, . . . or in any other manner.[56]

The adoption of the constitution was followed by extension to all ministers of the gospel of the right to perform marriages, formerly enjoyed only by Congregationalist ministers. In 1823 the Episcopalians succeeded at last in securing a charter for a college, Washington (now Trinity), and the Methodists similarly secured a charter for Wesleyan in 1831. The victory of the liberals for Church-State separation and religious freedom was practically complete.

The Long Struggle in Massachusetts

To understand the Massachusetts struggle against the Established Church we must go back to early colonial days. In 1555 the Religious Peace of Augsburg had made the religion of the State that of the ruling prince. This was the situation to which the Puritans were accustomed in England, and to which they objected, especially as England was under Anglican rulers except during the Commonwealth. It was perhaps not unnatural that, although they left England primarily to secure freedom to worship God without interruption and according to the dictates of mind and conscience, they should themselves adopt in their new home the old theory that the rulers had the right to determine the religion of the State. In this case, the majority of the people and their rulers being strong Puritans, a Puritan State Church was under the conditions of the time almost inevitable. Indeed, the people had never been strongly opposed to an Established Church as such. They were merely opposed to an Established Church which they considered based on principles inconsistent with the New Testament and not functioning for the religious welfare of the people.

In Massachusetts, as in most other parts of New England, the Congregational Church at the outbreak of the Revolution was still in most ways the strongest institution in the state. It was in some though not all respects as much "established" as the Church of England in the home country. When the Revolution came and the new government was formed, there were "resonant and high sounding clauses concerning the sanctity of religion and liberty, immediately followed by others denying religious liberty in any adequate sense to many creeds and sects." [57] There was no longer the formally and exclusively established and supported Church of earlier times, but Congregationalism continued to be definitely favored. It was a long time before Massachusetts, which had much influence on other states, was able to secure absolute equality before the law for all religious bodies.

The first major step toward religious freedom was taken in 1780, when a state constitution was adopted.[58] It contained a Declaration of Rights, largely the work of John Adams, which included a clause on religious freedom that showed markedly the influence of the Virginia declaration:

It is the right as well as the duty of all men in society, publicly, and at stated seasons, to worship the SUPREME BEING, the great Creator and Preserver of the universe. And no subject shall be hurt, molested, or restrained, in his person, liberty, or estate, for worshipping GOD in the manner and season most agreeable to the dictates of his own conscience; or for his religious profession or sentiments; provided he doth not disturb the public peace, or obstruct others in their religious worship.[59]

However, coupled with this provision was one (Article III) requiring the towns and villages to "make suitable provision at their own expense" for "the support and maintenance of public Protestant teachers of piety, religion, and morality in all cases where such provision shall not be made voluntarily." [60] The constitution also invested the legislature with "authority to enjoin upon all the subjects an attendance upon the instructions" of the Protestant teachers, "if there be any on whose instructions they can conscientiously and conveniently attend." It provided that each taxpayer's payment should be applied "to the support of the public teacher or teachers of his own religious sect or denomination, provided there be any on whose instruction he attends; otherwise it may be paid towards the support of the teacher or teachers of the parish or precinct in which the said moneys are raised." Finally, the constitution provided that "every denomination of Christians, demeaning themselves peaceably, and as good subjects of the commonwealth, shall be equally under the protection of the law: and no subordination of any one sect or denomination to another shall ever be established by law." [61]

A constitutional convention called in 1820 submitted to the voters proposed amendments which would have liberalized these provisions, principally by extending the support benefits to non-Protestant religious teachers and terminating compulsory attendance and public worship. The voters, however, defeated the amendments by a vote of about 20,000 to 11,000.[62] (This occurred at the time of the Dedham case and the struggle between the Unitarians and the Congregationalists, discussed in Chapter 18, to which the reader is referred.)

Final disestablishment was to come thirteen years later, in 1833, when, by a ratio of 10 to 1, the voters of Massachusetts adopted a constitutional amendment which finally separated Church and State in this old Puritan commonwealth.[63] It substituted for Article III of the 1780 constitution a section securing to all religious organizations the right to elect their pastors or religious teachers, to contract with them for their support, and to raise money for erecting and repairing houses for public worship, maintaining religious instruction, and paying necessary expenses. Every member of every religious society was authorized to dissolve his membership, after which he would no longer be liable for any of its debts.[64] In short, religious societies were thenceforth to be both self-governing and self-supporting.

The Other Original States [65]

In New Hampshire, the constitution adopted in 1783 [66] contained provisions on religion which followed largely Article III of the Massachusetts constitution. It restricted eligibility for service in the state legislature to Protestants, a restriction not removed until 1852. However, a proposal made in 1852 to omit the specific power granted to the legislature to authorize towns or religious societies to provide for "public Protestant teachers of piety, religion and morality" did not pass.[67]

The constitution now in force in New Hampshire provides that "Every individual has a natural and unalienable right to worship God according to dictates of his own conscience, and reason," and that "no person, of any one particular religious sect or denomination, shall ever be compelled to pay towards the support of the teacher or teachers of another persuasion, sect, or denomination." [68] There are, however, three reminders of the old Protestant days. First, the Bill of Rights still refers to "morality and piety, rightly grounded on evangelical principles," a phrase which was probably intended to imply Protestantism. Second, the only groups specifically stated as "equally under the protection of the law" are "every denomination of Christians," [69] thus apparently not including Jews, though of course as a matter of practice there is no legal discrimination against them. Third, the legislature has the power "to authorize, from time to time, the several towns, parishes, bodies corporate, or religious societies, within this state, to make adequate provision, at their own expense, for the support and maintenance of public Protestant teachers of piety, religion, and morality." [70] It will be noticed that this is only an authorization, not a direction; but even so it is inconsistent with the American tradition of the impartiality of the State in matters involving the religious connections of citizens.

The South Carolina constitution adopted in 1778 expressly stated that "The Christian Protestant religion shall be deemed, and is hereby constituted and declared to be, the established religion of this State." [71] It contained detailed provisions to carry out this declaration,[72] provisions probably without parallel in our national history. Nevertheless, because this Constitution so vividly depicts the difference between a state with established Protestantism as its religion and the present situation of separation of Church and State, it is worthwhile to set forth here in full the relevant provisions of the South Carolina Constitution of 1778:

That all persons and religious societies who acknowledge that there is one God, and a future state of rewards and punishments, and that God is publicly to be worshipped, shall be freely tolerated. The Christian Protestant religion shall be deemed, and is hereby constituted and declared to be, the established religion of this State. That all denominations of Christian Protestants in this State, demeaning themselves peaceably and faithfully, shall enjoy equal religious and civil privileges. To accomplish this desirable purpose without injury to the religious property of those societies of Christians which are by law already incorporated for the purpose of religious worship, and to put it fully into the power of every other society of Christian Protestants, either already formed or hereafter to be formed, to obtain the like incorporation, it is hereby constituted, appointed, and declared that the respective societies of the Church of England that are already formed in this State for the purpose of religious worship shall continue incorporate and hold the religious property now in their possession. And that whenever fifteen or more male persons, not under twenty-one years of age, professing the Christian Protestant religion, and agreeing to unite themselves in a society for the purposes of religious worship, they shall, (on complying with the terms hereinafter mentioned), be, and be constituted a church, and be esteemed and regarded in law as of the established religion of the State, and on a petition to the legislature shall be entitled to be incorporated and to enjoy equal privileges. That every society of Christians so formed shall give themselves a name or denomination by which they shall be called and known in law, and all that associate with them for the purposes of worship shall be esteemed as belonging to the society so called. But that previous to the establishment and incorporation of the respective societies of every denomination as aforesaid, and in order to entitle them thereto, each society so petitioning shall have agreed to and subscribed in a book the following five articles, without which no agreement or union of men upon pretence of religion shall entitle them to be incorporated and esteemed as a church of the established religion of this state:

1st. That there is one eternal God, and a future state of rewards and punishments.

2d. That God is publicly to be worshipped.

3d. That the Christian religion is the true religion.

4th. That the holy scriptures of the Old and New Testaments are of divine inspiration, and are the rule of faith and practice.

5th. That it is lawful and the duty of every man being thereunto called by those that govern, to bear witness to the truth.

Twelve years later a new constitution was adopted which called for complete religious freedom "without distinction or preference," [73] although it did continue the provision in the 1778 constitution that excluded clergymen from public office.

New Jersey had a better colonial record in the matter of toleration than most of the colonies. Quite naturally, therefore, its first constitution, adopted in 1776, declared that no person "shall be compelled to attend any place of worship, contrary to his own faith and judgment; nor shall any person, within this Colony, ever be obliged to pay tithes, taxes, or any other rates, for the purpose of building or repairing any other church or churches, place or places of worship, or for the maintenance of any minister or ministry, contrary to what he believes to be right, or has deliberately or voluntarily engaged himself to perform." [74] The constitution, however, did limit eligibility for public office to Protestants. Not until 1874 did the New Jersey constitution provide that "no religious test shall ever be required for any office or public trust; and no person shall be denied the enjoyment of any civil right merely on account of his religious principles." [75]

Delaware, which inherited a tradition of religious toleration from its long association with Pennsylvania, never had a regularly established church. Its first constitution, adopted in 1776, provided that there "shall be no establishment of any one religious sect in this State in preference to another." [76] It did, however, bar from holding political office not only clergymen of all faiths but all persons who did not subscribe to Trinitarian Christianity.[77] Full religious freedom was secured in 1792 with the adoption of a constitution forbidding any religious test for public office.[78]

Pennsylvania, too, in its original constitution adopted in 1776 secured religious freedom for all [79] but included a religious test for service in the state Assembly which required the legislator to profess belief "in one God" and to "acknowledge the Scriptures of the Old and New Testament to be given by Divine inspiration." [80] This disqualification of non-Christians was dropped in 1790.[81] The constitution of that year did, however, contain a provision that "no person, who acknowledges the being of a God and a future state of rewards and punishments, shall, on account of his religious sentiments, be disqualified to hold any office or place of trust or profit under this commonwealth," [82] thus excluding non-believers in God from the right to hold political office. This provision is still in the Pennsylvania constitution but is no longer of any practical effect since in 1961 a similar section in the Maryland constitution was declared by the United States Supreme Court to be unconstitutional.[83]

The Maryland constitution of 1776 likewise guaranteed religious freedom but excluded non-Christians from eligibility for public office, an exclusion which was not removed until 1826.

Georgia's first constitution was adopted in 1777. It guaranteed to all "the free exercise of religion" and provided that no person shall "unless by consent support any teacher or teachers except those of his own profession." [84] In 1798 a new constitution forbade all compulsory contributions to religion, even that of the taxpayer's own profession, and forbade too the denial of any civil right merely on account of religious principles.[85]

The Vermont constitution of 1777 followed closely the provisions regarding religion contained in the Pennsylvania constitution of 1776, with the exception that it required a belief in the Protestant religion as a prerequisite to service in public office.[86] In 1791 the state was admitted into the Federal Union and two years later revised its constitution, retaining the guarantees of freedom of religion and omitting all religious test oaths.[87]

Rhode Island, the home of American religious freedom, did not immediately formulate a state constitution but merely continued under the liberal charter of 1663.[88] In 1842 the state adopted a constitution of its own with declarations true to the best standards of a body politic inheriting Rhode Island's traditions.[89]

We have now dealt with the constitutional provisions of the thirteen original states in the field of religion and religious freedom as these were decided upon in the early days of the republic. A summary of the results [90] seems therefore in order:

Two out of thirteen, Virginia and Rhode Island, conceded full freedom.

One, New York, gave full freedom except for requiring naturalized citizens to abjure foreign allegiance and subjection in all matters ecclesiastical as well as civil.

Six, New Hampshire, Connecticut, New Jersey, Georgia, North and South Carolina, adhered to religious establishments.

Two, Delaware and Maryland, demanded Christianity.

Four, Pennsylvania, Delaware, North and South Carolina, required assent to the divine inspiration of the Bible.

Two, Pennsylvania and South Carolina, imposed a belief in heaven and hell.

Three, New York, Maryland, and South Carolina, excluded ministers from civil office.

Two, Pennsylvania and South Carolina, emphasized belief in one eternal God.

One, Delaware, required assent to the doctrine of the Trinity.

Five, New Hampshire, Massachusetts, Connecticut, Maryland, and South Carolina, insisted on Protestantism.

One, South Carolina, still referred to religious "toleration."

We have traced the beginnings of disestablishment and of religious freedom in the original thirteen states and in Vermont, the first to join them. When the Congregationalists finally capitulated in Massachusetts in 1833, religious freedom had been to all intents and purposes secured as a matter of constitutional right in all parts of the United States. There were a few minor legal injustices that needed to be ironed out, but the victory for complete legal separation between Church and State had been won. Furthermore, since most of the thirteen colonies had originally some State Church, it was natural that these, as public institutions, should not be taxed. This privilege was also gradually extended in colonial times to other churches, and, as it was increasingly realized that the churches rendered a public service, exemption became a regular procedure under the new state constitutions and statutes. Conditions differed with the times, and there were inconsistencies due to historical and local factors, but the above may be taken as in general a fair summary for the Revolutionary period. The overall picture shows freedom of public worship and religious expression gained everywhere and Church-State separation in most jurisdictions, but with some civil disabilities continued against Roman Catholics, especially with respect to office holding. This last was difficult to overcome because of the problem involved in papal allegiance. There were also one or two states where Jews were not legally eligible to some public offices.

Chapter 4

CONSTITUTIONAL PROVISIONS FOR RELIGIOUS FREEDOM AND CHURCH-STATE SEPARATION

Founders' Official Acts and Utterances Prior to the Constitution

Since the conditions existing at the time of the founding of any institution and the point of view of the founders always have an important influence on the institution's ideals and development, it is appropriate to consider the emerging Federal government's attitude toward the relation of Church and State and the cause of religious freedom at the time of the Revolutionary War and during the decade thereafter.

We may first consider the prayers, thanksgivings, and chaplaincies from the beginning of the Revolutionary period. The official minutes of the first session of the Continental Congress in 1774 show a proposal that the sessions be opened with prayer.[1] The motion was carried, over the opposition of John Jay and John Rutledge based on the diversity of the religious sentiments of the body.[2] The person nominated to deliver the prayer was the Reverend Jacob Duché,[3] an Anglican of Huguenot stock, who two years later was formally elected chaplain of Congress.[4] This initiation of Congressional chaplaincies was somewhat inauspicious in that Duché resigned shortly after his election, having, in the words of John Adams, "turned out an apostate and traitor"[5] who urged Washington to call for rescission of "the hasty and ill-advised Declaration of Independence."[6] Fortunately, his successors were ardent patriots.

The Continental Congress issued four fast-day proclamations prior to its first thanksgiving. Of these, perhaps the most significant was that issued July 12, 1775, for a fast day in all the united colonies, the first to represent all the colonies that were being molded into a nation.[7] It was with reference to this fast day that John Adams, writing to his wife from Philadelphia, said, "We have appointed a Continental fast. Millions will be upon their knees at once before their great Creator, imploring His forgiveness and blessing; His smiles on American Councils and arms."[8]

The first proclamation for a day of thanksgiving was issued by Congress in November, 1777, setting aside December 18 for "solemn thanksgiving and praise." It called upon all Americans to "join the penitent confession of their manifold sins," and to offer "their humble and earnest supplication that it may please God through the merits of Jesus Christ, mercifully to forgive and blot them out of remembrance." [9] This proclamation is also noticeable for its Trinitarian statement,[10] almost always omitted in later Federal and state proclamations so as to make them equally acceptable to all Christians, Jews, and other theists.

A decade later, at a crucial moment during the Federal Constitutional Convention in Philadelphia, the aged Franklin moved "that henceforth prayers imploring the assistance of Heaven, and its blessings on our deliberations, be held in this Assembly every morning before we proceed to business, and that one or more of the clergy of this city be requested to officiate in that service." [11] Madison's "Notes" on the Convention state that "After several unsuccessful attempts for silently postponing the motion by adjourning, the adjournment was at length carried, without any vote on the motion." [12]

Several reasons seem to have contributed to the failure to adopt Franklin's motion for opening prayer: (1) adoption at that late date would draw attention to the fact that there had been no prayers during the preceding sessions; (2) it might lead the public to believe that there were dissensions within the Convention; (3) the Convention had no funds to pay a clergyman; (4) the Convention was held in Philadelphia, a Quaker city, and Quaker usage frowned on public prayers; (5) there was a discord of opinion not only among the delegates to the Convention but among clergymen as well.[13]

Although the Constitutional Convention did not adopt Franklin's motion, the custom established by the Continental Congress of having its sessions opened with prayer was taken over by the Congress established by the Constitution and has continued to this day.

Also worthy of inclusion in this listing of the official utterances on religion and religious freedom by the founders of our republic prior to the Constitution are the Letter to the Inhabitants of Quebec, the Declaration of Independence, and the Northwest Ordinance of 1787. The Letter, drafted by John Dickinson [14] and adopted by the first Continental Congress in 1776, was an appeal to the Canadians to unite with the colonies in securing a redress of their grievances. It asserted that liberty of conscience in religion was not conferred by Parliament but was a gift of God.[15] It also sought to assure the Canadians that their Catholicism would not constitute a bar to complete amity with the Protestant colonies, pointing out that the union of the Swiss cantons "is composed of Roman Catholic and Protestant States, living in the utmost concord and peace with one another." [16] Two years later, the Congress sent a diplomatic mission to Canada with instructions to "declare that we hold sacred the rights of conscience and may promise to the whole people, solemnly in our name, the free and undisturbed exercise of their religion; and, to the clergy, the full, perfect and peaceable possession and enjoyment of all their estates." [17]

There are four references to God in the Declaration of Independence. He is referred to as "Nature's God," the "Creator," the "Supreme Judge of the world," and "Divine Providence." The Declaration may be accepted as evidence that the founders of the country, although most of them were neither catholic, in the historic sense of the word, in their theology nor evangelical in their attitude, were sympathetic with the fundamental theistic belief and with the moral and social teachings of the Gospels.

The Declaration was not only an epoch-making document in the sphere of politics; it was almost as important in its implications for religion because of its assertion that man, as such, has derived from his Maker certain rights which are basic, and which no government can either give or take away. Its direct and indirect influence on freedom, including religious freedom, was large. As one signer (Roman Catholic) wrote, "When I signed the Declaration of Independence I had in view, not only our independence from England, but the toleration of all sects professing the Christian religion, and communicating to them all equal rights." [18]

The Northwest Ordinance, adopted by the Continental Congress in 1787 to set up a government for the Northwest Territory, provided that "No person, demeaning himself in a peaceable and orderly manner, shall ever be molested on account of his mode of worship, or religious sentiment in the said territory." [19] It stated further that "Religion, morality and knowledge, being necessary to good government and the happiness of mankind, schools and the means of education shall forever be encouraged." [20]

Also worthy of mention in this listing of the official acts and utterances of the founders before the Constitution are the resolution of Congress in 1777 instructing the Committee on Commerce to import twenty thousand copies of the Bible [21] and its resolution of 1782 approving "the pious and laudable undertaking" of a printer named Robert Aitken [22] in publishing an American edition of the Holy Scriptures. [23]

In this same year (1782) Congress entered into its first treaty with a foreign nation, the Netherlands, declaring, significantly, in Article 4, that

there shall be an entire and perfect liberty of conscience allowed to the subjects and inhabitants of each party, and their families; and no one shall be molested in regard to his worship, provided he submits, as to the public demonstration of it, to the laws of the country. [24]

Similar provisions were inserted during the next three years in treaties with Sweden and Prussia. [25]

Another interesting event occurring between the time the United States gained its independence and the time it adopted the Constitution, concerned our relations with the Church of Rome. In July, 1783, the papal nuncio at Paris addressed a letter to Benjamin Franklin, then our minister there, requesting the consent of Congress to the appointment as a bishop or prefect apostolic in the United States of a person who might not be an American resident.[26] Such a possibility might arise if a fitting candidate were not yet available within the United States, but the letter assured Mr. Franklin that the appointee would be selected from "some foreign nation on close terms of friendship with the United States." [27]

The "foreign nation" intended was France,[28] and any plan such as the one proposed, which would have made American Catholics dependent on a French ecclesiastical intermediary, would certainly have been unacceptable to John Carroll and most of his American friends. The plan evidently had at least in part a political purpose and is frequently referred to by Catholic historians as representing a French intrigue in which the French minister to the United States was also involved.

The attitude of Congress, of vital importance to all subsequent American history, was shown in the following resolution adopted in May, 1784:

Resolved, That Doctor Franklin be desired to notify to the Apostolic Nuncio at Versaille, that Congress will always be pleased to testify their respect to his sovereign and state; but that the subject of his application to Doctor Franklin, being purely spiritual, it is without the jurisdiction and powers of Congress, who have no authority to permit or refuse it, these powers being reserved to the several states individually.[29]

The Continental Congress also showed its interest in religion in many other ways. Its records are full of references to "God," under many titles, to "Jesus Christ," the "Christian Religion," "God and the Constitution," and the "Free Protestant Colonies." [30] The religious sanction for its utterances and acts is emphasized. Its legislation not only dealt with political, economic, and military matters but included definite references to Sunday observance, prayer, morality, repentance for "sins," public worship, thanksgiving, Christian education in the states, attendance at divine services by officers and men of the army, and true religion.[31] The legislators undertook their task with a clear feeling of its importance and of the need of encouraging the religious spirit in the new nation, while at the same time avoiding favoritism to any particular Protestant denomination.

Founders' Official Acts and Utterances After Adoption of the Constitution

Besides the acts and utterances on religion and religious liberty that preceded the Constitution, there are a number of matters, in addition to the Constitution and the Bill of Rights, which have seemed of sufficient importance to be brought together for the later period, as they all throw light on the foundations of Church and State relations in this country. First in time was the divine service which was part of Washington's inauguration in 1789. By resolution adopted by both houses of Congress it was decided that after the administration of the oath of office to the president "divine services" should be held in St. Paul's Chapel, "performed by the Chaplain of Congress." [32] (It may be queried why an Episcopal church was chosen. The answer is probably threefold: it was the Church of the president; it was the Church of the chaplain; and St. Paul's was an unusually spacious edifice in the city and within half a mile of Federal Hall.[33])

In the first Congress that convened after the adoption of the Constitution, a resolution was introduced requesting the president to recommend to the people of the United States a day of thanksgiving and prayer, to be observed "by acknowledging with grateful hearts the many signal favours of Almighty God, especially by affording them an opportunity peacefully to establish a Constitution of Government for their safety and happiness," [34] The resolution was opposed on the ground that "it is a business with which Congress has nothing to do; it is a religious matter, and as such is proscribed to us." [35] Nevertheless, it was adopted, and President Washington issued a proclamation setting aside Thursday, November 26, 1789, as a day for national thanksgiving and urging all to "unite in most humbly offering our prayers and supplications to the great Lord and Ruler of Nations, and beseech him to pardon our national and other transgressions." [36]

Two of Washington's other proclamations of a religious character are also worth recording. On January 1, 1795, he proclaimed a day of prayer and thanksgiving when the prospect of another foreign war had decreased, and again a year later when the treaty with England was sustained. He also appointed February 19, 1795, a day of public thanksgiving and prayer in connection with the ending of the so-called Whiskey Insurrection in western Pennsylvania in the summer of 1794.

In 1798, when many felt that the ideas of the French Revolution might have a demoralizing and perhaps disastrous influence on the new republic, President John Adams, acting on his own initiative, appointed May 9 as a "day of solemn humiliation, fasting and prayer" that "our country may be protected from all dangers which threaten it." [37] He was a staunch Federalist, and his proclamation bears evidence of fear that the godless and socially radical ideas of the French Revolution, transplanted, as he thought, in large measure to the United States by Jefferson, might prove calamitous.[38] This proclamation can be understood only as we bear in mind the French influence of the time and the bitter controversy it provoked between the Federalists, who felt the proclamation should make Americans humble and prayerful for the removal of the threatened dangers, and the Antifederalists, who favored Jefferson and France and consequently would not in most cases recognize the day of prayer. Thus, more than in any case in our history outside the Civil War period, the proclamation proved a bone of contention.

Jefferson, when president, broke with the Washington-Adams tradition over the propriety of the Federal government's proclaiming days of national prayer and thanksgiving.[39] His reasons were set forth in a letter to a Presbyterian clergyman in 1808:

I consider the government of the United States as interdicted by the Constitution from intermeddling with religious institutions, their doctrines, discipline, or exercises. This results not only from the provision that no law shall be made respecting the establishment or free exercise of religion, but from that also which reserves to the States the powers not delegated to the United States. Certainly, no power to prescribe any religious exercise, or to assume authority in religious discipline, has been delegated to the General Government. It must then rest with the States, as far as it can be in any human authority. But it is only proposed that I should *recommend*, not prescribe a day of fasting and prayer. That is, that I should *indirectly* assume to the United States an authority over religious exercises, which the Constitution has directly precluded them from. It must be meant, too, that this recommendation is to carry some authority, and to be sanctioned by some penalty on those who disregard it; not indeed of fine and imprisonment, but of some degree of proscription, perhaps in public opinion. And does the change in the nature of the penalty make the recommendation less a *law* of conduct for those to whom it is directed? I do not believe it is for the interest of religion to invite the civil magistrate to direct its exercises, its discipline, or its doctrines; nor of the religious societies, that the General Government should be invested with the power of effecting any uniformity of time or matter among them. Fasting and prayer are religious exercises; the enjoining them an act of discipline. Every religious society has a right to determine for itself the times for these exercises, and the objects proper for them, according to their own particular tenets; and this right can never be safer than in their own hands, where the Constitution has deposited it.[40]

James Madison proclaimed several days for fasting and thanksgiving, although he had some scruples on the subject of his constitutional position in the matter. One case was of special significance. In 1812, in connection with the war, he appointed a national fast day for the people to pray, among other things, that "God would guide their public counsel," "animate their patriotism," and "bestow a blessing on their arms." [41] This created some opposition from Federalists, who did not believe the war justifiable and therefore considered the president's proclamation political in its significance and an impertinence. His views as to the propriety of Federal proclamations of days of prayer and thanksgiving are given in a letter written to Edward Livingston in 1822. In this he referred to his objection to having chaplains paid from the public treasury and added,

There has been another deviation from the strict principle in the Executive proclamations of fasts and festivals, so far, at least as they have spoken the language of *injunction*, or have lost sight of the equality of *all* religious sects in the eye of the Constitution. Whilst I was honored with the Executive trust, I found it necessary on more than one occasion to follow the example of predecessors. But I was always careful to make the Proclamation absolutely indiscriminate, and merely recommendatory; or, rather, mere *designations* of a day on which all who thought proper might *unite* in consecrating it to religious purposes, according to their own faith and forms. . . . I have no doubt that every new example will succeed, as every past one has done, in showing that religion and Government will both exist in greater purity the less they are mixed together.[42]

Thus, of the first four presidents of the United States, two deemed presidential proclamations of prayer and thanksgiving to be proper, while two held a contrary opinion. It should also be noted that on occasion such presidential proclamations were used, or at least were construed by many to have been used, for partisan political purposes, thus giving support to Madison's admonition "that religion and Government will both exist in greater purity the less they are mixed together." [43]

Besides the presidential proclamations for prayer and thanksgiving, reference should be made to two treaties with Tropoli, entered into by the United States in 1797 and 1805. The first provided as follows:

As the government of the United States is not, in any sense, founded on the Christian religion; as it has in itself no character of enmity against the laws, religion, or tranquility of Musselman; and as the said States never have entered into any way or act of hostility against any Mohometan nation, it is declared by the parties that no pretext arising from religious opinion shall ever produce an interruption of harmony existing between the two countries.[44]

However, eight years later, in a new treaty with Tripoli, the phrase "is not in any sense founded on the Christian religion" was omitted.[45]

Finally, reference should be made to the fact that the House of Representatives early in its history authorized the use of its hall for religious services,[46] and that even during the administration of Thomas Jefferson the Capitol was used for religious services.[47]

The Constitution of the United States

With this background of official acts and utterances, we can now consider the Constitution itself. It contains two fundamentally important provisions which deal directly with religious rights, namely, the forbidding of religious tests as qualifications for public office in the original Constitution,[48] and the guarantee of religious freedom in the Bill of Rights,[49] which followed three years later.

Although the Declaration of Independence of 1776 contains references to "Nature's God," the "Creator," and "Divine Providence," there are no such references in the Constitution a decade later. Its only incidental mentions of religion—as distinct from those in the Bill of Rights—are the clauses which except Sundays as days to be counted within which the president may exercise his veto rights on legislation,[50] the dating of the document at its close as "in the Year of our Lord one thousand seven hundred and eighty seven," [51] and the all-important clause ruling out all Federal religious tests.[52]

The absence of any reference to God in the Constitution was much criticized and was frequently mentioned by those who opposed its ratification in state conventions. President Timothy Dwight of Yale, who may be considered representative of the conservative Christian element in the country at the time, thought it "highly discreditable to us that we do not acknowledge God in our Constitution," and so informed his students at Yale two decades later. He attributed the omission to Jefferson's influence.[53]

Also of great constitutional importance was the following reference in the journal of the Convention under date of August 30, 1787:

"It was moved and seconded to add the following clause to the 20th article: —'but no religious test shall ever be required as a qualification to any office or public trust under the authority of the United States'; which passed unanimously in the affirmative." [54]

North Carolina was the only state that ultimately voted against the adoption of this clause, which seemed to meet general approval, although there was some anti-Catholic objection based on such arguments as that the pope might become president, and the dire effect of having Roman Catholics and pagans in office.[55] Referring to the significance of the clause, Justice Joseph Story said: "The Catholic and the Protestant, the Calvinist and the Arminian, the infidel and the Jew, may sit down to the Communion-table of the National Council, without any inquisition into their faith or mode of worship." [56]

In recent discussions of religious freedom and Church-State separation in the United States attention has been so much centered on the Bill of Rights that the importance of this provision in the original Constitution as a bulwark of Church-State separation has been largely overlooked. As a matter of fact it was and is important in preventing religious tests for Federal office—a stipulation later extended by the Supreme Court to all the states.[57] Because of its importance it will be dealt with in further detail in a later chapter.[58] Here it need be added only that it went far in thwarting any Church-State union even less than the establishment of a State Church in the United States. It would be almost impossible to establish such a Church, since no Church has more than a fifth of the population. Congress as constituted of men and women from all denominations could never unite in selecting any one body for this privilege. This has been so evident from the time of the founding of the government that it is one reason why the First Amendment must be interpreted more broadly than merely as preventing the State establishment of religion, which had already been made practically impossible.

James Madison proposed with Mr. Pinckney "to insert in the list of powers vested in Congress a power—'to establish an University, in which no preferences or distinctions should be allowed on account of religion.'" This proposal, to which Madison refers in his "Notes," was supported by James Wilson, but Gouverneur Morris stated, "It is not necessary. The exclusive power at the Seat of Government, will reach the object." [59] This question was lost by a vote of 6 to 4, with one state (Connecticut) divided.[60]

In view of the fact that there had been much diversity of opinion in the states represented on the subject of religious freedom, and that many of them were themselves still discussing the question of Church-State separation, the Constitutional Convention probably went as far as it could at the time. But the action already taken by Virginia, in doing away with the Episcopal Establishment and providing complete religious freedom, pointed the way clearly to the ultimate goal.

There is also evidence that the Constitutional Convention was not much concerned with the question of religion because it assumed that this was a matter under state rather than Federal jurisdiction. In the eighty-five *Federalist* papers, by Hamilton, Madison, and Jay, which appeared in the six months beginning in October, 1787, there is only one reference to religion or the Church. This is by Madison, who mentions "A zeal for different opinions concerning religion" as one of the "latent causes of faction" which appear in civil society.[61] The framers of the Constitution believed that the religious issue could best be left to the states, which had already begun, under the leadership of Virginia, to handle it constructively and wisely. Speaking in the Virginia convention in June, 1788, on Patrick Henry's objection that the new Constitution did not expressly protect religion, Madison said, "There is not a shadow of right in the general government to intermeddle with religion. Its least interference with it, would be a most flagrant usurpation." [62]

Also significant is the reply by President Washington to a letter from a group of Presbyterian churches in New England regarding the omission of any reference to the Christian religion in the Constitution:

I am persuaded [the president wrote], that the path of true piety is so plain, as to require but little direction. To this consideration we ought to ascribe the absence of any regulation respecting religion from the Magna Charta of our country. To the guidance of the Ministers of the Gospel, this important object is, perhaps, more properly committed. It will be your care to instruct the ignorant, and to reclaim the devious. And in the progress of morality and science, to which our Government will give every furtherance, we may confidently expect the advancement of true religion, and the completion of our happiness. [63]

The Bill of Rights

Bills of rights already existed in eight of the new states and at least four of them were used by Madison as a basis for drafting the one presently adopted by Congress. [64] On May 4, 1789, four days after the inauguration of President Washington, Madison announced to the House of Representatives, then assembled in Federal Hall, New York, that "he intended to bring on the subject of Amendments to the Constitution, on the fourth Monday of this month." It was well known that he had a bill of rights in mind, something that would protect the nation against the possible arbitrary acts of government. This is a matter which Jefferson also had always had much at heart.

On June 8 Madison urged the adoption of the Bill of Rights. It was no secret, he said, that many Americans, "respectable for their talents and respectable for the jealousy which they have for their liberty," were dissatisfied with the Constitution as it stood because it "did not contain effectual provisions against encroachments on particular rights, and those safeguards which they have been long accustomed to have interposed between them and the magistrate who exercises the sovereign power." "We ought not to disregard their inclination," he urged, "but, on principles of amity and moderation, conform to their wishes and expressly declare the great rights of mankind secured under this Constitution."

The House, after a full discussion, agreed upon the proposed amendments and sent them to the Senate. Discussion of differences between the two houses followed, and on September 25, 1789, the Senate concurred "in the amendments proposed by the House of Representatives to the amendments of the Senate."

The joint resolution embodying the Bill of Rights bore a preamble stating that it was issued because "the convention of a number of states" had "at the time of their adopting the Constitution, expressed a desire, in order to prevent misconstruction or abuse of its powers, that further declaratory and restrictive clauses should be added," and because "extending the grounds of public confidence in the government will best secure the beneficent ends" of its institution.[65]

The first of the amendments to the Constitution thus adopted by Congress in 1789 and ratified by the requisite number of states[66] in 1791[67] is of prime importance in connection with the relations of Church and State in the United States. It reads as follows: "Congress shall make no law respecting an establishment of religion, or prohibiting the free exercise thereof; or abridging the freedom of speech, or of the press; or the right of the people peaceably to assemble and to petition the Government for a redress of grievances."

These rights are interrelated. They are all of importance from the standpoint of the Churches. Freedom of speech is related to preaching, freedom of the press to religious journalism, freedom of assembly and petition to church meetings; but here we are mainly concerned with religious freedom and Church-State separation.

A careful study of the preliminaries in Congress leading up to the adoption of the epoch-making clause in behalf of religious freedom seems necessary. This is difficult to make with entire confidence in details because the records are meager and inadequately prepared and edited. It shows, however, that on June 8, 1789, Madison offered a series of proposed constitutional amendments for the approval of the House of Representatives. They included this statement to be added in Article I, Sections 9 and 10, of the original Constitution:

The civil rights of none shall be abridged on account of religious belief or worship, nor shall any national religion be established, nor shall the full and equal rights of conscience be in any manner, or on any pretext, infringed.

No State shall violate the equal rights of conscience, or the freedom of the press, or the trial by jury in criminal cases.[68]

The word "national" was added in the first clause to meet the scruples of states with an Established Church. It will be noticed that the last clause proposed to extend the religious guarantee to the states, thus going further than the later Federal Bill of Rights.

Madison's proposals were referred to the committee of the whole,[69] but on July 21 this committee was discharged from further consideration of the matter and the House appointed a representative Committee of Eleven,[70] including Madison, with a member from each state to consider both Madison's amendments and those suggested by the various states. The report of the special committee was the subject of full debate in the House on August 15, 1789.[71] The debate, is important for the understanding of the historical foundations of our religious freedom, and is therefore given here in full.[72]

AMENDMENTS TO THE CONSTITUTION

The House again went into a Committee of the whole on the proposed amendments to the constitution, Mr. BOUDINOT in the chair.

The fourth proposition being under consideration, as follows:

Article I, Section 9. Between paragraphs two and three insert "no religion shall be established by law, nor shall the equal rights of conscience be infringed."

Mr. SYLVESTER had some doubts of the propriety of the mode of expression used in this paragraph. He apprehended that it was liable to a construction different from what had been made by the committee. He feared it might be thought to have a tendency to abolish religion altogether.

Mr. VINING suggested the propriety of transposing the two members of the sentence.

Mr. GERRY said it would read better if it was, that no religious doctrine shall be established by law.

Mr. SHERMAN thought the amendment altogether unnecessary, inasmuch as Congress had no authority whatever delegated to them by the constitution to make religious establishments; he would, therefore, move to have it struck out.

Mr. (Daniel) CARROLL.—As the rights of conscience are, in their nature, of peculiar delicacy, and will little bear the gentlest touch of governmental hand; and as many sects have concurred in opinion that they are not well secured under the present constitution, he said he was much in favor of adopting the words. He thought it would tend more towards conciliating the minds of the people to the Government than almost any other amendment he had heard proposed. He would not contend with gentlemen about the phraseology, his object was to secure the substance in such a manner as to satisfy the wishes of the honest part of the community.

Mr. MADISON said, he apprehended the meaning of the words to be, that Congress should not establish a religion, and enforce the legal observation of it by law, nor compel men to worship God in any manner contrary to their conscience. Whether the words are necessary or not, he did not mean to say, but they had been required by some of the State Conventions, who seemed to entertain an opinion that under the clause of the constitution, which gave power to Congress to make all laws necessary and proper to carry into execution the constitution, and the laws made under it, enabled them to make laws of such a nature as might infringe the rights of conscience, and establish a national religion; to prevent these effects he presumed the amendment was intended, and he thought it as well expressed as the nature of the language would admit.

Mr. HUNTINGTON said that he feared, with the gentleman first up on this subject, that the words might be taken in such latitude as to be extremely hurtful to the cause of religion. He understood the amendment to mean what had been expressed by the gentleman from Virginia; but others might find it convenient to put another construction upon it. The ministers of their congregations to the Eastward were maintained by the contributions of those who belonged to their society; the expense of building meetinghouses was contributed in the same manner. These things were regulated by by-laws. If an action was brought before a Federal Court on any of these cases, the person who had neglected to perform his engagements could not be compelled to do it; for a support of ministers, or building of places of worship might be construed into a religious establishment.

By the charter of Rhode Island, no religion could be established by law; he could give a history of the effects of such a regulation; indeed the people were now enjoying the blessed fruits of it. He hoped, therefore, the amendment would be made in such a way as to secure the rights of conscience, and a free exercise of the rights of religion, but not to patronize those who professed no religion at all.

Mr. MADISON thought, if the word national was inserted before religion, it would satisfy the minds of honorable gentlemen. He believed that the people feared one sect might obtain a pre-eminence, or two combine together, and establish a religion to which they would compel others to conform. He thought if the word national was introduced, it would point the amendment directly to the object it was intended to prevent.

Mr. LIVERMORE was not satisfied with that amendment; but he did not wish them to dwell long on the subject. He thought it would be better if it was altered, and made to read in this manner, that Congress shall make no laws touching religion, or infringing the rights of conscience.

Mr. GERRY did not like the term national, proposed by the gentleman from Virginia, and he hoped it would not be adopted by the House. It brought to his mind some observations that had taken place in the conventions at the time they were considering the present constitution. It had been insisted upon by those who were called antifederalists, that this form of Government consolidated the Union; the honorable gentleman's motion shows that he considers it in the same light. Those who were called antifederalists at that time complained that they had injustice done them by the title, because they were in favor of a Federal Government, and the others were in favor of a national one; the federalists were for ratifying the constitution as it stood, and the others not until amendments were made. Their names then ought not to have been distinguished by federalists and antifederalists, but rats and antirats (evidently ratificationists and antiratificationists).

Mr. MADISON withdrew his motion, but observed that the words "no national religion shall be established by law," did not imply that the Government was a national one; the question was then taken on Livermore's motion, and passed the affirmative, thirty-one for, and twenty against it.

Throughout this momentous debate there were references to the "anxiety" felt by large sections of the people over the omission of a bill of rights from the Constitution. This was well expressed by Madison in the debate in the House, August 15:

I appeal to the gentlemen who have heard the voice of the country, to those who have attended the debates of the State conventions, whether the amendments now proposed are not those most strenuously required by the opponents to the constitution? . . . Have not the people been told that the rights of conscience, the freedom of speech, the liberty of the press, and trial by jury were in jeopardy? that they ought not to adopt the constitution until those important rights were secured to them?

The committee of eleven had also recommended adding a clause to the Constitution to the effect that "no person religiously scrupulous shall be compelled to bear arms," [73] a clause based on the proposals of Virginia and Carolina. This proposal was strongly supported [74] and favored on August 17, and the reasons for its final omission are not clear.

In the same report the Committee of Eleven included a recommendation, long urged by Madison. The *Journal* thus refers to this matter:

The committee then proceeded to the fifth proposition:
Article I, section 10, between the first and second paragraph, insert "no State shall infringe the equal rights of conscience, nor the freedom of speech or of the press, nor of the right of trial by jury in criminal cases."
Mr. TUCKER.—This is offered, I presume, as an amendment to the constitution of the United States, but it goes only to the alteration of the constitutions of particular States. It will be much better, I apprehend, to leave the State Governments to themselves, and not to interfere with them more than we already do; and that is thought by many to be rather too much. I therefore move, sir, to strike out these words.
Mr. Madison conceived this to be the most valuable amendment in the whole list. If there was any reason to restrain the Government of the United States from infringing upon these essential rights, it was equally necessary that they should be secured against the State Governments. He thought that if they provided against the one, it was as necessary to provide against the other, and was satisfied that it would be equally grateful to the people.
Mr. LIVERMORE had no great objection to the sentiment, but he thought it not well expressed. He wished to make it an affirmative proposition; "the equal rights of conscience, the freedom of speech or of the press, and the right of trial by jury in criminal cases, shall not be infringed by any State."

This transposition being agreed to, and Mr. TUCKER's motion being rejected, the clause was adopted.[75]

Unfortunately the clause thus approved by the House was among those "disagreed to" by the Senate on September 21, undoubtedly due mainly to state rights feelings.[76] It is interesting to note Livermore again supporting Madison on a broad-gauge proposal regarding religious freedom. It was not until the second quarter of the twentieth century that the substance of this proposal, at least in respect of freedom of conscience, speech and the press, became part of our Constitution, and this by the Supreme Court's interpretation of the Fourteenth Amendment.[77]

In the debate on August 18 and 23, Thomas Tucker of South Carolina proposed the addition of the word "other" between the words "No" and "religious Test" in Article VI; but this was finally "passed in the negative"—that is, voted down; a wise decision, for otherwise the oath or affirmation for officeholders provided for would have been designated specifically as a religious test, which it was not intended to be, but rather as an assurance of action taken with great solemnity as in the presence of God.

On August 19 Roger Sherman of Connecticut against pressed his idea that the amendment should not be inserted in the original Constitution but placed in separate articles in a supplement, and won his point, supported by Livermore and others. The next day, August 20, the "supplement" idea for all the amendments was adopted.

On motion of Fisher Ames of Massachusetts the amendment regarding religious freedom was altered so as to read, "Congress shall make no law establishing religion, or to prevent the free exercise thereof, or to infringe the rights of conscience."

The exact arrangement of the amendments was referred August 22 to a subcommittee consisting of Egbert Benson as chairman, with Roger Sherman and Theodore Sedgwick, "who were directed to arrange the said amendments and make report thereof." Evidently the committee's duties were similar to those of the committee "on style" of the original Constitution. Indeed the records refer to it in one place as the committee on "style and arrangement."

The next and final action of the House was taken two days later on August 24 when the *Journal* states that

Mr. Benson, from the committee appointed for the purpose, reported an arrangement of the articles of amendment to the constitution of the United States, as agreed to by the House on Friday last; also, a resolution prefixed to the same, which resolution was twice read and agreed to by the House as follows:

Resolved by the Senate and House of Representatives of the United States of America in Congress assembled, (two-thirds of both Houses deeming it necessary,)

That the following articles be proposed to the Legislatures of the several States as amendments to the constitution of the United States, all or any of which articles, when ratified by three-fourths of the said Legislatures, to be valid to all intents and purposes as part of the said constitution.

On the following day (August 25) the Senate received a communication from the House requesting its concurrence with the amendment adopted. A lively debate soon began. We fortunately have this record of the discussion on September 3:

On motion to amend article third, and to strike out these words: "religion, or prohibiting the free exercise thereof," and insert "one religious sect or society in preference to others:"
It passed in the negative.
On motion for reconsideration:
It passed in the affirmative.
On motion that article the third be striken out:
It passed in the negative.
On motion to adopt the following, in lieu of the third article: "Congress shall not make any law infringing the rights of conscience, or establishing any religious sect or society:"
It passed in the negative.
On motion to amend the third article, to read thus: "Congress shall make no law establishing any particular denomination of religion in preference to another, or prohibiting the free exercise thereof, nor shall the rights of conscience be infringed:"
It passed in the negative.[78]

This action was significant in showing that Congress was not satisfied with a proposal which merely prevented an advantage to any one denomination over others as far as Church-State separation was concerned. It wished to go further.

On September 9 the Senate "proceeded in the consideration of the resolve of the House of Representatives of the 24th of August, on Articles to be proposed to the legislatures of the several states as amendments to the constitution of the United States"; and more closely defined the establishment of religion clause, and combined this article (old III) with the following one, Article IV, producing the preliminary Senate form of the First Amendment:

On motion to amend article the third, to read as follows: "Congress shall make no law establishing articles of faith or a mode of worship, or prohibiting the free exercise of religion, or abridging the freedom of speech, or the press, or the right of the people peaceably to assemble, and petition to the government for the redress of grievances:"
It was passed in the affirmative.[79]

The abstract of the Senate records for September 21 show disagreement on some of the House propositions, and agreement on others; Article III, involving religious freedom, being one over the exact wording of which they disagreed.[80] It was therefore decided that the Senate "do concur with the" proposal of the House "that a conference be desired with the Senate on the subject matter of the amendments disagreed to." Oliver Ellsworth of Connecticut, Charles Carroll of Maryland, and William Paterson of New Jersey were appointed to represent the Senate in straightening out the points at issue; with James Madison of Virginia, Roger Sherman of Connecticut, and John Vining of Delaware chosen by the House—a strong joint committee, four of whom had been members of the Constitutional Convention. The inclusion of Carroll, a Roman Catholic, is significant.

The choice of the heads of the two delegations is also significant .Madison had proved himself a most earnest and intelligent advocate of Church-State separation and religious freedom, as we have repeatedly pointed out; and Ellsworth had written forcefully on the absurdity of giving any church a favored position or of curtailing religious liberty. Wiser choices could not have been made. Unfortunately the minutes of the committee's deliberations have not been preserved, if any were ever kept; but we can be reasonably sure, from experience in other situations, that Madison played the leading part in adjusting the Livermore formula so as to make it even more effective and more completely acceptable to the Senate.

The Senate *Journal* for Thursday, September 24, contains two important entries dealing with the subject. The first is a report from Senator Ellsworth representing the managers of the conference committee to the effect

That it will be proper for the House of Representatives to agree to the said amendments, proposed by the Senate, with an amendment to their fifth amendment, so that the third article shall read as follows: "Congress shall make no law respecting an establishment of religion, or prohibiting the free exercise thereof; or abridging the freedom of speech, or of the press; or the right of the people peaceably to assemble, and petition the government for a redress of grievances". . . .

The second is a direct message from the House received later the same day quoting the above action giving the vote on religious freedom which the conferees had accepted and which the House of Representatives had approved, but making their approval of the other Senate amendments dependent upon the acceptance of this new phraseology and a change in Article 8. The exact minute reads as follows:

A message from the House of Representatives:
Mr. Beckley, their Clerk, brought up the amendments to the "Articles to be

proposed to the legislatures of the several states, as amendments to the constitution of the United States;" and informed the Senate, that the House of Representatives had *receded* from their disagreement to the 1st, 3d, 5th, 6th, 7th, 9th, 10th, 11th, 14th, 15th, 17th, 20th, 21st, 22d, 23d, and 24th, amendments, insisted on by the Senate: provided that the "two articles, which, by the amendments of the Senate, are now proposed to be inserted as the third and eighth articles," shall be amended to read as followeth:

Art. 3. Congress shall make no law respecting an establishment of religion, or prohibiting the free exercise thereof; or abridging the freedom of speech, or of the press; or the right of the people peaceably to assemble, and petition the government for a redress of grievances.

The following day, September 25, it was

Resolved, That the Senate do concur in the amendments proposed by the House of Representatives to the amendments of the Senate.[81]

These compromises, as adopted by the House on September 24 and by the Senate on September 25, restored the religious clauses nearer to the original Livermore formula. They resulted in the present wording of Article I of the Bill of Rights.

The Congress adjourned September 29 after completing with honor its vitally important work.

The Meaning of the First Amendment

Beginning in the 1920's the United States Supreme Court began to hold that the various freedoms guaranteed by the First Amendment against infringement by Congress were equally guaranteed against infringement on the part of the states by the operation of the Fourteenth Amendment, which had become part of our Constitution in 1868.[82] That amendment forbids the states from depriving any person of "life, liberty or property without due process of law." The term "liberty," the Court has consistently held, must be construed to mean not merely physical freedom but also intellectual, spiritual, and aesthetic freedom.[83] Therefore a state may not, any more than Congress, prohibit the free exercise of religion[84] or abridge the freedom of speech,[85] press,[86] or assembly.[87]

This was a great advance in judicial protection of individual liberties, but the Court has gone even farther. It has held, in effect, that the term "liberty" in the Fourteenth Amendment also encompasses the freedom from a relationship between the Church and State which would violate the First Amendment if it were the Federal government that was involved.[88] In other words, just as the Fourteenth Amendment makes the free-exercise guarantee of the First

Amendment applicable to the states,[89] so too does it make the prohibition on laws respecting an establishment of religion.[90]

The importance of this holding can hardly be overestimated, for the opportunities and temptations for violation of Church-State separation are many times more numerous on the state than on the Federal level. The foremost arena of Church-State conflict today is in the field of education, whether with regard to religion in public education [91] or public financing of private religious educational institutions,[92] and under our system education is primarily a state rather than Federal responsibility.[93]

The tremendous expansion of the practical applicability of the no-establishment clause of the First Amendment has evoked in recent years a widespread professional and public interest in the meaning of that clause and in the intent of its drafters.[94] Naturally those who favor a closer co-operative relationship between governmental and religious institutions interpret the framers' intent quite narrowly and urge that they sought only to forbid legislation tending toward a formal union of a single Church and the national government to the exclusion of other Churches,[95] while those who favor the separation of Church and State to the farthest extent possible interpret the framers' intent broadly.[96] It is therefore no accident that the most vigorous defenders of a narrow interpretation are to be found among those associated with Roman Catholicism and the Catholic Church,[97] whose doctrine as late as 1964 characterized Church-State separation as "unfortunate." Conversely, secular groups such as the American Civil Liberties Union assert a broad interpretation.[98] It must not be supposed, however, that the narrow interpretation enjoys no support in non-Catholic and particularly academic circles.[99] Conversely, the broad interpretation is strongly urged within non-secular groups such as many Protestant and Jewish organizations.[100]

The issue came to the fore first in 1947 in the famous parochial school bus case, *Everson* v. *Board of Education*.[101] In that case, while upholding by a vote of 5 to 4 the validity of using tax-raised funds to transport children to parochial schools, the Court spelled out the meaning of the First Amendment in the following definitive language:

The "establishment of religion" clause of the First Amendment means at least this: Neither a state nor the Federal Government can set up a church. Neither can pass laws which aid one religion, aid all religions, or prefer one religion over another. Neither can force nor influence a person to go to or remain away from church against his will or force him to profess a belief or disbelief in any religion. No person can be punished for entertaining or professing religious beliefs or disbeliefs, for church attendance or non-attendance. No tax in any amount, large or small, can be levied to support any religious activities or institutions, whatever they may be called, or whatever form they may adopt to teach or practice religion. Neither a state nor the Federal Government can, openly or secretly, participate in the affairs of any religious organizations or groups and vice versa. In the words of Jefferson, the clause against establishment of religion by law was intended to erect "a wall of separation between Church and State." [102]

This statement, reiterated by the Supreme Court the following year in the Champaign released-time case, *McCollum* v. *Board of Education*,[103] showed clearly that the Court had adopted the broad interpretation of the no-establishment clause. Such an interpretation imposes an obligation of neutrality on government not merely as between different religions but also as between religion and non-religion, and indeed between religion and irreligion.

That, said the Supreme Court, is what the fathers of the Constitution and of the First Amendment intended. And they intended it not because they were hostile to religion but because they were convinced that the cause of religion could best be served if the government maintained a strict hands-off policy and a high and impregnable wall between Church and State. They were convinced too that the best way to keep from these shores the religious bloodshed, persecution, and intolerance that had plagued the Old World was to keep such a wall between Church and State in the New World.

This definitive interpretation of the no-establishment clause evoked considerable criticism from a number of sources.[104] It was argued that the Supreme Court has misread the Constitution and misinterpreted the intent of the framers. It was not, these critics asserted, the purpose of the First Amendment to divorce religion from government or to impose neutrality between believers and non-believers but only to meet in a practical manner the problems raised by a multiplicity of competing sects. This was done by requiring the government to be neutral as among the sects and forbidding it to favor one at the expense of the others. The amendment was not meant to bar the government from aiding and supporting religion and religious institutions so long as the aid and support were granted equally and without preference to some faiths and discrimination against others.[105]

The proof of their contention, said the critics of the Supreme Court's interpretation, was to be found in the history of our country and in the society about us. Throughout its history our governments, national and state, have co-operated with religion and shown friendliness to it. God is invoked in the Declaration of Independence and in practically every state constitution. Sunday, the Christian Sabbath, is universally observed as a day of rest. The sessions of Congress and of the state legislatures are invariably opened with prayer, in Congress by chaplains who are employed by the Federal government. We have chaplains in our armed forces and in our penal institutions. Oaths in courts of law are administered through use of the Bible. Public officials take an oath of office ending with "so help me God." Religious institutions are tax exempt throughout the nation. Our pledge of allegiance declares that we are a nation "under God." Our national motto is "In God We Trust" and is inscribed on our currency and on some of our postage stamps.

These and many other similar illustrations of governmental cooperation with religion, said the critics of the Everson-McCollum principle, show conclusively that the purpose of the First Amendment was not to erect an absolute, impenetrable wall between religion and government or to make our nation godless. The amendment, in their view, prohibits preferential treatment and imposes an obligation of neutrality on the part of government as among the different religious groups, but not as between religion and non-religion or as between God-fearers and atheists.

Four years after the McCollum decision, the Court, in the New York City released-time case of *Zorach* v. *Clauson*,[106] showed some retreat from the broad scope of the Everson-McCollum principle. "We are," said the Court, "a religious people whose institutions presuppose a Supreme Being." The First Amendment "does not say that in every and all respects there shall be a separation of Church and State." It requires only that "there shall be no concert or union or dependency one on the other."[107]

Nevertheless, and despite this language, it is now quite clear that the Court did not intend to repudiate the broad interpretation of the no-establishment clause announced in the Everson and McCollum cases. Even in the Zorach case [108] it expressly affirmed adherence to the McCollum decision, a decision which is consistent only with the broad interpretation of the First Amendment expressed in the Everson and McCollum cases. The Court also went out of its way to say that under the First Amendment "Government may not finance religious groups nor undertake religious instruction" [109]—a disability required only if the broad interpretation of the Everson and McCollum cases is accepted. In any event, whatever doubt may have been cast by the Zorach case was removed by later cases. In 1961 in the Sunday law case of *McGowan* v. *Maryland* [110] and the Maryland notary public oath case of *Torcaso* v. *Watkins* [111] the Court reiterated in full the definitive paragraph set forth in the Everson and McCollum cases, and in succeeding years in the New York Regents' prayer case, *Engel* v. *Vitale*,[112] and the Bible reading case of *Abington School District* v. *Schempp* [113] the Court, while it did not repeat the paragraph, applied it to bar prayer and Bible reading from the public schools. Thus, at least up to the present time the Supreme Court is committed to the broad interpretation of the First Amendment, which approximates Livermore's proposal that "Congress shall make no laws touching religion or infringing the rights of conscience."

Chapter 5

THE SUPREME COURT'S DECISIONS
IN CHURCH AND STATE

Having considered the factors leading to the adoption of the Federal constitutional provisions regarding religious freedom and Church-State separation, both in the text of the Constitution and in the First Amendment, and having considered too the evidence regarding the fathers' intent in respect to these provisions, we may appropriately summarize all the decisions of the United States Supreme Court interpreting and applying these provisions. Also included in this chapter will be a summary of those Supreme Court decisions which, while not specifically tied in with the Constitution, nevertheless concern the general subject of the relation of religion and government in the United States. Later chapters will from time to time refer to most of these decisions as part of the discussion of the specific subject being treated; they might, therefore, have been distributed throughout the rest of this book. Nevertheless, it was deemed preferable to place them all in one chapter so that the reader might understand the constitutional development of Church-State relations as reflected in the decisions of the Supreme Court.

Terrett v. *Tylor* (1815)[1]

The first case to reach the United States Supreme Court in the realm of Church and State arose out of the disestablishment of the Episcopal Church in Virginia. When Virginia became a state in 1776, its legislature passed a law confirming in the Church all its rights of ownership to the lands and other properties it then held. Twenty-five years later, in 1801, as the last step in the process of disestablishment, the legislature declared that the 1776 law was inconsistent with the state's bill of rights and constitution and was therefore void. It accordingly rescinded the charter of the Church as a corporation and directed that its glebe (parish) lands be sold and the proceeds used for the poor of the parish.

In *Terrett* v. *Taylor* the United States Supreme Court, in a decision written by Justice Joseph Story, held the 1801 law to be void and of no effect. The legislature of a state might, in its constitution or bill of rights, provide against compulsory attendance at church or payment of taxes in support of any particular sect. It could not, however, deny to members of a religious corporation the right to retain their corporate charter and continue to act as a corporation. Nor could it deny to the church the right to retain and use for religious purpose the property it had acquired over the years through purchase and the generosity of its donors. A law rescinding the lawfully granted corporate charter of a church and expropriating its lawfully held property violates the fundamental principles of natural justice and is therefore void.

It should be noted that this case was not decided under any specific section of the Federal Constitution or Bill of Rights. It was not claimed, nor did the Court hold, that the attempted rescission of the corporate charter granted by the English Crown to the Episcopal Church in Virginia or the attempted expropriations of its lands violated the clause of the First Amendment guaranteeing the free exercise of religion. The decision was based on the general principles of fundamental law which protect all corporations alike, including religious corporations.

Vidal v. *Girard's Executors* (1844)

The next case decided by the Supreme Court in which it considered the relationship between religion and the State likewise did not involve the First Amendment. Stephen Girard, a wealthy Philadelphia resident, died leaving a will in which he bequeathed a large sum of money to be used to establish a college for orphans. He declared that there be taught therein the secular subjects reading, writing, grammar, arithmetic, geography, astronomy, philosophy, foreign languages, and such other learning and science as might be found appropriate. However, he directed that "no ecclesiastic, missionary, or minister of any sect whatsoever" shall ever hold any office in the college or even be admitted to it as a visitor.

In making this restriction [he said in the will], I do not mean to cast any reflection upon any sect or person whatsoever; but, as there is such a multitude of sects, and such a diversity of opinion amongst them, I desire to keep the mind or minds of the orphans . . . free from the excitement which clashing doctrine and sectarian controversy is so apt to produce; my desire is that all the instructors and teachers in the college shall take pains to instil into the minds of the scholars, the purest principles of morality, so that on their entrance into active life, they may, from inclination and habit, evince benevolence towards their fellow-creatures, and a love of truth, sobriety, and industry, adopting at the same time such religious tenets as their matured reason may enable them to prefer.

Girard's heirs sought to upset this bequest and retained Daniel Webster for the purpose. Arguing before the Supreme Court, Webster charged that what Girard had sought to do was to make "a cruel experiment" to ascertain whether children can be brought up without religion. The exclusion of Christian clergymen and Christian teachings from the school, he asserted, was derogatory and hostile to the Christian religion, and since Christianity is part of the common law of Pennsylvania, his bequest should be declared void.

This the Court refused to do. Christianity, it said in an opinion by Justice Story, is part of the common law of Pennsylvania only in the qualified sense that its divine origin and truth are admitted, and therefore it is not to be maliciously and openly blasphemed against, to the annoyance of believers or the injury of the public. However, the guarantee of religious freedom contained in the state constitution is broad and comprehensive in its language, providing for the "complete protection of every variety of religious opinion . . . and must have been intended to extend equally to all sects, whether they were Jews or infidels."

It is not necessary, Justice Story continued, to decide whether it would be valid in Pennsylvania to leave property "for the establishment of a school or college for the propagation of Judaism, or Deism, or any other form of infidelity." There is no such provision in the present case, nor is there even any prohibition of the teaching of Christianity. The most that can be said is that the testator omitted to provide for religious instruction in his scheme of education, and this fact does not make the bequest void under the laws of Pennsylvania.

Permoli v. First Municipality of New Orleans (1845)

The city of New Orleans had enacted an ordinance giving to a certain chapel a monopoly on all funerals, forbidding the exposition of corpses in Roman Catholic churches other than the one specified in the ordinance and imposing a fine of $50 against any Catholic priest who officiated at a funeral at any other church or chapel. The Reverend B. Permoli, a Catholic priest, was fined for violating this ordinance and appealed to the United States Supreme Court. He contended that the imposition of the fine infringed upon the free exercise of religion guaranteed by the United States Constitution.

The Supreme Court dismissed the appeal. The Court, it said, has jurisdiction only if there has been a violation of the Federal Constitution or a law enacted by Congress. Nothing in the Constitution or the First Amendment makes any provision for the protection of the citizens of the respective states in their religious liberties. This is exclusively a matter for the states themselves.

The Northwest Ordinance of 1787 had provided that "no person demeaning himself in a peaceable manner, shall ever be molested on account of his mode of worship, or religious sentiments in the said territory." When that part of Louisiana which later was called New Orleans was organized as a territory in 1805, Congress ruled that all the residents were to enjoy the same rights as those who resided in the Northwest Territory. In 1811 Congress authorized the people of the territory to form a constitution and state government and directed that the constitution guarantee civil and religious liberty. The next year Congress admitted Louisiana as a state, but the act of admission provided that this guarantee should be deemed a fundamental condition of the state's admission to the Union.

Nevertheless, the Supreme Court held, it had no jurisdiction over the controversy. Once Louisiana was admitted as a state by the act of Congress, it was in all respects the equal of every other state, since the Constitution does not recognize different classes of states. Hence, no matter what might have happened before the act of Congress admitting Louisiana into the Union, once that had been accomplished the Federal government, including the judiciary, had no greater control of the state than over any other state. Since in respect to all other states the protection of the citizens' religious freedom is exclusively a matter for the states themselves, so too must it be in the case of Louisiana. (Of course, this case was decided before the Fourteenth Amendment was added to the Constitution.)

Watson v. Jones (1872)

This case arose out of the schism in the Presbyterian Church caused by the slavery issue. In 1861, at the outset of the Civil War, the General Assembly of the Presbyterian Church declared slavery to be sinful and threw its moral force on the side of the Union. The Presbytery of Louisville thereupon denounced as heretical the doctrines promulgated by the General Assembly. In turn, many within the Louisville churches attacked the action of the Presbytery and declared their loyalty to the General Assembly and its anti-slavery position.

The local churches were soon embroiled in the controversy. In some the pro-slavery members would be in the majority; in others they would be in the minority. In many cases the dispute would reach the courts, and one such involved the Walnut Street Church. The Kentucky state courts ruled in favor of the pro-slavery faction and adjudged that it had the legal right to possess and operate the church. The anti-slavery faction countered by bringing a suit in the Federal court, and this suit ultimately reached the United States Supreme Court under the name of *Watson* v. *Jones.*

The Court held that under the American system of jurisprudence and the limitations of the constitutional requirement of the separation of Church and State it had no power to decide for itself which of the two factions contesting for the Walnut Street building represented the true Presbyterian Church, and that it was required to abide by the decision of the appropriate ecclesiastical tribunal. Among strictly independent congregations, as in Congregational and Baptist churches, this appropriate tribunal is the majority of the congregants; in hierarchical church systems the tribunal is the highest ecclesiastical judicatory to which the particular church is subject, whether it be priest, bishop, pope, synod, or general assembly. Since in the present case the supreme church body was the General Assembly, and it had determined that the anti-slavery faction alone represented the true faith, that faction was legally entitled to the possession of the Walnut Street Church property.

The freedom and independence of churches would be in grave danger if the Supreme Court undertook to define religious heresy or orthodoxy or to decide which of two factions really represented the true faith. The Court expressed this thought in the following oft-quoted paragraph:

In this country the full and free right to entertain any religious belief, to practice any religious principle, and to teach any religious doctrine which does not violate the laws of morality and property, and which does not infringe personal rights, is conceded to all. The law knows no heresy, and is committed to the support of no dogma, the establishment of no sect. The right to organize voluntary religious associations to assist in the expression and dissemination of any religious doctrine, and to create tribunals for the decision of controverted questions of faith within the association, and for the ecclesiastical government of all the individual members, congregations, and officers within the general association, is unquestioned. All who unite themselves to such a body do so with an implied consent to this government, and are bound to submit to it. But it would be a vain consent and would lead to the total subversion of such religious bodies, if any one aggrieved by one of their decisions could appeal to the secular courts and have them reversed. It is of the essence of these religious unions, and of their right to establish tribunals for the decisions of questions arising among themselves, that those decisions should be binding in all cases of ecclesiastical cognizance, subject only to such appeals as the organism itself provides for.

Reynolds v. *United States* (1878)

This was the first of the Mormon cases. Congress had passed a law making it a criminal offense to commit bigamy in any of the territories under control of the Federal government. The defendant, charged with violating this law, asserted as a defense that he was a member of the Church of Jesus Christ of Latter Day Saints, commonly known as the Mormon Church, and that its doctrines required him to practice polygamy or plural marriage. He claimed further that enforcement of the law against him would violate his religious freedom as guaranteed by the First Amendment.

The Supreme Court rejected this contention and affirmed the conviction. The First Amendment, the Court said, came about as part of the history of the disestablishment of churches in America, and particularly as the next step after the successful struggle in Virginia against the General Assessment Bill and for the adoption of Jefferson's Bill Establishing Religious Freedom. Quoting Jefferson, the Court said that the purpose of the amendment was to build "a wall of separation between Church and State." The amendment deprived Congress of all power over beliefs, but it did not forbid its enacting laws aimed at actions which were in violation of social duties or subversive of good order.

Marriage, the Court held, is a relationship created, regulated, and protected by civil authority. The monogamous family is the basis of Western societal life, and it was never doubted that government had the power to preserve it by prohibiting polygamy. The fact that the defendant's religious convictions require him to practice polygamy no more immunizes him from the operation of the law than would a person's religious belief in human sacrifice immunize him from the operation of the laws against homicide. To permit religious beliefs to justify polygamy would be to make the professed doctrines of religious belief superior to the law of the land and would in effect permit every citizen to become a law unto himself. Effective government could hardly exist under such circumstances.

Davis v. Beason (1890)

In this case the Supreme Court upheld the constitutionality of a statute enacted by the territorial legislature of Idaho which required every person seeking to vote at a general election to take an oath that he was not a bigamist or polygamist and did not belong to any association demanding or encouraging bigamy or polygamy as a religious duty or otherwise. The effect of the law, of course, was to deny the franchise to all members of the Mormon Church.

Following the reasoning of *Reynolds* v. *United States*, the Court held that it was not the purpose of the First Amendment to prevent legislation for the punishment of acts inimical to the peace, good order, and morals of society.

With man's relations to his Maker, the obligations he may think they impose, and the manner in which he expresses those obligations government may not interfere, provided always that the laws of society, designed to secure its peace and prosperity, and the morals of its peoples are not violated. It cannot be seriously contended, however, that the whole punitive power of the government for acts recognized by general consent of the Christian world in modern times as proper matters for prohibitory legislation must be suspended in order that the tenets of a religious sect encouraging crime may be carried out without hindrance.

The Court said:

. . . Bigamy and polygamy are crimes by the laws of all civilized and Christian countries. They are crimes by the laws of the United States, and they are crimes by the laws of Idaho. They tend to destroy the purity of the marriage relation, to disturb the peace of families, to degrade woman and to debase man. Few crimes are more pernicious to the best interests of society and receive more general or more deserved punishment. To extend exemption from punishment for such crimes would be to shock the moral judgment of the community. To call their advocacy a tenet of religion is to offend the common sense of mankind. If they are crimes, then to teach, advise and counsel their practice is to aid in their commission, and such teaching and counseling are themselves criminal and proper subjects of punishment, as aiding and abetting crime are in all other cases.

The term "religion" has reference to one's views of his relations to his Creator, and to the obligations they impose of reverence for his being and character, and of obedience to his will. It is often confounded with the cultus or form of worship of a particular sect, but is distinguishable from the latter. The First Amendment to the Constitution, in declaring that Congress shall make no law respecting the establishment of religion, or forbidding the free exercise thereof, was intended to allow everyone under the jurisdiction of the United States to entertain such notions respecting his relations to his Maker and the duties they impose as may be approved by his judgment and conscience, and to exhibit his sentiments in such form of worship as he may think proper, not injurious to the equal rights of others, and to prohibit legislation for the support of any religious tenets, or the modes or worship of any sect. The oppressive measures adopted, and the cruelties and punishments inflicted by the governments of Europe for many ages, to compel parties to conform in their religious beliefs and modes of worship to the views of the most numerous sect, and the folly of attempting in that way to control the mental operations of persons and enforce an outward conformity to a prescribed standard, led to the adoption of the Amendment in question. It was never intended or supposed that the Amendment could be invoked as a protection against legislation for the punishment of acts inimical to the peace, good order and morals of society. With man's relations to his Maker and the obligations he may think they impose, and the manner in which an expression shall be made by him of his belief of those subjects, no interference can be permitted, provided always the laws of society, designed to secure its peace and prosperity, and the morals of its people are not interfered with. However free the exercise of religion may be, it must be subordinate to the criminal laws of the country, passed with reference to actions regarded by general consent as properly the subjects of punitive legislation. There have been sects which denied as part of their religious tenets that there should be any marriage tie, and advocated promiscuous intercourse of the sexes as prompted by the passions of their members. And history discloses the fact that the necessity of human sacrifices, on special occasions, has been a tenet of many sects. Should a sect of either of these kinds ever find its way into this country, swift punishment would follow the carrying into effect of its doctrines, and no heed would be given to the pretense that, as religious beliefs, their supporters could be protected in their exercise by the Constitution of the United States. Probably never before in the history of this country has it been seriously contended that the whole punitive power of the government, for acts recognized by the general consent of the Christian world in modern times as proper matters for prohibitory legislation, must be suspended in order that the tenets of a religious sect encouraging crime may be carried out without hindrance.

Church of Jesus Christ of Latter-Day Saints v. United States (1890)

This was the last of the Mormon Church cases. In it the Court upheld the constitutionality of a law adopted by Congress in 1887 which annulled the charter of the Church and declared all the property forfeited except a small portion used exclusively for worship.

Notwithstanding the stringent laws which Congress had enacted to bring an end to the "barbaric practice" of polygamy, and in spite of all other efforts, the Mormon Church continued to defy law in preaching, upholding, promoting, and defending polygamy. In these circumstances, the Court held, it was within the power of Congress to annul the charter of the Church and to seize its property so as to prevent its continued use for unlawful purposes.

Church of the Holy Trinity v. United States (1892)

Congress enacted a law prohibiting the importation of foreigners "under contract or agreement to perform labor in the United States." The question presented in this case was whether the law forbade a New York church from contracting with an English clergyman to migrate to the United States and act as its rector and pastor. The Court held it did not, for the evil at which the statute was aimed was the breakdown of domestic wage standards as result of the importation of large numbers of foreign manual laborers under contract to work off their passage at an agreed-on substandard rate. Congress had not intended the act to apply to individual contracts of a professional person such as a clergyman, which in no way aggravated the influx of cheap unskilled labor.

Moreover, the Court said, to apply the statute to the present situation would be an act of unfriendliness to religion, and no purpose of action against religion may be imputed to any legislation, state or national, because we are a religious people. From the commission to Christopher Columbus, which recited that "it is hoped by God's assistance some of the continents and the islands in the ocean will be discovered," to the Declaration of Independence, with its assertion that all men "are endowed by their Creator with certain unalienable rights," its appeal "to the Supreme Judge of the world," and its expression of "a firm reliance on the protection of Divine Providence"—all the major documents and declarations of American history emphasize and reiterate the religious nature of our people and our nation. An examination of American life, as expressed not only by its history, but also by its laws, its business, its customs, and its society, shows everywhere a recognition of this truth. The Court then, in a paragraph often quoted by those who dispute the claim that the Constitution requires strict separation of Church and State, lists many evidences in American life which indicate a cordial and close co-operative working relationship between the Church and the State.

The Court said:

If we pass beyond these matters to a view of American life as expressed by its laws, its business, its customs and its society, we find everywhere a clear recognition of the same truth. Among other matters note the following: The form of oath universally prevailing, concluding with an appeal to the Almighty; the custom of opening sessions of all deliberative bodies and most conventions with prayers; the prefatory words of all wills, "In the name of God, amen"; the laws respecting the observance of the Sabbath; with the general cessation of all secular business, and the closing of courts, Legislatures, and other similar public assemblies on that day; the churches and church organizations which abound in every city, town, and hamlet; the multitude of charitable organizations existing everywhere under Christian auspices; the gigantic missionary associations, with general support, and aiming to establish Christian missions in every quarter of the globe. These, and many other matters which might be noticed, add a volume of unofficial declarations to the mass of organic utterances that this is a Christian nation. In the face of all these, shall it be believed that a Congress of the United States intended to make it a misdemeanor for a church of this country to contract for the services of a Christian minister residing in another nation?

Bradfield v. Roberts (1899)

In the general appropriation act for the District of Columbia, adopted by Congress in 1897, was included an appropriation of $30,000 for the erection of two buildings on the grounds of two hospitals and to be operated as part of the hospitals. Accordingly, the commissioners of the District entered into a contract with the Providence Hospital corporation, chartered by Congress, to construct a building on the property of the hospital and pay a specified sum for each poor patient sent by the commissioners.

A taxpayer residing in the District brought suit to declare the contract unconstitutional and contrary to public policy, on the ground that the hospital was controlled and operated by an order of Catholic nuns under the auspices of the Catholic Church. The agreement, the plaintiff alleged, involved a principle and a precedent for the appropriation of funds of the United States for the use and support of religious societies that would be contrary to the First Amendment. It would also, he alleged, constitute a precedent for giving to religious societies a legal agency in carrying into effect a public and civil duty which would, if established, speedily obliterate the essential distinction between civil and religious functions.

The Court overruled these contentions and upheld the validity of the agreement. The hospital, the Court said, is a corporation, a legal entity, chartered by Congress. As such it is a purely secular agency and does not become a religious one merely because its members are Catholic nuns. Whether the individuals who compose the corporation under its charter happen to be all Roman Catholics, or all Methodists, or Presbyterians, or Unitarians, or members of any other religious organization or of none, is not of the slightest consequence to the law of its incorporation; nor can the individual beliefs upon religious matters of the various incorporators be inquired into.

The fact that the hospital is conducted under the auspices of the Roman Catholic Church is likewise immaterial. Under whatever auspices it is conducted, it still must be operated in accordance with the charter granted by Congress, i.e., as a secular corporation whose purpose it is to cure the sick of all faiths.

Jacobson v. Massachusetts (1905)

In this case the Supreme Court upheld, upon the principle of self-defense and paramount necessity, the constitutionality of a Massachusetts statute empowering communities to compel the vaccination of all residents against smallpox in the presence of a threatened epidemic. The statute was not attacked under the First Amendment because the Supreme Court had not yet decided that the religious-freedom guarantee of the amendment was applicable to the states as well as the Federal government. Nevertheless, the Court asserted in support of its decision that under the principle of self-defense and paramount necessity a person "may be compelled, by force if need be, against his will and without regard to his personal wishes or his pecuniary interests, or even his *religious* and political convictions, to take his place in the ranks of the army of his country and risk the chance of being shot down in its defense."

It is clear from this that had the plaintiff asserted that his religious convictions forbade vaccination the result would have been the same. The Supreme Court has in fact in later cases interpreted the decision in this case as holding that a person cannot claim freedom from compulsory vaccination on religious grounds.

Quick Bear v. *Leupp* (1908)

In this case the Supreme Court ruled that treaty and other funds held by the Federal government as trustee for Indians who were in fact the real owners could legally be disbursed to private, religious schools at the designation of the Indians to pay the cost of their tuition. This arrangement, the Court said, was not unconstitutional. Nor was there a violation of a declaration of policy adopted by Congress in 1897 that the Federal government "shall make no appropriation whatever for education in any sectarian schools." This declaration of policy, it was argued, was applicable on the ground that the actions of the United States were always to be undenominational and that, therefore, the government can never act in a sectarian capacity, either in the use of its own funds or in that of the funds of others, in respect to which it is a trustee.

The Court, however, refused to hold that Indians could not be allowed to use their own money to educate their children in the schools of their own choice simply because the government is necessarily undenominational, as it cannot make any law respecting an establishment of religion or prohibiting the free exercise thereof. Because the funds involved belonged to the Indians and not to the government, the Court upheld the validity of the contract made with the Bureau of Catholic Indian Missions for the education of the Indians in Catholic schools.

Arver v. *United States* (Selective Draft Law Cases) (1918)

One of the constitutional challenges to the Selective Draft Law of 1917, enacted as part of the World War I effort, was that the exemptions granted by it to ministers of religion, theological students, and members of religious denominations whose doctrines and discipline declared military service sinful rendered the law unconstitutional. The Court disposed of this contention with these words: "We pass without anything but statement the proposition that an establishment of a religion or an interference with the free exercise thereof repugnant to the First Amendment resulted from the exemption clauses of the act to which we at the outset referred, because we think its unsoundness is too apparent to require us to do more."

Meyer v. Nebraska (1923)

As an aftermath of American entry into World War I, a number of Midwestern states enacted laws aimed at the teaching of foreign languages to children, and particularly the German language. One of these states, Nebraska, made it a criminal offense for teachers in private, denominational, or parochial schools to teach in a language other than English or to teach a foreign language to a child who had not yet successfully passed the eight grade. In *Meyer* v. *Nebraska* the defendants were teachers in Lutheran and Reformed parochial schools who were convicted of teaching children the German language by the use of a collection of Biblical stories.

In reversing the conviction, the Supreme Court held that the term "liberty" in the Fourteenth Amendment's ban on state deprivation of "life, liberty, or property, without due process of law" included "not merely freedom from bodily restraint but also the right of the individual to contract, to engage in any of the common occupations of life, to acquire useful knowledge, to marry, establish a home and bring up children, to worship God according to the dictates of his own conscience, and generally to enjoy those privileges long recognized at common law as essential to the orderly pursuit of happiness by free men."

The Court then held that, though the ends sought to be achieved by the statute were commendable, they might not be effected by coercion in violation of the individual's "liberty" as thus defined. The desire to foster a homogeneous people with American ideals may not be effectuated by forbidding the lawful conduct of teaching a foreign language, at least in the absence of an emergency which would render knowledge by a child of some language other than English so clearly harmful as to justify abridgment of rights guaranteed by the Constitution.

Pierce v. *Society of Sisters* (1925)

The same post-World War I nationalism that gave rise to the anti-foreign-language laws invalidated in *Meyer* v. *Nebraska* was responsible for a statute enacted in Oregon which required all parents to send their children between the ages of eight and sixteen to public schools. The purpose and effect of this statute was to outlaw private and parochial schools. The constitutionality of the law was challenged by the owners and operators of two non-public schools, an order of nuns that operated parochial schools, and the owners of a private, secular school known as Hill Military Academy.

Under the doctrine of *Meyer* v. *Nebraska*, the Supreme Court held, it was clear that the Oregon law unreasonably interfered with the liberty of parents and guardians to direct the upbringing and education of children under their control. Rights guaranteed by the Constitution may not be abridged by legislation which has no reasonable relation to some purpose within the competence of the state. The fundamental theory of liberty upon which all governments in the United States repose excludes any general power of the state to standardize its children by forcing them to accept instruction from public teachers only. The child is not the mere creature of the state; those who nurture him and direct his destiny have the right, coupled with the high duty, to recognize and prepare him for additional obligations.

No question exists concerning the power of the state reasonably to regulate all schools; to inspect, supervise, and examine them and their teachers and pupils; to require that all children of proper age attend some school, that teachers be of good moral character and patriotic disposition, that certain studies plainly essential to good citizenship be taught, and that nothing be taught which is manifestly inimical to the public welfare. What, however, is not constitutionally permissible is to require that this teaching be given exclusively in public schools.

Cochran v. *Louisiana State Board of Education* (1930)

A statute of the state of Louisiana providing for the purchase of secular textbooks for use by school children, including children attending private and parochial schools, was attacked as unconstitutional. The basis for the attack was not that the expenditure constituted a violation of the principle of Church-State separation under the First Amendment, since it was then generally assumed that this mandate of the First Amendment applied only to the Federal government and not to the states. The attack was under the provision of the Fourteenth Amendment forbidding states to deprive any person of property without due process of law. The plaintiffs contended that a grant to private schools of textbooks purchased out of tax-raised funds was in effect a tax for a private, rather than a public, purpose and therefore a deprivation of the taxpayer's money without due process of law.

The Supreme Court overruled this contention and upheld the statute. The Louisiana Supreme Court had interpreted the statute as providing benefits not to the private schools but to the children of the state, those attending private and parochial schools as well as those attending public schools. The private schools were not the beneficiaries of the appropriations and obtained nothing from them, nor were they relieved of a single obligation because of the appropriations.

So interpreted, the United States Supreme Court held that the taxing power of the state had been used for a public and not a purely private purpose and therefore no violation of the Fourteenth Amendment had occurred.

United States v. Macintosh (1931)

A Canadian native, who had been ordained a Baptist minister and later became a professor of theology and chaplain at Yale University, applied for citizenship in the United States. Upon being asked whether he would bear arms in defense of the United States he answered that he would if he believed the war was morally justified but not if he believed it conflicted with the principles of Christianity, because he could not put allegiance to the government of any country before allegiance to the will of God. The naturalization court thereupon denied his application and its decision was affirmed by the Supreme Court.

We are, the Supreme Court said in its opinion, a Christian people, according to one another the equal right of religious freedom, and acknowledging with reverence the duty of obedience to the will of God. But we are also, a nation with the duty to survive, a nation whose Constitution contemplates war as well as peace, whose government must go forward upon the assumption, and safely can proceed upon no other, that the unqualified allegiance to the nation and submission and obedience to the laws of the land—those made for war as well as for peace—are not inconsistent with the will of God.

There is, the Court held, no constitutional right to be relieved of the duty to bear arms by reason of religious conviction. The privilege of conscientious objection is one granted by Congress and may freely be abolished by Congress at any time in its judgment. An alien, therefore, who in effect asserts that he will not serve in the armed forces even if Congress should terminate the privilege of conscientious objection has no right to citizenship.

(Note: This decision was overruled in *Girouard* v. *United States*, summarized below in this chapter.)

Hamilton v. *Regents of the University of California* (1934)

Students at the University of California, a state institution, were expelled because they refused on the ground of religious conviction to take required courses in military science and tactics. They appealed to the United States Supreme Court on the ground that the expulsion deprived them of liberty without due process of law in violation of the Fourteenth Amendment.

The term "liberty" in the amendment, the Court held, undoubtedly encompasses the right to entertain, adhere to, and teach religious beliefs. However, government, Federal and state, each in its own sphere, owes a duty to the people within its jurisdiction to preserve itself in adequate strength to maintain peace and order and to assure the just enforcement of law. Conversely, every citizen owes the reciprocal duty, according to his capacity, to support and defend the government against all its enemies. It is clear, therefore, that the regulation of the university requiring all able-bodied students under the age of twenty-four as a condition of their enrollment to take the prescribed courses in military science and tactics transgresses no constitutional rights of the students.

Lovell v. *Griffin* (1938)

This was the first of the many Jehovah's Witnesses cases to be decided by a Supreme Court opinion, although it was decided under the First Amendment guarantees of freedom of speech and press rather than of religion. The town of Griffin in Georgia had enacted an ordinance which prohibited the distribution of circulars on the streets without a written permit from the city manager. Amy Lovell, a Jehovah's Witness, distributed tracts of the sect without first obtaining such a permit.

The Supreme Court held that the ordinance was unconstitutional as a violation of the First Amendment's guarantee of freedom of speech and of the press. Its character was such as to strike at the very foundations of the freedom of the press by subjecting it to license and censorship. Liberty of the press, the Court said, is not limited to newspapers and periodicals but embraces pamphlets, leaflets, and every other type of publication which affords a vehicle of information and opinion.

Schneider v. Irvington, New Jersey (1939)

This too was a Jehovah's Witness case decided under the freedom of speech and press guarantees of the First Amendment. In this case the Supreme Court declared invalid an ordinance which, seeking to prevent littering of the streets, forbade the distribution of literature on the city streets. The constitutional method of preventing littering of the streets, the Supreme Court held, is to arrest the litterers, not to forbid the circulation of literature.

The Court also declared invalid an ordinance which prohibited the distribution of circulars from house to house without a license from the chief of police, who had authority to deny the license unless he was satisfied that the applicant was of good character and that there was no danger of fraud. This, the Court said, unconstitutionally makes liberty to communicate dependent upon the police chief's power of censorship.

Cantwell v. Connecticut (1940)

This was the first Jehovah's Witness case decided by the Supreme Court under the freedom-of-religion guarantee of the First Amendment, which, the Court held, was applicable to the states no less than to the Federal government. The case arose out of the action of a Witness, Jesse Cantwell, who accosted two pedestrians upon the streets of New Haven and with their permission played them a record on a portable phonograph he carried with him. The record contained an attack upon organized religions generally and upon the Roman Catholic religion in particular; the latter was stated to be an instrument of Satan that for fifteen hundred years had brought untold sorrow and suffering upon mankind by means of fraud and deception. No violence occurred, but Cantwell was arrested and convicted of inciting a breach of the peace.

Cantwell appealed to the United States Supreme Court, which reversed the conviction as an unconstitutional violation of his right to the free exercise of religion. While there can be no doubt, the Court said, that the state has the right to prevent breaches of the peace and to punish those who incite such breaches even out of religious consideration, the fact that a person resorts to exaggeration or villification in his missionary endeavors and thereby arouses public animosity may not render him subject to punishment in the absence of a clear and present menace to public peace. In the case at issue there was no assault or threat of bodily harm, no truculent bearing, no intentional discourtesy, no personal abuse—and therefore no clear and present danger to the public peace.

In the same case the Court also set aside the conviction of Cantwell for violating a statute forbidding the solicitation of funds without first obtaining a certificate from the secretary of the public welfare council, who could refuse it if he did not believe that the "cause is a religious one." This censorship of religion as a means of determining its right to survive by soliciting contributions, the Supreme Court held, is a denial of the religious freedom guaranteed by the First Amendment.

The Court said:

We hold that the statute, as construed and applied to the applicants, deprives them of their liberty without due process of law in contravention of the Fourteenth Amendment. The fundamental concept of liberty embodied in that Amendment embraces the liberties guaranteed by the First Amendment. The First Amendment declares that Congress shall make no law respecting an establishment of religion or prohibiting the free exercise thereof. The Fourteenth Amendment has rendered the legislatures of the states as incompetent as Congress to enact such laws. The constitutional inhibition of legislation on the subject of religion has a double aspect. On the one hand, it forestalls compulsion by law of the acceptance of any creed or the practice of any form of worship. Freedom of conscience and freedom to adhere to such religious organization or form of worship as the individual may choose cannot be restricted by law. On the other hand, it safeguards the free exercise of the chosen form of religion. Thus the Amendment embraces two concepts,— freedom to believe and freedom to act. The first is absolute but, in the nature of things, the second cannot be. Conduct remains subject to regulation for the protection of society. The freedom to act must have appropriate definition to preserve the enforcement of that protection. In every case the power to regulate must be so exercised as not, in attaining a permissible end, unduly to infringe the protected freedom. No one would contest the proposition that a state may not, by statute, wholly deny the right to preach or to disseminate religious views. Plainly such a previous and absolute restraint would violate the terms of the guarantee. It is equally clear that a state may by general and non-discriminatory legislation regulate the times, the places, and the manner of soliciting upon its streets, and of holding meetings thereon; and may in other respects safeguard the peace, good order and comfort of the community, without unconstitutionally invading the liberties protected by the Fourteenth Amendment. The appellants are right in their insistence that the Act in question is not such a regulation. If a certificate is procured, solicitation is permitted without restraint but, in the absence of a certificate, solicitation is altogether prohibited.

Minersville School District v. Gobitis (1940)

The children of Walter Gobitis, a member of Jehovah's Witnesses, were expelled from the public schools of Minersville, Pennsylvania, for their refusal to salute the national flag and pledge allegiance to it. Contending that the expulsions violated the First Amendment's guarantee of religious freedom since the doctrines of the sect forbade flag saluting and pledges of allegiance, Gobitis appealed to the Federal courts. The Supreme Court, however, held that the First Amendment had not been violated.

Religious liberty, the Court said, does not exempt citizens from obedience to general laws applicable to all and not designed to restrict religious beliefs. The purpose of the flag-salute regulation was to promote national unity and loyalty, and this certainly was within the proper scope of the powers of school boards. While many persons might doubt that compulsory flag saluting will be effective to promote unity and loyalty, this is a decision to be made by the duly elected school officials and not by the Supreme Court, else the Court would become "the school board of the country."

(Note: This decision was overruled in *West Virginia State Board of Education* v. *Barnette*, summarized below in this chapter.)

Cox v. New Hampshire (1941)

Some ninety Jehovah's Witnesses engaged in a parade in Manchester, New Hampshire, carrying signs reading "Religion is a Snare and a Racket," and "Serve God and Christ the King." The marchers also handed out leaflets announcing a meeting to be held at a later time.

The marchers neither received nor applied for a permit to hold the procession, and they were prosecuted for violating a state statute requiring a permit to hold a parade or procession on a public street. The Supreme Court of New Hampshire, in affirming the conviction, interpreted the statute to confer no power on the licensing official to consider the purpose of the parade or to censor the signs carried or literature distributed, but only to consider the time, place, and manner of the proposed parade so as "to prevent confusion by overlapping parades or processions, to secure convenient use of the streets by other travelers, and to minimize the risk of disorder."

So construed, the statute was held constitutional by the United States Supreme Court, which affirmed the Witnesses' conviction. The Court held that the necessity of avoiding disorder on the streets, which would inevitably result if two or more groups were to seek to parade on the same street at the same time, justifies the relatively minor restriction on religious liberty imposed by the statute.

Chaplinsky v. New Hampshire (1942)

In this case the Supreme Court affirmed the conviction of a Jehovah's Witness under a state statute making it a crime to "address any offensive, derisive or annoying word to any other person who is lawfully in any street or other public place, or call him by any offensive or derisive names." The evidence showed that the Witness, while being brought to a police station after citizens complained to a traffic officer of his tactics in distributing his literature, was met by the city marshal, to whom he said, "You are a God damned racketeer, [and] a damned Fascist and the whole government of Rochester are Fascists or agents of Fascists."

To the assertion that the conviction violated the defendant's freedom of religion, the Court expressed doubt "that cursing a public officer is the exercise of religion in any sense of the term." But even if the defendant's activities were religious, "they would not cloak him with immunity from the legal consequences for concomitant acts committed in violation of a valid criminal statute." The statute is not invalid as an unconstitutional abridgment of free speech, for "resort to epithets or to personal abuse is not in any proper sense communication of information or opinion safeguarded by the Constitution, and its punishment as a criminal act" raises no constitutional question.

Jones v. City of Opelika (1942)

Here the Supreme Court considered the constitutional validity of the application of city ordinances that imposed license taxes on bookselling in general against Jehovah's Witnesses who were distributing their religious literature. The license taxes, varying in amounts from $10 to $300 a year, were not shown to be so unreasonably high as to interfere seriously with the Witnesses' activities; but the Witnesses refused to pay them on the ground that the sale of their literature constituted an exercise of religion that could not constitutionally be taxed in any amount.

The Court sustained the validity of the city's action in enforcing the license tax ordinances against the Witnesses. The Court viewed the Witnesses' action as primarily commercial rather than religious, and therefore subject to the non-discriminatory taxes on commercial transactions. The Court held that when proponents of religious or social theories use the ordinary commercial methods of sales of articles to raise propaganda funds, it is a natural and proper exercise of the power of the state to charge reasonable fees for the privilege of canvassing.

(Note: This decision was set aside in Jones v. City of Opelika (2d). See below, this chapter.)

Murdock v. Pennsylvania (1943)

In this case the Supreme Court refused to follow the decision in Jones v.

City of Opelika and held that a tax ranging from $1.50 a day to $20.00 for three weeks for the privilege of canvassing or soliciting orders for articles could not constitutionally be applied to Jehovah's Witnesses who sold their religious literature from door to door.

It could hardly be denied, the Court said, that a tax laid specifically on the exercise of religion would be unconstitutional, yet the license tax imposed by the city of Jeannette was in substance just that. The Witnesses spread their interpretations of the Bible and their religious beliefs largely through the hand distribution of their literature by full- or part-time workers, each of whom is ordained by the society as a minister. They assert that they follow the example of Paul, teaching "publickly, and from house to house" (Acts 20:30), and take literally the mandate of the Scriptures, "Go ye into all the world, and preach the gospel to every creature" (Mark 16:15). In doing so they believe that they are obeying a commandment of God.

The hand distribution of religious tracts, the Court held, is an age-old form of missionary activity and occupies the same high estate under the First Amendment as do worship in churches and preaching from pulpits. Religious groups are not free from all the financial burdens of government. A tax on the income of one who engages in religious activities or a tax on property used in connection with those activities would be constitutional. But it is one thing to impose a tax on the income or property of a preacher and quite another to exact a tax from him for the privilege of delivering a sermon or delivering his message through printed material. A person cannot be compelled to purchase, through a license fee or a license tax, a privilege that is freely granted by the Constitution.

Jones v. *City of Opelika* (2d) (1943)

On the basis of the reasoning set forth in *Murdock* v. *Pennsylvania*, and on the same day that the Murdock decision was handed down, the Court set aside the decision in *Jones* v. *City of Opelika* and held the the ordinance involved in that case to be unconstitutional.

Martin v. *City of Struthers* (1943)

An ordinance of the city of Struthers, Ohio, forbade knocking on the door or ringing the doorbell of a residence to deliver a handbill to the occupant without prior invitation from him. The purpose of the ordinance was to prevent crime and assure privacy in an industrial community where many of the residents worked on night shifts and had to obtain their sleep during the day. The Supreme Court held the ordinance unconstitutional in its application against Jehovah's Witnesses who distributed their literature in this way, acting in accordance with their religious convictions.

West Virginia State Board of Education v. Barnette (1943)

In this case the Court overruled *Minersville School District* v. *Gobitis* and held that the guarantee of freedom of speech in the First Amendment forbade state or public school authorities from compelling children to salute the flag or pledge allegiance to it under penalty of expulsion from the public school. The guarantee of freedom of speech, the Court held, encompasses freedom not to speak and not to make any other symbolic expression, such as saluting. While public officials have the right to foster national unity and may use a symbolic ceremony to achieve this, they may not make participation in the ceremony compulsory.

To the argument that unwise laws should be eliminated through the electoral process rather than court action, the Court said that "One's right to life, liberty, and property, to free speech, a free press, freedom of worship and assembly, and other fundamental rights may not be submitted to vote; they depend on the outcome of no elections."

The Court concluded its opinion with the following eloquent words:

Struggles to coerce uniformity of sentiment in support of some end thought essential to their time and country have been waged by many good as well as by evil men. Nationalism is a relatively recent phenomenon but at other times and places the ends have been racial or territorial security, support of a dynasty or regime, and particular plans for saving souls. As first and moderate methods to attain unity have failed, those bent on its accomplishment must resort to an ever increasing severity. As governmental pressure toward unity becomes greater, so strife becomes more bitter as to whose unity it shall be. Probably no deeper division of our people could proceed from any provocation than from finding it necessary to choose what doctrine and whose program public educational officials shall compel youth to unite in embracing. Ultimate futility of such attempts to compel coherence is the lesson of every such effort from the Roman drive to stamp out Christianity as a disturber of its pagan unity, the Inquisition, as a means to religious and dynastic unity, the Siberian exiles as a means to Russian unity, down the fast failing efforts of our present totalitarian enemies. Those who begin coercive elimination of dissent soon find themselves exterminating dissenters. Compulsory unification of opinion achieves only the unanimity of the graveyard.

It seems trite but necessary to say that the First Amendment to our Constitution was designed to avoid these ends by avoiding these beginnings. There is no mysticism in the American concept of the State or of the nature or origin of its authority. We set up government by consent of the governed, and the Bill of Rights denies those in power any legal opportunity to coerce that consent. Authority here is to be controlled by public opinion, not public opinion by authority.

The case is made difficult not because the principles of its decision are obscure but because the flag involved is our own. Nevertheless, we apply the limitations of the Constitution with no fear that freedom to be intellectually and spiritually diverse or even contrary will disintegrate the social organization. To believe that patriotism will not flourish if patriotic ceremonies are voluntary and spontaneous instead of a compulsory routine is to make an unflattering estimate of the appeal of our institutions to free minds. We can have intellectual individualism and the rich cultural diversities that we owe to exceptional minds only at the price of occasional eccentricity and abnormal attitudes. When they are so harmless to others or to the State as those we deal with here, the price is not too great. But freedom to differ is not limited to things that do not matter much. That would be a mere shadow of freedom. The test of its substance is the right to differ as to things that touch the heart of the existing order.

If there is any fixed star in our constitutional constellation, it is that no official, high or petty, can prescribe what shall be orthodox in politics, nationalism, religion, or other matters of opinion or force citizens to confess by word or act their faith therein. If there are any circumstances which permit an exception, they do not now occur to us.

We think the action of the local authorities in compelling the flag salute and pledge transcends constitutional limitations on their power and invades the sphere of intellect and spirit which it is the purpose of the First Amendment to our Constitution to reserve from all official control.

Taylor v. *Mississippi* (1943)

This case involved the validity of a statute that made it a felony to preach or teach anything designed to encourage violence, sabotage, or disloyalty to the United States and the state of Mississippi or "to create an attitude of stubborn refusal to salute . . . the flag." The evidence showed that the defendant, in the course of interviews with several women whose sons had been killed in combat, stated that it was wrong to fight our enemies and that "the quicker people here quit bowing down and worshipping and saluting our flag and government, the sooner we would have peace." A second defendant published a pamphlet suggesting that the Roman Catholic Church was responsible for flag saluting. The third defendant (all were Jehovah's Witnesses) distributed a book replete with such sentences as "Satan influences public officials and others to compel little children to indulge in idolatrous practices by bowing down to some image or thing, such as saluting flags and hailing them, and which is in direct violation of God's commandment (Exodus 20:1-5)."

The Supreme Court held the convictions unconstitutional. If, the Court held, the Constitution bans enforcement of a flag salute regulation, it prohibits also the imposing of punishment for urging and advising that, on religious grounds, citizens refrain from saluting the flag. The Constitution protects the preacher and teacher of religion no less than the practitioner.

Jamison v. Texas (1943)

Following the decision of *Schneider* v. *Irvington*, the Supreme Court, in reversing the conviction of a Witness for violating an ordinance of Dallas that prohibited the distribution of handbills in city streets, ruled that a state "may not prohibit the distribution of handbills in the pursuit of a clearly religious activity merely because the handbills invite the purchase of books for the improved understanding of the religion or because the handbills seek in a lawful fashion to promote the raising of funds for religious purposes."

United States v. Ballard (1944)

Guy W., Edna W., and Donald Ballard, organizers of the "I am" movement, were indicted for using the mails to defraud. The indictments charged that the defendants had falsely and fraudulently represented "that Guy W. Ballard . . . alias Saint Germain, Jesus, George Washington . . . had been selected and designated . . . as a divine messenger"; that the words of "ascended masters and of the divine entity Saint Germain" would be communicated to the world through the "I Am" movement; that the Ballards had supernatural powers to heal the incurably ill—and that they had in fact cured hundreds of afflicted persons. According to the indictment, the Ballards knew that these representations were false, and made them solely for the purpose of obtaining for their own use the moneys of the credulous.

During the course of the trial it was testified that the Ballards had represented that the teachings of the "I Am" movement had been dictated from Heaven to the Ballards, who took down and transcribed them, and that Jesus had shaken hands with them. The Supreme Court held that the jury had no power to decide whether or not these statements were literally true, but only whether the defendants honestly believed them to be true. Under the constitutional principle of the separation of Church and State and religious freedom, neither a jury nor any other organ of state has the power or competence to pass on whether certain alleged religious experiences actually occurred. The jury could no more constitutionally decide that Guy Ballard did not shake hands with Jesus than they could constitutionally determine that Jesus did not walk on the sea. The test of religion under the Constitution is belief: that which is believed to be religiously true is religion, and constitutionally protected; that which is not believed to be true is not religion but fraud, and may be the subject of criminal prosecution.

Prince v. Massachusetts (1944)

The Massachusetts child labor law forbade boys under 12 and girls under eighteen to sell newspapers or periodicals on streets and in other public places. Mrs. Prince, a Jehovah's Witness, allowed her two young children and nine-year-old ward to accompany her on the streets and help her sell or distribute the literature of the sect. She was tried for violating the statute. It was testified that she and the children considered themselves ordained ministers and believed that it was their religious duty to perform this work and that neglect would bring condemnation "to everlasting destruction at Armageddon."

The Supreme Court acknowledged the "right of children to exercise their religion and of parents to give them religious training and to encourage them in the practice of religious belief, as against predominant sentiment and assertion of state power voicing it." It also recognized that "the custody, care and nurture of the child reside first in the parents, whose primary function and freedom include preparation for obligations the state can neither supply nor hinder."

Nevertheless, the conviction was upheld. The state, the Court said, has a strong interest in protecting the health and welfare of children and where necessary may constitutionally override the religious conscience of the parents. The evils that may come from child labor, including the sale of publications on public streets, are sufficiently serious to justify state intervention and prohibition despite any claim of religious liberty.

In its opinion the Court said:

. . . It is cardinal with us that the custody, care and nurture of the child reside first in the parents, whose primary function and freedom include preparation for obligations the state can neither supply nor hinder. And it is in recognition of this that [our] decisions have respected the private realm of family life which the state cannot enter.

But the family itself is not beyond regulation in the public interest, as against a claim of religious liberty. And neither rights of religion nor rights of parenthood are beyond limitation. Acting to guard the general interest in youth's well being, the state as parens patriae may restrict the parent's control by requiring school attendance, regulating or prohibiting the child's labor, and in many other ways. Its authority is not nullified merely because the parent grounds his claim to control the child's course of conduct on religion or conscience. Thus, he cannot claim freedom from compulsory vaccination for the child more than for himself on religious grounds. The right to practice religion freely does not include liberty to expose the community or the child to communicable disease or the latter to ill health of death. The catalogue need not be lengthened. It is sufficient to show what indeed appellant hardly disputes, that the state has a wide range of power for limiting parental freedom and authority in things affecting the child's welfare; and that this includes, to some extent, matters of conscience and religious conviction.

* * * * *

The state's authority over children's activities is broader than over the actions of adults. This is peculiarly true of public activities and in matters of employment. A democratic society rests, for its continuance, upon the healthy, well-rounded growth of young people into full maturity as citizens, with all that implies. It may secure this against impeding restraints and dangers, within a broad range of selection. Among evils most appropriate for such action are the crippling effects of child employment, more especially in public places, and the possible harms arising from other activities subject to all the diverse influences of the street. It is too late now to doubt that legislation appropriately designed to reach such evils is within the state's police power, whether against the parent's claim to control of the child or one that religious scruples dictate contrary action.

Follett v. Town of McCormick (1944)

The principle of *Murdock* v. *Pennsylvania,* that a state may not tax the privilege of canvassing or soliciting orders for religious literature when engaged in as an act of religion, was held applicable in this case even where the Jehovah's Witness was not an itinerant colporteur or evangelist but resided permanently in the town that imposed the license tax and earned his livelihood exclusively by selling religious literature. Preachers of the more orthodox faiths, the Court pointed out, are not engaged in commercial undertakings merely because they are dependent on their calling for a living, nor because they reside permanently in the community in which they preach, and the same is constitutionally true of such unorthodox faiths as that of Jehovah's Witnesses.

In re Summers (1945)

In this case the Supreme Court upheld the constitutional power of a state (Illinois) to deny admission to the bar of an otherwise qualified applicant who was a conscientious objector to war and who therefore would not serve in the state militia if called upon to do so in accordance with the provisions of the state constitution. The power of a state to deny a free college education to conscientious objectors who refuse to enroll for military training was upheld in *Hamilton* v. *Regents of the University of California.* This decision, the

Court held, applies equally to the denial of the privilege of practicing law, particularly since a lawyer is an officer of the court who is charged with the administration of justice and must take an oath to support the state constitution.

Girouard v. United States (1946)

Overruling *United States* v. *Macintosh*, the Supreme Court held that religiously motivated refusal to bear arms does not manifest a lack of attachment to the principles of the Constitution. Accordingly the naturalization court had no power to deny citizenship to an applicant, otherwise qualified, who for religious reasons refused to swear that he would bear arms in defense of the nation.

The decision was not based on constitutional grounds, but only on the ground that Congress had not intended to make religiously motivated pacifism a bar to citizenship.

(Note: The present Immigration and Naturalization Law, enacted after this decision, requires applicants for citizenship to take an oath of willingness to bear arms, but expressly exempts conscientious objectors from this requirement.)

Marsh v. Alabama (1946)

The state of Alabama has a law making it a crime to enter or remain on private premises after one has been warned by the owner not to do so. This law was applied against a Jehovah's Witness who distributed religious literature in the streets of a company-owned town in disregard of a company rule, posted in store windows, reading "This is Private Property, and Without Written Permission, No Street or House Vendor, Agent or Solicitation of Any Kind Will Be Permitted."

The town, a suburb of Mobile, Alabama, known as Chickasaw, was entirely owned by the Gulf Shipbuilding Corporation. Except for that fact it had all the characteristics of any other town; it consisted of residences, streets, sewers, and a "business block" and had as town policeman a deputy county sheriff. All residents of the town were company employees and their families, but the streets of the town were open for traveling by all persons.

In holding that the statute could not constitutionally be enforced against the Witness, the Court ruled that the decisions declaring that a state may not prohibit the dissemination of religious literature in the publicly owned streets of the usual town are equally applicable to a case involving the privately owned streets of a company town.

Everson v. *Board of Education* (1947)

This is the famous parochial school bus case. Here the Court held that the First Amendment's ban on laws respecting an establishment of religion is applicable to the states by reason of the Fourteenth Amendment. It also held that under the ban neither the Federal government nor a state may aid religion. Nevertheless, it ruled that a state (New Jersey) could constitutionally finance bus transportation of children to parochial as well as public schools. The purpose of the program, said the Court, was to protect children from traffic hazards and the dangers of the road. Such a program is constitutional; it does not become unconstitutional merely because an incidental benefit is conferred upon churches by reason of the fact that if the state did not pay for the transportation the churches might have to (or lose some of their children to the public schools).

The New Jersey statute, the Court held, must not be struck down if it is within the state's constitutional power even though it approaches the verge of that power. New Jersey could not constitutionally contribute tax-raised funds to the support of an institution which teaches the tenets and faith of any Church. This does not mean, however, that it may not protect the children from traffic accidents through providing them with free transportation to schools, any more than that it may not do so by stationing policemen near schools, private and parochial as well as public.

The Court said:

We must consider the New Jersey statute in accordance with the . . . limitations imposed by the First Amendment. But we must not strike that state statute down if it is within the state's constitutional power even though it approaches the verge of that power. New Jersey cannot consistently with the "establishment of religion" clause of the First Amendment contribute tax-raised funds to the support of an institution which teaches the tenets and faith of any church. On the other hand, other language of the amendment commands that New Jersey cannot exclude individual Catholics, Lutherans, Mohammedans, Baptists, Jews, Methodists, Non-believers, Presbyterians, or the members of any other faith, because of their faith, or lack of it, from receiving the benefits of public welfare legislation. While we do not mean to intimate that a state could not provide transportation only to children attending public schools, we must be careful, in protecting the citizens of New Jersey against state-established churches, to be sure that we do not inadvertently prohibit New Jersey from extending its general State law benefits to all its citizens without regard to their religious belief.

Measured by these standards, we cannot say that the First Amendment prohibits New Jersey from spending tax-raised funds to pay the bus fares of parochial school pupils as a part of a general program under which it pays the fares of pupils attending public and other schools. It is undoubtedly true that children are helped to get to church schools. There is even a possibility that some of the children might not be sent to the church schools if the parents were compelled to pay their children's bus fares out of their own pockets when transportation to a public school would have been paid for by the State. The same possibility exists where the state requires a local transit company to provide reduced fares to school children including those attending parochial schools, or where a municipally owned transportation system undertakes to carry all school children free of charge. Moreover, state-paid policemen, detailed to protect children going to and from church schools from the very real hazards of traffic, would serve much the same purpose and accomplish much the same result as state provisions intended to guarantee free transportation of a kind which the state deems to be best for the school children's welfare. And parents might refuse to risk their children to the serious danger of traffic accidents going to and from parochial schools, the approaches to which were not protected by policemen. Similarly, parents might be reluctant to permit their children to attend schools which the state had cut off from such general government services as ordinary police and fire protection, connections for sewage disposal, public highways and sidewalks. Of course, cutting off church schools from these services, so separate and so indisputably marked off from the religious function, would make it far more difficult for the schools to operate. But such is obviously not the purpose of the First Amendment. That Amendment requires the state to be a neutral in its relations with groups of religious believers and non-believers; it does not require the state to be their adversary. State power is no more to be used so as to handicap religions, than it is to favor them.

This Court has said that parents may, in the discharge of their duty under state compulsory education laws, send their children to a religious rather than a public school if the school meets the secular educational requirements which the state has power to impose. It appears that these parochial schools meet New Jersey's requirements. The State contributes no money to the schools. It does not support them. Its legislation, as applied, does no more than provide a general program to help parents get their children, regardless of their religion, safely and expeditiously to and from accredited schools.

The First Amendment has erected a wall between church and state. That wall must be kept high and impregnable. We could not approve the slightest breach. New Jersey has not breached it here.

McCollum v. Board of Education (1948)

The Champaign, Illinois, Board of Education granted permission to the interfaith Champaign Council on Religious Education to offer classes in religious instruction to the children attending the city's public schools. Classes were made up of pupils whose parents signed printed cards requesting that their children be permitted to attend; they were held weekly for thirty or forty-five minutes, depending upon the grades. They were conducted by teachers engaged by the Council at no expense to the city, but the instructors were subject to the approval of the superintendent of schools. The classes were taught in separate religious groups in the regular school classrooms during school hours. Students who did not choose to take the religious instruction were required to leave their classrooms and go to some other place in the school building to pursue their secular studies. On the other hand, students who were released from secular studies were required to be present at the religious classes.

In a suit by the mother of a student challenging the constitutional validity of this system, the Supreme Court held that this use of tax-supported property for religious instruction and the close cooperation between the school authorities and the religious council in promoting religious education violated the First Amendment's ban on laws respecting an establishment of religion.

The plaintiff contended that (1) in actual practice certain Protestant groups had obtained an overshadowing advantage in the propagation of their faiths over other Protestant sects; (2) the religious education program was voluntary in name only because in fact subtle pressures were brought to bear on the students to force them to participate in it; and (3) the power given the school superintendent to reject teachers selected by religious groups and the power given the local Council on Religious Education to determine which religious faiths should participate in the program was a prior censorship of religion.

The Court, however, did not find it necessary to pass on these contentions, for it was of the view that even if they could not be upheld the plaintiff was entitled to prevail.

Expressly reiterating the principle announced in *Everson* v. *Board of Education* that the state may not pass laws that aid all religions, the Court held the Champaign system of released time unconstitutional because the operation of the state's compulsory education system assisted and was integrated with the program of religious instruction carried on by separate religious sects. The Court declared that the state might not consistently with the First and Fourteenth amendments utilize its public school system to aid any or all religious faiths or sects in the dissemination of their doctrines or ideals.

Moreover, the Court said, not only were the state's tax-supported public school buildings used for the dissemination of religious doctrines, but the state also afforded sectarian groups invaluable aid in that it helped to provide pupils for their religious classes through the use of the compulsory public school machinery. This was not separation of Church and State.

To hold [the Court said] that a state cannot consistently with the First and Fourteenth Amendments utilize its public school system to aid any or all religious faiths or sects in the dissemination of their doctrines and ideals does not, as counsel urge, manifest a governmental hostility to religion or religious teachings. A manifestation of such hostility would be at war with our national tradition as embodied in the First Amendment's guaranty of the free exercise of religion. For the First Amendment rests upon the premise that both religion and government can best work to achieve their lofty aims if each is left free from the other within its respective sphere. Or, as we said in the Everson case, the First Amendment has erected a wall between Church and State which must be kept high and impregnable.

Niemotko v. Maryland (1951)

The city of Havre de Grace, Maryland, allowed use of its park for public meetings, including those of religious groups, but by custom a permit was required. In this case the city council questioned the representatives of Jehovah's Witnesses, who had requested a license, about their views on saluting the flag, the Roman Catholic Church, service in the armed forces, and similar matters in no way related to public order or public convenience in use of the park. Apparently because of their unsatisfactory answers to these questions, the Witnesses were denied a permit. They nevertheless went ahead with their planned meeting, and when two of them attempted to speak, they were arrested for disturbing the peace.

The Supreme Court reversed the conviction on the ground that the unlimited power of censorship exercised by the city officials violated the First Amendment. The right to equal protection of the laws, in the exercise of freedom of speech and of religion, cannot be made to depend upon the whims or personal opinions of a local governing body.

Kunz v. New York (1951)

Here the Supreme Court held that the city of New York could not deny a Baptist missionary, Carl Kunz, the right to preach in the public streets or parks even though he engaged in scurrilous attacks on Catholics and Jews, charging that "the Catholic Church makes merchandise out of souls," that Catholicism is "a religion of the devil" and the Pope "the anti-Christ," and denouncing the Jews as "Christ-killers" who "should have been burnt in incinerators" as garbage. If such preachings actually incite to violence, the Court held, Kunz could be criminally prosecuted, but he could not in advance be denied the right to preach in the public streets or parks.

A city ordinance, the Court held, which authorizes the police commissioner to deny a license or revoke one already granted to a person who has ridiculed or denounced other religious beliefs in his meetings but which sets forth no appropriate standards to guide the commissioner's determination constitutes unbridled advance censorship and is unconstitutional.

Zorach v. Clauson (1952)

The Supreme Court here refused to extend the decision in *McCollum* v. *Board of Education* to outlaw the the New York City system of released time for religious education, which was at issue in the Zorach case. The difference between the Champaign and the New York systems was that in the former the public school authorities were deeply involved in the religious-education programs. Not only was the instruction given within the public school buildings during school hours, but the school authorities undertook a general supervision of the program. In New York, on the other hand, public school involvement was minimal. All the school authorities did, according to the Court, was to release from their regular secular studies, for one hour a week, those children who, without urging or pressure by the school authorities, wished to partake of religious instruction in churches or church schools off the public school premises. The school authorities assumed no further responsibility in respect to the program.

This, said the Court, is distinguishable from the Champaign program. Here all that is involved is no more than an adjustment of the public school schedule to accommodate the religious needs of the children. While the principle of the McCollum case was reaffirmed, it was not to be extended to the present situation.

We are, said the Court, a religious people whose institutions presuppose a Supreme Being. When the state encourages religious instruction or co-operates with religious authorities by adjusting the schedule of public events to sectarian needs, it follows the best of our traditions. For it then respects the religious nature of our people and accommodates the public service to their spiritual needs. Government may not finance religious groups nor undertake religious instruction nor blend secular and sectarian education nor use secular institutions to force one or some religion on any person. But it can close the public school doors or suspend its operations as to those who want to repair to their religious sanctuary for worship or instruction. No more than that was undertaken in New York, and therefore the action was constitutional.

Burstyn v. Wilson (1952)

Involved in this case was the motion picture *The Miracle*, a forty-minute Italian-language film relating the tale of a simple peasant girl who is seduced

by a bearded stranger she imagines to be St. Joseph and who later gives birth
to a baby she believes to have been divinely conceived.

New York has a statute requiring that all commercially exhibited films
receive a license from the Department of Education. The statute further provides that licenses shall be denied to films that are obscene, immoral, crime-
inciting, or "sacrilegious." *The Miracle* had been duly granted a license, but
later the Department of Education reversed itself and revoked the license on
the ground that the film was sacrilegious, presumably because it cast doubt on
the authenticity of the Biblical account of the conception and birth of Jesus.

Overruling a 1915 decision, the Supreme Court first held that motion pictures are protected by the First Amendment. It then held that the interest of
the state of New York in seeing to it that no religion be treated with contempt, mockery, and ridicule does not justify prior restraints upon the expression of views. It is not, said the Court, the business of government in our
nation to suppress real or imagined attacks upon a particular religious doctrine,
whether they appear in publications, speeches, or motion pictures. Moreover,
the term "sacrilegious" was not defined by the New York statute, nor was it
narrowly limited by the New York courts. Thus the censor (Department of
Education) was set adrift upon a boundless sea amid a myriad of conflicting
currents of religious views, with no charts but those provided by the most
vocal and powerful orthodoxies. This circumstance did not accord with the
guarantees of the First and Fourteenth amendments, and the action of the
Department of Education in revoking the license was therefore unconstitutional.

Kedroff v. *St. Nicholas Cathedral* (1952)

This case, known as the Russian Orthodox Church case, followed and applied
the principles that had been announced in *Watson* v. *Jones*. After the Bolshevik
Revolution in Russia, most of the Russian Orthodox churchmen in the United
States, asserting that the Moscow Patriarchate was under the domination of the
Soviet state, declared themselves independent of the Patriarchate in respect to
the administration of church affairs in America. They established the "Russian
Church in America" to care for the faithful until such time as the Patriarchate
should regain full freedom of action and thus resume its rightful status as
supreme authority of the Russian Orthodox religion.

A minority of churchmen in the United States retained their allegiance to
the Patriarchate, and the dispute between the two factions gave rise to more
than a quarter-century of court litigation, which is still going on. In New
York the state legislature sought to resolve the controversy by enacting a statute which declared that the Russian Church in America was the true Russian

Orthodox Church and therefore entitled to obtain possession of all Russian Orthodox Church property in New York. This included St. Nicholas Cathedral, the seat of the Church in New York City, which the Russian Church sought to obtain from the Metropolitan Benjamin, who had been designated by the Moscow Patriarchate as Archbishop of North America.

When the case reached the United States Supreme Court, the Court held the statute unconstitutional. A state is no more allowed than the Federal government to enact a law impairing the separation of Church and State or infringing upon religious freedom. Separation of Church and State and religious freedom mean that government has no capacity to intervene in ecclesiastical controversies or to determine which faith is true and which is false or which faction in a church schism represents the true faith and which is heretical. Under the Constitution such determination can be made only by ecclesiastical tribunals, and the determination of the highest ecclesiastical authority of the particular religion (in this case the Moscow Patriarchate) must be accepted by the secular government.

Fowler v. Rhode Island (1955)

The city of Pawtucket, Rhode Island, had an ordinance forbidding political or religious meetings in any public park, but the ordinance had been interpreted by the authorities as not forbidding church services in the parks. Catholics had held mass in a park and Protestants could conduct church services there without violating the ordinance. However, when Jehovah's Witnesses held a public meeting in the park, the minister who addressed the assemblage was arrested for violating the ordinance.

The Supreme Court reversed the conviction on the ground that by treating the religious services of Jehovah's Witnesses differently from those of other faiths, the city was discriminating against them. The services of Jehovah's Witnesses are different from and undoubtedly less ritualistic than those of other religious groups. But it is not the business of the state to say that what is a religious practice or activity for one group is not religion under the protection of the First Amendment. Nor is it within the competence of government to approve, disapprove, classify, regulate, or in any manner control sermons delivered at religious meetings. To call the words which one minister speaks to his congregation a sermon, immune from regulation, and the words of another minister an address, subject to regulation, is an indirect way of preferring one religion over another and is barred by the Constitution.

The Sunday Law Cases (1961)
(McGowan v. Maryland; Two Guys from Harrison-Allentown, Inc. v. McGinley; Gallagher v. Crown Kosher Super Market of Massachusetts; Braunfeld v. Brown)

The first two of these cases involved owners of highway discount department stores which were open for business seven days a week. The other two involved stores owned by Orthodox Jews who, because of their religious convictions, kept their stores closed on Saturdays, which is the Jewish Sabbath. The four cases involved the Sunday closing laws of three states, Massachusetts, Pennsylvania, and Maryland. In all four cases the statutes were attacked on three principal grounds: (1) that Sunday laws violate the constitutional prohibition against establishment of religion, (2) that they infringe upon religious liberty, and (3) that they deny the merchants equal protection of the laws in violation of the Fourteenth Amendment.

The Supreme Court overruled all three contentions and upheld the constitutionality of all three statutes. In all four cases the prevailing opinions were written by Chief Justice Earl Warren. In meeting the attack based upon the principle of separation of Church and State he said that if the present purpose of a Sunday law is to use the State's coercive power to aid religion it would be unconstitutional and in violation of the no establishment clause of the First Amendment. He conceded further that this indeed was the original purpose of the three Sunday laws under attack. There was no question, he said, that historically these Sunday laws were enacted during colonial times as religious laws whose purpose was to insure the observance of the Christian Sabbath as a religious obligation. However, he held, the religious origin of these statutes did not require that they be held invalid today, if in fact, the religious purpose was no longer in effect.

This, he said, was the case in respect to these laws. The present purpose of the legislature is to set aside a day not for religious observance but for rest, relaxation and family togetherness and the motivation is therefore secular rather than religious. As evidence to support this conclusion the Chief Justice pointed out that, for example, the Maryland statute permits such Sunday activities as the operation of bathing beaches, amusement parks and even pin ball and slot machines as well as the sale of alcoholic beverages and the performance of professional sports. Such exemptions from the law obviously go directly contrary to the religious purpose and thus indicate clearly that the purpose of the statute is not religious but secular.

Since these are today welfare or secular statutes, the fact that to a certain extent their operation coincides with religious purposes does not make them religious laws. Said the Chief Justice:

In light of the evolution of our Sunday Closing Laws through the centuries, and of their more or less recent emphasis upon secular considerations, it is not difficult to discern that as presently written and administered, most of them, at least, are of a secular rather than of a religious character, and that presently they bear no relationship to establishment of religion as those words are used in the Constitution of the United States.

Throughout this century and longer, both the federal and state governments have oriented their activities very largely toward improvement of the health, safety, recreation and general well-being of our citizens. Numerous laws affecting public health, safety factors in industry, laws affecting hours and conditions of labor of women and children, week-end diversion at parks and beaches, and cultural activities of various kinds, now point the way toward the good life for all. Sunday Closing Laws, like those before us, have become part and parcel of this great governmental concern wholly apart from their original purposes or connotations. The present purpose and effect of most of them is to provide a uniform day of rest for all citizens; the fact that this day is Sunday, a day of particular significance for the dominant Christian sects, does not bar the State from achieving its secular goals. To say that the States cannot prescribe Sunday as a day of rest for these purposes solely because centuries ago such laws had their genesis in religion would give a constitutional interpretation of hostility to the public welfare rather than one of mere separation of church and State.

The Chief Justice referred to the *Everson* case in which the Court in 1947 upheld a New Jersey statute providing for transportation of children at public expense to parochial and private schools as well as public schools. The purpose of that statute, the Chief Justice said, was to protect children from the hazards of traffic and the fact that indirectly the parochial schools benefited thereby did not transform what was basically a secular or welfare law into a prohibited law respecting an establishment of religion. For the same reason, he said, the fact that the Christian religion may benefit by the state's decision to choose Sunday as a day in which people are required to abstain from labor and to rest and relax, does not transform these purely secular and welfare laws into a law prohibited by the First Amendment.

The Court also rejected the claim of the two discount houses that the Sunday laws violated their religious liberty. The Chief Justice asserted that the discount houses could not even raise the issue of religious liberty. They alleged only economic injury, not any infringement of their own religious freedoms due to Sunday closings; in fact, there is nothing in the record to show what their religious beliefs are.

The Court did concede that the Jewish Sabbath observers had standing to assert violation of religious freedom since the operation of the compulsory Sunday law hindered their observance of their own Sabbath by imposing upon them an economic hardship. Nevertheless, six of the nine justices held that the statutes were constitutional even as against these Sabbath observers.

The freedom to hold religious beliefs and opinions, the Chief Justice said, is absolute. However, he continued, what was involved in the present cases is not freedom to hold religious beliefs or opinions but freedom to *act*, and such freedom, even when motivated by religious convictions, is not totally free from legislative restrictions. Thus, for example, the fact that polygamy may be a positive command of the Mormon religion does not prevent the government from declaring it illegal and making its practice criminal. Similarly, the Court in the past had upheld a statute making it a crime for a girl under the age of eighteen years to sell newspapers or periodicals in public despite the fact that a child of Jehovah's Witnesses faith felt that it was her religious duty to perform this work.

In the present case, Chief Justice Warren asserted that the statutes did not even go as far as those involved in the polygamy and child labor cases, for there they forbade conduct which religion commanded, whereas in the present case the Jewish religion does not command engaging in business on Sunday. The restriction on religious freedom is merely indirect and consequential and the Court should not strike down what it found to be a welfare law merely because of this indirect burden on the exercise of religion. "If the State regulates conduct by enacting a general law within its power, the purpose and effect of which is to advance the State's secular goals, the statute is valid despite its indirect burden on religious observance unless a State may accomplish its purpose by means which do not impose such a burden."

It was argued in the briefs that the States of Pennsylvania and Massachusetts could in fact accomplish their purpose of securing one day rest in every seven without imposing such a burden upon Sabbatarians. For example, the State could enact a law, as many States have done, requiring one day of rest each week for all workers but leaving it up to each employer to decide which day shall be the day of rest. Or the State could, as a number of States do in fact, designate Sunday as the day of rest but provide an exemption for those whose religious convictions compel them to observe a day other than Sunday as their day of rest. The majority of the Court, however, rejected this argument stating that the Court could not judge arbitrary and unreasonable the refusal of the States to use this method of achieving their purpose.

The Chief Justice said:

A number of States provide such an exemption, and this may well be the wiser solution to the problem. But our concern is not with the wisdom of legislation but with its constitutional limitation. Thus, reason and experience teach that to permit the exemption might well undermine the State's goal of providing a day that, as best possible, eliminates the atmosphere of commercial noise and activity. Although not dispositive of the issue, enforcement problems would be more difficult since there would be two or more days to police rather than one and it would be more difficult to observe whether violations were occurring.

Additional problems might also be presented by a regulation of this sort. To allow only people who rest on a day other than Sunday to keep their businesses open on that day might well provide these people with an economic advantage over their competitors who must remain closed on that day; this might cause the Sunday-observers to complain that their religions are being discriminated against. With this competitive advantage existing; there could well be the temptation for some, in order to keep their businesses on Sunday, to assert that they have religious convictions which compel them to close their businesses on what had formerly been their least profitable day. This might make necessary a state-conducted inquiry into the sincerity of the individual's religious beliefs, a practice which a State might believe would itself run afoul of the spirit of constitutionally protected religious guarantees. Finally, in order to keep the disruption of the day at a minimum, exempted employers would probably have to hire employees who themselves qualified for the exemption because of their own religious beliefs, a practice which a State might feel to be opposed to its general policy prohibiting religious discrimination in hiring. For all these reasons, we cannot say that the Pennsylvania statute before us is invalid, either on its face or as applied.

The third ground upon which the Sunday law was challenged in all the cases was that the crazy-quilt pattern of exclusions, exceptions and exemptions in the various statutes bear no semblance of reason and being arbitrary constituted denial of due process and of the equal protection of the laws. For example, in Massachusetts, it was legal to sell fish and foodstuffs at wholesale but not at retail; to dig for clams but not to dredge for oysters. In Pennsylvania, it was permissible to fish on Sundays from public waters but not on private property without the consent of the owner. In Maryland, merchandise customarily sold at beaches and amusement parks could be sold there on Sundays, but the same articles could not be sold on Sundays in places other than beaches and amusement parks. These and many other illustrations were cited to support the argument that the Sunday laws were completely irrational and act unequally, all of which made them unconstitutional and in violation of the Fourteenth Amendment.

In rejecting this challenge, the majority opinion reflects the almost unbroken practice of the Supreme Court since the Roosevelt Court Reform campaign in 1937, not to interfere with state social welfare legislation on the ground that it is arbitrary or a deprivation of property without due process of law. Once the Court determined that Sunday laws are not religious laws but social welfare laws, it would not interfere with the legislature's discretion on which practices should be prohibited and which permitted in these laws. The Court felt that it could not say without a shadow of doubt that there could be no reason or rationale underlying the inclusions and exclusions of the various statutes. Chief Justice Warren said:

Although no precise formula has been developed, the Court has held that the Fourteenth Amendment permits the States a wide scope of discretion in enacting laws which affect some groups of citizens differently than others. The constitutional safeguard is offended only if the classification rests on grounds wholly irrelevant to the achievement of the State's objective. State legislatures are presumed to have acted within their constitutional power despite the fact that, in practice, their laws result in some inequality. A statutory discrimination will not be set aside if any state of facts reasonably may be conceived to justify it.

It would seem that a legislature could reasonably find that the Sunday sale of the exempted commodities was necessary either for the health of the populace or for the enhancement of the recreational atmosphere of the day—that a family which takes a Sunday ride into the country will need gasoline for the automobile and may find pleasant a soft drink or fresh fruit; that those who go to the beach may wish ice cream or some other item normally sold there; that some people will prefer alcoholic beverages or games of chance to add to their relaxation; that newspapers and drug products should always be available to the public.

The record is barren of any indication that this apparently reasonable basis does not exist, that the statutory distinctions are invidious, that local tradition and custom might not rationally call for this legislative treatment. . . . Likewise, the fact that these exemptions exist and deny some vendors and operators the day of rest and recreation contemplated by the legislature does not render the statute violative of equal protection since there would appear to be many valid reasons for these exemptions as stated above, and no evidence to dispel them.

Torcaso v. Watkins (1961)

This case involved a resident of Maryland who had been appointed by the governor to the office of notary public but had been denied his commission because he would not swear that he believed in the existence of God, a requirement imposed by the state constitution on all holders of public office.

The Maryland supreme court had upheld the requirement on the ground that the interpretation of the no-establishment clause set forth in the cases of *Everson* v. *Board of Education* and *McCollum* v. *Board of Education* had been repudiated by the United States Supreme Court in *Zorach* v. *Clauson*. But this, the Supreme Court held, was erroneous. The Court's opinion in the Zorach case specifically said that "We follow the McCollum case." Nothing in the Zorach decision indicates that the government, state or Federal, may restore the historically and constitutionally discredited policy of probing religious beliefs by test oaths or limiting public offices to persons who have or profess a belief in some particular kind of religion. The Maryland religious test for public office violates the no-establishment and religious-freedom clauses and is therefore unconstitutional.

Engel v. Vitale (1962)

The New York State Board of Regents formulated a "non-sectarian" prayer and recommended that it be recited daily in the public schools of the state. The prayer read, "Almighty God, we acknowledge our dependence upon Thee, and we beg Thy blessings upon us, our parents, our teachers, and our country." A number of school boards adopted the recommendation, one of these being the board of New Hyde Park on Long Island. Shortly after the practice of reciting the Regents' prayer at the beginning of each school day was instituted, the parents of ten pupils brought suit on the ground that use of this official prayer in the public schools was contrary to the beliefs, religions, or religious practices of both themselves and their children. The basis of the suit was that the practice violated the no-establishment clause of the First Amendment, made applicable to the states by the Fourteenth Amendment.

By a vote of 6 to 1, the Supreme Court held the practice unconstitutional as violative of the First Amendment's ban on establishment of religion. The majority opinion was written by Justice Black, who had written the majority opinions in the Everson case (upholding parochial school bus transportation), the McCollum case (invalidating released-time programs on public school premises), and the Torcaso case (invalidating religious tests for public officials), and who had dissented in Zorach v. Clauson (upholding the released-time programs off public school premises).

We think [said Justice Black for the majority], that by using its public school system to encourage recitation of the Regents' prayer, the State of New York has adopted a practice wholly inconsistent with the Establishment Clause. There can, of course, be no doubt that New York's program of daily classroom invocation of God's blessings as prescribed in the Regents' prayer is a religious activity. It is a solemn avowal of divine faith and supplication for the blessings of the Almighty.

The state laws requiring or permitting use of the prayer, continued Justice Black, must be struck down because "the constitutional prohibition against laws respecting an establishment of religion must at least mean that in this country it is no part of the business of government to compose official prayers for any group of the American people to recite as part of a religious program carried on by the government."

The history of government-sponsored prayer both in the Old World and in the New has been a history of oppressions, coercion, and conflict. When our Constitution was written,

. . . people knew, some of them from bitter experience, that one of the greatest dangers of freedom of the individual to worship in his own way lay in the Government's placing its official stamp of approval upon one particular kind of prayer or one particular form of religious service. . . . The First Amendment was added to the Constitution to stand as a guarantee that neither the power nor the prestige of the Federal Government would be used to control, support or influence the kinds of prayer the American people can say. . . . Under that Amendment's prohibition against governmental establishment of religion, as reinforced by the provisions of the Fourteenth Amendment, government in this country, be it state or federal, is without power to prescribe by law any particular form of prayer which is to be used as an official prayer in carrying on any program of governmentally-sponsored religious activity.

The Court rejected the argument that since the prayer is "non-denominational" and since pupils may remain silent or be excused from the room if they so request there is no constitutional violation. The Court's opinion stated,

Neither the fact that the prayer may be denominationally neutral nor the fact that its observance on the part of the students is voluntary can serve to free it from the limitations of the Establishment Clause, as it might from the Free Exercise Clause of the First Amendment, both of which are operative against the States by virtue of the Fourteenth Amendment. . . . The Establishment Clause, unlike the Free Exercise Clause, does not depend upon any showing of direct governmental compulsion and is violated by the enactment of laws which establish an official religion whether these laws operate directly to coerce nonobserving individuals or not. . . . The Establishment Clause . . . stands as an expression of principle on the part of the Founders of our Constitution that religion is too personal, too sacred, too holy, to permit its "unhallowed perversion" by a civil magistrate. Another purpose of the Establishment Clause rested upon an awareness of the historical fact that governmentally-established religion and religious persecutions go hand in hand. . . . The New York laws officially prescribing the Regents' prayer are inconsistent with both the purposes of the Establishment Clause and with the Establishment Clause itself.

Nothing, Justice Black said, could be more wrong than the argument that to apply the Constitution in such a way as to prohibit state laws respecting an establishment of religious services in public schools is to indicate a hostility toward religion or toward prayer. Men who had faith in the power of prayer were the leaders of the fight for the adoption of our Constitution and Bill of Rights.

It is neither sacrilegious nor antireligious to say that each separate government in this country should stay out of the business of writing or sanctioning official prayers and leave that purely religious function to the people themselves and to those the people choose to look to for religious guidance.

Justice Black concluded the opinion by disposing of the assertion that the recitation of the Regents' prayer constituted at most a minor infringement on the separation of Church and State:

It is true that New York's establishment of its Regents' prayer as an officially approved religious doctrine of that state does not amount to a total establishment of one particular religious sect to the exclusion of all others—that, indeed, the governmental endorsement of that prayer seems relatively insignificant when compared to the governmental encroachments upon religion which were commonplace two hundred years ago. To those who may subscribe to the view that because the Regents' official prayer is so brief and general there can be no danger to religious freedom in its governmental establishment, however, it may be appropriate to say in the words of James Madison, the author of the First Amendment:

"It is proper to take alarm at the first experiment on our liberties. . . . Who does not see that the same authority which can establish Christianity in exclusion of all other religions may establish with the same ease any particular sect of Christians, in exclusion of all other sects? That the same authority which can force a citizen to contribute three pence only of his property for the support of any one establishment, may force him to conform to any other establishment in all cases whatsoever?"

Abington School District v. *Schempp; Murray* v. *Curlett*
(THE BIBLE READING DECISION) (1963)

One decision was rendered in these two cases. The first (the Schempp case) came from Pennsylvania, the other (*Murray* v. *Curlett*) from Maryland. The Schempp case challenged the validity of a Pennsylvania law requiring the reading without comment of ten verses from the Holy Bible on the opening of public school each day. The statute provided that any child shall be excused from participation or attendance at the written request of his parent or guardian. In the Murray case no statute was involved. The suit, brought by an avowed atheist, challenged the daily Bible reading and Lord's Prayer recitation which had been practiced in the Baltimore public schools pursuant to a rule of the city board of school commissioners which had been promulgated in

1905. The Pennsylvania suit had been brought in a Federal district court, and the three judges unanimously ruled the statute unconstitutional. The Maryland suit had been brought in the state courts, and the state's highest court, by a vote of 4 to 3, upheld the practice.

The opinion of the United States Supreme Court was written by Justice Clark and concurred in by all the other members of the Court except Justice Stewart.

It is true, said Justice Clark, that religion has been closely identified with our history and government. The fact that the founding fathers believed devotedly that there is a God and that the inalienable rights of man are rooted in Him is clearly evidenced in their writings, from the Mayflower Compact to the Constitution itself. Today our oaths of office, from the president's to an alderman's, end with the supplication "So help me God." Congress opens with a prayer, and the crier of the Supreme Court itself invokes the grace of God in declaring the sessions of the Court open. Some 64 per cent of Americans have church membership and only 3 per cent profess no religion whatever.

However, the opinion continues, it is equally true that religious freedom is embedded in our public and private life. Freedom to worship is indispensable in a country whose people come from the four quarters of the earth and have brought with them a diversity of religious opinions. Under this ideal of religious freedom it has long been recognized that government must be neutral and, while protecting all, must prefer none and disparage none.

The Court's opinion then examines the various earlier decisions interpreting the provision in the First Amendment that "Congress shall make no law respecting an establishment of religion or prohibiting the free exercise thereof." As early as 1940 the Court had stated in the case of *Cantwell* v. *Connecticut* that the "fundamental concept of liberty," protected against state infringement by the Fourteenth Amendment, embraces the liberties guaranteed by the First Amendment, including the provision against establishment or prohibition of the free exercise of religion. A large number of cases since then have repeatedly held that the ban on establishment is applicable to the states as it is to the Federal government, and this principle was again reaffirmed in this case.

Reaffirmed too was the Court's rejection of the contention that the establishment clause forbids only governmental preference of one religion over another. Ever since the Everson (parochial school bus) case of 1947, it has been the law that under the First Amendment "neither a state nor the Federal government can pass laws which aid one religion, aid all religions, or prefer one religion over another." In the light of the Court's consistent interpretation of the clause the contentions of those who question its history, logic, and efficacy "seem entirely untenable and of value only as academic exercises."

There is, the Court's opinion continues, an overlapping between the no-establishment and free-exercise clauses of the amendment.

> . . . The Establishment Clause has been directly considered by this Court eight times in the past score of years and, with only one Justice dissenting on the point, it has consistently held that the clause withdrew all legislative power respecting religious belief or the expression thereof. The test may be stated as follows: what are the purpose and the primary effect of the enactment? If either is the advancement or inhibition of religion then the enactment exceeds the scope of legislative power as circumscribed by the Constitution. That is to say that to withstand the strictures of the Establishment Clause *there must be a secular legislative purpose* and a primary effect that neither advances nor inhibits religion. . . . The Free Exercise Clause, likewise considered many times here, withdraws from legislative power, state and federal, the exertion of any restraint on the free exercise of religion. Its purpose is to secure religious liberty in the individual by prohibiting any invasions thereof by civil authority. Hence it is necessary in a free exercise case for one to show the coercive effect of the enactment as it operates against him in the practice of his religion. The distinction between the two clauses is apparent— a violation of the Free Exercise Clause is predicated on coercion while the Establishment Clause violation need not be so attended.

Applying these principles to the cases before it, the Court found that, since the challenged exercises were of a religious character, they were unconstitutional, as was the statute that required them. Religious exercises that are prescribed as part of the curricular activities of students who are required by law to attend school violate the First Amendment's ban on laws respecting an establishment of religion.

In the Maryland case it was argued by the school authorities that (unlike the finding of the trial court in the Pennsylvania case) the purpose of the morning program was not religious but secular, in that it sought to promote moral values, contradict the materialistic trends of our times, perpetuate our institutions, and teach literature. But, Justice Clark said,

> even if its purpose is not strictly religious, it is sought to be accomplished through readings, without comment, from the Bible. Surely the place of the Bible as an instrument of religion cannot be gainsaid, and the State's recognition of the pervading religious character of the ceremony is evident from the rule's specific permission of the alternative use of the Catholic Douay version as well as the recent amendment permitting nonattendance at the exercises. None of these factors is consistent with the contention that the Bible is here used either as an instrument for non-religious moral inspiration or as a reference for the teaching of secular subjects.

The invalidity of the practices is not mitigated by the fact that individual students may absent themselves upon parental request, for that fact is no defense to a challenge under the establishment clause. Nor is it a defense that the religious practices here may be relatively minor encroachments on the First Amendent. "The breach of neutrality that is today a trickling stream may all too soon become a raging torrent and, in the words of Madison, 'it is proper to take alarm at the first experiment on our liberties.'"

The banning of religious exercises does not establish a "religion of secularism," nor does it manifest a hostility to religion. Nor does this decision mean that the study of the Bible for its literary and historic qualities, or the study of religion presented objectively as part of a secular program of education, would necessarily violate the First Amendment. What are banned by this decision are only "religious exercises, required by the States in violation of the command of the First Amendment that the Government maintain strict neutrality, neither aiding nor opposing religion."

Finally, the Court's opinion rejects the contention that the concept of neutrality, which does not permit a state to require a religious exercise even with the consent of the majority of those affected, collides with the majority's right to the free exercise of religion. The free-exercise clause has never meant that a majority could use the machinery of the State to practice its beliefs. Freedom of worship is not dependent upon the outcome of any election.

The place of religion in our society [the opinion concludes], is an exalted one, achieved through a long tradition of reliance on the home, the church and the inviolable citadel of the individual heart and mind. We have come to recognize through bitter experience that it is not within the power of government to invade that citadel, whether its purpose or effect be to aid or oppose, to advance or retard. In the relationship between man and religion, the State is firmly committed to a position of neutrality.

Sherbert v. Verner (1963)

A member of the Seventh Day Adventist Church was discharged by her employer because she would not work on Saturday, the Sabbath day of her faith. When she was unable to obtain other employment because, from conscientious scruples, she would not take Saturday work, she filed a claim for unemployment compensation benefits under the compensation law of the state (South Carolina). The law disqualified from benefits a person who "without good cause" refused to take a suitable position offered him. The state unemployment compensation commission ruled that the claimant's refusal to accept a position requiring Saturday work was "without good cause" and therefore she was not entitled to unemployment benefits. The ruling was affirmed by the state courts, and the claimant appealed to the United States Supreme Court.

With two justices dissenting, the Supreme Court reversed the decision and ruled that the denial of benefits to the claimant constituted an infringement of her constitutional rights under the First Amendment. The disqualification for benefits imposed a burden on the free exercise of religion. The consequence of such a disqualification to religious principles and practices, the Court continued, may be only an indirect result of the state's action; but this fact does not necessarily render it immune from invalidation under the amendment. Here not only was the claimant's declared ineligibility for benefits derived solely from the practice of her religion, but the pressure upon her to forgo that practice was unmistakable. The ruling forced her to choose between following the precepts of her religion and forfeiting benefits, on the one hand, and abandoning one of the precepts of her religion in order to accept work, on the other. Governmental imposition of such a choice puts the same kind of burden upon the free exercise of religion as would a fine imposed against claimant for her Saturday worship.

Chapter 6

EFFECTS OF CONSTITUTIONAL FREEDOM
ON THE CHURCHES

We have examined in a previous chapter the Federal Constitution and its amendments that bear directly on religious freedom. Attention has been called to the fact that these constitutional provisions—especially those prior to the Fourteenth Amendment—still left open most matters for the individual states to adjust in their relationship to the Churches, more particularly in the field of religious education and matters affecting church property.

All the original thirteen states, with the exception of Massachusetts, Rhode Island, and Connecticut, had drafted new constitutions of their own liking by 1777—a year after the Declaration of Independence and twelve years before the confederation had passed into the republic under its new Federal Constitution. Massachusetts followed suit in 1780. These actions were in accordance with the resolution of the Continental Congress, passed in May, 1776, urging the colonies to form new governments "such as shall best conduce to the happiness and safety of their constituents." [1]

It is now necessary to study the organization of the states after the Declaration of Independence, both prior to and following the adoption of the Federal Constitution. What provisions did these now self-governing former colonies, having thrown off all European allegiance, put in their constitutions regarding religious freedom, and what laws were adopted which facilitated the establishment of voluntary religious bodies?

In general it may be said that in New England Church-State relations were at first not materially altered. Not until 1818 did Connecticut throw off her old alliance with Congregationalism, and Massachusetts was even slower—1833. However, a more liberal tendency was noticed after the Revolution.

In the middle states, where the population was more heterogeneous and people were accustomed to a considerable degree of religious freedom, the states nevertheless did not attain complete neutrality in religious matters for several decades.

In the South the Church of England, transformed into the Protestant Episcopal Church of the United States, soon lost its privileged status, but with the exception of Virginia, where Jefferson and his colleagues had accomplished such an important victory for total religious freedom, the Church was still a matter of state concern.[2] These developments have been considered state by state in a previous chapter.

States' Insistence on Federal Religious-Freedom Guarantees

The adoption of the Federal Constitution did not in and of itself abolish the various religious restrictions and provisions legally in force in the different states. Each state was free to do as it wished in regard to liberty of worship, Church establishment, taxation of property used for religious purposes, and religious tests for state officers. The states carried over the special institutions in force in 1789 and used their own time and method in making such changes as they desired.[3]

The Constitution, as drafted and approved by the Constitutional Convention, had to be submitted to the various states for their approval. And, as was natural under the circumstances, the interest in constitutional religious issues proved very much greater in the state conventions than in the Federal discussions. In most of the state conventions there was much debate both on the clause that "no religions test shall ever be required as a qualification to any office or public trust under the United States" and on the absence of any further guarantee of religious liberty. The question of a religious test for public office, including the historical background leading up to the constitutional prohibition of such tests, will be taken up in detail in a later chapter in this book.[4] Here we will consider only the omission of any guarantee of religious freedom. This omission might well have shipwrecked the Constitution had it not been for the assurance of Washington and other leaders that a bill of rights would be approved by the Congress of the United States when it first met. Indeed, five of the thirteen states definitely urged or suggested, in ratifying the Constitution, an amendment to this effect[5]; and in Pennsylvania, which ratified the Constitution in December, 1787, by a small majority without any specific recommendation regarding religious freedom, the minority issued a strong address entitled "Reasons of Dissent." In it various amendments were proposed, including the following:

The right of conscience shall be held inviolable, and neither the legislative, executive, nor judicial powers of the United States shall have authority to alter, abrogate, or infringe any part of the constitutions of the several States, which provide for the preservation of liberty in matters of religion.[6]

Let us now take up some other significant state actions in turn.

The case of New Hampshire is specially important. It was the ninth state to ratify, June 21, 1788, and this action completed the requisite number of states favoring ratification for inaugurating the government on the basis of the new Constitution. New Hampshire proposed twelve amendments, of which the eleventh had historic significance: "Congress shall make no laws touching religion, or to infringe the rights of conscience." This was proposed by a committee of which Samuel Livermore was chairman, and, as we have seen, it was he who was to propose the basis of the religious-freedom motion in the first Congress.[7]

The Virginia convention, in June, 1788, was the scene of the most memorable debates on the subject of the necessity of a bill of rights. These had been preceded by certain important actions. For instance, the General Committee of the Baptists, meeting six weeks earlier, resolved that the new Federal Constitution did not make "sufficient provision for the secure enjoyment of religious liberty."[8] Elder John Leland, who had been an ardent advocate of religious liberty, was nominated as a delegate to the Virginia convention from Orange County but withdrew in favor of James Madison, who had been the consistent champion not only of the Baptists but of other dissenting churches who wished to have their rights safeguarded. Some of the smaller religious bodies, such as the Associated Presbyterian Church and the Associated Reformed Church, agreed to abstain from all voting until the Federal Constitution was amended so as to acknowledge the sovereignty of God and the subservience of the state to Christ's kingdom.[9] The climax of the convention came in the debate between James Madison, supporting the Constitution, and Patrick Henry, who opposed its ratification without an amendment guaranteeing religious freedom. Madison took the ground that there was no specific power in the Federal government to infringe upon religious liberty, which was safe in the hands of the states. Patrick Henry replied with the effective speech referred to where we discussed his contribution to religious freedom.[10]

Edmund Randolph also engaged in the debate, taking his well-known position that the variety of sects in the United States would preclude the establishment of any one to the prejudice of others and would forever prevent and attempts to infringe religious liberty. Henry was again in the fray, demanding that it be guaranteed. Randolph answered in the spirit of Madison: "Will he not be contented with the answer that has been frequently given to that objection? . . . No part of the Constitution, even if strictly construed, will justify a conclusion that the general government can take away or impair the freedom of religion."[11]

Madison's theory was of course the one that, as no power had been expressly given the Congress to legislate concerning religion, the power did not exist in the Federal government. This power as well as that of dealing with religious freedom were in his judgment safely left to the states.

After brief debate Virginia ratified the Constitution. The convention recommended, however, among other amendments, one which is substantially a repetition, somewhat strengthened, of a clause in the bill of rights adopted by the colony just prior to the Declaration of Independence:

That religion, or the duty which we owe to our Creator, and the manner of discharging it, can be directed only by reason and conviction, not by force or violence; and therefore all men have an equal, natural and unalienable right to the free exercise of religion, according to the dictates of conscience, and that no particular religious sect or society might be favored or established by law in preference to others.[12]

This clause, with its emphasis on complete religious freedom and not mere toleration, and its advocacy of Church-State separation, was to prove of special significance for the Federal Bill of Rights.

The convention of New York, meeting in June and July, adopted the Constitution by a small majority—three votes—but with certain recommendations, including one to the effect

That the people have an equal, natural, and unalienable right freely and peaceably to exercise their religion, according to the dictates of conscience; and that no religious sect or society ought to be favored or established by law in preference of others.[13]

The North Carolina convention, met in July of 1788, insisted that a guarantee of religious freedom should be added to the Federal Constitution. Among the leaders in this movement was the Reverend Henry Abbot, a Baptist minister who had been a member of both conventions at Halifax in 1776. A strong opponent of any form of establishment, it is he to whom tradition assigns the authorship of the religious-liberty guarantee of the North Carolina Declaration of Rights. Another leader was General William Lenoir, a much respected Revolutionary patriot.[14] This was a very characteristic combination of forces urging a religious-freedom guarantee. There was a good deal of debate over the ratification of the Constitution, due largely to the absence of such a guarantee. Some feared the Congress, with its treaty-making power, might agree with the papacy to adopt the Roman Catholic religion; some feared that "pagans" might be elected Senators and Representatives; others felt that men might take oaths merely "by Jupiter," or "by Minerva." To these arguments James Iredell, later a justice of the United States Supreme Court, who opposed the evils of religious persecution and believed in religious liberty, replied that Congress wished to establish general religious liberty but had no authority to interfere in the state. General Samuel Johnston said,

A Jew, a Mahometan or a pagan could get office only in one of two ways: either the American people would have to lay aside the Christian religion altogether, or such persons would have to acquire confidence and esteem by good conduct and the practice of virtue.[15]

Equally true was the statement of another layman, William Lancaster, who was strongly for religious liberty:

But let us remember that we form a government for millions not yet in existence. I have not the art of divination. In the course of four or five hundred years I do not know how it will work. This is most certain, that Papists may occupy that chair, and Mahometans may take it. I see nothing against it.[16]

General Lenoir criticized the proposed Constitution because it contained "no provision against the infringement of the rights of conscience; that ecclesiastical courts might be established which would be destructive to our citizens," [17] and so on.

After much discussion the state convention resolved "Neither to ratify nor to reject the Constitution" (it acted affirmatively in November), but voted

That a declaration of rights, asserting and securing from encroachment the great principles of civil and religious liberty, and the unalienable rights of the people . . . ought to be laid before Congress and the convention of the States that shall or may be called for the purpose of amending the said Constitution. . . .[18]

This declaration included an assertion of "an equal, natural and unalienable right to the free exercise of religion according to the dictates of conscience. . . ." [19]

Rhode Island was the last to ratify—May 29, 1790—but only with a declaration of principles of which the fourth is practically verbatim the same as that adopted in Virginia.[20] The convention did not, however, recommend any specific amendment dealing with religious liberty.

Sufficient has been said to show how seriously the leaders of public opinion in the period of the framing of the Constitution took the question of the guarantees of religious freedom. Generally delegates to state constitutional conventions, who were fairly representative of intelligent contemporary public opinion, took one of three views, which may be summarized as follows:

1. Most thought the provisions in the Federal Constitution suitable and adequate.

2. There were others, almost equally numerous, who felt that the guarantees

did not go far enough and who wished to have them extended so as to cover the points later incorporated in the first section of the Bill of Rights.

3. There were those who felt that it was dangerous to guarantee religious freedom, believing that it would interfere with Church establishments in the states which had them. These were in general strong Protestants who feared the possible influence not only of sectarianism but also of the Church of Rome. They regretted that the Constitution had not shown more definitely the inherited Christian point of view of the Reformation. This was the smallest of the three groups.

Probably the solution reached was, all things considered, the best, namely, that the Constitution, with its guarantee against religious tests for Federal offices, should be ratified; that further guarantees of religious freedom should be incorporated in the Bill of Rights, as was demanded by several states [21] and was promptly done; and that little by little these guarantees, originally intended to cover only Federal cases, should be extended to include the whole nation. The latter has been actually accomplished, partly by state constitutional action, partly by the Fourteenth Amendment and its interpretation by the Federal courts.

Religious-Freedom Guarantees of New States

The First Amendment, stating that "Congress shall make no law respecting an establishment of religion, or prohibiting the free exercise thereof," was not in the early decades of the republic interpreted as including the states in its scope. Yet, as a matter of fact, the tradition of Church and State separation and of entire religious freedom, as shown in the debates on these subjects in the formation of our state and national governments, was so strong that after the necessary adjustments from colonies to states had been made, the spirit of the provisions of the Virginia bill for religious freedom and of the similar clauses of the Federal Constitution and its Bill of Rights was, with a few exceptions,[22] in force in all the states.

We have dealt with the constitutional progress of religious freedom in the thirteen original states.[23] The scope of this book does not make it possible to consider the history of the subject in each of the remaining thirty-seven states. We must, however, take up here the requirements made by Congress in representative cases, after the republic was well established, to insure religious freedom in the new states which it created from the public domain secured by treaty from various foreign powers. In early days each of the original states was permitted to carry over or modify its own laws with such provisions regarding freedom of conscience and religion and its establishment as it might desire. But when new states wished to be admitted to the Union their constitutions had to be approved by Congress, and Congress after the beginning of the nineteenth century required that states have adequate guarantees of religious freedom.

Ohio. The case of Ohio, the first state admitted in the nineteenth century, is particularly significant. The Ordinance of 1787 for the government of the Northwest Territory[24] is rightly regarded as one of the fundamental documents in the history of American religious freedom. Its guarantees in this and many other respects were taken as precedents in drafting legislation for other areas, and it insured religious liberty in all the states later carved out of the original Northwest Territory. These included Ohio, Illinois, Indiana, Michigan, Wisconsin, and much of Minnesota—that is, the region east of the Mississippi and north of the Ohio rivers.

When Congress in 1802 passed the enabling act authorizing the admission of Ohio as a state it was with the specific understanding that its "constitution and State government . . . shall be republican, and not repugnant to the ordinance"[25] referred to. If the constitution presented to Congress had included a State Church or the disqualification of Roman Catholics or Jews for public office or citizenship it certainly would not have met this test.

The state constitution adopted later the same year was one of the most comprehensive of any up to that time in its guarantees of religious freedom. The closing sentence reproduced the wording on this subject in the Ordinance of 1787. The full statement, which was repeated with only a few modifications in the constitution of 1851 and not modified in the latest revision—that of 1912—reads as follows:

Sec. 3. That all men have a natural and indefeasible right to worship Almighty God according to the dictates of their conscience; that no human authority can, in any case whatever, control or interfere with the rights of conscience; that no man shall be compelled to attend, erect, or support any place of worship, or to maintain any ministry, against his consent; and that no preference shall ever be given by law to any religious society or mode of worship, and no religious test shall be required, as a qualification to any office of trust or profit. But religion, morality, and knowledge being essentially necessary to the good government and the happiness of mankind, schools and the means of instruction shall forever be encouraged by legislative provision, not inconsistent with the rights of conscience.[26]

The first sentence shows the influence of several of the early constitutions, notably those of the United States, New Jersey, and Georgia. The reference to the "natural and indefeasible right to worship Almighty God" is one of the most characteristic of religious-freedom guarantees in state constitutions. Of the twelve states admitted to the Union between Connecticut (1791) and

Michigan (1837) eight used this terminology, and three others asserted the same right in other words.[27]

Louisiana. Religious freedom was assured by the Louisiana Territorial Act of 1804 and by the third section of an act of Congress in February, 1811, to the effect that the constitution of the state to be formed out of the Territory of Orleans should "contain the fundamental principles of civil and religious liberty." The act of the following year admitting the state into the Union provided that "all the conditions and terms contained in said third section should be considered, deemed and taken as fundamental conditions and terms, upon which the said State is incorporated into the Union." [28]

Florida. The treaty by which Spain ceded Florida—that is, both east and west Florida—to the United States, concluded in 1819 and proclaimed in 1821, contains full guarantees of religious freedom for the people of this newly acquired territory. Article V reads, "The inhabitants of the ceded territories shall be secured in the free exercise of their religion, without any restriction. . . ." [29]

This is historically significant because of the Roman Catholic background of the state due to its early association with Spain, and the fact that the St. Augustine parish, founded in 1565, is the oldest in the United States. The form of Church-State union which existed during much of the colonial period does not seem to have been encouraging.[30] Under the brief English rule (1763-83), however, freedom of religion was guaranteed, though Roman Catholics maintained that officials interpreted it unfairly to their interests.[31] When Congress established the Territory of Florida in 1821 this guarantee was reaffirmed.[32]

When the third step was taken, by which Florida became a state, the constitution drafted by the delegates of the territory in 1838 and duly submitted to Congress was accepted because it was "republican" in character, and provided in its Bill of Rights

That all men have a natural and unalienable right to worship Almighty God according to the dictates of their own conscience; and that no preference shall ever be given by law to any religious establishment or mode of worship in this State.[33]

To bring this brief survey up to date, and to show the continuity and expansion of religious-freedom guarantees characteristic of our states, the provision on the subject in the latest Florida constitution, that of 1885, is here given:

The free exercise and enjoyment of religious profession and worship shall for ever be allowed in this State, and no person shall be rendered incompetent as a witness on account of his religious opinions; but the liberty of conscience hereby secured shall not be so construed as to justify licentiousness or practices subversive of, or inconsistent with, the peace or moral safety of the State or society.

No preference shall be given by law to any church, sect or mode of worship, and no money shall ever be taken from the public treasury directly or indirectly in aid of any church, sect or religious denomination, or in aid of any sectarian institution.[34]

Texas. The case of Texas is particularly interesting. Owing to its early association with Mexico, it had inherited a Roman Catholic tradition. The Church was duly established by law; but by the treaty of annexation, whereby the Republic of Texas was incorporated into the United States, religious freedom was guaranteed, and by the first state constitution, that of 1845, the Roman Catholic religion was reduced from the high privilege of being the only national church to a level and an equality with every other denomination.[35]

California. California was ceded to the United States by the Treaty of Guadalupe Hidalgo in 1848 at the close of the Mexican War. It had come under the jurisdiction of Mexico in 1822 but had remained practically autonomous. The next quarter of a century was marked by the influx of Americans, the decline of the missions, and dissatisfaction with Mexican rule. The last of these culminated in the revolt led by an American officer, John C. Frémont, and occupation by United States naval and military forces during the Mexican War. California was proclaimed part of the United States by Commodore Sloat in July, 1846.

A constitution was drafted in 1849 with a Declaration of Rights containing this guarantee of religious freedom:

Section 4. The free exercise and enjoyment of religious profession and worship, without discrimination or preference, shall forever be allowed in this State; and no person shall be rendered incompetent to be a witness on account of his opinions on matters of religious belief; but the liberty of conscience hereby secured shall not be so construed as to excuse acts of licentiousness, or justify practices inconsistent with the peace or safety of this State.[36]

This provision in substantially the same form was retained in the constitution of 1879, so California started its career with guarantees of religious freedom.

In the period from the end of the eighteenth century to the close of the Civil War most of the new states admitted, being carved from the Northwest Territory or influenced by the Ordinance of 1787 or the act of 1804 admitting the lands of the Louisiana Purchase to territorial status, had agreements as to religious freedom. After the Civil War—owing partly to these same influences and partly to the desire to prevent the spread of Mormon polygamy—new states were in most cases admitted under a Federal compact providing a religious-freedom guarantee.

For instance, the admission of Nevada in 1864 required in the enabling act that the constitutional convention should provide "That perfect toleration of religious sentiment shall be secured, and that no inhabitant of said State shall ever be molested in person or property on account of his or her mode of religious worship." [37] This clause was followed in the cases of Arizona, Idaho, New Mexico, North Dakota, South Dakota, Utah (with the addition for the first time of a guarantee against "polygamous and plural marriages"), Washington, and Wyoming—states which have all incorporated a religious-freedom ordinance into their constitutions, agreeing never to modify it without consent of Congress.[38]

Lack of space precludes a more detailed examination into the text and origin of state constitutional provisions securing religious freedom and the separation of Church and State. The development may be summarized by noting that when, during the second quarter of the twentieth century, the Supreme Court ruled that under the Fourteenth Amendment the states were subject to the same restrictions in respect to religious liberty[39] and Church-State separation[40] as were imposed upon the Federal government by the First Amendment, the Court was simply giving Federal constitutional substance to what was in any event in effect in all the states.[41]

Attempted Exclusion of Clergymen from Public Office

The only very early evidence that reveals concern over the wisdom of having clergymen active in the American Federal government is an action taken by the Continental Congress under date of July 25, 1778. We are told that "a motion was made, that the sense of the house be taken, whether it is proper that Congress should appoint any person of an ecclesiastical character to any civil office under the United States." Evidently, however, there was relatively little interest in the matter; when the previous question was put it was carried, and the issue was never again brought forward.[42] But on the state scene as distinguished from the national one the question was often sharply raised.

In the early days of the republic some of the Eastern and many of the Southern states, in their belief that Church and State should be kept separate, provided in their constitutions that ministers of religion should not be elected to membership in their legislatures or to certain other offices. This stricture was partly to prevent the undue influence of any denomination in state political affairs, and partly to prevent clergymen from being drawn away from their important ministerial tasks. It was felt by some that New England ministers in particular had been unduly active in political life—the Congregationalists as supporters of the status quo, and the Baptists and some other dissenters in demanding legislative changes. It is also not improbable that the activity of some clergymen in slave states in behalf of emancipation had created a reaction. For these and other reasons, and especially from fear lest the principle of Church and State separation be compromised, constitutional provisions for preventing ministers from holding important political offices were sought. Thirteen states had such provisions—or about half of those admitted to the Union in the first half-century after independence. Except for New York they all were Southern or border states.

The earliest was North Carolina (1776), with its strong Scotch-Irish Presbyterian background. Here the constitution provided

That no clergyman, or preacher of the gospel, of any denomination, shall be capable of being a member of either the Senate, House of Commons, or Council of State, while he continues in the exercise of the pastoral function.[43]

This section was dropped in the revision of 1868.

New York went further in its constitution of 1777 (Article 39) by making clergymen of all denominations ineligible for any public office. This provision, which lasted until nearly the middle of the nineteenth century, is here given in full:

And whereas the ministers of the gospel are, by their profession, dedicated to the service of God and the cure of souls, and ought not to be diverted from the great duties of their function; therefore, no minister of the gospel or priest of any denomination whatsoever, shall at any time hereafter, under any pretence or description whatever, be eligible to, or capable of holding, any civil or military office or place within this State.[44]

South Carolina[45] (1778-1868), followed by Mississippi (1817-32) and Texas (1866-68), had virtually the same form, with only minor changes. Delaware accomplished the same major purpose in its constitution of 1792 by excluding ministers from "holding any civil office in this State," a prohibition which was discontinued in 1831.[46] Maryland had this same provision until 1864.[47]

Virginia and Georgia[48] had similar restrictions in Revolutionary constitutions. The constitution of Kentucky, adopted in 1799, continued in the revision of 1850 and dropped only in 1890 a prohibition with the same objective but applying only to the office of governor.

The wording of the first Louisiana constitution is interesting:

No person *while he continues to exercise the functions* of a clergyman, priest or teacher of any religious persuasion, society or sect, shall be eligible to the general assembly or to any office of profit or trust under this State.[49]

It seems not unlikely that this proviso was added because of the influence of a former Jesuit priest, Eligius Fromentin, a jurist, who represented Louisiana in the United States Senate from 1813 to 1819.[50]

Two states continue to disqualify ministers from certain offices: Maryland[51] and Tennessee[52]; and in each case the disqualification applies only to membership in the state legislature.

The opinion of James Madison on the subject is contained in his "Remarks on Mr. Jefferson's draught of a constitution" for Virginia, prepared in October, 1788:

Does not the exclusion of Ministers of the Gospel as such violate a fundamental principle of liberty by punishing a religious profession with the privation of a civil right? does it [not] violate another article of the plan itself which exempts religion from the cognizance of Civil power? does it not violate justice by at once taking away a right and prohibiting a compensation for it? does it not in fine violate impartiality by shutting the door ag[st] the Ministers of one Religion and leaving it open for those of every other?[53]

Jefferson later came to much the same position as Madison on this matter and dropped his objection to granting full civil rights to clergymen.

There have been a few ministers of religion in Congress and in civil positions under the Federal government—and there is no law to prevent their serving—but very few in comparison with the number of Roman Catholic clergy in the parliaments of some States on the continent of Europe, or the number of Anglican bishops who hold membership ex officio in the House of Lords. Among those whose names come readily to mind are the Reverend Manasseh Cutler (Congregationalist), a member of Congress from 1801 to 1805; the Reverend Henry Augustus Mühlenberg (Lutheran), a member of Congress from 1829 to 1839, twice candidate of the Democratic party for governor of Pennsylvania, and minister to Austria from 1838 to 1840; the Reverend Owen Lovejoy (Congregationalist), a highly influential anti-slavery member from 1856 to 1864; the Reverend Samuel J. Barrows (Unitarian), a member of Congress from 1896 to 1898; the Reverend Henry van Dyke (Presbyterian), minister to the Netherlands, 1913 to 1917; the Reverend Adam Clayton Powell (Baptist), now a member of Congress; the Honorable Elbert Thomas (Mormon), long a missionary of the Church of Latter Day Saints in Japan and later a respected member of the United States Senate; and Monsignor Francis Haas, long with the Catholic University of America, who held many important posts under the Federal government in connection with the settlement of labor disputes and securing fair industrial practices.

Perhaps the most interesting case of a clergyman's being elected to national political office in the early years of the republic was that of the Reverend Gabriel Richard, a French priest of the Roman Catholic Church, who played a large part in the early religious, philanthropic, and educational life of Michigan.[54] His long interest in public matters resulted in his being elected in 1823 a delegate to Congress from Michigan territory. This is believed to be the only instance in which a priest has held a seat in the House. He won over many candidates, receiving large non-Catholic support, and gave to the Church the salary he received from the government. In Congress he made a notable speech advocating a bill for the opening of a post road from Chicago to Detroit. He was greatly respected by all. Henry Clay held him in especially high esteem, frequently repeating his friend's arguments to the House when the latter's English was defective. He was again a candidate for election in 1826 but failed, chiefly because of the opposition of a prominent trustee of his Church who had opposed his policies.[55]

These examples are cited merely to show that the separation of Church and State in America is no legal impediment to having a minister of religion of any denomination hold public office, except for the minor restrictions noted in Maryland and Tennessee. In general it has seemed more consistent with the ideals of religious freedom to make no legal distinction between the civil rights of laymen and clergymen in the matter of holding office, leaving the decision in each case to the individual concerned or the restrictions, if any, of his communion, and to the judgment of the electorate. In this respect the change that has come over public opinion as expressed in constitutions is somewhat similar to that regarding belief in God as a requirement for election to certain public offices.

We shall deal later with the part played by clergymen in fighting political corruption in modern times.[56]

Development of Higher Education

Colleges and schools were both profoundly influenced by the development of the American republic. It will for obvious reasons be more convenient to deal with schools when we come to consider the beginnings of non-sectarian public education.[57]

Suffice it here to say that the Federal Constitution made no provision for education. This was assumed to be a state matter, and the Constitutional Convention did not even discuss it except for a passing reference to the possibility of establishing a national university. After the Constitution came into force, colonial systems of education continued for some time about as they had in the past. In most cases the states permitted the dominating Church, such as the Congregationalists in Massachusetts and other parts of New England, to go on supplying most of the education through the old academies, but little by little they developed new institutions or systems of education of their own. New York took the lead in 1795 by passing an "Act for the Encouragement of Schools," but nothing approaching the modern highly organized state systems of public tax-supported education was adopted until several decades later, during the governorship of De Witt Clinton. Pennsylvania followed (1834), and then Massachusetts (1837), Connecticut (1838) and North Carolina (1839). With this preliminary comment about the state school movement, which was later in origin than the state university movement, we shall here confine ourselves to the field of higher education, taking special account of changes as they affected the Churches and their institutions.

At the time of the Revolution there were about twenty-five hundred graduates of the nine colleges then existing in the American colonies.[58] These men played an important part in the Revolution, the overwhelming majority favoring the patriotic cause.[59] The effect of the war and of the founding of the new government on higher education in the United States was manifold, both in developing education under state auspices and in modifying education in privately controlled institutions. Perhaps the most significant results were these:

1. Several state universities were established. The first was the University of North Carolina in 1789.[60] It did not differ greatly in atmosphere from the older colleges. Its president during most of the first third of the century was a Presbyterian minister, the Reverend Joseph Caldwell, who insisted on regular attendance by students at religious worship and on orthodox religious instruction. He had strong support from the legislature.[61]

South Carolina did not follow until 1801, when South Carolina College was established at Columbia. This state was slow in developing a strong state university, partly because so many South Carolinians, more than from any other colony, went to England for their higher education, especially at the Inns of Court, attended by over one hundred Americans from 1750 to 1780.[62]

The university, however, attained considerable renown because of the identification with it from 1821 to 1834 of Thomas Cooper, an erratic but able and distinguished liberal philosopher and publicist who was a friend of Jefferson. He represented what to some was a cold form of Unitarianism, and at times a hard materialism. To have a thoroughly unorthodox person known to be especially opposed to the powerful Presbyterian clergy as the president of a

Southern state institution was sure to cause Church-State difficulties. These began with his appointment and continued at intervals throughout his administration. In 1822-23 his attacks on a "hired clergy," and especially on the Presbyterian "priesthood," were largely responsible for presentments against him by grand juries in two upstate counties.[63] The legislature was persuaded to investigate. He defended himself, taking the ground that it was not within the power of the legislature or state university trustees to engage in a religious controversy. His trial before the trustees was held in the hall of the state House of Representatives in December, 1832. Although exonerated, he resigned the presidency the following year.[64]

Other state universities followed that of South Carolina. Most important were the University of Virginia (1819) and the University of Michigan (1837). The attitude taken by the founder of the first, Thomas Jefferson—to keep the university secular and free from Church control but at the same time to provide the inspiration of religion to its students—has been discussed in an earlier chapter.[65]

The case of the University of Pennsylvania is particularly significant. In some ways it can be considered our first state university, for in 1779 the old Academy or College of Philadelphia—so closely identified with Franklin's views—was adopted as a state institution and given a new charter by the legislature of the commonwealth of Pennsylvania. The board of trustees was reorganized so that, of the twenty-four trustees, the old number of self-perpetuating members, six should be ex officio state officers; six the senior ministers of the principal religious denominations of the city, including the Roman Catholic—a most significant departure from tradition; and twelve eminent citizens—Franklin, Mühlenberg, and others.[66] The name of the institution was changed to the University of the State of Pennsylvania; the lesser seal of the state was adopted for it; the trustees, as state officials, were expected to take an oath of allegiance to the state,[67] and their election became subject to confirmation by the legislature, or to rejection within six months.[68] This plan, involving the university title with state connection, was here first used in the United States. But to satisfy the old provost and trustees of the college, who had opposed the 1779 charter as unfair to them, a new act was passed combining the old college and the new state university into the modern University of Pennsylvania, with a board of trustees made up half of the old board of the college and half of members chosen by the trustees of the state university, all under the presidency of the governor.[69]

2. A movement was started for the establishment in Washington of a national university under the Federal government and consequently without connection with any Church. Strangely enough, the only question regarding

education which arose in the Federal Constitutional Convention was whether it would be possible under the Constitution for the Federal government to establish a university at the capital. Charles Pinckney was specially interested in the project, and Washington in the first draft of his "Farewell Address" had planned to include a reference to it. Special attention was given to the plan after the death of the president, who bequeathed certain valuable securities, which the commonwealth of Virginia had given him in recognition of his public services, for the establishment of a national university.[70]

The presidents after Washington, including Jefferson, Madison, and John Quincy Adams, all favored the carrying out of this plan, though Jefferson thought that an amendment to the Constitution would be necessary to permit money to be appropriated for the purpose by the Federal government. In spite of these endorsements the idea slumbered from that time until recently, being supported by most leaders of public education in the West and opposed by most of the more conservative educational leaders of the Eastern universities.

The only direct ventures of importance by the government in the field of higher education—prior to the establishment of Howard University primarily for Negroes in 1867—were the starting of the military and naval academies, at West Point and Annapolis, in 1802 and 1845 respectively; but as these were for the training of officers for the government there was no objection. These academies have beautiful chapels erected by Federal grants. Services are conducted by official chaplains and are regularly attended by cadets and midshipmen. The chapel at the Air Force Academy, established at Colorado Springs in 1958, has, however, been the subject of considerable controversy because of its unconventional design.

3. Schools of law began to be set up. William and Mary College had the first chair of law in this country, established in 1779, and widely influential in Virginia. The trustees of Columbia College voted in 1784 to establish a law school with three professorships, but it was not until James Kent became a professor there in 1793 that any effective beginning was made. He resigned after a few years of effort and did not return to teaching until 1823, when he began the lecturing career which resulted in his epoch-making *Commentaries on American Law* (1826-27). This became the generally recognized supplement to Blackstone insofar as American law under the judicial decisions and legislation of this country modified the English tradition.[71]

4. The making of grants by the Federal government to promote higher education in the states gained headway through the adoption by Congress in 1787 of the ordinance for the government of the Northwest Territory. This document stated that "the means of education shall forever be encouraged." It provided that Lot 16 is each township should be given for purposes of

education, and that up to two complete townships should be given for purposes of a university. This laid the basis for the policy of public financial support for higher educational institutions under state auspices as distinct from those of the Church. From 1800 on most of the states admitted to the Union received land for the purpose of founding a university.[72]

The act of the legislature of the Northwest Territory of 1802, establishing a university and granting it two townships of land, exerted a marked influence throughout the West and North, as did also the provision that the university should be governed by a board of trustees which should not be a close corporation, the successors of the first incumbents being chosen by the legislature. No limit was placed upon the amount of property which the university might own. Thus, Ohio University at Athens became in fact a truly state institution with large possibilities for development.[73]

5. The curriculum broadened and greater tolerance developed. The old college curriculum of the colonial period had been made up mostly of the classics and mathematics, with a little Christian philosophy. Now other subjects were added that would be specially valuable in a new and democratic State, such as botany, economics, applied science, modern languages, and political science. These courses, representing new fields of college study and new methods of teaching, greatly broadened the academic outlook and tended to develop more tolerance in matters of religion. In addition, more foreign-born scholars, in keeping with Jefferson's views, began to be found on college faculties.[74]

6. The gradual nationalization of the Northern universities did much to break down both sectional and denominational prejudices. The older universities, such as Harvard, Yale, and Columbia, had up to the Revolution drawn men mainly from their own and the bordering colonies; but as a result of the development of national spirit and the improvement of means of communication these and other institutions began to take on a national aspect early in the nineteenth century, accepting students from all over the nation.[75]

7. Roman Catholic colleges and universities were founded. Prior to the Revolution all the colleges and universities in the United States were under Protestant auspices. Outside of Maryland there would not have been a constituency adequate to support a Catholic institution, and it is doubtful whether one could have been established in view of existing laws and public opinion. Under a new government, however, with entire separation of Church and State and equal rights for all religious bodies, a Roman Catholic institution became natural and inevitable. The first one was founded in 1789 in Georgetown, then part of the state of Maryland, now in the District of Columbia, through the efforts of the Reverend John Carroll, afterward Archbishop of

Baltimore.[76] The incorporated Catholic clergy of Maryland selected certain trustees from their own number and gave them full power to choose a president and professors. The college was opened in 1791. In 1805 it was handed over to the control of the Society of Jesus.[77]

8. New colleges, both denominational and undenominational, came into being. Up to 1789 there had been established only seventeen institutions generally considered of college or university rank. From that time on the number increased decade by decade up to the Civil War period.[78] The great majority were denominational foundations; although the State was beginning to provide institutions of higher learning of its own, all sections of the country continued a century ago to look for higher education mainly to institutions founded, though not always directed, by the Churches.[79]

We see from the above that the major activity in the United States up to the mid-nineteenth century in the field of higher education was under the leadership of the state governments and of the Churches, or of institutions founded by the Churches. The period of establishing great independent and undenominational foundations by individual philanthropists did not begin until the second third of the century, Cornell being incorporated in 1865 and Johns Hopkins in 1867. Nor did the Federal government establish any university, in spite of much discussion of the project, or do anything directly for higher education, except through the military and naval academies at West Point and Annapolis and through grants of land from the public domain to the new state governments in the West, for the purpose of establishing universities or colleges. Higher education was considered mainly the province of the various states or of the different religious denominations.

The Beginnings of Co-operation Among Religious Groups

The absence of a State Church under the republic, the religious guarantees of the Constitution and its Bill of Rights, and the general spirit of democracy which was increasing in this country soon developed a degree of mutual respect and even of co-operation among religious bodies that was remarkable.[80] In 1786 we find the president, with members of his cabinet and of Congress, attending a dinner in connection with the dedication of the first Roman Catholic church in New York City. As these persons were almost all Protestants, here was evidence of a new spirit of unity that was due very largely to the broad-minded and patriotic attitude of Bishop John Carroll. Further evidence was the development in 1790 of the First Day or Sunday School Society in Philadelphia, with directors from Episcopal, Roman Catholic, Quaker, and other communions. Another manifestation of the new spirit was the attempt by Governor William Livingston in his late years to compose a

prayer to comprehend and conciliate college students of every Christian denomination, formed entirely of texts and phrases of Scripture. Madison felt
that even this was inconsistent with true religious freedom, since some students
might object to any set form of prayer.[81]

Even before the close of the Revolutionary War, an attempt was made to
provide a college that would be conducted on a broad basis without denominational tests—Transylvania College, founded in 1780, in the region later to
be named Kentucky. The Virginia legislature stated that there should be no
religious tests and no special privilege for any sect; but the Presbyterians, the
leading force in the institution's establishment, soon got control of it. This
continued until 1816, when a Unitarian, the distinguished Reverend Horace
Holley, was put in as president. At his death ten years later, however, the
college returned to Presbyterian control.[82]

Equally important was the tendency of the older colleges and universities
to appeal to more students outside their own sectarian connections. Yale,
though still Congregational, attracted a growing number of Episcopalians, and
King's College, though founded under Anglican auspices, opened even its
professorships to all denominations. When in 1784 the state legislature appropriately and significantly changed its name to Columbia University it was
stipulated "that no Professor shall in any way whatsoever be accounted ineligible for or by reason of any religious tenet or tenets that he may or shall
profess, or be compelled by any by-law or otherwise to take any religious
test-oath whatsoever." [83] Similarly, when somewhat later (1819) what is now
Colgate University was chartered by the state of New York, though founded
by Baptists, largely with a view to advancing their cause, it was provided that
"if the said Society shall at any time pass any law or regulation effecting the
rights of conscience, the said corporation shall cease and be void." [84] This
was in accordance with the Baptists' historic stand for religious freedom, but
it was significant of the growing liberalism in the early national period that
such a proviso should be inserted in a charter obtained from the state.

In 1795 a new type of institution of higher learning, Union College in
Schenectady, New York, was chartered by the state legislature, with the definite purpose of supplying higher education under "Christian" auspices to
meet the needs of all the religious denominations near what was then the
Western frontier, and with the charter provision that no religious denomination should at any time have a majority on the board of trustees. This fellowship of the Churches was responsible for the "Union" name. The institution
was destined to be the precursor of many American colleges founded through
that co-operation of different groups which the spirit of the new Federal
Constitution encouraged.[85]

In the late winter of 1797 a meeting of the ministers of different denominations residing in and near Philadelphia was held to congratulate Washington on the occasion of his retirement from public life. The bringing together of religious groups was in and of itself characteristic, and symptomatic of other meetings held elsewhere in this early national period. Washington, replying to their address, said,

Believing, as I do, that religion and morality are the essential pillars of civil society, I view, with unspeakable pleasure, that harmony and brotherly love, which characterize the clergy of different denominations as well in this, as in other parts of the United States; exhibiting to the world a new and interesting spectacle, at once the pride of our country and the surest basis of universal harmony.[86]

And so the movement for co-operation among the Churches developed. But not long after this time (the first quarter of the nineteenth century) the picture changed, and although Protestant co-operation continued, especially in supporting agencies to help Christianize the West, the growth of Irish immigration was to create unfortunate clashes between Catholics and Protestants.

The Development of Churches Independent of the State

It is appropriate at this point to quote a few typical statements made during the early years of our republic on the effect on religion and the Churches of the Federal and state provisions for religious liberty and Church-State separation.

In Thomas Jefferson's *Notes on Virginia*, written in 1781-82, when the controversy over an assessment in behalf of the Christian churches was acute in his native state, there is a passage noting the good effect of having Church-State separation:

. . . Our sister States of Pennsylvania and New York, however, have long subsisted without any establishment at all. The experiment was new and doubtful when they made it. It has answered beyond conception. They flourish infinitely. Religion is well supported; of various kinds, indeed, but all good enough; all sufficient to preserve peace and order; or if a sect arises, whose tenets would subvert morals, good sense has fair play, and reasons and laughs it out of doors, without suffering the State to be troubled with it. They do not hang more malefactors than we do. They are not more disturbed with religious dissensions. On the contrary, their harmony is unparalleled, and can be ascribed to nothing but their unbounded tolerance, because there is no other circumstance in which they differ from every nation on earth. They have made the happy discovery, that the way to silence religious disputes, is to take no notice of them. . . .[87]

Madison, writing to Edward Livingston in 1822, refers to the fact that, as far as Virginia is concerned,

It is impossible to deny that religion prevails with more zeal and a more exemplary priesthood than it ever did when established and patronized by public authority. We are teaching the world the great truth that Governments do better without kings and nobles than with them. The merit will be doubled by the other lesson that Religion flourishes in greater purity, without than with the aid of government.[88]

The following year, writing to Edward Everett, Madison said,

Prior to the Revolution, the Episcopal Church was established by law in this State. On the Declaration of Independence it was left, with all other sects, to a self-support. And no doubt exists that there is much more of religion among us now than there ever was before the change, and particularly in the sect which enjoyed the legal patronage. This proves rather more than that the law is not necessary to the support of religion.[89]

Similarly, a discriminating Scotch visitor to this country, writing on his return in 1844, called attention to the good effects of the voluntary principle of church support in the United States. This was largely due, he was convinced, to the fact that American churches had been from the first so largely dependent on their own efforts, since the money sent from abroad for religious purposes was mainly for the evangelization of the Indians and for the support of colleges. He called to mind that even in those colonies which had an establishment the State did not support their churches adequately, while in all cases dissenters had to rely exclusively on their own efforts.[90]

Under the new arrangements made by the states in the early decades after the adoption of the Constitution all the Churches became self-governing (except as the Roman Catholic Church continued to be dependent upon Rome) and self-supporting—and both factors in the end greatly strengthened their work. A new sense of responsibility became apparent, with that of the laity much increased. Both developments had been prepared for in the colonial period, partly by the Congregational principle, which had a broad influence, and partly by the necessities of the case due to the long distance from Europe. Whatever the causes, it is clear that voluntary rather than State support of the Churches has had many advantages. It has been responsible for the developing of a larger sense of responsibility on the part of the laity for church welfare and the spread of religion; the removal of constant difficulties—the cause of many serious conflicts abroad—which come through securing State support and through administering State supervision and control; the giving to every man the right to aid only that form of worship which appeals to his mind and conscience. All in all, it has proved an inestimable boon both to the Churches and to the American people.

Part Two

THE ESTABLISHMENT AND
ADJUSTMENT OF CHURCHES
INDEPENDENT OF THE STATE

Chapter 7

EARLY NATIONAL INFLUENCES ON CHURCHES

The Great Revival and the Christian Education of the Western Frontier

The early decades of the nineteenth century were marked by two major factors, the development of a strong national feeling in the United States and the opening of the West. Both factors affected the churches, and the churches responded effectively to both. Indeed, the national feeling developed largely out of the very fact that the West existed, and that it was not made up of a group of territories belonging to separate states—though part of it had been acquired in the eighteenth century by separate seaboard colonies—but was all now, thanks to the Ordinance of 1787 and Jefferson's purchase of Louisiana, the possession of a nation which included many diverse states. We will find the interplay of these two factors in almost all the events of the period that we shall outline.

The large additions to the national domain, most of which were followed by extensive colonization, were a challenge to the Christian Church, which it heeded in a heroic way. Its missionaries, thanks largely to the religious impetus created by the Great Awakening of 1740 to 1790 and the Second Awakening or Revival of 1799 to 1803, which was on a broader scale, had been actively working on the changing Western frontier in considerable numbers since the days of George Whitefield. They were actuated by Christian zeal and worked in the spirit of the Ordinance of 1787 for the government of the Northwest Territory, which was the major basis for controlling the nation's new land in the West. This emphasized the importance of "religion, morality and knowledge" and provided for religious freedom. The frontier was crude, turbulent, and godless. Evangelical Protestantism, more than any other single force, tamed it.[1] The organized religious forces of the nation responded by starting schools, churches, and benevolent institutions in large numbers. As a result, the Churches mainly provided, for decades, such secondary and higher education as the frontier communities commanded, as well as their best standards of personal and social morality. The impress of the Churches is still noticeably felt in the old "Christian colleges" extending from Oberlin in Ohio to Whitman in Washington, and in the villages and towns of the Middle West. To appreciate the importance of these movements we must remember that at the close of the first third of the last century about a third of the population of the United States was on the frontier.[2] It was this large group that appealed to the imagination of the Christian forces of the East.

The careful student of American social history must be impressed by the many influences for social betterment which developed out of the religious awakening at the turn of the century. The year 1798 or 1799 may be taken as the time of its beginning. The major "revival" lasted until 1803, but its work continued much longer. Henry Adams, writing of the second administration of James Madison, says that "Religious interest and even excitement was seen almost everywhere, both in the older and in the newer parts of the country." [3] This revival had a profound influence in making Christianity a factor in national life. Timothy Dwight, president of Yale College, and many others in the clergy, although unsympathetic to the new democratic revolution and leaders in the campaign against French atheism and indifference, nevertheless found it necessary to meet the challenge of a real moral crisis in the nation and became exponents of a "new theology." [4] They realized that, though Calvin was right in teaching that God was supreme, He could do His work effectively only through willing men, and that the old doctrine of divine election must pass into the background and its implications be broadened. As a result of this changed emphasis, strengthened by the rise of Unitarianism and Methodism with their Arminian tendencies, and by other factors, little by little the Christian world realized that all men who truly sought salvation might attain it. The new prophets laid emphasis not only on a vital faith but on works and helped the Church to become much more "activist" in outlook. This meant more interest in human efforts to improve the individual and society. In the end it resulted in a Church which could better serve the higher moral and educational interests of the State.

The most extensive results of the new movement in theology and of the revival were seen along the Western frontier. Here the Methodists and the Presbyterians were the leading factors. The camp meeting—a peculiar form of American religious service, frequently marked by emotional excesses, including a spirit of religious intolerance—first became known in the winter of 1799-1800 in Kentucky, and from that time on for several years there was a remarkable upsurge of religious interest. In thirty years the Presbyterian Church increased its membership about fourfold, the Congregational churches twofold, the Baptist churches threefold, and the Methodist churches most of all, about sevenfold.[5]

The Methodists, with their emphasis on loyalty to Christ, rather than on dogmatic explanations, and on human freedom were both directly and indirectly highly influential. They made many converts to their own denomination and helped modify the rigid views of election and predestination held by Calvin's followers among Presbyterians, Congregationalists, and other groups. The contribution of the Baptists to education in the West did not compare with that of Presbyterians and Congregationalists, nor were they as effective evangelists as the Methodists, but they did a highly important work for religion and moral standards among the rough frontiersmen and in the villages and towns.[6]

Other churches also played an important part—the Roman Catholics, for example, especially through their earlier Indian missions. Nevertheless, during the early decades of the republic their clergy were generally too engrossed in effecting their national organization, adjusting it to American conditions, and caring for the urban sections of the East, which were receiving large immigration from Europe,[7] to carry on the vigorous type of missionary campaign in the West which we find later. Indeed, under the leadership of Archbishop John Hughes of New York the Church was trying to hold immigrants in the Eastern towns and cities, where they could be better cared for by the relatively small number of priests available; hence the Western states, and especially their rural sections, were neglected. However, much was accomplished under difficult circumstances in the central West, which had not, prior to the turn of the century, been much affected by early Catholic influences either from Louisiana in the south or from Canada in the north. It was sufficient to show that the Church could, though with some difficulty, adjust itself to the American Constitutional provisions for separation of Church and State, and to the parity of all law-abiding religious groups in the eyes of the State.

Not only did the Church influence the West, but the democratic life of "the frontier" had a profound influence on religion in this country. It resulted in several very characteristic American denominations, of which the Disciples of Christ was probably the most typical; was responsible for the camp-meeting movement; encouraged evangelism and the evangelistic attitude; strengthened the movement to democratic church administration; and in many other ways affected American church life.[8]

The part played by the Christian Church in laying the foundations for public education in the West was one of the greatest contributions to the republic, and it began in earnest in this period. The Church, both Protestant and Catholic, had done some previous work in educating the Indians, and the pastor in early pioneer communities had often taken on the duties of the teacher, but the organized work for public education under Christian auspices did not become effective until the formation of the national missionary organizations in the decade beginning in 1815.

The Roman Catholic Church was still largely engrossed in meeting the needs of the small Catholic groups and the new immigrants on the seaboard. Protestantism, however, was strongly enough entrenched there to take up the task of Christian education on a large scale in the West. There its influence was primarily in supplying Bibles and an elementary literature for school work; in establishing schools, academies, and colleges; and in giving aid to the public school movement. The pioneers carried with them the educational traditions of the seaboard, with its interest in education generally tied in with the religious heritage. Further impetus was given by the Ordinance of 1787 for the government of the Northwest Territory, which became the basic law for all the older states west of the Alleghenies. It contained an impressive statement, already quoted,[9] indicating the importance of closely related religious, moral, and mental education. Moreover, the preamble declared that one purpose of the ordinance was "extending the fundamental principles of civil and religious liberty." These declarations, together with the grants of land made for educational purposes by Congress, meant that the new states were to lay great emphasis on education, and that religion and religious freedom were considered of basic importance.

The Churches exercised a large influence on education through the founding of institutions and the providing of educational leadership in the days when public education was not yet strong enough to stand alone.[10] It is significant and interesting to note that in 1829, of the forty-three recognized colleges and universities then in the United States, all except four—Harvard University, Western University at Pittsburgh, and the state universities of South Carolina and Virginia—had clergymen as presidents or as heads with other titles. Men trained in these colleges were the ones who laid the foundation of education— at least of secondary and higher education—in the West.[11]

The Alien and Sedition Acts of 1798

The Alien and Sedition Acts, put through Congress by the Federalist party at a time when war was threatened with France, have generally been considered by historians as efforts to insure a Federalist victory at the polls against the Jeffersonian Republicans, and thus to save the country from the influence of radical French political thought. This was doubtless the major reason for their enactment, but underlying it was the fear of the weakening of Protestantism through the increasing Irish Catholic immigration, on the one hand, and, on the other, through the free views of religion brewing in France as a result of the teachings of science and of reaction against what seemed to many to be the rigid conservatism of the Roman Catholic Church.

The first of the new laws, passed in June, 1798, decreed that aliens must reside in the country fourteen years before naturalization, instead of five years, and must declare their intention of becoming citizens five years in advance. This "Act concerning aliens" was repealed in 1802 by the Jeffersonian Republicans.

A second act, also passed in June of 1798, which continued two years but was not renewed, gave the president the power to deport aliens if he thought them dangerous to the public peace. This extreme measure, whose constitutionality and wisdom were both debated, passed Congress by a close vote but was not put into effect.[12]

The third act, that of July 6, empowered the president in time of war to arrest, imprison, or banish aliens with whose country the United States was at war. It was not enforced, but it so frightened many aliens that they left the country.

In addition to these alien acts was the Sedition Act of July 14, which made it a high misdemeanor "unlawfully to combine and conspire" to oppose legal measures of the government, to interfere with any officer in the discharge of duty, or to engage in or abet "insurrection, riot, unlawful assembly or combination," the penalty being not over $5,000 and imprisonment up to five years. The law also made the publication of false or malicious writings against the United States, the president, or Congress punishable by fine and imprisonment. It has generally been considered that the Sedition Act was both unwise and unconstitutional, though ten citizens, all Antifederalists, were fined and imprisoned under it.[13]

When Jefferson came to power he pardoned all sufferers under the act, adding in a letter written in July, 1804, "I discharged every person under punishment or prosecution under the Sedition Law, because I considered and now consider that law to be a nullity as absolute and palpable as if Congress had ordered us to fall down and worship a golden image." [14]

The passage of the Sedition Law signed the death warrant of the Federalist party and brought the Jeffersonians to power. In due time this was to have its broad influence in removing the vestiges of State-Churchism which remained in Massachusetts, Connecticut, and some other states.

The Alien and Sedition Laws are important events in the development of "Nativism" and "Know-Nothingism" in this country. They represented the conservative Protestant antagonism to the influence of Latin countries and to the foreigner when not a Protestant. The later Know-Nothingism had its genesis in the prejudices nursed by the Federalists against foreign-born citizens and in their intolerance of their fellow citizens professing the Roman Catholic faith, and this can be traced back to the Alien Acts.[15]

The Influence of Jeffersonianism

It is difficult for us at this distance of time to appreciate the alarm felt in conservative Church circles over the re-entrance of Thomas Jefferson into public life after his retirement to Monticello, by his election to the vice-presidency in 1796 and the presidency in 1800. This was especially manifest in the New England states of Connecticut and Massachusetts, where the Congregational Church was still established and where Jefferson was looked upon as representing the ideals of the French Revolution—radicalism in matters political and social, and atheism, or at least agnosticism, in religion.

Most of the Thanksgiving Day sermons preached in Congregational churches in Massachusetts from 1795 on for a few years denounced Jeffersonianism and frequently by contrast praised the Federalist party.[16] The Reverend Timothy Dwight, a stanch defender of the old "standing order" and often referred to as the "pope of Connecticut," was particularly virulent in his attacks on Jefferson.[17] Dwight identified him very definitely with French Jacobinism. His baccalaureate address to the students of Yale in 1797 and his Fourth of July sermon in New Haven in 1798, entitled "The Duty of Americans at the Present Crisis," were characteristic. They show him as violently opposed to Jeffersonianism with its sympathy for much in French radicalism as his successor of today in a conservative college or church position would be to Russian Communism of the Marxian type. He believed that it implied atheism, personal immorality, public license, and all kinds of social disorder. "Shall our sons," he exclaimed, "become the sons of Voltaire and the dragoons of Marat . . . ?"

Next to the orthodox Congregationalists of New England, the Episcopal leaders in Virginia were among Jefferson's most bitter opponents, although after the first decade of the nineteenth century the Episcopal clergy of Connecticut supported his party as being the only way they could break the strangle hold of the established Congregational Church, always in close alliance with the Federalists. In other religious bodies there was considerable opposition to Jefferson because of his radical theological and social views; but as he was an ardent advocate of religious freedom, which he had done so much to secure in Virginia, many dissenting sects, including especially the rank and file of Baptists and Methodists, gave him support in the hope of disestablishing the Church.[18]

It was largely due to the influence of Jefferson's views that Massachusetts in 1800 repealed laws, passed in 1780, for the support of worship and the settling of ministers. Later, when the Republicans (Jeffersonians) were in power, they adopted the Religious Freedom Act of 1811, by which any person who should show a certificate that he belonged to a religious society, either incorporated or unincorporated, other than the regularly established society of the town or parish was exempt from paying taxes for the support of the Establishment.[19] This law [20] led ultimately to the overthrow of the Congregational Establishment in 1833.

But although Jefferson was a thoroughgoing liberal in his political and religious outlook, it became increasingly evident to open-minded people that he was not an iconoclast either in his statesmanship or in his religion. In particular, as his years in the presidency went on, the Churches, which had been much offended and frightened by his unorthodox views, came to realize that he was not an atheist—indeed, that he emphasized the importance to the nation of faith in God.

The Rise of Humanitarianism

Another influence of the time which was ultimately to affect greatly the relations between Church and State was the rise of humanitarianism. This movement manifested itself in the Christianizing and educating of the West, which has already been considered. It expressed itself too in many other fields of activity, in most of which the Churches played a prominent role. Later in the century the State was to enter these fields, with conflicts of interest between Church and State often resulting.

In the eighteenth century "charity," outside of orphanages and hospitals, and "education" had been largely personal or church affairs. Many schools and colleges had been established, for the most part under church auspices, but not until nearly the close of the century were any important organizations to meet broad social needs established in this country.

The new movement had many causes. The major European influences were the development, on the one hand, by French philosophers of the Enlightenment, of the theories of the natural rights of man and of human progress, and, on the other, of the Methodist movement—both equally interested in very different ways of improving the common man's lot. In this country the leading influences were the Great Awakening and its successor, the Great Revival of 1797-1803, and the establishment of the new nation with its manifold needs.

From the close of the Revolutionary War until the opening of the Civil War numerous educational and philanthropic institutions sprang up throughout the United States, but headquartered mostly in New York, Boston, and Philadelphia. In addition to institutions formed to provide for theological, missionary, and religious training and other educational purposes, there were those established to counteract vice,[21] care for the relief of the destitute, heal the sick, promote peace among nations, educate and train the blind, deaf, dumb, and other handicapped children and adults, improve the conditions of seamen, promote the observance of the Sabbath, abolish slavery, oppose lotteries and other forms of gambling, etc.[22]

Along with the founding of philanthropic institutions in the various states went a humanizing of the laws, especially in such matters as the care of the handicapped, the abolition of imprisonment for debt, and the limitation of the death penalty. Pennsylvania prior to the Revolution required a jury trial before anyone could be deprived of life, liberty, or estate, and whereas in the time of Blackstone 160 crimes were punishable by death, in 1794 death was restricted to deliberate homicide.[23] This is characteristic of the more humane laws that were being adopted almost everywhere in the United States.

The humanitarian influence lasted for several decades, reaching its climax in the anti-slavery movement. It developed a sense of brotherhood among the citizens of the new nation and was an important factor in making the period after the War of 1812, and especially the years from 1817 to 1824, "the Era of Good Feeling," covering the two terms of Monroe's presidency. The leaders of the Churches took a large part in all phases of this movement (except perhaps in the early effort to secure industrial rights for workers,[24] a field which the Church was not to enter actively until the last quarter of the century, when the situation became much more acute); many important benevolent movements and institutions were "cradled" in the Church.

The War of 1812 and the Rise of the Peace Movement

The War of 1812 was not popular among most of the religious leaders of New England, even though in numerous ways the section prospered as a result of it, and much diversification of its industrial life resulted. Enlistments were discouraged by many religious leaders, especially Connecticut Congregationalists, and the president's requisitions for militia were declined by some states. A proposed vote of thanks to a naval hero failed to pass in the Massachusetts legislature, being rejected on the ground that it was "not becoming a moral and religious people." [25] Victories of England and her allies in the European war against the France of Napoleon were celebrated. The more thoughtful clergymen of the time were not sympathetic with the "War Hawks." These were chiefly younger members of Congress from the West and South who wished through a military victory to prevent the Indians friendly to Great Britain from pursuing an aggressive policy on the Northwestern frontier, and to secure the Floridas from Spain and Canada from Great Britain. They encouraged President Madison in his warlike plans. They had a good talking point in Great

Britain's policy of "impressing" from American ships on the high seas deserters from the Royal Navy and other British subjects, especially as some Americans were victims of this high-handedness.

The Roman Catholic Church was in a difficult position, owing to the fact that the papacy was in captivity and ecclesiastical business with foreign countries was virtually at a standstill, but the Catholics in the United States were entirely loyal to the government. Certain groups, such as the Irish element, gave it strong support, partly for patriotic reasons, partly because of inherited antagonism to England, and partly out of love of a good fight.[26]

A highly important result of the War of 1812 was that it gave birth to the first peace societies. These were founded in 1815: one in New York through the activities of an earnest Christian layman, David Low Dodge, who in 1812 had published *War Inconsistent with the Religion of Christ*; the other by two Unitarian ministers in Boston, Noah Worcester and William Ellery Channing. Several additional societies were formed in the years immediately following, and united in 1828 in the American Peace Society, an organization with a most honorable history. William Ladd became the active leader of this movement, which was partly a reaction against the War of 1812 and the Napoleonic Wars and partly an expression of the determination of a high-minded group of Christian humanitarians to influence public opinion in government against war as contrary to the ideas of Christian ethics and human brotherhood. It is interesting to note that in 1833 the American Peace Society, which was largely supported by church leaders, petitioned the Massachusetts legislature in favor of the idea of a congress of nations, and that the New York Peace Society similarly petitioned the Federal government in 1837.[27]

After these societies had been in existence for about twenty years, there arose a division of opinion to which we have become accustomed in recent years between those who believed "that all war was contrary to the spirit of the Gospel and inconsistent with Christianity" and those who believed in a less radical policy. This question of the so-called Gospel decision split the society.[28]

The Effects of Immigration, Urbanization, and Industrialization

Few new factors that entered American life in the decades after the formation of the government were to have a greater effect on Church-State problems than the increased immigration from Europe, and especially from Roman Catholic Europe. This began in earnest after 1815, the year which saw the close of the Napoleonic Wars with the Battle of Waterloo, and of the War of 1812, between Great Britain and the United States. In 1820, when regular immigration statistics of our government began to be published, some 8,385 aliens gained entrance. By 1840 the number for the year had increased to 84,066, and in 1850 it was 369,980, a record not to be surpassed for twenty years.[29]

It was the Irish immigration[30] that was to create the most serious Church-State problem. The importance of meeting the needs of the recently arrived Irish Catholics, mostly drawn from the little-educated rural laboring population made desperately poor by the potato blight, was more responsible than any other factor for the development of parochial schools[31] and for the controversy over the Bible in public schools.[32]

Perhaps the most marked influence of Irish immigration on Church-State relations was the fact that it caused the rise of the Nativist movement in America, which had many serious repercussions.[33] Besides, the large new supply of cheap labor from Europe, overwhelmingly Roman Catholic, was directly and indirectly an economic and social factor of importance. It not only made possible the development of transportation in the West but created many of the problems connected with labor and industry.[34]

The arrival of a considerable number of Jews in this country also raised certain problems of Church-State relations, but large-scale Jewish immigration did not take place until the closing decades of the nineteenth century, there being only about 200,000 Jews in the United States at the end of the Civil War.[35]

Closely related to the increase of immigration was the urban drift. When the republic was founded, more than 95 per cent of the population was agrarian. By 1830 the urban population, that is, persons living in towns over 8,000, had gone up to 6.7 per cent and by 1850 to 12.5 per cent.[36] Later it advanced until today more than two-thirds of our population is urban.[37]

This urban development had certain interesting Church-State bearings. As Bishop John Hughes was determined to have the Church keep in close touch with the newly arrived immigrants from Europe, especially from Ireland, he strongly opposed their going west to take up an agricultural life. Hence their concentration in the large cities of the East. There they identified themselves with the party of the Jefferson-Jackson tradition, which had been opposed to the Alien and Sedition Acts and was in general more favorable to liberal ideas than its opponents. A resulting development was the problem of the Irish boss, whose political organization came to be a demoralizing factor in most large cities. The new immigrants were not responsible for the founding of Tammany Hall and similar "machines," but they soon made a large contribution to their growth. The rural West became increasingly antagonistic to the great cities of the East, and many splits along Protestant-Catholic, urban-rural, and what came to be Republican and Democratic groups followed.

Urbanization affected Church-State relations in many other ways. It strengthened enormously the interest in what has come to be known as the social gospel, which became concerned with such matters as labor conditions, the ethics of trade, the Americanization of the immigrant, the prevention of "pauperism," the problem of temperance, the improvement of city hospitals and prisons, and social welfare institutions. The Churches began to realize that urbanization carried with it evils and difficulties which personal evangelization alone could not meet; there must be a brave attempt to influence public opinion and legislation. These issues, as well as the problem of the immigration of large numbers of Jews from Europe, became much more acute after the Civil War, but they first came to the surface as matters in which Church and State were mutually interested in the second quarter of the nineteenth century.

Industrialization, which appeared in the United States after the Revolution, was likewise to influence Church-State relations profoundly. With its tendency to stratify society and to obliterate men's sense of local community, industrialization made the workers feel dependent for advance mainly on their labor organizations. These were not related to the Church and were often hostile to it. The workers therefore began by the middle of the nineteenth century to look rather to public agitation and to the State for protection. The effects are seen in such movements as the ten-hour-day agitation of the 1820's, the passage of the first child labor law by Pennsylvania in 1848, and the slowly but steadily increasing demands of labor for State protection. The discussions of slavery were a preparation for interference by the State in labor conditions. This found its first striking demonstration in the Civil War and in the Reconstruction amendments to the Constitution, which most of the Northern Churches strongly supported, but for the ordinary laborers in industry it was not to reach its climax until many decades later.

The new industrial movement, associated as it was with congested living conditions in urban centers, was destined to throw the old American stock into close relation and competition with European and French-Canadian immigrants. For the first time Protestant-Catholic misunderstandings were raised in serious form. They not infrequently resulted in conflicts in which the State had to interfere to prevent grave trouble, but ultimately—especially through the contacts of the public school—a larger toleration was reached. In a word, under the new conditions of life the old church-and-minister control was largely superseded by that of new factors, including especially public authority, until the Church could partly regain its hold by readjusting its outlook, as described in another chapter.[38]

The Rise of Jacksonian Democracy

The inauguration of Andrew Jackson as president of the United States in 1829 brought to the office for the first time a man of the people—an opponent of concentrated wealth and of special privileges. It was natural that Jackson should stoutly oppose special favors for any religious body, and that he should stand for the principle of strict separation of Church and State and of religious freedom, even opposing the issuance of a Thanksgiving Day proclamation.[39]

Jackson was bitterly opposed by the Churches with aristocratic and Federalist backgrounds, such as the Episcopalians and Congregationalists. To the old representatives of the Establishment or of the Standing Order he seemed too radical, too close to the people; but since he was a good Presbyterian no such effective campaign could be made against him from the standpoint of orthodoxy as had been made against Jefferson a quarter of a century before. Baptists, Methodists, and other groups close to the people, as well as some branches of his own Church, were inclined to follow him (though his participation in a well-known duel in 1817 outraged the feelings of many religious groups).[40]

The Beards, in *The Rise of American Civilization*, state the situation clearly:

> Conforming to the restless spirit of Jacksonian Democracy was a remarkable growth in the Methodist and Baptist churches, especially in the West and Southwest. Undoubtedly, J. Franklin Jameson is right in relating the extension of political equality with the prosperity of the religious bodies that reject the Calvinist doctrine of election for the favored few. How could Jacksonian Democrats who exalted the masses of farmers and mechanics believe in a system of theology which condemned most of them to hell in advance without a hearing and reserved heaven for a select aristocracy favored of God? Of course the Presbyterians also flourished during the middle period, as the Scotch-Irish population increased, but the followers of John Calvin did not maintain the relative strength which they commanded in the colonial age.[41]

Jackson's presidency lasted only from 1829 to 1837, but the movement he represented began well before the first date—indeed, it had some of its roots in the ideals of Jefferson—and its influence lasted many years after the second. It stood for the rights of man as man; for the restoration of political control to plain citizens rather than its retention by entrenched well-to-do Federalists; for the dominant influence of the frontier and the towns with their democratic life and new industries rather than that of the old-established seaboard plantations and their gentry; for emphasis on a vigorous Americanism, especially to meet the needs of the large number of recently arrived immigrants; for the extension of the suffrage and of public education; for the larger influence of the workingmen; for the passing of major control from men trained in the conservatively conducted Episcopal and Congregational Churches of Virginia and Massachusetts to the evangelical denominations such as the Methodists, Baptists, and Western Presbyterians.

Indirectly Jackson, by the impetus he gave the cause of democracy, greatly stimulated Protestant churches of the evangelical type, as well as strengthening the view that the rank and file of people, as distinct from the higher ecclesi-astics, had the right to govern their own church affairs. Some idea of the change in the electorate, for which he was mainly responsible, may be seen by noting the influence of his election to the presidency in 1828. In 1824 the aggregate presidential vote was only 356,000; in 1836 it was a million and a half; and in 1840 it was nearly two and a half million—seven times as much as only sixteen years earlier.[42] The electorate, originally largely limited to men owning property or paying taxes, had been extended remarkably. This meant that the various Churches close to the masses of the people, such as the Baptist and the Methodist, which had received no favors from the State in the colonial and Revolutionary periods, having never been established anywhere and being somewhat looked down upon by the old ruling classes, were coming into their own. Their members were to have a much larger influence in determining public policy in general and, more specifically, in wiping out all survivals of old Church-State connections. In a word, the democratic movement in the State would inevitably stimulate the democratic movement in the Churches and change the public attitude toward them. Congregationalists would no longer dominate public opinion in New England, nor would Episcopalians in the South.

Jackson's views of democracy were thus influenced by his religion, and on the whole he had strong support from Church people, outside of those of the more conservative social groups, especially in New England and New York.[43] A goodly number of the latter accused him, as they had Jefferson, of being anti-religious—and for several reasons: his general liberalism and independence, his opposition to the anti-Sunday mail campaign, and his refusal to issue the usual fast-day proclamation. His attitude on these and similar matters was due not to a lack of respect for religion but to his determination to keep religion out of politics and to advance the cause of democracy. His unsympathetic atti-tude toward the protection of the rights of the Cherokee Indians, in whose welfare the missionary societies were so deeply interested, is harder to explain.

The Early Co-operation in Behalf of the Indians

The first official recognition [44] given by the Federal government to missionary work among the Indians was a recommendation made by Secretary of War Henry Knox in 1789 that missionaries be sent to the frontiers to conciliate the Indians and cause them to be attached to the interests of the United States.[45] General Knox pointed out that while conciliatory efforts to pacify the Indians might be expensive they were nevertheless more economical than coercive methods.[46]

Missionaries were frequently used in making treaties with the Indians and in quieting disturbances.[47] Jefferson gave the Indians miscellaneous agricultural implements and occasionally made small financial contributions from public funds for the support of missions among them. These grants, coming from the fund provided by Congress in 1802, were for the civilizing of the Indians,[48] and similar grants were made during later administrations.[49] The missionary boards aided and abetted the contributions from government. Several denominations had followed the Moravians and the Quakers in establishing special work among the Indians—the Baptists in 1807, the American Board in 1810, the Episcopalians in 1815, and the Methodists in 1816. Some of these hesitated later, because of the importance of maintaining the separation of Church and State, to accept the responsibility of having their missionaries serve as Indian agents, but most did not seem to think there was anything inconsistent or dangerous in accepting grants of money from the Federal government.[50]

While the relations between Church and State over Indian questions were on the whole friendly during the early years of the republic, there were times of serious friction between the two great powers dealing with the Indians. The most critical single situation in the early period had to do with the Cherokee Nation and the successful efforts of the state of Georgia to have the Cherokees removed from lands which the white citizens of the state wished for their own use.

Early in the eighteenth century the Cherokees occupied, or claimed, all the territory south of the Ohio River and west of the Great Kanawha, and including the northern sections of Georgia and Alabama. But owing to the western migration of white settlers and the resulting Cherokee wars, by 1819 the tribe had through various treaties given up all its possessions except those in the South—mostly in Georgia. Here they determined to make a stand and to have their clear rights under the treaty of 1791 with the United States observed. With the active guidance of missionaries from New England, and with the aid of the Federal authorities, they had so far developed the arts of civilization that in 1827 they organized a government with a written constitution.[51]

But Georgia wanted the rich lands of the tribe, in which gold had been found. The state was undoubtedly in a difficult position, having what was virtually an independent Indian nation in its midst. In 1828 and 1829 it extended its laws to cover the Indians and demanded the withdrawal of the Cherokees to some western reservation and the handing over of their lands to the state.[52] A bitter legal fight ensued. The Supreme Court of the United States was repeatedly appealed to, as the Cherokees could get no help from President Jackson.[53]

The plight of the Cherokees in their conflict with the state of Georgia was much before Congress, especially in the twenties and early thirties.[54] The progress of the tribe in the arts of civilization and the cruelties involved in the attempt of Georgia to dispossess them from what remained of their ancestral lands [55] made a strong appeal to the Christian people of the country. However, neither the warm support given to the Cherokees' cause by Christian leaders [56] nor intervention by the Supreme Court [57] was strong enough—particularly in view of the fact that President Jackson's sympathies were with the state of Georgia[58]—to win justice for them.[59] In December, 1835, a treaty ceding their lands in Georgia was signed at the old Cherokee capital of New Echot by representatives of a minority of the tribe. It was ratified by the Senate by a small margin and was proclaimed by the president in May, 1836. Accepting $5,000,000 and 7,000,000 acres land west of the Mississippi, some 15,000 started their sad trek in 1838—the "trial of tears" to Oklahoma, but only after a tragic experience with concentration camps and armed force, thus bringing to an end a story which makes Americans of today blush with shame.[60]

Chapter 8

PROTESTANT ADJUSTMENTS TO AMERICAN CHURCH-STATE CONDITIONS

In the period immediately after independence, and especially after the adoption of the Constitution, the various Churches [1] had to adjust to new political conditions. It was a time when, freed from political connection with Europe and from the limitations of old colonial bounds, national Churches or denominations were being established as voluntary associations and were rapidly developing. These had, generally speaking, democratic constitutions giving large powers to the laity and frequently showed the influence of the American federal principle in their form of organization. Some Churches were of a purely local character, and the state organization created no problem. But others were nation-wide, and their missionary work was almost world-wide. This latter difficulty was met and has generally continued to be met by the incorporation of the controlling denominational organization in the state which was the home of its national office.

It is important to study the corporate development of American religious bodies, always remembering that the regulation of church property, as far as such regulation is permissible in the Constitution, is a state rather than a Federal responsibility. As a great American jurist, Justice Joseph Story, stated over a century ago, "The whole power over the subject of religion is left exclusively to the State governments, to be acted upon according to their justice and the State Constitutions." [2] This was prior to the adoption of the Fourteenth Amendment, but it still holds substantially true, for the Constitution, through the Bill of Rights adopted in 1791, says that "the powers not delegated by the Constitution to the States nor prohibited by it to the States, are reserved to the States respectively, or to the people." [3]

This provision was highly important, since now for the first time education, which was not so much as mentioned in the original Federal Constitution, and the control of churches, if any was needed, became state matters. Indeed, education—because of preoccupation with political matters, lack of general interest in public education in many colonies, the desire not to start denominational feeling, and other factors—was only once referred to in all the debates of the Constitutional Convention. That was when a question was asked as to the power under the new Constitution to establish a national university at the seat of government, and the chair ruled that the Federal government would have such power.[4]

We shall see that the churches, being placed on an equality before the law and without any financial help from the State [5] except exemption from taxation of property essential for church purposes,[6] began to thrive as "free churches in a free state." With the final action by Connecticut in 1818 and by Massachusetts in 1833 severing all connection between the Congregational churches and the state, the principle of Church-State separation became one of the accepted principles of political philosophy in the United States.[7]

Let us turn now to the leading Protestant bodies and consider their organization or reorganization under the republic, taking them up, as nearly as possible, in the order of their development as self-governing bodies after the Revolution, rather than in that of the establishment of their work in the colonies. Later chapters will consider similar steps in the history of the Roman Catholics [8] and of the Jews.[9]

The Methodists

Prior to the Revolution there had been no such thing in America as a Wesleyan or Methodist Church.[10] Its beginnings in what is now the United States go back to 1766 when Philip Embury, a Wesleyan "local preacher" from Ireland, began to preach in New York City and formed a society now known as the John Street Church, generally considered the first organized Methodist congregation in the country. In 1769 John Wesley sent over two itinerant preachers, and in 1771 two others.[11]

John Wesley's political conservatism constituted a difficulty for patriotic Methodists to overcome in the early days of the movement in this country. His *Calm Address to the American Colonists*, issued in 1777, was not calculated to make him and his followers popular in America. Many Methodist ministers suffered persecution for taking the British side, but it was understandable in view of Wesley's attitude and of the fact that they had not at the time any independent American organization. There was not even a yearly conference for colonial Methodists until 1773, and another decade passed before foundations were laid for an effective organization of American Methodism.

The first result of the treaty of peace of 1783, as far as a new religious organization was concerned, was the establishment of the Methodist Episcopal

Church in America. Up to this time American Methodism had been a part of the "Wesleyan Connection," partly Church of England and partly somewhat separate.[12] The conference to consider the organization of American Methodism, known as the Christmas Conference, was held in Baltimore late in December, 1784, when the denomination numbered 83 preachers and nearly 15,000 members.[13]

The most important questions and answers of the 1784 conference, from our standpoint, were the following:

Ques. 2. What can be done in order to [insure] the future union of the Methodists?

Ans. During the life of the Rev. Mr. Wesley, we acknowledge ourselves his sons in the gospel, ready in matters belonging to church government to obey his commands. And we do engage, after his death, to do everything that we judge consistent with the cause of religion in America and the political interests of these States to preserve and promote our union with the Methodists in Europe.

Ques. 3. As the ecclesiastical as well as civil affairs of these United States have passed through a very considerable change by the Revolution, what plan of church government shall we hereafter pursue?

Ans. We will form ourselves into an Episcopal Church, under the superintendents, elders, deacons, and helpers, according to the form of ordination annexed to our liturgy and the Form of Discipline set forth in these minutes.[14]

The new Church was loyal to the republic from its earliest days even though John Wesley had opposed independence. In 1789 the Reverend Dr. Thomas Coke and Francis Asbury, who had been appointed by Wesley as "Joint Superintendents," wrote to President Washington to express the Methodists' confidence in him, "for the preservation of those civil and religious liberties which have been transmitted to us by the providence of God and the glorious Revolution . . . ," and prayed that he might he enabled to advance "the happiness and prosperity of the United States." [15]

In 1791 there was sympathetic correspondence between Dr. Coke and Bishop William White of the Episcopal Church for union of their two Churches, and in 1792 at the General Convention of the Episcopal Church such a plan passed the House of Bishops but failed in the House of Clerical and Lay Delegates.[16] In the same year the first of the General Conferences was held. The General Conference was the highest authority in the Church. It became from now on a regular quadrennial event and did much to encourage unity, *esprit de corps*, and missionary zeal. Missionary outreach became one of the marked characteristics of the denomination, whose preaching of free grace and personal responsibility was extremely effective in Christianizing the frontier.[17]

The Methodist Protestant Church was established in 1830. Its principal

departures were in doing away with episcopacy and admitting lay representation in the conferences of the Church. The later separation of the Methodist
churches over slavery, which was not so much either a secession or an expulsion
of the Southern churches but rather a bisection of the Church along territorial
lines, came to an end in 1939 with the reunion of the two bodies and their
joinder by the Methodist Protestant Church.[18]

The Presbyterians

Most of the early Presbyterians in the American colonies were of Scotch
or Scotch-Irish descent. They came especially from Ulster in the decade after
the woolen industry there was destroyed by a law enacted in 1699—which
prevented exportation to any country except England and limited even this—
and other factors interfered with their prosperity. They were also opposed to
being assessed for the support of the Episcopal Church; and so for economic
and religious reasons many decided to emigrate. In 1718 the first considerable
body, consisting of from six to eight hundred, arrived in Boston. They scattered,
so that by the end of the colonial period there were some five hundred distinct
Scotch and Scotch-Irish communities in the American colonies.[19] They played
an important part in the movement for national unity and independence and
influenced the form of our republican government.[20] As "dissenters" in Virginia
and some other states, they were in the forefront of the battle for religious
freedom, being especially concerned to prevent an Episcopal establishment.
Samuel Davies,[21] the founder of the Hanover Presbytery, was the leader of the
group of ministers, mostly Presbyterian and Baptist, who helped to stimulate
Jefferson, Madison, and others to secure religious liberty and ultimately the
overthrow of the established Anglican Church in Virginia.

The Presbyterian Church in the United States was always interested both in
education and in evangelism and laid great emphasis on a well-trained ministry.
The members of the Church played a notable part in the Revolution. The
names of the Reverend John Witherspoon,[22] president of Princeton College
and a prominent member of the Continental Congress, the Reverend George
Duffield, one of the two chaplains of the Congress, and many others establish
the record of Presbyterian ministers for loyalty to the colonial cause.

The Synod of New York and Philadelphia of the Presbyterian Church was
one of the most influential of all colonial institutions in the development of
a centralized national conscience. It instigated the method by which, through
a republican form of organization, the collective wisdom of the entire Church,
both lay and clerical, could be focused on church affairs [23] and doubtless had
some effect on the American form of government.

A delegated General Assembly of the Presbyterian Church in the United

States of America was provided for by the Synod of 1786. The Church was subdivided into synods, and these in turn into presbyteries.[24] The synod ordered the preparation of "a book of discipline and government" accommodated to the state of the Presbyterian Church in America.[25] The Church had an inherited tradition of self-government with a federal ecclesiastical system of its own, and was accustomed to look on its General Synod as its servant rather than its master. The first meeting of the new General Assembly was appropriately held in Philadelphia in 1789.

The Presbyterian Church quite naturally, therefore, took the lead among the previously existing Churches in adjusting its constitution to the needs of the new government. It found, for instance, that changes in the Westminster Catechism would have to be made to eliminate the principle of State-Churchism and to proclaim the doctrine of religious liberty and of the legal equality of all Christian denominations. The most important change was that made in Chapter XXIII regarding civil magistrates.[26] Provisions in the original text of 1647 recognizing the authority and the duty of the civil magistrates to intervene in the Church in order to preserve unity and peace and to suppress blasphemies and heresies were eliminated in the American text of 1788. Instead the duty of the civil magistrates was defined as being limited to the protection of the Church without preference to any denomination of Christians.[27]

The closing clause of this chapter, formerly reading "they may lawfully be called to account, and proceeded against by the censures of the Church and by the power of the Civil Magistrate," was modified by the omission of the last eight words to show that the State had no power to control the Church and the internal affairs of its members.[28] Furthermore, the American edition of the Westminster *Larger Catechism*, in its answer to question 109, deleted "tolerating a false religion" as a sin forbidden in the second commandment, in Christ's summary of the law,[29] a significant change in the interest of tolerance.

The Presbyterian Church as thus constituted in this country was not, however, long to remain united. Schisms and divisions appeared, due especially to the very conservative groups, such as the "Old School," some of which secured control of the General Assembly in 1837, wishing to have their own denominational agencies instead of continuing to support an undenominational movement like the American Board. It read out the "New School" group, which represented nearly half of its ministry and membership. This division lasted until 1870. In the meantime the Presbyterians had been further split, north and south, over slavery.

Such were the beginnings of organized American Presbyterianism after independence. It represented a sturdy group of citizens with a Calvinist background and profound belief in the Christian religion and its Bible as of fundamental importance for the developing nation, to whose effective evangelization and religious education it stood ready to consecrate all its power.

The Episcopalians

The Episcopal Church was more affected by the American Revolution than almost any other, partly because it gained its independence from the English Church, though remaining in communion with it, and partly because in the Northern states it lost so many strong leaders who sympathized with the British government and consequently fled to loyal British colonies, especially Nova Scotia or other parts of Canada.

During most of the colonial period there had been almost everywhere, except in parts of the South and a few large seaboard towns, strong opposition in the colonies to the Episcopal Church. In New England and some other parts of the country it was thought to be an intruder. Its liturgy, ceremonies, and traditions were considered inconsistent with the ideals of the Reformation, with which the overwhelming body of settlers sympathized. Outside of New England the Anglican Church generally had either the support or the sympathy of governors and higher officials sent over from England, but this made it increasingly unpopular among the rank and file of people as the Revolution approached. During the entire colonial period it was without bishops,[30] in spite of earnest petitions that they be appointed.[31] These did not succeed, largely because of non-Episcopal American opposition.[32] Presbyterians, Congregationalists, and Baptists all feared that bishops would mean a State Church with tithes and other distasteful features. They also realized the English bishops, being sworn supporters of the crown, would be unlikely to take the side of the colonies in political issues. Consequently, Episcopalianism was not self-propagating in America, since no one could be confirmed and no minister could be ordained here. Such Americans as became clergymen had to go to England for ordination, and the rite of confirmation was practically disregarded—all sincere, baptized Christians of mature years being admitted to the communion.

By the time of the Revolution there were about 250 ministers and 300 churches.[33] Their situation became particularly difficult from the standpoint of Church-State relations. They were connected with the Established Church in England and by their oath of allegiance had bound themselves to the crown. Consequently, they felt that they had to continue their prayers for the king and the royal family. This issue became acute, especially in New England. For instance, the General Court of Massachusetts passed an act in March, 1777, forbidding expressions in preaching or praying which might discountenance popular support of colonial independence. A fine of fifty pounds was stipulated for violation of the act.[34] Similar acts were passed in some of the other colonies.[35]

Other matters besides the question of prayers created difficulties. For instance, should the Episcopal minister keep the fast days and observe the thanksgiving days appointed by Congress? Was he willing to read the Declaration of Independence or take up a collection for clothing for the rebel soldiers? Such questions were raised in many places.[36] Episcopal clergymen who did any of these things or otherwise showed sympathy for the cause of independence were likely to find themselves dismissed or to have their stipend diminished or completely stopped.[37] On the other hand, clergymen who showed any sign of antipathy to the cause of independence were often assaulted by the Sons of Liberty, put in jail, waylaid and beaten, had overripe vegetables thrown at them, and suffered other indignities.[38]

Political independence separated the churches from the English episcopate and from the supervision of the Bishop of London. At the same time financial support ceased, and the disestablishment of the Church in the Southern states put them in a difficult financial situation, as they lost in some cases much of their revenue and property. Then, too, the independent establishment of the Methodists reduced their ranks, as did the flight of the Tories, especially in New York and New England. Tens of thousands of British sympathizers—most of them affiliated with the Church of England—left the United States. This weakened a Church which was already none too popular in most parts of the country. The Tories who remained had to swear loyalty to the new State by signing a formal test-act document. They were obliged to swear allegiance before "the everlasting God" and agree to give no aid to Britain. So the Episcopal Church entered the regime of independence depleted by migration and with many of its remaining members ill-affected toward the new regime and for a time denied the vote.[39]

The position of the Church was more difficult than ever, for it was not until the passing of the Enabling Act of 1784 that men could be ordained for service in America without taking the oath of allegiance to the British crown. This was of course impossible for Americans, and at the same time the supply of clergymen from England entirely ceased.

A prime necessity to strengthen the Church and to fit it for growth in the new nation was to secure American bishops. Connecticut took the lead. In 1784, Samuel Seabury, who had been selected by its clergy, was consecrated in Aberdeen by non-juring bishops. He had been unable to secure consecration in England because the established Anglican Church did not feel that it could consecrate bishops outside of England in an independent State where prayers for the president were being substituted for prayers for the king, and where bishops could not swear allegiance to the crown. To Seabury's persistence and resourcefulness belongs the credit of overcoming all obstacles and domesticating the Anglican episcopate in America; but it was the Reverend William White, the rector of Christ Church, Philadelphia, and first Bishop of Pennsylvania, who did more than anyone else to make the Church part and parcel of American life. Seabury had not been sympathetic with the cause of the American Revolution, whereas White, who had been chaplain of the Continental Congress, was an ardent patriot. He was mainly responsible for arranging for the General Convention of 1789, which organized the Protestant Episcopal Church in the United States.

This outcome became possible because the petition addressed to the English episcopate in 1785, asking that its members consecrate bishops elected by conventions in different American states, had resulted in an act of Parliament authorizing the consecration of three American bishops, who united with Bishop Seabury in establishing the succession of American bishops. Prior to this time, the members of the Episcopal Church in several of the states considered it necessary to secure certificates from state authorities of the legitimacy under a republican constitution of their form of government. It was thought that such certificates would meet objections to securing the desired consecration of bishops in England. Indeed, the authorities of the Church of England had suggested to the representatives of the American Episcopal Church the importance of the certification. Certificates were thus secured from Pennsylvania, New York, and Virginia.[40] The governors of the states, apparently reluctant to indicate any right to certify the legitimacy of any Church, issued certificates which simply said that the clergy and members of the Episcopal Church as of any other Church were entitled to the free exercise of religion and could adopt any lawful means to keep a succession of religious teachers or in any other way practice their religious professions.

It became evident after independence had been won that the various Episcopal churches in the former colonies had to unite on some form of organization independent of control from England and yet maintain the historic episcopate. Some groundwork had already been laid, but the major step was the important General Convention of 1789,[41] which adopted canons that, with relatively few modifications, have continued to this time.

The Thirty-Nine Articles of Religion from the English *Prayer Book* were not finally revised until 1801, when certain important changes were made. For example, the old statement about the throne was omitted:

The Queen's (King's) Majesty hath the chief power in this realm of England and other of her (his) dominions, unto whom the chief government of all estates of this realm, whether they be ecclesiastical or civil, in all causes doth appertain, and it is not, nor ought to be, subject to any foreign jurisdiction.[42]

In place of this the following was substituted:

The power of the civil magistrate extendeth to all men, as well clergy as laity, in all things temporal; but hath no authority in things purely spiritual. And we hold it to be the duty of all men who are professors of the gospel, to pay respectful obedience to the civil authority, regularly and legitimately constituted.[43]

This article is still in force and represents the attitude of the Church and its membership.

The Episcopal Church was now well organized and implemented on a national scale for its work in the new republic. It was entirely self-governing, having broken all administrative ties with England though continuing in regular communion with all branches of the Anglican Church. It was in a position to carry on as a missionary body and to make all further adjustments in the various states that might seem advisable or necessary.[44]

The Universalists

The rise of Universalism as a separate denomination soon after the formation of the American republic was not without significance to our study of Church-State relationships. Its principal doctrine was and is the belief that all men will ultimately be saved, a theory which had its relation to the democratic ideal of opportunity and progress. There were ministers of various orthodox churches who held Universalist views from an early date. But these were individual cases. Universalism as a denomination goes back to the landing in New Jersey in 1770 of the Reverend John Murray. He preached in several Eastern colonies and settled in 1774 in Gloucester, Massachusetts. Here, in 1780, he built the first American Universalist Church. It stood for the view that Church and State should be kept separate, denying the right of human authority to regulate conscience by law.

There was soon trouble with the local Congregational Church and resulting lawsuits. The contention of the opponents was that Mr. Murray's congregation did not represent a church or religious society, "not being incorporated by any order of authority known in the commonwealth—but a mere jumble of detached members,"[45] and consequently that those who attended its place of worship should support financially the regular Congregational church.[46] The court, however, decided to the contrary. Its decision, which permitted the Universalist congregation to employ and support its own minister, was of importance not only to the new denomination but to Episcopalians, Baptists, and other groups. It later became necessary, however, for the Gloucester Universalists to obtain an act of incorporation from the state to make their position absolutely secure.[47]

Not until 1790, however, at a meeting of seven Universalist preachers and ten laymen in Philadelphia, did Universalism become organized to render national service. The meeting was honored by the attendance of Dr. Benjamin Rush, who was sympathetic to its purposes. The convention adopted articles of faith, a plan of church government, and various recommendations to their churches.[48] The meeting was also notable for its declaration that the holding of slaves was "inconsistent with the union of the human race in a common Saviour, and the obligations to mutual and universal love which flow from that union."[49]

Thus was established an American denomination, which, although not large numerically and not credited with as many men of distinction as the closely related Unitarian Church (with which it was to unite in 1961), has nevertheless proved a leaven in modifying the views of many denominations on the subjects of predestination and hell, and in enlarging their interpretation of human brotherhood.

The Evangelical and Reformed Church

The churches of German origin found it in many ways more difficult to adjust themselves effectively to new conditions under the republic than did any other religious bodies, not excepting the Roman Catholic. For one thing, their relationship to their Church authorities in Germany or Holland was almost as close as that of Roman Catholics to Rome. Moreover, those in control had had much less experience in adjusting the Church to conditions outside their own world.

The German Reformed Church, later called the Reformed Church in the United States, and to be distinguished from the Reformed Church in America —the Dutch branch—was the first to organize on an American basis after the Revolution. It traces its origin to the German immigration at the end of the seventeenth century and the early eighteenth. The cause of the migration was largely historical, growing out of conditions following the Peace of Westphalia (1648) at the close of the Thirty Years' War, when State-Churchism triumphed: each German State was to be Protestant or Catholic, and only Lutherans, Roman Catholics, and Reformed were recognized. As a result, Mennonites, Schwenkfelders, Moravians, and other groups migrated to America, as did members of the Reformed Church from some Catholic-controlled States.[50]

The Church of the Palatinate, with Heidelberg as its center, took a special interest in the settlers and sent over many useful ministers—to such an extent, indeed, that it became extremely difficult for the Reformed Church in this country to become independent of German influence and self-determining in its policy and administration. The Church also had close relations with the Dutch Reformed Church, which had shown the immigrants much kindness on their way through Holland and which continued to help it financially. For some time the Dutch synods virtually took charge of the American Reformed churches, especially after the effort to combine both Reformed Churches with the Presbyterian Church had failed in the middle of the eighteenth century.[51]

Most of the ministers of the "coetus," or synod, of the Reformed Church were earnest advocates of independence, and the Germans of Pennsylvania were active in organizing militia companies. However, the Church was then too dependent upon Holland for support to become an effective American religious body, and it was not until 1793 that the Church separated formally from Holland and became an independent body, although the word "German" was not dropped from the official title until 1869.[52]

In 1800 the first church of what came to be known as the Evangelical Association was formed among the Germans in Pennsylvania as a result of the preaching of Jacob Albright, an American-born German who was distressed at the lack of vital religion among his people. He held a small council in 1803 of "Evangelical and Christian friends,"[53] and in 1807 the name "The Newly Formed Methodist Conference" was adopted, and Albright became its first presiding elder. In 1816, at a "general conference," the denomination known as "The Evangelical Association" came into being. Later, owing to differences of opinion leading to much litigation in the American courts,[54] which reached a climax in the years 1887-93, a small group seceded and formed the United Evangelical Church. Negotiations resulted in the healing of the breach in 1922 and the assumption of the name of the Evangelical Church. In 1934 it agreed to unite with the Reformed Church as the Evangelical and Reformed Church, a union fully consummated in 1941.[55]

In 1957 the Evangelical and Reformed Church united with the General Council of the Congregational Christian Churches to form the United Church of Christ.[56]

The Dutch Reformed

Another communion deeply affected by the establishment of the independent government of the United States was the Dutch Reformed Church.[57] Its position among the Dutch settlers was not unlike that of the Presbyterian

Church among the Scotch settlers and the German Reformed among immigrants from Germany. It was definitely favorable to the independence movement, and many families which have rendered important service to America have come from this religious stock: the Stuyvesants, Roosevelts, Livingstons, Frelinghuysens, Schuylers, Brinkerhoffs, Van Rensselaers, Van Dycks, and others. These families came from New York and New Jersey, in which the Dutch Reformed Church was strongest.[58]

In October, 1764, the Dutch Reformed Church in this country, through the New York coetus, informed the Classis of Amsterdam, the highest governing authority of the Church, that it must have its independence. "We believe," it said, "that any subordination to a Church, which is destitute of all power (being under another civil government) is plainly contrary to the Netherlands Church constitution." [59]

While the adoption of the Union Convention in 1771 provided for the substantial independence demanded by the coetus,[60] it was not until 1794 that the Dutch Reformed Church in the United States became to all intents and purposes free to develop as an independent national body. It reissued the old version of the Heidelberg Catechism in 1795 but published an English translation in 1810. English, first used in its services in New York in 1763, now became increasingly the language of the Church in America, though in some rural parishes Dutch continued until about 1820.[61] The Church is now known as the Reformed Church in America, with approximately nine hundred churches and a quarter of a million members.[62]

The United Brethren in Christ

The United Brethren in Christ [63] represent a movement less dependent upon Germany than the other non-Lutheran Churches of German origin in the United States. This group had a definite founder in the United States, the Reverend Philip William Otterbein, a member of the Reformed Church born in Germany. He arrived in America in 1752 to work among the German congregations in the colonies, especially in Pennsylvania.

In 1785 the New or Evangelical Reformed Church accepted as its basis twenty-eight rules formulated by Otterbein. They provided that every minister connected with the congregation "care, to the best of his ability, for the various churches in Pennsylvania, Maryland, and Virginia, which churches, under the superintendence of William Otterbein, stand in fraternal unity with us."

The next important step was the holding of the first formal conference, in 1789. It was attended by seven of the fourteen ministers connected actively with the movement, nine being of German Reformed antecedents and five of

Mennonite. Among the latter was Martin Boehm, whose strongly evangelical preaching had caused Otterbein, when meeting him twenty-three years earlier, to exclaim *"Wir sind Brüder."* Thus the coming denomination was given its name, which was formally adopted at a conference in 1800 as the United Brethren in Christ. At this latter meeting Otterbein and Boehm were both elected bishops, and at subsequent conferences re-elected, and the new denomination, with its evangelistic and democratic tone, was fully launched.

The Church has generally worked in close co-operation with the Methodists. It followed them in its condemnation of slavery, support of temperance and Sunday observance, and opposition to secret societies. It was strengthened when the union with the Evangelical Church was consummated in 1946, thus forming the Evangelical United Brethren Church. Today its approximately 440 churches have three-quarters of a million members.[64]

The Congregationalists

No group played a larger part in the early development of our country than the Congregationalists. At the time of the Revolution they formed the biggest denomination in the United States. It dominated all of New England except Rhode Island, where Baptists and Quakers were stronger. The adoption of the Halfway Covenant in 1662, which permitted a partial church membership for those believers who could not claim any definite religious experience, had broadened its base (although its opponents felt that this resulted in many "halfway Christians"); it had gained about 25,000 adherents in the second third of the eighteenth century through the Great Awakening.[65]

New England Congregationalism was intensely patriotic during the Revolution. Indeed, the attitude of its leaders had done much to bring the Revolution about. The election sermons preached in Boston and other centers had become increasingly outspoken in behalf of the colonial cause. The great New England universities, Harvard and Yale, had been founded and nourished by Congregationalists and were national centers of patriotic sentiment. Furthermore, the fact that Congregationalism, with its Calvinistic inheritance of responsibility for public conditions, was the State Church in almost all of New England and that its ministers went *pari passu* with the sentiment of its colonial assemblies was another important explanation for Congregationalist patriotic inclinations.[66]

The Congregational churches adjusted themselves without serious difficulty to the new national conditions. Owing to their democratic organization and their emphasis on self-government, they represented, in spite of their devotion in New England to their inherited Church-State tradition, a liberty-loving people. Furthermore, latent in this denomination was an early English tradition of independence. For instance, Robert Browne, one of Congregationalism's great leaders, began to make his views on the subject public as early as 1580. To him a body of Christians administering their own church affairs, and choosing and ordaining their own pastors, was the ideal form of ecclesiastical organization, and the Church was to be entirely independent of the State.

The West developed rapidly after the passing of the Ordinance of 1787 regarding the Northwest Territory and the settlement of Marietta, Ohio, the following year. The extreme separatist tendencies of the different Congregational churches made it difficult, however, for them to unite nationally in missionary service. Indeed, the Congregationalists had nothing that could be called a national organization until the founding of the highly important American Board of Commissioners for Foreign Missions, which received its charter from the state of Massachusetts in 1810 and was the first national religious society of its type.

We have been considering the essential character of the Congregational churches, their organization and influence in the early decades of the republic. Let us now turn to the reverse of the picture. The only conspicuous influence of American independence on Congregationalism was that it was little by little disestablished in New England, the process not being completed in Massachusetts until 1833. This change produced its temporary difficulties but in the end strengthened rather than weakened the religious influence of all the Churches.

In June, 1957, the General Council of the Congregational Christian Churches united with the Evangelical and Reformed Church to form the United Church of Christ.[67] A number of individual Congregationalist churches, acting through Kenneth W. Greenawalt, a prominent lawyer and Congregationalist layman, brought suit to prevent the merger on the ground that Congregationalist churches are independent and autonomous and that therefore the Council had no authority to enter into the union. The suits, however, proved unsuccessful and the merger went into effect.[68]

The Friends (Quakers)

The Friends [69]—or Quakers, as they are most commonly called—were a larger denomination in proportion to total population in colonial times than they are today. In the beginning of the eighteenth century they were, after the Congregationalists, among the most numerous groups. Even at the outbreak of the Revolutionary War, although they had relatively decreased somewhat because of immigration and other factors, they stood fifth in numbers among

Church organizations, being exceeded only by the Congregationalists, Presbyterians, Baptists, and Anglicans.[70]

In 1756 the Quakers, who had been a dominant force in Pennsylvania political life, vacated their seats in the Pennsylvania Assembly, and others declined to be candidates for their positions. The society discouraged members from holding political office from that time on during the colonial period.[71] In most other colonies they had had a hard time to secure the right of suffrage. In New Jersey they acquired it first in 1713; in New York, in 1735.[72]

The Revolution brought serious problems, owing to the society's anti-war convictions. The Friends were sympathetic with the desire of Americans to obtain redress of grievances, but most of them remained neutral so as to avoid all warlike measures. They provided the first considerable group of "conscientious objectors" in our history. Since they refused to serve in the army or militia, they were frequently suspected of Tory sympathies, and their property was seized to pay for substitutes or lost by their refusing to pay war taxes. They were also virtually shut out of teaching school in Pennsylvania, for during the war the Assembly required a patriotic test oath of all teachers. Even some of the useful Friends' schools were closed. There was, however, especially in Philadelphia, a group known as free or fighting Quakers who erected a special meetinghouse of their own. The extent to which the members of the society were embarrassed by the conflict between patriotism and religious principle is shown by the public discussions of the time; by the fact that their quarterly meetings were not infrequently forbidden on the ground that they were "centers of plotting" against the American government; and by the further fact that fines against them for various charges involving their patriotism amounted during the war to about £35,000.[73]

The founding of the new government affected the Quakers less than most groups because of the local democratic form of organization to which they were already accustomed.

Essentially Quakerism is a very simple, personal religion which has made a point of carrying over its beliefs into life and work. It has remained faithful to the principles of George Fox, its seventeenth-century founder, who emphasized the "inner light." Simplicity of life and worship, opposition to war and oaths, kindness to sufferers and outcasts, the separation of Church and State, and other features have since marked its society. Speaking generally, it has kept itself from interference in public affairs, except as it has consistently opposed war and advocated social welfare projects and minority rights. Indeed, the Friends Committee on National Legislation operates actively and effectively in Washington in support of peace, equality, and social justice, although it is not technically an organic part of the Friends' denomination.[74]

The Baptists

The beginning of the Baptist Church in the United States goes back to Roger Williams, whose work for religious freedom has been described in an earlier chapter.[75] The leaders of the Church in the second half of the seventeenth century and in the eighteenth century were strong advocates of religious freedom, partly on principle, and partly because they were persecuted by the Established Churches in Massachusetts, Virginia, and elsewhere. Besides Williams, John Clarke,[76] Isaac Backus,[77] and John Leland [78]—all Baptist ministers or teachers—were among those responsible for making complete separation of Church and State a cardinal principle of the communion, and a potent American ideal. In spite of such leaders as these, the Established Churches, both Congregational and Anglican, considered most Baptists uneducated, and somewhat dangerous fanatics who cared little about law and order.[79] Outside of Providence and a few other centers, the Baptists did not reach many of the educated classes. Unquestionably, however, they did much to maintain and develop an interest in religion, especially in small communities. The denomination had no strong central organization and represented many different separatist tendencies.

Baptists gained the respect of Benjamin Franklin largely because they had no formal theological creeds. They did not even publish their Articles of Faith, thinking that they had reached no finality in this matter and that they might find new truth. It was this point of view that gained Franklin's commendation: "This modesty in a sect is perhaps a single instance in the history of mankind, every sect supposing itself in possession of all truth, and that those who differ are so far in the wrong." [80]

The Baptists were aided by the Great Awakening in the second third of the eighteenth century and by the growth of the independence movement from 1774 on, as many as nineteen associations being organized.[81] These almost without exception became centers for advancing the cause of civil and religious liberty, which were considered two sides of the same shield.

The Baptists were quick to adjust themselves to the new conditions brought about by the Revolution, for the freedom, both civil and religious, involved was most congenial to them. Their congregational system did not, to be sure, seem at first to demand a national organization, but they formed associations and general committees in various cities, counties, and states.

Soon they began to organize on a national basis, one of their reasons being to have a stronger position from which to secure complete religious freedom in the states. Finally, in 1814, representatives of eleven of the eighteen states then in the Union, meeting in Philadelphia, organized the General Missionary

Convention of the Baptist Denomination of the United States of America for Foreign Missions.[82] By the time of the second convention, in 1817, a national educational and home missions movement [83] had developed, and in 1832 the Baptist Home Missionary Society was established.

On the whole, the Baptists have remained remarkably faithful to the tradition established by Roger Williams and his followers. Operating through the Joint Baptist Committee on Public Affairs, established in 1939 for the express purpose of maintaining the Baptist witness of separation of Church and State and religious liberty, they have opposed many infractions of separation and religious freedom,[84] particularly in respect to government aid to sectarian institutions. For example, at the request of the Southern Baptist Convention, the Hill-Burton Act was revised in 1958 to permit a church to accept a loan instead of a grant of Federal funds to a sectarian hospital, although a few Baptist hospitals under private boards continue to accept grants.[85]

The Unitarians [86]

Unitarianism, as a form of religious belief emphasizing the unity of God and denying Trinitarianism as an explanation of the Godhead, is an ancient belief. Some trace the beginning of the Unitarian Church in this country to the adoption by King's Chapel, Boston, in 1785, of a new form of liturgy from which all references to the Trinity were dropped. There were other movements in and around Boston in the early days of the nineteenth century as a result of which the Unitarian Church, as a separate denomination, was gradually developed. The date generally taken as representing the beginning of the independent denomination in the United States is 1819, when William Ellery Channing of Boston delivered a sermon in Baltimore, stating beliefs generally accepted by those members of the Congregational and other Churches who denied the Trinitarian doctrine.

In 1825 the American Unitarian Association was formed. From that time until the end of the century Unitarianism was a great factor in broadening the social interests of the churches; in promoting independent thinking on theological, civic, educational, and other matters; in advancing the welfare of the Negro; and in urging various reforms on the State. From its earliest days the Unitarians have been strong supporters of religious freedom and of the importance of the Church's aiding the State through the encouragement of social reform.

Although the Unitarians represented much more of an intellectual and social elite, they shared many views with the Universalists. The denomination had in the last century such outstanding thinkers, after Channing, as Ralph Waldo

Emerson, Theodore Parker, and Charles W. Eliot, as well as many of the leaders both of the abolition movement and of the New England literary revival. In 1865 its churches, which had always maintained the congregational form of government, formed a national conference and became active in extending the influence of the denomination. Their purpose was to appeal to those who wished to unite "pure religion and perfect liberty." The covenant in general use expresses the main emphases of Unitarianism: "In the love of truth, and in the spirit of Jesus, we unite for the worship of God and the service of men." In this spirit the Church has always emphasized the vital importance of tolerance, though, according to some, occasionally lapsing into intolerance in its attitude toward those religious bodies which lay stress on dogmatic beliefs.

In 1961 the American Unitarian Association merged with the Universalist Church of America to form the Unitarian Universalist Association.[87]

The Lutherans [88]

The Lutherans had more difficulty than most Protestant groups in adjusting themselves to the new conditions, in large measure because of the continued devotion of most of them to the German or to some Scandinavian language.

The first important step in adapting to American conditions was taken in 1748, when a synod—originally called the United Pastors, but later the Ministerium of Pennsylvania—was organized in Philadelphia. This led ultimately to the independence of the Lutheran Church in the United States, which at the outbreak of the Revolution included more than a hundred congregations in Pennsylvania and about a third of that number in the other colonies.[89]

Other steps forward were the organization of the New York Synod, 1785, and the introduction of lay delegates into an American Ministerium for the first time in New York in 1792. Intermarriage with other non-Lutheran Protestant stock, such as Huguenots and Presbyterians, now became more frequent; theological tests were made less rigid; the Church united increasingly with the general evangelical movement after about 1810;[90] and the Synod of Ohio and adjoining states was formed in 1818.

During this period the language question was uppermost. *A Hymn and Prayer Book for the Use of such Lutheran Churches as use the English Language,* the "first mode" of the current book, was published in 1795; English was adopted by the New York Ministerium in 1807. St. John's English Lutheran Church was founded in Philadelphia in 1810 after St. Michael's, by a narrow majority, had declined to call a third pastor who would conduct services in English.[91] Ten years later dissension arose in the new parish, and the matter was carried to the courts, where the German party lost.[92] A similar controversy arose in Lancaster, where the Lutheran congregation refused to contribute to the treasury of the synod until young men were educated to preach in English.

The beginnings of a union movement are seen in the action of the powerful Ministerium of Pennsylvania in 1818, when it passed a resolution to the effect that "in its judgment, it would be well if the different Evangelical Lutheran Synods in the United States were to stand in some way or other, in true union with one another. . . ." This movement resulted in the organization of the General Synod.[93]

In 1918 the United Lutheran Church in the United States was formed by the merger of the General Synod, the General Council, and the United Synod of the South, a body created as a result of Civil War controversies. It placed its forty-five synods on the same doctrinal basis, committed them to the same general practices, and made possible common action in the fields of general benevolence and missionary work. The merger was followed in twelve years by the union in the American Lutheran Church of three heretofore separate groups—the Joint Synod of Ohio, the Iowa Synod, and the Buffalo Synod.[94]

In 1960, at a constituting convention in Minneapolis, Minnesota, the Evangelical Lutheran Church and the United Evangelical Lutheran Church merged with the American Lutheran Church, under the latter name, to bring together Lutherans of Danish, German, and Norwegian heritage. Independent of this is the Lutheran Church in America, organized in June, 1962, by the consolidation of the American Evangelical Lutheran Church, the Augustana Evangelical Lutheran Church, the Finnish Evangelical Lutheran Church, and the United Lutheran Church in America. With more than three million baptized members, the new body is the largest of the Lutheran churches in the United States.

In general there has been much progress toward unity and full Americanization among Lutherans of different national origins. But in spite of a constantly increasing minority which feels that the Church has a large responsibility for social and political conditions, Lutherans have in the main continued their European tradition of aloofness from any active participation as churchmen in the affairs of State. They have not until quite recently been specially interested in the problems of religious freedom.

The Disciples of Christ [95]

No religious body is more definitely an American product than the Disciples of Christ (sometimes known as Churches of Christ or Christian Churches);

this small denomination has had two of its members, James A. Garfield and Lyndon B. Johnson, occupy the office of the presidency of the United States.[96] It is therefore natural that the denomination should have been committed to the ideal of religious freedom. It developed on the frontier and was an attempt to restore primitive Christianity. The movement that resulted in its foundation goes back to the great religious revival which took place in the Appalachian region in the early years of the nineteenth century. Five ministers of the Presbyterian Church in Ohio and Kentucky who wanted to preach what they believed to be the simple truths of Christianity felt outraged because the Presbyterian Synod had taken action against one of their number for his creedal views. The synod felt that old-time Calvinism must be maintained at all hazards, while this group was opposed to hard-and-fast denominational creedalism and was interested in a simpler form of doctrine based entirely on New Testament preaching. It consequently withdrew from the synod, stating that its members would take the Bible as the standard of faith and rule of life to the exclusion of all man-made creeds and would adopt the name "Christian." This they believed to be of divine authority, and better than all sectarian and denominational designations. From the first they sought union with all who believed in Jesus Christ.[97]

In addition to this group of "Christians," a second and equally important stream came into the movement through the Reverend Thomas Campbell, a Scotch Presbyterian, who arrived in the United States in 1807. Campbell became a Presbyterian minister in western Pennsylvania, where he invited all Christians so disposed and duly prepared, without any reference to denominational conditions, to unite in the communion. As a result, the presbytery found him worthy of censure, and he appealed to the Associate Synod of North America.[98]

The synod released him from censure but believed that the feeling against him on account of his liberal spirit made it advisable for him to withdraw, which he did. There was then formed what was known as "The Christian Association of Washington, Pa." This was in 1809. It issued a "Declaration and Address," whose purpose it was to do away with denominationalism.[99]

When Alexander Campbell, co-founder with his father of the Disciples of Christ, arrived in the autumn of 1809, he approved the document, but stated that to be true to their principles the Disciples would have to give up the requirement of infant baptism and some other practices.

This denomination represented a new effort on the part of frontier Christians to gather into a single group the religious people who, coming from many churches and traditions, had been molded to a common pattern by the West.[100]

The group represented by the "Christians" and the group represented by

Alexander Campbell—the "Disciples" or "Campbellites"—finding, after talks and conferences on various occasions, that they had virtual identity of spirit and purposes, consummated a union in 1832 in Lexington, Kentucky, with the Bible as the only basis of their creed.[101]

Some favored the old name "Christians"; Campbell, the name "Disciples." So it happens that the group is sometimes known as "Christians," sometimes as "Disciples of Christ," while some, who refused to accept the merger, persist in the name "The Christian Church."

Thus came into being an organization which now numbers almost two million, principally in the Middle West and Southwest. It is the type of independent organization which, with its ideas of freedom and lack of ecclesiastical authority or State connection, could never have arisen prior to the organization of the republic. "Each local church is under Christ, a self-governing unit." It is also characteristic of one stream or wing of American religious thought which has resulted in the "community church movement"—namely, the feeling that dogmatic beliefs are much less important than uniting in worship and service in the spirit of Christ.[102]

The Mennonites

The Mennonites are such small, independent, and loosely related groups that it is hard to give a definite date for their reorganization after the Revolution. They derived their name from one Menno Simons, a Dutch reformer living in Zurich. These industrious, peace-loving, and mostly rural groups repudiate oaths, lawsuits, the holding of office, and the bearing of arms—a position still persistently held by a majority of members. Although originating in Switzerland, where they separated from the Zwinglian State Church because they rejected infant baptism, they gained many followers in neighboring countries, especially in Germany and the Netherlands.

Their first settlement on our shores was at Germantown, Pennsylvania, in 1683.[103] In the next seventy years several thousand Mennonites had reached eastern Pennsylvania, coming mostly from South Germany and Switzerland. For the most part they held firmly during the Revolution to their principle of non-resistance.[104] Special taxes and fines were therefore imposed upon them for their pacifist views. Some paid and rendered noncombatant service. Others served prison sentences rather than contribute in any way to the cause of war. When the Pennsylvania Assembly set up a Revolutionary government and required an oath of renunciation and allegiance, many, though in no sense Tories at heart, declined to submit. One result was a considerable migration to Canada. Here they and the Quakers still form the leading religious pacifist groups. Those who remained finally succeeded in securing documents of privilege both from the colonial Assembly of Pennsylvania and from the Continental Congress exempting them from military service.[105]

The formation of the American government seems to have effected less change in the Mennonite Church than in any other American religious body. Even more than some other German religious groups, the Mennonites constitute the exception to the rule that the formation of the American government profoundly influenced in a relatively short time the organized religious bodies of the nation.

The most conservative members of this conservative group have been and still are the Amish people of Pennsylvania. Some idea of their opposition to all liberalism may be shown by the names of their two principal bodies: the Old Amish Order, which still uses only the German language and accepts no innovations, and Conservative Amish, the less extreme group, which holds services in both German and English.

The Effects of Independence on the Protestant Churches

As we study the general effect on the Protestant churches of the establishment of a new and independent republican form of government in place of the old colonies, we notice certain characteristics of what is sometimes called "American religion."

1. The political separation from Europe and the winning of independence inevitably encouraged denominationalism with its advantages and disadvantages. Every group could have a Church of its own liking, as all Churches were now independent of the State. As a result, some entirely new denominations were established and some old denominations organically divided. The tendency to divide and multiply denominations was accentuated by several factors: the spirit of freedom that was prevalent; the life of the frontier with its isolated communities; the growing split over slavery, which brought about the division of the larger Protestant churches, with the exception of the Episcopal, into Northern and Southern branches; the Second Awakening, which developed in the first few years of the nineteenth century, and the growing revival of religion and independent conviction that followed it; and the immigration of groups from northern Europe with strong national traditions and feelings.[106]

2. The support of the Churches—except for a few Germanic-language groups which continued to receive help from abroad—became entirely a voluntary matter. State subsidies were a thing of the past.[107] The change in support was quite in keeping with the Protestant point of view that religion is a personal matter in which the State as such has no direct concern other than to see

that laws and conditions are fair and friendly without favoritism to any de-nominational group.[108]

3. The emphasis on evangelism became noticeable. The new freedom and the new responsibility, combined with the opening up of new territories, resulted in much emphasis on evangelistic effort. That this was sometimes accompanied by extremes cannot be doubted, but on the whole the missionary zeal that developed was a healthy sign.

4. The Churches became more democratic in their organization and administration, with a larger amount of power given to the laity. This was the case everywhere, although in the Roman Catholic Church the hierarchy and priesthood succeeded in retaining all authority in matters of doctrine and ecclesiastical polity.[109] As far as local trusteeship of property is concerned, there was a long struggle where the Roman Catholic Church maintained its old tradition, but probably in no other place in the world has lay opinion had as much influence in Catholic circles as in the United States.

5. The forces of religion and of religious toleration were definitely strengthened in most parts of the country. Notable have been the removal of remaining barriers against the Jews; the growth of interdenominational societies among Protestants; the starting of denominations which minimized doctrinal barriers, such as the Methodists and the Disciples of Christ; and the integration of American Catholics into national life, in spite of the beginnings of certain threatening anti-Catholic disturbances which arose with the large immigration, especially Irish, in the second third of the nineteenth century.

Francis J. Grund, a Bohemian-born American publicist, published in 1837 *The Americans in Their Moral, Social and Political Relations*, in which he noted the American tendency of extreme independence in church matters. He wrote that "For America, every clergyman may be said to do business on his own account, and under his own firm." [110] Here are three additional exceptionally revealing quotations from his book on the status of religion and the churches in the United States in the 'thirties of the last century.

. . . Although the most perfect tolerance exists with regard to particular creeds, yet it is absolutely necessary that a man should belong to some persuasion or other, lest his fellow-citizens should consider him an outcast from society. The Jews are tolerated in America with the same liberality as any denomination of Christians; but if a person were to call himself a Deist or an Atheist, it would excite universal execration. Yet there are religious denominations in the United States whose creeds are very nearly verging on Deism; but taking their arguments from the Bible, and calling themselves followers of Christ, they and their doctrines are tolerated, together with their form of worship.[111]

The religious habits of the Americans form not only the basis of their private and public morals, but have become so thoroughly interwoven with their whole course of legislation, that it would be impossible to change them, without affecting the very essence of their government.[112]

. . . The Americans look upon religion as a promoter of civil and political liberty; and have, therefore, transferred to it a large portion of the affection which they cherish for the institutions of their country . . .[113]

These, then, were the major effects of American independence on the Protestant churches and the adjustments made by them. But Catholics and Jews likewise found it necessary to make adjustments to American Church-State conditions, as the next two chapters will indicate.

...

Chapter 9

ROMAN CATHOLIC ADJUSTMENTS TO
AMERICAN CHURCH-STATE CONDITIONS

The Roman Catholic Church[1] waged a long fight in the United States against laws and public opinion which interfered with its standing and with the complete equality of its members in political rights and privileges. In the struggle leaders in the Church found it advisable to modify some of the traditional attitudes on matters it did not consider fundamental, so as to adjust itself to the American requirement of separation of Church and State and of equal treatment by the State of all law-abiding religious bodies.

The Colonial Background of Difficulties

Most of the early American settlers came from England, and, as is well known, Protestant England found its principal enemies in Catholic France and Spain. Successive British sovereigns and parliaments from the time of Elizabeth to George III, by the passage of various laws—some of a penal character—sought to weaken the Roman Catholic faith in England and even to eradicate it. In so doing they showed intolerance and at times cruelty. The people of England, however, had a right to be disturbed at some of the actions of the popes and of the Roman Catholic Church in early centuries, and it is not difficult to see why the "No Popery" battle cry received popular support.[2]

So the colonists inherited from England and Germany strong opposition to the abuses and claims of Rome. Many of the colonial charters, and their own later legislative enactments, contained severe restrictions against "Papists," whose numbers outside Maryland were extremely limited. Even Maryland, which in the early days had developed a spirit of toleration under its Roman Catholic proprietors, in 1654 repealed its Toleration Act of five years earlier and enacted a law to the effect that "none who profess to exercise the Popish religion, commonly known by the name of Roman Catholic religion, can be protected in this province." [3] For a considerable period here and elsewhere Roman Catholics were excluded from office holding. Indeed, in the beginning of the eighteenth century Rhode Island and Pennsylvania were the only ones of the original thirteen colonies in which Roman Catholics could enjoy a large measure of religious and civil rights.[4] Elsewhere, except for the four years of the reign of the Catholic king, James II, they were legally denied the essentials of religious freedom and were generally required to pay toward the support of the locally established church.[5] The Puritans were inclined to favor John Cotton's well-known dictum that "it was toleration that made the world anti-Christian."

The Quebec Act of 1774, by which Roman Catholics were given protection by the British in Quebec and in the region west of the Ohio, fanned the flame.[6] Protestant Americans feared that this would ultimately mean an end to their liberties, which they believed were bound up with the Christianity of the Bible—a book the Roman Catholic Church did not then encourage its lay members to read and would not indeed allow them to read in the King James and Geneva versions most common in the colonies. The widespread attack on the Quebec Act shows the determination of most of the people in the American colonies at the outbreak of the Revolution to oppose the spread of Roman Catholicism among them. Except for Franklin, Jefferson, and Washington, few colonial leaders failed to denounce Catholics in some degree at one time or another. The press was uniformly hostile especially because of its fears that Quebec Roman Catholicism would spread south.[7]

Prior to the middle of the eighteenth century "Pope Day"—the anniversary of the Gunpowder Plot on November 5—was observed in some places in Massachusetts and other colonies, the pope in effigy with the devil being paraded through the streets of New England towns. It was in many ways the counterpart of Guy Fawkes Day in England, and its celebration frequently ended with "the burning of the pope." President Washington had no sympathy with this extreme anti-Catholic propaganda and favored toleration. He issued a well-known order condemning the custom as "ridiculous and childish."

It is probably needless to go into further details. The Roman Catholics in what is now the United States were, speaking generally, badly treated prior to the Revolution.[8]

Early Steps in Organizing the Church—Leadership of John Carroll

The American Revolution and the start of the United States government resulted in many changes in political conditions which proved helpful to the Roman Catholic Church. It had to overcome much prejudice and opposition in almost all the colonies, due partly to historical reasons; to the tie-up of the colony with an Establishment, or at least with laws favoring Protestants; or to the feeling that it owed "allegiance to a foreign prince"—the pope. From 1757 to the Revolution, the vicar apostolic of London had held jurisdiction for the Church of Rome over all the colonies and islands in America that were subject to the British Empire.[9] There was, however, no one in the colonies who could administer the rite of confirmation. Thus thousands of Roman Catholics could not be adequately cared for. Appointment of a prefect or bishop residing in the colonies was opposed by the Catholics themselves for fear it might bring violent persecution by civil authorities who were not sympathetic with the Church. (It should be noted, however, that there was also strong and for many years successful opposition to the appointment of an Anglican bishop, indicating that American antagonism to "prelacy" was by no means limited to Roman Catholic prelacy.)

In addition to the passing of the Quebec Act, the suppression of the Jesuit order had further complicated the situation, since many of the priests in America were members of that order. In spite, however, of the presence of European priests, a large group of Roman Catholics favored independence, of whom the most conspicuous representative was Charles Carroll of Carrollton, a signer of the Declaration of Independence. During the war there seems to have been almost no connection between the Church in America and its authorities in Europe, and when the war was over and the colonies separated from Great Britain the vicar apostolic of London declared that he would no longer exercise jurisdiction in what were often referred to as the "Thirteen Provinces of America." [10]

Although the principle of religious freedom made progress during the Revolution, the state constitutions and the laws passed under them still often discriminated against Roman Catholics. Only four of the new states (Pennsylvania, Delaware, Virginia, and Maryland) early abolished the old laws and allowed Roman Catholics absolute equality with other Christians.[11] The other states in one way or another insisted that Protestantism should be supported, or provided that Protestants should not be denied the enjoyment of civil rights, without referring to Catholics, or adopted a constitutional clause to the effect that the truth of the Protestant religion must be accepted by all who wished to hold office in the state.[12] In New York, which was typical, the oath preventing Roman Catholics from becoming citizens with the right of holding office was not removed until 1806.[13]

The disclaimer of jurisdiction by the London vicar apostolic [14] did not change the position of the American laymen against appointment of a native bishop, but the clergy of Maryland and Pennsylvania, after meetings held in

1783 and 1784, petitioned Rome for the appointment of an American superior with power to administer confirmation, grant faculties and dispensations, bless oils, and exercise other privileges which were not strictly episcopal in character.[15] Complying with this petition, Pope Pius VI appointed the Reverend John Carroll of Maryland superior of the Catholic clergy in the United States with power to administer the rite of confirmation.[16]

Carroll's appointment was an extraordinarily fortunate one, from the standpoint both of the Church and of the new State. A devoted Catholic and an ardent patriot, respected and trusted by Washington, he was ideally fitted for his very difficult and delicate task of organizing the churches of the Roman communion in the United States. As a representative of the Catholic Church, he had also been able to exert considerable influence in France in favor of aid during the Revolutionary War. But the great thing about Carroll was his noble character and his breadth of view, which made him honored by all who knew him.

Carroll's appointment was of momentous significance. Its effect was to give the American Church a quasi-independent position, subject only to Rome and without any connection to Great Britain.

The following year Carroll was made prefect apostolic, and the final act necessary to place the Church on a firm basis in the United States was his election to the bishopric. This was effected in 1788, by the nomination of twenty-four of the twenty-six priests assembled and entitled to present a name to the pope from America. The bull confirming his election was issued the next year, and Carroll was consecrated in England in the summer of 1790 by the senior vicar apostolic. The Roman Catholic Church was now able to undertake its work in the new republic under favorable auspices and theoretically on a basis of legal equality with all other religious bodies. This was a condition which had not existed anywhere for more than a thousand years, since the Church here was not a State Church, nor a merely tolerated Church, nor a persecuted Church. It was, in the view of the State, merely one of a large number of religious bodies treated with impartiality by the Federal government and soon to receive equal treatment in all the states.

Some idea of the more tolerant spirit toward Roman Catholics which came with independence can be seen from the fact that in 1786 the president, along with members of Congress, attended a dinner celebrating the dedication of St. Peter's, the first Roman Catholic church to be erected in New York City. It is also illustrated by the situation in Boston, headquarters of American Puritanism. During the colonial period there was no Roman Catholic parish in New England, and in Massachusetts none would have been allowed. But on All Saints' Day, 1788, a French priest in Boston celebrated mass in the old

French Huguenot Church, now considered "the first Catholic Church in New England." The mass did not have to be celebrated secretly but was duly described in the press.[17] In 1799 subscriptions were opened for a new church, as the old one on School Street was no longer fit for divine service. Representative Protestants, headed by President John Adams, subscribed $11,000, about a third of the total. The church was dedicated in 1803, and the Roman Catholics, having persuaded most of Boston's representative citizens that they were doing highly useful work and were loyal to the government of the United States, were now in a position to serve recent immigrants and others appealed to by their polity and form of worship.[18]

Nevertheless anti-Catholic bigotry was by no means dead. It was largely fear of Catholic growth that resulted, during the administration of the Federalist president, John Adams, in the enactment of the Alien and Sedition Laws, which gave the president authority to expel from the United States aliens suspected of disaffection, and the Naturalization Act of 1798, which required residence of fourteen years in this country to obtain citizenship.

The extremes of those advocating a "Native American" policy were largely responsible for the overthrow of the Federalists in 1800, when John Adams was defeated by Thomas Jefferson, one of the Jeffersonian planks being "freedom of religion and opposition to all manoeuvres to bring about a legal ascendancy of one sect over another." [19] As the nineteenth century began, under the influence of the bills of rights and with a liberal in the presidency, anti-Catholic prejudice died down. State Churches and discriminatory laws against Catholics were gradually dropped.

The patriotism, breadth, and character of Father Carroll, as first bishop of the Roman Catholic Church in the United States, from 1789 on, probably did as much as anything else to create a more favorable public attitude during the first two decades of the new century. But religious peace was not to last long. The day of violent anti-Catholic demonstrations, absurd outbreaks of fanaticism against convents and nuns, publication of scandalous books by alleged ex-nuns and ex-priests, etc., was still ahead. This movement, which reached its climax in the thirties and forties, was led mostly by irresponsible persons, though occasionally men of character and standing, such as Samuel F. B. Morse, took part. His work entitled *A Foreign Conspiracy against the Liberties of the United States* was an important book in the controversy, and he wrote or edited several other works of the same character.

Anti-Catholicism can be explained largely by the fact that, theoretically at least, democracy—such as we have in the United States, where the final appeal is to the vote of the people—is inconsistent with absolutism, and to many the power of the pope as final authority in the field of "morals" as well as of religion seemed to involve a possible basis of serious conflict between the two powers.

The old theory of St. Augustine, which the Church adopted, states that there are two societies, one spiritual and supernatural (the City of God) the other temporal and natural (the State) and that both derive their power from God, but it is exceedingly difficult to draw a sharp line between the two. In most cases—perhaps three-fourths—the division is clear, but in the remaining fourth, where it is not, fear arises among non-Catholics. The trouble is aggravated by the fact that the constitution of the Roman Catholic Church is based on an authoritarian central government, albeit in some respects its life, its constituency, and the parish clergy are democratic in the best sense of the word, whereas the Constitution of the American State is republican, with checks and balances between the Federal government and the states and among the legislative, executive, and judicial departments. In other words, there is a broad distribution of powers in our American democracy, whereas in the Roman Catholic Church final authority is in the hands of a pope elected by cardinals in whose choice the rank and file of people have no say. No one should quarrel with those who wish this form of government in the field of "religion"—and it *is* the choice of millions of intelligent people—but when the Church claims through the pope final authority also in "morals," in which the State as well is vitally concerned, there is a basis for possible difficulty, because the word may be extended to include the broad field of social ethics, of direct concern to the modern State. Although the vocal opponents of Roman Catholicism as a factor in American life are often very unfair and frequently cannot give sound reasons for their attitude, their underlying fear is due to the fact that the Church does concentrate ultimate power in a single person. They apply to the Church what Harold Laski has applied to the body politic: the conviction that "There will never be liberty in any state where there is excessive concentration of power at the center." [20]

The Provincial and Plenary Councils of Baltimore [21]

Bishop Carroll's diocesan synod of 1791—attended by the bishop and twenty-two priests—laid the foundations for a strong Roman Catholic Church in the United States. We are now to consider the first seven provincial councils of Baltimore which legislated for practically the whole Catholic population of the republic. These have added importance because their acts were approved by the first plenary council of 1852 and its successors. We shall deal only with those which have an important direct or indirect bearing on the subjects discussed in this volume, Church-State relations and religious freedom.

The first provincial council of Baltimore was held in 1829, attended by one archbishop and four bishops. It enacted that:

None are to be married until they know the Christian doctrine. Slaves, however, need know only the principal truths if more cannot be acquired.

In mixed marriages the non-Catholic must promise to bring up the offspring as Catholics.

Vernacular hymns and prayers are encouraged at evening service.

The Douai English Version of the Bible is to be used.

The faithful are to be warned against improper theaters, dances and novels.

The control of Church property should be consigned to the bishop whenever possible so as to avoid the abuses of lay trustees, who are not allowed either to institute or dismiss a pastor.

Latin must be used in the sacraments and the burial service, but a ceremonial in English is to be drawn up.[22]

The council thought so highly of the acts of the synod of 1791 taken under Carroll's leadership that it voted to have them reprinted at the head of those it passed.

The second council was held in 1833, attended by one archbishop and nine bishops. Various American dioceses were set up. Indian missions were entrusted to the Jesuits.

The third council in 1837 brought together one archbishop and eight bishops. It was decreed that ecclesiastics should not bring ecclesiastical cases before civil tribunals but that ecclesiastical property was to be secured by the best means the civil law afforded.

The fourth council in 1840 issued decrees signed by one archbishop and twelve bishops. Temperance societies were recommended. Pastors were to see that children frequenting public schools did not use the Protestant version of the Bible, or sing sectarian hymns; and must use their influence against the introduction of these practices into public schools. Bishops were to control ecclesiastical property.

In 1843 the fifth council was held, attended by one archbishop and sixteen bishops. It was decreed that laymen were not to deliver orations in the churches.

The sixth council of 1846 was attended by one archbishop and twenty-two bishops. "The Blessed Virgin Mary Conceived Without Sin" was chosen as the patron of the United States.

The seventh council in 1849 was attended by two archbishops and twenty-three bishops. Priests were forbidden to assist at the marriages of those who had already had a ceremony performed by a Protestant minister, or who intended to have such a ceremony. A national council was proposed to be held in Baltimore by apostolic authority.

These seven councils were practically, even though not formally, plenary councils of the Church in the United States. This is not true of later provincial councils.

The first plenary council of Baltimore was solemnly opened in May, 1952; its sessions were attended by six archbishops and thirty-five bishops.

They professed their allegiance to the Pope, as the definitely constituted head of the Church, and declared their belief in the entire Catholic faith as explained by ecumenical councils and the constitutions of the Roman pontiffs.

They decreed that the enactments of the seven provincial councils of Baltimore were obligatory for all the dioceses of the United States. The bishops were exhorted to choose consultors from among their clergy and to ask their advice in the government of the diocese.

Bishops should appoint censors for books relating to religion.

Bishops were exhorted to have a Catholic school in every parish with teachers paid from the parochial funds.

Laymen were directed to take no part in the administration of church affairs without the consent of the bishop.

Bishops were to use their influence with the civil authorities to prevent anyone in the army or navy from being obliged to attend the religious service repugnant to his conscience.

These and other decrees were duly approved by the papacy, the cardinal prefect stating that the Holy See tolerated relaxations of the common law of the Church for grave reasons only, but that every effort was to be made to bring about the observance of the universal discipline.

The second plenary council was held in 1866; President Andrew Johnson was among the auditors at the last solemn session. The decrees were signed by seven archbishops and thirty-nine bishops, or their procurators, and two abbots.

The council devoted much attention to the "errors" of the time, such as Unitarianism, Transcendentalism, Pantheism, spiritualism, indifferentism, etc. They warned against the teaching that one religion is as good as another provided one be honest and just to his neighbor. They provided for diocesan synods in which the bishop alone was to be legislator and judge. Methods for the nominations to the papacy for American sees were decided upon.

Much attention was given to the matter of preaching, and it was decreed that priests were not to mingle political and civil matters with religious doctrines in their sermons, or to attack public legislators. They were to avoid having recourse to civil tribunals as far as possible.

The decrees of the seven provincial councils of Baltimore against the abuses of lay trustees and the best method of securing church property by civil sanction were reenacted.

Pastors were instructed to keep registers of baptisms, confirmations, marriages, and funerals, all except the last named to be in Latin.

Teachers belonging to religious congregations should be employed, as far as possible, in parochial schools, which should be erected in every parish. Catechism classes should be instituted in the churches for public school children.

The idea of a Catholic university in the United States was favored.

Evidence of the result of the Civil War is seen in the decree commending both secular and regular priests to further the conversion of Negroes.

The large emigration from southern and western Germany was responsible for the provision that in dioceses with many Germans, seminarians should learn enough German to hear confessions, this being in keeping with the Church's policy to care for immigrants in their own language, in addition to the Latin Mass, until they could be Americanized.

The third plenary council was held in 1884, being presided over by Archbishop Gibbons as apostolic delegate.

Much attention was given to the matter of filling vacant sees. It was decided that when a see becomes vacant the archbishop should call together the consultors and irremovable rectors of the diocese, and that they should choose three names to be forwarded to Rome as well as to the other bishops of the province. The latter were to discuss the candidates and if desired they could reject the names proposed by the clergy and substitute others, but they must give their reasons when sending their recommendations to Rome.

Diocesan consultors must be at least two in number, and should be four or six, the consultors being chosen by the bishop, half at his own option, and half by clerical nomination.

Detailed arrangements were made for so-called irremovable rectors, pastors who could not be removed except for a canonical cause and who were to be chosen by examination, the bishop being allowed to give a vacant, irremovable rectorship only to a candidate who has received the approving votes of the examiners.

Priests were not to bring an action against another cleric before a civil tribunal about temporal matters without written permission from the bishop, and never regarding ecclesiastical affairs, which pertain only to the Church authorities.

Catholics who were married before a sectarian minister were excommunicated.

Detailed arrangements for the education of clerics were adopted, beginning with the preparatory seminaries, where the pupils were to be taught Christian doctrine, English, and at least one other language, and must learn to speak and write Latin; Greek, natural science, music, and the usual branches of profane learning being included in the curriculum. These seminaries were to be followed by the greater seminaries, with two years devoted to philosophical and four to theological courses. The Catholic university project was to be advanced entirely under the management of the episcopate, but some students should continue to be sent to Rome, Louvain, and Innsbruck.

Much attention was given to ways in which the parochial schools could be made more efficient, and it was stated that it was desirable that they should be free.

As to the control of Church property, it was decreed that the bishop is the guardian and supreme administrator of all diocesan property. Where lay trustees are necessary, only those members of the congregation have a voice who are twenty-one years of age, have fulfilled the "Paschal Precept" (i.e., Easter Communion), have paid for a seat in the church during the past year, have sent their children to Catholic schools, and belong to no prohibited society. The pastor was to be ex officio president of the board.

This council adopted an important statement regarding the attitude of the Church toward the American government. It breathes the spirit of Archbishop Gibbons, in many ways the most influential member of the council, who frequently gave expression to the view that the American Constitution with the democratic provisions of its Bill of Rights was one to which devout Catholics could give loyal assent. The statement referred to has added weight because it was in a pastoral letter adopted at the close of the council.

We think we can claim to be acquainted with the laws, institutions and spirit of the Catholic Church, and with the laws, institutions and spirit of our country; and we emphatically declare that there is no antagonism between them. . . . We believe that our country's heroes were the instruments of the God of Nations in establishing this home of freedom; to both the Almighty and to His instruments in the work we look with greatful reverence; and to maintain the inheritance of freedom which they have left us, should it ever—which God forbid—be imperiled, our Catholic citizens will be found to stand forward, as one man, ready to pledge anew "their lives, their fortunes, and their sacred honor. . . ."[23]

The above quotations from the acts of these councils should suffice to show the broad and statesmanlike way in which the Roman Catholic Church organized in the United States and undertook to make its contribution to national life. Church action on the specific problems of Church trusteeship and incorporation need to be dealt with more at length. But it should be noted first that the councils were held mostly in the period of large foreign immigration; and it would be difficult to overestimate the constructive part the Church played at that time in meeting the needs of the immigrant and in helping him to make the necessary adjustments to American traditions and ideals.

The Trusteeship Controversy

Even in the early days of the republic the historical theory of the Catholic Church was well known: that as an organization the Church was essentially independent of the civil power and was anxious to control its own policy in matters where its interests were thought to be at stake. So it had to fight hard for legal recognition, since the American legal theory inherited from England is that tenure of property requires the approval of civil authority and that every corporation is at least to some degree the creation of the civil law.[24] From the standpoint of canon law,

The Church is a juridical person which owns all the temporalities that are required for divine worship. Consequently the real owner of the parish church is the parish itself. . . . Especially must the false notion be eliminated that the parishioners are the owners of the parish church. Such an idea may suit a Protestant community, but does not agree with the fundamental principles of the Catholic Church.[25]

This theory had implications that involved difficulties and much ill feeling. The growing opposition by Protestants to transplanting Roman Catholicism to the United States without some modification of its policies took various forms, of which perhaps the most important at this time, next to fear of the papacy, was objection to the European system of exclusive ecclesiastical control of Church property. This seemed to be autocratic and made many fear that the Church would prove an enemy to democratic institutions. Even many Catholic laymen did not wish exclusively ecclesiastical control of Church property but advocated some form of trusteeship in which the congregation should be represented. Such a compromise was in accordance with the method generally provided in the various states following the lead of New York, which adopted a general incorporation act in 1784. This early caused difficulties in the most important Roman Catholic parish in the state, that of St. Peter's, New York City. "The Trustees of the Roman Catholic Church in the City of New York"— five Catholics—were duly incorporated under the law. But these men, all laymen, wanted as a priest one who was a good preacher, laying relatively little emphasis on his sacerdotal qualifications and ignoring the priest whom the prefect apostolic, John Carroll, had given the faculty for the church.

The trustees claimed the right "not only to choose such a parish priest as is agreeable to them, but [of] discharging him at pleasure, and that after such election, the bishop or other ecclesiastical superior cannot hinder from exercising the usual function." [26] To this Carroll replied, "If ever the principles thus laid down should become predominant, the unity and catholicity of our Church would be at an end; and it would be formed into distinct and independent societies, nearly in the same manner as the congregation Presbyterians of our neighboring New England States." [27]

Carroll was faced with similar troubles in Philadelphia. In 1797 he was forced to excommunicate a German priest for denying his jurisdiction and maintaining that "The power of ecclesiastical ministry and government is derived to pastors from the community or congregation of the people." [28]

Priests coming from abroad caused Bishop Carroll special difficulty. In one case a German Franciscan took possession of certain property of a Catholic priest, who had died before being able to build a church on it, and defied the authority of Bishop Carroll; whereupon the case came before a Pennsylvania court, which in 1798 rendered a decision favorable to the bishop. The court said,

The Bishop of Baltimore has the sole episcopal authority over the Catholic Church of the United States. Every Catholic congregation within the United States is subject to his inspection; and without authority from him, no Catholic priest can exercise any pastoral functions over any congregation within the United States. . . . [29]

This was a valuable precedent but not always followed. Indeed, much difficulty was caused by this and scores of similar cases of "lay trusteeism" in the United States.

In New York, the 1784 act was superseded in 1813 by a new act for the incorporation of religious societies.[30] Its purpose appeared to be to place control of the temporal affairs of churches (including the Roman Catholic churches) in the hands of the majority of the persons who form the churches. In fact, it was even interpreted as placing a church corporation on a plane of equality with all other corporations by making the members the corporation and reducing the trustees to the position of a mere board of directors.[31] Naturally, the act was distasteful to the Catholic Church.[32]

Aside from the effects of American democratizing influences, the trusteeship problem was considerably complicated by the conflicts which arose between Irish and French, and German and English groups, and among other national divisions with the Church itself. For example, a particularly serious situation arose in Norfolk, Virginia, where, in the early days of the nineteenth century, there was no legislative provision for incorporation of religious societies. Church property was consequently held by incorporated trustees in fee simple, the conveyance being "for and in behalf of the Trustees of the Roman Catholic Society of the Borough of Norfolk." [33] A French priest sent to the parish in the winter of 1815-16 had a hard time because, although duly appointed by the bishop, he was treated by the trustees as a hired servant. The bishop supported his objections to this attitude, authorizing him to abolish the trustees and to choose personally from time to time certain members of the corporation whom he thought best fitted to help him manage the temporal affairs of the parish. The old trustees protested in a letter to Archbishop Leonard Neale, Carroll's successor. His reply was as follows:

In the Catholic Church none but Bishops have the power of appointing or removing subordinate pastors within their respective dioceses, and whatever goes to contradict that, goes to subvert episcopal authority, and to establish a system which must eventually deluge the public with confusion and disorder.

Hence I conclude, that the trustees and vestrymen in the Catholic congregations of this diocese should only be such as are appointed by the pastor to assist him in the administration of temporal concerns, not to suppose him amenable to their authority with degradation to his character as to their appointed pastor, who is solely amenable to his bishop.[34]

The situation became so serious that in 1818 Archbishop Ambrose Maréchal, Archbishop Neale's successor, sent a report to Rome explaining to the Sacred Congregation that the principal cause of the trouble was the American people's devotion to civil liberty, under which "absolutely all magistrates, whether high or low," are selected by popular vote. The report continues,

. . . all sects of Protestants, who constitute the greater part of the people, are ruled by the same principles and accordingly elect or dismiss, at their pleasure, their pastors. Now the Catholics living in their society, are evidently exposed to the danger of admitting the same principles of ecclesiastical rule, and by the artifices of impious priests, who cater to their pride, are easily led to believe that they also have the right to elect and dismiss their pastors as they please.[35]

At about the same time a bitter dispute was taking place in Philadelphia because of the action of the lay trustees of St. Mary's Cathedral in electing Reverend William Hogan pastor and because of the newly appointed bishop's efforts to remove him. In 1823 the Hoganites petitioned the Pennsylvania legislature to pass a law requiring lay members of a congregation to choose their own pastors and forbidding appointments by the hierarchy.[36] The legislature, in spite of the latter's opposition, passed the requested bill, but it was vetoed by the governor.

The first provisional council of Baltimore, held in 1829, gave serious consideration to the question of lay domination. The majority expressed strong condemnation of any asserted right by laymen to appoint or dismiss pastors or to build churches independent of direction by the local bishop.[37]

There was no more vigorous opponent of the American lay trustee system than the Bishop of New York, John Hughes.[38] He appealed to the churches of his diocese to give up voluntarily their civil right to hold church property. As his legal position was at least questionable, he had introduced into the legislature in 1852 a measure which would permit the holding of property by ecclesiastical authorities. Protestant opposition was so strong that the bill was defeated. One church in Buffalo—which preferred the lay trustee plan, to which it was accustomed—found its trustees excommunicated by Hughes, now archbishop, since the church had defied the interdict of the new diocesan when he attempted to secure the surrender of the trustees. The latter petitioned the legislature to have the old law of 1784 rigidly enforced. The legislature replied by adopting in 1855 the Putnam Bill, designed to make the clerical holding of church property illegal. However, the state officials did not try to enforce this law, and it was repealed in 1863. Non-enforcement was also the reaction in the case of similar bills passed by other legislatures, but the whole controversy created much ill feeling. This was increased by the Vatican's sending to America a papal nuncio, Archbishop Bedini, empowered to settle the most serious trustee conflicts in New York and Philadelphia. His visit resulted in mob riots; the burning of his effigy; attacks on churches and their priests; revival of the anti-nunnery campaign, especially in the South; violent utterances against the nuncio in the Senate of the United States, resulting in a request to the president that he submit to the Senate information regarding the archbishop's visit; a recrudescence of emotional, and often vulgar and ill-informed, anti-Catholic literature; lurid attacks on the confessional as an alleged cause of immorality, and on the motives of the hierarchy; and the coming to the fore of dangerous anti-Catholic agitators.

We shall deal later with the development and present status of trusteeship in New York State, which in this matter set certain precedents for the nation.[39]

Convent Problems and Protestant Prejudice

The period after about 1825 was one in which religious prejudice played a large part on the American scene. It was due to many causes; perhaps the most important were the fear of injury to our democratic institutions as a result of the large Catholic immigration from Europe, and anxiety over influencing the religious character of the expanding West. The newly established "religious press" was largely responsible for much misinformation and bitterness on both sides. By 1827 there were thirty Protestant periodicals, all anti-Catholic in tone. The formation of the American Bible Society in 1816, which was undenominational but Protestant in its aims and support, and of the various national Protestant missionary and educational societies meant that Protestantism was prepared to strengthen its position and to oppose, if need be, what it considered "the enemy at the gates." On the other hand, the Roman Catholics, with their increasingly effective national organization and the founding, in 1822, of their first journal, the *United States Catholic Miscellany,* were ready to battle for what they believed to be their rights. The religious press became very bitter in the thirties, some of the newly established publications, such as *The Protestant* and *Priestcraft Unmasked,* going beyond all bounds of decency in their denunciations of Roman Catholicism.[40]

The discussions proceeded apace, not only in the press but in the pulpit, and public forums were held in different parts of the country where subjects like "Is Popery Compatible with Civil Liberty?" were debated. The New York Protestant Association, established in 1831, was specially active in promoting these debates, some of which accomplished a useful purpose, though most were too extreme to be wholesome and helpful. At least two series of debates in the period attracted wide attention: those in 1833 between the Reverend (later Archbishop) John Hughes and the Reverend Professor John Breckenridge of the Princeton (Presbyterian) Seminary and in 1837 between Bishop John Purcell and the Reverend Dr. Alexander Campbell, one of the founders in Cincinnati of the Disciples of Christ. The major problem was recognized as the same, namely, "Is the Roman Catholic religion, in any or all of its principles or doctrines, inimical to civil or religious liberty?"[41]

The controversy, after several years of agitation, came to a head in Massachusetts in 1834, when a young girl who had been dismissed from a menial position in the Ursuline Convent in Charlestown began telling lurid tales of her convent life. These stirred up much public indignation, strengthened by reports in the Boston newspapers that a nun had mysteriously disappeared from the same convent under suspicious circumstances. The convent was attended by the daughters of some prominent Boston Unitarian families, who were dissatisfied with the rigid religious teaching in the public schools. Later investigation showed that the woman in question, a Miss Harrison, had been temporarily mentally deranged; but the tinder had been set for an explosion of public anger. It was fanned by extreme anti-Catholic sermons by the Reverend Lyman Beecher and other ministers who should have been wiser.[42]

The convent situation became so serious that the selectmen visited the convent on the morning of August 11 and prepared a report stating that Miss Harrison, who had returned, was "entirely satisfied with her present situation, it being that of her own choice; and that she had no desire or wish to alter it." Unfortunately this report did not appear in the Boston papers until the following morning; by that time the convent was in flames. On the night of August 11 a mob of forty or fifty men, partly disguised and bearing "No Popery" and "Down with the Cross" banners, approached the convent and demanded that they be shown the secreted nun, whom they believed to have been placed in some dungeon. They were told to return the next day when the children would not be disturbed. But they decided on action that night, and while fire companies stood helplessly by, the mob's leaders broke into the convent and applied the torch. The building, from which the sixty pupils had been hurried to safety by a back door, became a smoldering ruin. The town selectmen, who early in the evening had been notified of the threatened trouble that evening, took no preventive measures other than to have the town's one policeman on hand, believing that that would be sufficient to forestall any serious disturbance. The next evening another mob burned fences, trees, and everything else they could lay their hands on within the convent grounds. Only the presence of troops prevented the burning of a nearby Catholic church.

The mob action was universally condemned. On the day after the fire there was a mass meeting of Protestants presided over by the mayor in Faneuil Hall. It adopted resolutions denouncing the burning as "a base and cowardly act" [43] and appointed an influential committee to try to bring to justice those responsible, and to consider raising a fund to reimburse the convent. A reward was offered for the apprehension of the culprits.[44]

Even editors of the religious press which had been denouncing convents were repentant. But the trial of those responsible showed intense anti-Catholic feeling with the usual efforts to prove the immorality of convent life. The attempt of the attorney general to have jurors questioned as to their prejudice against Roman Catholicism was not successful. After twenty hours' deliberation the jury delivered a verdict of acquittal. It was received with "thunderous applause." The state legislature soon became involved when Bishop Fenwick petitioned for funds to rebuild the convent. Since there was evidently a difficult question of Church-State relations involved, the request was referred to a committee, which early in 1835 presented two reports. The majority recommended that the funds be granted, though denying the right of the Ursulines to reimbursement; the minority bitterly attacked Roman Catholicism and recommended no compensation. The majority report was defeated overwhelmingly—412 to 67.

In March, 1839, the Massachusetts legislature passed an act making the community responsible for damages under circumstances such as that of the burning of the Ursuline Convent, but since the measure was not retroactive the Ursulines did not get any damages.[45] Later efforts at repayment, in 1842, were equally unsuccessful. In 1846 an inadequate sum was voted and refused; and in 1853 and 1854 attempts to adjust matters on a fairer basis failed, so that particular issue was considered dead.[46]

Organization of Parochial Schools

One of the reasons for the development of the Roman Catholic parochial school system was that Roman Catholics felt they could not conscientiously subject their children to instruction conducted mainly by Protestant teachers, with a Protestant point of view, and with opening exercises of an undenominational religious character. Another was that they felt that no secular public school could or would give adequate attention to religious teaching. This teaching is to the devout Roman Catholic basic—as it is to earnest Protestants. The former, however, also felt that Sunday instruction in church, voluntary Bible classes in religion, and home influences are not adequate to give a thorough grounding in religion; this not only must be taught by qualified Roman Catholics regularly in the school but must permeate all teaching. The school must make God the center.

Consequently, in starting the parochial school movement, Roman Catholics were sincerely interested in having all their children taught in school the Christian religion as the Church of Rome understood it; but since this proved impossible under the American view of the public school system, the logic of the situation seemed to them to demand the creation of their own schools.

The first parochial school was erected in 1782 by St. Mary's Church, Philadelphia, then the largest and richest Roman Catholic parish in what is now the United States. It is considered the "Mother School" of the parochial school system in the English-speaking colonies and states.[47] But the idea was not carried out in many places for several decades. Indeed, the real development of the system on a national scale did not come until half a century later. It was first officially sanctioned in Baltimore in 1829 and was developed soon thereafter in New York and Massachusetts, an almost inevitable result of the enormous Roman Catholic immigration at that time.[48]

The problem became particularly acute in the Eastern states with the large influx of Irish Catholics after 1830,[49] and especially after the potato famine in 1848, when the Catholic population arriving from Ireland in one decade was sufficient to double the number of Catholics in the United States.[50]

Roman Catholic schools, which up to about 1840 had generally been developed under diocesan influences, added more during the period of immigration to the cause of Roman Catholic education than during all the previous decades. In this progress the religious teaching communities or orders were the most important single factor. The first of these orders, known as the Sisters of Charity, was established by Mother Elizabeth Seton in 1809 at Emmitsburg, Maryland. It is to the teaching orders that the Church is mainly indebted for the success of the movement, for they provided an inexpensive, devoted, and fairly well-trained group of teachers. At the beginning of the period of the great immigration there were thirteen religious communities in the United States engaged in parish school work, but as the immigration advanced toward the middle of the century some twenty-five more were added, most of them branches of European orders.[51] All but six of the new group were sisterhoods. In this respect the parochial schools are like the public schools; most of the teachers are women.

As far back as 1829 the first provincial council of Baltimore adopted a canon declaring it necessary that Catholic schools be established to avoid the danger of loss of faith on the part of Catholic children.

The second provincial council, in 1833, carried the development of parochial schools farther by appointing a standing committee to supervise the preparation of textbooks for Catholic schools. At the fourth provincial council pastors were directed to prevent Catholic pupils in the public schools from being made to join in the use of the "Protestant Bible" and hymns and prayers.[52]

When we reflect that the Roman Catholic immigrants were mostly of the less privileged portion of the population, and that many of them were day laborers earning only a dollar a day, their unselfishness in developing this new system commands our admiration. By the year 1840 there were two hundred Catholic parish schools in the United States, many of them west of the Alleghenies.[53] Now there are about sixty times as many—a really amazing growth in a century and a quarter.

The organization of parochial schools was stimulated by the anti-Catholic feeling, especially in the large Eastern centers of immigration, where unfortunate incidents were common. The Charlestown burning, and subsequent trial and legislative hearings, raised the "No Popery" campaign to a national issue. Attacks on Catholic churches and other property became so common that armed guards were frequently posted to protect them. Insurance companies even refused to insure Catholic buildings unless they were constructed of non-inflammable materials. Anti-Catholic literature increased. Rebecca Reed's *Six Months in a Convent*, although itself rather colorless, formed the basis of national discussion; it was her stories, exaggerated as they passed from mouth to mouth, that had led to the Charlestown attack. Other much more sensational "revelations" followed, by "ex-nuns," "ex-priests," and Protestant extremists. Of these the most famous was Maria Monk's *Awful Disclosures of the Hotel Dieu Nunnery of Montreal*, published in 1836 and reprinted in large editions totaling 300,000 copies in a quarter of a century. It was a lurid, unreliable, and later discredited account of the alleged immoralities and cruelties of convent life by an unbalanced woman. She was later arrested for picking the pockets of her temporary companion in a New York house of ill fame and died shortly afterwards in prison.[54]

In the same year (1836) the powerful American Society to Promote the Principles of the Protestant Reformation, generally spoken of as the Protestant Reformation Society, was established to put on a national basis the work of the old New York Protestant Association. Its work was both to "convert Papists to Christianity" and to carry on organized work through auxiliaries, lecturers, tracts, and the religious press against the Roman Catholic Church.

It became evident that Catholics had to develop a vigorous campaign in behalf of the type of education they favored, and in support of their views of religion, if their Church was not to lose in the struggle. Bishop John Hughes was to prove the most vigorous leader in this movement, and New York, where he became bishop in 1842 and archbishop in 1850, was to be the center of his activity.[55]

Roman Catholic Immigration and the "Protestant Bible" in Schools

In the late thirties the anti-Catholic movement became more serious as the conviction spread that the foreign Catholic immigrants, arriving in larger and larger numbers, were in alliance with their Church to overthrow the government of the country. The pope, assisted by the Roman Catholic rulers of Europe, was seen as trying to capture the Mississippi Valley for the future headquarters of the Church. Two missionary societies—the Society for the Propagation of the Faith, formed at Lyons, France, in 1822, and the Leopold Association of Austria-Hungary, formed in 1829—were specially feared because of their active interest in trying to convert the newly settled West to Catholicism and their large contribution to the cause.[56]

The fear of the political designs of the papacy was given a semblance of respectability by no less a person than Samuel F. B. Morse. In 1834, under the pen name of "Brutus," he wrote a series of articles in the Protestant *Observer* on "A Foreign Conspiracy against the Liberties of the United States," followed the next year by a similar series in the New York *Journal of Commerce* on "Imminent Dangers to the Free Institutions of the United States through Foreign Immigration." The main argument was that the purpose of the pope and of the societies named was not merely religious but political. The articles asserted that if the papacy and its great ally, Austria, were to survive they must have Catholic immigrants enter the country in sufficient numbers to strangle liberty and democracy and to convert America to "popery," thereby saving the decaying monarchies and paving the way for the papacy and despotism in America. Referring to the Leopold Association in his "Foreign Conspiracy," Morse asserted that the nefarious "plot" to conquer the United States must be killed. Roman Catholic schools and officers of government, and lenient immigration laws, must be discontinued, "Nativism" must be encouraged, and Protestants must unite to conquer the West.[57]

The Reverend Lyman Beecher was another man of education and standing who was greatly stirred by what he believed to be papal plans to conquer and control the United States. Specially fearful of the influence of Roman Catholic schools as proselyting agencies, in his *Plea for the West* (1832) he popularized this issue and the method of avoiding the feared calamity, namely, Protestant schools and colleges.[58]

The "Nativist" attitude had been growing so strong that it was inevitable that it should get actively into politics. It had a successful beginning in New

York City in 1837, when the mayor and the entire Common Council were elected by the New York Native Americans. This and similar associations which opposed foreign officeholders and voters, as well as free immigration, were virtually aggressive Protestant groups convinced that unrestricted immigration and foreign influence were linked with Roman Catholicism. Other agencies, such as the American Bible Society, pledged themselves to labor until the Scriptures—that is, what the Catholics called the Protestant Bible—were read in every classroom in the country. The struggle over this issue became particularly acute in New York City, where the public schools at the time were under the control of an association, formed in 1805, which had as one of its stated purposes "to inculcate the sublime truths of religion and morality contained in the Holy Scriptures." [59] The Public School Society from 1813 on had its own funds supplemented by the allocation of part of the state's common school fund administered by the Common Council. By 1840 it had acquired a virtual monopoly of the school facilities of the city, operating nearly one hundred schools. The Roman Catholics had ground for complaint, since not only was the King James Version of the Bible alone used, but some of the textbooks, especially those in history, were both unfair and disrespectful to their Church. They protested strongly, both to the society and to the Board of Aldermen of the city.

This situation attracted the attention of the governor of the state, William H. Seward, an Episcopalian. In his message to the legislature in January, 1840, Seward said that many immigrant children were being kept from these public schools because of the sectarian nature of the instruction. He went farther and advocated, in the interest of such children, the "establishment of schools in which they may be instructed by teachers speaking the same language with themselves and professing the same faith." [60]

The few existing Catholic parochial schools petitioned the Common Council for a share of the state funds. This was unanimously denied, the council having evidently been impressed by the argument of the Public School Society that if the request were granted it would be followed by others from other religious groups, and that in the end sectarian instruction would displace general education in the schools of the city. The issue was thus made clear and it brought to the fore Bishop Hughes as a vigorous advocate of the Catholic position. After much public discussion in which both sides went to extremes, the Common Council appointed a committee to reconsider the whole matter. In the following year the committee's report, advocating the rejection of the Roman Catholic financial claims, was adopted by a vote of 15 to 1.[61]

Bishop Hughes replied by securing a petition to the state legislature prepared by a committee of citizens advocating—what he evidently considered the lesser of two evils—a completely secular system of state-controlled education, so that New York City would not be at the mercy of the Public School Society. Governor Seward again entered the fray in behalf of his plan for state aid to sectarian schools, stating that some twenty thousand children in the city— mostly the children of immigrants—were being kept out of school by the type of Protestant instruction afforded.

The legislature decided to ask the secretary of state, who also served as superintendent of state schools, to study the matter. He recommended that in place of the old society a responsible school commissioner should be elected in each ward. The matter became an important issue in the fall elections of 1841. The Whigs nominated a ticket pledged to support the existing system and opposed to sectarian schools; the Democrats officially tried to avoid the issue, although a majority of their candidates for the legislature took, as individuals, the same position.

Fearing that the situation as it stood was hopeless, Bishop Hughes called a meeting four days before the election, and Catholics were urged to support a group of independent candidates whose names were submitted before the meeting adjourned. This action, whatever its intent, brought the Church into politics and was resented. The day after the famous Carroll Hall meeting the Democratic candidates unanimously announced their opposition to any change in the public school system.[62] The votes showed Whigs, 15,980; Democrats, 15,690; Catholic party, 2,200; Nativist party, 470. The Roman Catholic group was in a hopelessly small minority, but the Democrats could win if they adjusted their politics to attract it. As a result, the legislature, having a Democratic majority with the upstate vote, passed a bill which practically extended the state school system to New York City. But the state superintendent was a strong Protestant who favored the daily Bible reading, and Bishop Hughes consequently decided that the only way out was to build up the parochial school system. He was, however, able to secure some temporary relief through the action of the ward school commissioners, so that by 1844 the Bible reading practice had been given up in thirty-one schools in dominantly Catholic wards.[63]

Similar agitation took place in Philadelphia, Newark, Boston, and other cities, arousing much bitter controversy on the Church-State issue. In some cases Roman Catholic children were expelled from school or otherwise punished for refusing to participate in the opening religious exercises. It should be remembered that from their standpoint—or at least that of their parents— the Bible read in the schools (King James Version) was a "sectarian" book, an opinion which Protestants denied.

While the New York controversy was at its height, anti-Catholic organizations were being strengthened all over the country, specially by the American Protestant Union, founded in 1841 and headed by Samuel F. B. Morse. It was opposed to the "subjugation of our country to the control of the Pope of Rome, and his adherents, and [was] for the preservation of our civil and religious institutions." [64]

The fear of the growing "foreign" Catholic influence was so great that in 1843 the American Republican party was formed. Its printed *Songster* of this year well shows the purpose and spirit of this group. For instance:

> Then strike up "Hail Columbia!" boys, our free and happy land,
> We'll startle knavish partisans and break the Jesuit's band.
> We'll snap the reins, spurn party chains and priestly politics
> We swear it by our father's [sic] graves—our sires of Seventy six! [65]

In its various utterances the party laid emphasis on extending the naturalization laws so that a foreigner would have to reside in the United States twenty-one years before voting; continuing the Bible in the schools; restricting office holding to native Americans; preventing all union between Church and State; and demanding the "right to worship the God of our fathers according to the dictates of our own consciences, without the restraints of a Romish priest, or the threats of a Hellish Inquisition." [66]

The following year (1844) this party made a deal with the Whigs, who were naturally inclined toward Nativism, to support Henry Clay and Theodore Frelinghuysen on the national ticket in return for support of local American Republican candidates in some places, especially New York and Pennsylvania. The Whigs lost the national election, but their new allies swept New York City and most of Philadelphia. This victory gave them encouragement to organize independently on a national scale, which they did July 4, 1845, changing the party name from Native Republican to Native American.

Among the early results of the Nativist movement were many discussions in Congress on tightening the naturalization laws. Petitions came in in large numbers from Nativist anti-Catholic sources,[67] but when the matter came before the House of Representatives in December, 1845, a few statements as to the "Papal plot" to subdue the country by sending over millions of immigrants from the despotic countries of Europe were so extreme as to create a revulsion. The agitation then died down until renewed by the advocates of Know-Nothingism. The title of a book published in 1846 shows the spirit of this movement: *The Great American Battle; or The Contest between Christianity and Political Romanism.*[68]

Unfortunately it was a battle in more ways than one, as the Philadelphia riots of 1844 showed disastrously. They had many causes, of which the most important was the liberal attitude of the school board in 1843, allowing children to read the Bible from their own version, as urged by Bishop Francis Patrick Kenrick. The American Protestant Association made this a vital issue. Mass meetings were held, conflicts between Irishmen and "Natives" occurred, Irish homes were destroyed, the Catholic churches of St. Michael and St. Augustine in the suburb of Kensington were burned, and mob rioting was so extensive that the bishop, to prevent further outrages, ordered all his churches in the city closed the following Sunday. Thereafter serious trouble ceased for two months, to be revived by the excitement of the celebration of July 4. Unwise action by the pastor of the Church of St. Philip Neri in another suburb, Southwark, caused riots in which several people were killed. The church was broken open, and only the presence of the militia, the mayor, and the governor prevented its being burned.[69]

When rumors of the Philadelphia riots reached New York, Bishop Hughes advocated defense of the Catholic churches and took firm ground. "We might forbear from harming the intruder into *our house* until the last, but his *first* violence to our church should be promptly and decisively repelled." [70] The bishop put large groups of armed men around each church with instructions to keep the peace as long as possible, but if necessary to defend the churches at all costs. This firm stand and the co-operation of the authorities prevented serious trouble.[71]

On the whole, the years immediately preceding 1850 witnessed a slight decline of anti-Catholic agitation of an extreme form; the Protestant societies devoted their attention more to religious education, to attempts at conversion, and to efforts to safeguard the freedom of Protestants. This was a period when the anti-slavery agitation was uppermost in people's minds. But with the Compromise of 1850, which seemed to settle the most acute aspects of the slavery question for some time, the aggressive Protestant forces again took over. The Roman Catholic Church made some blunders, due chiefly to the earnest but narrow loyalty of its ablest representative, Bishop Hughes of New York. For instance, speaking in St. Patrick's Cathedral on "The Decline of Protestantism and Its Causes," he said,

Everybody should know that we have for our mission to convert the world— including the inhabitants of the United States,—the people of the cities, and the people of the country, the officers of the navy and marines, commanders of the army, the Legislatures, the Senate, the Cabinet, the President, and all! [72]

This was at least outspoken, but it seemed to many to be an unwise way of stating at that particular time and place the mission of the Church. Under the lead of the *Freeman's Journal,* the official organ of the bishop, and probably inspired by him, the Church went into action in a dozen states, petitioning the legislatures for a division of the public school fund and for laws against the required reading of the "Protestant Bible." In many instances Roman Catholic citizens threatened to defeat at the polls candidates who would not accept these and similar demands. The Protestants were equally active in lobbying, but *against* the Catholic demands, their principal agent being the American and Foreign Christian Union. This organization declared that the Bible would not be expelled from the classroom of the public schools "so long as a piece of Plymouth Rock remains big enough to make a gun flint out of." [73] Fortunately, America recognized that courts of law rather than guns were the appropriate means to resolve the issue of Bible reading in the public schools.

Nativism, Know-Nothingism, and the American Party

The formation of the anti-Catholic "Know-Nothing" party in the 1850's was partly the cause and partly the result of a wave of Nativist hysteria which swept the country, and which had not been experienced since the days of the Alien and Sedition Laws of 1798.[74] A striking evidence of the strong feeling was the furor occasioned in 1852 when the pope sent a block of marble to be placed in the Washington Monument at the capital. Mass meetings of protest were held, and finally, two years later, a mob forced its way into the shed where it was stored, secured the block, and, carrying it away, threw it into the Potomac River.[75]

The election in 1852 of Franklin Pierce, a Democrat, with the support of Catholic and foreign-born elements, and his naming of a Catholic, James Campbell, as postmaster general and of several foreign-born Democrats to diplomatic posts, alarmed the Whigs and Nativists. To them, here was clear evidence that the Roman Catholic Church was in politics. This was believed to be particularly the case with the Irish, tens of thousands of whom migrated to America after the potato blight of 1846-47 and became politically firmly entrenched and sometimes turbulent, especially in New England and New York.

In consequence, the most famous of Nativist parties, the Know-Nothings, appeared. Article II of its constitution provided that

The object of this organization shall be to resist the insidious policy of the Church of Rome, and other foreign influence against the institutions of our country by placing in all offices in the gift of the people, or by appointment, none but native-born Protestant citizens.[76]

The Know-Nothing party grew out of a "patriotic" society established in New York in 1849 known as the Order of the Star Spangled Banner. It had been foreshadowed for two decades by many similar organizations, such as the Native American Democratic Association and the Order of the Sons of America, whose followers virtually pooled their anti-Catholic and Nativist interests in the new party.

The Know-Nothings became a nationally organized secret political organization, employing ritual, high-sounding titles, passwords, initiation ceremonies, and grades or degrees of membership. No one was eligible unless he was born in the United States of Protestant parents and was not married to a Roman Catholic. Every candidate was required to answer the question "Are you willing to use your influence and vote only for native-born American citizens for all offices of honor, trust or profit in the gift of the people, the exclusion of all foreigners and Roman Catholics in particular, and without regard to party predilections?" [77]

As is well known, the new party secured its name from the common answer to questions from outsiders, namely, "I don't know." The *Know-Nothing Almanac* stated its comprehensive purpose: "Anti-Romanism, Anti-Bedinism, Anti-Pope's Toeism, Anti-Nunneryism, Anti-Winking Virginism, Anti-Jesuitism, and Anti-the-Whole-Sacerdotal-Hierarchism with all its humbugging mummeries. Know-Nothingism is for light, liberty, education and absolute freedom of conscience, with a strong devotion to one's native soil." [78]

The significance of these slanders will be understood by all readers except perhaps the reference to Bedinism, which was so called because of the visit to America in 1853 of a papal legate, Archbishop Cajetan Bedini, for the purpose of attending to certain property and other matters which concerned the Church. His visit was the occasion for many disturbances on the part of the Know-Nothings. The police had to be called out to protect him as a result of hostile demonstrations in several places, especially Baltimore and Cincinnati. In Cincinnati an effigy of the nuncio was burned, and threats were made against Roman Catholic churches and clergy.

But Know-Nothing mobs were not confined to the route of his tour. Even in upper New England there were serious disorders. A priest was tarred and feathered in Maine, and in New Hampshire a mob tore down the American flag from the front of a priest's house and wrecked the inside of his chapel. In Brooklyn, New York, several thousand people escorted an anti-Catholic preacher through the streets. A free fight occurred between them and another mob—this time of Irish Catholics. In an election riot in Kentucky between the Know-Nothings and the Catholics twenty-two lives were lost and much property destroyed, in spite of police efforts.[79]

Fortunately, most responsible public men saw the grave evils and injustices of the situation and its entire incompatibility with American traditions and

ideals of religious freedom. Abraham Lincoln, writing in 1855 to his friend
Joshua Speed, said,

> . . . I am not a Know Nothing; that is certain. How could I be? How can any
> one who abhors the oppression of Negroes be in favor of degrading classes of
> white people? Our progress in degeneracy appears to me to be pretty rapid. As a
> nation we began by declaring that "all men are created equal." We now practically
> read it "all men are created equal, except Negroes." When the Know-Nothings
> get control, it will read "all men are created equal, except Negroes and foreigners
> and Catholics." When it comes to this, I shall prefer emigrating to some country
> where they make no pretense of loving liberty—to Russia, for instance, where
> despotism can be taken pure, and without the base alloy of hypocrisy.[80]

In 1854 the Know-Nothing party felt strong enough with its effective
national and state organization to enter the political field actively. In the fall
of that year it carried Massachusetts, Delaware, and—after a combination
with the Whigs—Pennsylvania. In Massachusetts it elected the governor, all
state officers, every member of the Senate, and all but 2 of the 378 members
of the House.[81]

This Know-Nothing legislature passed laws restricting officeholding to
native-born citizens, requiring twenty-one years' residence for the voting
privilege; directing daily Bible reading in the schools "in the common English
version"; and appointing a "Nunnery Committee" to report on "such theological
seminaries, boarding schools, academies, nunneries, convents, and other institutions of like character as they may deem necessary." [82] The committee's
activities were scandalous, and the legislature ended its tour and expelled its
chairman from membership in the House.

The next year Rhode Island, New Hampshire, Connecticut, Maryland, and
Kentucky were also in the Know-Nothing or "American" column, and in many
other states the party elected candidates or held the balance of power. But in
spite of these amazing successes, when given power in various states, it could
not or did not carry out much of its program. In Connecticut, for example,
its major achievement was passing a law requiring corporate rather than individual holding of church property and a literacy test for voters. In Congress,
the Know-Nothing party in 1855 had forty-three members in the House and
five in the Senate, as well as some sympathy from an even larger number of
Republicans who had been members of its secret "lodges." [83] But it accomplished almost nothing definite, although it created considerable interest in
restricting immigration and extending the naturalization period.

As a result of failures in the field of constructive effort, of extreme attitudes
and lawlessness, of the ridicule of the party's secrecy, of dissensions within,
and especially of the return of slavery as the major political issue, the Know-

Nothings did not survive in many places as an effective party after 1856,[84] and this in spite of the fact that at one time they claimed a million members.[85]

The Development of the Church as a Public Power in the United States

It is difficult today, when Church statistics show a Catholic population of more than 42,000,000 persons, or nearly one in four of our inhabitants, to realize its amazing growth since the close of the American Revolution, when its membership could be counted in five figures, being probably less than 30,000. Many causes have contributed to this progress, of which, humanly speaking, the large immigration from Europe, especially from Ireland, Germany and Austria, and Italy, was the most important and the large birth rate was a subsidiary factor. But corresponding to the increase in numbers was an increase in effective organization, showing the power of the Church to adjust itself to new conditions. A few dates tell the story.

Mother school of the parochial schools in the United States, Philadelphia, 1782.

Reverend John Carroll appointed superior of the missions in the United States, 1784.

First diocese, Baltimore, 1789.

First college, Georgetown, 1789.

Reverend John Carroll consecrated first bishop, 1790.

First Roman Catholic Diocesan Synod in the United States, Baltimore, 1791.

First archdiocese, Baltimore, 1808.

Baltimore Cathedral completed, 1821.

United States Catholic Miscellany established, 1822.

First Plenary Council, Baltimore, 1852.

American College at Louvain founded, 1857.

American College at Rome founded, 1859.

Second Plenary Council decrees that a parochial school be established in every parish, 1866.

Knights of Columbus organized, 1882.

Catholic University of America founded, 1889.

Apostolic delegation to the United States established, 1893.

Roman Catholic Church in the United States outgrows its missionary status as an activity of the Sacred Congregation for Propagating the Faith, becoming largely self-governing under the control of the papacy—*Sapienti Consilio,* 1908.

Catholic Encyclopedia published, 1914.
National Catholic Welfare Conference established, 1919.
Archdiocese of Washington (D.C.) established, 1947.
Number of Roman Catholic archbishops and bishops exceeds 225, 1963.

Every state in this growth has been marked by intense devotion on the part
of members of the Church, who have generally shown their capacity to be
loyal to Rome in matters of religion and ethics while being loyal to the
United States government in political matters.

Chapter 10

JEWISH ADJUSTMENTS TO AMERICAN
CHURCH-STATE CONDITIONS

Colonial Conditions

Prior to the Revolution there were only scattered groups of Jews in the North American colonies, and in the decades immediately following they did not increase to any large extent. That they had a hard time in colonial America must not blind us to the fact that on the whole their lot here was better than in most parts of Europe. Owing to historic factors, prejudice against them was deep set, and it was not until the American and French revolutions had vindicated the rights of man that they were to be treated anywhere exactly like other citizens.

The early status of the Jews in most of the colonies may be gathered from correspondence of the middle seventeenth century between the directors of the West India Company in Amsterdam and Governor Peter Stuyvesant. In 1655 the directors wrote to the governor turning down his request "that the new territories should not be further invaded by people of the Jewish race." [1] While the directors recognized the difficulties that Stuyvesant had pointed out would result from the entry into New Netherlands of Portuguese Jews from Brazil, nevertheless in view of the considerable loss sustained by them in the taking of Brazil and also because of the large amount of capital which they had invested in the Company, it was decided to allow them to settle in New Netherlands, provided that they supported their poor and did not allow them to become a burden on the Company. [2]

Stuyvesant was quite unhappy with this decision and protested it, but to no avail. The next year the directors wrote him reaffirming their decision. [3] A short time later they wrote again to reprimand him for forbidding the Jews to trade in certain areas and to purchase real estate, although they agreed that Jews were not to be employed in public service or permitted to open retail shops. [4]

Under the English rule there were ups and downs, but we find a Jewish school in 1755 and several Jewish voters in 1761. Not, however, until the state constitution of 1777 did Jews receive full rights in New York. (There are no accurate statistics as to the number of Jews in the thirteen original colonies, but it probably at no time exceeded one thousand.[5])

For most of the colonial period, Jews were under political disabilities nearly everywhere. Even Rhode Island slipped from its early tradition of tolerance during part of the eighteenth century. However, although they were not given full constitutional rights, ways were found by which they were permitted to become prominent in intercolonial commerce, and occasionally men of standing were elected to serve in the colonial assemblies—of Georgia, South Carolina, and Pennsylvania,[6] for example, and probably in other colonies. They were also sometimes granted exemptions from duties inconsistent with their religious scruples, as in the case of one Hart Jacobs, who was exempted from military service on Friday nights, the Jewish Sabbath.[7]

The status of Jews in most colonies was somewhat improved after the passing of the parliamentary Act of 1740, which provided that foreigners who had been resident in the British colonies for seven years could be naturalized. For Jews an oath of fidelity on the Old Testament was considered sufficient.[8] After the outbreak of the Revolution the franchise was gradually extended so that within a few decades the Jews had the vote everywhere, although the right to hold office was won with more difficulty.

Among the colonies the conditions of the Jews were best in Massachusetts and South Carolina. The situation in the latter colony was quite remarkable. The constitution of 1669, largely through Locke's influence, merely required everyone to have a religion,[9] and an early naturalization law in 1697—later repealed—made Jews eligible. Charleston had the second Jewish synagogue in America in 1755.[10] (The first was Shearith Israel—"the Remnant of Israel"— in New York City.) In 1774 Francis Salvador, Jr., was elected to the First Provincial Congress from South Carolina, the first Jew in American history, and probably the first Jew in the modern world, to serve in an elective office.[11]

The Georgia situation was somewhat similar. The charter of 1735 gave liberty of conscience to all "except Papists," [12] and Jews were given some early land grants. In Savannah, which was a Jewish center, a few minor public offices were filled by Jews from 1765 to 1768,[13] and a cemetery, always a special desideratum of the Jews, was provided for in 1773. Perhaps these colonial conditions favorable to the Jews laid foundations for the election of a Jew, David Emanuel, to be governor of Georgia in the early republican period, 1801. He was the first of many Jews to hold the honor of governorship in the United States.[14]

Other colonies where conditions, on the whole, were encouraging were Rhode Island and Pennsylvania. Roger Williams planned to open his colonies even to pagans, Jews, and Turks, and in 1665 a statute provided that "all men of competante estates, and of civill conversation" who submitted to the civil magistrates "though of different judgments," were eligible to vote or hold office.[15] Unfortunately, when the statutes were published in 1719 the words "professing Christianity" were added after "all men," and the Roman Catholics were also excepted. The Jews, although tolerated to a larger extent than Roman Catholics, had more difficulty in Rhode Island than in Massachusetts. Indeed, a distinguished Newport Jew, one Aaron Lopez, being denied naturalization in Rhode Island in 1762, found it necessary to go over the border to Massachusetts, where he was naturalized without serious difficulty.[16]

In Pennsylvania the laws of 1682 provided for complete toleration for all "who profess and acknowledge the one Almighty and Eternal God, to be the Creator, Upholder, and Ruler of the World,"[17] thus admitting Jews but excluding agnostics and atheists. Nevertheless, voting and office holding were restricted to Christians, and at times to Protestant Christians. A Jewish burial ground was permitted in Philadelphia in 1738 and a congregation was established in 1747, but there was no synagogue until the time of the Revolution.

In western New Jersey, probably owing to the influence of William Penn, one of the incorporators, no one was to be disturbed "for the sake of his opinion, judgment, or worship towards God."[18]

Adjustments to the Conditions of the New Government

The Jews in most cases had favored the Revolutionary movement; many of them in Newport and other Jewish centers both volunteered for war service and gave liberally to the colonial cause. Being a small minority, they naturally were strong supporters of religious freedom, but as they represented scattered groups in a few urban centers, it was a long time before they profited in any large way by the new movement in American life. However, with the founding of the new American Federal State several difficult adjustments were made, the most difficult and important being the removal of all civil disabilities. Public opinion in the republic and the influence of the spirit of the Declaration of Independence and the other charters of American freedom resulted in the gradual elimination of the religious disabilities of Jews in the various states. These had been of different types; a majority of the thirteen original colonies had at least confined voting and office holding to Christians—generally then understood to be those who did not deny the Trinity—in some places excluding Roman Catholics.

Because the Jews played an honorable part in the Revolution and in the founding of the government and because American constitutional freedom fitted in well with their needs and ideals, they adjusted themselves without serious difficulty to the new conditions. The patriotic attitude of Haym Salomon during the Revolution and of such leaders as Rabbi Gershon Seixas in the early days of the republic helped them. Rabbi Seixas was one of fourteen clergymen to participate in Washington's inauguration, and on Thanksgiving Day, 1789, he preached the first English sermon known in connection with such a public occasion in America.[19]

The most interesting document in connection with the Jews and the formation of our government was the exchange of letters between the important Hebrew congregation in Newport and President Washington. This resulted from the president's visit in 1790, when a moving address was delivered to him on behalf of the Jews of the city, in which they said, in part,

Deprived, as we have hitherto been, of invaluable rights of free citizens, we now—with a deep sense of gratitude to the Almighty Disposer of all events—behold a government erected by the majesty of the people, a government which gives no sanction to bigotry and no assistance to persecution, but generously affording to all liberty of conscience and immunities of citizenship, deeming every one, of whatever nation, tongue or language, equal parts of the great governmental machine. This so ample and extensive Federal Union, whose base is philanthropy, mutual confidence and public virtue, we cannot but acknowledge to be the work of the great God, who rules the armies of the heavens and among the inhabitants of the earth, doing whatever deemeth to Him good.[20]

Washington's reply included the following well-known paragraph:

The citizens of the United States of America have the right to applaud themselves for having given to mankind examples of an enlarged and liberal policy worthy of imitation. All possess alike liberty of conscience and immunities of citizenship. It is now no more that toleration is spoken of as if it were by the indulgence of one class of people that another enjoyed the exercise of their inherent natural rights, for happily the Government of the United States, which gives to bigotry no sanction, to persecution no assistance, requires only that they who live under its protection should demean themselves as good citizens in giving it on all occasions their effectual support.[21]

Jefferson and Madison showed the same tolerant and sympathetic spirit as Washington in their attitude toward the Jews. In 1818 Jefferson wrote the following in a letter to Rabbi Mordecai M. Noah:

Your sect, by its sufferings, has furnished a remarkable proof of the universal spirit of religious intolerance inherent in every sect, disclaimed by all while feeble, and practised by all when in power. Our laws have applied the only antidote to the vice, protecting our religious as they do our civil rights, by putting all men on an equal footing. But more remains to be done; for although we are free by the law, we are not so in practice; public opinion erects itself into an inquisition, and exercises its office with as much fanaticism as fans the flames of an auto da fé. The prejudice still scowling on your section of our religion, although the elder one, cannot be unfelt by yourselves; it is to be hoped that individual dispositions will at length mold themselves to the model of the law, and consider the moral basis on which all our religions rest as the rallying point which united them in a common interest.[22]

Similarly, in 1820 Madison wrote to Dr. De La Motta of the Savannah synagogue:

Among the features peculiar to the political system of the United States, is the perfect equality of rights which it secures to every religious sect. And it is particularly pleasing to observe in the good citizenship of such as have been most distrusted and oppressed elsewhere a happy illustration of the safety and success of this experiment of a just and benignant policy. Equal laws, protecting equal rights, are found, as they ought to be presumed, the best guarantee of loyalty and love of country; as well as best calculated to cherish that mutual respect and good-will at length mold themselves to the model of the law, and consider the moral harmony, and most favorable to the advancement of truth. The account you give of the Jews of your congregation bring them fully within the scope of these observations.[23]

The few Jews in America in colonial and Revolutionary times had been mainly Sephardim, of Spanish and Portuguese origin, or from Holland, where they had also inherited cultural traditions. After 1820, the second wave of Jewish immigration, that of German Jews, began; it became heavy in the two decades before the Civil War. They and their co-religionists in Poland were Ashkenazim Jews. This immigration continued until the closing years of the century, when the Jewish immigrants were coming mainly from Russia and eastern and southeastern Europe. It was clear that the Jews had come to stay and that they were capable of rendering important contributions to American life.

Conditions were developing auspiciously for the integration of Jews into American life, but probably no one in the Revolutionary period ever envisioned the time when they would form such a large and important element in our population as they do today. There were, however, still two or three states, notably North Carolina and Maryland, with constitutional restrictions designed to prevent their holding office, although generally, where men of standing were concerned, these were not strictly observed. A notable instance was that of Jacob Henry, a respected member of the legislature of North Carolina. In 1809 an attempt was made to have his seat declared vacant on the ground that he was a Jew. It failed, largely because of the effective speech he made in his own behalf.[24] He took the ground that any provisions in the state constitution inconsistent with its bill of rights must be considered annulled—a basic argument of broad application. It was not until 1835 that a new constitution, ratified the next year, did away with the Protestant requirement for officeholding, which affected Catholics and Jews alike, and not until 1868 that some minor disabilities involving Jews were removed. One of the causes of difficulty here and elsewhere was the old English common-law doctrine that practically no one but a Christian was a competent witness in court.[25]

The Battle for Political Rights in Maryland

The most bitter and most instructive American struggle for religious liberty for the Jews took place in Maryland. As was customary at the time, its constitution adopted in 1776 contained a Declaration of Rights. However, while recognizing the "duty of every man to worship God in such manner as he thinks most acceptable to him," this declaration did give the legislature the power to lay "a general and equal tax, for the support of the Christian religion," and made "a declaration of a belief in the Christian religion" a requirement for "any office of trust or profit" under the state.[26] These provisions were naturally considered by the Jews prejudicial to their basic rights and interests in a free state. But the one serious effort made to enforce the tax—in 1785— was defeated.[27]

Efforts made in 1797 to have the disqualification against Jews' holding office removed were without effect. They were repeated in subsequent years. A generation passed before the final adoption of the "Jew Bill" in 1826, and not until the middle of the century did a constitutional revision specifically forbid all discrimination among persons believing in the existence of God. This discrimination against non-theists, in turn, was not removed until the United States Supreme Court's decision in 1961 in the case of *Torcaso* v. *Watkins*.[28]

The struggle for religious liberty in Maryland produced several heroes whose names have been almost forgotten. The most important, Thomas Kennedy,[29] was a devout Christian of Scotch Presbyterian stock, who felt that the discrimination against Jews in the constitution of the state, by limiting office holding to Christians, was inconsistent with American ideals of religious liberty and with the spirit of Christianity.

Kennedy came to this country as a boy with his immigrant parents from Scotland. He was a profound admirer of Thomas Jefferson's contributions to the cause of liberty, both political and religious. In 1817 he was elected a delegate to the Assembly, and in December of the following year he introduced a resolution for the appointment of a committee to consider the justice and expedience of "placing the Jewish inhabitants on an equal footing with the Christian." [30]

The committee, so appointed, was headed by Kennedy. Less than two weeks later it issued a report, prepared by him, asserting that religion is purely a personal matter between the individual and his God, and that no human tribunal can take cognizance of it. As part of its report, the committee submitted for consideration of the Assembly "An Act to extend to the sect of people professing the Jewish religion, the same rights and privileges that are enjoyed by Christians." [31] The crux of the proposal was that "no religious test, declaration or subscription of opinion as to religion, shall be required from any person of the sect called Jews, as a qualification to hold or exercise any office or employment of profit or trust in this state." [32] Further, every oath administered to a Jew "shall be administered on the five books of Moses, agreeably to the religious education of that people, and not otherwise." [33]

In opening the debate in favor of the bill, Kennedy delivered an eloquent address, of which the following paragraph is typical:

> There is only one opponent that I fear at this time, and that is PREJUDICE— our prejudices, Mr. Speaker, are dear to us, we all know and feel the force of our political prejudices, but our religious prejudices are still more strong, still more dear; they cling to us through life, and scarcely leave us on the bed of death, and it is not the prejudice of a generation, of an age or of a century, that we have now to encounter. No, it is the prejudice which has passed from father to son, for almost eighteen hundred years.[34]

Nevertheless, when a vote was taken in January, 1819, the bill was defeated 50 to 24. The following year it was again introduced and again defeated, this time by a vote of 47 to 20. When Kennedy returned to his home in Washington County his action in introducing his bill to remove the disqualification of Jews from office holding was violently attacked. He was assailed as "an enemy of Christianity"; he was called Judas Iscariot; it was asserted that he was "one half Jew and the other half not a Christian." [35]

In 1822 his bill finally passed the House of Delegates, but under the laws of the state confirmatory action at a subsequent session was necessary for any modification of the constitution. Consequently, the proposal became the major issue in the election of 1823.

Furious opposition to the bill was renewed, especially in the Protestant "religious" journals, which stated that there was a death struggle on between orthodox Christianity, as represented by the provisions in the old constitution, and the "Unitarian views" presented by Mr. Kennedy. The proposed amendment failed to receive the necessary confirmatory vote.

In Kennedy's home county a so-called "Christian ticket" was now put into the field, with one Benjamin Galloway as a candidate in opposition to the earnest advocate of Jewish political freedom. Galloway frankly proclaimed that he wanted only Christian support, not that of "Jews, Deists, Mohammedans, or Unitarians." [36] He published a manifesto in the *Washington County Herald* appealing for the defeat of the "Jew Bill" and of its advocates—Kennedy and his associates.[37]

The prejudice created by Galloway's campaign caused Kennedy to be defeated for re-election. Some of the most representative newspapers in the state expressed deep regret at this outcome. In the forthcoming session, when Kennedy was not a member of the House, the bill was again defeated, by a vote of 44 to 28, although the Senate, all of whose members Kennedy had interviewed in the meantime, passed the bill 8 to 6. This latter fact gave him encouragement to run as an independent candidate, which he did in the next year's campaign and won.

The matter had now become something of a national issue. Papers all over the country, North and South, called on Maryland to redeem itself and put the state in line with the American tradition of equality of Jew and Christian in all political rights.[38]

As a result of the agitation the bill passed at the 1825 session, but it required confirmation by a second legislature. There was another determined effort in the next session, and on January 5, 1826, the Assembly finally voted 45 to 32 for a bill similar to Kennedy's, presented in the Senate by Reverdy Johnson, later one of the country's leading lawyers. It was characteristic of Kennedy, who had carried the brunt of the whole battle, that he gladly withdrew his own bill when it seemed that the cause would be better advanced by accepting the Senate substitute. The bill, having been duly passed by two legislatures as required for constitutional change, became a law in 1826. Jews were soon elected to office in the state and the well-known Baltimore Hebrew Congregation was duly incorporated.

In 1851 the constitution of Maryland was revised and a new Article 34 was adopted which read as follows:

Art. 34. That no other test or qualification ought to be required, on admission to any office of trust or profit, than such oath of office as may be prescribed by this constitution, or by the laws of the State, and a declaration of belief in the Christian religion; and if the party shall profess to be a Jew, the declaration shall be of his belief in a future state of rewards and punishments.[39]

In the revision of 1864 the article regarding tests of qualifications for office was modified to read,

Art. 37. That no other test or qualification ought to be required on admission to any office of trust or profit than such oath of allegiance and fidelity to this State and the United States as may be prescribed by this constitution, and such oath of office and qualification as may be prescribed by this constitution, or by the laws of the State, and a declaration of belief in the Christian religion, or in the existence of God, and in a future state of rewards and punishments.[40]

It will be noticed that a slight distinction was still made between Jews and Christians, though Jews were no longer mentioned by name. This was unacceptable as virtually making a difference in the law between two religious groups and was modified in the constitution of 1867, whose Bill of Rights reads,

That no religious test ought ever to be required as a qualification for any office of profit or trust in this State, other than a declaration of belief in the existence of God; nor shall the Legislature prescribe any other oath of office than the oath prescribed by this Constitution.[41]

The constitution was now acceptable to all religious groups except the small number of agnostics and atheists. The United States Supreme Court decision in *Torcaso* v. *Watkins*[42] made the constitution acceptable even to these.

Other Adjustments to Conditions Under the New Governments

The last memorable battle over Jewish political rights took place in North Carolina, where the complete emancipation of the Jews did not take effect until 1868. Up to that time a clause debarred from holding office any "person who shall deny the being of God or the Divine Authority of both the Old and the New Testament." The last portion was then eliminated.[43] Final success was due largely to the efforts of Isaac Leeser, rabbi of the leading synagogue in Philadelphia.

A matter of special difficulty for American Jews, as they tried to adjust themselves to life in the American republic, and one in which they were specially interested, was that of the change from Hebrew to English in religious services. The beginnings of this are found in 1824, when the Reformed Society of Israelites was established in South Carolina with the express purpose of altering customs and ceremonies so as to fit the Jewish synagogue better into American conditions. It wished to have the major part of the service, including the reading of the Bible, in English and to have English sermons. In 1830

Leeser, a rabbi of the Sephardic tradition, began preaching in English in a Philadelphia synagogue. This made a deep impression, since he was a man of broad influence. Leeser was the founder of the Board of Delegates of American Israelites, which brought together Jews from different parts of the country, and editor of *The Occident*, pioneer in American Jewish periodical literature. In 1845 he published a translation of the Old Testament which became a standard version for American Jews.[44] Although an adherent of the Orthodox faith, he is classed as an enlightened Conservative. It was largely owing to influences stemming from his group that Reform congregations were established in Philadelphia in 1842 and in New York (Temple Emanu-El) in 1845. These emphasized the use of English in Bible reading, preaching, and the conduct of the service.[45]

An even more independent and forceful leader was Rabbi Isaac Mayer Wise, who in 1847 became rabbi of a Jewish congregation in Albany and later moved to Cincinnati, where he established *The American Israelite* and developed various plans for unifying and organizing in a progressive spirit the Jews in America. Thus the Union of American Hebrew Congregations—a movement begun in 1848 but not realized until 1873—the Hebrew Union College, and the Central Conference of American Rabbis were founded.[46] With the establishment of these institutions, and of the Independent Order of B'nai B'rith in 1843, we find leaders of "Reform Judaism" and their most representative congregations becoming well adjusted to American life.

A decade later came a petition from Jewish citizens in Washington, D.C., requesting the passage of an act enabling them to build a synagogue in the capital. "I understand," explained Senator Lewis Cass of Michigan, in presenting the petition to the Senate in 1856, "that the existing law in this district makes provision . . . only in relation to Christian denominations. Such a distinction is an act of gross injustice, and if continued after our attention is directed to it, would be a disgrace to our jurisprudence." Senators agreed to refer the petition to the Committee on the District of Columbia, and the defect in the law was soon remedied.[47]

An important incident in the development of Jewish adjustments in America was the so-called "Keiley case." It had to do with the appointment by President Cleveland in 1885 of Anthony M. Keiley of Virginia to be minister to Austria-Hungary, an appointment which that government declared to be unacceptable, solely on the ground that Keiley's wife was Jewish.

The essential facts are these: In May, 1885, Secretary of State Thomas F. Bayard notified the Austro-Hungarian minister in Washington of the president's selection of Mr. Keiley. The following day Count Gustave Kalnóky, minister of foreign affairs of Austria-Hungary, informed its minister in Washington, Baron Schaeffer, that "The position of a foreign envoy wedded to a Jewess by civil marriage would be untenable and even impossible in Vienna." The baron accordingly informed our secretary of state that the appointment was looked upon with disfavor by his government. The resulting situation from the American constitutional and political standpoint was intolerable. Secretary Bayard wrote to Baron Schaeffer:

> The supreme law of this land expressly declares that "no religious test shall ever be required as a qualification to any office or public trust under the United States," and by the same authority it is declared that "Congress shall make no law respecting an establishment of religion or prohibiting the free exercise thereof." . . .
>
> It is not within the power of the President nor of the Congress, nor of any judicial tribunal in the United States, to take or even hear testimony, or in any mode to inquire into or decide upon the religious belief of any official, and the proposition to allow this to be done by any foreign Government is necessarily and *a fortiori* inadmissible.
>
> To suffer an infraction of this essential principle would lead to a disfranchisement of our citizens because of their religious belief, and thus impair or destroy the most important end which our constitution of Government was intended to secure. Religious liberty is the chief corner-stone of the American system of government, and provisions for its security are imbedded in the written charter and interwoven in the moral fabric of its laws.[48]

President Cleveland in his subsequent annual message to Congress in December, 1855, stated that the arguments of the Austro-Hungarian government

> . . . could not be acquiesced in, without violation of my oath of office and the precepts of the Constitution, since they necessarily involved a limitation in favor of a foreign government upon the right of selection by the Executive, and required such an application of a religious test as a qualification for office under the United States as would have resulted in the practical disfranchisement of a large class of our citizens and the abandonment of a vital principle of our Government.[49]

Notwithstanding these protests, the Austro-Hungarian government persisted in its refusal to accept Keiley and requested our government to designate another ambassador in his place. Keiley, being advised of this action, thereupon resigned his mission,[50] thus bringing the incident to a rather unsatisfactory conclusion.

Other questions involving Jewish adaptation to American conditions will be discussed later. It is sufficient in closing this chapter to note that no group of people in America is more appreciative of the religious liberty which they enjoy here than are the Jews.

Chapter 11

THE CHURCH AND NATIONAL ISSUES ARISING
BEFORE THE CIVIL WAR

The greatest moral issue that faced the nation during the first half of the nineteenth century was the slavery question, and the Church was of course deeply involved in it. There were, however, other less prominent but nonetheless important national issues during this period in which the Church played a significant role, sometimes trying to direct or stimulate, sometimes to restrain, the arm of government. Among these were (1) the anti-dueling campaign, (2) the Sunday mail controversy, (3) the anti-Masonic campaign, (4) the anti-lottery campaign, (5) religious journalism, (6) temperance and liquor control, (7) the Mormon theocracy and independence, (8) non-sectarian public education, and (9) the diplomatic representation at the Vatican.

The Anti-Dueling Campaign

There had been sporadic opposition to dueling from the seventeenth century on, and some of the fathers of the republic—notably Washington, Franklin, and Jefferson—opposed it. But they accomplished relatively little. The duel continued to be a recognized method of settling disputes in certain parts of the American colonies, especially those where cavalier or other aristocratic European traditions were strong. It was actively resisted by the organized Protestant forces of the country. Their position was largely responsible for the adoption in various states—especially after the killing of Alexander Hamilton by Aaron Burr in 1804—of constitutional provisions against dueling and statutes making it illegal. These generally made anyone who challenged or accepted a challenge to fight a duel incapable of holding, or being elected to, any position under the state government, and in other ways tried to discourage the custom.

In his Hamilton commemoration oration before the New York State Society of the Cincinnati in July, 1804, the Reverend John M. Mason, then one of the leading Protestant ministers of the country, gave nation-wide impetus to the effort to secure anti-dueling legislation. He assailed dueling as "a custom which has no origin but superstition, no ailment but depravity, no reason but in madness." "My countrymen," he declaimed, "the land is defiled with blood unrighteously shed. Its cry, disregarded on earth, has gone up to the throne of God; and this day does our punishment reveal our sin. It is time for us to awake." [1]

The same year the Reverend Timothy Dwight, the influential president of Yale College, preached a sermon in the college chapel on "The Folly, Guilt, and Mischief of Duelling." [2] This was twice printed in 1805 and had a wide circulation. It was also preached in the old Presbyterian Church in New York City. Occasioned by the Burr-Hamilton duel, it was significant both because of the preacher's important standing and because Aaron Burr was his first cousin.

About the same time the Reverend Eliphalet Nott, afterward president of Union College and one of the most representative ministers of religion in the United States, preached a sermon in the North Dutch Church, Albany, in which he referred to the same event, and assailed dueling as a "barbarous custom" and "the most guilty practice that ever disgraced a Christian nation." [3]

These opinions well expressed the enlightened opinion of numerous public men early in the last century on the evils of the duel of honor, and they did much to create a general sentiment in opposition to its continuance. But it was a sermon [4] preached by Lyman Beecher on New Year's Day, 1806, advocating that citizens refuse to vote for any duelist, that did more than anything else to stir up the American people against dueling and to bring about legislation to prevent it. [5] In it he said,

Duelling is a great national sin. With the exception of a small section of the Union, the whole land is defiled with blood. From the lakes of the North to the plains of Georgia is heard the voice of lamentation and woe—the cries of the widow and fatherless. This work of desolation is performed often by men in office, by the appointed guardians of life and liberty. On the floor of Congress challenges have been threatened, if not given, and thus powder and ball have been introduced as the auxiliaries of deliberation and argument. [6]

It was not unnatural, in view of the special influence of the Beecher family in Connecticut and their identification with the anti-dueling cause, that Connecticut should have been the first of the states to go on record against dueling. Its constitution of 1818 included conviction for dueling, along with bribery, forgery, and other offenses, as disqualifying a person from being an elector—that is, voter. [7]

Many anti-dueling societies were established in the South in 1825-26. John

England, the eminent Roman Catholic Bishop of Charleston, was one of the active sponsors of the South Carolina Anti-Duelling Association. In November, 1827, he delivered an address in the cathedral of Charleston before the members of the association "On the Origin and History of Duelling," a work which had a broad influence.[8] But public opinion in that state, where the code of honor between gentlemen was strong, was not easily roused to the point of forcing dueling to be made illegal. This was first effected by the Reconstruction constitution of 1868.[9] Nevertheless, the movement against dueling was growing in the South, its stronghold.

Today a majority of the states, twenty-six out of fifty, have constitutional provisions against dueling. They are generally one of three types; disqualifying duelists from office holding and the franchise, making duels illegal, or specifically authorizing the legislature to pass appropriate legislation to prevent the practice.[10] Sometimes two or more of these provisions have been adopted. In other states there is no mention of dueling in the constitution, since the custom has entirely disappeared—an encouraging example of the effect of an awakened public opinion in which the Church played a large part.

The Sunday Mail Controversy

The friction between Church and State over the matter of Sunday observance will be dealt with later in this volume.[11] Here we are concerned with a single manifestation of this controversy, the question of the Sunday mails. It went back to the fact that all the American colonies had laws against Sunday travel —reflections of old English laws on the same subject—which were only gradually modified under the republic. This created a good deal of trouble with the United States government because of the carrying of the mails. The question of mail delivery on Sundays became a matter of Congressional discussion. By an act of April 30, 1810, "to regulate the post office establishment," post offices were required to be open "every day on which a mail or bag, or other packet or parcel of letters shall arrive." Soon after the passage of the new act Congress began to receive strong remonstrances.[12]

For twenty years the question of keeping the post offices open on Sunday for the delivery of mail was frequently before Congress. Congress was flooded with protests, petitions, and counter-petitions condemning and approving the practice.[13] In January, 1829, the Senate Committee on Post Office and Post Roads, to which petitions for discontinuing the Sunday mails were referred, issued a report adverse to the proposal. The report, presented by Senator Richard M. Johnson, later to be vice-president of the United States, said in part,

We are aware that a variety of sentiment exists among the good citizens of this nation on the subject of the Sabbath day; and our Government is designed for the protection of one, as much as for another. . . .

With these different religious views the committee are of opinion that Congress cannot interfere. It is not the legitimate province of the Legislature to determine what religion is true, or what is false. Our Government is a civil and not a religious institution. Our constitution recognizes in every person the right to choose his own religion, and to enjoy it freely, without molestation. Whatever may be the religious sentiments of citizens, and however variant, they are alike entitled to protection from the Government, so long as they do not invade the rights of others.

The transportation of the mail on the first day of the week, it is believed, does not interfere with the rights of conscience. The petitioners for its discontinuance appear to be actuated from a religious zeal, which may be commendable if confined to its proper sphere; but they assume a position better suited to an ecclesiastical than to a civil institution.

They appear, in many instances, to lay it down as an axiom, that the practice is a violation of the law of God. Should Congress, in their legislative capacity, adopt the sentiment, it would establish the principle that the Legislature is a proper tribunal to determine what are the laws of God. It would involve a legislative decision in a religious controversy, and on a point in which good citizens may honestly differ in opinion, without disturbing the peace of society, or endangering its liberties. If this principle is once introduced, it will be impossible to define its bounds. Among all the religious persecutions with which almost every page of modern history is stained, no victim ever suffered but for the violation of what Government denominated the law of God. To prevent a similar train of evils in this country, the constitution has wisely withheld from our Government the power of defining the divine law. It is a right reserved to each citizen; and while he respects the equal rights of others, he cannot be held amenable to any human tribunal for his conclusions.[14]

A contrary minority report was presented by William McCreery, stating in part,

All Christian nations acknowledge the first day of the week to be the Sabbath. Almost every State in this Union has, by positive legislation, not only recognized this day as sacred, but has forbidden its profanation under penalties imposed by law.

It was never considered by any of those States as an encroachment upon the rights of conscience, or as an improper interference with the opinions of the few, to guard the sacredness of that portion of time acknowledged to be holy by the many. . . .

The petitioners ask the enactment of no law establishing the first day of the week as the Christian Sabbath; they only ask the extension and application to one Department of Government of a principle which is recognized, and has, since the foundation of our Government, been acknowledged in every other Department. The principle embraced in the petitions has been recognized by Congress, by adjourning over the first day of the week. At the first session of the first Congress a law was passed establishing judicial courts, and in that law Sunday is exempted from the days on which that court may commence its sessions. All the other Executive Departments of Government are closed on that day. Congress has never, by this, considered itself as expounding the moral law, or as introducing any religious coercion into our civil institutions, or making any innovation on the religious rights of the citizens, or setting by legislation any theological question that may exist between Jews, Sabbatarians, and other denominations.[15]

A number of state legislatures submitted memorials to Congress endorsing the majority report. The resolution of the Indiana legislature is typical: It said,

That we view all attempts to introduce sectarian influence into the councils of the nation as a violation of both the letter and the spirit of the Constitution of the United States and of this State, and at the same time dangerous to our civil and religious liberties.

That all legislative interference in matters of religion is contrary to the genius of Christianity and that there are no doctrines or observances inculcated by the Christian religion which require the arm of civil power either to enforce or to sustain them.

That we consider every connection between church and state at all times dangerous to civil and religious liberty.

Apparently Senator Johnson's arguments had carried weight. The attempt to prevent the "Sunday mail" failed.

The Senate report, based on the theory that our government is "a civil and not a religious institution," made Senator Johnson a national hero of the more liberal-minded and radical groups, to whom he also appealed by his opposition to imprisonment for debt. Among his ardent supporters was the then notorious Frances Wright, who believed that Johnson had struck a heavy blow at a union of Church and State. The mail question, she asserted, "betrayed the whole soul of priestcraft. . . . A standard is reared under which all the party-coloured bands of orthodoxy may rally into one phalanx."[16] Many radical and workingmen's papers joined in her attack.[17]

The Anti-Masonic Campaign

As we have shown,[18] Freemasonry was a factor in uniting the colonies and in laying the foundations of separation of Church and State. It held an honorable position among the fathers of the nation, and Church and Masonic membership by the same person was not considered inconsistent by Protestants. However, an organized anti-Masonic movement, beginning with the Morgan trials in western New York in 1826, secured the active support of many religious bodies and, as it developed into the first national third party, brought churches into a political controversy. Although the Roman Catholic Church had been long opposed to Freemasonry (its members were subject to excommunication if they joined the society, and Pope Clement XII issued the first papal pronouncement against it in 1738),[19] the extreme Protestant opposition came much later. There had always been some suspicion of secret societies among Americans but the fact that George Washington and many of the founders of the nation were Masons led to their being generally accepted and honored. It took the kidnapping and alleged slaying in 1826 of William Morgan, a bricklayer of Batavia, New York, because of the report that he was about to publish a revelation of Masonic secrets, to cause a vigorous campaign against the order. Because of its secrecy people came to believe that it was trying to control the State, and to do so in a way inimical to Christianity.[20] And so Masonry was drawn into the Church-State issue.

The Morgan incident and the ensuing public discussion resulted in a serious decrease in Masonic membership. The churches became aroused, partly because a secret society of this character was felt to be dangerous in a democracy and partly because interest in Masonry was believed to detract attention from the Church and religion. Masons were in many cases excluded from admission to church membership and from participation in the communion, while pastors who were Masons were barred from some pulpits.[21]

The anti-Masonic movement grew in strength and entered the political arena,[22] electing governors in Pennsylvania and Vermont and securing seven electoral votes—all from Vermont[23]—for William Wirt, its candidate for the presidency in the election of 1832. However, its life as an independent party was short; by 1838 it had merged with the Whigs.[24]

The elements which made up the Nativist parties of the future were largely behind political Antimasonry. Extreme groups of Protestants saw similarities between Masons and Roman Catholics in their emphasis on ritual and secrecy (whether oath or confessional). "Popery and Freemasonry" were denounced together; both were declared to have something of the Inquisition about them and to be dangerous to democratic institutions. The Antimasons were, in the opinion of many, determined to have the control of the State captured by Protestant Christian protagonists. They carried this religious emphasis in public life so far that they were frequently charged with trying to tie up politics with religion.[25]

Opposition to the Masons died down before the middle of the last century, but it has occasionally revived. For instance, in 1868 the National Christian Association was founded in Aurora, Illinois, with the special object of opposing secret societies or orders such as the Masons and the Jesuits, as well as Mormons, atheists, spiritualists, and advocates of free love. From 1867 to 1871 it published a weekly journal, *The Christian Cynosure.*

In these ways the active identification of large portions of the American Church with the Antimasonic cause resulted in organized religion's becoming confused with politics in the public mind.

The Anti-Lottery Campaign

Lotteries were accepted as a matter of course in colonial times, and many churches and educational institutions profited from them. Among the colleges were Harvard, Yale, and the College of New Jersey. Among the churches were several prominent Episcopal and Presbyterian churches in Pennsylvania.[26] Faneuil Hall in Boston, "the cradle of American liberty," was rebuilt in 1761 after the fire, with the help of a public lottery, and the Continental Congress in 1776 authorized a lottery for the benefit of soldiers in the field.[27] The Church raised no effective voice of opposition. At late as 1775 the handsome First Baptist Church of Providence, where Brown University holds its commencements, was built largely with the proceeds from a lottery.[28]

It was not until the nineteenth century was well under way that, as a result of the growing Christian conscience in social matters and the development of private philanthropy, the movement against this form of gambling received wide statutory recognition. Anti-lottery legislation was adopted by New York in 1821, and lotteries were suppressed by both New York and Massachusetts in 1833. Other states followed their example[29]: Connecticut in 1834, Maryland shortly afterward, and Virginia in 1850.

In these efforts against lotteries the Church played a leading role. In New York, for example, the Reverend Dr. John M. Mason, professor in the Union Theological Seminary, wrote a series of influential papers entitled "Considerations of Lots," in which he based his argument against lotteries on the theological ground that all things are determined by Divine Providence.[30] In Pennsylvania a few years later (1834) clergymen participated prominently in the formation of the Society for the Suppression of Lotteries. At the same time an important book[31] was published detailing the bad moral and public effects of lotteries, especially in Pennsylvania, but also to some extent in the twenty other states where they were legal.[32]

Religious Journalism

Religious journalism in this country,[33] as distinct from secular, goes back to Boston in the period of the Great Awakening, when *The Christian History* appeared for two years, 1743-45. The first definitely denominational periodical was the *Arminian Magazine*, which appeared in 1789-90 under the editorship of two great Methodist leaders, Thomas Coke and Francis Asbury. It was followed by similar periodicals published in behalf and often under the official auspices of the Baptist, Unitarian, Universalist, Episcopalian, Presbyterian, Congregational, and Roman Catholic Churches. These publications were for the most part interested not merely in religious faith and church work but also to some extent in the issues of the day such as Deism, education and slavery— the last-named splitting the periodicals of the North and South into two hostile camps.[34]

Perhaps the most noteworthy of the early strictly religious periodicals was *The Churchman* of New York City. From 1804 until the present it has been an effective and on the whole representative organ of the liberal elements in the Protestant Episcopal Church, and it has appeared without interruption except during the War of 1812 and the Civil War. Recently it has become undenominational, though its editor continues to be an Episcopalian. It has fearlessly attacked public abuses and been a strong supporter of the separation of Church and State, but not always tolerant of the ecclesiastical views of others.

During the first third of the nineteenth century a number of other denominational publications were established: the Baptist *Christian Watchman* and *Christian Reflector*, later merged into the *Watchman and Reflector*,[35] the Presbyterian *New York Observer*, the Unitarian *Christian Register*, and the Methodist *Christian Advocate* and *Zion's Herald*.

In addition, there arose other publications that developed into the strong modern undenominational Protestant religious press of which *The Christian Century* is the most conspicuous example. In 1806 this somewhat broader type of religious journalism received an able recruit in the person of the Reverend John Mitchell Mason, who, as we have seen, was one of the early opponents of lotteries. Mason projected the *Christian Magazine*, but even broader in its scope, and perhaps the most influential in its public policy, was the monthly *Panoplist* of Boston, edited from its foundation in 1805 to 1810 by the Reverend Jedidiah Morse. From 1810 to 1820 Jeremiah Evarts was the editor. Evarts was an active and respected layman who was secretary of the American Board of Commissioners for Foreign Missions, and editor of its *Missionary Herald*, with which the *Panoplist* was merged in 1821. He was deeply interested in having the Christian churches contribute to the amelioration of the nation's social and political ills. In some matters, such as protecting the rights of the Cherokee Indians, the problems of temperance, and Sunday rest, he was the national spokesman of America's Christian conscience.[36]

Roman Catholic journalism in the United States really began with *The Shamrock*, or *Hibernian Chronicle*, published in New York from 1810 to 1817.[37] Its purpose, which may be taken as characteristic of most of the nineteenth-century Catholic papers in the United States, was in the main to vindicate the fame of Ireland and the truth and purity of the Roman Catholic Church.[38] *The United States Catholic Miscellany*, the first continuing Catholic newspaper in the United States,[39] was published by Bishop John England of Charleston, South Carolina, in 1822.[40]

With the second quarter of the century and the large influx of Roman Catholic immigrants came a great development of the Catholic press. *The Truth Teller*, which appeared in New York in 1823, was perhaps the most prominent journal. It merged in 1855 with the *Irish American*. In 1830 came the "first strictly Catholic magazine," the *Metropolitan*, or *Catholic Monthly Magazine* of Baltimore. This was followed in 1839 by the *Catholic Register*, which soon combined with the well-known *Freeman's Journal*, established the following year, and was for several years under the control of Bishop John Hughes.

Perhaps the three leading Catholic magazines[41] published today are, in the order of their establishment, *The Catholic World*, *America*, and *The Commonweal*. The first was founded in 1865 and is thus a century old. It is issued monthly by the Paulist Fathers and publishes articles dealing with current problems from a Catholic viewpoint. *America*, founded in 1909, appears weekly. Published by the Jesuits, it is probably the major Catholic periodical in the United States, occupying a position in Catholicism similar to that of *The Christian Century* in Protestantism, although more conservative even in respect to Catholicism than *The Christian Century* is in respect to Protestantism. The counterpart within Catholicism of *The Christian Century* in relation to liberalism is the weekly *The Commonweal*. Founded in 1924, it is a journal of opinion published and edited by Catholic laymen. This magazine has won the respect of Protestant and Jewish leaders, and though its circulation is relatively small, its influence today is considerable.

In general, Roman Catholic religious journalism in this country[42] has concerned itself mainly with advancing the interests of the Church and defending it against misunderstanding and abuse. This defense was particularly important in the middle of the last century when the Know-Nothings and the Nativists were so active. The two political and social matters which have in the past most attracted its attention have been the cause of free Ireland and the attempt to secure public financial support for parochial schools. While the establishment of Ireland as a free and independent republic has removed that matter as an issue for discussion in the Catholic press, the cause of public financial support for parochial schools remains as the subject which probably more than any other fills the pages of Catholic publications, and on which there is a practical unanimity of approach.

For a long time the Catholic press confined itself almost exclusively to matters which directly and closely concerned the Church and Catholicism. Since, however, the conclusion of World War II, it has increasingly expanded the scope of its coverage to include all major political and public issues. Today there is no discernible difference between the amount of space devoted to such subjects as peace, disarmament, unemployment, foreign aid, racial discrimination, etc., in the Protestant *Churchman* and *Christian Century* and the amount in the Catholic *America* and *Commonweal*.

The Occident, founded in 1843 and long edited by Isaac Leeser, was the pioneer in Jewish periodical literature.[43] It interested itself in public issues and is credited with large influence in the ultimate victory which made Jews for the first time eligible for public office under the constitution of North Carolina.

The Roman Catholic diocesan weeklies have no counterpart in the Protestant world. They are newspapers serving their constituency in much the same way that small-town secular weeklies meet local needs. They give the news of the locality, the state, the nation, and the world, with emphasis on items of special interest to Catholics and also contain much church and religious material. The special articles are provided for the most part by the National Catholic Welfare Conference with its "News Service" and *Catholic Action*, or one of their related organizations. Through these papers the Church strongly influences public opinion.

Somewhat similar to the Roman Catholic diocesan weeklies are the Anglo-Jewish (as distinguished from Yiddish) weeklies published in all the major cities of the United States. One of them at least, the *National Jewish Post* (published in Indianapolis), is nation-wide in its circulation, but practically all the others are limited in their readership and in the subjects covered. Unlike the Catholic diocesan weeklies, the Anglo-Jewish papers are generally independently owned and controlled.[44]

Temperance and Liquor Control

The effective temperance movement in this country began with the publication in 1785 of Dr. Benjamin Rush's *Inquiry into the Effects of Ardent*

Spirits on the Human Body and Mind. This gave a good scientific basis for temperance instruction and, because of the author's standing as a patriot and physician, it carried weight. He was not an advocate of prohibition by State action but believed that the Churches should take the lead in promoting temperance.[46] In 1811 he presented a thousand copies of his *Inquiry* to the General Assembly of the Presbyterian Church, which the following year adopted a report placing the assembly behind the temperance movement. The Methodist General Conference and the Congregational Associations of Massachusetts and Connecticut followed suit. In 1826 the American Society for the Promotion of Temperance was organized, Protestant ministers taking the lead in its advocacy and providing seven of the sixteen members of its first board. In 1836 a more radical organization, known as the American Temperance Union, was formed by a merger of various societies. It adopted the principle of total abstinence. Stimulated by these groups the frontier churches did much to advance the temperance cause.

It was probably the Reverend Lyman Beecher, the father of Henry Ward Beecher, who did more to promote the temperance cause—which ultimately resulted in prohibition—than anyone else in the second quarter of the nineteenth century. His *Six Sermons on the Nature, Occasions, Signs, Evils and Remedy of Intemperance,* first preached in Litchfield, Connecticut, ran through many editions from 1827 on. Their teachings became part of the general ethical equipment of the Christian preachers and revivalists who spread through the growing Middle West at this time.[47]

Father Theobald Mathew, an earnest Irish priest, was another great temperance leader. After founding his Total Abstinence Society in Ireland in 1838, Mathew spent two years—1849-51—lecturing in this country and had a profound influence; nearly 500,000 Catholic Americans are said to have taken the pledge during his visit.[48] Largely as a result of the movement he started, the Catholic Total Abstinence Union was formed in 1872. Two years later the Women's Christian Temperance Union was formed, and under the able leadership of Miss Emma Willard it became a national force in uniting the women of most Protestant churches behind the total abstinence and prohibition movement.[49]

In 1837 Neal Dow, who had inherited from his Quaker upbringing a strong opposition to the liquor traffic, established, with the backing of leading Protestant ministers, the Maine State Temperance Society. Its purpose was to control the policy of the state legislature in matters dealing with the liquor evil. This society secured the first definite legal prohibition of intoxicating liquors in the United States, brought about by the Maine law of 1851 which prohibited their manufacture, sale, or keeping for sale. In the following four years, twelve states in New England and in the North Central Division and two Western states adopted similar laws. Many Protestant groups supported the legislation, but Roman Catholics, Episcopalians, Lutherans, and some others, who were for temperance but not for prohibition, held aloof.

Mormon Theocracy and Independence

The Mormons, or "The Church of Jesus Christ of Latter Day Saints," represent in their way the nearest approach to a theocracy on a large scale which this country has known since early Puritan days. They were founded as an independent sect in 1830, in Fayette, New York, as a result of the revelations to Joseph Smith as reported in his *Book of Mormon*. The founder was an extraordinary person, combining religious enthusiasm, an eye for business, capacity for leadership, imagination, and some dramatic instincts. His followers, moving West, became a missionary body attracting large numbers of adherents in Ohio, Missouri, Illinois, and elsewhere and suffering severe persecution, especially in the last two named states. In Jackson County, Missouri, in 1834, a mass meeting of several hundred citizens demanded that they move away, razed the printing shop of their newspaper, and tarred a Mormon bishop. The Mormons appealed to Governor Daniel Dunklin for troops. They asserted that "no republican will suffer the liberty of the press and liberty of conscience to be silenced by a mob," and that "every officer, civil and military, with a very few exceptions, has pledged his life and honor to force us from the country, dead or alive." [50]

Failing to get from the governor satisfactory action protecting them and their rights, they addressed a petition to President Jackson, saying that no sect had endured such persecution since the Declaration of Independence; that they were suffering unjustly, as the county court records carried no name of a Mormon in connection with any crime; and praying that they be restored to their lands in Jackson County and protected by armed force. Secretary of War Lewis Cass replied that the laws of Missouri had been violated, not those of the United States, and that the latter could interfere only if the state applied for help on the ground that an insurrection existed. A petition to Congress was answered in the same way through the judiciary committee.[51]

Thwarted in their attempt to gain legal protection, the Mormons organized a militia of their own in 1838, incurring Missouri's armed opposition. Governor Lillburn W. Boggs sent a dispatch, since known as the "Boggs Exterminating Order," in which he said, ". . . The Mormons must be treated as enemies and must be exterminated, or driven from the state if necessary, for the public good. Their outrages are beyond all human description." [52] A few days later occurred the massacre of Haun's Mill, in which seventeen Mormons were killed or mortally wounded.[53]

In 1839, driven out of Missouri where they had become a political factor because they voted practically as a unit, the Mormons laid out and established an incorporated colony of many thousand people at Nauvoo (first called Commerce), Illinois. This was in effect an independent, self-governing theocracy under their "Prophet," who acted as head of the administrative, judicial, and military departments.[54] Here again they came into serious conflict with the neighboring communities.

The charter secured from the Illinois legislature, through Mormon influence with the Whig party, contained clauses assuring all religious sects freedom of speech and worship, but was really contrived to deliver all control into the hands of Smith, and to create a situation which made it improbable that any non-Mormons would settle in the city.[55]

Smith, as mayor, lieutenant general of the armed Nauvoo Legion, chief justice, etc., was virtually a dictator, though technically a legal one under his extraordinary charter. He was also head of the Mormon Church, prophet, president of Nauvoo University, a rich real estate speculator, political boss, husband of twenty-eight "celestial wives," and a candidate, in 1844, for the presidency of the United States on a remarkable platform which he signed as "the friend of the people and of unadulterated freedom." [56]

Things came to a head in the struggle between the non-Mormon citizens of the county and some anti-Smith Mormons on the one hand, and the organized forces under Smith on the other. In June, 1834, the state militia had to be called out to secure the surrender of the Legion—a striking example of a Church-State conflict in a limited area but in an extreme form. Joseph Smith and his brother were arrested for treason and while awaiting trial were killed by a mob.[57]

After Smith's death in 1844 and a brief interregnum, Brigham Young, president of the council, succeeded him as president of the Church. He led his followers west to Salt Lake Valley in 1846-47 and established "the State of Deseret"—"land of the honey bee." He administered the government autocratically through his church position, and without any regular authorization. He appointed all civil and ecclesiastical officers. Later (1850-54), by appointment of the president of the United States, he served as first governor of what was named officially the Territory of Utah. He also continued as president of the Church. Under the Mormon system the Church is the only channel of divine revelation, so that when polygamy was first proclaimed by Brigham Young, in 1852, to be a doctrine of the Church, the government was unwilling to grant Utah's application for statehood.

The story of the Church-State battle over this question and of the closely related legal phase of the polygamy issue will be considered later.[58]

Non-Sectarian Public Education

Public education of all of the people at public expense had scarcely been dreamed of in the Europe of three centuries ago.[59] Such education as a matter of public right under direct State, rather than Church, auspices was not known until it was tried in the Massachusetts of the seventeenth century. From the breakup of the Roman Empire until the 1600's the Church had been the dominant factor in all forms of institutional life, especially intellectual, moral, and social; hence it was natural that education had been considered primarily a function of the Church or of endowed institutions closely related to it and having a definitely religious character. American public education, secular but not anti-religious in character, grew out of the ideals nurtured by the Reformation. It is "the child of American Protestantism," [60] and was born in the Calvinistic tradition of Geneva.

The Massachusetts School Law of 1647 established the first system of public education in the American colonies. On their own initiative, some towns had established schools, and a law had been adopted by the colony in 1642 calling for the instruction of children in reading; but this was the first general school law. "It being one chief project of the old deluder, Satan," it stated, "to keep men from the knowledge of the Scriptures, as in former times by keeping them [the Scriptures] in an unknown tongue, so in these later times by persuading from the use of tongues [i.e., from learning to read]" and in order that the true sense and meaning of the original might not be clouded by false glosses of saintly-seeming deceivers, every township having 50 or more householders shall appoint a teacher to instruct children in reading and writing. In the event the township shall increase to 100 families, it shall set up a grammar school, and failure to do so shall subject it to a penalty.[61]

Such was the beginning of public education in North America under Massachusetts leadership. Since New England until very modern times continued to lead in the evolution of the American public school system, its experience in developing Church-State relations is particularly important. Each little New England town was originally established as a religious republic, with the Church in complete control. It was the State acting as the servant of the Church which enacted the laws of 1642 and 1647, requiring the towns to maintain schools for religious purposes.[62]

There was a close connection between the religious town which controlled church affairs and the civil town which looked after roads, fences, taxes, and defense—the constituency of both being one and the same, and the meetings of both being held at first in the meetinghouse. When the schools were established it was natural that the colony legislature placed them under the civil, as involving taxes and being a public service, rather than under the religious town, even though they were religious in origin. From this religious beginning the civil school, and the civil school town and township, with all our elaborate school administrative machinery, were later evolved.

The erection of a town hall, separate from the meetinghouse, was the first step in the process. School affairs were now discussed at the town hall instead of in the church. Town taxes, instead of church taxes, were voted for buildings and maintenance. The minister continued to certificate the grammar school master until the close of the colonial period, but the power to certificate elementary school teachers passed to the town authorities early in the eighteenth century. By 1800 all that the minister, as the surviving representative of church control, had left to him was the right to accompany the town authorities in the visitation of the schools. Thus gradually but certainly did the earlier religious schools pass from the control of the Church and become a state responsibility. When our national government and the different state governments were established, the states were ready to accept, in principle at least, the theory gradually worked out in New England that schools are State institutions and should be under the control of the State.[63]

Throughout the colonial period there was never a time when Massachusetts did not apply the principle that it was the function of the State to promote religion and when the majority did not believe that taxation for religious purposes was justified.[64]

In all the schools, whether tax supported or not, and in Harvard College, which received many grants from the state, the teaching of religious subjects and the developing of a religious spirit were considered of fundamental importance. During this period toleration had been established for all except Roman Catholics, though all taxpayers had to support the religious worship approved by the majority of each town, except that Episcopalians might have their tax transferred to their own minister, and Quakers and Baptists, if members of a regular church society, were exempted out of respect for their conscientious scruples.[65]

There was some modification of this attitude after the American Revolution, although the 1780 constitution authorized the legislature to "require the several towns, parishes, precincts and other bodies politic, or religious societies, to make suitable provision, at their own expense, for the institution of the public worship of God, and for the support and maintenance of public Protestant teachers of piety, religion and morality, in all cases where such provision shall not be made voluntarily," and "to enjoin upon all the subjects an attendance upon the instruction of the public teachers aforesaid, at stated times and seasons, if there be any upon whose instructions they can conscientiously and conveniently attend." [66]

The practice of catechizing in the schools and the character of many of the textbooks of this period indicate clearly the sectarian quality of the instruction. Not until the educational law of 1827 were the school committees having power over textbooks forbidden to direct the purchase or use of any books "which are calculated to favour any particular religious sect or tenet." [67]

Several factors profoundly affected the interest in public education at this time: the popular Democratic presidential administrations of Andrew Jackson, the gradual freeing of the suffrage from property qualifications, the large immigration of European laborers ignorant of English and of our democratic traditions, the rapid growth of urban industrial centers, and the need of providing schools in the newly settled states of the Middle West. These and other factors attracted national attention to the problem of education in the second quarter of the nineteenth century. It was realized that the Churches and privately endowed or supported institutions were entirely inadequate to the task. Massachusetts took the lead in the resulting movement for greatly strengthening the public schools and for making attendance at some school obligatory for all children of certain ages.

In 1837 Massachusetts set up the first state board of education in the United States, and Horace Mann was elected by the board to be its secretary.[68] He was a man of untiring energy, great ability, and boundless enthusiasm for public education. Under his leadership the state developed a compulsory education system of secular schools under state auspices, which became particularly effective after 1842 when the legislature adopted the principle of compulsory education. By 1855 this system, as well as the increased membership in the Roman Catholic Church and other non-Congregational churches and the influence of Unitarian ideas, brought about complete elimination from publicly supported schools of sectarian as distinct from religious instruction.[69]

In his *First Report* to the Massachusetts Board of Education, delivered in 1838, Mann indicated that his strong opposition to sectarian teaching in the schools was coupled with an equally strong belief in moral instruction. The "entire exclusion of religious teaching, though justifiable under the circumstances," he said, "enhances and magnifies a thousand fold the indispensableness of moral instruction and training." He deplored the fact that in only six of the almost three thousand schools investigated did the textbooks teach "the beautiful and sublime truths of ethics and of natural religion." [70]

In this and some subsequent reports Mann had specially in mind the attempt of the American Sunday School Union to have its "select library," approved by the Union at its annual meeting in 1837, accepted for use in the schools. Both he and the governor of Massachusetts declared this to be a sectarian proposal. The Union's agent, Frederick A. Packard, pressed in particular the acceptance of Abbott's *Child at Home*, and there followed the famous Packard-Mann correspondence, as published in the *Boston Recorder* in 1838. Packard contended that this book was Christian but not sectarian, while the secretary of the Board of Education showed that its doctrinal basis regarding the last judgment, sin, and other matters represented orthodox doctrines not accepted by such religious groups as the Unitarians and Universalists. Mann felt that since the schools had children of all denominations in attendance they must, while supporting the fundamental religious and ethical truths of the Bible, decline to teach anything in the way of sectarian doctrines. He won, and it was an important victory.[71]

In his final report (1848) Mann set forth in great detail his views on the role of the Bible and religious education in the public schools:

I believed then (1837), as now, that sectarian books and sectarian instruction, if their encroachment were not resisted, would prove the overthrow of the schools.

I believed then, as now, that religious instruction in our schools, to the extent which the Constitution and the laws of the State allowed and prescribed, was indispensable to their highest welfare, and essential to the vitality of moral education.

I avail myself of this, the last opportunity which I may ever have, to say in regard to all affirmations or intimations that I have ever attempted to exclude religious instruction from the schools, or to exclude the Bible from the schools, or to impair the force of that volume, that they are now, and always have been, without substance or semblance of truth.

Our system earnestly inculcates all Christian morals; it founds its morals on the basis of religion; it welcomes the religion of the Bible; and in receiving the Bible, it allows it to do what it is allowed to do in no other system, to speak for itself.

Mann went on to say that the religious education which a child receives at school

. . . is imparted for the purpose of enabling him to judge for himself, according to the dictates of his own reason and conscience, what his religious obligations are and whither they lead. But if a man is taxed to support a school, where religious doctrines are inculcated which he believes to be false, and which he believes that God condemns, then he is excluded from the school by divine law, at the same time that he is compelled to support it by human law. This is a double wrong.[72]

Mann's efforts led to the removal of denominational sectarianism from the public schools, thus making them generally acceptable to Protestants, but not to Roman Catholics. As a result the Roman Catholics in Boston, as in New York and other places, developed parochial schools of their own, and in at least one place, Lowell, secured public support for their schools.[73] The town required that these schools meet three tests: (1) that the instructors be examined as to their qualifications by the committee, and receive their appointments from them; (2) that the books, exercises, and studies be prescribed and regulated by the committee, and that no other be taught or allowed; (3) that these schools be placed, as respects the examination, inspection, and general supervision of the committee, on precisely the same footing with the other schools of the town.[74]

Public opinion was coming around definitely, however, to the position since generally maintained in all American states: that public school money should not be applied to any sectarian institution. By 1855 the Massachusetts constitution was amended so as to forbid the appropriation of funds "to any religious sect for the maintenance, exclusively, of its own schools." [75] In 1917 the constitution provision was strengthened by forbidding the grant of public funds for the "founding, maintaining or aiding any school or institution of learning, whether under public control or otherwise, wherein any denominational doctrine is inculcated." [76]

In Connecticut the development was much like that in Massachusetts. Regular religious instruction was part of the accepted program of the colonial schools.[77] It continued, only slightly modified so as to be on a simple non-sectarian basis, in the tax-supported schools of the early days after the establishment of the state; but not until after Church and State were separated by the constitution of 1818 did the movement for public schools entirely divorced from the local Congregational churches become strong. The early efforts to secure efficiently directed non-sectarian public education go back to Henry Barnard, who as a member of the Connecticut legislature in 1838 secured the passing of an act to provide for the better supervision of the common schools. That year Barnard became the secretary of the state Board of Education and did for his state the same type of work that Horace Mann was doing at the same time for Massachusetts. His work in Connecticut, and later in Rhode Island and Wisconsin, and as the first United States Commissioner of Education and founder and editor of the *American Journal of Education*, was of epoch-making importance in building up the non-sectarian public school system of the United States.

Little by little definite religious instruction was given up in the Connecticut schools. By about the middle of the century all formal religious instruction had been generally eliminated, leaving only formal Bible reading, hymns, and prayers, as opening and closing exercises.[78]

In Virginia the history of education [79] goes back to the establishment of the College of William and Mary in 1693. However, the constitution of 1776 had nothing to say about education, as was true even of the constitution of 1830. This shows how backward the state was in providing a system of public education, in spite of the far-seeing efforts of Thomas Jefferson, who in 1779 introduced into the Virginia Assembly his "Bill for the more general diffusion of knowledge." [80]

Under this plan every county was to be divided into districts so that all children, girls as well as boys, would be enabled to attend the schools established in each for three years, "tuition gratis," to learn reading, writing, arithmetic, and history. By a system of scholarships the best boys in the local schools were to be chosen to attend the grammar schools, and from the grammar schools the best scholars to attend William and Mary College, their expenses being met from the public funds.[81] The plan was the most ambitious one for public education separated from Church devised in the United States in the first half-century after independence; but nothing came of it as far as Virginia was concerned.

In 1796 Virginia passed her first school law, entitled "An Act to Establish Public Schools." Instruction was to be free for three years, and thereafter tuition was to be paid. But the plan was optional and consequently ineffective.

In 1803 a charter was secured for an academy, given statutory existence in 1819 as the University of Virginia.[82] Under Jefferson's leadership, this institution stood for the separation of Church and State in public education. Nevertheless, as late as 1843, the governor's message to the legislature stated that after nearly thirty years of effort to advance public education there was provision for only sixty days of schooling for about half the indigent white children of the state. There was not yet any state provision for Negro education.

The constitution of 1851 was the first to mention education. It imposed a capitation tax on white persons for the purposes of education in primary and free schools, a provision which was retained in the revision of 1864.

During all this period the various religious bodies, especially the Anglicans and Presbyterians, supplied most of the worthwhile education in the state through their academies, of which some 317, with 9,060 pupils, were reported in 1850.[83] The Presbyterians seem to have first conceived popular education in a large way without reference to a strictly denominational emphasis. It was not until the law of 1870 that the basis of a really effective state school system, with a state superintendent and an ex officio state Board of Education, was established under the leadership of Dr. William H. Ruffner, a Presbyterian minister, who showed himself to be a man of uncommon good sense, energy, and vision.[84]

In New York, an act was passed in 1795 for the encouragement of schools. Societies were then organized to provide free schools in many places where public education did not exist, or to promote the movement to have such schools started and supported by the state. In 1805 a permanent state school fund was created, and in 1812 a state system of schools was authorized under a superintendent of common schools. De Witt Clinton, governor of the state from 1817 to 1823 and from 1825 to 1828, was a strong advocate of public education at state expense, believing that a system of tax-supported schools was "the palladium of our freedom" and that it should care for the children of the state for ten years. "Upon education," he said, "we must rely for the purity, the preservation, and the perpetuation of republican government." [85]

In New York City, under an act passed by the state legislature in 1813, the commissioners of the school fund were directed to distribute its income, plus an equal amount to be raised by tax on the city, to the trustees of various named institutions, "and of such incorporated religious societies, in said city as now support or hereafter shall establish charity schools." The distribution was to be based on the number of children from four to fifteen years old, taught free therein during the preceding year.[86] The New York Free School Society, organized in 1805, began to receive grants from public funds two years later and in 1825 became the sole recipient of public funds for education in the city, grants to church schools being discontinued. Up to this time such grants had persisted, though decreasing in number and amount.

In 1825 the New York Free School Society changed its name to the Public School Society of New York and was permitted to levy a tax. It provided some "non-sectarian" religious instruction, but because this was based on the King James translation of the Bible it was unsatisfactory to Roman Catholics. This situation continued until 1842, when a city board of education was created, and the society handed over to it its buildings and property. In 1853 the society was disbanded.[87]

In 1840 Governor Seward recommended that "foreign children" have schools with teachers of their own faith and language, and this statement was interpreted as favoring public funds for parochial schools.[88] In the same year Bishop Hughes appealed for public aid for seven New York City parochial schools which were doing an important work among the Irish and other immigrant children. When his request was denied by the corporation of the city, he presented it to the state legislature, where it passed the Assembly but was voted down by the Senate.[89]

In 1841 the state superintendent advocated in his annual report applying to the city of New York the principle of local control by which "each district suits itself, by having such religious instruction in its school as is congenial to the opinions of its inhabitants." [90] But the city decided that "religious instruction is no part of the common school education." [91] Not until after the close of the Civil War was a comprehensive system of universal free education established in the state.

Pennsylvania was only a few years behind New York. In 1834 its legislature passed an act to establish a general system of education for public schools.[92] The Pennsylvania Society for the Promotion of Public Schools was very active.

In the South, North Carolina with its vigorous and democratic Scotch-Irish population took the lead in setting up democratic common schools, creating a permanent school fund in 1825, and passing a public school law in 1839. But state schools, as distinct from private and denominational ones, were not organized in anything like an effective system until the appointment in 1853 of a state superintendent of public schools.[93]

From 1844 on, all states amending their constitutions, and new states when admitted to the Union (except West Virginia, which later corrected the omission), decreed in their fundamental laws against any diversion of public funds to denominational purposes.[94] The state constitution framers were in the great majority of cases sympathetic with the cause of religion but anxious to keep the functions of Church and State distinct.

By 1860 all Northern states and several Southern ones had laid the foundations of the American system of public schools free for pupils and free from denominational control. Some grants from public funds were still being made to church and private schools, mostly on the secondary level, but the movement for a completely public-controlled public school system had become well established, with laws in most states permitting public taxation to support it. There had also been progress in the development of public high schools, normal schools, and state universities, as well as in finding responsible superintendents and boards of education. The framework of the American system had been laid in the East, Middle West, and upper South, and the superstructure was to be erected all over the country as soon as the Civil War and its immediate aftermath had passed.

This brief survey of the development of public education in the most representative states shows that the beginning of the movement for an adequate public school system goes back to the thirties and forties of the nineteenth century. It was the enormous Irish immigration of the middle of the century, with the growing urbanization that accompanied it, that contributed more than any other new factor to the determination to develop a public school system which, while entirely undenominational, should conserve all that was considered best in the American educational tradition as formed mainly under New England leadership.

Although Massachusetts and some other states, faced by the wave of European immigration, took the necessary steps a generation earlier, the importance from a national standpoint of an adequate system of public schools under state auspices was not fully realized until after absorption in the Civil War was a thing of the past and the Union had been restored. The most striking and effective presentation of this view, and of the danger of giving public moneys to parochial schools, was expressed by President Grant in his address in 1875 to the Army of the Tennessee at Des Moines, Iowa:

Let us all labor to add all needful guarantees for the security of free thought, free speech, a free press, pure morals, unfettered religious sentiments, and of equal rights and privileges to all men, irrespective of nationality, color or religion. Encourage free schools and resolve that not one dollar appropriated for their support shall be appropriated to the support of any sectarian schools. Resolve that neither the state nor the nation, nor both combined, shall support institutions of learning other than those sufficient to afford every child growing up in the land the opportunity of a good common school education, unmixed with sectarian, pagan or atheistical dogma. Leave the matter of religion to the family altar, the church, and the private school, supported entirely by private contributions. Keep the Church and State forever separate.[95]

The following year, in the Hayes-Tilden presidential controversy, the matter came prominently to the fore when the Republican national platform called for an amendment to the Federal Constitution forbidding "the application of any public funds or property for the benefit of any school or institution under sectarian control."[96] When James G. Blaine submitted the proposed amendment in a strengthened form to Congress in August, 1876, it failed to receive the necessary two-thirds majority in a strictly party vote, the Republicans voting for it and the Democrats against it.[97] The exact wording of the proposed amendment was as follows:

No State shall make any law respecting an establishment of religion, or prohibiting the free exercise thereof; and no religious test shall ever be required as a qualification to any office or public trust under any State. No public property, and no public revenue of, nor any loan of credit by or under the authority of, the United States, or any State, Territory, District or municipal corporation, shall be appropriated to, or made or used for, the support of any school, educational or other institution, under the control of any religious or anti-religious sect, organization, or denomination, or to promote its interests or tenets. This article shall not be construed to prohibit the reading of the Bible in any school or institution; and it shall not have the effect to impair rights of property already vested. Congress shall have power, by appropriate legislation to provide for the prevention and punishment of violations of this article.[98]

Although the Blaine amendment was not passed by Congress, the overwhelming majority of its members were clearly in favor of a public school system divorced entirely from religious affiliations. Practically every state entering the Union since this time has been required as a condition of admission to agree, by an ordinance irrevocable without the consent of the United States and of the people of the new state, that provision be made "for the establishment and maintenance of a system of public schools, which shall be open to all the children of the state and free from sectarian control." [99]

The question of maintaining the separation of Church and State in education, in respect both to religious practice in the public schools and to the grant of government funds to sectarian schools, will be considered further in this book. At the present time it represents one of the most critical domestic issues facing the American people.

Diplomatic Representation at the Vatican

The question of diplomatic representation at the Vatican points up one of the most interesting historical phases in American Church-State relations. In 1797 a native of Rome by the name of John B. Sartori was commissioned as the first consul to represent the United States in the papal dominions.[100] Though technically only a consular representative, he was, through the courtesy of the papal government, permitted to exercise the functions of a diplomatic official.[101] The question of diplomatic representation had arisen as early as 1779. John Adams wrote the Continental Congress that he hoped it would "never send a minister to His Holiness" or receive a Catholic nuncio to this country.[102] About seventy years passed before a duly commissioned American diplomatic agent was appointed, and the appointment was due to the enthusiasm created in 1846 by the election of Pius IX to succeed Gregory XVI as pope. His election was very popular in this country, for it was believed at the time that he was a liberal who would work for greater freedom. He started his administration by various reforms of a most encouraging character, releasing political prisoners, granting more freedom to the press, establishing a constitution, making improvements in the field of public works, and even placing a box at the Vatican to receive complaints.[103]

Apparently the first definite proposal that formal diplomatic relations be established between the United States and the government of the Papal States was in a dispatch to the secretary of state in June, 1847, when the American consul at Rome stated that high officials of the papal government and the pope himself had expressed to him the desire that such relations be formally inaugurated.[104] In November of the same year, the New York *Herald* recommended diplomatic representation at the papal court as the fittest manifestation of American sympathy and admiration.[105] Mass meetings were held in New York and Philadelphia expressing admiration for the efforts of the new pope to ameliorate the condition of the Italian people,[106] and a resolution was adopted by the Louisiana legislature stating that it would be a source of gratification should the United States government open diplomatic relations with the court of Rome.[107]

In his message to Congress in December, 1847, President Polk proposed the opening of diplomatic relations with the Papal States. "The interesting political events now in progress in these States," he said, "as well as a just regard to our commercial interests have in my opinion rendered such a measure highly expedient." [108]

The proposal met with a warm debate in Congress. It was opposed on the ground that under our Constitution the government could have nothing to do with ecclesiastical matters; that there were no American commercial interests to protect in the Roman States; that the recognition would strengthen the hands of the Jesuits; and for other reasons.[109] There were, in addition, accusations that the president was playing politics, trying to seek the Roman Catholic vote. In the end, however, both houses voted overwhelmingly to finance the sending of a chargé d'affaires to Rome.[110]

The first chargé was Jacob L. Martin, a former Protestant who had become a convert to Roman Catholicism. His instructions from Secretary of State James Buchanan, dated April, 1848, stated,

> There is one consideration which you ought always to keep in view in your intercourse with the Papal authorities. Most, if not all the Governments which have Diplomatic Representatives at Rome are connected with the Pope as the head of the Catholic Church. In this respect the Government of the United States occupies an entirely different position. It possesses no power whatever over the question of religion. All denominations of Christians stand on the same footing in this country,—and every man enjoys the inestimable right of worshiping his God according to the dictates of his own conscience. Your efforts, therefore, will be devoted exclusively to the cultivation of the most friendly civil relations with the Papal Government, and to the extension of the commence between the two countries. You will carefully avoid even the appearance of interfering in ecclesiastical questions, whether these relate to the United States or any other portion of the world. It might be proper, should you deem it advisable, to make these views known, on some suitable occasion, to the Papal Government; so that there may be no mistake or misunderstanding on this subject.[111]

During the twenty years of this diplomatic relationship matters moved on the whole quietly, without serious difficulties. There were important incidents, such as that in connection with the coming to the United States of Monsignor Cajetan Bedini, then papal nuncio to Brazil, and the question of his exact status as an apostolic delegate; the virtual recognition by the Papal States of the Southern Confederacy; the important part played by the American legation in protecting Vatican property at the time of Garibaldi's entrance into Rome; the saving by the American minister in 1849 of two thousand copies of a Protestant edition of the Bible published in Italian and ordered destroyed;[112] and the refusal by the Washington Monument Association in 1852 of a block of marble for the monument sent by the pope.[113] There was also at the time considerable discussion of the possible removal of the pope to the United States,[114] but as far as known, this was never seriously considered by our government.

The most difficult matter that arose in connection with American representation at Rome had to do with Protestant worship within the walls of the Holy City. Such worship outside an embassy chapel apparently seemed to the papacy inconsistent with the idea of Rome as the hallowed center of the one Universal Church—a jurisdiction which should according to this view be exclusively Catholic.[115] In 1850, intervention by the American minister at the Vatican was necessary after the police ordered the discontinuance of a Protestant service being conducted for American citizens.[116]

Following this there were persistent rumors that all services under Protestant auspices were being discontinued. It is true that many voices were raised in Rome against continuing them, but as long as they were held in the legation and it was not conducted as a Protestant missionary propaganda institution but was merely for the use of American Protestant worshipers, there was no real trouble. But when property was taken outside the legation to accommodate the two or three hundred American visitors who frequently attended services, serious difficulties followed, especially as the English and Scotch had to go outside the walls of Rome to conduct their Protestant services other than those in the English legation chapel.[117] To enable the American chapel, set up in an apartment outside the legation, to go on providing for American citizens of the Protestant faith, the American minister to the Vatican found it necessary, in 1866, to place the arms of the American legation over the building which housed an apartment hired by an American Protestant clergyman for use as a chapel.[118]

As a result of this difficulty, which had been exaggerated in the public mind, growing sympathy with the aspirations of Italians for a united Italy, and other factors, Congress refused to appropriate any more money for a Roman mission, and it ceased to exist in 1867, without any specific action formally discontinuing it. Apparently both President Andrew Johnson and Secretary Seward favored this disposition of a delicate matter, and no formal message of explanation was sent to the supreme pontiff.[119]

Thus ended this interesting chapter in American Church-State relations. It should be noted that during the existence of the American ministry to the Vatican there was no reciprocal representation of the Papal States at Washington.

Yet at this time—prior to the fall of Rome in 1870 and its becoming the capital of Italy the following year—the pope continued to exercise temporal as well as spiritual authority in the Papal States, which since 1860 had been reduced to a very small area. The temporal power of course disappeared from 1870 until the Lateran Treaty and Concordat with Italy in 1929 recognized the political independence of Vatican City, a small territory of slightly over one hundred acres with a population then of about one thousand people.

It was the impending outbreak of World War II that revived the idea of formal representation at the Vatican. In 1939, after the start of the war, President Roosevelt sent his Christmas letter of greeting to Pope Pius XII, saying that he was planning to appoint a personal representative to the papacy, and accompanied it with a statement that he would remain for the duration of the war, so that "our parallel endeavors for peace and the alleviation of suffering may be assisted."[120] The proposal was, on the whole, favorably received at first by the secular press of the country. This reaction was due in part to the State Department's letting it be known that the president's choice for this mission—Mr. Myron C. Taylor, an Episcopalian personally acquainted with the pope and a man of high reputation—would have merely the title of "Personal Representative of the President of the United States of America to His Holiness, Pope Pius XII." It was also announced that his appointment did "not constitute the inauguration of formal diplomatic relations with the Vatican," though it carried the rank of envoy extraordinary, and that he would serve without personal compensation.

Mr. Taylor was not regarded by this country as a member of the regular diplomatic service of the government, who had to be nominated to and confirmed by the Senate. In keeping with this understanding he was not formally accredited by the State Department to the Vatican. He was thought of as the representative of our chief executive in a world crisis to the individual head of the Roman Catholic Church, not as a full-fledged American ambassador to Vatican City.

Simultaneously with the sending of the letter to the pope, the president sent letters to Dr. George A. Buttrick, president of the Federal Council of Churches of Christ in America, as a Protestant leader, and to Rabbi Cyrus Alder, president of the Jewish Theological Seminary of America, expressing the hope that each would, "from time to time, come to Washington to discuss the problems which all of us have on our minds, in order that our parallel endeavors for peace and the alleviation of suffering may be assisted." [121] The press release issued by the White House created the impression that similar Christmas greetings had been sent by the president to the pope and these two religious leaders. However, when the full text of the letter to the pope became known, the Protestant press began to be increasingly critical of the project because of fear of its ultimate implications. *The Christian Century*, the most representative journal of liberal Protestantism, immediately attacked it as an entering wedge to the establishing of regular diplomatic relations between the Vatican and the American government. In the judgment of the editor, such action would be inconsistent with our inherited independence of Church and State. In his first editorial he said,

> To strip away all camouflage, the President has, in reality, established diplomatic relations with the Vatican without legal authority. He has done so, we believe, not as a peace move but as a political move. Roman Catholics will be greatly pleased and can be counted on to remember it at the polls. Protestants and Jews are expected to be diverted by the sop in the invitations to Dr. Buttrick and Dr. Adler, and to forget it long before November. In that expectation we predict that the President will be disappointed. The American majority does not want to see relations established between this government and any religious body, and it will hold Mr. Roosevelt responsible for having tried to do this under the nearly sacrosanct cover of a campaign for peace.[122]

Restrained but nevertheless vigorous protests were issued also by representatives of the Baptist,[123] Lutheran, and Seventh Day Adventist Churches who, after a visit to the White House, stated that they were assured by the president "that the appointment was a temporary expedient and grew out of the vast influence exerted by the Vatican over the large populations within the confines of those countries now engaged in war." [124] They reiterated their commitment to the principle of the absolute separation of Church and State and their opposition to a permanent ambassadorial relationship with the Vatican.

A month after the Christmas letters, the Executive Committee of the Federal Council of Churches issued the following "Declaration of Attitude and Policy":

> If the appointment should unfortunately prove a stepping-stone to a permanent diplomatic relationship, we should feel obliged in good conscience to oppose it, as a violation of the principle of separation of governmental function and religious function, which is a basic American policy and which both history and conscience approve, and as an ultimate injury to all faiths.
> We assume, however, unless events disprove us, that the appointment is strictly temporary, unofficial, and centrally concerned with efforts for world peace. We can

see ways in which it may help to bring peace and to avert wholesale bloodshed and a continuing disaster to civilization.[125]

As time passed, the Protestant churches became more and more restive and expressed strong disapproval of any permanent policy of diplomatic interchange between this government and the Holy See.[126] A recurring theme was the demand that the relationship be terminated at the earliest possible date. Nevertheless, Mr. Taylor's presence at the Vatican continued after the death of President Roosevelt and resulted in 1946 in a visit to President Truman by a delegation representing the Federal Council of Churches and nine major Protestant denominations. The president assured the delegation that the appointment was a temporary expedient to give him the fullest opportunity to contribute to the peace and would certainly terminate with the signing of the peace treaty if not earlier. Two years later, in March, 1948, the president again reiterated his pledge that Mr. Taylor's mission would be terminated when peace was made, and he stated unqualifiedly that this would be his policy so long as he remained in office. In January of 1950 Mr. Taylor resigned. Despite the pledge of two years earlier, President Truman, in September, 1950, disclosed that he was contemplating sending an official ambassador to the Vatican.[127]

This announcement provoked a strong reaction from the Protestant churches. A consultation among the heads of the major denominations, including large bodies not affiliated with the Federal Council, led to the formulation of a document entitled "A Brief in Support of Maintaining a Valuable American Tradition." [128] The brief was approved by the General Board of the National Council of Churches of Christ in the United States, which had been formed in the interim to succeed the Federal Council, at its first regular meeting in January, 1951, and was sent to the president and the secretary of state. President Truman's reply was to offer the post of ambassador to the Vatican to Charles P. Taft of Cincinnati, a former president of the Federal Council and a member of the General Board of the National Council. Mr. Taft declined the appointment and urged President Truman to give up the idea.[129] This the president was unwilling to do, and in October, 1951, he submitted to the Senate the name of General Mark W. Clark as ambassador to the Vatican.

Simultaneously, the president issued the following statement to the press to explain his action:

The President has decided that it is in the national interest for the United States to maintain diplomatic representation at the Vatican.

He has therefore nominated General Mark W. Clark as Ambassador to the State of Vatican City.

During and after the war the Taylor mission performed an extremely useful service, not only in the field of diplomacy but in the amelioration of human suffering. That service is set forth in official correspondence published from time to time.

The President feels that the purpose of diplomacy and humanitarianism will be served by this appointment.

It is well known that the Vatican is vigorously engaged in the struggle against Communism. Direct diplomatic relations will assist in coordinating the effort to combat the Communist menace.

Thirty-seven other nations have for a great many years maintained at the Vatican diplomatic representatives.[130]

General Clark's name had been submitted to the Senate but a few hours before the scheduled adjournment of Congress and there was therefore no time to act upon it. Hence, the submission had no immediate practical effect other than to raise a storm of controversy.[131] Practically every major Protestant organization and publication in the country expressed strong opposition. The National Council of Churches appointed a special committee under the chairmanship of Dr. Franklin Clark Fry, president of the United Lutheran Churches of America, to mobilize public opinion against the appointment. Protestants and Other Americans United for Separation of Church and State, which had been organized four years earlier in part to oppose diplomatic representation at the Vatican, entered the fray with the announcement that it had launched a nation-wide campaign to block confirmation of the appointment of General Clark. Among the Jewish organizations only the American Jewish Congress publicly declared itself in opposition to the appointment and urged the president to withdraw it,[132] although by and large American Jews were likewise against it.

The campaign of opposition proved extremely effective. Communications to the president were six to one against the appointment, and leaders of both houses of Congress assured the Protestant organizations that the appointment would not be confirmed. Less than three months after his name was submitted to the Senate, General Clark announced that he had requested the president to withdraw the nomination, which the latter "reluctantly" did. Although the president stated that he had not given up the idea and would submit another name, he left the White House a year later without doing so.

That the administration of President Dwight D. Eisenhower had no intention of reviving the controversy was shown when it submitted its first budget to Congress for foreign service personnel without any item for a Vatican envoy. The issue remained dormant until the presidential campaign of 1960, when the fact that a leading candidate for the Democratic nomination, John F. Kennedy, was a Roman Catholic threatened to revive it. However, very early in the campaign for the nomination, Senator Kennedy declared that he favored strict

Church-State separation and was "flatly opposed" to the sending of a United States ambassador to the Vatican.[133] This announcement was accepted by the Protestant churches and the potentially explosive issue was again laid to rest, at least temporarily. Whether it will be revived by President Lyndon Johnson or a future president, only time can tell.

Chapter 12

THE CHURCH AND SLAVERY

The Colonial Background

The first opponents of slavery in North America were religious leaders and groups in Pennsylvania—Quakers, Mennonites, and Dunkers. No other group was as fearless and active in denouncing slavery as the Quakers. The first published protest against the institution on this continent was by the monthly meeting of Friends in Germantown, Pennsylvania, in 1688. In 1693 the Philadelphia Yearly Meeting—the most influential of its kind in America—declared that it should be the policy of Friends to buy no slaves "except to set free." It was also agreed that they should aim to release their own slaves "after a reasonable time of service . . . and during the time they have them, to teach them to read, and give them a Christian Education." [1] In 1776 Pennsylvania Quakers went even farther and virtually decided to expel from membership those who did not emancipate their slaves. Before the end of the century slaves of Quakers had practically all been set free.

In New England, probably the earliest published attack on slavery was Samuel Sewall's tract, written in 1700 for the Society for the Propagation of the Gospel under the suggestive title *The Selling of Joseph*.[2] Ten years later, the Reverend Cotton Mather published his *Essays to Do Good*, full of objections to slavery and so clear-cut in denunciation of its injustice that the American Tract Society, reprinting it more than a century later, had to expurgate it to make it pass without undue criticism at a time when the slavery question was being debated.[3]

In Rhode Island and the neighboring colonies there had been a good deal of domestic slavery in colonial days, Negro servants being frequently found in the larger towns. The Puritans felt that they themselves were "God's elect," and it was not until their inherited Calvinism was modified in the course of the eighteenth century that any real sense of universal brotherhood developed among them. Respectable church people in Rhode Island saw nothing inconsistent in sending ships to Africa with rum and having them come back laden with slaves. But in Newport, the leading New England center of the slave trade, the Reverend Samuel Hopkins fired the first effective gun in the anti-slavery campaign. He was the earliest of the New England ministers to preach against slavery in an outspoken way. He delivered a powerful sermon on the subject in 1770 and published in 1776, with a dedication to the Continental Congress, his *Dialogue concerning the Slavery of the Africans; showing it to be the duty and interest of the American States to emancipate all their African Slaves.*[4]

In the South the Established Church in the early days could not break away easily from an old English law ruling that a slave who had been baptized became free. There was consequently a good deal of opposition to baptism on the ground that it would encourage manumission. But the Virginia Assembly in 1667, in the hope of encouraging "the propagation of Christianity," cleared up this matter by adopting resolutions to the effect that baptism did not alter the status of an individual as to his bondage or freedom. Maryland in 1671 definitely approved slave baptism. Such actions tended to lay the foundations for the Christian teaching of the slaves, and indirectly for a more humane treatment of them. Little by little anti-slavery sentiment appeared in some quarters, until at the time of the Revolution, with ideas of human rights in the air, considerable opinion in favor of the ultimate freeing of slaves had developed.[5]

The Revolutionary and Early Federal Periods

During the Revolutionary period and shortly thereafter some voices in the South, notably those of Jefferson[6] and George Wythe,[7] spoke up against the institution of slavery and demanded abolition. They remained largely unheeded, primarily because the economic system of the South made slavery financially profitable. In New England practical steps toward the abolition of slavery began in Rhode Island[8] just before the outbreak of the Revolution, and these steps were soon taken by Vermont.[9]

Pennsylvania, the Quaker stronghold, adopted measures for gradual abolition in 1780. More significant was the action of Massachusetts, where in 1781 a Negro sued his master for freedom on the ground that the state constitution, following the wording of the Declaration of Independence, stated that "All men are born free and equal." The success of this suit ended slavery in that state.[10] A similar decision was handed down in New Hampshire, and by the time the Federal Constitution was adopted, emancipation and abolition had spread to Connecticut, Rhode Island, New York, and New Jersey.

For many reasons the year 1787 was eventful in the slavery conflict. It saw the reinvigoration, under the presidency of Benjamin Franklin (who had long noticed the inconsistency between advocating liberty and permitting slavery[11]), of the Society for Promoting the Abolition of Slavery, established a decade earlier and the prototype of many similar societies, North and South. It was also a partial defeat for the opponents of slavery in the Constitutional Convention and a notable victory in Congress with the prohibition of slavery in the Northwest Ordinance.

As usual, the Quakers took an honorable lead in the matter. As early as March, 1790, they petitioned Congress against slavery. The same action was taken by the Pennsylvania Society for Promoting the Abolition of Slavery, which had been much influenced by the Quaker view that the traffic in slaves was unchristian. These were the earliest petitions to Congress on the matter.[12]

Three factors greatly impressed the churches during this early national period and led to their taking an anti-slavery stand. There were, first, the "Great Revival," which strengthened the religious note and quickened the conscience of the evangelical groups in American Protestantism; second, the arguments in behalf of the liberation of the slaves as a Christian duty advocated by the Quakers, especially in Pennsylvania, and by the Reverend Samuel Hopkins, the Reverend William Ellery Channing, and other Congregational and Unitarian ministers in New England, and by the new peace societies in various states; and third, the influence of the "rights of man" ideas which had been incorporated in the Declaration of Independence, the Federal Bill of Rights, and the state constitutions.

Of the church groups, other than the Quakers, the Methodists were the earliest, after the separation from England, to take a definite anti-slavery attitude.[13] This is not surprising in view of the fact that their ministers were very close to the masses of the people and relatively little influenced by the aristocrats of the South who profited particularly by slavery. Beginning with a conference held in Baltimore in 1790, Methodists asserted that "slavery is contrary to the laws of God" and took steps to discipline through exclusion members who refused to emancipate their slaves within specified periods of years.[14] However, Methodists residing in the Carolinas and Georgia were expressly exempted from the prohibition,[15] and in 1808 the rule which forbade slaveholding among private members of the Church was dropped, leaving only the traffic in slaves as illegal.[16]

A similar ambivalent position was taken by the Baptists. In 1789 the General Committee of the Church adopted a resolution declaring slavery to be "a violent deprivation of the rights of nature and inconsistent with a republican government"[17] and calling on its members to "make use of every legal measure to extirpate this horrid evil from the land."[18] Nevertheless, the majority of Baptists soon reconciled themselves to slavery as an institution which "they were powerless to abolish, but which they would do everything in their power to mitigate by humane treatment and Christian instruction."[19] Indeed, while the Northern Baptists continued to issue statements deploring slavery, some of their Southern brethren sought to justify it on the basis of Old Testament teaching and lack of specific prohibition in the New Testament.

The Presbyterians too combined an outright condemnation of slavery as an institution with demands for action which were much more modest. For example, in 1818 the resolution of the General Assembly of the Presbyterian Church in the U.S.A. expressed the view that slavery was "a gross violation of the most precious and sacred rights of human nature" and "utterly inconsistent with the law of God." But to implement this condemnation it went no farther than to call upon its members to support the society formed for colonizing Africa with free Negroes of the United States, permit their slaves to attend gospel services, encourage their instruction in the Christian religion, and refrain from treating them cruelly.[20]

Among the Protestant denominations only the Congregationalists [21] and the Unitarians, whose memberships were largely restricted to New England, were uncompromising in their opposition to slavery during the years from Independence to 1830. The Episcopal Church (and the Roman Catholic Church as well [22]) took no official action on the issue in this period.

The Beginnings of Effective Anti-Slavery Sentiment

By the early thirties the positions of both North and South began to harden perceptibly on the slavery issue. In the South, the old view had been that slavery was an unfortunate, unwise, and unchristian institution, which in some way and at some time must be superseded by a system of labor more in keeping with the humane conception of human dignity enshrined in the Declaration of Independence. But this was slowly yielding, especially in South Carolina and the deep South, to the view that it was an ideal system with divine sanction, and essential for the economic and political welfare of the South.[23] In the North, at the same time, anti-slavery sentiment was growing steadily, especially in church circles, even though simultaneously a strong effort was made to prevent a split between the two sections of the country.[24]

The fifteen years from 1830 on were years in which the Church in the North, speaking generally, identified itself more actively in the anti-slavery cause—giving it growing support, including that of the most prominent of its martyrs, the Reverend Elijah Lovejoy.[25] There were at this time two somewhat divergent movements in the interest of the Negro. Both were led by Christian laymen and ministers. Little by little the two groups separated into the more conservative "Colonizationists" and the more radical "Abolitionists." [26]

The American Colonization Society, founded in 1816, was interested in removing the American Negro, and more particularly the free Negro, to Africa. Its early advocates included many of the most representative and public-spirited men of both North and South, with strong support in the border states. They believed that if they could develop a movement to have the free Negroes return to their "native home," a large migration might follow which would greatly reduce the seriousness of the slavery problem in this country. The Colonization Society's efforts accomplished some good, but they reached only a few thousand people. Owing to the difficulties of transportation and other factors, the project could not be considered a major solution of the problem, so that after 1833 the main stress of American philanthropists was transferred to more radical measures.

The other movement was interested in securing the complete abolition of slavery in the United States. This more radical group felt that the efforts of the colonizers were merely a palliative that distracted attention from the major issue. Its members were greatly encouraged by the movement for the abolition of slavery in the British Empire. As the *New York Evangelist* said, "Let us imitate our British brethren and open the floodgates of light on this dark subject." [27] In New York a group proposed a plan for an American Anti-Slavery Society, but this did not assume definite form until the news arrived that the slaves in the West Indies were about to be emancipated. The New England Anti-Slavery Society had been formed two years before (1831); but the new organization was national in scope and was interested in having other sectional societies formed, from which delegates might come to the national organization. The new society launched the *Emancipator*, published anti-slavery pamphlets, and circularized the country with information about the British movement. It came out for *"immediate* emancipation," interpreting the words, however, rather broadly to gain support for any measure "if it be promptly commenced with the honest determination of urging it on to its completion. . . . In fine, it is *immediate* emancipation which is gradually accomplished." [28] Even more outspoken against the evils of slavery was William Lloyd Garrison's *Liberator*, which conducted an unceasing campaign for abolition from 1831 until after the passing of the Thirteenth Amendment in 1866.

From 1834 on, the situation even in the North became serious. Especially in the large cities conflicts between slavery and anti-slavery groups were not uncommon. The congregation in the Chatham Street Chapel in New York, where the New York Anti-Slavery Society had recently been organized, was expelled. Other churches were attacked, and St. Philip's Episcopal Church (colored) was nearly torn down. Such events were especially prevalent in the summer of 1834, when the conditions of the city were so serious that all the local troops were under arms. [29] But rural regions were not free from trouble. Typical of extreme cases was that of a Methodist preacher in North-field, New Hampshire, in 1835. While at prayer during the course of a meeting he was conducting for the anti-slavery society, he was dragged from his knees by virtue of a deputy sheriff's warrant accusing him of being "an idle and disorderly person . . . a common railer and brawler, going about . . . disturbing the common peace." [30] This time he was discharged, but a few months later, while addressing another meeting in a neighboring town, he was arrested in the pulpit and tried the same day. The sentence was three months' hard labor in the house of correction.

Many committees denounced abolitionists as much as they did slaveholders, and in 1834 a group, following in the footsteps of the Reverend Lyman Beecher, founded the American Union for the Relief and Improvement of the Colored Race. Its purpose was to avoid the extremes connected with Garrison and most of the abolitionists, on the one hand, and the tendency of many Northerners to support the growing sentiment of the South in maintaining the status quo, on the other. This American Union, in which many clergymen were active, advocated a "conciliating spirit, a Bible spirit," and expressed the belief that "the hopes of the friends of the peaceful abolition of slavery in the United States depend upon securing the concurrence of slaveholders, procured by an appeal to their humane and Christian principles.[31]

Garrison became increasingly radical. He started out by presenting the abolition cause from a Christian and Church standpoint, emphasizing that liberty is "a gift of God and nature." [32] Later he became an opponent of the Church and was opposed by it in turn because of his violence of utterance rather than because of his ultimate goal. His movement, which had become more and more extreme, became separated from the mainstream of American Christianity. He called the Methodist Church a "cage of unclean birds and a synagogue of Satan"; ministers were "Dumb Dogs" (D.D.'s). Even the New England Congregationalists were "at the head of the most implacable foes of God and man," while the Presbyterian Church was anathema.[33] Garrison's tirades against the Church were so bitter that at one time no church in Boston would open its doors for the annual meeting of his society.[34]

Garrison's sincerity of purpose and unselfishness have been increasingly recognized. He was the embodiment of devotion to a cause, even though his intense interest in it led him to many violent statements. He placed abolition ahead of union, thus opposing Lincoln's views and policy. He was not, however, an advocate of force. Indeed, with the notable exception of John Brown's raid in 1859, the abolitionists—of whom many were Quakers—did not use force.[35]

The American Anti-Slavery Society, established in 1833 and having as one of its major objects "to influence Congress" to abolish slavery in the District of Columbia,[36] was particularly influential at this time among the Presbyterians, Congregationalists, Methodists, and Baptists. More than two-thirds of all the abolitionists in New England were either Methodists or Baptists, these being groups very close to the needs of the common man.[37] In fact, an analysis of the delegates to the New England Anti-Slavery Society meeting of 1835 shows that two-thirds were ministers, and of these about two-thirds were Methodists,[38] although some of the most effective leaders were also found among the Congregational and Unitarian ministers.[39]

A mammoth memorial to Congress, two hundred feet long, bearing among its signers the names of 3,050 New England clergymen and beginning "In the name of the Almighty God," was presented against the proposed extension of the domain of slavery. In a few months 125 separate remonstrances came from the ministers of the New England states.[40]

In 1834 a nation-wide petition campaign against slavery was inaugurated, with Protestant clergymen again taking a prominent role. John C. Calhoun, then in the Senate, charged that the petitions represented a Northern conspiracy against the "peculiar institution" of the South, and he moved against their reception. His motion failed, but the discussion attracted considerable attention to the anti-slavery cause. In the House a similar motion was referred to a special committee, which recommended that "all petitions relating . . . to the subject of slavery or the abolition of slavery, shall, without being either printed or referred, be laid upon the table, and . . . no further action whatever shall be had thereon." [41]

This form of parliamentary obstruction, which certainly contradicted the provision in the Bill of Rights guaranteeing the right of petition, was known as the "Pinckney Gag," and it was repeated in various sessions until 1840, when it was made a standing rule of the House. The issue did much to unite the North in favor of abolitionism. Petitions which the Anti-Slavery Society with its clerical agents had done so much to encourage were received and automatically laid on the table. The matter was fought in both houses of Congress. Its major result was to identify abolitionism with the constitutional rights of citizens as laid down in the Bill of Rights.

The Two Decades Before the Civil War

At the beginning of the second third of the nineteenth century four groups of churches had the largest influence in the South: the Methodists, who were the first to separate (1844) over slavery; the Baptists, who separated in 1845; the Presbyterians, who divided in 1858 and 1861; and the Episcopalians, whose Southern members carried on their work independently during the war years but never completely broke their organic unity. The first three were the most numerous bodies; the Episcopal Church, though it had lost its pre-eminence after the Revolutionary period, continued to be highly influential among the planter aristocracy, which held so much political prestige and power. The Roman Catholics, because division would have been inconsistent with the genius of their Church, did not divide. A study of the slavery crisis as shown by the discussions and actions of these five bodies and of certain related groups is one of the most illuminating in the history of Church-State relations in the United States.

In 1833 the first Methodist abolition society was formed in New York. It was followed in 1835 by the establishment of similar societies by the New England and New Hampshire Methodist conferences. On the other hand, the Ohio Conference in 1835 declared against abolition. The line of cleavage between New England and most of the rest of the country was becoming clear, and it was inevitable that the matter would come before the next General Conference. This was held in Cincinnati in 1836 and was forced to consider abolitionism, which was advocated in an uncompromising way by a New England delegate. After discussion, in which serious differences of opinion appeared, the conference voted 120 to 14 against abolition and for a disclaimer of any "right, wish, or intention to interfere with the civil and political relation between master and slave as it exists in the slave-holding States of this Union." [42]

This setback did not deter the activities of the New England "radicals" within the Methodist Church. In 1843 the New England Conference adopted a resolution that "slave-holding is sin; that every slave-holder is a sinner, and ought not to be admitted to the pulpit or the communion; that the Methodist Episcopal Church is responsible for slavery within its pale." [43]

It was now obvious that a crisis within the denomination was inevitable, and, with the resulting division of the major historic body of American Methodism, it took place at the General Conference of 1844[44] The break came upon the announcement of Bishop James O. Andrew that he had inherited some slaves and that emancipation was "impracticable." [45] After considerable debate, the Ohio delegation introduced a resolution that "it is the sense of this General Conference that he desist from the exercise of this office so long as this impediment remains." [46] The resolution carried by a vote of 111 to 69, almost entirely along geographic lines.[47] Adoption of this resolution led to adoption of another resolution sanctioning the departure of the Southern churches from the General Conference and their setting up a Methodist Episcopal Church South with jurisdiction and control of the assets of the Methodist Episcopal Church in the Southern states.[48]

The invitation was accepted by the Southern churches. The following year they voted at their annual conferences to set up an independent General Conference of the Methodist Episcopal Church South.[49] Almost a century was to pass before the division within the Methodist Church was healed.

The Baptists too sought at first to avoid a division on the slavery issue.[50] The triennial Convention of 1841, held in Baltimore, decided not to discuss the issue. This was in keeping with the resolution of the Baptist Board of Missions passed in the winter of 1839-40, asserting the neutrality of the board on the slavery question. But it was clear that such a situation could not last. Not long afterward the Board of Foreign Missions took an increasingly active attitude against slaveholding missionaries, and it was generally understood in the South that slaveholders would be excluded from appointments as missionaries, agents, or officers of the board. This policy was in effect approved by the board in 1845, with the result that the various Southern state conventions formally withdrew and organized a Southern Baptist Convention.[51]

A similar schism took place within the Presbyterian Church, leading ultimately to the formation of the Presbyterian Church in the Confederate States.[52] On the other hand, the Congregationalists, Unitarians, and Quakers, all of whom were largely concentrated in New England and the middle Atlantic states north of the Mason-Dixon line, were able to maintain their anti-slavery positions without changing their organizational structures.

The Protestant Church which found itself in the most difficult position as the war approached was the Episcopal. It was one of the few Protestant Churches which had not, prior to the war, directly opposed Negro slavery.[53] The reasons why the Episcopal Church was not clear-cut on the slavery issue are not hard to find. The Church was then absorbed in the threatened split between evangelical low churchmen and high churchmen influenced by the Tractarian movement. It had also not fully overcome the prejudice and disabilities inherited from the Revolution and was deeply interested in strengthening its position in the East and South and carrying out missionary work in the West. Then too it had inherited, from its Church of England past, a feeling that Church and State held two very distinct spheres and that the Church should not get too much entangled in political questions. Finally, it was at the time relatively stronger in the South than in the North, and in the South its membership was largely of the slaveholding group, while in the North it had only begun to regain the public standing lost in the Revolutionary War becaust so many of its clergy were Tories.[54]

Like the Episcopalians, the Disciples of Christ did not suffer any formal separation between North and South on the slavery issue or the resulting Civil War, but for a different reason. The Disciples were primarily interested in personal religion and evangelization, not in political and social reform. The same was in large measure true of the Lutheran Church, which on the whole maintained its historic position of serving the State almost entirely through its religious and moral efforts to transform individual lives rather than to influence corporately its public policy, and it thus stood much more apart from the slavery issue than did most Protestant bodies.[55]

The attitude of the Roman Catholic Church in the period immediately preceding the Civil War differs from that of most other religious bodies. It held practically aloof from the discussion of slavery—then and indeed throughout the war [56]—an attitude due to historic and practical reasons. It found slavery in the world, and, although it worked steadily for the alleviation of the condition of slaves and most of its leaders did not favor slavery, the Church did not officially condemn the system.[57]

The Church in America was in a particularly difficult position, for it had no evidence that the modern papacy had condemned slavery as such.[58] Gregory XVI's apostolic letter on slavery issued in 1839 had been a strong denunciation of the *slave trade* but had had nothing whatever to say against domestic slavery. The Catholic prelates in the United States concurred with Bishop John England of South Carolina, who drew a distinction between the slave trade, as already prohibited by this country and by the European nations, and domestic slavery. He said, "The Pope neither mentions nor alludes to this latter in his Apostolic Letter, which is directed, as were those of his predecessors, solely and exclusively against the former." [59]

It may be said that in general the Roman Catholic Church had inherited the position that slavery under American conditions would be tolerated but that every possible effort should be made to ameliorate the condition of slaves. On the one hand, slavery was not the "God-given institution" of some Southern advocates; on the other hand, forced speedy abolition did not seem the wisest policy. Such was the general attitude of the Church as the war came on.

The Jews played a considerable part in the Civil War, but in the agitation over slavery which preceded it they were not very active. In general they conformed in attitude to the pattern of their community. They were naturally sympathetic with freedom, but the supporters of slavery, both Christian and Jewish, could turn to many Old Testament texts and incidents that seemed to give it as an institution sanction under some circumstances, though stressing the need for humane treatment of slaves.[60]

The War Years

The Northern churches, almost without exception, came out definitely for the Union cause and against slavery during the period of the Civil War, while the Southern churches with at least equal fervor and unanimity backed the cause of the Confederacy. In most cases the declarations of the Northern churches in support of the Union were based on the immorality of slavery.[61] One exception during the early part of the war was found among the Lutherans, whose Church generally considers it its duty to support the established government in any crisis. When the General Synod met in 1861, it sent a committee to President Lincoln communicating resolutions characterizing "the rebellion against the constitutional government of this land" as "most wicked in its inception, inhuman in its prosecution, oppressive in its aims, and destructive in its results to the highest interests of morality and religion." [62] It also practically read out of the Church the Southern synods which opposed the Federal government. Unlike most religious bodies however, it did not do this on the issue of slavery but because of the "open sympathy and active cooperation they have given to the cause of treason and insurrection" [63]—things which always stirred the politically loyal Lutheran Church. The division was not fully healed until 1918.

Another exception was the Episcopal Church, whose Triennial Convention of 1862 adopted strong resolutions in favor of supporting the Union without specifically discussing the slavery issue.[64] The Southern dioceses absented themselves from this convention—although their names were read on the roll call—and formed the Protestant Episcopal Church in the Confederate States. However, they returned to the next Triennial Convention, held in 1865 shortly after the close of the war.[65]

During the Civil War there were several small denominations in the North that on the whole remained true to their non-resistance or pacifist principles. These included the Quakers and Mennonites—the two most numerous groups— and the Dunkers (German Baptist Brethren), Shakers, Schwenkfelders, Christadelphians, Rogerenes, Amana Society (Community of True Inspiration), and certain Catholic orders, particularly the Benedictines.[66] But none of them were favorable to slavery, and all of them together represented only a very small percentage of the total population. Hence, it is safe to say that during the war, and especially after the issuing of the Emancipation Proclamation, the Northern Protestant Churches increasingly supported both the war and the anti-slavery emphasis.

The attitude of the Quakers toward war service, war taxes, and fines received much attention both within and without the denomination. Their position was difficult because they were and had always been outspoken opponents of slavery. But they wished it abolished by peaceful means and could not sanction a resort to force even to do away with such a recognized evil. Toward military service they maintained on the whole their historic stance; few were actually in the armed forces. Similarly, they were nearly unanimous in op-posing fines for non-performance of military service.[67] In regard to the pay-ment of taxes, much of which went for war purposes, there was less unanimity. Most adopted a compromise position which sanctioned the payment of all lawfully levied taxes without "making any impractical distinctions."[68]

Among the most interesting Church-State issues during the war were several involving the attempt by Union officers in reconquered territory to control Southern Protestant churches and their services. A famous case of this sort arose in 1862 after the Episcopal Church in the Southern states in its revision of the *Prayer Book* had changed the prayers so as to make them for the Con-federacy, instead of for the United States and its president. General Benjamin F. Butler issued an order to the effect that "The omission, in the service of the Protestant Episcopal Church in New Orleans, of the Prayers for the President of the United States, would be regarded as evidence of hostility to the Government of the United States."[69] There was much discussion, ending in the forcible closing of some churches and the arrest of their rectors. The latter were sent north as military prisoners, but on their arrival in New York they were at once set at liberty.[70]

In another case, in Mississippi, a young Union officer led an Episcopal clergyman to the door for omitting the usual prayer for the president. Then, entering the pulpit, he read in the hearing of the Southern congregation the regular *Prayer Book* prayer "for the President of the United States, and all in Civil Authority."[71]

In one state, Alabama, the bishop and the clergy were inhibited for their failure to observe the order. The churches were closed and armed guards sta-tioned at the doors. The bishop, however, wrote a letter on the subject to Pres-ident Johnson, and this produced an immediate revocation of the obnoxious order.

Presbyterians in Missouri also had their troubles. In the fall of 1862 a pastor in St. Louis refused to declare himself for the Union and baptized a child with the name of a Confederate general. A provost marshal arrested him, taking control of the church. He protested to the attorney general. The matter was brought to the attention of President Lincoln, who wrote to General Curtis,

I tell you frankly I believe he does sympathize with the rebels, but the question remains whether such a man, of unquestioned good moral character . . . can, with safety to the government, be exiled upon the suspicions of his secret sympathies. . . . I must add that the United States Government must not . . . undertake to run the churches. When an individual in a church or out of it becomes dangerous to the public interest, he must be checked. . . . It will not do for the United States to appoint trustees, supervisors, or other agents for the churches.[72]

A somewhat similar question arose in connection with the Methodist churches in Southern communities occupied by Union troops. In 1862 a War Department order, signed by the secretary of war, directed the commanding generals of the departments in the South to place at the disposal of Northern bishops "all houses of worship belonging to the Methodist Episcopal Church, South, in which a loyal minister does not officiate." Memphis, Tennessee, was one of the places where this issue of what group should control a church was specially acute. Lincoln's orders were clear-cut. He wrote to the military commander,

I am now told that . . . the military put one set of men out of and another set of men into the building. This, if true is most extraordinary. I say again, if there be no military need of the building leave it alone, neither putting one set in or out of it, except on finding some one preaching or practicing treason, in which case lay hands on him, just as if he were doing the same thing in any other building, or in the street or highway.[73]

The Roman Catholic Church during the war continued to refrain from taking sides as a Church on the slavery question. Thousands of its members served in both armies. Naturally, however, since the South had relatively few of the recent immigrants from Ireland, Germany, and the Latin countries of continental Europe, it was much stronger in the North. Consequently most of the hierarchy supported the Union side, which commended itself to the Catholic mind with its emphasis on the support of legitimate government and on constitutional law. It was interested in removing the evils of slavery, but abolitionism, which seemed a radical and disruptive doctrine, had no appeal. The prevalent point of view of the Church was expressed in a letter written by Archbishop Hughes to the secretary of war in October, 1861:

The Catholics, so far as I know, whether of native or foreign birth, are willing to fight to death for the support of the constitution, the Government, and the laws of the country. But if it should be understood that, with or without knowing it, they are to fight for the abolition of slavery then, indeed, they will turn away in disgust from the discharge of what would otherwise be a patriotic duty.[74]

The Jews, being a minority group, have generally sympathized with other minority groups like the Negroes, because they were both seeking recognition and the removal of disqualifications imposed on them. This fact gave special zeal to the Northern Jews during the war—a zeal in opposition to the extension of slavery and in behalf of Negro enfranchisement and progress.

The Jews of the North made an excellent record during the war, as did also those of the South in their natural devotion to the Confederacy. There were about 6,000 Jewish soldiers in the Northern army alone, though the total Jewish population in the entire country was only about 150,000.[75] In the

South they were relatively most prominent at this time in cities like Savannah and New Orleans. New Orleans gave the Confederacy its secretary of state, the distinguished jurist Judah P. Benjamin.

An unfortunate incident early in the war threatened the friendly feeling between this group and the State. It came soon after the Congressional authorization of Jewish chaplains in 1861. In November, 1862, General Ulysses S. Grant issued instructions to General Hurlbut to refuse permits to pass south of Jackson, Tennessee. He added, "The Israelites especially should be kept out." Later orders to General Webster referred to the Jews as "an intolerable nuisance." He also officially reported to Washington that "the Jews roam through the country contrary to the government regulations." Finally, in a general order in December, he expelled all Jews "from his Department within 24 hours." [76] Probably the persons referred to were merely peddlers—who in that time and section were mainly Jews—but the form of the order discriminated against Jews as a group, a thing which of course could not be tolerated under our American system.

Protests and appeals made to President Lincoln had the necessary effect. The president notified General Halleck that the obnoxious order should be revoked, and he, in turn, notified General Grant. Halleck wrote to Grant,

> It may be proper to give you some explanation of the revocation of your order expelling all Jews from your department. The President has no objection to your expelling traitors and Jew peddlers, which, I suppose, was the object of your order; but as it in terms proscribed an entire religious class, some of whom are fighting in our ranks, the President deemed it necessary to revoke it.[77]

The Postwar Activities

The part played by the Church after emancipation in fitting the slave for his civil responsibilities was of national importance. Indeed, the education of the Southern Negro in its early stages after the war was due mainly to the missionary zeal of the Northern churches. In many ways this formed the most constructive work for the Negro during the decade of Reconstruction. It left its permanent impress for good on the South, not only through the institutions founded and the freedman trained, but through stimulating public education by convincing the South that the former slave was capable of education and would profit by it. The Congregational Church, which stood behind the American Missionary Association, was a specially important factor in this movement. It had produced many anti-slavery leaders and now did much of the educational work which in other countries would have been undertaken under similar circumstances by the State. It is necessary only to mention some of the institutions which it founded or fostered: Atlanta University, 1865; Fisk University, 1866; Talladega College, 1867; Hampton Institute, 1868. Howard University, chartered by Congress in 1867, should also be mentioned, for, though mainly supported by the government and undenominational, it grew out of a missionary meeting in the First Congregational Church in Washington in 1866; has had from the first a definitely Christian purpose; has generally had a minister of religion as its president; and has received much help from the American Missionary Association, especially for its School of Religion.

It should be remembered that a few Southern schools for Negroes, of which Tuskegee Institute is a conspicuous example, arose in the Southern states through the action of their own citizens, and that the Reconstruction legislatures, in which the colored people played such a large part, did much, in spite of corruption and extravagance in other fields, to encourage Negro education. But in the earliest days of emancipation no factor was more helpful than that of the Negro schools founded by the Christian people of the North and supported by frequent visits of their officers to the Northern churches. On the whole, the Church was probably the greatest single factor in the decade after the Civil War in educating the former slave for effective citizenship.

Today, of course, the task facing the United States is no longer supplying Negroes with schools for the education of their children but assuring every child the constitutional right to a full and equal education in a non-segregated public school. In this task the Church is playing a significant role.[78]

Part Three

MODERN AND CONTEMPORARY
PROBLEMS AND THEIR SOLUTION

Chapter 13

NATIONAL ISSUES AFTER THE CIVIL WAR

The Rise of Social Christianity

The "social gospel" arose in America at the end of the Civil War, occasioned mainly by certain acute industrial problems which came to the fore in connection with immigration, urbanization, and the development of the industrial system. Its roots are clearly in the teachings of the Old Testament prophets, the pages of the Gospels, and the thought and activities of the Christian Church. The Church through most of its history has victories to its credit against social abuses. In the Middle Ages, through the guild system, the "truce of God," hostels, hospitals, and other activities, it made Christianity the greatest power for unity and civilization in Europe. Christianity was not satisfied merely with fitting the individual for eternal life; it was also concerned with the realization of the Kingdom of God on earth.[1] Such ideas were held and demonstrated in this country by the framers of the Puritan commonwealths, but it is to Unitarianism, with its insistence on meeting the actual social needs of humanity, that we are perhaps most indebted for emphases in teaching which led to the effective beginnings of the movement that made the "social gospel" a national force. Unitarianism was the principal seedbed in which the ideological roots of social Christianity found themselves most at home, though the Quakers of Pennsylvania preceded it in some fields.[2]

In 1826 the Unitarians started in Boston "a ministry at large to the unchurched classes" which was not only the first example of religious social service in America but the first serious effort on the part of a religious body to cope with the social and religious problems of the submerged population of a sizable city.[3] The fact is that a social conscience was coming into being, especially in and around Boston. Congregationalists were affected as well as Unitarians; so, too, were other denominations.

There were many reasons for this development among the American churches. The writings of such English Christian Socialists as Frederick Denison Maurice and Charles Kingsley had a deep influence, especially in Episcopal Church circles.[4] Other foreign factors affecting the American churches were the European industrial revolutions in the late forties; the philosophic, social, and scientific thought that came from Germany (Kant and his successors), where Americans had begun to go for advanced studies; the theory of evolution, which in its accepted form dates back to Darwin's *Origin of Species* (1859); and Utilitarianism, which, though not as powerful a force in America as in England, nevertheless helped the movement for social reform through legislation, and especially for alleviating the burdens of the working classes.

But it was not until the slaves had been liberated by the Civil War that "the social impulse of Christianity" was set free to devote itself to the relief of the new industrial conditions which the war had helped to create. Up to that time public interests of the Church had been mainly absorbed in the question of slavery; now religion became the most powerful drive behind the humanitarian movements of the age.[5] When Henry Ward Beecher wrote in his *Sermon on Christian Character*, published in 1869, that all the details of human life were to be influenced by Christianity, the social gospel was starting to come into being. People began to think of the Kingdom of God as having to do with this world as well as the next.

Articles by Christian ministers appeared in papers and magazines on prisons, boys' clubs, workingmen's clubs, co-operatives, child labor, the ethics of trade, and the improving of factory conditions.

Social Christianity was now being popularized, and by nothing so much as the simple books of the Reverend Charles M. Sheldon, effective Congregational pastor of Topeka, Kansas, from 1889 on. The most significant of his books, *In His Steps: What Would Jesus Do?* first published in 1896, had an amazing circulation and influence. It is believed that more copies of it were printed than of any other book written in this country; by 1925 an estimated eight million copies.[6] The author tried to answer the question "What would Jesus do in solving the problems of present political, economic and social life?" *In His Steps* was preceded by a book by the well-known English journalist William T. Snead entitled *If Christ Came to Chicago* (1893). This book had a large influence on the reform of municipal conditions; more than 200,000 copies were sold. Its revelation of the crime and graft in which police and politicians were involved so aroused public opinion that the Civil Federation of Chicago was formed and did much to improve local conditions.[7]

The Brotherhood of the Kingdom was established by the Reverend Walter Rauschenbusch and some other Baptists in 1892. Among its aims were the following:

Every member shall lay stress on the social aims of Christianity, and shall endeavor to make Christ's teaching concerning wealth operative in the church.

On the other hand, each member shall take pains to keep in contact with the common people, and to infuse the religious spirit into the efforts for social amelioration.[8]

From this time on for many years Rauschenbusch was the leading exponent of the social gospel in the United States. He was most influential through his writings, and his fame will probably last longer than that of any of his contemporaries in the field of what became known as social Christianity and Christian socialism.

Professor Rauschenbusch's *Christianity and the Social Crisis* appeared in 1907. Later he summed up the views of those who wished to reform "our semi-Christian social order," in a single sentence in his *Christianizing the Social Order*, which appeared in 1912: "My sole desire has been to summon the Christian passion for justice and the Christian powers of love and mercy to do their share in redeeming our social order from its inherent wrongs."[9] Rauschenbusch's books were translated into French, Norwegian, Finnish, Swedish, Russian, Chinese, Japanese, and German and were undoubtedly the most significant religious publications in the United States if not in the English language in the first two decades of the new century.[10]

Rauschenbusch's presentation of facts and arguments made it impossible for the Church to keep out of the field of political and social reform.[11] Moral and social reform became one of the major activities of the Church. Of course, concern for public morality was not a new thing in American religion. The old election sermons in New England frequently took public morals as their theme, but it was then more an individual than a corporate matter. Now, societies founded either under Church auspices or by Christian leaders, for crime prevention, settlement houses, social welfare conferences, movements of all kinds to eliminate the abuses connected with the saloon, gambling, immigration, Mormon polygamy, etc.,[12] became common.

Social Christianity had now become official with most representative churches. During the first decade or so of the twentieth century most of the larger religious bodies also appointed social service agencies or commissions. A strong and aggressive minority, conscious of the social ills of the nation and the responsibility of the Church to help relieve them, had forced the issue. The Presbyterians took the lead, with the work of the Reverend Charles Stelzle, who was called in 1903 to "a special mission to working men" by the Home Missions Board and became to all intents and purposes the "Department of Church and Labor" of the Protestant churches. He established the Labor Temple in New York and provided a clearing house for information on all sorts of social problems and the relation of the Church to them.

The National Council of Congregational Churches and the General Convention of the Protestant Episcopal Church took official cognizance of the labor

problem at their meetings in 1901. The latter appointed a standing committee on the relations of capital and labor, and the General Convention of
1910 reconstituted the committee into a Joint Commission on Social Service,
which from 1913 on became a permanent body.[13] In 1907 the Methodist
Church, North, organized the Methodist Federation for Social Service, whose
purpose it was to deepen within the Church the sense of social obligation and
opportunity, to study social problems from the Christian point of view, and
to promote social service in the spirit of Jesus Christ.[14]

In 1908, at the Baltimore Conference, the Church adopted its highly influential "Social Creed of Methodism." Its program of social study and reform
has been a marked characteristic of its work ever since, and especially after
1912, when the Reverend Harry F. Ward, an outspoken liberal and later
professor of Christian ethics at the Union Theological Seminary, became the
Federation's secretary.

In 1908 the American Unitarian Society voted to establish a Department
of Social and Public Service. The National Baptist Convention in this same
year, which was the year of its founding, took official cognizance of social
problems, and three years later this influential Church provided for a Department of Social Service and Brotherhood. The Y.M.C.A. and the Y.W.C.A.
and other Christian organizations added to the impetus of this movement, which
by the time of the opening of World War I was typical of American
Protestantism. The Salvation Army also deserves mention. Founded in London
in 1865 by William Booth, a Methodist minister, it gained little foothold in
this country until 1889 and was not incorporated in New York until ten
years later. In spite of its emotionalism and unconventional methods, its work
among "down and outs," prisoners, drunkards, and the outcast gained it much
respect. Its lodging houses, soup kitchens, and workrooms became as characteristic as its gospel hymns, bands, and evangelical services. The Army and
its offshoot, the Volunteers of America, must be considered among the important Christian social welfare agencies of our large towns and cities.

The churches, as national organizations or other groups, or as local parishes,
or through their individual members, have a right to air their grievances
regarding the body politic or the body social, and to proclaim their panaceas,
and the arm of the law will seldom try to interfere. This means that the cause
of social reform is enormously stimulated, especially in a nation whose dominant religious emphasis inherited so much from the Puritan reformers of
Cromwell's day. This interest has more recently been prodded from a very
different source, the great papal encyclicals on social reform, particularly the
two issued during the short reign of John XXIII, *Mater et Magister*, and
Pacem in Terris. It may, in fact, be said that the rationale of the social gospel
is summed up in the words of the latter encyclical, issued at Christmas, 1962:

Every man has the right to life, to bodily integrity, and to the means which are necessary and suitable for proper development of life. These are primarily food, clothing, shelter, rest, medical care, and finally the social services. Therefore a human being also has the right to security in cases of sickness, inability to work, widowhood, old age, unemployment, or in any other case in which he is deprived of the means of subsistence through no fault of his own.

The Question of Polygamy (The Mormons)

We have already dealt with the origins and early struggles of the Mormons.[15] Here we consider exclusively the question of polygamy, which became acute shortly after the middle of the nineteenth century.

This custom was euphemistically called "plural marriage." It was probably never indulged in by more than a small percentage of the Mormon population, but Brigham Young married in all twenty-seven women and left seventeen wives surviving. He was an amazingly effective organizer of a highly successful and thrifty co-operative community, which was virtually a theocracy under his control. The desert was made to "blossom as the rose," but his polygamous ideas and practices and his dictatorial methods resulted in much friction with the government—thus maintaining the reputation for conflict which his predecessor, Joseph Smith, had begun.

As early as 1862 the Federal government, stimulated by Christian public opinion, undertook to stamp out the polygamy evil, which was openly practiced, and defended on the ground of a divine revelation, by Mormons. In this year the first of several Federal laws forbidding it—the Morrill Act, "to punish and prevent the practice of polygamy in the Territories"—was adopted, and a vigorous effort was begun to have the law enforced. The Mormon Church and its adherents fought this law in the courts, but the decision of the Supreme Court of the United States in 1878 (*Reynolds* v. *United States*[16]) held that Congress could constitutionally prohibit polygamy even where practiced because of religious beliefs.

Notwithstanding this and other Supreme Court anti-polygamy decisions (which have been summarized in Chapter 5), the Mormons persisted in its practice. The Federal government became thoroughly aroused. In 1879 it even attempted to enlist the service of other countries in the crusade against polygamy. A circular letter was sent to the American ministers in Europe, asking them to call the attention of the governments to which they were accredited to the American enactments against polygamy, and requesting that they prevent the preaching of Mormonism and the emigration of professed Mormons to the United States.[17]

In 1882 Congress passed the Edmunds Act, which punished actual polygamy by disfranchisement, imprisonment, and other penalties. Five years later the corporation of the Church of Jesus Christ of Latter Day Saints was dissolved by the Federal government. Effective resistance was no longer possible. Hundreds of polygamists suffered fines and imprisonment, over one thousand were disfranchised, and much of the property of the Church was confiscated. In 1890 the head of the Church, President Wilford Woodruff, issued a pronunciamento against polygamous marriages, stating that he would submit to the Federal law and advising all Mormons "to refrain from contracting any marriage forbidden by the law of the land." [18] His action was promptly approved by a general conference of Mormon representatives, who accepted his "declaration concerning plural marriages as authoritative and binding." [19] The matter was not, however, conclusively settled until 1896, when the Territory of Utah was admitted as a state under a constitution whose third article reads,

The following ordinance shall be irrevocable without the consent of the United States and the people of the state: Perfect tolerance of religious sentiment is guaranteed. No inhabitant of this state shall ever be molested in person or property on account of his or her mode of religious worship; but polygamous or plural marriages are forever prohibited.[20]

Thus came to an end a memorable controversy which had aroused the Christian people of the nation. Polygamy was contrary, they felt, to the Jewish-Christian moral code of the Bible, on which the ideals and law of the land were largely based.

The Campaign Against Public Gambling

Perhaps the most important of the early campaigns of American churches against gambling was the one which resulted in the overthrow of the Louisiana lottery. This campaign had its effective beginning in 1890, when Congress authorized the postmaster general to prohibit the use of the mails for lottery purposes,[21] and lasted until 1894, when the lottery was overthrown.

The Louisiana lottery was developed in New Orleans soon after the Civil War, chartered by the legislature in 1868 for twenty-five years. It was given a reputable exterior by the association with it of men of known personal integrity and commanding position. It has been estimated that within twenty-five years about $300 million, drawn from the whole country, passed through New Orleans.[22] The lottery had a state charter, which was about to expire when the movement in opposition to it became articulate in 1891. The "lottery crowd" was said to have offered a provisional gift of $1,250,000 a year for the Louisiana state schools if the lottery, which under its tax-exempt franchise brought the state regularly $40,000 a year, were continued for another twenty-five-year period.[23]

Under the leadership of Protestant clergymen, including the Reverend Lyman Abbott, editor of *Christian Union*, Bishop Phillips Brooks, and the Reverend Dr. Everett Hale, a campaign against the renewal was instituted and came to a successful conclusion when the Louisiana citizens, by a majority of 40,000, decided against renewing the lottery franchise.[24]

The lottery interests thereupon moved out of Louisiana. The new postal regulations, under the act of Congress of 1890, forbade the distribution of tickets and other lottery material through the mail, but they were transported by express all over the country and were advertised in theater programs, newspapers, almanacs, etc. The railroads and express companies had a financial stake and were profiting by the closing of the mails. Evidently nothing would stop the lottery evil except a stringent national law which would prohibit under severe penalty the sending by any means of lottery tickets, money, or material from one state to another, or from another country into our own. To secure such a law was now the purpose of the group which had led the successful campaign against the Louisiana lottery and which now had its headquarters in Boston. A national movement was started by an appeal sent to about two hundred of the country's best-known citizens by the leading clergymen of Boston and some other representative molders of public opinion. It resulted in a petition signed by thirty-eight bishops of the Episcopal Church, twenty-seven college and university presidents, Cardinal Gibbons and three archbishops, ten Methodist clergymen, the governors of eight states, and others.

In February, 1894, the memorial favoring national legislation against the lottery evil, with an accompanying bill, was presented to the Senate by Senator George F. Hoar. It passed the Senate unanimously three months later but was held up for some time in the House, as unanimous consent could not be secured for its consideration in spite of an overwhelming sentiment in its favor. There followed a national mail campaign which was extraordinary for its time. Religious newspaper subscription rolls, church registers, college catalogs, and other lists were secured, and about twenty thousand documents a week were sent out, all concentrated on securing favorable action in the House. The religious press of the country was particularly active, all religious papers with as many as five thousand subscribers being sent documents wrapped and stamped, with the request that they be forwarded to the leading men and women on their lists.[25] Effort was particularly concentrated on the clergy of nine states whose Representatives in Congress were not favorable. Finally the Lottery Act passed in 1895, making it a Federal crime to import, transmit through the mails, or transfer across state lines any lottery or gambling tickets or advertisements of lotteries or games of chance.

The campaign against the Louisiana lottery was but one of many similar successful state and local campaigns against various forms of gambling carried through under the leadership of the International Reform Federation, the Watch and Ward Society of New England, and like organizations whose main support had come from the Protestant Church group. Among other successful campaigns was the defeat in Maryland, in 1938, of a proposed amendment to the constitution which would have legalized lotteries. Public opinion credited the Council of Churches and Christian Education of Maryland with a large share of this success.

While the leadership in the anti-gambling campaigns, nationally and locally, has been in the Protestant groups, prominent Roman Catholic clerics co-operated in the early days of the struggle. The memorial against the lottery evil and in favor of a Federal anti-lottery law presented to Congress in 1894 contained among its many Christian leaders the names of Cardinal James Gibbons and three Roman Catholic archbishops. As late as 1941 Cardinal O'Connell of Boston joined forces with Protestant church leaders and a number of Jewish clergymen in successfully opposing a proposal introduced in the Massachusetts legislature to conduct a state lottery as a means of raising revenue.[26] Other ecclesiastics, like Archbishop Curley,[27] also spoke out strongly against the gambling craze. Such dioceses as Buffalo, Pittsburgh, Albany, and Fall River took action against it, banning it from all church activities.

It should be noted that Roman Catholic dogma does not forbid gambling or deem it in all cases immoral. According to the *Catholic Encyclopedia* a lottery is morally objectionable only "if carried to excess, as it tends to develop the gambling spirit and distract people from earning a livelihood by honest work. However, if there is no fraud of any sort in the transaction, and if there is some sort of proportion between the price of a ticket and the value of a chance of gaining a prize, a lottery cannot be condemned as in itself immoral." According to the column "Theology for Everyman," appearing in the *Pilot*, official organ of the Boston archdiocese, "No one can be accused of sin merely because he plays cards for money, or because he buys lottery tickets, or because he lays wagers on races or other athletic contests. It is quite possible that actions such as these may take place in completely unobjectionable circumstances and may serve the purpose of harmless, or even helpful recreation."

Because there is no doctrinal prohibition of gambling in Roman Catholic teaching, it became possible for many financially hard-pressed parishes to resort to bingo as a means of raising funds for church purposes. The annual *Official Catholic Directory* began to print full-page colored advertisements by manufacturers of equipment used in bingo. In city after city the Catholic churches took up bingo as a major fund-raising device. In Cincinnati in one year alone (1939) some thirty Catholic churches netted a profit of almost a million and a half dollars out of bingo played by about two and a half million players in local churches. Today, a quarter of a century later, the amount has undoubtedly multiplied, not only in Cincinnati but in many other major cities.

It must not be supposed that this development was welcomed by Roman Catholic churchmen. Many have had grave reservations and some have actively opposed it, and still do. But on the whole the Church has accepted it, perhaps as a necessity. Not only have bishops and priests ceased joining their Protestant colleagues in fighting for anti-lottery laws, but on the contrary they have become the most active and articulate supporters of legislation allowing bingo or similar games of chance where the beneficiary is a religious or charitable organization.

The consequences of this change of position are vividly illustrated by the situation in one state, New York, over a period of fifteen years. In 1942 the New York City police commissioner issued a statement to the effect that bingo and similar games would be deemed unlawful except when conducted under the auspices of the Church. Mayor Fiorello H. La Guardia disagreed with the opinion. "If a game is unlawful," he said, "the ultimate disposal of the funds, or the auspices under which the game is operated, or the place where the game is operated, does not make an unlawful game lawful. If bingo is unlawful in one place, it cannot be lawful in another." Archbishop (now Cardinal) Francis Spellman stated that such gambling would be discontinued while the legal status of the matter was further probed before the courts, but he simultaneously intensified pressure for the enactment of a law permitting bingo.

The pressure was partly successful. The next year the state legislature passed but Governor Thomas E. Dewey vetoed a bill which would have authorized local governing bodies, upon petition of 5 per cent of the local voters, to issue permits for the operation of bingo games by religious, social, fraternal, civic, and educational organizations. The governor based his disapproval of the bill on three main grounds. He felt that it was "clearly unconstitutional"; that it did not effectively bar professional promoters, who might take over an obscure fraternal organization and operate a central bingo game, transmitting the play to assembly halls throughout the state; and that the provision for voter petitions would annually stir up bitter political and moral issues in many localities.[28] The governor quoted an amendment to the state constitution adopted in 1939 which so clearly seemed to bar bingo that in the New York *Times'* opinion the only way to make this form of gambling legal in the state would be a further constitutional change.

Undaunted, the Church kept on trying to obtain enactment of permissive legislation. Meanwhile, efforts were continued to prevail upon police officials not to enforce the anti-gambling laws against churches sponsoring bingo. In New York City in 1954 a high police official was demoted and shortly thereafter resigned after arousing a storm of protest for his strict enforcement of the anti-gambling law against bingo playing in Roman Catholic churches.[29]

In the end, the efforts of the Catholic Church proved successful; the state constitution was amended and permissive legislation was passed in New York. Indeed, for Governor Averell Harriman this procedure was too slow; he preferred the enactment of legislation without waiting for any constitutional amendment. In his annual message to the state legislature in 1957 he stated,

Two years ago I recommended that statutory provisions be made for churches and other bona fide charitable organizations to conduct games of bingo, provided that the entire proceeds were devoted to charitable purposes. There was precedent for such statutory action, but the [Republican controlled] Legislature chose to follow the slower process of constitutional amendment to attain the same end.

I call your attention to the fact that the amendment passed in 1955 must be passed again this year, if action is again not to be deferred for two years. In addition, I urge that the legislation needed to implement the constitutional change should be enacted at this session so that there may be no delay if the people approve the amendment at the polls this fall.

A word should be added concerning the Jewish position on this issue. In general, rabbinic and synagogue organizations have kept aloof from the struggle. However, in 1955 both the New York Board of Rabbis and the United Synagogue, the latter representing the synagogues affiliated with the Conservative branch of Judaism, by formal resolution disapproved the use of bingo and other games of chance as a means to raise funds for synagogue and religious school purposes.[30] (In 1963, two Conservative synagogues discontinued bingo after being warned that failure to do so would result in their expulsion from the United Synagogue.) In 1958 the Reform congregational organization followed suit.[31] None of these groups, however, expressed any opinion as to the desirability of legislation either prohibiting or permitting bingo for the benefit of religious and charitable agencies. Probably the views expressed by these three organizations represent the position of American Jewry, in respect to both what was said and what was left unsaid.

Political Corruption and Good Government

Although our great national religious bodies have deeply interested themselves in various social reforms and features of good government, the fight against entrenched political corruption, as far as the Church is concerned, has been carried on mainly by individual members, and by ministers and local ministerial groups in various municipalities. Probably the most impressive and illuminating case is that of the Reverend Charles H. Parkhurst, D.D.,[32] whose work was the main factor in the overthrow of the corrupt Tammany Hall administration in New York in November, 1894.

Dr. Parkhurst, pastor of the Madison Square Presbyterian Church, became president of the Society for the Prevention of Crime in 1891. The society had been organized in 1878 and for thirteen years had tried to work in conjunction with the police. The new president, however, accepted the office on condition that henceforth it should deal with the police as its "arch-antagonist, making with it no alliance and giving it no quarter." [33]

What is generally considered the beginning of the campaign against Tammany Hall was the sermon preached in the Madison Square Church by Dr. Parkhurst in February, 1892. In it he attacked the municipal life of the city as "thoroughly rotten." He called the city officials "polluted harpies" and "a lying, perjured, rum-soaked, and libidinous lot." [34]

Many individuals and some organizations and publications supported Dr. Parkhurst, but he was generally reviled by men in office and by those in league with them. They took the ground that he should confine his activities to preaching the gospel and keep out of politics. Tammany was furious, and the reforming pastor even received a presentment from the grand jury declaring that his charges, especially those against the district attorney in office, were unfounded and that their author had "no evidence upon which to base them, except alleged newspaper reports, which in the form published had no foundation." [35] The presentment added that the charges "can only serve to create a feeling of unwarranted distrust in the minds of the community with regard to the integrity of public officials, and tend only to hinder prompt administration of justice." Thereupon Dr. Parkhurst decided to get evidence at first hand. In three weeks, with the aid of a detective and friends, he obtained 284 affidavits, which he presented to the grand jury, stating that his sole object was "to secure in the general mind an indictment against the Police Department." [36]

Dr. Parkhurst's evidence of illegal open saloons, gambling places, houses of prostitution, "protection" by the police, etc., could not be refuted. It resulted in a sudden change in front and a presentment by the grand jury against the Police Department. This was the beginning of a movement that led to the overthrow of the corrupt Tammany administration. The next steps need not be recounted here. It should be enough to have shown how a great reform movement began with the courageous attitude of a single minister of the gospel. That his action was unconventional, that it was much more characteristic of an Old Testament prophet than of a modern clergyman, cannot be denied; but it was extremely effective.

Others who followed in the tradition of Dr. Parkhurst were Dr. Graham Taylor,[37] working through the Chicago Commons and in other ways to clean up one of the worst wards in Chicago, and Norman Thomas, who before becoming the national leader of the Socialist party was, as the minister of a Presbyterian church, active in municipal reform in New York. Rabbi Louis Mann of Chicago and Rabbi Stephen S. Wise [38] of New York may be taken as representative of the many Jewish rabbis, especially of Reform Judaism, who have identified their synagogues with liberal public causes in the interest of good government and social welfare.

Christian Science Healing

Christian Scientists feel that they have a right to have their sick treated in such ways as commend themselves to their judgment and conscience, and that any interference with this right is an interference with the Constitutional guarantees of religious freedom.

The legislative debate over Christian Science began a few years after the publication, in 1875, of Mrs. Mary Baker Eddy's textbook *Science and Health with Key to the Scriptures*. It was most acute during the first two decades of this century, when, on the one hand, bills were introduced into practically all state and territorial legislatures to forbid the professional practice of the "healing" of disease without drugs and, on the other hand, bills were introduced designed to recognize spiritual healing as a legitimate method of curing disease. Public opinion was specially inflamed in 1902, following the indictment in White Plains, New York, of three Christian Science practitioners after the death of a child under conditions which seemed to show neglect. Mrs. Eddy then advised that "until public thought becomes better acquainted with Christian Science, the Christian Scientist shall decline to doctor infectious or contagious diseases." [39]

The opposition to Christian Science, as far as legislation was concerned, came mainly from medical practitioners. Usually the form of opposition chosen was the introduction of a bill to regulate the practice of medicine but containing a definition of medical practice so broad as to include Christian Science healing. The purpose was to eliminate Christian Science healers who could not meet the tests of the standard training required of medical practitioners, the point being that the practitioners of this new cult could not conscientiously attend the regular medical schools, where most diseases were treated as being due to physical causes.

The campaign of the Christian Scientists to obtain legislative recognition of their rights has been uniformly successful. Within a half-century after Mrs. Eddy's death in 1910 practically every state in the Union acted to give them adequate protection.[40] It must be remembered, however, that the Christian Scientists have secured their rights by strenuous efforts—by creating public opinion favorable to their cause; by submitting drafts of bills to the legislatures; and by taking cases to the courts. For our purpose in this study the important thing is that when the Christian Scientists have considered their religious freedom to be at stake, statutes and the courts in general have given them their desired relief as long as laws for the protection of public health, especially in the case of communicable diseases, are not infringed. Typical is the action of the Ohio legislature in 1949 in amending its statute providing a license for the practice of medicine.[41] The amendment stipulates that treatment of human ills through prayer alone by a practitioner of the Christian Science Church, in accordance with its tenets and creed, shall not be regarded as the practice of medicine.

Other legislation involving difficulties between the Christian Science Church and the State which are not yet fully settled has to do with such matters as vaccination, the physical examination and medical treatment of pupils in Church schools, the incorporation of churches, the exemption of Christian Scientists from school health instruction, and workmen's compensation benefits.

The National Prohibition Amendment

With the Internal Revenue Act of 1862, passed under the pressure of need for money to carry on the war, Congress adopted the principle of licensing the liquor business, which thus received in a measure the sanction of the Federal government and was organized as an effective national industry. Similar taxes had been enforced during the Revolution and the War of 1812, but they had been removed soon after these wars were over. The new excise taxes now came to be thought of as part of the regular revenue policy of the government. The open saloon increasingly prospered, especially in the large cities, where it became a center of political corruption and of moral degradation.

The situation was serious, and as early as 1865 a convention was held that brought together various organizations in a new body, the National Temperance Society and Publication House. "Crusades" against saloons were organized, especially by women. In 1869 the National Prohibition party was formed, committed to "the total prohibition of the manufacturing, importation and traffic of intoxicating beverages."[42] The Protestant churches, led by the Methodists, were behind this and similar movements, of which the most effective at the time was the Women's Christian Temperance Union, established in 1874.

In 1893 the Anti-Saloon League was organized in Oberlin, Ohio, one of the strongest Protestant religious centers of the Middle West. It soon described itself as "the church in action against the saloon." [43] Largely as a result of its efforts, a wave of prohibitory legislation began in 1907, so that by 1919 thirty-three states had by statute or constitutional provision prohibited the liquor traffic.

The movement for a nation-wide amendment was greatly stimulated by World War I, and the Eighteenth Amendment, proposed in 1917, was ratified by the necessary thirty-six states in 1919 and later by ten others.[44] The resulting Federal prohibition could not have been brought about had it not been for the larger Protestant churches. The movement had the support of many other forces—educational, medical, industrial, social welfare, and religious—but undoubtedly the energy and political activity which carried it to success were supplied in large measure by the Methodist Board of Temperance, Prohibition, and Public Morals.

This board, established in 1916, organized and implemented inherited interest of Methodists in doing away with the evils of the liquor traffic. At the General Conference of 1883 drunkenness was declared to be an "immorality," and rules were adopted for proceeding against members drinking spiritous liquors.[45]

Three years later (1886) the General Conference decided to agitate actively the question of prohibition, and the Book of Discipline was amended to provide that anyone who engaged in the manufacture or sale of intoxicating liquor as a beverage should be dealt with as in cases of immorality.[46] In 1888 the permanent Committee on Temperance and Prohibition was established.

The liquor dealers of the country realized that the members of the various Methodist churches were their most effective opponents. In 1914 the secretary of the Liquor Dealers' Association said, "It is only necessary to read the list of those preachers who are active in the present propaganda for legislative prohibition to realize that it is the Methodist Church which is obsessed with the ambition to gain control of the government." [47]

The wording of this statement is extreme, but there can be no question that the Methodist Church, as the largest Protestant group in the country and containing many able and sincere propagandists, did exert almost a controlling influence in favor of having the government—both Federal and state—ban intoxicating liquor for beverage use. From then until the final repeal of the prohibition amendment in 1933 the primary public interest of the Methodist, and also the Baptist, Church was for the Eighteenth Amendment. This was particularly the case in the South, where both Churches were so powerful. Speaking of their influence and that of some other Protestant groups at this time in prohibition, and incidentally in the anti-evolution and various other restrictive legislation of a puritanic type, a foreign publicist who had been studying Southern conditions said that "during the 1920's clergymen may almost be said to have dominated the South."[48]

The Federal Council of Churches was heartily in favor of prohibition, but it never took such an extreme stand for it as did the Methodist and Baptist groups. It did not denounce those who conscientiously opposed prohibition. Throughout the discussion it laid special emphasis on the importance of removing abuses in administration, and continued to emphasize the vital importance of temperance and temperance education.[49]

On the whole it is clear that most of the Christian churches, except the Episcopalian and the Roman Catholic, favored the prohibition amendment and its enforcement. The movement was undoubtedly actuated by high idealism and was designed to deal with a great national evil. Nevertheless, the more thoughtful elements in the community—outside of the leaders of Methodism and some other denominations—increasingly believed that the specific plan adopted to bring about a temperate nation was not the wisest, and in 1933 the prohibition amendment was repealed. It was charged by the supporters of prohibition that repeal was effected by the Liberty League and other groups which carried on high-powered propaganda with the financial backing of a small group of very rich men.[50] That such a movement existed cannot be doubted, but it never would have succeeded had not the majority of thoughtful American citizens felt that, in spite of the serious evils of the liquor trade, the Eighteenth Amendment was not, in the existing state of public opinion, the wisest way to overcome them. Indeed, the high-pressure methods used to secure the adoption of Federal Constitutional prohibition did not give the nation great confidence in the plan of direct action by the Church in State matters.

The Industrial Strikes—Capital and Labor

There have been few if any important strikes or trials of labor "agitators" in the past half-century in which many ministers of religion and some churches have not become directly or indirectly involved. As a result, Church and State have frequently come into conflict. Speaking very generally, during the first third of the twentieth century the pastors of conservative churches in large towns, with a few notable exceptions, were inclined to side with capital and the "ruling classes" in local disputes, but independent pastors, including many Roman Catholic priests, in industrial regions, in increasing numbers have been siding with labor—specially where the living conditions among workingmen have been on a deplorably low economic scale. Today there is a growing tendency for the more liberal churches, especially through their national organizations, to support the labor unions in all reasonable demands as long as the strikers observe the law. The Mooney-Billings case of 1916 in connection with the Preparedness Day parade bombings in San Francisco, the case of the Scottsboro Negro boys charged with rape in 1931, and the case of the Harlan, Kentucky, miners in the same year are examples.[51] The Sacco-Vanzetti murder case in Boston, in 1920, was so complicated that relatively few Church bodies took specific action on it.

Cases in which individual clergymen took part in industrial conflicts—generally on the side of labor but opposing violence—became frequent toward the close of the nineteenth century. Roman Catholic priests were then often active in trying to protect the rights of miners and factory workers. Protestant ministers also played their part. The Reverend W. H. Cawardine, a Methodist pastor in Pullman, Illinois, was an early representative of this group. His flaying of the Pullman Corporation for the strike of 1894 received much attention.[52] The Reverend Alexander F. Irwine, a Congregationalist, was active in many industrial conflicts near the turn of the century.[53] These are merely instances taken at random.

Roman Catholic priests, and even members of the hierarchy, have played a creditable part in helping to settle industrial disputes through membership on boards of mediation and arbitration. It may be sufficient to mention the names of Archbishop Ireland for his part in helping to settle two railroad strikes in the Northwest in 1894; of Bishop John L. Spalding, who served in 1902 as a member of President Theodore Roosevelt's Anthracite Coal Commission which settled the serious coal strikes of that year; and of Monsignor Francis J. Haas, who was active for many years after 1935 as a Federal labor conciliator. Similarly, the Reverend John P. Boland, pastor of a Roman Catholic church in Buffalo, served for some years as chairman of the New York State Labor Relations Board. Several Protestant ministers of prominence, such as the Reverend Albert E. Day of California, formerly vice-president of the Federal Council of Churches, and Bishop G. Bromley Oxnam, also served as referees in labor disputes by appointment of the National War Labor Board.

Probably no single industrial dispute in the history of the United States will show more clearly the attitude of churches, both local and national, than the steel strike of 1919. The long hours of labor, recognition of the union, and conditions of work were the major issues, though wages in certain grades in the industry were also unsatisfactory. Public opinion was particularly concerned about the twelve-hour day, which a report of a committee of the stockholders of the Steel Corporation had shown to be required of more than 50 per cent of the employees in rolling mills and furnaces. This committee recommended a reduction in hours, but the Finance Committee refused at the time to grant the request. The struggle became serious, with freedom of speech and assembly denied, and there was much bitterness. At McKeesport, Pennsylvania, alone 3,000 men were sworn in as special police subject to instant call; and on the first day of the strike some 365,000 men throughout the nation stayed away from work.[54]

A representative Protestant group, the Inter-Church World Movement, began an investigation three weeks after the opening of the strike in September, 1919, and transmitted its report to President Wilson in January of the following year, after a careful investigation by experts in the field and the taking of much testimony. The group found the conditions—especially the twelve-hour day seven days a week—most serious but believed that they were "remediable without the inauguration of anything even resembling social revolution." [55]

The Social Service Commission of the Federal Council of Churches of Christ co-operated closely with the Inter-Church World Movement in its survey, and in June, 1923, its Research Department published a pamphlet entitled *The Twelve-Hour Day in the Steel Industry*. It dealt with the social consequences of this system with its long hours seven days a week, and with the practicability of its abolition. Further evidence of co-operation among the churches is the fact that three of the leading groups, namely, the Commission on the Church and Social Service of the Federal Council of Churches (Protestant), the Social Action Department of the National Catholic Welfare Conference (Roman Catholic), and the Social Justice Commission of the Central Conference of American Rabbis (Jewish), issued a joint statement on the situation in June, 1923. This assailed the report of the special investigating committee of the American Iron and Steel Institute, which had declined to abolish the two-shift twelve-hours-a-day system—the action being mainly based on economic grounds.[56] However, later that same year, responding to the force of public opinion, which the churches had done much to develop, the twelve-hour shift was abolished in the steel industry.

Of the serious industrial strikes which characterized the period between the two world wars the most significant from the standpoint of church relations after the steel strike was that in the cotton mills at Gastonia, North Carolina, in 1929. It offered an example of the relatively recent intrusion of Communism as an important factor in industrial disputes. This was one of the rather few large-scale strikes in which the local churches, because of their extreme social conservatism, had no important part either in preventing the conditions that produced the strike or in bringing about settlement.

The strike began on April 1, 1929. It was organized by an experienced strike leader from New Bedford, Massachusetts, Fred E. Beal, who formed a secret union. A public meeting attended by a thousand mill hands was held on March 30, and on April 1 practically the entire working force walked out. The strike was under the leadership of the National Textile Workers Union, which stood for elimination of all piecework, a minimum standard weekly wage of twenty dollars, the forty-hour week, abolition of the doubling up of work, decent sanitary and housing conditions, recognition of the union, and other matters deemed to be fundamental. It regarded the methods of the old United Textile Workers as class collaboration with the mill owners, whereas the new union was a militant, fighting one. It condemned the general economic system and took the ground that the strike was the opening wedge in the South for the organization of all its textile workers.[57]

Some twenty-three outside representatives of Communist organizations took part, and the *Daily Worker* was widely distributed. The strike was consequently interpreted as a Communist struggle. It had no connection with the churches. At first the strikers did not attack religion, but they became more and more radical as the conflict moved from the economic into the political sphere. Soon there were clashes between strikers and police, and the National Guard was called out. Attempts were made to get its members to join the workers, but without success. Mass picketing was resorted to. After two weeks, however, the strike seemed to have been defeated, and by May 1 the number of strikers had decreased from two thousand to two hundred.

Circulars were distributed by the mill management branding the strikers as un-American and atheistic. One of the circulars said,

Our Religion, Our Morals, Our Common Decency, Our Government, and the very Foundations of Modern Civilization, all that we are now and all that we plan for our children is in danger. Communism will destroy the efforts of Christians of 2,000 years. Do we want it? Will we have it? No!! It must go from the Southland.[58]

The officials of the American Federation of Labor and of the United Textile Workers repudiated any connection with the strike, which they considered Communistic in character and purpose. But the strikers who remained became more aggressive, with a tent colony which became increasingly extreme in its views. In June, when rumors of a raid on the strike center were rife, there was a serious clash. One striker and four policemen, including the chief of police, were wounded, and the latter died the following day. Thus ended the Communist challenge to Gastonia. The attitude of the strikers now became merely one of defense.

It is worth noting that none of the religious associations or organizations adopted any resolutions or engaged in any institutional action with regard to the strike.[59] They were quiescent. In spite of the actions of religious bodies outside, the local churches retained their old tradition of keeping "out of politics," but in general they were unsympathetic to the strike. The ministers were of a markedly conservative type. Sermon topics during the strike, as they appeared in the Gastonia *Gazette*, were almost all on theological or Biblical themes, with little or no reference to the local crisis. The chief approach by the ministers to the problem was intensified evangelism. They are said to have opposed mob terrorism and police brutality against strikers less, if anything, than they opposed the Communists.

As a result of this disturbance Beal and fourteen other strike leaders were arrested and put in jail. To secure a jury took nine days and the examination of 408 veniremen. They were examined as to their beliefs about trade unions, religion, the sanctity of private property, and other matters. The panel chosen consisted of seven workers, four tenant farmers, and one grocery clerk—all but two church members.[60]

During the trial there were many serious local disorders, creating a reign of terror in the country. A speaking platform used by the Communists was destroyed by dynamite. A prominent supporter of the strike was murdered in the presence of at least fifty persons, yet no conviction of the murderer was ever secured. A newspaperman, writing of the long series of criminal actions and trials, said, "In every case where strikers were put on trial strikers were convicted; in not one case where anti-unionists or officers were accused has there been a conviction." [61]

A second trial was for an alleged unlawful conspiracy among strikers which the state alleged had resulted in the murder of the chief of police, but as a matter of fact the issue of Communism was always in the foreground, especially the question of the admissibility of evidence as to Communist views on religion and other matters. The judge in the second trial admitted testimony on religious belief in determining the credibility of witnesses, the atheism of Communists being used against them. Religion also entered into the final summations by the attorneys for the prosecution and by the solicitor representing the state. Biblical references were almost as common as they were in the Scopes trial. The jury brought in a verdict of guilty, with sentences varying from five to twenty years in different cases. The defendants forfeited the bail which had been posted for them and fled to Russia. Beal, the leader, became disillusioned in Russia, returned to the United States, and served a prison sentence in North Carolina until January, 1942, when he was paroled.

The rest of the story is that the trials resulted in the rout of the Communists; company unions were formed after the strike; and the mills enlisted in 1929 the services of the four ministers to endorse applicants before they could be hired as mill hands. In the opinion of the mill management, this plan, continued for a decade, worked well. Monthly conferences were held between the mill superintendent and the village pastors, and the mills did more than ever to help finance and support the churches. Efforts were also made, through trained workers, "to offset the incoming tides of materalism, unbelief, and anti-Americanism." [62] General conditions in the mills, however, remained much the same until improvements were brought about by the National Recovery Act of 1933.

Later Roman Catholic Adjustments to American Democracy

Although the Roman Catholic Church throughout the world is one in its creed and one in its loyalty to the pope in matters of faith and morals, there have been two somewhat divergent tendencies in its modern development, one conservative, the other liberal. The conservative is pretty well summed up in the word "ultramontanism." The term came into use after the Vatican Council in the middle of the last century to indicate those who agreed with Rome without qualification in matters of doctrine, discipline, and policy and were not willing to allow much scope for national differences or for any considerable measure of what has come to be called self-determination.

The liberal tendency has been called modernism on its theological side, liberalism on its social side, and both strands in this country have been summed up in European thought in the word "Americanism." By far the most outstanding exponent of the liberal tendency was the late Pope John XXIII, who in the brief four years of his reign probably did more than any other pope to point the Church toward the need of adjusting to and meeting the problems of modern civilization.

In the United States the more liberal view has been taken from the earliest times of the republic; a view due partly to its being a new country, partly to its democracy, and partly to its Constitutional separation of Church and State. These factors all influenced the first bishop of the hierarchy in the United States and the first Archbishop of Baltimore, John Carroll, who had a strong desire to adjust Roman Catholicism to the democratic traditions of America. He was not very popular with Rome because of his feeling that the Americans should nominate their own bishops, his friendly attitude toward Protestants, his deep interest in the cause of civil and religious liberty, and other reasons. His general open-minded attitude was continued by John England, first Bishop of Charleston, whose standing as an American patriot may be seen in his being invited to address the United States Congress in 1826.

These men and others like them had constant difficulties with some members of the hierarchy who were more wedded to the past and less broad-minded and tolerant. The outstanding leaders of the group that was fighting to maintain the Church in strict keeping with European Catholic practice were Archbishop John Hughes, an ecclesiastic of great force of character who, failing to secure financial grants from the State for Catholic parochial schools, fought many features of the public school system and encouraged tendencies that resulted in keeping Roman Catholics as a group largely apart from their Protestant fellow citizens; Bernard McQuaid, Bishop of Rochester, leader of the opposition to many of Cardinal Gibbons' more liberal views; and Francis Cardinal Spellman of New York, long-time leader of the conservative wing of Roman Catholicism in America.

The liberal-minded leaders following Archbishop Carroll and Bishop England were entirely loyal to the Church and its head but believed this loyalty consistent with certain adaptations—which did not compromise fundamental matters of belief—directed toward making the Church more effective and more influential in the American democracy of the nineteenth century. The main representatives of this group after the middle of the nineteenth century were different in type and background, but all were men who deserve respect. They were Isaac Thomas Hecker, Archbishop Ireland, and Cardinal Gibbons.

Hecker,[63] who came from a German Protestant background, joined the Roman Catholic Church in 1844 after a brief stay with the Brook Farm group of transcendentalists. He entered the Redemptorist order, was ordained abroad in 1849, and came to America with four fellow Redemptorists in 1851 to work among immigrant Catholics in the large cities. He became well known for his lectures on Catholic truth and was particularly effective in presenting the claims of the Church to non-Catholics.

Hecker and four of his associates—also Americans and Protestants by birth—had some difficulties with the rector major of the order in Rome, for they believed that the Church would be relatively ineffectual in the United States unless it adopted methods of work and appeal more suited to the country and the time. Acting as the agent of his associates, Hecker went to Rome in the hope of getting permission to establish a Redemptorist novitiate in America. Instead he was expelled from membership, the stated cause being that he had made the journey to Rome to promote his views without sufficient authorization. The pope dispensed him and his companions from their vows and authorized them to form a new congregation devoted to missionary work in the United States. As a result, we have the highly influential preaching order of the Paulist Fathers—legally known as the Missionary Society of St.

Paul the Apostle in the State of New York—founded in 1858, an order small in numbers but strong in intellectual and spiritual qualities.

Hecker, who edited the influential *Catholic World* from 1865 until his death, was an ardent American, deeply interested in democracy and anxious to adjust the Church to American condition.[64] His views became known to the world at large in January, 1899, through their being condemned in an apostolic letter known as *Testem Benevolentiae* addressed to Cardinal Gibbons by Leo XIII. This refers to the preface of the French translation of *The Life of Father Hecker* (by Father Walter Elliott), a book which, with its introduction by Archbishop Ireland, had great impact in France. Groups of liberal-minded French Catholics were disturbed by the facts that their clergy were hostile to the republic and in sympathy with the monarchists; that they kept aloof from modern methods and modern thought; and that they put too little emphasis on individual conviction and activity, and too much on the routine of religious observances. Largely because Hecker's views fitted so well with their own and had become so influential abroad, when his biography was translated into French in seemed important to the papacy to disavow its views, especially as Monsignor O'Connell had given them some support at the Catholic Congress in Freibourg in 1897.

The apostolic letter took the position that in keeping with the teachings of the Vatican Council the Church must constantly adhere to the same doctrine in the same sense and in the same way, though modifications in the rules of the Christian life might, in the judgment of the Church, be made from time to time. The idea that the individual could follow his own bent in keeping with modern ideas of civil liberty could not be allowed. The views which were condemned included the alleged insistence on interior initiative in the spiritual life as distinct from direction by the Church; the tendency to give too much heed to natural virtues in place of supernatural ones; the feeling that the vows of religious orders tended to interfere with true liberty; and the minimizing of certain features of Catholic doctrine.[65]

The general effect of the encyclical, with its condemnation of "modernism" and "Americanism," was to retard substantially the adjustment of Roman Catholicism to democratic conditions,[66] an effect which lasted until the ascension of John XXIII.

John Ireland,[67] Archbishop of St. Paul, was one of the most vigorous and admirable leaders produced by the Roman Catholic Church in this country. Born in Ireland he came to America, settled in St. Paul, and was ordained a priest in time to serve as a chaplain in the Union army.

When he left the army after being stricken with fever, he returned to St. Paul but continued the tradition of his old connection through the Grand Army of the Republic, in which he was always prominent. As pastor and, after 1884, bishop of the Catholic cathedral in the leading city of the North-west, he waged a lively campaign against the liquor interests and was instrumental in organizing total abstinence societies, though he never advocated prohibition. He also took the lead in many other public causes, especially as a strong opponent of political corruption and as a stanch defender of American principles.

He was particularly identified with two movements. The first was the attempt —in contrast to Bishop Hughes' efforts—to get Catholic immigrants to leave the congested cities of the East and move to the West. The second had to do with the public schools. The gist of his plan was outlined in an address before the National Education Association in 1890,[68] in which he urged a compromise: the state would pay for the secular instruction at parish schools, which should be inspected by the state and be free, the teaching being conducted by the denomination concerned. This was the plan put into effect at Faribault (from which it got its name) and at Stillwater—parochial buildings being leased to the city, which paid their running expenses. The religious instruction and devotions both before and after the regular school hours were under local pastors. Here was an honest attempt to solve the Church-State problem in the field of education.

Ireland was generally also a strong supporter of organized labor. He discussed its problems with breadth and force, fearlessly taking sides when such action seemed to him justified, as in his support of President Cleveland in the railroad strike in 1894. His independence was shown in many other ways, as when he condemned Tammany Hall, interested himself in the membership of the New York State Board of Regents, and opposed Bryanism and the adoption of bimetallism. In fact, he was always in politics, but always with clean hands and a definitely high purpose, and never in a way that identified him with petty matters.

Cardinal James Gibbons did perhaps more than any other person in the past hundred years to commend the Roman Catholic Church to the people of the United States, and to interpret its views and adjust its work so as to make them effective under the conditions of religious freedom in our American democracy. Ordained a priest in 1861, he ministered as chaplain to Federal and Confederate soldiers alike near Fort McHenry in Maryland, although his sympathies were with the Union cause. In 1868, at the age of thirty-four, he was consecrated a bishop, the youngest of twelve hundred Catholic bishops. Seven years later he became Bishop of Baltimore.

The proximity of Baltimore to Washington helped Gibbons to become the intimate friend of Presidents Cleveland, Theodore Roosevelt, and Taft. He had friendly relations too with all the other American presidents during his lifetime. Though not a partisan in national affairs, he took the deepest interest in helping to create wise public opinion on important issues. He organized and presided over the important Third Plenary Council of Baltimore in 1884, guiding it into taking a strong stand in behalf of American civil institutions. Later he took a leading part in the establishment of the Catholic University at Washington, which he served as head for its beginning until his death.

In 1887, after going abroad to receive the red biretta at the hands of his sympathetic friend Leo XIII, he preached a sermon in Rome declaring that the great progress of the Catholic Church in this country was in large part due to the liberty guaranteed by the American Constitution. He expressed his gratitude at being the citizen of a country "where the civil government holds over us the aegis of its protection, without interfering with us in the legitimate exercise of our sublime mission as ministers of the gospel of Christ." [69]

On this visit he devoted much attention to securing ecclesiastical support for the labor movement. His influence enabled him to receive the assurance that the Knights of Labor would not be condemned in the United States, and he secured the lifting of the ban against them in Canada. His plea addressed to the prefect of the Propaganda was published and created a remarkable impression, as did his efforts to prevent condemnation by the Church of Henry George's *Progress and Poverty*.

In the last decade of the nineteenth century Cardinal Gibbons identified himself actively with the experiments Archbishop Ireland was making for co-operation between the Church and the public school authorities. He even favored the reading of the Bible in the public schools if no other form of religious instruction could be provided, a position which did not receive the acceptance of most Roman Catholic bishops and priests until a half-century later.[70]

On the desirability of separation of Church and State in the United States, he had this to say in an article published in 1909:

American Catholics rejoice in our separation of Church and State, and I can conceive no combination of circumstances likely to arise which would make a union desirable to either Church or State. We know the blessings of our arrangement; it gives us liberty and binds together priests and people in a union better than Church and State. Other countries, other manners; we do not believe our system adapted to all conditions. We leave it to Church and State in other lands to solve their problems for their own best interests. For ourselves, we thank God that we live in America, "in this happy country of ours," to quote Mr. Roosevelt, where "religion and liberty are natural allies." [71]

This extract has been often quoted to show Roman Catholic commitment to the American principle of Church-State separation. It was echoed only a few years ago by Archbishop McNicholas of Cincinnati:

No group in America is seeking union of church and state; and least of all the Catholics. We deny absolutely and without any qualification that the Catholic Bishops of the United States are seeking a union of church and state by any endeavors whatsoever, either proximate or remote. If tomorrow Catholics constituted a majority of our country, they would not seek a union of church and state. They would then as now, uphold the Constitution and all its Amendments, recognizing the moral obligation imposed on all Catholics to observe and defend the Constitution and its Amendments.

It is also appropriate to quote at this point from an address delivered at Loyola University in March, 1960, by Archbishop Egidio Vagnozzi, apostolic delegate to the United States:

In practice, the Church will not interfere, and has not interfered, in local situations where the separation between Church and State may be considered the greater and more general good.

In considering freedom as applied to religious belief and worship, it is well to remind ourselves that the very concept of complete separation between Church and State is a relatively modern idea. Even some of the largest Protestant denominations were born out of a stricter and more nationalistic interpretation of a close relationship between religion and the civil power.

In the practical field of relations with civil powers, the Catholic Church shows, with reciprocal international agreements called Concordats, a considerable variety of provisions in particular questions, depending on local traditions, customs and practices. In fact, it is extremely difficult to define the neat line of demarcation between the domain of the Church and that of the State. Actually, even in some traditionally and predominantly Catholic countries, no preferential juridical recognition is granted to the Catholic Church.

As far as the United States is concerned, I feel that it is a true interpretation of the feelings of the Hierarchy and of American Catholics in general to say that they are well satisfied with their Constitution and pleased with the fundamental freedom enjoyed by their Church; in fact, they believe that this freedom is to a large extent responsible for the expansion and consolidation of the Church in this great country.

Whether they remain a minority or become a majority, I am sure that American Catholics will not jeopardize their cherished religious freedom in exchange for a privileged position.

These statements indicate perhaps better than anything else Catholic adjustments to American democracy.[72]

Chapter 14

ADJUSTMENT TO RACIAL AND RELIGIOUS
MINORITY NEEDS

Race Relations—The Negro

The early activities of the Church in the field of race relations as they affect the Negro were in the long struggle against slavery. These culminated in the Civil War and the adoption of the Thirteenth Amendment abolishing slavery. The second step, which indeed began while the struggle against slavery was still in progress, was to improve the lot of the individual Negro, primarily through education which would enable him effectively to discharge the responsibilities of his newly acquired citizenship and also to rise on the economic ladder. The third stage was to seek through political and legal means to protect the Negro from the physical, political, and economic consequences of anti-Negro bias, such as lynching, racial discrimination in voting and employment, etc. The fourth and contemporary stage is co-operation with the Negro in his struggle to break down the barriers of racial segregation and achieve full equality in a color-blind society.

The first two stages have already been discussed.[1] The third can be said to have taken place during the two decades between the first administration of Franklin D. Roosevelt and the historic decision of the Supreme Court in 1954 declaring racial segregation in the public schools to be unconstitutional.[2] Illustrative of the activities of the Church in this third stage was the statement submitted to Congress in 1934 in behalf of the Federal Council of Churches by its president, Dr. Samuel McCrea Cavert, in favor of legislation to make lynching a Federal crime.[3] It was during this same year that the Catholic Interracial Council was established in New York.[4] (Eleven years earlier the Federal Council of Churches had appointed a Committee on the Church and Race Relations and had established Race Relations Sunday.)

During World War II, partly as a result of Supreme Court decisions protecting Negro rights and partly because of the labor shortage and the liberal attitude of President Franklin D. Roosevelt, the recognition of interracial justice made great progress. This stirred up reactionary forces in various parts of the country. Unfortunate clashes occurred in urban centers, where the Negro population was disturbed and often indignant, especially because of discrimination in the armed forces and inadequate housing and recreation facilities at home. Much was said and said truly of the inconsistency between our condemnation of Nazi racialism and our all too prevalent superior attitude toward blacks.

In the new movement of protest led by the militant National Association for the Advancement of Colored People (the NAACP), an important part was played by Negro urban churches and their ministers in securing support for the Association, and at the same time for the Urban League with its similar objectives—though mainly concerned with the Negro's rights in industry rather than in government—and with more conservative methods. Similarly in this period the churches, led by the Federal Council of Churches and the National Catholic Welfare Conference, and supported by such other agencies as the Y.W.C.A. and the Methodist women of the South, became much more active in demanding the abolition of all discrimination against Negroes as Negroes.[5] These efforts reached their climax in March, 1946. At a special meeting of the Federal Council held in Columbus, Ohio, a report on "The Church and Race," prepared by a national commission which had long studied the subject, was adopted after careful consideration and without dissenting vote. It included the following statement under the subheading "The Church Must Choose":

The Federal Council of the Churches of Christ in America hereby renounce the pattern of segregation in race relations as unnecessary and undesirable and a violation of the Gospel of love and human brotherhood. Having taken this action, the Federal Council requests its constituent communions to do likewise. As proof of their sincerity in this renunciation they will work for a non-segregated Church and a non-segregated society.[6]

Notwithstanding this statement, the churches made little progress in eliminating segregation either within their own ranks or in the community at large. It was the decision of the Supreme Court in 1954 outlawing public school segregation [7] that marked the beginning of a determined effort to remove this evil from democratic America. For some six or seven years the struggle was largely confined to the courts, but progress was slow and the Negro community became impatient. The feeling grew among the Negroes that they could not depend even upon the well-meaning white liberals but must rely more and more upon their own militancy. On February 1, 1960, in Greensboro, North Carolina, four Negro college students sat down at a lunch counter and demanded service. When they were refused on the ground that only whites were welcome, they continued sitting. Thus began, modestly and almost accidentally, a Negro protest movement that was to spread throughout the nation, north as well as south, and become the major domestic issue of the sixties. Sit-ins, kneel-ins, freedom rides, picketing, and demonstrations swept the country.

It was a movement by the Negroes for the Negroes, and in it the leadership was taken by Negro clergymen. The first of these was the Reverend Adam Clayton Powell, Jr., minister of the largest Negro church in America, who entered politics as a Congressman from Harlem, the Negro section in New York City. Although some of Mr. Powell's activities, both political and social, aroused considerable criticism, he nevertheless was the first Negro clergyman to adopt a militant approach to the problem of racial segregation and discrimination. The real leadership, however, quickly passed to the Reverend Martin Luther King, Jr., and his associates. In every community it was the local Negro minister who led the protest, and the demonstration invariably started in the local church. The singing of hymns and the recitation of prayers were an indispensable part of every such demonstration. Even the most extreme of the Negro protesters, who called themselves Black Muslims and rejected Christianity, resorted to religion—the Islamic faith—in their protest. All in all, the Negro's struggle for freedom and equality during the sixties has been a struggle fought under the leadership of Negro clergymen and through the instrumentality of the Negro churches.

The non-Negro Church expressed its support and offered its co-operation. The National Council of Churches established, under the chairmanship of Presiding Bishop Arthur Lichtenberger of the Protestant Episcopal Church, a special Commission on Race and Religion, committed to support and press for civil rights legislation. Similar commitments were made by official bodies of Roman Catholics and Jews. After a conference held by President Kennedy with almost 250 religious leaders in June, 1963, an interreligious committee was formed under the chairmanship of J. Irwin Miller, president of the National Council of Churches, to battle racial discrimination throughout the United States.[8] Nevertheless, the leadership in the struggle has remained within the Negro community under the inspiration and guidance of its religious leaders.

Anti-Semitism

It is not necessary here to enter into the long story of anti-Semitism in Europe. Suffice it to say that though in the early Roman Empire, before the rise of the Christian Church to power, Jews were frequently discriminated against and persecuted because of their religion, which kept them as a group apart. Yet, after the destruction of the temple in A.D. 70 had resulted in their dispersion over the world, they began to enjoy virtually the rights of citizenship under the constitution of Caracalla in A.D. 212. But these rights were lost in the medieval world, partly because of the attitude of the Church, which was based in great measure on the connection of Jews with the crucifixion, and on their unwillingness to accept Christianity; partly because the medieval conception of citizenship rested not so much on State allegiance as on membership in some largely self-governing corporation or guild, or on privileged estate; partly because of the false accusation of "ritual murder," a charge also made by the Romans against the Christians in earlier days; and partly because of economic factors. It was in the later Middle Ages, beginning with the period of the Crusades and the terrible slaughter of Jews on the way to Palestine, climaxed at the capture of Jerusalem in 1099, that the restrictions on the Jews and their persecution reached their worst, with the ghetto, yellow badge, economic restrictions, expulsions, and other indignities. Many of the extreme discriminations and cruelties were opposed by the Church, especially by some of the popes; but the record of "Christian" Europe was on the whole far from good, and all too often foul slanders and rumors were accepted by the multitude, the Jews being even thought to be in league with the devil. Speaking generally, not until the era introduced by the American and French revolutions and the rise of the so-called secular State did the Jews regain the right which they once held under the Roman Empire to be treated like others before the law.[9]

Organized anti-Semitism, as it is known today, did not appear in the United States on any large scale until toward the close of the nineteenth century, following the wave of Jewish immigration that set in at that time. Up to then it had been mainly a matter of social ostracism, and of criticism of certain personal traits and economic tendencies that were considered by some groups to characterize most Jews. The so-called "Protocols of the Elders of Zion," now known to be spurious and to have been devised in the interest of anti-Semitism, did not appear in this country until after the first decade of the twentieth century. The whole movement seems to have been associated with the wave of reaction which followed World War I.[10]

The publication in *The Dearborn Independent*, sponsored by Henry Ford, of the "Protocols" in 1920 gave them much publicity, and the prejudice and bitterness they stirred up were great. The antagonism of the *Independent* toward the Jew was fanned by the revived Ku Klux Klan, but the anti-Semitic movement was somewhat interrupted by Henry Ford's retraction, made in 1927. The anti-Jewish movement subsided for a few years only to be reactivated by the depression and the rise of Nazi anti-Semitism.

Many groups, in their legitimate opposition to Marxian Communism, fell into the grievous error of trying to show that this has an inevitable connection with Jewish thought. Consequently there developed the dangerous movement misleadingly named "The Christian Front." Father Charles Coughlin was closely related to this group, and it was a source of some surprise that he was allowed by his Church to continue long in his agitation. He had his counterparts in Protestantism. Perhaps the most notorious was a Baptist minister, formerly allied with the political machine of the late Huey Long and more recently identified with various other movements of a Fascist tendency, the Reverend Gerald L. K. Smith of Detroit. Another militant leader of Nativist views was the Reverend Gerald B. Winrod.

The official utterances of responsible agencies and spokesmen of the Roman Catholic and Protestant Churches in this country uniformly condemn anti-Semitism, both on patriotic and on Christian grounds. One of the major functions of the National Conference of Christians and Jews, whose membership combines Protestants, Roman Catholics, and Jews, has been to combat anti-Semitism. The terrible persecution suffered by Jews under Hitler and his campaign to exterminate them shocked American Christianity and impelled the Churches to examine their own works, customs, and practices. For example, during the early sixties each of the three major faiths undertook to examine its own textbooks, used in the religious schools, to ascertain to what degree they treat other faiths unfairly.[11] In this and many other ways the Churches in the United States expressed their unanimous belief that anti-Semitism is immoral and sinful.[12]

Anti-Roman Catholicism

During the Civil War period, slavery was the supreme issue in the Protestant Churches. Hence anti-Catholic agitation was in abeyance. It was not until the most violent years of political reconstruction after the war were over that the anti-Catholic movement, developed earlier by the "Nativist" agitation and "Know-Nothingism," again came to the front. The fears behind this recurring movement were just then given an objective basis in the minds of many people by two authoritative pronouncements of great importance: the *Syllabus of Errors*[13] of Pope Pius IX in 1864, and the Vatican Decree of 1870.[14] Among the "errors" condemned in the *Syllabus* were statements such as these:

15. Every man is free to embrace and profess that religion which, guided by the light of reason, he shall consider true.

24. The Church has not the power of using force, nor has she any temporal power, direct or indirect.

27. The sacred ministers of the Church and the Roman pontiff are to be absolutely excluded from every charge and dominion over temporal affairs.

42. In the case of conflicting laws enacted by the two powers, the civil law prevails.

45. The entire government of public schools in which the youth of a Christian state is education, except (to a certain extent) in the case of episcopal seminaries, may and ought to appertain to the civil power, and belong to it so far that no other authority whatsoever shall be recognized as having any right to interfere in the discipline of the schools, the arrangements of the studies, the conferring of degrees, in the choice or approval of the teachers.

47. The best theory of civil society requires that popular schools open to children of every class of the people, and, generally, all public institutes intended for instruction in letters and philosophical sciences and for carrying on the education of youth, should be freed from all ecclesiastical authority, control and interference, and should be fully subjected to the civil and political power at the pleasure of the rulers, and according to the standard of the prevalent opinions of the age.

48. Catholics may approve of the system of educating youth, unconnected with Catholic faith and the power of the Church, and which regards the knowledge of merely natural things, and only, or at least primarily, the ends of earthly social life.

67. By the law of nature, the marriage tie is not indissoluble, and in many cases divorce properly so called may be decreed by the civil authority.

80. The Roman Pontiff can, and ought to, reconcile himself, and come to terms with progress, liberalism and modern civilization.[15]

The latent anti-Roman Catholic feeling in the country was given additional stimulus by the Vatican Decree of Papal Infallibility of 1870. Many thoughtful people who had no sympathy with the Know-Nothing and Ku Klux groups were alarmed at the concentration in the hands of the pope of so much power over members of the Church the world over. They feared that his declared supremacy in his ex cathedra utterances in the field of "morals" as well as of religion might bring friction between the American democracy and the papacy. "The Roman Pontiff cannot err in defining matters of faith and morals" was the passage from the decree which caused so many misgivings in its possible application to pronouncements bearing on American social legislation.[16]

Almost as significant from the standpoint of possible Church-State friction was the constitution adopted by the same council on the Church of Christ, or, as it is often called, on the Pope of Rome.

When, therefore, anyone says that the Pope of Rome has only the office of supervision or of guidance, and not the complete and highest power of jurisdiction over the entire Church not merely in matters of faith and morals, but also in matters which concern the discipline and administration of the Church throughout the entire world, or that the pope has only the chief share, but not the entire fullness of this highest power, or that his power is not actual and immediate either over all and individual Churches, or over all and individual clergy and faithful let him be anathema.

The *Syllabus*, the Vatican Decree, and other factors resulted in a growing anti-Catholic spirit during the 1870's. It first manifested itself prominently in national politics during the Cleveland-Blaine campaign for the presidency in 1884.[17]

The infusion of the religious issue in the campaign was due to a variety of causes connected with desperate attempts to win votes. An effort was made to draw away Irish Catholics from their traditional support of the Democratic party, on the ground that Grover Cleveland, who was the son of a Presbyterian minister, was "a Presbyterian bigot," while James G. Blaine's mother was a Roman Catholic. Even so influential a journal as the *Irish World* ardently supported the Republican ticket.

On October 9, the eleventh hour in the campaign, when it looked altogether probable that Blaine would carry the pivotal state of New York, the Reverend Samuel D. Burchard, a Presbyterian minister, in the course of a speech advocating Blaine's election at a great rally at the Fifth Avenue Hotel in New York, referred to his opponents as the party of "rum, Romanism and rebellion." This charge was bitterly resented by the Democrats, especially as it was not disowned by Blaine. It proved a boomerang. Cleveland carried New York, but only by a plurality of 1,047 votes in a total of more than a million. Blaine himself felt that the Reverend Dr. Burchard's unfortunate remark lost him enough Roman Catholic votes to turn the scales against him, and thus the introduction of the religious issue into the campaign brought failure.[18]

Three years after the 1884 presidential campaign, the American Protective Association, commonly known as A.P.A., was founded in Iowa. The central idea that brought the seven initiators together was opposition to Roman Catholicism, and among the association's definite aims were the curbing of immigration and the preservation of the public schools from what was considered the Catholic purpose to thwart their activity.[19]

The association received a great stimulus as a result of the panic of 1893, when the scarcity of jobs brought about a campaign in favor of the native American and in opposition to the immigrant, especially the Roman Catholic. As usual, the association flourished in the rural Protestant areas and was in part a movement antagonistic to the urban Catholic population, which had been demanding a share in the public school funds. Its million votes went almost entirely to the Republican party because of fear of the Church connections of the Democrats, who under Irish leadership had secured the almost solid Roman Catholic vote.

This movement[20] died down after the McKinley campaign of 1896, which split its forces, but there arose in the next decade another that was equally threatening. In 1908 the first American Catholic missionary congress met in

Chicago, the largest body of prelates, priests, and laymen ever brought together in the New World. It was followed by the appointment of two additional cardinals for America. These and other events caused alarm in some Protestant circles. Inflamed by *Tom Watson's Magazine, The Menace,* and other journals, various organizations were established to combat what was considered to be the danger to American institutions from a large group of people holding allegiance to the pope. One was launched, according to its own statement, "in the belief that the Roman Catholic Political Machine, in its political intrigues and its interference with established American institutions, is the deadliest enemy to our civilization and liberties." [21]

Another incident which contributed to tension between Protestants and Roman Catholics involved Bellamy Storer, who was in turn minister or ambassador of the United States to Belgium, Spain, and Austria-Hungary, all strongly Catholic countries, during the administrations of William McKinley and Theodore Roosevelt. Storer and his wife were devout Catholics, who desired, among other things, to have the American government prevent the sending of Protestant missionaries to the Philippines, and more especially to secure the advancement of Archbishop Ireland to be a cardinal.[22] Mr. Storer apparently misinterpreted the devotion of Governor Theodore Roosevelt to the archbishop, and his assurance that he would personally be pleased to see the latter given the cardinal's hat, as a formal authorization to the ambassador to request the appointment. After Roosevelt became president Storer called on the pope and delivered what he believed to be the president's suggestion. The fact of the interview reached the press, and Mr. Roosevelt wrote his ambassador to be more careful in the future.[23] Storer's approach to the Vatican in the name of Roosevelt was fruitless; to Roosevelt's disappointment, Ireland was not named a cardinal at the consistory of December, 1905, and three months later Storer was asked to resign his ambassadorship.

There was some introduction of the religious issue in the Taft presidential campaign in 1908. Taft was opposed by some Protestants because he was a Unitarian and, perhaps paradoxically, because he was thought to have been over-friendly to the Roman Catholic Church in the Philippines and in his negotiations at Rome with the Vatican.[24] However, the most serious instance of religious intrusion in a presidential campaign occurred in 1928 [25] at a time when the revived Ku Klux Klan was at the height of its power.

The Ku Klux Klan started in 1866 with the idea of saving the white civilization of the South by overthrowing the "carpetbag" and Negro regimes. Its nomenclature, white-hooded garb, night parades, and secret rites appealed to a large Protestant group of the South, especially in the rural regions; but not until its revival in 1921 in Atlanta, Georgia, did its Nordic racial propaganda include a strong anti-Jewish and anti-Catholic program.[26] The Klan began to become a national factor in 1920, when it engaged professional promoters. "Native, white, Protestant supremacy" became its watchword. The fact that the pope was an Italian, and that some twenty thousand or more Roman Catholic priests in the United States owed spiritual allegiance to him, was made much of. The Klan propaganda emphasized the fact that the pope was a political autocrat and that the Roman Catholics were gaining in political power. The growth of the Knights of Columbus (founded in New Haven, Connecticut, in 1882) and of the Roman Catholic Church frightened the Klan members. They circularized a bogus oath attributed to the Knights, passed from mouth to mouth stories of rifles buried under Catholic churches and under halls of the Knights, and made tens of thousands of ignorant people believe that the government was in danger of being seized by the hierarchy.

The work of the Klan came to a head in the presidential campaign of 1928, but it was almost equally prominent in 1924 in opposing the candidacy of Governor Alfred E. Smith, a Roman Catholic, for the nomination at the Democratic convention in Madison Square Garden, New York. The Committee on Resolutions was almost evenly divided as to whether the Ku Klux Klan should be condemned by name; the Ku Kluxers—supported by certain politicians in the interest of party harmony—finally secured elimination of the resolution that would have done so. These groups supported William Gibbs McAdoo, who, though not a member of the Klan, had differed from his opponent, Governor Smith, in not wishing to have opposition to it referred to specifically and so secured large Klan support. The division was so violent between the two groups that a compromise candidate, John W. Davis, was finally selected. In accepting the nomination he did not specifically name the Klan but clearly referred to it in his statements denouncing intolerance, bigotry, and race prejudice. In August he said, "I am unalterably opposed to the evident purpose of the secret organization known as the Ku Klux Klan, as disclosed by its public acts."[27] Both Democrats and Republicans found it expedient that year to reaffirm the constitutional guarantee of religious liberty, following the precedent of the Democratic platform of 1896.[28]

As the election of 1928 approached, it became increasingly clear that the Democratic candidate would probably be Governor Smith. In April and May, 1928, the *Atlantic Monthly* published an exchange of letters between Charles Clinton Marshall, a New York Episcopalian and lawyer of high standing, and Governor Smith. Mr. Marshall took the ground that there existed an irreconcilable opposition between the root principles of the Roman Catholic Church and the American democratic State. The reply, entitled "Catholic and Patriot; Governor Smith Replies," had an introductory note by the editor, Ellery Sedgwick:

This is an historic incident, historic for the country and for the Church. Now for the first time in the republic's history, under a constitution which forever forbids religious tests as qualifications for office, a candidate for the Presidency has been subjected to public questioning as to how he can give undivided allegiance to this country when his church restricts the freedom of his choice; and the candidate has answered—answered not deviously and with indirection, but straight-forwardly, bravely, with the clear ring of candor.[29]

The exchange of letters and the literature it produced, especially Mr. Marshall's book, *The Roman Catholic Church in the Modern State*,[30] and the replies of the Reverend Dr. John A. Ryan[31] and others, are important in the annals of American Church-State relations.

As expected, Governor Smith was nominated by an overwhelming majority, even though the Southern Baptist Convention, representing nearly four million people, had by unanimous vote warned the Democratic party against nominating him,[32] and Senator J. Thomas Heflin charged that Smith's candidacy was "the crowning effort of the Roman Catholic hierarchy to gain control of the United States." [33]

And so the battle went on. Prohibition was the major issue for the Methodists and some other Protestant groups,[34] but the alleged Roman Catholic "menace" was always in the background. Although the Anti-Saloon League was un-doubtedly the dominant force against Smith, it did not actively take up the religious issue. There were further grounds of opposition to the former governor of New York based on his Tammany affiliations[35] and other matters, but the religious issue played a considerable part. On the whole, though Gov-ernor Smith, who was not elected, referred to it only two or three times in his campaign, the general effect on intelligent American voters was to impress them with the fact that the Roman Catholic Church as such was not being used as a national political weapon.

The most encouraging single thing about the controversy in 1928 was that it caused no recorded acts of physical violence or bloodshed. This shows that the United States had learned one of the fundamental lessons of a democratic government. Another indirect good result was the organization, under the leadership of former Secretary of War Newton D. Baker representing the Protestants, Professor Carlton Hayes, the Roman Catholics, and Roger Straus, the Jews, of the National Conference of Christians and Jews, which has ever since been a potent factor in seeking to prevent intolerance in this country.

The Klan has become considerably less aggressively anti-Catholic in recent years; indeed, in 1957 a major Klan organization in the South opened its membership rolls to Roman Catholics. However, some of its fellow travelers among ministers of Protestant denominations continued much of its spirit, especially Gerald L. K. Smith and Gerald B. Winrod, editor of *The Defender Magazine,* both considered extreme Nativist leaders. Smith has been a presidential candidate. Winrod was a candidate for the Senate under Republican auspices in Kansas in 1938 but was defeated, largely by a campaign in behalf of tolerance by a group of Kansas ministers.

The religious issue returned to the national political scene in 1960 with the nomination of Senator John F. Kennedy, a Roman Catholic, for the presidency.[36] However, the intensity and bitterness were much less than in the 1928 campaign. The American people had undergone considerable education in interreligious relations in the intervening thirty-two years. In addition, Kennedy faced the issue frankly and early in his campaign. He disarmed many of his opponents by declaring unequivocally his commitment to the principle of the separation of Church and State and his opposition to the use of Federal funds for parochial schools and the exchange of ambassadors with the Vatican, two specific points that most excited Protestants.

The turning point in the campaign in respect to the religious question was an address made by Mr. Kennedy to some four hundred members of the Ministers Association of Greater Houston, Texas, on September 13, 1960, and, perhaps even more important, the answers given by him to the ministers' questions after the formal address. Because of the importance of the event, we set forth here the full report as issued by the Religious News Service.

"Whatever issue may come before me as President—on birth control, divorce, censorship, gambling or any other subject—I will make my decision in accordance with what my conscience tells me to be the national interest, and without regard to outside religious pressures or dictates," he declared.

Sen. Kennedy said he did not speak for the Catholic Church on public matters and the Church did not speak for him.

The Democratic nominee's remarks were contained in a prepared speech he delivered to the ministers. At the end of the address, he answered questions from the floor. He was applauded frequently during the talk and the question period.

Sen. Kennedy said he believed in an America where no religious body seeks to impose its will directly or indirectly upon the general populace or the public acts of its officials—and where religious liberty is so indivisible that an act against one Church is treated as an act against all.

"For," he continued, "while this year it may be a Catholic against whom the finger of suspicion is pointed, in other years it has been, and may someday be again, a Jew—or a Quaker—or a Unitarian—or a Baptist."

The Senator said the Presidency should not be "humbled" by making it the instrument of a single religious group, nor "tarnished" by withholding it from the members of any religious group.

In his address, Sen. Kennedy replied to the attack made against him by a group of Protestants headed by Dr. Norman Vincent Peale, pastor of Marble Collegiate Reformed Church, New York. The group had charged that a Roman Catholic President would be unable to withstand "pressure" from the hierarchy.

Such groups, he said, were seeking to "subvert" Article VI of the Constitution which declares that there shall be no religious test for office.

"If they disagree with that safeguard," he added, "they should be openly working to repeal it."

Mr. Kennedy asked to be judged on the basis of his 14 years in Congress and not on the basis of quotations taken "out of context" from the statement of Catholic Church leaders in other countries that he said were "rarely relevant" to the situation in the United States.

Pamphlets and publications which use these statements, he said, always omit the 1948 statement of the American bishops which endorses Church-State separation.

The Senator said he did not intend to disavow his Church or his views in order to win the election.

"If I should lose on the real issues," he declared, "I shall return to my seat in the Senate satisfied that I tried my best and was fairly judged.

"But if this election is decided on the basis that 40,000,000 Americans lost their chance of being President on the day they were baptized, it is the whole nation that will be the loser in the eyes of Catholics and non-Catholics around the world, in the eyes of history, and in the eyes of our people."

Also of great importance was a statement on "Religious Liberty in Relation to the 1960 National Campaign," issued in September, 1960, by more than a hundred American religious leaders of all faiths, lay and clerical, including Bishop G. Bromley Oxnam, Dr. Reinhold Niebuhr, Bishop James A. Pike, Cardinal Richard Cushing, Bishop Arthur Lichtenberger, and Rabbi Dr. Maurice N. Eisendrath. The statement is too long to be quoted in full, but the ten principles suggested as guidelines for action by voters in the 1960 campaign are equally relevant to all future elections in which one or more of the candidates may be affiliated with a minority religion or no religion at all, and therefore they merit being set forth here.

1. The exclusion of members of any family of any faith from public office on the basis of religious affiliation violates the fundamental conditions of a free democratic society, as expressed in the spirit and letter of our Constitution.

There must be no second-class citizenship in the United States, whether it be based on religion, race, class, or national origin.

2. The religious faith of a person of integrity will influence his private and his public conduct. The relevance of faith to his personal spiritual life is a private matter. His religious faith can give him an insight, independence, and composure that will enable him to make dispassionate judgments in the crisis of public life, and lead the nation to a more creative fulfillment of its destiny.

The bearing of the religious view of any candidate of any party upon his decisions in public office is a public matter. Inquiry regarding this relevancy is an exercise of responsible citizenship, if conducted in such a way as not to violate the constitutional prohibition against any religious test for public office.

3. No citizen in public office dare be false either to his conscience or to his oath of office.

Both his conscience and his oath impose responsibilities sacred under the law of God. If he cannot reconcile the responsibilities entailed by his oath with his conscience, then he must resign, lest he fail his nation and his God.

4. The fact that a major religious group has so far never furnished the nation with a candidate who won election to a particular public office does not obligate the voters to elect a candidate of that faith to that office solely to demonstrate our devotion to democracy.

This would establish a religious test for public office much narrower than the one complained of, and contrary to the obvious intent of the Constitution. It would, furthermore, focus attention on a marginal qualification rather than on the essential qualities of personal integrity, leadership capacity, and policies relating to central issues.

5. No religious organization should seek to influence and dominate public officials for its own institutional advantage.

The exercise of public office must always be in the public interest, and serve the welfare of the whole community, local or national. The rights and liberties of each and every voluntary association must be respected and protected as long as they do not infringe upon the like rights of others.

6. Every person of every faith must be accorded full religious liberty, and no person should be coerced into accepting any religious belief or practice. No religious group should be given special preference or advantage by the state, nor be allowed to use state agencies for the restriction of other faiths.

7. A candidate's faith, and his affirmations of it, as they bear upon his responsibilities in public office, should be viewed in their best light rather than their worst, and the response and expectation of the nation should be such as will encourage him to attain the highest spiritual and moral realization which his own faith can inspire.

8. Just as the choice of candidates for public office should be based upon integrity, leadership, and convictions on basic issues, so the public officer after his election is obligated to make his appointments to subordinate positions on a non-discriminatory basis, using competence and record rather than religious affiliation as the criteria of selection.

9. The President's participation in important national and community religious functions can be a fine symbol of the common concern for the spiritual welfare of the nation. But if for reasons of his own he feels that participation in a particular religious ceremony is not in order, it would be contrary to the civic character of the American Presidency for him to feel obligated to accept the invitation.

Participation in special religious ceremonials is an aspect of the Presidency that is secondary in importance to matters of Constitutional responsibility, such as the conduct of foreign affairs, the governing of the nation, and the execution of the laws, and it must be weighed in proportion to these functions in any estimate of a candidate's suitability for that office.

10. Every public official who is a member of a religious group should, of course, take into consideration the spiritual and moral principles of his faith, in confronting the decisions he must make. But in our pluralistic society he will recognize that the values in historic faiths other than his own must be brought to bear upon the problems of the day. He alone, under the judgment of God, can fully appraise the force and applicability of all such values and advice for his situation, and he should seek to apply all in such a way as to enhance and undergird the best interests of the nation.

Because of these and other factors the deplorable experience of 1928 was not repeated in 1960.

It cannot, of course, be assumed that Mr. Kennedy's religion was not an important factor in the campaign.[37] Undoubtedly there were many who voted against him solely or primarily because he was a Roman Catholic, although it is equally probable that many others voted for him just for that reason. On the whole, the election of Mr. Kennedy marked a new era in interreligious relations in the United States. It is unlikely that in the future either major party will again be reluctant to nominate an otherwise acceptable candidate solely because he is a Roman Catholic. Indeed, probably both parties will often seek to "balance" their tickets by nominating a Roman Catholic for either the presidency or the vice-presidency so as, hopefully, to attract Roman Catholic voters or at least not alienate them. It may be suggested that such a development is as unfortunate as the exclusion of Roman Catholics from these nominations; in either case, religion is deemed a factor in eligibility for political office in violation of the spirit of the principle of Church-State separation.

The Irish Question and American Politics

Irish Catholic political agitation showed itself in this country in several ways.

First and foremost, it aided the cause of Irish freedom.[38] The political question of Irish freedom was one which the hierarchy and priesthood of the Roman Catholic Church in the United States considered of vital importance and promoted almost unceasingly for years. As a result, the Church-State problem was considerably complicated, for most Protestants believed that Roman Catholics as such, in spite of many legitimate civil and social grievances, had already secured religious freedom in Ireland, and that the agitation had as a major ultimate purpose the setting up of an independent Roman Catholic

State which would be unfriendly to England and Protestantism. However, the Irish Free State (Eire), when it came into existence, though recognizing the "special position of the Catholic Church as the guardian of the faith professed by the majority of the citizens," granted "freedom of conscience, and the free practice and profession of religion to all." Furthermore, all religions existing in the country at the time the constitution went into force were recognized, and it was stipulated that no religion might be endowed by the State or subjected to disability of a discriminatory character [39]—relatively liberal provisions in view of the fact that about 93 per cent of the population of the new State were of the same religious body.

The agitation by the Catholic press, and to some extent by the priesthood, lasted until Ireland gained legal recognition of her freedom by the treaty of 1921 with Great Britain. Thereafter this form of political activity on the part of the Church became mostly a thing of the past.

Second, it opposed England.[40] A striking example of this aspect of the problem was the refusal of an Irish militia regiment in New York to parade in honor of the Prince of Wales when he visited here in 1860.[41] Another was the defeat of the Anglo-American Treaty of Arbitration in 1897, due mainly to Irish influence in the United States Senate. Fortunately, since the granting of freedom to the Catholic portion of Ireland after World War I this feeling of hostility to England on the part of Irish-Americans has largely disappeared, and in World War II many prelates of Irish descent supported Great Britain.

Third, it promoted the interests of the Democratic party, which first concerned itself with the Irish cause. Thus the Irish vote was handed over almost solidly, and until recent years often under ecclesiastical leadership, to a single party,[42] just as for decades the Negro vote went almost solidly to the Republicans. However, the Negro vote shifted practically en masse to the Democratic party after Franklin D. Roosevelt became president, and likewise a substantial portion of the Irish Catholic vote left the Democratic party to support Dwight D. Eisenhower, although it probably returned (whether temporarily or not it is too early to say) to support Senator Kennedy.

Co-Religionists in Other Countries

Concern for the welfare of co-religionists in other countries has created frequent contacts—sometimes of friction but more often of co-operation—between American Churches and the government. They have been confined principally to two fields: the protection of American missionaries and their property and interests, especially in Asia, and the prevention of persecution in Europe. Difficulty in the first field has occurred especially in places where there has been a lack of law and order, or where the government in control has been totalitarian, or unsympathetic to a given religious group, as with the Portuguese colonics in Africa and their Protestant missions, or certain Mohammedan countries and all Christian groups.

In the early days of American Protestant missions it was assumed that the Churches could and should depend for the protection of property on the diplomatic support of the American government, and if necessary on the influence of the American navy. But in the last forty years a strong conviction has grown up that the Church should not rely on armed protection from the American State. In 1928 the Foreign Missionary Conference of North America declared that ". . . force for the protection of missionaries is in general a serious hindrance to missionary work and . . . the effort should be made to secure for those missionaries desiring it, the privilege of waiving their right to such protection." [43]

In general Protestant missionary societies, believing in the separation of the functions of Church and State, have not favored having their missionaries assume political posts, as distinct from service on various educational, relief, and other social welfare commissions, without at least temporarily giving up their official connection with the home society. In the early days this policy was extended to disapproval of accepting financial grants for missionary educational work from foreign governments, especially when these were ruling native peoples. It was feared that missionaries might side with the government as opposed to the native population in whose interest they had gone to the foreign field.

The issue of religious freedom as related to the American Protestant churches working in Latin America has been raised in a serious way by the actions of the Catholic hierarchy. We have various treaties with these countries, generally treaties of amity or friendship, which give our citizens liberty of conscience and worship.[44] These countries also generally give Protestants the protection of their laws providing for religious toleration, though perhaps half of them have some more or less close links with the Roman Catholic Church. Mexico, Brazil, Chile, Uruguay, and Cuba are among those in which the two powers have been separated. It is true that the overwhelming majority of the people throughout South and Central America are Catholic. But American Protestant missionaries claim the same right as American Catholic priests to the sympathetic help of the American State Department in obtaining visas and in protecting their legal rights to carry on their work.

The American Catholic hierarchy's protest against Protestant missionary work in Mexico and in Central and South America were made guardedly but clearly in the statement on "Victory and Peace" issued November, 1942, by the members of the administrative board of the National Catholic Welfare Conference in the name of all archbishops and bishops of the United States:

> Citizens of these countries are bound to us by the closest bonds of religion. They are not merely our neighbors; they are our brothers professing the same faith. Every effort made to rob them of their Catholic religion or to ridicule it or to offer them a substitute for it is deeply resented by the peoples of these countries and by American Catholics. These efforts prove to be a disturbing factor in our international relations.[45]

The Federal Council of Churches issued a reply in which it asserted that the principle of religious liberty and the recognition of the rights of religious minorities in the United States and throughout the world, entitled the Protestant churches to continue their missionary activities in Latin America and that these activities did not constitute a peril to the good relations between the United States and the nations of Latin America.[46]

To this *America*, the national Jesuit weekly, responded with an editorial. The constitutional freedom of religion enjoyed in the United States, it said, was not generally enjoyed in Latin America, where only Uruguay granted complete separation of Church and State. The Catholic bishops' statement, it continued, was really only a plea to Protestant missionaries not to attempt to embarrass the Latin Americans in their Catholic faith and thereby disturb our international relations and directly make for disunity in the Western Hemisphere.[47]

It is impossible in this volume to enter into a detailed discussion of the treatment of Protestant missionaries in Latin American countries and the repercussions in the United States. We will merely mention briefly the situation in Colombia, where the situation has probably been most grave. Protestant missionaries and churches there have been the victims of violence, discrimination, and persecution. The extent of the harassment has varied from year to year and place to place, but it has always been present in a significant degree.[48] Illustrative incidents may be mentioned: the closing of a number of Protestant schools by the government inspector in 1954 (although the nation's president thereafter ordered that they be reopened); an assertion by the National Association of Evangelicals in 1955 that some twenty Protestants had been murdered in a recent new outbreak of religious persecution; continued reports of the stoning of Protestant churches and assaults upon clergymen; a report appearing in the New York *Times* on January 23, 1956, asserting that pressures, both subtle and violent, against Protestants in Colombia were mounting steadily and that in the small villages in the interior, Catholic priests, who were the highest local authorities, incited the population against Protestants so that many missionaries were assaulted and churches were burned (a report vigorously

denied by Catholic spokesmen in the United States); the refusal to allow the
evangelist the Reverend Dr. Billy Graham to hold a public evangelical service
in January, 1962, on the ground that under the Colombian constitution only
the Roman Catholic Church was allowed to propagandize.[49] Many similar incidents could be cited.

There followed protests by Protestants and others to the United States Department of State and other governmental agencies, and demands that American government funds be withheld from Colombia.[50] Protestant-Catholic
relations in the United States were exacerbated. However, a hopeful sign that
the situation may be improving is indicated by a report given in December,
1962, to the National Council of Churches' Division of Foreign Missions by
its Latin American expert. Colombia's attorney general had recently ruled, he
said, that the country's constitutional guarantee of religious liberty applied to
all religious groups unless they violated "Christian morals" of the country's
laws, and religious proselytism and the dissemination of religious literature
were permissible throughout the land.[51]

Closely connected with the protection of missionaries in foreign lands is
the plight of Christians and Jews in other parts of the world where American
churches believe they are being persecuted or oppressed and therefore demand
effective protests by our government. Notable among such oppressed groups in
earlier years were the Armenians, in whose welfare American Protestants were
especially interested; the Irish, about whom American Roman Catholics of
Irish extraction were greatly concerned; and the Jews in Russia, Turkey,
Rumania, Poland, and Nazi Germany, whose persecution outraged not only
American Jews but all people of good will.

In addition, there is today considerable bitterness, particularly among American Catholics, regarding the restrictions upon religious liberty and freedom
of worship in Communist-controlled countries. A host of books, articles, and
lectures on religion behind the Iron Curtain have been produced in America
under Catholic sponsorship reflecting the views of the Catholic Church and
all painting the picture in dark colors.[52] Cardinal Mindszenty, Archbishop
Stepinac and other Roman Catholic priests and prelates imprisoned behind the
Iron Curtain are considered martyrs to the cause of religious freedom. Provisions in the constitution of Soviet Russia and the other Russian satellite countries purporting to assure freedom of worship as well as protestations from
official governmental sources are discounted. Great weight is placed upon
reports by émigrés from eastern Europe and Catholic missionaries coming out
of Communist China, and upon information originating from underground
sources, all of which belie the constitutional provisions and official statements
and indicate a reign of terror not only against the Roman Catholic Church

but against all churches and religions. How, Catholics ask with a logic difficult to meet, can one expect freedom of religion from a political system that deems religion an enemy of the people and is committed to its extirpation?

Catholics have been particularly grieved at the relative Protestant silence on the persecution of Roman Catholics behind the Iron Curtain. They contrast this with the Protestants' vigorous objections to persecution of Protestants in Spain, in Colombia, and in other Catholic-influenced countries. They ask whether the Protestants are not applying a double standard and whether religious persecution and infringements upon freedom of worship are less horrendous when committed by non-Catholic states than when committed by Catholic states.

It is indisputable that Protestants are generally a good deal less pessimistic than Catholics about the status of religion in Communist countries. Protestant clergymen who visit Soviet Russia return with reports that are considerably more charitable to the Communists in respect to their treatment of religion than can be found in Catholic publications. They are more likely than are the Catholics to give credence to the declarations of churchmen inside Soviet Russia that they do enjoy freedom of worship and are not subject to persecution by the government.

Protestants can hardly be under any illusions as to the Communist view of religion and the ultimate Communist goal in respect to religion. Nor can they be unaware of the violent anti-religious activities of the revolutionary Soviet government or of the Communist governments in the satellite countries. Many Protestants, however, find some measure of justification for this state of affairs in the reactionary policies and practices of the Orthodox Church in Russia during the czarist era and of the Roman Catholic Church in eastern Europe in the period between the wars. They look at Mindszenty, Stepinac, and the other Roman Catholic prelates not as religious martyrs but as political activists. They are inclined to believe that Russia's obvious desire to reach a rapprochement with the West will cause it to subordinate its long-term goal of eliminating religion and for an indefinite period to ameliorate the condition of the churches and of religion behind the Iron Curtain.

A rather startling development in respect to the status and treatment of the Roman Catholic Church in the Communist countries of Europe (though not of Asia or Cuba) was the reported effort on the part of both the Vatican and Soviet Russia during the reign of Pope John XXIII to improve relations between the two powers. Undoubtedly, a direct result of this has been the easing somewhat of restrictions on Roman Catholic bishops and priests behind the Iron Curtain. To what extent the effort to better relations between the Vatican and Soviet Russia will be continued by Paul VI it is too early to tell. Should the present pope carry forward the policy initiated by his predecessor—a policy almost diametrically opposite that of Pius XII, John's predecessor—it is safe to predict that the situation of the Roman Catholic Church and its bishops and priests in European Communist countries will continue to improve.

Closely related to the problem of overseas religious missionaries is that of the use of religious agencies in carrying out the program of the Peace Corps. The Peace Corps was established in 1961 as a pool of trained men and women sent overseas by the United States or through private institutions and organizations to help foreign countries meet their urgent needs for skilled manpower. Shortly after the Corps was established, its director, R. Sargent Shriver, Jr., announced that twelve of its initial projects would be carried out through contracts with private and voluntary agencies, half of them religious agencies. With Federal funds, they would engage in teaching, agriculture, and community development in Asia, Africa, and Latin America. However, the director said, no religious group would receive Peace Corps funds unless it forswore all proselyting on the project it undertook.[53]

The announcement brought forth protests, first from the United Presbyterian Church in the U.S.A. and the American Jewish Congress,[54] and then by other, principally Protestant, organizations and spokesmen, much as the Baptist Joint Committee on Public Affairs,[55] the National Association of Evangelicals,[56] and the National Lutheran Council.[57] The position taken by these groups was endorsed editorially by *The Christian Century* [58] and the New York *Times*.[59] The objection to participation by religious groups and missionary societies in Peace Corps projects was based on the belief that their use of government funds would violate the principle of Church-State separation, and that the groups would confuse their governmental obligations with their missionary zeal, thereby imperiling the success of the Peace Corps program.[60] The resolution adopted by the American Jewish Congress in June, 1961, stated in part,

Any use by the religious groups of government funds or of Peace Corps personnel in their church-sponsored projects would, we believe, violate the constitutional mandate of separation of Church and State.

Any requirement of religious belief or affiliation among Peace Corps personnel, or any veto power in the selection of Peace Corps volunteers by religious bodies, would violate the constitutional prohibition against religious tests for public office.

Any effort, whether deliberate or coincidental, on the part of church groups either to spread their religious beliefs or enhance their good name through participation in the Peace Corps program overseas would violate the constitutional mandate against use of governmental funds or personnel to promote religious teachings or practices.

There is grave danger that such groups, because of their long tradition of proselytising activity, will confuse their governmental obligations with their missionary zeal. There is also grave danger that the operations of the Peace Corps may be severely handicapped by the presence of church groups as participants. It is not unlikely that many citizens of the countries where such Peace Corps projects are launched will view the program with suspicion as being motivated not so much by the goal of furthering the cause of peace as by promoting the missionary ends of the church groups involved.

The protests proved effective. In December, 1961, the director of the Peace Corps announced that it would sign no contracts with Church-related agencies.[61] No reason was given for this reversal of policy other than a belief that it would be a mistake for the Peace Corps to sponsor projects conducted by Church-related groups.[62]

The Movement for Protecting Minority Rights and Improving Interfaith Relations

During the past half-century, especially since the close of World War I, various national agencies or divisions of agencies have been devoted to the cause of promoting religious liberty, protecting the rights of religious minorities, and improving relationships among religious groups in the United States. Among the most significant of these are the Religious Liberty Association of America, the American Civil Liberties Union, the National Conference of Christians and Jews, the Fund for the Republic's Center for the Study of Democratic Institutions, the Joint Baptist Committee on Public Affairs, Protestants and Other Americans United for Separation of Church and State, the Department of Religious Liberty of the National Council of Churches, the Synagogue Council of America and its constituents, and the Jewish civic organizations—the American Jewish Congress, the American Jewish Committee, and the Anti-Defamation League of B'nai B'rith.

The Religious Liberty Association of America came into existence in 1888 under the name of the National Religious Association. With headquarters in Takoma Park, Washington, D.C., it works in close co-operation with the Seventh Day Adventist movement. Indeed, it came into being in connection with a discussion in Congress providing for a Sunday rest law.

The association has taken a broad interest in the whole problem of religious liberty in this country and publishes a quarterly "Magazine of Religious Freedom" entitled *Liberty*. As it has nine affiliated regional associations and a representative in each state, it keeps in touch with all proposed legislation that seems to infringe on the basic religious-freedom guarantees of our government. It has been particularly active in opposing restrictive Sunday legislation, because the Seventh Day Adventists, for what they believe to be Biblical reasons, observe Saturday instead of Sunday as the holy day. It has filed briefs *amicus curiae* ("friend of the court") in suits involving infringement of religious liberty or the separation of Church and State.[63] A statement of principles, aims, and objectives issued in 1936 sets forth its basic philosophy in the following short paragraph:

> The Association holds that the State may properly enact laws regulating the relationship of man to his fellow man, but that it has no right to pass measures which have to do with man's relationship to God or religion. The right to disbelieve may be as sacred as the right to believe. The right to dissent should be sacredly guarded.[64]

The American Civil Liberties Union was born out of the attacks made on civil liberties, especially freedom of speech, in the early days of World War I. The former American Union Against Militarism created a civil liberties bureau that soon became independent and in 1920 expanded into the present American Civil Liberties Union. This ably conducted organization has dealt with all sorts of subjects involving civil liberties under the American Constitution—censorship of radio, press and moving pictures; civil rights of employers, organized labor, and unorganized workers; defense of racial, religious, and radical minorities; freedom of speech on the platform, and in schools and colleges; and the rights of conscientious objectors under conscription laws. The organization takes the ground that the law has a right to step in when overt acts dangerous to the State arise but not when some individual or group merely made a radical utterance. Its position on civil liberty is that of Thomas Jefferson, who said, "It is time enough for the rightful purpose of civil government for its officers to interfere when principles break out into overt acts against peace and good order." [65]

The efforts of the Union have been mainly before the courts, where its attorneys volunteer their services. Among the important religious-liberty and Church-State cases in which it has participated either as *amicus curiae* or by providing counsel for the plaintiffs are the Everson parochial school bus case, the McCollum and *Zorach* v. *Clauson* released-time cases, the Maryland notary public oath case (*Torcaso* v. *Watkins*), the Regents' prayer case (*Engel* v. *Vitale*), and the Bible-Lord's Prayer case (Schempp and Murray).

The National Conference of Christians and Jews, originally called the National Conference of Protestants, Catholics and Jews, was established in 1928 to provide an effective agency in which individuals from the three main religious groups in the country might work together on matters of common concern in their various communities. Dr. S. Parkes Cadman, long president of the Federal Council, the Honorable Newton D. Baker, formerly secretary of war, and Charles Evans Hughes, later chief justice of the Supreme Court, were among the leaders in the movement. The conference early took as one of its key sayings the words of Mr. Hughes: "When we lose the right to be different, we lose the right to be free." It has consequently upheld from the first the right of men to differ in their religious beliefs, but it has stood for something more than tolerance, namely, for a sympathetic understanding of religious views different from one's own. As stated by the first Protestant co-chairman of the conference, the Honorable Newton D. Baker, "The aim of the National Conference of Christians and Jews is to moderate—and finally to eliminate—a system of prejudices which disfigures and distorts our business, social, and political relations." [66]

In the past the conference was subject to considerable criticism because of its avoidance of what it called "controversial issues." However, under the dynamic leadership of its present president, Dr. Lewis Webster Jones, the Conference has during the past five years adopted an entirely different approach to interreligious conflict. It has assumed as one of its principal functions the task of providing a forum where representatives of the major faiths, and often persons of no religious affiliation, can freely and frankly explore even the most sensitive of public issues that divide them. These interreligious "dialogues" and other conference activities, especially those conducted by its project, Religious Freedom and Public Affairs, have proved extremely helpful in alleviating friction and conflict among the religious groups over such controversial questions as religion in the public schools, government aid to church schools, birth control, and censorship.[67] Mention should also be made of one of the most valuable operations of the conference, its daily *Religious News Service*, by far the most comprehensive source of current information on matters of Church and State.

Also engaged actively in providing forums for the exchange of views on controversial issues in the area of Church and State is the Center for the Study of Democratic Institutions established by the Fund for the Republic. Its face-to-face discussions have helped ameliorate interreligious tensions, and the books and pamphlets that have come out of them (particularly the paperback *Religion in America*, edited by John Cogley) have become valuable additions to the literature of the field of Church-State and interreligious relations.[68]

The organization Protestants and Other Americans United for Separation of Church and State (POAU) came about as a result of the Supreme Court's decision in the Everson parochial school bus case. It was launched under the leadership of Dr. Joseph M. Dawson, executive director of the Baptist Joint

Committee on Public Relations, in January, 1948, by the issuance of a manifesto signed by John A. Mackay, president of Princeton Theological Seminary; Edwin McNeill Poteat, president of Colgate-Rochester Divinity School; Methodist Bishop G. Bromley Oxnam; Louie D. Newton, president of the Southern Baptist Convention; and Charles Clayton Morrison, editor emeritus of *The Christian Century*.[69] The manifesto set forth the immediate objectives of the new organization: enlightenment of public opinion on religious liberty, prevention of further breaches in the wall of separation between Church and State, opposition to diplomatic relations with the Vatican, repeal of laws granting public funds to church schools, invoking the aid of the courts in maintaining the separation of Church and State, opposition to Federal aid to parochial schools, and protection of the public schools from sectarian domination.[70]

POAU has taken tremendous strides since its formation. It owns two spacious, well-equipped buildings in Washington and maintains a full-time paid staff headed by Glenn L. Archer, formerly dean of the Law School of Washburn University in Kansas, and Dr. Stanley R. Lowell. It publishes a monthly newsletter, has established active functioning chapters in many of the major American cities, and helps in the financing of litigation aimed at preventing the use of public funds for sectarian institutions.[71] Its program and activities are strongly opposed by spokesmen for the Roman Catholic Church, who charge it with being motivated by anti-Catholic bigotry.[72]

Like the POAU, the Department of Religious Liberty of the National Council of Churches grew out of concern with what was deemed the aggressive policies of the Roman Catholic Church in American political and national life. It was organized by a group of Protestant clergymen, including, besides Dr. John McKay and Bishop Oxnam, Dr. H. S. Coffin, Bishops O'Connell and Peabody, and the Reverend Roswell Barnes. This informal group sponsored studies of individual communities in which Roman Catholic influence was felt to be dominant. It also sponsored a book by Dr. James H. Nichols, published in 1951 under the title *Democracy and the Churches*. In 1948 the group combined with the Joint Committee for Religious Liberty of the Federal Council of Churches, and in 1952 its name was changed to Department of Religious Liberty of the National Council of Churches.

The first executive director of the Department was Dr. Claud Nelson, who served until 1960, when he was succeeded by the present director, the Reverend Dean M. Kelley. The activities of the Department have included opposition to the "Christian Amendment" and to Federal funds for parochial schools, and defense of the Supreme Court's decisions in the field of Church-State relations.[73]

The Baptist Joint Committee on Public Affairs (formerly Baptist Joint

Conference Committee on Public Relations), under the leadership first of Dr. Joseph M. Dawson and then of Dr. C. Emanuel Carlson, has been active in struggling for religious liberty and preserving the separation of Church and State. Its activities have included the filing of a brief *amicus curiae* in the McCollum released-time case, the issuance of a monthly newsletter on Church-State affairs, the opposition through testimony before Congressional committees and through public education to Federal aid to parochial schools and to an exchange of ambassadors with the Vatican.[74]

In discussing Protestant efforts toward religious liberty it is appropriate at this point to set forth the latest statement on the subject on the part of the Protestant Churches throughout the world. This is the statement adopted by the Third Assembly of the World Council of Churches at New Delhi, India, on December 4, 1961.

1. Mankind is threatened by many forces which curtail or deny freedom. There is accordingly urgent need to reinvigorate efforts to ensure that every person has opportunity for the responsible exercise of religious freedom.

2. Christians see religious liberty as a consequence of God's creative work, of his redemption of man in Christ and his calling of men into his service. God's redemptive dealing with men is not coercive. Accordingly human attempts by legal enactment or by pressure of social custom to coerce or to eliminate faith are violations of the fundamental ways of God with men. The freedom which God has given in Christ implies a free response to God's love, and the responsibility to serve fellow-men at the point of deepest need.

3. Holding a distinctive Christian basis for religious liberty, we regard this right as fundamental for men everywhere.

4. We reaffirm the Declaration on Religious Liberty adopted by the World Council of Churches and the International Missionary Council in August-September 1948, and hold to its provisions. We recognize the Universal Declaration of Human Rights, proclaimed by the United Nations in December 1948, as an important instrument in promoting respect for and observance of human rights and fundamental freedoms.

5. Although freedoms of every kind are inter-related, religious liberty may be considered as a distinctive human right, which all men may exercise no matter what their faith. The article on religious freedom in the Universal Declaration is an acceptable standard, always provided that it be given a comprehensive interpretation.

> Everyone has the right to freedom of thought, conscience and religion; this right includes freedom to change his religion or belief, and freedom, either alone or in community with others and in public or private, to manifest his religion or belief in teaching, practice, worship and observance

6. The recognition of the inherent dignity and of the equal and inalienable rights of all members of the human family requires that the general standard here

declared should be given explicit expression in every aspect of society. Without seeking to be inclusive, we illustrate as follows:

7. Freedom of thought, conscience and belief, even considered as inner freedom, requires freedom of access to reliable information.

8. Freedom to manifest one's religion or belief, in public or in private and alone or in community with others, is essential to the expression of inner freedom.

  a. It includes freedom to worship according to one's chosen form, in public or in private

  b. It includes freedom to teach, whether by formal or informal instruction as well as preaching with a view to propagating one's faith and persuading others to accept it.

  c. It includes freedom to practise religion or belief, whether by performance of acts of mercy or by the expression in word or deed of the implications of belief in social, economic and political matters, both domestic and international.

  d. It includes freedom of observance by following religious customs or by participating in religious rites in the family or in public meeting.

9. Religious liberty includes freedom to change one's religion or belief without consequent social, economic and political disabilities. Implicit in this right is the right freely to maintain one's belief or disbelief without external coercion or disability.

10. The exercise of religious liberty involves other human rights. The Universal Declaration proclaims, among others, the right to freedom of peaceful assembly and association; the right to freedom of opinion and expression including freedom to seek, receive and impart information and ideas through any media and regardless of frontiers; the prior right of parents to choose the kind of education that shall be given to their children; freedom to participate in choosing the desired form of government and in freely electing officials; freedom from the retroactive application of penal law; and freedom to leave and to return to one's country and to seek asylum elsewhere.

11. The freedom with which Christ has set us free calls forth responsibility for the rights of others. The civil freedom which we claim in the name of Christ must be freely available for all to exercise responsibly. It is the corresponding obligation of governments and of society to ensure the exercise of these civil rights without discrimination. It is for the churches in their own life and witness recognizing their own past failures in this regard to play their indispensable role in promoting the realization of religious liberty for all men.

The Roman Catholic Church too is concerned with the question of religious liberty. With the vigorous backing of the American Bishops, Vatican Council II has been considering a resolution upholding the principle of religious liberty. While this resolution, if adopted, would not go as far as the statement adopted by the World Council of Churches, it nevertheless would be an historic landmark in Roman Catholic adjustments to democratic values, and particularly to the American concept of freedom of conscience.

One of the most significant developments in the Church-State field during the past fifteen years has been the active part played in it by Jewish organizations, religious and civic. The major Jewish religious agencies are affiliated with the Synagogue Council of America, which acts as a co-ordinating body for them. The constituents of the Council are the Central Conference of American Rabbis, the Rabbinical Assembly, and the Rabbinical Council, representing respectively the Reform, Conservative, and Orthodox rabbinical bodies, and the Union of American Hebrew Congregations, the United Synagogue of America, and the Union of Orthodox Jewish Congregations of America, representing respectively the Reform, Conservative, and Orthodox synagogue organizations.

The chief Jewish civic organizations operating in the field are the American Jewish Congress, the American Jewish Committee, and the Anti-Defamation League of B'nai B'rith.[75] In addition to these national organizations, local Jewish community councils have been established in practically all the major cities in the United States. In 1944 these national and local organizations formed an overall co-ordinating council under the title of the National Community Relations Advisory Council, choosing as its executive director Isaiah Minkoff, who has continued to act in that capacity since then.[76]

In 1948 the Synagogue Council of America and the National Community Relations Council formed a Joint Advisory Committee on Religion and the Public School (later changed to Joint Advisory Committee on Religion and the State), and it is through this committee (whose present executive secretary is Philip Jacobson) that the largest part of Jewish activity in the field of Church and State has taken place. Through this committee, for example, the Jewish organizations filed friend-of-the-court briefs in the McCollum, Sunday law, Regents' prayer, and Bible reading cases in the United States Supreme Court, although in the last three cases separate briefs were filed jointly by the American Jewish Committee and the Anti-Defamation League, inasmuch as these two organizations had withdrawn from the National Community Relations Advisory Council in 1952.[77]

Chapter 15

ADJUSTMENTS IN PUBLIC EDUCATION

The Major Issues Involved

Many of the major issues in the United States between Church and State have been in the educational field. The American public's firm belief in the capacity of education—especially public education—to solve the complicated problems facing democracy has resulted in an enormous development in public schools (of which a good example is the increase in high schools between 1880 and 1960 from 800 to 25,784).[1] Through constitutional enactment, legislation, and court decisions the country has registered its determination to develop a system of public schools in harmony with American ideals, and with no loss of that religious freedom and the resulting Church independence which the founders of the republic incorporated in the Bill of Rights.

At the outset it is essential to understand the constitutional status of the public school as detached from every religious organization, and the constitutional provision in many states prohibiting grants from public taxation to any form of parochial or denominational school. These specific provisions are found primarily in the state constitutions and bills of rights, since general education is not a matter transferred by the states to the national government under the Federal Constitution but is reserved to the states, whose representatives in Congress have, however, authorized certain educational projects and financial appropriations in the interest of education by the United States. The principal exceptions are in such obvious cases as the education of army, navy, marine, and air officers, and of the reservation Indians, who have been considered the special "wards of the nation." The Federal government has also, and increasingly, aided other forms of public education through such agencies as the land-grant colleges, the National Youth Administration, the National Defense Education Act and the College Aid (higher education facilities) Act of 1963; but neither Congress nor the president nor any political party has ever adopted as a policy the transfer of major responsibility for the general conduct of public education from the community and the state to the nation as a whole. It must be constantly explained to visitors from abroad

351

that American public schools are conducted *not* by Washington but by thousands of towns and villages scattered through the country under the general constitutional and statutory provisions of their respective states. These are and of course must continue to be consistent with the provisions regarding religious freedom in the Federal Constitution.

Typical of the state constitutional provisions requiring the maintenance of a common public school and forbidding the use of tax-raised funds for sectarian schools are those in the Arizona constitution of 1912 and the New York constitution of 1938.[2]

Arizona (1912), Article XI

Sec. 1. [Public school system] The Legislature shall enact such laws as shall provide for the establishment and maintenance of a general and uniform public school system. . . .

Sec. 2. [Supervision of school system] The general conduct and supervision of the public school system shall be vested in a State Board of Education, a State Superintendent of Public Instruction, county school superintendents, and such governing boards for the State institutions as may be provided by law.

. . . .

Sec. 7. [Sectarian instruction] No sectarian instruction shall be imparted in any school or state educational institution that may be established under this Constitution, and no religious or political test or qualification shall ever be required as a condition of admission into any public educational institution of the State, as teacher, student, or pupil; but the liberty of conscience hereby secured shall not be so construed as to justify practices or conduct inconsistent with the good order, peace, morality, or safety of the State, or with the rights of others.

Article IX

Sec. 10. [Aid to sectarian schools] No tax shall be laid or appropriation of public money made in aid of any church, or private or sectarian school, or any public service corporation.

New York (1938), Article XI

Sec. 1. [Common schools] The legislature shall provide for the maintenance and support of a system of free common schools, wherein all the children of this state may be educated.

. . . .

Sec. 3. [Common school, literature and the United States deposit funds] The capital of the common school fund, the capital of the literature fund, and the capital of the United States deposit fund shall be respectively preserved inviolate and the revenue of the said funds shall be applied to the support of common schools and libraries.

Sec. 4. [Use of public property or money in aid of denominational schools prohibited; transportation of children authorized] Neither the state nor any sub-division thereof shall use its property or credit or any public money, or authorize or permit either to be used, directly or indirectly, in aid or maintenance, other than for examination or inspection, of any school or institution of learning wholly or in part under the control or direction of any religious denomination, or in which any denominational tenet or doctrine is taught, but the legislature may provide for the transportation of children to and from any school or institution of learning.

It is also relevant and interesting to set forth the provisions of the two latest states to be admitted to the Union, Alaska and Hawaii.

Alaska (1959), Article I

Sec. 4. [Freedom of Religion] No law shall be made respecting an establish-ment of religion, or prohibiting the free exercise thereof.

Article VII

Sec. 1. [Public Education] The legislature shall by general law establish and maintain a system of public schools open to all children of the State, and may provide for other public educational institutions. Schools and institutions so estab-lished shall be free from sectarian control. No money shall be paid from public funds for the direct benefit of any religious or other private educational institution.

Hawaii (1959), Article I

Sec. 3. [Freedom of Religion, Speech, Press, Assembly and Petition] No law shall be enacted respecting an establishment of religion or prohibiting the free exer-cise thereof, or abridging the freedom of speech or of the press, or the right of the people peaceably to assembly and to petition the government for a redress of grievances.

Article VI

Sec. 6. [Appropriation for Private Purposes Prohibited] No tax shall be levied or appropriation of public money or property made, nor shall the public credit be used directly or indirectly, except for a public purpose. No grant shall be made in violation of Section 3 of Article I of this constitution.

Article IX

Sec. 1. [Public Education] The State shall provide for the establishment, sup-port and control of a statewide system of public schools free from sectarian control, a state university, public libraries and other educational institutions as far as may be deemed desirable, including physical facilities therefor. There shall be no segre-gation in public educational institutions because of race, religion or ancestry; nor shall public funds be appropriated for the support or benefit of any sectarian or private educational institution.

Beginning with Massachusetts in 1855, within about sixty years over thirty states adopted constitutional provisions forbidding the granting of public funds —in some cases with a few minor specified exceptions such as orphan asylums— to any denominational or sectarian institution.[3] The movement was greatly accelerated by the effort of President Grant in 1875 to secure a Federal constitutional amendment on the subject.[4] This was generally thought unnecessary and undesirable, but the Federal government has shown repeatedly by later actions its determination that none of its educational grants or appropriations should be made to denominational or sectarian institutions at the elementary and secondary school level. Furthermore, in view of the guarantees of the Federal Constitution, the special provisions in some states against financial contributions from public funds to parochial or denominational schools, and the general provisions in the other states regarding public school education under public control, it seems unlikely that any law proposing to give direct financial aid to other than the regular public schools would pass the courts.

From a study of the constitutions quoted and similar constitutional provisions in other states, five general conclusions emerge:

1. Though the Federal government, under the interpretations of the Fourteenth Amendment by the Supreme Court, protects religious freedom[5] and the separation of Church and States in the states,[6] all matters involving the administration and curriculum of American public schools, except for a few groups like the Indians, are cared for by the states.

2. State constitutions lay great emphasis on public education under the control of duly elected or appointed state officials, but without any attempt to force pupils to attend public schools as distinct from private or parochial schools.

3. Almost all states by constitution or statute have tried to prevent any state funds from reaching parochial or denominational schools, though they provide exemption of taxation for such schools, and in some instances and under specified conditions permit free bus transportation, free textbooks, free lunches, and free medical care for their pupils.

4. Sectarian or denominational teaching in public schools was specifically prohibited by most states even before it was ruled unconstitutional by the Supreme Court in the McCollum case,[7] and there has been much difference in state legal requirements on reading the Bible and repeating the Lord's Prayer at school exercises,[8] although this matter is now settled by the Supreme Court decision in the Schempp-Murray cases.[9]

5. Freedom of conscience in religious beliefs and worship is everywhere protected.

It is clear that these provisions have come to be considered part of the American creed. They cannot be altered without state constitutional changes, and these in turn are subject to being ruled out if inconsistent with the guarantees of religious freedom in the Federal Constitution.

It is realized that the public school in a democracy is almost necessarily a secular institution, being intended for pupils of all religious groups. This, however, does not and should not imply that it is anti-religious, and a people with our background should not and would not permit it to become anti-religious. Many people would go farther, believing that every public school should show its sympathy with a spiritual outlook that involves recognition of the existence of God as the creator of the world and of man, and the Judaeo-Christian teaching of our duty to Him and to our neighbors. These are the foundations of our national creed based on the Declaration of Independence, the spirit of the Constitution, the Ordinance of 1787, the decisions of our higher courts, and the papers of Washington, Jefferson, Lincoln, and our other great statesmen. What it all means is that the State, which is essentially a lay body, without trying to cover all education, and leaving certain vital tasks to Church and home, undertakes during a few hours each day to give mental and moral discipline, and instruction in certain secular subjects deemed essential for all future citizens—the process being carried out in an atmosphere of social idealism.[10]

The history of the inauguration and development of the public school system, which in the early days often involved a struggle with the Church, has already been treated.[11] Here we are concerned with problems that are still more or less acute, made so partly by the activity of various religious pressure groups and partly by the determination of most thoughtful people in the United States to keep Church and State separate, yet at the same time to see that our public schools co-operate in wise and legal ways with the moral forces represented by the Church (including the synagogue) and the home. It is generally conceded that neither the parochial school nor the Sunday school, nor both of these historic institutions together, important as they are, nor the modern vacation Bible school, can completely solve the problem of aiding the Church and home in providing religious education for the young. Many believe, therefore, that the pupils of our public schools desiring religious instruction must be reached by some specific and effective additional plan.

The two general plans which have received the most consideration are (1) religious education in the public school curriculum, generally as an option, and (2) religious education by churches for pupils desiring it, generally outside public school buildings.

Religious Education in the School Curriculum

The question of adequate religious education in a democracy is both highly important and very complicated. The general absence of religion in the curriculum of the public schools, where most of our future citizens receive the major part of their education, means that large groups of youth not reached by the churches have no regular religious instruction. The situation is more serious than most people realize. It is a result of our transfer from Church to State during the past century and a half of the major task of molding the minds and characters of our children, and of the belief of many that this transfer involves not only public neutrality in the whole field of religion but public indifference.

In general, Americans are almost equally concerned about two things: that sectarianism in every form shall be kept out of our public schools, and that the schools shall not be dominated by irreligion, which would be out of keeping with the best American tradition.

There is and has for many years been a widespread belief that the fundamental data of religion must be made known to public school pupils in school as part of the school curriculum. Five different types of proposals have been put forward to achieve this end. While some of them have apparently been ruled out by the Supreme Court's decision in the McCollum and later cases, it nonetheless seems worthwhile to describe them, for they contain ideas which when modified to meet Supreme Court requirements may provide bases for constitutionally and otherwise sound educational projects. The first might be called the "common denominator" or "three faiths" plan; the second, the interdenominational Christian education plan; the third, the "historical" method plan; the fourth, the incidental study of religion through the general liberal arts courses; and the fifth, the ethical teaching plan.

Under the common denominator plan [12] representatives of the Protestant, Roman Catholic, and Jewish faiths agree on certain fundamental statements regarding the religious and moral teachings common to all three groups which will be taught as an optional course—conscientious objectors being excused. The proponents of this plan assert that it at least shows that the importance of religion as a subject of study is recognized.[13] Simple bibliographies refer pupils to books recommended for further study, if desired.

The plan has been tried on a small scale in a few places. Whether it would pass the courts is at best uncertain. In any case, a major difficulty—though perhaps not insuperable—is to get agreement on the part of all concerned as to the content of the instruction. Some states with a large rural population have made successful attempts to issue syllabi of Bible study, for which credit is given in optional high school courses. For instance, the state board of education of Virginia issued in 1933 a series of courses in the Old Testament and in New Testament history and literature with the title *Official Syllabus of Bible Study for High School Pupils*. The commission in charge of planning the series included the state superintendent of education, a Protestant minister, a Roman Catholic priest, a Jewish layman, the president of a college, and two university professors. The courses proposed had the unanimous approval of this committee. Special attention was called to the fact that references were provided from the King James, Douay, and Leeser (Jewish) versions.[14]

It will be noticed that this plan requires the co-operation not only of Protestants and Catholics, as in England, but also, in many sections of the country, of Jews. This is likely to be difficult to obtain in most cases because of the position taken by the major Jewish organizations against this method of religious education. The Statement of Policy and Position, entitled "Safeguarding Religious Liberty," issued by the Synagogue Council of America and the National Community Relations Advisory Council through their Joint Advisory Committee, has this to say on the subject:

> We are opposed to any public school program that seeks to inculcate as doctrine a body of principles, beliefs or concepts that is represented as the "common core" of several or all religious faiths. The effort to extract from the religions current among us such a common denominator or "common core" can lead only to a watering down, a vitiation, of all that is spiritually meaningful in every religious faith. We submit, moreover, that attempts at religious inculcation in the public schools, even of articles of faith drawn from all religions and endorsed by representatives of all, violate the traditional American principle of separation of church and state.

Thus, for example, after the Zorach decision of 1952, representatives of the Protestant Council of New York, the Roman Catholic Archdiocese, and the New York Board of Rabbis (the latter with extreme reluctance) for months attempted jointly to work out an acceptable "common core" program for use in the New York City public schools. The endeavor finally came to an end when the Board of Rabbis decided to inform the Protestant and Catholic representatives and the city Board of Education that agreement on a program was impossible and that no useful purpose would be served by continuing the effort to arrive at it.[15] In Indianapolis, on the other hand, a "common core" program based on the Ten Commandments was agreed upon by a Protestant minister, a Catholic priest, and a rabbi (here, too, the latter with extreme reluctance) but was not introduced into the public schools because the attorney for the Board of Education advised the board that it violated the Constitution.[16]

The proposal has also been criticized by the American Council on Education on the ground that it "suggests a watering-down of the several faiths to the point where common essentials appear" and that this "might easily lead to a new sect—a public school sect—which would take its place alongside the existing faiths and compete with them." [17]

A modification of the plan outlined, which has much to commend it for older high school students in some communities, would be to have each of the three faiths prepare a statement, entirely constructive in character, regarding its own history and tenets. If it were elected by all it would enable each group to learn the point of view of the other two groups. This would give a minimum of instruction on the basic facts of religion, to be supplemented outside the school by such classes as the different churches might wish.

The interdenominational Christian education plan has been tried out in a number of communities in Illinois, Ohio, Vermont, and the South, especially communities with a relatively homogeneous Protestant population. Typical was the city of Elgin, Illinois, where the plan was put into effect in 1938.[18] The students were given the religious education work in the classroom, under trained teachers but on an interdenominational basis. The classes gave instruction in the fundamental teachings of the Bible, especially the outstanding characters of the New Testament, the later leaders of the Church, and the truths of Christianity. They took place one day a week and were preceded by a devotional service led by one of the children, with the singing of hymns. The objective of the classes was "to release the dynamic of the Christian religion" in the lives of the boys and girls, "in order that they may consciously experience and gladly share that 'abundant life' which is the portion of those who keep their values straight." The ultimate purpose was to provide through religion a basis for strong character. The budget, which amounted to nearly $10,000 a year, was raised by the seventeen Protestant churches represented in the Council of Christian Education. It was believed by those connected with the movement that it did much to encourage higher ideals and standards of conduct. However, the Supreme Court's decision in the McCollum case would seem quite clearly to make this plan unconstitutional if the instruction is held within the public school buildings.

The purpose of the third, or historical method, plan is to have an objective course in the history and teachings of religion given to all pupils in high schools, and thus to recognize the important role religion in forming the ethics and culture of our day. There is no sectarian religious instruction, but merely a frank recognition of the part which religion has played in the formation of our literature, history, government, art, moral standards, etc. The plan has been put into effect without offense in many high schools—indeed, to teach history leaving out religion entirely is quite impossible. Some advocate an extension of this plan. For instance, such a book as *The Bibles of the World*, giving the sacred scriptures of all nations, with brief introductions, might be used as a textbook. It would not take the place of denominational instruction in Church Sunday school or at home but would give students in simple form the story of the growth of religion from that of primitive people through polytheism to Christian theism. It would be an introduction to the more thorough courses in the history of religion and comparative religions as provided in colleges and universities.[19] It would also show that there is no necessary antithesis between religion and science. Many thoughtful people think that some such emphasis in instruction is important to prevent the growth of materialism and secularism.[20]

The advocates of the plan are constantly calling attention to the fact that the boasted neutrality of the American public school in the matter of religion tends to be interpreted by many as an endorsement of anti-religious secularism. The students become exposed to all the major social forces of the nation except religion and consequently tend to think that the State does not consider it a matter of importance. This group believes that the home and the Church, especially those denominations that are not authoritarian in character, seem incapable of providing ample religious instruction—as distinct from facilities for worship, which most of its supporters think the school should not provide. Thus the only choices, they believe, are (1) the development by Protestants, as well as Catholics, of parochial schools, and (2) the objective teaching by qualified teachers, using the historical method, of the basic facts of religion in the public school curriculum. Recognizing the social values to democracy of the public school in which all groups meet, they dismiss the parochial school alternative as an undesirable general solution and accept the plan of objective teaching by the historical method. They believe that religious subject matter, as distinct from religious devotion, should not be separated from other subjects of instruction but should be a part of public education, omitting of course any attempt at denominational indoctrination—which should be left entirely to the Church, the church schools, and the home. They also believe that, though doctrinal teaching would be unconstitutional in public education, there is nothing contrary to the Constitution in imparting the facts about the origin, history, and meaning of religion, treated historically, to Jew, Catholic, Protestant, and agnostic alike.[21]

The fourth plan, the incidental study of religion through the general liberal arts courses,[22] is related to the preceding. It is advocated by those who do not believe that religion with a view to indoctrination can properly under our Constitution be specifically taught as a school course but who think that it is unfair to religion and to society to have it entirely taboo in general school teaching. The plan encompasses adequate objective references by teachers to religious subject matter in the study of such subjects as history, literature (including the Bible), social sciences, music and art, and in community service. Its proponents hold that the Judaeo-Christian tradition is an essential basis of our democracy, that it should therefore not be disregarded in public education, and that due regard should be paid the Bible, not in special Bible-study classes, but as part of the literature program. In their view such teaching would not be unconstitutional, under Supreme Court decisions, if conducted by regular public school teachers specially trained for the purpose. They would be merely imparting knowledge about religion to those wishing it, just as in a course in government the policies of Republicans, Democrats, Socialists, and Communists might all be presented without any attempt to convert a high school student to any political party.

This view is supported by the opinion of the Supreme Court in the Schempp-Murray cases. The Court emphasized that its decision banning devotional Bible reading and recitation of the Lord's Prayer did not mean that the study of the Bible for its literary and historic qualities, or the study of religion presented objectively as part of a secular program of education, would necessarily violate the First Amendment.

Various other ingenious modifications of this historical or cultural teaching of religion have been proposed. For example, at Hunter High School, New York—a tax-supported institution—a class in the "Problems of Democracy" has paid special attention to the historical place of the Church and its role in national life today. The course has included visits to a Jewish temple and to Catholic and Protestant churches, and at each of these a minister of the faith traced its history and basic beliefs. One of the results has been the discovery that the great religious bodies hold many truths in common.[23] Similar plans have been tried in other high schools, and by some Protestant churches.

The study of various communities where an attempt has been made to introduce courses bearing on religion in public schools makes clear that certain things should be borne in mind when and if such experiments are made in the future. These seem to be the basic requirements:

1. That all plans for courses dealing with religious subjects should be strictly in keeping with the constitution and laws of the state and the nation and with our historic American separation of Church and State.
2. That arrangements for such courses should be made after informal consultation with local Protestant, Catholic, and Jewish groups.
3. That all courses should be of a scholarly character and taught objectively by well-trained teachers.

4. That the point of view of teachers in all courses should be undenominational and should show, when occasion arises, the common factors underlying religion considered historically.

5. That there should be no attempt to teach dogma, and no theological indoctrination—leaving these to be left entirely to the Church, the religious school, and the home.

6. That courses should show the contributions of religion to our modern civilization and culture.

7. That the obligations of democracy to religion for its origin, growth, and present status in this country should be clearly brought out.

8. That religious literature, especially that of the Bible, should be emphasized, each student being allowed to use the version favored by his religious group.

9. That instruction should stress the importance of the Church (including the synagogue) and its institutions as a factor in local life.

10. That the influence and responsibility of the churches in meeting modern national and international problems should receive due attention.

11. That religion should be broadly considered as fundamentally not only the worship of God but also the service of one's fellow men—truths taught in both Old and New Testament and in the fundamental American charters.

12. That the needs of high school students especially should be considered.

13. That tolerance and religious freedom should be emphasized.

14. That the courses should be optional.

This discussion has considered only the debatable proposal that optional courses in religion, even though restricted to its literary significance and its historical contributions to thought, culture, and social welfare, should be provided by public school authorities. The plan suggested was therefore necessarily confined to a minimal basis which might receive general support in some communities, and would offer little more than the historic framework for religious teaching in home, church, and religious school. It would not take the place of the latter but would at most provide an introduction to an understanding of the meaning and significance of religion and the part it plays in the modern world. When we come to discuss the development of religious courses by voluntary action on "dismissed" time and given outside school buildings, we shall be confronted by no such limitations of content and scope.

The Champaign, Illinois (McCollum), Case

The decision by which the Supreme Court invalidated the Champaign, Illinois, plan for religious instruction in the public schools has already been summarized in Chapter 5 of this book. Here we will consider only the reactions to the decision and some of its consequences.

The decision was expected by many constitutional lawyers. It disappointed most Roman Catholics [24] and Protestant Evangelicals but was praised by most Jewish agencies, by *The Christian Century,* Unitarians, and other liberal Christian groups, and even by many Baptists, who saw its importance from the standpoint of Church-State separation. The executive head of the International Council of Religious Education, which has done so much to advance the weekday religious education plan in America, expressed the views of many thoughtful religious leaders. He was naturally disappointed at the McCollum case decision but stated that the Protestant Churches should do three things: seek clarification of the law, help weekday systems to conform to the law, and find other and more effective ways that are definitely constitutional to combat increasing secularism.[25]

Unfortunately much of the discussion of the decision by the general public, and especially by those who opposed it, was based not on the constitutional questions involved but on the desirability of weekday religious education from the standpoint of inculcating in public school children some knowledge of religion. There was, however, a general recognition by responsible religious leaders that the form of religious instruction in public school buildings by the churches must be abandoned and some "dismissed-time" or other constitutional plan substituted as aid to home and Church in preventing the education of future citizens from being too dominantly secular.

A study published by the National Education Association in the early summer of 1949 entitled *The Status of Religious Education in the Public Schools* showed that the states were adjusting their programs of religious education to conform to the McCollum decision. For example, the Michigan State Board of Education ordered all released-time classes stopped in that state. Oregon required religious education classes to be moved away from public school buildings. South Carolina—one of the most conservative states—announced that credit toward graduation would no longer be given for Bible study classes, and teachers would no longer be certified by the state for Bible teaching. Ohio left the whole matter to local discretion after taking account of the McCollum decision. At least six states announced that no changes were necessary, chiefly because their classes in religion were not held on school property.

Today, more than fifteen years after the McCollum decision, it appears that on the whole both the public schools and the churches have adjusted to it. Religious instruction of the type given in Champaign is no longer carried on within public schools in the large cities, although it may be continuing in some rural communities, particularly in the South.[26]

The decision itself is still the subject of considerable criticism,[27] particularly on the part of spokesmen of the Roman Catholic Church,[28] because of its strict application of the principle of Church-State separation and the recognition—later proved true—that the effect of the decision would extend far beyond the banning of religious instruction within public school buildings during school hours. Thus, in November, 1948, the bishops, speaking through the National Catholic Welfare Conference, issued an important statement in which they asserted that the First Amendment was adopted simply to prevent governmental establishment or preference of one sect over others. The statement then continued,

If this practical policy be describe by the loose metaphor "a wall of separation between Church and State," that term must be understood in a definite and typically American sense. It would be an utter distortion of American history and law to make that practical policy involve the indifference to religion and the exclusion of cooperation between religion and government implied in the term "separation of Church and State" as it has become the shibboleth of doctrinaire secularism. . . .

We, therefore, hope and pray that the novel interpretation of the First Amendment recently adopted by the Supreme Court will in due process be revised. To that end we shall peacefully, patiently and perseveringly work. . . .

We call upon our Catholic people to seek in their faith an inspiration and a guide in making an informed contribution to good citizenship. We urge members of the legal profession in particular to develop and apply their special competence in this field. We stand ready to cooperate in fairness and charity with all who believe in God and are devoted to freedom under God to avert the impending danger of a judicial "establishment of secularism" that would ban God from public life.[29]

Religious Education Outside Public School Buildings (Released and Dismissed Time)

The McCollum decision outlawed released-time religious instruction during school hours on public school premises. But did it also outlaw such instruction if not conducted on public school premises? The Board of Education and the Council of Religious Education in Champaign, where the suit originally arose, assumed that it did, for they discontinued all religious instruction during public school hours and substituted after-school-hours instruction.[30] Other public school authorities agreed, but the overwhelming majority either took a contrary position or decided to wait for further clarification by the Supreme Court.[31] In any event, in most communities where released-time religious instruction was conducted during school time off school premises, the programs were continued, in the belief that they were lawful. Before we reach the legal question, however, something should be said of the history and extent of the released-time movement.[32]

There has been considerable confusion as to the exact meaning of the terms "released time" and "dismissed time." Some use the former to describe a program under which during the school day those children wishing to participate in religious instruction may do so, returning to their secular studies at the conclusion of their religious instruction. The term "dismissed time" is used when the period of religious instruction is the last period of the school day, so that in effect the children participating in the religious classes are "dismissed" form their secular studies while the non-participating children remain under the usual closing hour. Others make no distinction based on the time of excusal and use "released time" to encompass both situations, while "dismissed time" is used to describe a plan under which all the children are dismissed early with the expectation, but not requirement, that they will attend religious classes. This latter definition seems preferable, since as far as constitutionality is concerned it would seem to make no difference at what time the participating children are excused, the sole constitutional issue being whether the fact that the non-participating children must remain in class tends to make the program coercive.

Co-operative weekday church schools, which had their origin in France after the overthrow of the old regime in 1882,[33] were first effectively organized in this country in Gary, Indiana, in 1914 by an able superintendent of schools, Dr. William A. Wirt. The released-time plan, as there developed, did not involve some of the later dangers pointed out by the Supreme Court in the McCollum case. Superintendent Wirt, originator of the plan, insisted that the custody of a pupil was not to be shared between school and church either on school or church property or on the streets. Ignoring this precaution, ecclesiastics began to exercise some of their functions upon school grounds—for example, by making announcements and giving directions to children, in some instances assembling children of a given faith preparatory to guiding them in a body to the weekday church school. An equally real, though less obvious, crossing of the line occurred when public school teachers assisted in the promotion work of the churches in school hours and upon school grounds, and when records of attendance, work, and conduct at the weekday class in religion were submitted to and kept by the state school.

Released-time classes were officially recognized in about three hundred towns during the twenty years following the Gary experiment. Groups of churches and ministerial associations secured the co-operation of boards of education and superintendents of schools in permitting classes in religious education during school hours. Classes were started as a result of the belief of educational leaders that it is difficult to provided adequate character education without some religious training, and surveys showed that large percentages of the children in this country were not reached by Sunday schools.[34] The following statement, preceding a resolution of the Board of Education in Rochester, New York, in authorizing the starting of the program, is significant:

The importance of religious instruction, both to the individual and to the country, is generally recognized. By common consent, however, the free public-school system of this country cannot teach religion. The responsibility for such instruction must rest upon the home and the church, but the public school can and should cooperate to the limit of its power with the home and the church, to the end that the greatest possible number of our boys and girls may receive effective religious instruction.[35]

After this plan had been in force for some years, a committee was appointed to survey the results and make recommendations. A summary of these follows:

Excuses to attend religious instruction should not be granted below the third grade; among the reasons mentioned for eliminating first and second-grade pupils were the problem of control of traffic and the loss of school time in the case of many first-grade pupils who were attending half-day sessions.

All religious instruction classes are to be so organized that pupils from a single school grade shall be excused at the same time and avoid disturbing the same group more than once a week.

Assure careful checking of attendance at the religious instruction centers and place responsibility for absences after the pupil has left the public school upon the church school, which, in turn, will report to the parents.

Responsibility for the conduct of pupils either on the way to the classes or during the classes rests upon the religious instruction center. If a pupil's conduct is such as to reflect upon his school, permission to go should be cancelled.

A uniform practice should be adopted as to the time allowed for religious instruction. Forty-five minutes is recommended, this to include the time necessary quested to make regular reports to the board of education.[36]
for preparation to leave the school. This involves the presence of "centers" which are near enough to require no more than 15 or 20 minutes of the pupil's time for transfer from the school. In the semi-departmental school the period would coincide with the regular class period.

It is considered unnecessary to have "consent" cards signed anew each year.

It is recommended that the board of education set a definite limit to the number of pupils to be placed in charge of one teacher; 100 or more is too large a number for adequate control and efficient instruction.

Pupils should not be taken from the schools until adequate control and instruction are provided for them in the religious classes.

The committee recommends that the religious instruction authorities be re-

These recommendations have been set forth in detail because they indicate how a released-time program can best operate effectively without either violating constitutional prohibitions or unduly interfering with the regular school curriculum and operations.

The influential International Council of Religious Education reported in 1943 that the general plan of releasing children for weekday religious instruction which it endorses had been legalized in some way in forty-one states.[37]

In the early summer of 1949 the National Education Association published *The Status of Religious Education in the Public Schools.* This showed only four states—Maryland, Nevada, New Hampshire, and Wyoming—and the District of Columbia and Alaska reporting no religious education programs releated to the public schools or their pupils. Of the 2,639 school systems reporting—urban, town, village, and county units—708 or 26.8 per cent showed that they were co-operating to some degree in or providing formal religious instruction; only 15.3 per cent had classes in public school buildings during school hours. The largest group, 68.1 per cent, reported individual pupils released to attend classes away from the school—the public school keeping a record in about half the cases. About 14 per cent of all pupils covered by the survey were enrolled in some form of religious education class. Of the systems reporting, 11.8 per cent stated that for one or more reasons—in 52.3 per cent of these because of the United States Supreme Court decision in the McCollum case—they had given up their religious education program. These facts show the actual situation as it was early in 1949; the questionnaires for these studies had been sent out in December, 1948.[38]

Today, fifteen years after this study by the N.E.A., the legal system remains on the whole unchanged. However, there are no accurate figures as to either the number of school systems participating in programs for weekday religious instruction or the number of children enrolled in them. Estimates of the former have gone as high as three thousand and of the latter as high as three million.[39] (In 1962, the last year for which exact figures are available, there were 38,836,610 children enrolled in the nation's public elementary and secondary schools.[40]) It is probable that both these figures are too high and that an estimate of perhaps fifteen hundred school systems and between one and a half and two million children would not be far off.[41]

Professor Richard B. Dierenfeld, of the University of Minnesota, on the basis of a nation-wide survey made in 1961, estimated that about 30 per cent of the school districts co-operated in a program of released-time religious instruction.[42]

More significant that absolute figures is the question whether enrollment has increased in recent years, and if so whether the increase has kept up with the rise in the public school population. The answer is that probably neither has happened. In New York City, when the program was first introduced in 1941, 110,000 children enrolled. In 1963, after more than two decades, the enrollees numbered 103,605.[43]

It is hard to say how effective the weekday religious classes and schools have been,[44] but they have undoubtedly accomplished something in "dispelling spiritual illiteracy." The schools are mainly in small cities and towns, though some large cities, such as Chicago, Milwaukee, Kansas City, Rochester, Boston, New York City, St. Louis, and Pittsburgh, have adopted the plan. But it must not be thought that released time has been universally favored in American cities. Thus in San Diego, California, the Board of Education, after nearly a year's trial in ten schools, declined in 1947 to expand or continue the released-time program. Among the nine grounds stated were these:

Religious training is the special and particular sphere of the church. . . .

The year's trial of "released time for religious education" has demonstrated that the program interferes with the progress of school work during the entire day, increases the work of principals and teachers, and results in certain confusion and loss of time to all children in the grade, both those who are released and those who remain. The evidence does not show growth of character or desirable behavior beyond that of the children who did not participate in the released time program. The results do not justify a continuation or extension of the plan.

The request for a continuation of the "released time program" falls short of having the support of all the people or even of all the churches or church people.[45]

The validity under the United States Constitution of the released-time plan where the religious instruction is not held on public school premises and public school authorities are not directly involved in its operation was upheld by the Supreme Court in the case of *Zorach* v. *Clauson,* which has already been summarized in Chapter 5 of this book. The case involved the New York City released-time program, which had been established in 1941 pursuant to the McLaughlin-Coudert Law[46] passed by the state legislature in the previous year, with the backing of many representative citizens and public organizations. The law provided that "Absence from required attendance shall be permitted only for causes allowed by the general rules and practices of the public schools. Absence for religious observance and education shall be permitted under rules that the commissioner shall establish."[47]

After the law was adopted, Dr. Ernest E. Cole, the commissioner of education, announced the following rules:

1. Absence of a pupil from school during school hours for religious observance and education to be had outside the school building and grounds will be excused upon the request in writing signed by the parent or guardian of the pupil.

2. The courses in religious observance and education must be maintained and operated by or under the control of a duly constituted religious body or of duly constituted religious bodies.

3. Pupils must be registered for the courses and a copy of the registration filed with the local public school authorities.

4. Reports of attendance of pupils upon such courses shall be filed with the principal or teacher at the end of each week.

5. Such absence shall be for not more than one hour each week at the close of a session at a time to be fixed by the local school authorities.

6. In the event that more than one school for religious observance and education is maintained in any district, the hour for absence for each particular school in such district shall be the same for all such religious schools.[48]

The State Council of Churches, which supported the law and was pledged to aid in making it effective, was disappointed that this departmental ruling restricted the hours of instruction to the close of morning or afternoon sessions. It also felt that not permitting the religious instruction in school buildings might prevent the carrying out of the plan in some rural districts. Furthermore, since the wording of the law appeared to make the provision for religious education merely permissive, some boards of education did not seem disposed to put it into effect. In spite of these criticisms the New York experiment was on such a large scale as to attract national attention.

The introduction of the program in New York City was greeted with strong reactions on both sides. For example, there was a discussion at the meeting of the New York Kindergarten 6-B Teachers Association in the spring of 1941, where able speakers denounced the law as inimical to constitutional liberty and others with equal vigor supported it.[49] The released-time discussion was opened by Dr. Everett Ross Clinchy, then president of the National Conference of Christians and Jews, who spoke in favor of the plan. He asserted that voluntary religious instruction on released time was not a threat to our constitutional liberties but that the existing lack of religious education among large elements of the population was a threat to them. He advocated co-operation in carrying out the plan, believing that it would benefit both the churches and the schools and would moderate tendencies to bigotry. The associate superintendent of schools of New York City argued that religious education must be an integral part of the total education of every child and that released time might in spite of its difficulties be one of the ways of making this possible.[50]

Dr. Clinchy was opposed by Dr. Kenneth Leslie, editor of *The Protestant Digest*, who said that it was an "administrative bridge" between the State and the Church and would become "an effective weapon in the hands of clerical-fascism to develop a State-supported church school system and ultimately a church-controlled State." He suggested that, instead of continuing the plan then in use, a complete holiday be given on Wednesdays for children to go to religious classes if they or their parents so wished. Further opposition to the plan, on the ground that it was an opening wedge to public support of parochial schools and an interference with regular school work, was voiced by the principal of the Samuel J. Tilden High School. He felt that there was ample opportunity for religious schools on Saturday or Sunday, or after school hours.[51] These were the major differences of opinion which arose regarding the plan.

How the plan actually operated also became the subject of considerable dispute. The Greater New York Coordinating Committee on Released Time declared itself well satisfied with both the operation of the program and its results. So did the public school authorities. On the other hand, many private citizens as well as the United Parents Association and the Public Education Association[52] were of the opinion that there were many infractions of the rules and regulations established by Commissioner of Education Coles in 1940 as well as of those promulgated by the New York City Board of Education the following year.

Although the petition in the case of *Zorach* v. *Clauson* asserted that in practice the rules and regulations were disregarded, and that in fact pressures were often exerted by teachers upon children to enroll for religious instruction,[53] these issues were not decided either by the New York courts[54] or by the Supreme Court.[55] The courts held that if in fact this was true, the appropriate remedy was to protest to the public school authorities, who would order the offensive conduct to be discontinued and would, in the proper case, discipline the offending teacher. But the deviations from the rules and regulations did not, the courts held, affect the validity of the program as prescribed by the statute and the regulations.[56]

The Supreme Court's upholding of the constitutionality of the released-time plan has, of course, not settled the strongly held difference of opinion as to its wisdom and desirability. In particular, Protestant, Jewish, and Roman Catholic attitudes toward religious education for public school pupils differ on the subject of the released- and dismissed-time projects.

Protestant churches played the major part in developing the plan and have given it official support through actions by many ministerial and church associations.[57] They believe that with suitable regulations it constitutes an apparently constitutional way of meeting, at least in part, the Roman Catholic charge that public education is godless, and that parochial schools provide the only substitute, in view of the fact that the American public will not permit religious indoctrination, by priests or other authorized teachers of any religious communion, in public schools. The overwhelming commitment of the Protestant churches to the released-time plan is evidenced by the fact that the constituents of the National Council of Churches voted unanimously to authorize that body to file a brief as "friend of the court" in the Zorach case urging the Supreme Court to uphold the constitutionality of the New York City program.

The Roman Catholic Church has devoted its major attention in religious education to building up its parochial schools. It has generally felt that all supplementing of public school education by special religious instruction outside of school hours was both inadequat eand unsatisfactory. This view is well expressed by Father Richard Gabel, the historian and exponent of the movement to secure aid from public funds for church or parochial schools which are open to the public without charge. In 1937 he wrote,

. . . Catholics desire all children in a Catholic school under the Catholic teachers. Mere religious instruction does not suffice for it is necessary "also that every other subject taught, be permeated with Christian piety" and "that religion may be in very truth the foundation and crown of the youth's enire training" in elementary, intermediate and higher institutions, as the Encyclical *Christian Education of Youth* puts it.[58]

More recently, however, the Church has in many communities indicated strong interest in the released-time plan as a means of providing some religious education to Roman Catholic children who do not attend parochial schools. In New York City this is especially the case. Here, statistics show that 80 per cent of the children released for religious instruction are Roman Catholics who go or are taken to nearby churches or parochial schools for religious instruction.[59] The same is substantially true in other large cities, such as Chicago and Pittsburgh. On the other hand, in some cities, like Philadelphia, the Church has shown no interest in introducing the program and has concentrated its efforts in providing parochial school education for Roman Catholic children. Nevertheless, even in dioceses where the Church does not seek the introduction or avail itself of a released-time program, it strongly favors the principles upon which such programs are based.[60] The Church has been practically unanimous in its condemnation of the McCollum[61] decision and its praise of the Zorach decision.[62]

The Jewish attitude toward released time is almost universally unfavorable.[63] The reasons were stated in a study conducted by the American Jewish Congress which reached the conclusion that the dangers and disadvantages outweigh "by far" the benefits. It listed four objections: it is a threat to the principle of Church-State separation; public school authorities often put pressure on children to attend the courses; Jewish children occasionally attend Christian classes regularly for fear of disclosing their religious differences; and the amount of religious instruction that can be given is negligible.[64]

The position of the Jewish organization in respect to released and dismissed time has been stated by the Joint Advisory Committee of the Synagogue Council and the National Community Relations Council:

We believe that Jewish communities are justified in objecting to released time or dismissal time programs.

Inherent in dismissal time are many, though not all, of the faults of released time. Nevertheless, when confronted with the necessity of a choice, we regard dismissal time as less objectionable.

When a program of released time or dismissal time is in effect, or may be adopted, the Jewish community should insist upon the following safeguards against possible abuses:

1. No religious instruction shall be given on public school premises;

2. The administrative machinery of the public school system shall not be employed to record or encourage attendance at religious instruction centers of students who avail themselves of either program;

3. There shall be no proselytizing on school premises;

4. All children participating in such programs shall be dismissed together, and all grouping, separation, or identification by religion or by participating or non-participation in such programs shall be avoided;

5. Children shall not be assembled on public school premises for the purpose of being led to religious instruction centers nor shall any representative of such religious instruction center meet the children on such premises to facilitate the operation of either program.[65]

Bible Reading and Prayer Recitation

It is interesting to note that Congress specially approved the publication of what is generally known as the Revolutionary Bible.[66] This edition of the Authorized Version was published by Robert Aitken in Philadelphia in 1782. It was the first English Bible published on the American continent.

The Bible is not usually read at the opening exercises of Congress today, there being merely a prayer. But its reading by the public has been frequently urged by government officials, as when President Wilson made his public appeal for funds to give the Scriptures to all soldiers and sailors of the nation in World War I, and when President Franklin D. Roosevelt issued his message in behalf of Universal Bible Sunday, in which he said, "We know that the ancient truths of the Bible will prevail over all error because they constitute the teachings of God." [67]

Prior to the late thirties of the nineteenth century there was no serious objection by large groups to the then common practice of reading the King James Version of the Bible at the opening exercises in public schools. Only one state in the Union during the first hundred years made such reading obligatory by statute—Massachusetts, in 1826. Elsewhere it was merely continued from colonial tradition or agreed to by the local school authorities. The Massachusetts legislation was not emulated by any other American state until the twentieth century, when twelve states followed suit in the two decades following 1913.[68]

The first strong objection to the practice arose in certain Eastern cities which in the second quarter of the nineteenth century acquired through immigration a large Roman Catholic population. The controversy was particularly acute about the middle of the century, when the Roman Catholics were using the Bible reading as an effective argument in favor of developing their own parochial schools.[69] The public issue of the question of Bible reading in the public schools has historically been closely related to the development of the Roman Catholic parochial school movement. Opposition to the practice was considered second in importance only to the vital need of providing an education under Church auspices for the millions of immigrants arriving from Ireland, Germany, and other parts of Europe. This strong opposition, as we shall shortly see, was completely reversed after the McCollum case, so that by the time public school devotional Bible reading was declared unconstitutional by the Supreme Court in the Schempp-Murray decision of 1963, the Roman Catholic Church had become its strongest defender.

The extent of devotional Bible reading in the public schools at the time of the Court's decision cannot be estimated with any certainty. A summary in 1934[70] showed that the practice of Bible reading in the public schools was specifically permitted by statute in seven states and allowed by court or administrative decisions in a few others; considered optional in thirteen through the lack of any definite state law on the subject; prohibited in eleven, generally by interpretation by courts or educational authorities of state constitution guarantees of religious freedom, and/or the protection of public education from denominational instruction; and required in eleven and the District of Columbia. A survey made in 1946 by the National Education Association showed that thirteen states, including the District of Columbia, required Bible reading in all public schools; twenty-five states permitted it; and in eight states no public schools read the Bible.[71] By 1963, it was probable that somewhere between a third and a half of the public schools in the nation opened their daily sessions with reading without comment from the Bible. This estimate is supported by a study made in 1961 by Professor Richard H. Dierenfeld of the University of Minnesota, which indicated that in about 42 per cent of the school districts Bible reading was conducted regularly.[72]

In general the opposition to Bible reading in the schools has in the past come from four very different groups: the Roman Catholics, the Jews, agnostics and atheists, and certain Protestants who believed that there are inherent dangers in such reading as inconsistent with Church and State separation in the United States.

The Roman Catholics objected mainly because the King James Version, which is generally used, is not the version approved by their Church. As is well known, they early adopted for use in this country the Douay (Rheims) Version as revised by Bishop Challoner in 1750. Roman Catholics asserted that the King James Version, having been made in England after the Reformation, inclines to a Protestant as distinct from a Catholic point of view, though freely granting that it has great literary beauty and significance and is deeply rooted in the literature of the language. The Roman Catholics frankly conceded, however, that even if the Douay-Rheims or other version satisfactory to them were substituted for the King James it would not result in their discontinuing their effort to build up a separate parochial school system. Indeed, the Douay Version was permitted in some places[73] without substantially altering the Church's position. In New York City, where Bible reading was required until 1963, it had become common for teachers to use this version in schools with a predominantly Roman Catholic constituency, just as the Old Testament alone was commonly used in the city public schools in Jewish districts. Even when the Douay Bible was used, the Roman Catholics generally were not satisfied. They asserted, with justice, that Bible reading alone, if considered from the standpoint of religious instruction, was entirely inadequate.

After the McCollum case, however, the Roman Catholic Church changed its position completely. Apparently convinced that the danger to its faithful from secularism had become more threatening than that from Protestantism or indifferentism, it vigorously opposed what it called the godlessness of the American public educational system. The extent and intensity of this change of position was to become apparent from its reaction to the Supreme Court's 1962 decision in *Engel* v. *Vitale*,[74] declaring unconstitutional the public school recitation of the New York Regents' Prayer, and its decision the following year invalidating Bible reading and recitation of the Lord's Prayer in the public schools.[75]

The point of view of the Jews regarding Bible reading in public schools is based partly on their desire to maintain complete separation between Church and State and partly on their fear that through the Bible Christological ideas which they cannot approve will be taught to their children.[76] They believe that the reading, being usually hurried and perfunctory, hurts rather than helps the cause of religious culture. They lay emphasis on the fact that if there is Bible reading it virtually amounts to a compulsory attendance at a religious service, which all would agree would be out of keeping with American traditions.[77] Jewish opposition to the practice was shown concretely by the submission of the Synagogue Council and National Community Relations Advisory Council of a brief *amicus curiae* in the Schempp-Murray case.

At least prior to the Regents' Prayer decision, Protestant groups and spokesmen overwhelmingly favored devotional Bible reading in the public schools. They felt that Bible reading is in the great American tradition and that its reading in the schools constituted at least a symbol of our allegiance to God. There were, however, even then dissenting voices within the Protestant Church.[78] After the decision in *Engel* v. *Vitale* these voices became louder.[79] Statements against devotional Bible reading in the public schools were issued by the United Church of Christ and the United Presbyterian Church[80] as well as other denominations. Most significant of all was the statement "The Churches and the Public Schools" adopted by the General Board of the National Council of Churches (with only the Greek Orthodox Church dissenting) on June 7, 1963. The paragraph dealing with Bible reading stated,

> The full treatment of some regular school subjects requires the use of the Bible as a source book. In such studies—including those related to character development—the use of the Bible has a valid educational purpose. But neither true religion nor good education is dependent upon the devotional use of the Bible in the public school program.[81]

It was not until 1963 that the Supreme Court passed upon the constitutionality of devotional Bible reading in the public schools. Before then the issue had been presented to many state courts with varying results.[82] The suits were usually brought by parents of Catholic children in the public schools who charged that the practice violated either state constitutional or statutory provisions forbidding sectarian teachings in the schools.[83] The issue in these cases, therefore, was whether the Bible, or more accurately the King James Version, was a "sectarian" book. In the majority of cases, the state courts held that the Bible was not sectarian and its reading in the public schools therefore not illegal.[84] Although the constitutionality of Bible reading in the public schools has now been authoritatively determined by the Supreme Court for all the states, it is nevertheless worthwhile to quote from two decisions, one of which upheld the practice and the other declared it illegal. Both were decided in 1910. These quotations set forth eloquently the arguments for and against Bible reading in the public schools.

In a decision upholding Bible reading the Supreme Court of Kentucky said,

> There is perhaps no book that is so widely used and so highly respected as the Bible. No other that has been translated into as many tongues. No other that has

had such marked influence upon the habits and life of the world. It is not the least of its marvelous attributes that it is so catholic that every seeming phase of belief finds comfort in its comprehensive precepts. Many translations of it, and of parts of it, have been made from time to time since two or three centuries before the beginning of the Christian era. And since the discovery of the art of printing and the manufacture of paper in the sixteenth century a great many editions of it have been printed. . . .

That the Bible, or any particular edition, has been adopted by one or more denominations as authentic, or by them asserted to be inspired, cannot make it a sectarian book. The book itself, to be sectarian, must show that it teaches the peculiar dogmas of a sect as such, and not alone that it is so comprehensive as to include them by the partial interpretation of its adherents. It is not the authorship, nor mechanical composition of the book, nor the use of it, but its contents that give it its character. The history of a religion including its teachings and claim of authority, as for example, the writings of Confucius or Mohammed, might be profitably studied. Why may not also the wisdom of Solomon and the life of Christ? If the same things were in any other book than the Bible, it would not be doubted that it was within the discretion of the school boards and teachers whether it was expedient to include them in the common school course of study without violating the impartiality of the law concerning religious beliefs.[85]

On the other hand, the majority opinion of the Illinois Supreme Court in a similar case said,

Christianity is a religion. The Catholic church and the various Protestant churches are sects of that religion. These two versions of the Scriptures are the basis of the religion of the respective sects. Protestants will not accept the Douay Bible as representing the inspired word of God. As to them it is a sectarian book containing errors and matter which is not entitled to their respect as a part of the Scriptures. It is consistent with the Catholic faith but not the Protestant. Conversely, Catholics will not accept King James' version, as to them it is a sectarian book inconsistent in many particulars with their faith, teaching what they do not believe. The differences may seem to many so slight as to be immaterial, yet Protestants are not found to be more willing to have the Douay Bible read as a regular exercise in the schools to which they are required to send their children, than are Catholics to have the King James' version read in schools which their children must attend.

The reading of the Bible in school is instruction. Religious instruction is the object of such reading, but whether it is so or not, religious instruction is accomplished by it. The Bible has its place in the school, if it is read there at all, as the living word of God, entitled to honor and reverence. Its words are entitled to be received as authoritative, and final. The reading or hearing of such words cannot fail to impress deeply the pupils' minds. It is intended and ought to so impress them. They cannot hear the Scriptures read without being instructed as to the divinity of Jesus Christ, the Trinity, the resurrection, baptism, predestination, a future state of punishments and rewards, the authority of the priesthood, the obligation and effect of the sacraments, and many other doctrines about which the various sects do not agree. Granting that instruction on these subjects is desirable, yet the sects do not agree on which instruction shall be given. Any instruction on any one of the subjects is necessarily sectarian, because, while it may be consistent with the doctrines of one or many of the sects, it will be inconsistent with the doctrines of one or more of them. The petitioners are Catholics. They are compelled by law to contribute to the maintenance of this school. What right have the teachers of the school to teach those children religious doctrine different from that which they are taught by their parents? Why should the state compel them to unlearn the Lord's Prayer as taught in their homes and by their Church and use the Lord's Prayer as taught by another sect? If Catholic children may be compelled to read the King James' version of the Bible in schools taught by Protestant teachers, the same law will authorize Catholic teachers to compel Protestant children to read the Catholic version. The same law which subjects Catholic children to Protestant influences will subject the children of Protestants to Catholic control where the Catholics predominate. In one part of the state the King James' version of the Bible may be read in the public schools, in another the Douay Bible, while in school districts where the sects are somewhat evenly divided, a religious contest may be expected at each election of a school director to determine which sect shall prevail in the school. Our Constitution has wisely provided against any such contest by excluding sectarian instruction altogether from the school.[86]

When, in 1948, the Supreme Court decided in the McCollum case that public school practices in respect to religion were subject to the restrictions of the First Amendment, it was immediately recognized by many that sooner or later the constitutionality of public school Bible reading would be decided by the Supreme Court. Such a case did reach the Court in 1952 in a suit challenging the New Jersey statute requiring daily Bible reading in the schools. However, by the time the case was argued in Washington, the plaintiff's child had already been graduated from the school she had attended, and the Court dismissed the suit for that reason without passing on the constitutional issue.[87] Before the Court again had the opportunity to decide the question it was faced with a challenge to prayer recitation in the public schools.

The practice of prayer recitation was widespread, though not quite as widespread as that of Bible reading. The prayer most often recited was the Lord's Prayer, and while in most cases the state courts had ruled that like the Bible itself the Lord's Prayer was non-sectarian, there were many who disagreed with this view. This, in any event, appeared to be the case in New York. For that reason in November, 1951, the New York State Board of Regents proposed what it considered a truly nonsectarian prayer for daily recitation in the public schools of the state. It issued a "policy statement" asserting that American people have always been religious, that a program of religious inspiration in the schools will assure that the children will acquire "respect for lawful authority and obedience to law [and that] each of them will be properly prepared to follow the faith of his or her father, as he or she receives the same at mother's knee or father's side and as such faith is expounded and strengthened by his or her religious leaders." [88]

The "policy statement" then went on, "We believe that at the commencement of each school day the act of allegiance to the flag might well be joined with this act of reverence to God: 'Almighty God, we acknowledge our dependence upon Thee, and we beg Thy blessings upon us, our parents, our teachers and our country.' " [89]

The announcement aroused a storm of controversy. The proposal was opposed by *The Christian Century*, which deemed the practice ineffectual and the prayer "likely to deteriorate quickly into an empty formality with little, if any, spiritual significance." [90] The leaders of the Lutheran Church of Our Redeemer in Peekskill charged that Christ's name had "deliberately been omitted to mollify non-Christian elements," and that the prayer "therefore is a denial of Christ and His prescription for a proper prayer. As such it is not a prayer but an abomination and a blasphemy." [91]

Opposition, but of course for different reasons, was also voiced by all the major Jewish organizations, including the American Jewish Congress, the Synagogue Council of America, and the New York Board of Rabbis,[92] as well as such non-sectarian organizations as the American Civil Liberties Union, the New York Teachers Guild, the United Parents Association, and the Citizens Union.[93]

On the other hand, strong support came from most Protestant and Catholic church leaders, such as the Reverend Norman Vincent Peale, Dr. Ralph Sockman, Charles H. Tuttle, Bishop William Scully of Albany and Monsignor John S. Middleton, secretary for education of the New York Archdiocese.[94] The *Tablet*, official organ of the Brooklyn Catholic Diocese, quickly became the most passionate defender of the proposal, and John F. Brosnan, a member of the Board of Regents and an important Catholic layman, speaking before the Friendly Sons of St. Patrick, charged that "the only criticism came from those who do not believe in God." [95]

The Regents' proposal was not mandatory; it was merely a recommendation which local school boards were free to adopt or not. In New York City, after a stormy public hearing, the Board of Education decided not to institute recitation of the prayer in the public schools of the city but compromised instead on the daily recitation of the fourth stanza of the patriotic hymn

"America." ("Our father's God, to Thee, Author of Liberty, to Thee we sing. Long may our land be bright with freedom's holy light, protect us by Thy might, great God our King.")

No survey appears to have been taken to determine how many school boards did adopt the Regents' prayer. A reasonable estimate is that not more than 10 per cent did so. However, among those that did was the school board in New Hyde Park, a Long Island suburb of New York. With the aid of the New York Civil Liberties Union, a group of parents of children in the public schools of that community brought suit in the state courts to declare the practice unconstitutional. All the New York courts ruled against them, holding the practice to be valid so long as no compulsion was used to cause any child to participate in the recitation.[96]

By a vote of 6 to 1 the Supreme Court reversed the holdings of the New York courts and held the practice unconstitutional. The decision, *Engel* v. *Vitale*, has already been summarized in Chapter 5. Here, however, it is necessary to relate some of the reaction to the dcision on its announcement.

Supreme Court decisions that arouse furor are hardly unprecedented. Throughout its history, the Court has witnessed reactions of outrage to this or that decision, generally accompanied by demands to amend the Constitution, impeach the justices, or restrict the powers or jurisdiction of the Court. The furor, however, which greeted *Engel* v. *Vitale* was probably unusual in its intensity. The decision was deplored and condemned on and off the floor of Congress,[97] and Senators and Representatives immediately began to sponsor resolutions for amendments to the Constitution to nullify the decision. Senator Robert C. Byrd asked whether "we, too, are ready to embrace the foul concept of atheism," [98] and Representative L. Mendel Rivers asserted that "The court has now officially stated its disbelief in God Almighty." [99] The Conference of State Governors, which happened to be meeting at the time, adopted a resolution, with only the governor of New York abstaining and none dissenting, deploring the decision and calling for a constitutional amendment to overrule it.[100]

Among the clergy too the reaction was violent. Cardinal Spellman of New York stated that he was "shocked and frightened that the Supreme Court has declared unconstitutional a simple and voluntary declaration of belief in God by public school children. The decision strikes at the very heart of the Godly tradition in which America's children have for so long been raised." [101] The Reverend Dr. Billy Graham, the popular evangelist, asserted that "This is another step toward the secularization of the United States. The framers of our Constitution meant we were to have freedom of religion, not freedom from religion." [102] Methodist Bishop Fred Corson condemned the decision and

Episcopal Bishop James A. Pike of California, in testimony before the Senate Judiciary Committee, called for the adoption of a constitutional amendment to overrule it.[103]

So severe was some of the criticism that one of the justices of the Supreme Court, Tom C. Clark, found it necessary in a public address to defend the decision and express the view that many who had criticized it had not read it or fully understood it.[104]

Nevertheless, it should not be assumed that the reaction was universally unfavorable. President John F. Kennedy, himself a practicing Roman Catholic, said in answer to a question at his news conference,

The Supreme Court has made its judgment. Some will disagree and others will agree. In the efforts we're making to maintain our constitutional principles, we will have to abide by what the Supreme Court says. We have a very easy remedy here, and that is to pray ourselves. We can pray a good deal more at home and attend our churches with fidelity and emphasize the true meaning of prayer in the lives of our children. I hope, as a result of that decision, all Americans will give prayer a greater emphasis.[105]

Within Protestantism too there were important voices in support of the decision and opposing a constitutional amendment to overrule it: those of *The Christian Century*, the Joint Baptist Committee on Public Affairs, the Reverend Eugene Carson Blake, formerly president of the National Council of Churches, and the Reverend Martin Luther King, spiritual leader of the Negro movement for equality.[106] A group of prominent Protestant leaders, including the dean of Harvard Divinity School, joined in a statement supporting the decision and expressing opposition to any constitutional amendment seeking to abrogate it. A similar statement, signed by 132 deans and professors of law and political science, of all faiths and none, was submitted to the Senate Judiciary Committee holding hearings on proposals for a constitutional amendment.[107] And, as was to be expected, the Jewish organizations and rabbis were practically unanimous in their support of the Supreme Court's ruling.[108] Perhaps more surprising was its endorsement by many of the major newspapers in the nation, such as the New York *Times*, the New York *Herald Tribune*, the Washington *Post*, the St. Louis *Post-Dispatch*, and others.[109]

While the initial reaction to the Regents' prayer decision was overwhelmingly adverse, it was relatively short-lived. After a few days of testimony, the Senate Judiciary Committee discontinued further hearings and appeared to have lost all interest in a constitutional amendment. The controversy evoked by the decision did serve one important purpose; it caused millions of people who had previously taken the principle of separation of Church and State more or less for granted to give serious thought to its meaning and implications. The result was seen in the public reaction when, almost a year to the day after the Regents' prayer decision, the Court, on June 14, 1963, in the combined case of *Abington School District* v. *Schempp* and *Murray* v. *Curlett* (called, for short, the Schempp-Murray case) held unconstitutional the daily devotional Bible reading and recitation of the Lord's Prayer in the public schools.

The Schempp case[110] challenged the validity of a Pennsylvania law requiring the reading without comment of ten verses from the Holy Bible on the opening of public school each day. The statute provided that any child must be excused from participation or attendance at the written request of his parent or guardian.

At the trial it was shown that each morning, in the particular high school attended by the plaintiff's children, the Bible reading exercises were broadcast into each homeroom through an intercommunication system. This was followed by recitation of the Lord's Prayer, in which the students were asked to join. The exercises were closed with the flag salute and announcements of various kinds relating to school activities. The evidence showed that, although the school furnished only the King James (Protestant) Version of the Bible, the student selected to do the reading could use a different version, and at times the Douay (Catholic) and Jewish versions were used. There were no prefatory statements, no questions asked or solicited, no comments or explanations made, and no interpretation given at or during the exercises. The students and parents were advised that the students might absent themselves from the classroom if they so elected.

The plaintiff (a Unitarian) testified that the literal reading of the Bible was contrary to his religious beliefs and teachings, but that he did not seek to have his children excused because he felt their relationships with their teachers and classmates would be adversely affected.

Expert testimony was introduced at the trial by both sides. On behalf of the plaintiff, Dr. Solomon Grayzel, editor of the Jewish Publication Society, which published the English translations of the Bible accepted by Jews, testified that there were marked differences between the Jewish Holy Scriptures and the Christian Holy Bible, and that the latter was deemed sectarian and unacceptable to Jews. For the defendants, testimony was given by Dr. Luther A. Weigle, formerly dean of Yale Divinity College, to the effect that the Bible was "non-sectarian" although he later qualified this statement by stating that he used the term to mean non-sectarian within the Christian faith.

The trial court, consisting of three Federal judges, unanimously held that the reading of the verses, even without comment, possessed a devotional and religious character and constituted in effect a religious observance. The practice was therefore held unconstitutional and its discontinuance decreed.

In the Murray case no statute was involved. The suit, brought by an avowed atheist, challenged the daily Bible reading and Lord's Prayer recitation practiced in the Baltimore public schools pursuant to a rule of the city board of school commissioners which had been promulgated in 1905. No trial was held in the Murray case; the Maryland trial court dismissed the complaint, and the state's highest court, by a vote of 4 to 3, upheld the dismissal.

The Supreme Court's decision, which has been summarized in Chapter 5, hardly came as a surprise.[111] In the light of its ruling in *Engel* v. *Vitale,* no other decision seemed possible. Only one of the nine members of the Court dissented, Justice Potter Stewart; he had likewise dissented in *Engel* v. *Vitale.* What was somewhat surprising was the difference in public reaction that greeted the two cases. In remarkable contrast to the earlier decision, the initial reaction to the Schempp-Murray ruling was generally favorable. Leading Protestant spokesmen and practically all Jewish spokesmen expressed themselves in favor of the decision. So, too, did many of the major newspapers and commentators in the nation.

There were, of course, strong voices in opposition; many of those who had voiced dissatisfaction with the Regents' prayer decision, such as the Reverend Dr. Billy Graham, Bishop James A. Pike, and Bishop Fred Corson, likewise criticized the ruling in the Schempp-Murray case. Three of the five American Roman Catholic cardinals, who were at the time in Rome preparing to participate in the election of a successor to Pope John XXIII, spoke forcefully against it. Cardinal J. Francis McIntyre of Los Angeles stated that the decision "can only mean that our American heritage of philosophy, of religion and of freedom are being abandoned in imitation of Soviet philosophy, of Soviet materialism and of Soviet-regimented liberty." Cardinal Richard Cushing of Boston expressed the view that the Communists must be taking great pleasure in the decision, and Cardinal Francis Spellman of New York asserted that no one who believes in God could approve such a decision.

Commenting on Cardinal Spellman's statement, James O'Gara, managing editor of *The Commonweal* said in the July 5, 1963, issue of that publication, "This view clearly seems to fly in the face of obvious facts; unless one is to say that the officials of such bodies as the National Council of Churches are atheists, it is obvious that there are believers who support the decision." While *The Commonweal* is a liberal magazine published by laymen and therefore perhaps not representative of general Church thinking, it is nevertheless true that on the whole Roman Catholic reaction, while almost uniformly unsympathetic to the Schempp-Murray ruling, was considerably more moderate than it had been a year earlier. Even the Jesuit weekly *America,* which had been bitter in its opposition to the Regents' prayer decision and was critical of the Schempp-Murray decision, opposed any amendment to the Constitution to overrule it. In view of such opposition, it would seem doubtful that any amendment to the Constitution in respect to religion in the public schools would be adopted.

Nevertheless, one member of Congress at least was undaunted. Representative Frank J. Becker of New York undertook what appeared to be a one-man crusade to overrule the Bible-prayer decisions by constitutional amendment. He prevailed upon the ninety-odd Congressmen who had introduced separate measures to join in supporting one measure (H.J. Res. 693, 88th Cong.) which reads as follows:

Section 1. Nothing in this Constitution shall be deemed to prohibit the offering, reading from, or listening to prayers or Biblical Scriptures, if participation therein is on a voluntary basis, in any governmental or public school, institution, or place.

Section 2. Nothing in this Constitution shall be deemed to prohibit making reference to belief in, reliance upon, or invoking the aid of God or a Supreme Being, in any governmental or public document, proceeding, activity, ceremony, school, institution, or place or upon any coinage, currency, or obligation of the United States.

Section 3. Nothing in this Article shall constitute an establishment of religion.

In urging support for this measure, Congressman Becker stated that "the urgency of this matter leaves no alternative if we are to prevent the advocates of a godless society to accomplish in the United States that which the Communists have accomplished in Soviet Russia." At the present writing it cannot be predicted with certainty whether Congressman Becker's effort will succeed or fail. Although almost 150 members of Congress have expressed support for the measure, as have also some state legislatures, it is more probable that the effort will not succeed and that the Court's decision will not be nullified.

Christmas and Other Holiday Observances

Related to the question of Bible reading and prayer recitation is the subject of Christmas and other religious holiday observances in the public school. These may vary from the singing of simple Christmas carols to the presentation of elaborate nativity and crucifixion plays, as well as the exhibition on school property of lifelike crèches or manger scenes.

The problem has become acute in recent years in communities or schools where there is a substantial Jewish minority.[112] While most Christians and even persons unaffiliated with any faith in the past generally found nothing wrong in public school celebrations of Christmas, Jewish parents in increasing numbers have often found them offensive. They point out that, unlike Thanksgiving and Washington's Birthday, Christmas and Easter are Christian holidays, celebrating the birth and death of the founder of the Christian faith. They assert that celebration of these holidays in the public schools causes discomfort and embarrassment to their children, and that if the children choose not to participate in the celebrations they are isolated and often scorned by their classmates.

In a number of communities protests against Christmas and, less often, Easter celebrations in the public schools have erupted into serious incidents of interreligious tension and misunderstanding.[113] The protesting Jewish parents have been charged with being bigoted and anti-religious. The celebrations have been defended on the ground that the United States is a Christian nation and that therefore its traditions and customs should properly be reflected in the public school program. They have also been defended on the ground that, notwithstanding its religious origin, Christmas has in fact become a national holiday in the same category as Thanksgiving Day and Washington's Birthday.

Many thoughtful school officials have not been convinced of the adequacy of these defenses and have in fact sought to eliminate or at least diminish the more theological aspects of Christmas celebrations. Others have tried to meet the problem by introducing into the schools a celebration of the Jewish holiday of Hanukah, or Festival of Lights, which commemorates the successful war of the Maccabees against the Seleucids for the right to practice their faith during the second century before Christ. Because this holiday generally falls about the same time as Christmas, it is often possible to have a December school program which celebrates jointly both Christmas and Hanukah. In this way many school authorities believe that they are acting fairly and removing the feeling of isolation and non-belonging suffered by Jewish children if Christmas alone is celebrated.

Undoubtedly their belief is shared by many Jewish parents. Some consider joint Christmas-Hanukah celebrations an acceptable if not ideal compromise and solution to a difficult problem. Others go even farther and welcome such celebrations in the belief that they are valuable as aspects of intercultural education and help improve interfaith relations. Most Jewish parents, however, and all major Jewish organizations are opposed in principle to joint holiday celebrations. The statement of principles entitled "Safeguarding Religious Liberty" issued by the Synagogue Council and the National Community Relations Advisory Council has this to say on the subject:

> We are opposed to the observance of religious festivals in the public elementary and high schools because in our view such observance constitutes a violation of the traditional American principle of the separation of church and state.
>
> Joint religious observances, such as Christmas-Hanukah and Easter-Passover, are in our opinion no less a breach of the principle of separation of church and

state and violate the conscience of many religious persons, Jews and Christians alike.

Where religious holiday observances are nevertheless held in public schools, Jewish children have a right to refrain from participation. We recommend that local Jewish communities take such action as may be appropriate to safeguard this right of non-participation.

These organizations are likewise opposed to the exhibition on public property of the symbols usually associated with Christmas, such as manger scenes. On this subject, their statement of principles has the following to say:

We oppose the erection of religious statues or the placing of religious symbols on publicly-owned property. Public parks, city halls, governmental office buildings and similar premises are purchased and maintained out of taxes imposed upon all persons, irrespective of their religious beliefs or affiliations. The presence on such premises of religious statues or symbols constitutes in effect a dedication of the premises to one sect or creed to the exclusion of others. The expenditure of governmental funds or the use of governmental property for religious purposes, moreover, is a serious impairment of the principle of separation of church and state. Experience has shown that the placing of religious statues or symbols on public property divides the community along religious lines and brings about interreligious disharmony and acrimony.

These evils are substantially aggravated when religious statues or symbols are placed on public school premises. In such cases, sensitive and defenseless children, rather than mature adults, are principally affected. Moreover, attendance at school is not voluntary but is by compulsion of law. To compel children to obtain their secular education in an atmosphere charged with a religion violative of their beliefs is to deny them their full religious liberty as well as to breach the relationship of confidence and trust that should mark their school experience.

The question of the legality of religious holiday celebrations as part of public school programs and the exhibition of religious symbols on public school property has never reached the Supreme Court for decision. Two state courts have passed on it. In Florida a court held it unconstitutional to present Christmas nativity and Easter crucifixion plays as parts of religious holiday observances in the public schools,[114] while in New York a court held that it was not unconstitutional to allow a crèche to be placed on the public school lawn during the Christmas vacation period when the children do not attend the school.[115]

Incidental References to Religion in Textbooks

It is recognized that no well-balanced cultural curriculum can possibly eliminate all references to religion. Religion has been so identified with the ideals and achievements of the human race that to leave it entirely out of historical or social studies is impossible. This fact creates some difficulty, for competent and conscientious teachers may occasionally and unwittingly color the presentation of important events in history, such as the Reformation, or the relations of Church and State in the Middle Ages, by their own religious convictions. American public high schools have nevertheless been increasingly successful in treating the fundamental facts of secular history that involve religious controversies or influences without bias or emotional appeal. This seems to be true of Protestant, Catholic, and Jewish teachers alike.

An early incident illustrating the difficulties that have arisen in our public schools because of references to religion or religious history goes back more than a century to the time when Bishop John Hughes of New York was carrying on his vigorous campaign to secure a share of the school fund for Catholic schools, and, when this proved impossible, to build up the separate parochial school system. The incident dates from a period when the public schools, as State-controlled institutions, were just coming into being, and when the Public School Society, a private organization, controlled their work.

At a general meeting of Roman Catholics held in September, 1840, a petition to the Board of Aldermen was adopted, asking that a portion of the common school fund be allotted to the Catholic schools. Conscientious Catholics, it said, could not send their children to the schools of the Public School Society because, among other reasons, many of the books in use contained passages unfair to and critical of Catholics. On this point the petition stated that

. . . many of the selections in their elementary reading lessons contain matter prejudicial to the Catholic name and character. The term "popery" is repeatedly found in them. This term is known and employed as one of insult and contempt toward the Catholic religion, and it passes into the minds of children with the feelings of which it is the outward expression. Both the historical and religious portions of the reading-lessons are selected from Protestant writers, whose prejudices against the Catholic religion render them unworthy of confidence in the mind of your petitioners, at least so far as their own children are concerned. . . .

They [petitioners] will quote the passage as one instance, taken from "Putnam's Sequel," p. 296.

"Huss, John, a zealous reformer from popery, who lived in Bohemia toward the close of the fourteenth, and the beginning of the fifteenth centuries. He was bold and persevering; but at length, trusting to the *deceitful Catholics*, he was by them brought to trial, condemned as heretic, and burnt at the stake."

The Public School Society may be excused for not knowing the historical inaccuracies of this passage; but surely assistance of the Catholic clergy could not have been necessary to an understanding of the word "deceitful," as applied to all who profess the religion of your petitioners. . . .[116]

The Public School Society, which had originally denied that the books contained anything reasonably objectionable to Catholics but had later retracted the denial, replied to the petition by asserting that their strenuous and long-continued efforts to induce the Catholic clergy to co-operate in an expurgation of the books had proved unavailing. Accordingly, they undertook the task themselves and the work was near completion. Even uncompleted, the Society's reply stated, there was now less matter objectionable to Roman Catholics in the textbooks used in New York City public schools than in those of any other school in the state, public or private.

This assertion did not satisfy Bishop Hughes. At an open hearing held by the Aldermen ten days later, he made a long address, in which he said,

. . . I defy you to find a reading-book in either public or private seminary, that in respect to Catholics is not full of ignorance. Not a book. For if it were clear of this, it would not be popular; and if they [the Public School Society] refer to this then, they refer to a standard which we repudiate. But it must be remembered those people can send their children to those schools or keep them at home. They are not TAXED for their support. But here we are. It is the public money which is here used to preserve the black blots which have been attempted to be fixed on the Catholic name. They say again (and it is an idea that will go exceedingly well with the public at large, for it will show how amiable and conciliating are these gentlemen)—that they have submitted the books to us as though we have nothing to do but to mark out a passage, and it will disappear. But are we to take the odium of erasing passages which they hold to be true? Have they the right to make such an offer? And if we spend the necessary time in reviewing the books to discover passages to be expurgated, have they given us a pledge that they will do it, or that they will not even then keep them in? . . .[117]

In defense of the Public School Society, one of its members, Hiram Ketchum, asserted that he was certain that Calvinists, Methodist, Democrats, Whigs, and many other religious and political groups would in combing through the textbooks find here and there a passage to which they could take exception. Were all these books removed, there would be no public school system at all.[118]

After the conclusion of the hearing, the trustees of the Public School Society offered to remove from the classroom texts all matters which might be deemed offensive to Roman Catholics and also to exclude from the school libraries any book which might have the general tendency of prejudicing the mind of the reader against the tenets or practices of the Roman Catholic Church. They undertook further to make every effort to prevent any occurrence in the schools which might be calculated to wound the feelings of Roman Catholic children, or to impair their confidence in or diminish their respect for the religion of their parents.[119]

In January, 1841, on the report of a committee which had considered all the evidence, and had also visited the public schools, the Board of Aldermen denied the petition of the Roman Catholics.[120] And so this particular controversy came to an end. It illustrates an inherent difficulty in the matter of public school teaching—that of being scrupulously fair to the facts of history without causing unnecessary offense to any religious group. It is clear that in this instance there were references in the textbooks of the time to which the Roman Catholics could legitimately take objection, and that the most serious were eliminated. It is also true that it would have been very difficult to have European history of the Reformation period, for example, taught in the schools objectively either by scholarly Catholic or Protestant teachers in a way to have entirely satisfied Bishop Hughes. Fortunately today, with the more tolerant attitude of both public school authorities and religious leaders, there is relatively little difficulty.

Roman Catholics have not been the only ones to object to their treatment in books used in the public schools. In 1930 an Episcopalian clergyman in New York City complained that a textbook in modern history, written by two Catholic professors, Carleton Hayes and Parker Moon, was pro-Catholic and anti-Protestant. The chairman of the Board of Education, a Roman Catholic, referred the letter of complaint to the superintendent of schools, a Presbyterian, who banned the book. In the meantime, the authors had, apparently independently, brought out a revised edition in which there were a few minor changes of phraseology, such as the use of Protestant "denominations" instead of "sects," the elimination of references to Henry VIII and Calvin as "Protestant Popes," and the tempering of criticisms of Luther. The book was now unobjectionable to the authorities and was restored to the list of approved texts.

Jews, too, have complained that books used in the public schools sometimes are anti-Semitic in their treatment of Jews or of the Jewish faith. Dickens' *Oliver Twist* and Shakespeare's *Merchant of Venice* have been particularly objected to on this ground. There is some basis for the charges, but advocates of these classics maintain that they should be retained in public school libraries or used in classrooms because of their literary distinctions. They point out that if merely incidental criticisms of religious views or types, whether of Protestants, Catholics, or Jews, are considered sufficient ground for keeping a book out of a public school library it might result in many exclusions, in the narrowing of the literary and historical "exposure" of youth, and in the development of an unfortunate censorship complex.[121]

This summary should give a fairly good idea of the difficulties involved in selecting public school textbooks and in teaching certain subjects in which the views and acts of the Church cannot be entirely disregarded. It is manifestly impossible to deal with the great problems of history and sociology, or to study the classics of literature, to say nothing of ethics and philosophy, without considering religion in general and Christianity in particular. Hence, there are from time to time complaints from Protestant, Jewish, and Catholic sources, as well as from the agnostic group, that the doctrines of some form of religion are being covertly introduced for propaganda purposes. It is obviously impossible to understand the world in which we live unless something of the history of Christianity and its relations to society and the State are taken into account. The same is, of course, true of the teaching of the theory of evolution, a matter dealt with later in this chapter.

Use of Public School Buildings for Religious Purposes

The use of public school buildings for religious meetings, worship, and instruction at times when they are not being used for regular school instruction has often been a matter of controversy between Church and State authorities. The state regulations differ considerably.[122] In some, the school authorities are given wide discretion in the use of public school buildings after school hours or during weekends. In others, they are authorized to allow such use for civil, cultural, and educational meetings but are expressly forbidden to permit it for religious purposes. In states having no express statute on the subject, the courts have differed. In some it has been held that, under their general power to manage and control the school system and its plant, public school authorities have implied power to allow its use, at least where there is no resulting cost to the school system. As a court in Kansas stated,

It is not an essential part of our school system that the public obtain no benefit from the buildings it has erected except during the hours they are occupied by the pupils. The movement for the use of school buildings for civic centers is generally recognized as a wholesome one.

Other state courts, however, have ruled that the business of school authorities is to run the schools and not to rent real estate.[123]

Where use of school buildings for non-school purposes is permitted either by statute or by court decision, and there is no express provision either permitting or forbidding use for religious purposes, the state courts are divided. A few have held that such use is permissible even where it is gratuitous. Typical is the following statement from a decision by the Iowa Supreme Court:

The use of a public school building for Sabbath schools, religious meetings . . . which, of necessity, must be occasional and temporary, is not so palpably a violation of the fundamental law as to justify the courts in interfering. Especially is this so where, as in the case at bar, abundant provision is made for securing any damages which the taxpayers may suffer by reason of the use of the house for the purposes named. With such precaution the amount of taxes any one would be compelled to pay by reason of such use would never amount to any appreciable sum. . . . Such occasional use does not convert the schoolhouse into a building of worship, within the meaning of the Constitution.[124]

On the other hand, some courts have held that allowing a church free use of public school buildings is in effect making a gift to the church and therefore violates constitutional prohibitions against use of public funds or property for sectarian purposes. In Florida the courts have taken a compromise position: such use is allowable if it is temporary, as, for example, while a local church is being repaired after sustaining damage by fire,[125] but is not allowable where its duration is permanent or indefinite.[126] The question has never yet reached the United States Supreme Court and therefore it cannot be authoritatively stated whether or not the free use of public school property for religious purposes would violate the First Amendment's ban on laws respecting an establishment of religion.

The Shared-Time Plan

Related to the problem of use of public school buildings by churches is what has become known as the shared-time plan.[127] The shared-time proposal would divide the Catholic child's school time between public and parochial schools. For such religiously neutral subjects as languages, mathematics, physics, chemistry, gymnasium, vocational training, etc., the child would go to the public school. For subjects which the Church feels must be taught with a religious orientation—history, literature, social sciences, etc.—the child would go to the parochial school. The benefit the Church would receive by this procedure would come from its being relieved of the costly budget items of expensive equipment as well as the salaries of teachers teaching the religiously neutral subjects.

The plan is not limited to Catholic schools. Protestant church schools and Jewish all-day schools could likewise take advantage of it. However, 90 per cent of the children attending non-public schools are Catholic children enrolled in parochial schools, so that for all practical purposes this is a plan for the aid of the Catholic Church.[128]

The plan would not work in most elementary schools, since these do not have departmentalized instruction. It could work in high schools, but only about one out of every five children attending parochial schools attends a Catholic high school, so that the benefits to the Catholic school system would appear to be quite limited. On the other hand, if the plan were adopted it is likely that more Catholic parochial school children would continue in Catholic high schools, on the shared-time basis. The plan also could be used in junior high schools, although the Catholic school system is not now set up on a junior high school basis.

Shared time must not be confused with released time. The latter refers to releasing children from secular education to take *religious instruction*. Shared time merely divides the places (public and parochial schools) where the children are to take *secular* instruction. Since the Supreme Court in the Zorach case ruled even released time off public school premises to be constitutional, it seems unlikely that shared time would be held unconstitutional. In order, however, to put the plan in effect, it would in most states be necessary to change the school law.

In 1963, Congressman Adam Clayton Powell of New York introduced a bill in Congress (H.R. 6074, 88th Cong.) for the appropriation of five million dollars annually for three years to finance experimental shared time programs. Hearings were held on this bill in February, 1964, at which the National Education Association presented the results of a preliminary study it had made which showed that a total of 35 states had one or more school systems with a shared-time program in operation. The study showed that the overwhelming majority of these programs were in the Midwest. In Michigan 42 school districts participated; in Ohio, 36; in Illinois, 26; and in Wisconsin, 25. The only non-Midwestern state with a substantial number of districts participating was Pennsylvania, with 31. The study also revealed the following significant information.

1. The typical (median) shared-time program had been in operation for eight years. The range was from one year in 18 districts to 40 or more years in Houghton, Michigan, and Ludington, Michigan.
2. The number of parochial-school pupils enrolled part time in the 135 public school systems totaled 7,237, and this was equal to 2.8 percent of the full-time enrollment of these public school systems.
3. The subjects most frequently offered to parochial-school pupils were those which were very expensive to offer, or for which qualified teachers were scarce. The subjects most frequently offered in these shared-time arrangements of the 135 school systems were as follows:
    Industrial Arts, offered by 65%
    Home Economics, offered by 39%
    Instrumental Music, offered by 34%
    Physical Education, offered by 15%
    Physics, offered by 12%

Advanced science and/or mathematics, offered by 10%

Modern foreign languages, offered by 10%

4. None of the following subjects were taught on a shared-time basis by more than two of the 135 reporting districts:

World History	Social Studies
Sociology	Problems of Democracy
Economics	Dramatics
English	

Perhaps the best way to show the actual operations of a shared time program is to set forth the agreement entered into in 1963 between the Philadelphia public school authorities and the Diocesan school authorities in that city for participation by Catholic parochial school pupils in the classes given at the city's technical high schools. The agreement reads as follows:

SHARED TIME PROGRAM

I. General Philosophy
  A. The pupils assigned to the Technical High Schools for shop instruction will remain on the sending school rolls, but a record of school membership on appropriate forms for purposes of state reimbursement will be kept for each "shared time" pupil in a Technical High School.
  B. Tenth Grade pupils only will be assigned on the initial program.
  C. Pupils will be assigned, by the sending schools, to various trades in the Technical High Schools according to the number of pupil stations open in a trade at the Tenth Grade level as reported by the Technical High School Principal after all properly qualified applicants from public schools have been accommodated.
  D. The Technical High Schools will inform the Associate Superintendent in charge of Secondary Schools of the available facilities, such as trades, numbers, morning or afternoon session. The Associate Superintendent in charge of Secondary Schools will send this information to the Superintendent of Diocesan Schools.
  E. The pupils choice of trade will be the responsibility of the Diocesan school coordinator. There will be only one choice indicated to the Technical Schools.

II. Organization
  A. Each Diocesan High School will have one person assigned to coordinate the program with the Technical High School to which that school's students will go on a shared time basis.
  B. Each Technical High School will have a coordinator to act as liaison person between his school and a sending school.
  C. Classes in the Technical High School will be three clock hours per day, five days per week.

    D. Diocesan pupils will report either at 8:30 A.M. or 12:15 P.M. to their assigned trade classes in the Technical School according to the availability of work stations.

    E. School year and school holidays for Diocesan pupils, while enrolled for trade classes in the Technical High School, will be the same as for full time Technical school pupils. However, the decision as to the observance of vacations or holidays not in the public school calendar will rest with the coordinator in the Diocesan school or his superior.

    F. Reports of progress, behavior, and attendance will be sent to the home school at the time of the scheduled issuance of reports to parents in the Technical High School.

    G. Graduation requirements will be the responsibility of the sending school.

    H. Transportation between Diocesan school and Technical High School will be the responsibility of the individual pupils or of the sending school.

    I. Lunch facilities may be used when space is available, if in the opinion of the sending school, this is desired.

    J. Diocesan coordinator will be notified of the various shop requirements such as, financial expenses, kits, proper uniforms or clothing, safety protection where necessary.

    K. There will be only one admissions date established by the Technical High School in cooperation with the Diocesan High School. There will be no mid-year admission since the program will be on an annual basis.

    L. Change of trade
        1. May be recommended by either Diocesan coordinator with permission of parent or by Technical school coordinator to Diocesan coordinator.

    M. In summation, the Diocesan pupils will be treated the same as any other pupils in the Technical School during their presence in the school.

III. Admissions
    A. Requirements
        1. Entrance examination, in keeping with the admissions requirements of the Technical High School.

    B. Admissions Committee of the Technical High School will notify Technical School Principal of the following:
        1. Vacancies available according to trade, boys or girls, time of day.
        2. Names of applicants who have qualified.

    C. The Technical High School will notify the Diocesan High Schools from which applicants for "shared time" enrollment have come of those pupils who have qualified for admission.

    D. Each Diocesan high school will make the decision as to which pupils will be enrolled in the "Shared Time Program" and send the names to the Technical High School in which they have qualified for admission.

IV. Removal of pupil from Technical High School
    A. A Technical High School may request removal of pupil.
    B. Sending school may request removal of pupil.

C. All removals will be arranged between the coordinators of the schools concerned after consultation with their principals.

Approved:

ALLEN H. WETTER
Superintendent
Phila. Public Schools
(RT. REV. MSGR.) EDWARD T. HUGHES
Superintendent
Phila. Diocesan Schools

WM. M. DUNCAN
Associate Superintendent
Phila. Public Schools

The Roman Catholic Church has expressed sympathetic interest in the plan and seems to be favorably inclined toward it.[129] The same is true of the National Council of Churches and many Protestant clergymen, who look to it as a means of breaking the long-standing impasse on Federal aid to education.[130] The Jewish groups have on the whole been opposed to it.[131]

The public school superintendents who responded to the N. E. A. survey stated the following advantages of shared time programs (in the order of frequency mentioned):

1. This type of co-operation results in good relationships between the parochial and the public schools, and in greater support of the public schools by Catholics.
2. Many parochial schools do not have the financial resources to provide sufficiently comprehensive programs to meet the many diverse needs of Catholic children and youth. Courses of study in industrial arts, vocational education, and business education are expensive to offer, and qualified teachers of such fields are difficult to find.
3. By tradition the public schools are free and open to all the children of all the people, and there is no logic in refusing to accept parochial-school pupils on a part-time basis; also, parents of parochial-school pupils help pay for public schools and their children are entitled to at least some of the benefits.
4. Sometimes the classrooms, teachers, and facilities available in the public school can accommodate extra pupils at little or no added cost; in such cases, there is no good reason for not accepting pupils from parochial schools.

The disadvantages expressed by the superintendents were as follows:

1. In such cases pupils serve two masters and pupil control is sometimes a problem; some of these pupils think the public school authorities have no right to discipline them.
2. There is no state reimbursement for part-time pupils.
3. Part-time attendance by large numbers of parochial-school pupils presents difficult problems of scheduling, transportation, record keeping, and participation in student activities.
4. There are conflicts between two types of grading systems.

At the same hearing on Congressman Powell's bill, Francis Keppel, United States Commissioner of Education, submitted a statement which included the following explanation of the rationale of shared time programs:

The rationale for these programs has usually expressed itself in terms of the need for developing closely knit ties within the community so that the entire community, not just a part, may share the benefit of common attendance at the public school and come to identify the public school as its own. Children who normally attend a private school can attend the public school on a part-time basis and receive experience in working together with others of different religious backgrounds. At the same time, public school children receive the opportunity to work with and know private school children. Thus, dual enrollment acts to bridge social, economic, and religious differences within the community. And it also may serve to develop greater popular support for education—for example, to ease the passage of bond issues by lessening the objection of parents of nonpublic school children to what they regard as "double taxation." Through these programs, their children have the opportunity to attend public school on a part-time as well as on a full-time basis.

On the national level, the principal reason advanced for supporting dual enrollment is to expand educational opportunities to all children and thus improve our overall educational system. Private schools have found it increasingly difficult to maintain a well-rounded curriculum, particularly in providing special education for gifted children and for the culturally deprived and for others requiring the use of costly scientific and technical training. There is a definite national need to strengthen and support such essential educational programs.

The arguments against the plan were stated in the following editorial in *The Christian Century* of March 14, 1962:

The latest proposed solution to the current dispute over federal aid to parochial schools—"shared time"—has a long, hard row ahead of it. Under the shared time plan pupils from parochial schools would take such "neutral" subjects as science, mathematics and physical education in the public schools. They would study religion and other courses the churches prefer to teach in their church schools. Any proposal which could conceivably provide an acceptable compromise in the present debate over the use of public funds for religious purposes is worth considering and the National Council of Churches' commission on general Christian education is correct in recommending to councils of churches that the plan be studied. At first glance, however, the counts against the shared time proposal seem too many and too weighty to encourage hope that this is the long-awaited solution of a many-faceted problem. In avoiding the constitutional barriers to public relief for parochial schools, the shared time plan runs into others which are equally obstinate. It is not likely—to give examples of such obstacles—that the administrators of public schools will look favorably on a plan which would so thoroughly fragment education and so completely disrupt the wholeness of academic schedules. The turmoil which would be stirred up by the coming and going of students, the division of classes, the scattering of records would seriously weaken both the public and parochial schools. More important, the divorcing of history, the humanities, the arts and social studies—which the church schools would certainly want to pre-empt for their students—from the sciences, mathematics, athletics and manual training would create an intolerable dichotomy for both religious and secular educations. . . . A shared time program would stimulate a wild and vigorous growth of church schools in denominations in which they do not now exist. Such a proliferation of parochial schools would eventually destroy the public school system.

General Freedom of Teachers and Teaching: Nuns

There is at times friction in certain communities where, in spite of the intended impartiality of the law, an active political group tries to secure a majority of Roman Catholic teachers or a Roman Catholic principal. On the other hand, there is occasional difficulty because of the opposition of some Protestants to Roman Catholic teachers. For instance, in communities where the Ku Klux Klan has been prominent and fundamentalism rampant, Roman Catholic teachers have at times been discriminated against, as was especially the case in the mid-1920's.[132] In this connection—though it should not be considered a discrimination but rather a reasonable attempt to prevent the identification of a public school with any one religious body—statutes and regulations have been adopted in several states to prohibit the wearing of a religious habit by teachers while engaged in the performance of their duties.

Apparently the first action of this type was by the Pennsylvania legislature in 1895. The state supreme court declared the law constitutional, on the ground that it was directed against acts and not against beliefs.[133] Similarly the New York Court of Appeals in 1906 upheld as reasonable a regulation of the state superintendent forbidding Catholic sisters to wear a distinctive garb.[134] The question has never come before the Supreme Court of the United States.

In some states nuns wearing their religious garb are permitted as public school teachers.[135] Speaking generally, there is no more valid objection to an eligible nun's being employed as a teacher than to a Protestant minister's being so employed. They stand on the same footing from a public school standpoint. But Protestant ministers engaged as teachers seldom wear a distinctive habit, and it is the appearance of the nuns in their regular garb that causes comment and even criticism, because it is a constant reminder to the pupils of the Church connection of their teachers and is likely to cause misunderstanding. The practice has been especially prevalent in a number of midwestern states, including Ohio, Kentucky, Missouri, New Mexico, and North Dakota.[136] In the last-named state, after the state supreme court held it legal for nuns to be employed as public school teachers and to wear their garb while teaching, a referendum was held in 1948 which determined that public school teachers should not be permitted to wear religious garb while engaged in their teaching duties. Thereafter the Catholic bishops of the state announced that the seventy-four nuns teaching in the public schools would not be required to wear religious garb but could wear "modest dress" while teaching, and accordingly their employment was continued.

To insure entire impartiality in the selection of public school teachers as far as religion is concerned some states have adopted stringent legislation. For example, New York in 1932 enacted a law to the effect that no person seeking employment in the public schools may be questioned regarding his or her religion or religious affiliation.[137] Many states have laws which expressly forbid discrimination in public employment, including public school employment, on grounds of religion. Even in the absence of such laws, the Supreme Court decision in *Torcaso* v. *Watkins*, summarized in Chapter 5, would appear to make such discrimination unconstitutional, even against atheists and agnostics, although, of course, any public school teacher abusing her trust by proselyting for her particular religion or against all religion would properly be subject to discipline and dismissal.

Teaching of Evolution in Public Schools—The Scopes Trial

The teaching of evolution in the public schools developed in the 1920's into a controversy in which the churches and the public were much concerned. It was not so much a struggle between Church and State, as such, as a difference of opinion between certain groups in both Church and State on a matter in which religion was deeply involved.

The issue came to a head in 1925 in the so-called Scopes trial, at Dayton, Tennessee. The legislature that year passed an act making it unlawful for any publicly employed teacher to teach "any theory that denies the story of the divine creation of man as taught in the Bible, and to teach instead that man descended from a lower order of animals." [138] This legislation was mainly due to the fundamentalist and Ku Klux Klan influence prevalent in the central South at that time.[139]

John Thomas Scopes was a teacher in 1925 in the high school of Dayton, Tennessee, who could not support the antievolution doctrine recently adopted by the legislature. He used an authorized textbook in biology which stated that

. . . the earth was once a hot, molten mass, too hot for plant or animal life to exist upon it; the earth cooled, the sea formed, and a little germ of one cell organism was formed in the sea; this kept evolving till it got to be a pretty good sized animal, then came on to be a land animal, and it kept evolving and from this was man.[140]

Stimulated by friends, he taught these views as his own. As a result, he was arrested, and one of the most amusing, amazing, and pathetic trials in the history of American education took place. On the one side was William-Jennings Bryan, sincere and earnest, but narrow-minded theologically, leading the forces of fundamentalism, antievolution, and reaction. On the other side were Clarence Darrow, a well-known agnostic, Arthur Garfield Hays, active in the American Civil Liberties Union, and others, protesting that the law was archaic and unconstitutional.

Bryan sought to prove that the Biblical account of creation in all its details was inspired by God. He claimed that the world was created in 4004 B.C., this being according to the chronology of Archbishop Ussher, who died in 1656. The idea that it was hundreds of millions of years old seemed to him preposterous in view of the statements in the Book of Genesis. He believed that Eve was actually and literally made out of Adam's rib. He took the ground that this was a fight between religion on the one hand and agnosticism or atheism on the other.

Darrow and his associates showed the inconsistencies in the Bible and the gaps between the Old Testament and modern science. They maintained that the law was unconstitutional on the ground that it fostered a specific type of ism. They pointed out that the state constitution promised that "no preference shall ever be given by law to any religious establishment" and that "it shall be the duty of the general assembly in all future periods of this Government to cherish literature and science." [141] The defense also held that the statute was vague in that it did not state what Bible translation was to be adopted or what was meant by forbidding the "teaching" of evolution. Did it mean that it should not be taught as a fact, or that it should not be taught even by way of information as a theory? In general, the prosecution took the ground that since the public owned the school and paid the teacher, it had a right to determine what the teacher should teach, while the defense upheld the idea that, although the state could determine what subjects should be taught, it could not demand that they be taught falsely, and that evolution in a general sense was accepted by modern science.[142]

A large amount of expert testimony on scientific and theological opinion was introduced by the defense, including that of eminent scientists who were also Christian believers. This was carried by the press all through the country and did much to inform the public on the theory of evolution. But it was lost on judge and jury. Judgment was rendered against the defendant and a fine was imposed as punishment.

The argument on the appeal was heard in June, 1926, by the Supreme Court of Tennessee. Great emphasis was laid on the preference shown by the law for the fundamentalist churches, on the fact that the law went beyond legislative power by a requirement of teachers to falsify the general conclusions of science, and on the indefiniteness of the law. The court found a way out without offending public sensibilities. Determined to prevent an appeal to the Supreme Court of the United States, it decided that, though the law was not contrary to the Constitution, the conviction should be reversed on the ground that the fine had been improperly imposed by the judge.[143] Although long on the books, the statute has become a dead letter, whereas the interest in the scientific theory of evolution has been greatly increased by the discussions that accompanied the trial of the case.

Somewhat akin to the religious outlook of the opponents of the teaching of evolution in the public schools is the opposition to compulsory vaccination laws for school children. Such laws exist in many states to prevent the spread of smallpox. Occasionally parents refuse to have their children comply with the law, basing their opposition on medical or religious grounds. With the former we are not concerned here, but the latter brings up an interesting example of possible Church-State conflict. For example, in December, 1939, the Associated Press carried a dispatch from Pittsburgh that a family was moving from Pennsylvania to California to avoid compliance with the state vaccination law.[144] The father of a public school child stated that he had religious scruples against it. According to press reports, he had been arrested seven times because of his refusal to obey it. The child went to school, but the authorities refused to admit him because he had not been vaccinated and refused to be. It appeared that the boy's father was a fundamentalist, at least in believing the verbal inerrancy of the Bible. The vaccination law seemed to him to be contrary to the teaching of St. Paul: "Know ye not that ye are the temple of God, and that the Spirit of God dwelleth in you? If any man defile the temple of God, him shall God destroy; for the temple of God is holy, which temple ye are" (1 Corinthians 3:15, 17). In other words, some anti-vaccinationists base their opposition to the required inoculation of public school pupils on the same ground as the antievolutionists we have been discussing—their interpretation of a Bible which they consider verbally inspired even in scientific matters. The decision of the Supreme Court in *Jacobson* v. *Massachusetts* (summarized in Chapter 5) as construed in later decisions, makes it quite clear that such religious objections do not excuse refusal to comply with compulsory vaccination laws.

Compulsory Salute to the Flag in Public Schools [145]

This simple mark of patriotism frequently creates tension between certain unconventional or extreme elements in the Church and the authorities of the State. The newspapers before World War II were full of reports of the children who were in difficulty with the public school superintendents, and occasionally with the police, because they refused to salute the flag. They were followers of Pastor Charles T. Russell, founder of the International Bible Students Association and of the Watch Tower and Bible Society, Inc. (1884). The latter has been known since 1931 as Jehovah's Witnesses, a somewhat extreme Protestant group organized with Judge Joseph F. Rutherford as president.[146] It has no churches or regular religious services but spreads its conception of the Christian gospel by tracts, public mass meetings, phonograph records, radio, and other forms of publicity. Its members generally use halls for meetings in substandard sections of a community.[147]

Their propaganda usually takes the form of a house-to-house visitation. They sometimes carry a phonograph and reproduces some of the utterances of Pastor Russell or Judge Rutherford, and they sell or give away free the literature of their sect. The records and publications contain prophecies of the expected end of the world, together with exhortations to repentance and denunciations of most forms of organized religion, and more particularly of the Roman Catholic Church. The government of the United States, at least in peacetime, also has come in for its share of abuse. A literal view of Old Testament prophecies, which they apply to definite present and coming events in the ecclesiastical and political world, is their stock in trade.

The extreme view of the group—which does not wish to be classed as a denomination—is thus officially stated in the *Year Book of Jehovah's Witnesses* for 1938:

Satan attempts to lull to complete silence everything that would expose him and his wicked operations. For that reason the religionists, Catholics, Protestants, Jews and others, all agree to say nothing that might provoke a controversy. They have induced the public press and the radio to refuse the publication of any truth concerning God's kingdom on the ground that it is controversial. They invoke every unrighteous rule against Jehovah's witnesses in their desperate attempt to keep the people in ignorance of everything pertaining to the kingdom of God, and this they do for the reason that they know the truth when told exposes the duplicity and crookedness of Satan and his religious agents.

Upon the false pretext of having peace those religionists insist that Jehovah's witnesses shall not be permitted to inform the people of God's kingdom, declaring that the Kingdom message is subversive and seditious; the very thing that religionists charged against Jesus when he was on the earth. The earthly ruling powers make laws which declare that the testimony given by Jehovah's witnesses concerning

God and his kingdom is seditious and liable to cause a breach of the peace and therefore should be suppressed.[148]

This group has become principally known to the public for its refusal on conscientious grounds to salute the flag. Its religious leaders have taught that this act is unchristian because it partakes of idolatrous worship. To Jehovah's Witnesses saluting the flag would be a violation of the commandment "Thou shalt have no other Gods before me. Thou shalt not make unto thee any graven image or any likeness of anything that is in heaven above, or that is in the earth beneath, or that is in the water under the earth. Thou shalt not bow down thyself to them nor serve them. . . ."[149] Moreover, they believe that to salute the flag ascribes salvation to it, whereas salvation is of Jehovah God.[150]

Probably no other American religious organization since the early days of the Mormons has experienced as much persecution as have the Witnesses. The Department of Justice has on file some 335 instances of mob violence in forty-four states during the one year 1940, involving 1,488 men, women, and children who were connected with this sect of zealots.[151] The intolerance against them has been mostly in small communities, where they are particularly active. Except on the single issue of the flag salute, their attitude toward the State is one of respectful obedience to all "righteous laws." They are opposed to military training but in general have observed the draft.

The peak of the violence came in May and June, 1940. Some of the most serious cases occurred in places as widely separated as Flagstaff, Arizona; Crocker, Missouri; Beaumont, Texas; Greenville, Illinois; and Kennebunk, Maine, although they were not as frequent in the East and far West as in other parts of the country. In one or two instances the sheriffs refused protection. There were cases where women were beaten, where mobs yelled "Damn the law!" when members of the sect were arrested and put in prison without charges against them, where papers in small communities approved of violence, where large numbers of automobiles belonging to the Witnesses were wrecked, where halls in which meetings were held were attacked, and so on.[152]

The expulsion of Jehovah's Witnesses children from the public schools for refusing to salute the flag was challenged in the state courts in the thirties and early forties with conflicting results. The issue reached the Supreme Court in the famous case involving the Gobitis children.

The court history of the case [153] goes back to 1938, when a Federal judge in Pennsylvania ordered the reinstatement, in a Minersville school, of certain pupils who had been expelled in 1935 because of their failure, on account of religious scruples as members of Jehovah's Witnesses, to comply with a school board regulation that made the salute to the flag compulsory. At the trial the former pupils (twelve and thirteen years of age), who were supported by their parents, stated that they had "dedicated" themselves to God and considered homage to the flag or other object contrary to this supreme allegiance. They were willing to "stand in respectful silence," but not to "bow down to a graven image." Judge Albert B. Maris delivered an opinion in which he stated that he could personally see no "religious significance" in the salute to the flag, but that if the members of the family concerned conscientiously believed that it had such significance they were entitled to their belief under the Constitution. In giving his reasons for differing from the decisions of some courts in other states on the matter, he said,

In so holding it appears to us that the courts overlooked the fundamental principle of religious liberty, namely, that no man, even though he be a school director or a judge, is empowered to censor another's religious convictions or set bounds to the areas of human conduct in which those convictions should be permitted to control his actions, unless compelled to do so by an overriding public necessity, which properly requires the exercise of the police powers.[154]

The case was carried to the Federal Circuit Court of Appeals, where a unanimous decision supported the district court.[155] The school authorities appealed the decision to the Supreme Court, where, contrary to the expectation of many thoughtful people, the decisions of the district and circuit courts supporting the rights of the Gobitis children were overruled in an 8-1 decision. (See *Minersville School District* v. *Gobitis* in Chapter 5.)

Justice Harlan Fiske Stone, later chief justice, in a dissenting opinion which was soon to influence the Court to reverse itself, took the ground that the rights of religious freedom involved were so important that the lower courts should be upheld. It is thought by some that the serious international situation at the time, and the consequent need of supporting patriotism and law observance, as well as the extreme character of the Witnesses' views, interpretations, and actions, played some part in the majority opinion. It was criticized by many legal authorities, by some religious and secular journals, and by various agencies interested in upholding civil liberties, as running counter to the principle of religious freedom.[156] For instance, the Jesuit weekly *America*—in spite of the Witnesses' attacks on the Roman Catholic Church—criticized the decision on the ground that it gave legislatures unrestrained powers,[157] while *The Christian Century* ended an editorial entitled "The Court Abdicates" with the words "Courts that will not protect even Jehovah's Witnesses will not long protect anybody."[158]

As a result of the decision of the Court, the conscientious members of this extreme group were placed for the time being in a difficult position. In at least one place in New York State the Witnesses provided schools of their own, following the public school curriculum in all respects except for substituting the reading of the Bible for the flag salute. In another place, Pontiac, Michigan, a modified pledge of allegiance to the United States was adopted omitting the word "flag." The probate judge warned the parents that if they would not accept "the very gracious ruling of the school board and train the children better in Americanism, it will be the obligation of the court to take the children out of the homes long enough to give them environment and training to understand what Americanism is." [159]

The Gobitis decision proved to be short lived. Three years later the Supreme Court reversed itself. In the case of *West Virginia State Board of Education* v. *Barnette* (see Chapter 5) it held that children could not be expelled from school or otherwise compelled to salute the flag against their conscience. The change in the Supreme Court's attitude was the result of the addition to the Court of two new members and the change in point of view of three of those who had taken part in the earlier majority opinion. The action of Justice Black, Douglas, and Murphy, in reversing an opinion they had only recently held, is believed to be without precedent in the history of the United States Supreme Court. It is an important milestone in the history of religious liberty.

Religion at State Universities [160]

Although state universities must, under our separation of Church and State, be entirely detached from any religious body, there is nothing that prevents their offering elective courses in religion. These are in fact rather frequent, especially courses in comparative religion and the history of religion. Indeed, in some cases extensive groups of courses on religion are included in the catalogue and usually count toward a degree.

The state universities differ considerably in what might be called their attitude toward religion. Some, like the University of Wisconsin, have maintained a very strict separation, and the religious forces have until recently had considerable difficulty in getting any strong foothold. As late as 1942 its Board of Regents seriously discussed whether the University Press could properly publish a volume recommended by the Department of Philosophy on *The Religious Availability of Whitehead's God*.[161] The book was published as proposed. Other state universities in the South and in Iowa and Oregon have been sympathetic to religion.

One of the interesting educational developments in Church-State relations is the founding during the past forty years of schools of religion or kindred organizations at several state universities. This movement has been closely related to the work of the Council of Religion in Higher Education.

The first proposal for anything approaching a "department of religion" at a state university was a statute adopted by the state legislature of South Carolina in its session of 1864-65 to the effect that "A school of mental and moral philosophy, sacred literature, and evidences of Christianity" should be one of the departments of the university.[102] The university had long had a "Professor of Sacred Literature and Evidences of Christianity," but there is no evidence that the proposed "school" was ever developed.

The first effective step toward a real school of religion at a state university was taken fifty years later at the state university of Iowa. Its life has been influenced from its foundation by ideals inherited from the universities and colleges of New England, and it has always had on its faculty men deeply interested in religion. The plan was formulated in the years from 1921 to 1924 through the co-operation of members of the faculty, local pastors, the university secretary of the Council of the Church Boards of Education, the Y.M.C.A., and other groups. It was proposed to establish a school of religion whose governing board would be "constituted in such a way as to secure the cooperative efforts of the religious bodies of the State and of the University in the support and control of the School." [163] The plan was approved by the president of the university and the state board of education.

A faculty was selected, including a Jewish, a Catholic, and a Protestant professor, and an administrative director. The school, in addition to offering its regular courses, undertook to aid in the extracurricular religious life of the campus, and a professor was added in 1930 with the primary purpose of developing the laboratory side of the enterprise.

Since 1933 the work of the school has been well integrated into the life of the university. It co-operated with the department of philosophy in providing a regular freshman course entitled "Religion and Ethics." The project was so wisely administered, in taking steps only when representatives of the three groups were unanimous about them, that it has had the hearty support of the university board and most of the members of the faculty.

The Hawaii School of Religion was made possible in 1930 through the co-operation of the various Protestant denominations and the Roman Catholic Church in the territory. It serves virtually as the department of religion at the university, offering courses in such subjects as problems in religious thought, Christian Church history, comparative study of religions, and the teachings of Jesus. It is controlled, under its constitution, by a board of trustees of not fewer than thirteen mmbers, of whom one representing the faculty of the university is nominated by the university, nine representing the Protestant Churches are appointed by the Collegiate Religious Education Commission, and three are appointed by the Roman Catholic Church. The Protestant teachers in the school are elected by the Commission, the Catholic members are appointed by the bishop of the diocese, and the administrative officers are chosen by the board of trustees.[164]

An especially interesting type of organization to promote religion and social welfare at a state university is at the Southern Branch of the University of California in Los Angeles and at nearby Los Angeles City College. The so-called University Religious Conference is a corporation composed of what it considers the leading religious groups in the United States, namely, Baptist, Congregational, Disciples of Christ, Lutheran, Methodist, Presbyterian, Unitarian, Jewish, Church of Jesus Christ of Latter Day Saints (Mormons), Roman Catholic (archdiocese of Los Angeles), and Episcopal (diocese of Los Angeles and San Diego). Each of these bodies and the Y.M.C.A. are officially represented on the board of trustees, and the officers of the corporation rotate each year among four trustees representing officially the Roman Catholics, Episcopalians, Jews, and Protestant denominations. Various racial groups are also generally represented on the board. The conference carries on two types of activity—religious work, through the various agents supported by the denominations, and united community work. These denominations own in common property adjoining the campus of the university with a suitable building where each has its own offices, and they rent from the archdiocese a building for similar use at the college. They support a common budget and engage in certain enterprises for their mutual benefit and for community service. In the community program emphasis is placed on increasing understanding among Jewish, Protestant, and Catholic citizens of the area. This is accomplished through an extensive and well-organized program of addresses, round tables, and other activities, and through welfare work for children and youth.[165]

Such are typical ways, outside the usual Y.M.C.A., Newman Clubs (Catholic), branches of Hillel (Jewish), and similar student organizations, and student pastors supported by the leading religious groups, by which the cause of religion is advanced at state universities with the active co-operation and sometimes with the financial support of the university. When the university is officially involved a special effort is made to have the work of high grade and equally acceptable to the three faiths. The various experiments recorded are evidence that it is practicable, although there are differing views as to whether all these activities are fully compatible with the principle of Church-State separation. The question has not yet been decided by the Supreme Court and until it is no definitive answer can be given.

Public and Public School Libraries

Church-State problems have on occasion risen in connection with modern public libraries.[166] Usually they come about because some religious group feels that a particular book available at some public library is offensive to it.[167] For example, the Committee on Publications of the Board of Directors of the First

Church of Christ Scientist in Boston (the "Mother Church") was believed to be active in trying to suppress Edwin F. Dakin's *Mrs. Eddy: The Biography of a Virginal Mind* (1930) by working in co-operation with similar committees in the states and advocating a boycott of bookstores which sold the volume.[168] Their efforts caused the book to be removed from some public libraries and to be placed on the reserve shelves in others, where it was inaccessible to the general public.

Such a book, critical in some ways of the founder of Christian Science and of its tenets, is considered by Christian Scientists to be obnoxious and to come under the provision of their *Church Manual* to the effect that "A member of the Church shall not patronize a publishing house or bookstore that has for sale obnoxious books" [169]—a rule easily interpreted by loyal adherents of the Church to discourage their using public libraries where books severely critical of their movement may be found.[170] The publishers of the book, Charles Scribner's Sons, were faced with a serious drive to "smother" it as a result of pressure by Christian Scientists to have it removed from sale by booksellers and taken out of general circulation in public libraries. In this way the Scientists almost duplicated in intention, but not in success, the experience of twenty years earlier (1909), when Georgine Milmines' biography of Mrs. Eddy, which ran serially in *McClure's Magazine*, was so removed from general circulation as to be today a very rare volume.

These efforts of course disregarded the spirit if not the letter of the First Amendment to the Constitution. Cases of friction between public libraries and Christian Scientists still occur occasionally, especially when the Scientists oppose the purchase and circulation of biographies of Mrs. Eddy which give an unfavorable impression of certain aspects of her career. Such incidents followed the publication of Lyman P. Powell's *Mary Baker Eddy* in 1930. Fundamentalists also caused some trouble a few years ago in protesting against scientific books which accepted the Darwinian theory.

The question of the version of Bible to be provided by public libraries occasionally comes up for discussion. Naturally in most parts of the country where only one Bible is provided it is the King James Version, because it is accepted by a majority of Americans and because of its associations with English literature and with the history of this country. It seems reasonable, however, where there are numbers of Roman Catholics or Jews, to provide versions satisfactory to them—for the Roman Catholics the Douay-Challoner Version, or the admirable 1941 revision of the English Bible by a commission appointed by the American hierarchy, and for the Jews the Leeser Version. This procedure usually avoids all difficulty. Indeed, all three versions should be available in all public libraries of any importance.

There has been at least one important case before the courts on the question of the Bible in a library supported by public funds. It arose in connection with the Selma High School in California and was decided by the state supreme court in 1924. The local school board adopted a resolution authorizing the purchase of twelve copies of the King James Version for the library of the schools. Complainants, who apparently were Roman Catholic sympathizers, brought suit, believing that this action was contrary to the constitution and statutes of the state.

This is apparently the first time that the issue of sectarian influence was squarely raised before the highest court of a state in the matter of placing the Bible in a public school library. The court, by unanimous decision, held (1) that the King James Version of the Bible is not a sectarian book and (2) that neither the constitution nor the statutes would be violated by placing any version of the Bible in a public school library.[171]

A serious case that has more recently arisen with reference to school library censorship is connected with the canceling by certain public school boards in New York, New Jersey, and elsewhere of subscriptions to *The Nation* because of a series of articles it had published by Paul Blanshard dealing in a critical way with the position taken by the Roman Catholic Church on various matters such as divorce, birth control, etc. (later made into the influential book *American Freedom and Catholic Power*). The New York state education commissioner supported the school board in its view that it had the right and responsibility of deciding what publications may be included in school libraries, and thus the right to exclude *The Nation*.[172]

The American Library Association has discussed ways of preventing religious censorship by groups in public library boards. It has even considered publishing black lists of librarians yielding to undue pressure. At the annual meeting in 1948 the president of the association warned his hearers that censorship was destroying intellectual freedom. He asked,

Should a small religious minority be allowed to keep off the shelves of a library a biography of their founder that does not depict her as they feel she should be depicted? Should copies of *The Nation* ever be removed from library shelves? Should libraries in the South fail to have current books on the race problem or novels on the problem that may be offensive to perhaps even a majority of their constituents? Should witch hunts for subversive books persuade librarians not to stock a book because it is friendly to Russia or a communistic idea? The answer to all these questions is, of course, an emphatic no.[173]

Chapter 16

ADJUSTMENTS IN THE CHURCH EDUCATION FIELD

Parochial Schools as Substitute for Public Schools

It is important at the outset to define what we mean by the term "public school" as distinguished from one that is private or parochial. A Massachusetts court in 1866 held that "public" or "common" school referred, under the legislation of the state, to schools which are (1) "supported by general taxation," (2) "open to all free of expense," (3) "under the immediate control and superintendence of agents appointed by the voters of each town or city."[1] The inference is that all schools that do not meet this threefold test are not public. Consequently parochial and other private schools, even though they meet the second test, cannot be considered strictly public institutions because they are not supported by taxation and are not under public control. This inference seems sound, for it is a fundamental thesis of democracy that the people through their own duly chosen agents alone have the right to determine the policy of publicly supported institutions or agencies, be they the Federal army and navy, or state forests, or local fire departments, or teachers' colleges, or elementary schools.

The only serious problems in Church-State relations as far as Church schools are concerned is provided by the efficient parochial school system of the Roman Catholic Church, whose purpose and development have already been discussed.[2] The question here is the demand of many of its advocates that it receive financial aid from the State, either directly, by a share of the school fund, or indirectly through free bus transportation, free textbooks, or other services for its pupils. These desired forms of aid will be discussed from various points of view later in this chapter. They can be understood only as we remember that some Roman Catholics have openly opposed the public schools on account of their allegedly "godless" character, and many conscientiously criticize them. An extreme example is the book by the Reverend Paul L. Blakely, S.J., *May an American Oppose the Public School?* with the imprimatur of Cardinal Hayes. He favored only schools in which textbooks, teachers, and curriculum are regulated by the Roman Catholic Church, quoting from the encyclical on education of Pope Pius XI to support his views. The Lutherans, whose parochial school system stands second in importance, do not object to paying taxes for the public schools and do not wish subsidies for their own schools. But as they give up their foreign language services the tendency is for their parochial schools to decrease in relative significance.

Of other Church groups the Episcopalians, the Friends, the Seventh Day Adventists, and the Jews perhaps have relatively the largest number of denominational schools. The Friends' schools are mainly confined to a few states; those of the Episcopalians are mainly private schools for persons who can afford to pay fairly large tuition fees.

The exact number of children attending each type or denomination of private and parochial schools cannot be estimated with certainty. The figures for 1960, the last year for which full statistics are available, show that there were then 117,637 public and 17,635 non-public elementary and secondary schools in the nation.[3] *The Official Catholic Directory* for that year indicates that 12,805 Roman Catholic elementary and secondary schools were then in operation. However, since these schools almost invariably have a much higher student enrollment per school than do other non-public schools, it is certain that the proportion of Catholic children attending non-public schools is much greater than would be indicated by the figures. For the same year (1960) the records of the United States Office of Education show that there were 43,927,801 children of school age (five to seventeen) in the United States, of which 36,146,846 were enrolled in public schools. The difference between these figures is 7,780,-955, and of these *The Official Catholic Directory* shows that 5,130,195 were enrolled in Catholic schools. (By 1963 the figure had increased to approximately 5,450,000.) When it is realized that many children do not enter school until they are six and that some children of school age attend no school at all, the frequent estimate that 90 per cent of children enrolled in non-public schools attend Roman Catholic schools is seen to be substantially correct.

The development of parochial schools on a national scale goes back to the First Plenary Council of Baltimore, which has been discussed in an earlier chapter.[4] Bishop John Hughes was then the most vigorous of Roman Catholic leaders. He bitterly attacked the public school system. He tried hard, with the backing of Governor William H. Seward, an Episcopalian, to secure the support of Church schools by the New York legislature. He complained that if this were not forthcoming Catholics would be subject to "a second taxation, required not by the laws of the land, but the no less imperious demands of their conscience." When his efforts to secure state support through political action failed, he turned his forceful, fighting personality into the movement to build up the parochial school system.

The decisions of the plenary councils between 1852 and 1884 laid the foundations for the remarkable development of Roman Catholic parochial schools which has since taken place. In general the position of the hierarchy has remained at least theoretically the same: Catholic parents are required to send their children to parochial schools when these are available, unless a dispensation is secured from the bishop. The press frequently contains admonitions to the faithful on the subject. For instance, in the fall of 1942 the Bishop of Mobile (Alabama) issued an annual warning that "the sacraments are to be denied to all parents not sending their children to the Catholic school." In the same year, the *Catholic Week* reminded its readers that "no priest of the diocese, be he pastor or curate, can grant this dispensation [of excuse]. It must come only from Bishop Toolen." But, said the *Week*, "if their [parents'] reasons are sufficiently weighty, he will grant the dispensation." [5]

Probably, however, there are many dioceses where these provisions are not strictly observed, and certainly millions of Catholic children are in the public schools. It is frequently estimated that one out of every two Catholic children of school age attends a public school.[6] However, one reason is that the parochial schools do not have room for all the Catholic children seeking to attend; they commonly have long waiting lists of parents who would like to enroll their children.

The following sections of the Canon Law, quoted by Justice Jackson in his dissenting opinion in the Everson case, shows how important Church-controlled education is in Roman Catholic doctrine.

1215. Catholic children are to be educated in schools where not only nothing contrary to Catholic faith and morals is taught, but rather in schools where religious and moral training occupy the first place. * * * (Canon 1372.)

1216. In every elementary school the children must, according to their age, be instructed in Christian doctrine.

The young people who attend the higher schools are to receive a deeper religious knowledge, and the bishops shall appoint priests qualified for such work by their learning and piety. (Canon 1373.)

1217. Catholic children shall not attend non-Catholic, indifferent, schools that are mixed, that is to say, schools open to Catholic and non-Catholics alike. The bishop of the diocese only has the right, in harmony with the instructions of the Holy See, to decide under what circumstances, and with what safeguards to prevent loss of faith, it may be tolerated that Catholic children go to such schools.

1224. The religious teaching of youth in any schools is subject to the authority and inspection of the Church.

The local Ordinaries have the right and duty to watch that nothing is taught contrary to faith or good morals, in any of the schools of their territory.

They, moreover, have the right to approve the books of Christian doctrine and the teachers of religion, and to demand, for the sake of safeguarding religion and morals, the removal of teachers and books. (Canon 1381.) (Woywod, Rev. Stanislaus, The New Canon Law, under imprimatur of Most Rev. Francis J. Spellman, Archbishop of New York and others, 1940.)

Although parochial schools have existed and flourished in this country for well over a century, there are many who still question their desirability. It is therefore appropriate to set forth here the principal arguments that have been advanced for and against these schools.

Reasons Given for Parochial Schools

They represent the conscientious wishes of a large and important element of the population to advance at much personal sacrifice the cause of religion and education in ways they think best.

They save taxpayers large amounts of money that would otherwise have to be expended in supplying extra accommodation in public schools.

They encourage discipline, moral standards, and especially the religious faith of those patronizing them.

Their standards, though differing widely, average about the same as those of the public schools, and the states can, if they will, make and enforce requirements as to teacher standards, health conditions, inclusion of courses in American history and government, etc.

Their teachers on the whole are men and women of character, unselfishness, and devotion who make a lifework of their profession.

They form a natural early training ground for the priesthood and other religious professions.

They provide a social outlet for the work and interests of the normal parish and a bond among its members.

They have provided a useful transition factor between European and American life and have helped to keep this country in touch with the main cultural tradition of western Europe.

Reasons Given Against Parochial Schools

They separate a large segment of the population from a great American "educational melting pot" in which they could both give and get much of value, and they consequently encourage a cult of "separateness" that is unfortunate. They weaken the public schools by drawing away the educational interests of many citizens from the public schools.

They employ mainly as teachers nuns living in Roman Catholic convents and detached from the mainstream of American life, who are trained to look unsympathetically at the Protestant religious viewpoint of most Americans.

They are constantly endeavoring to get financial help from public taxation, a plan which most Americans believe to be unconstitutional and fraught with grave dangers to our inherited freedoms.

Their teachers are not encouraged by training to undertake either independent thinking or democratic action, being taught that they must teach and do what the Church demands. Their high character is therefore to be balanced against a tendency to narrowness and subservience.

Their teaching, though loyal to the republic, is consequently likely to be so dominated by theological and ecclesiastical authoritarianism as not to fit pupils adequately to discuss impartially and independently in the classroom the great social and political problems which face the country.

They devote so much time to matters theological, ecclesiastical, and religious, and to old-time disciplinary subjects, as to leave too little time for the modern studies. Or to put it another way, they tend to emphasize the European background rather than conditions of present-day America.

They or their superiors object so much to state inspection and standardization that such state laws as exist on this subject are likely to go by default.

They tend to present American history inaccurately. For example, a study of nine high school texts prepared by Roman Catholic authors for use in their parochial schools showed an overemphasis on Roman Catholic contributions and the minimizing or overlooking of non-Catholic contributions. The net result is a warped understanding of the history of the nation, which reacts unfavorably on Catholic attitudes toward non-Catholics. In one of the texts examined, at least a third of the book was devoted to Roman Catholic matters, while no other religious body was mentioned in the section on our national period, though the Catholic Church here at the time was relatively small and uninfluential. Probably the regular public school textbooks occasionally err on the other side, but they are almost never guilty of the systematic minimizing of Roman Catholic influence.

The Rights of Private and Parochial Schools

There have been several cases in which the question of freedom in education, especially the right of parents to select their own schools, has come before the higher courts in the United States. Most of these were brought up for decision as to their constitutionality by religious groups to protect themselves against laws in western states which, in the interest of "Americanism," tried to interfere in one way or another with Church schools, even going so far as to require public school attendance of all children. Strangely enough, this movement in America came to a head before the development of the totalitarian State in Europe. It was led by vigorous and conscientious but sometimes extreme Protestants, who feared that the parochial schools of the Roman Catholic Church might prove inimical to democracy by educating a group apart, with supreme allegiance to Rome.

The courts have generally decided, as stated by the Supreme Court of Ohio as early as 1877, that it is not the "public policy of the state that the children of the state shall not receive any education in any other schools than in one of the public schools established by itself." [7] This would seem a reasonable position, but, to prevent advocates of a superpatriotic type from making it illegal for parents to educate their children in parochial or private schools, one state, Kentucky, in 1891 adopted an addition to its Bill of Rights reading, "Nor shall any man be compelled to send his child to any school to which he may be conscientiously opposed." [8] The following year (1892) the voters of Wisconsin repealed the Bennett law of 1889, to which the Lutherans and Roman Catholics had strenuously objected, because it required the elementary education of children to be in the English language.

There have been two especially important cases before the Supreme Court of the United States on this issue of freedom in education. The first was *Meyer* v. *Nebraska* in 1923, in which the Court reversed the conviction of one Robert T. Meyer, a teacher in a school maintained by the Zion Evangelical Lutheran Congregation, for unlawfully teaching the subject of reading in the German language, from a collection of Bible stories, to children who had not passed the eighth grade of elementary school, in violation of a 1919 statute which forbade such teaching (see Chapter 5).

The second was the famous Oregon parochial school case of 1925, entitled *Pierce* v. *Society of Sisters* (see Chapter 5). This decision held unconstitutional a law requiring that all children between the ages of eight and sixteen (with a few exceptions) attend public school. It in no way cast any doubt upon the power of the State to require that all children receive a basic secular education in some school, and later decisions of the Court specifically upheld this power even where the parents claimed that compulsory secular education violated their religious beliefs.

Such a case, for example, was *People* v. *Donner*,[9] decided in 1951. A number of extremely orthodox Jewish parents sent their children to a small religious school in which they learned only Bible, the Talmud, and elementary Jewish law, all taught exclusively in Yiddish and Hebrew. When they were prosecuted for violating the state's compulsory school attendance law, which required that all children receive secular instruction in ten common branches of learning for a period equivalent to the time spent for that purpose in public schools, they asserted that this law violated their religious freedom—according to their interpretation of Jewish law, all systematic, secular education is forbidden. The Supreme Court refused to review their conviction, thus in effect affirming it.[10]

Nor does the Pierce case cast any doubt on the right of the State to inspect parochial schools to assure that they comply with minimum standards. In fact, however, such inspection is often purely perfunctory if undertaken at all. A study of the supervision of sectarian (i.e., parochial and other denominational) schools by public school authorities was published by the National Education Association in 1946. With five states not heard from, the results are given from the then remaining forty-three states, the territories of Alaska and Hawaii, and the District of Columbia. There is generally the requirement that English be the medium of instruction in all privately conducted schools. Similarly, three-fourths of the states provide by law that education in parochial schools shall be equivalent to that in public schools. The following are the more important findings of the study showing the situation in the states in which private and sectarian schools are inspected in the matters mentioned: term equivalent to public schools, 20; certification of teachers, 15; registration with state department, 14; state-approved course of study, 19; U.S. Constitution, American history, civics, etc., in curriculum, 21; physiology and hygiene included, 19; hygiene and effects of narcotics taught, 18; standards for facilities and equipment, 15; attendance records filed, 27. Seven other states require inspection in most of these matters when formal state approval is sought.[11]

Attempted Adjustments to Public Education

The position of the Roman Catholic Church in the United States is that parochial schools should receive financial support from government because they are public schools in that they serve the public interest by admitting students irrespective of their religion; that parochial schools by their educational work save the taxpayers much money contributed by the Church for their erection and support; that the sincere Roman Catholic is now in a position of having to pay what he considers "double taxation," when he does not use the public schools; that the First Amendment to the Constitution does not prevent financial aid to religious bodies so long as this is given impartially, that in adopting it Congress had in mind mainly to prevent the establishment of a single Church for the Federal union; that the phrase "separation of Church and State" does not exist in the Constitution or any of its amendments; that the support of religious schools by government, frequent in colonial days and in the early days of the republic, does not and should not involve government control.[12]

The Church has been unable to win general acceptance of this position and has accordingly found it necessary to seek alternative plans under which some part of the financial burden of maintaining parochial school education would be undertaken by the State. The plan which at present seems to have attracted the most attention is the shared-time plan, discussed in the preceding chapter, but this is still mainly only in the talking stage, although here and there a few experimental efforts have been made to put it into effect. An earlier, more widespread effort was the so-called Faribault plan. It was the subject of considerable controversy within the Roman Catholic community and has remained a source of Protestant-Catholic tension and litigation.

The Faribault plan [13] is identified with the name of Archbishop John Ireland, who accepted the traditional Catholic doctrine that the education of the child belongs primarily to the parent and the Church but frankly conceded that the State as an agent of the parents has the right and duty of imparting instruction as well as the power of compulsory education.

As a result of his efforts, in 1891 the Catholic schools at Faribault and Stillwater, Minnesota, were in large measure placed under the control of the public school boards during the regular school hours, and the members of the religious societies, who were engaged as teachers, were listed on the payroll as public school teachers, receiving salaries just as teachers in regular public schools did. After hearing mass in the parish church, the children were marched to the schools, which were technically leased to the public school authorities. At the close of the regular public school day, the children were instructed in their catechism for an hour and then dismissed. No textbooks objected to by the archbishop were used, although both the teachers and the pupils were subject to examination by the school board.[14]

The Faribault plan was defended by many Catholics as a necessary compromise, while others attacked it as violating the decisions of the plenary councils. In 1892 the Congregation of the Propaganda in Rome issued a decision stating that "The Decrees of the Baltimore Councils in respect to parochial schools remaining in full force, the agreement entered into by Archbishop Ireland relative to the schools of Faribault and Stillwater, in view of all the circumstances, may be tolerated." [15]

This rather ambiguous decision did not settle the controversy. Later in the same year, the first apostolic delegate to the United States, Archbishop Francesco Satolli, came to this country and quickly became embroiled in the general furor regarding parochial and public school education as well as the specifics of the Faribault plan. He issued a statement which not only indicated tolerance of that plan but also apparently approved enrolling Catholic children in public schools in particular localities if the bishop found that this could be done with-out endangering their faith.[16] The statement appeared to nullify the rulings of the Baltimore councils, but it was for all practical purposes rescinded by a letter sent the following year (1893) by the pope to Cardinal Gibbons stating emphatically that "the decrees which the Baltimore Councils . . . have enacted concerning parochial schools . . . are to be steadfastly observed." [17]

This letter, unqualified and unambiguous as it was, put an end at least to the present time of any appreciable effort within the Catholic Church to legalize in principle the enrolling of Catholic children in public schools for full instruction. Moreover, the language of the letter would seem to rule im-permissible the compromise represented by the Faribault plan. Nevertheless, in many small rural communities, particularly in the Midwest and the South, Catholic and public school officials entered into arrangements which were in effect the Faribault plan.[18]

The pattern was generally uniform. The local priest leased the parochial school building to the public school authorities, sometimes for a nominal rental such as one dollar a year. The teaching staff, usually consisting of nuns, became technically public school teachers on the public payroll but remained at the school unless they were transferred by their ecclesiastical superiors to another school. Mass was conducted in the parish church, generally on the same premises as the school, before school officially opened, and catechism was taught at the end of the school day, by the same teachers who earlier taught secular subjects. All in all, there was no difference in the appearance of the school and little difference in its operation after its technical transfer to the public school board. Indeed, in some cases the same school remained listed in Catholic Church records as a parochial school while listed in public school records as a public school.[19]

This situation has given rise to considerable controversy and litigation, often bitter, as in North College Hill, Ohio, and Dixon, New Mexico. The organiza-tion Protestants and Other Americans United (POAU) has made it a special project to challenge in the courts the legality of these schools, which it calls "captive schools." With rare exceptions, the courts have held the arrangements to be unconstitutional and illegal and have ordered them discontinued.[20] How-ever, POAU claims that they are still in effect in many communities. Because the North College Hill controversy was the first to receive national attention and in many respects is typical, it will be set forth in some detail here.[21]

The situation began to be acute in 1940 when St. Mary Margaret Parochial School in North College Hill, a small suburb of Cincinnati, with its teaching staff of eight nuns, was incorporated into the local public educational system by a board of education in which the Catholics had secured a majority of one.

The school was leased for $3,500 a year, paid to the archbishop, an amount ultimately increased to $6,000. Although the school continued to be operated on the old parochial lines, its name was changed to the Grace Avenue School.

Owing to local indignation at the arrangement, so inconsistent with American public school traditions and with the constitutional separation of Church and State, the Catholic candidates were defeated in the election of 1942 and the new board of education terminated the arrangement. For the next four years the parochial school, though receiving no public funds, continued in existence, supported as it had been originally by the Roman Catholics.

In 1945, however, a normal slight non-Catholic majority in the school district of about 7,500 people relaxed its vigilance and lost, the main issue being the incorporation of the school. A strong point was made by the Citizens School League of the fact that under Ohio law a subvention from the state is made according to the number of pupils attending a public school, and that this subvention would be increased by the addition of the parochial school pupils.

Increased tension resulted when it appeared that not only was the parochial school building to be rented again for public school purposes, at an increased rental, the church retaining the basement for its own uses, but an attempt was being made to place it, and to some extent all the other schools in the school district, under Roman Catholic domination. It was this more than the leasing of the parochial school that stirred up the community. The crisis came over the appointment of new teachers, whose nomination under Ohio law was vested in the superintendent. As he declined to be interfered with in the matter, or to turn over his teacher correspondence file to the board, he was charged with insubordination, and at its meeting in February, 1947, the board voted not to renew his appointment when it expired in July. When this decision became known some seven-hundred students of the schools went on strike. The situation seemed so serious that the National Education Association investigated, severely criticized the school board, and upheld the superintendent, Dr. Cook, a former professor of education at the University of Cincinnati. The Ohio Education Association black-listed the school as "an unprofessional place" for teachers to work.

The N.E.A. made an eight-point indictment, including the board's "unwarranted action" in refusing to re-employ Dr. Cook, its ignoring the protest "of the great majority" of students and teachers, and its conducting "the affairs of the board in such a way that large sections of the community have been divided on religious grounds." As to the continuing character of the school as of the Roman Catholic parochial type, the report stated,

This school enrolled only Catholic pupils and was taught largely by Catholic Sisters, wearing the garb of their religious order. It was conducted as a sectarian school, but paid for out of public funds. Sectarian religious instruction was given each day as a regular part of the school program. The symbolic decorations of the building were of a sectarian nature. The Sisters were paid from public funds under contract with the local board of education.[22]

The school board met in April in a public session, with about a thousand persons reported as attending in the large school gymnasium. The School Improvement Association, which supported the non-Catholic minority on the board, and other citizens offered petitions for the reinstatement of Superintendent Cook, but the petitions were not considered. This created indignation, which grew still hotter when letters were received from twenty-nine of the thirty-three regular teachers in the schools resigning in protest. In the discussion that followed a fracas broke out that resulted in the arrest of several persons in the protesting group. The whole situation was so serious that it threatened to spread its ill feeling over a wide area. The tension was reflected in the action of various non-Catholic organizations in the Cincinnati area. For example, the Council of Churches of Greater Cincinnati, at a meeting attended by large numbers of ministers and laymen, commended the action of certain taxpayers who had brought suit in the Common Pleas Court to recover the money which they felt had been illegally paid from public funds for the rental of the parochial school. Furthermore, it authorized its headquarters committee to oppose the use of public funds "for the establishment and maintenance of sectarian religious schools or the teaching of sectarian religious belief or practice in public schools." [23]

The next important move came in June, when, yielding to public opinion at a large mass meeting, the Roman Catholic majority of three board members resigned. The Protestant minority did the same, thus throwing the administration of the schools into the hands of Probate Judge Chase M. Davies of Cincinnati. After a public hearing he offered the superintendency again to Dr. Cook for a three-year term and the latter accepted it.

In November, by a vote of about 2,400 to 1,600 two Protestants were elected to the school board for the vacancies then to be filled. The election was interesting for two reasons: it brought nearly all the voters to the polls, and it showed that though the town was fairly evenly divided between the two major religious groups a large number of Catholics, believing that the former Catholic members had been wrong in trying to conduct the schools in a way inconsistent with our constitutional Church-State separation, voted for the Protestant candidates.[24]

Thus the situation was restored to a constitutional basis in keeping with the American tradition. Judge Davies appointed a new board of education of five members, of whom four were Protestants and one was a much respected Catholic who had shown himself a moderate in school matters. The Catholic later resigned for reasons not connected with the school situation. After the November elections all the members of the board were Protestants, and for the first time in years a Protestant mayor and city council were chosen. The arrangement between the parish and the public school system was discontinued, and the Grace Avenue School became again the St. Mary Margaret parochial school.

Non-Catholic Parochial Schools

Among the Protestant Churches the one that has most nearly approximated the Roman Catholic parochial school system is the Lutheran Church. Indeed, it may be considered in many ways the effective founder of the modern parochial school system of general education under religious auspices, having adopted it before the Council of Trent. The Catholic Church had developed the external schools conducted by monasteries, episcopal and cathedral schools, guild schools, city schools, and many other useful types of education, but it was the early Lutherans, confronted by their special problems in northern Europe, who most clearly emphasized the parish unit as the basis for humanistic education in addition to religious training. Therefore, since Luther's time the parochial school has been a characteristic Lutheran institution.

When the Germans began to settle in the American colonies in considerable numbers during the eighteenth century they always emphasized the schooling of their children. All the German sects, which were particularly strong in Pennsylvania, had their parochial schools—that is, schools including the ordinary branches of education in addition to religion. The ministers were frequently the schoolmasters. By 1750 all the congregations in Pennsylvania but one reported flourishing schools. These developed to such an extent that when the Pennsylvania Assembly in 1796 took steps to introduce free schools the Ministerium of Pennsylvania addressed a petition to it on the subject, fearing that the plan might injure the existing educational system. By 1820 there were 206 parochial schools and 84 congregations.[25]

Throughout the first half of the nineteenth century these parochial Lutheran schools were flourishing in the Ministerium of Pennsylvania and that of New York, but the absence of a seminary for the training of teachers, the growth of free public schools, and the gradual substitution of English for German as the language taught in the home, resulted in the decline of the system in the East. The same plan, however, was taken up very actively by the Evangelical

Lutheran Synod of Missouri, Ohio, and Other States, established by the Lutherans who sailed from Germany in 1838.[26] Nine years later the Lutheran Church-Missouri Synod was formed and among its purposes, according to Article III of its constitution, was "The training of teachers. . . . The publication of school books. . . . The furtherance of Christian parochial schools." [27] The first president of the Synod, Dr. Carl F. W. Walther, stated that "Next to the public ministry, the chief means of preserving and spreading our Church is the solicitous promotion of our parochial School system." [28] By 1857 there were 114 schools.[29] By 1927 the Synod had 1,354 parochial schools, and today the number has increased to 1,456.[30]

There are certain clearly marked characteristics of the Lutheran school system:

The predominance of men teachers over women. In this the Lutheran system, following the German tradition, is differentiated from the public school system of this country and from the Roman Catholic parochial schools.

The great emphasis on thorough Lutheran-religious instruction. Otherwise the main features of the public school curriculum are reproduced.

The regular instruction in German or one of the Scandinavian or other European languages with which the Church group is connected. This emphasis is declining.

The concentration of responsibility for the parochial school on the parish itself, which elects a committee, of which the pastor is generally chairman, to look after the school.

The thorough preparation of teachers at Lutheran colleges or teachers' seminaries.

The continued success of the Lutheran school movement in the North Central states, and at the same time its decline in the Eastern states, where English has become the dominant language of the home.

The frequent opposition to compromising denominational convictions by uniting to support weekday schools under combined Protestant auspices for the purpose of teaching "a general Protestant religion" after regular school hours.[31]

The providing of instruction at low cost, or free, at the expense of the congregation.[32]

The enthusiasm and loyal support of members of the churches, who normally send their children to their schools.

The dependence entirely on self-support and the unwillingness of the Church to ask for any support from public funds. In this respect there is a striking difference between the supporters of the Roman Catholic and the Lutheran schools.

The Jews in the United States have been highly appreciative of the opportunities of the American public school system, and the overwhelming majority of Jews have availed themselves of its privilege. They have, however, supplemented this secular education by various forms of Jewish education. Some of them go much farther than most Protestant groups have gone in providing for adequate background religious instruction. This movement goes back to the early synagogue schools, and to the general Jewish Sunday school, not affiliated with any synagogue, as first established in Philadelphia in 1838. It has been particularly strong since 1910, when the Bureau of Jewish Education (now called the Jewish Education Committee) was established in New York. This was the first time that an American Jewish community recognized its responsibilities to provide adequate educational facilities in keeping with Jewish history for its boys and girls. More than twenty-five other Jewish communities have since followed the New York lead by establishing a competent central community agency devoted to Jewish education.[33]

This agency was conceived on a broad plan to advance the religious education of Jewish youth. It had little sympathy with the one-day-a-week Sunday school idea, which it thought inadequate, or with the ordinary parochial school that included both secular and religious subjects, which it felt removed the Jewish youth too much from the rank and file of other Americans. It favored a communal school, not affiliated with any one congregation, to provide instruction in Hebrew, the Bible, and Jewish history. The idea was to build largely on the basis of the so-called Talmud Torahs—weekday schools unaffiliated with any specific congregations.[34] However, in recent years the independent Talmud Torah has largely disappeared, at least outside New York City, to be replaced by the after-hours religious schools connected with specific congregations. There is hardly a synagogue today outside New York City, whether Reform, Conservative, or Orthodox, that does not have its own religious school.[35]

In addition, there has been lately a great rise in the number of Jewish children attending day schools, the equivalent of Catholic parochial schools, where both religious and secular subjects are taught. In 1936 only 3,000 Jewish children attended such schools; in 1963 it was estimated that more than 50,000 Jewish children were enrolled in them.[36] Despite this increase, it is unlikely that they represent a major tendency of American Judaism or that more than a small percentage of Jewish children will receive their secular education in non-public schools.

Direct Aid to Parochial Schools

There has been, and there is today perhaps more than ever, considerable opposition by Roman Catholics in the United States to being called upon to support two systems of education—the public schools maintained by the State and the parochial schools maintained by the parish or other Church unit. They feel that since their schools, to which they contribute generously, are open to public inspection and provide instruction free or practically so, they should be exempt from paying taxes to support the so-called "public" or "free common schools," or else receive State grants-in-aid for their parochial schools. They take the position that, whereas the modern public school system of the United States, which derived much of its inspiration from Prussia, is fairly well adapted if adequately supplemented by Church or home to train citizens as such, it is prevented by its secularity from meeting the higher spiritual needs of youth. To the Catholic the civil government cannot truly educate youth in the full and deeper meaning of the term, because all such education will be inadequate except when it is under the direction and control of the Church or of those committed to the viewpoint of the Church.

There have been three groups in the Roman Catholic Church concerned with aid from tax funds for parochial schools. The first, represented in general by the hierarchy and priesthood, and most of the laity, believes that such grants are legitimate and strongly favors them; the second, represented by a small group of liberals, recognizes that such grants may be unconstitutional federally under recent opinions of the Supreme Court and are definitely unconstitutional under the constitutions or statutes of most of the states; the third group, also a small but thoughtful one, holds a somewhat intermediate position, believing that such grants are legitimate and have some precedents in American history but that it is unwise to press the issue at this time because of the strong public opinion among non-Catholic citizens against grants from tax funds to any schools conducted by religious bodies. The first group has probably always been the largest, but within the past three or four years—more specifically since the issuance on March 2, 1961, of an authoritative statement by the National Catholic Welfare Conference [37]—its dominance has become so manifest that one today rarely hears either of the other two views expressed by recognized Roman Catholic spokesmen.[38]

The maintenance of separate schools by the Church is a costly matter when large numbers in many centers are involved. In spite of their devotion to their Church, Roman Catholics probably would not be able to meet the expense were it not that they can make use of a celibate clergy of various orders, and of many nuns who are increasingly receiving special training for such work.

The question of financial aid to parochial schools has created much friction in some parts of the country, especially in large urban centers where Roman Catholics have a well-developed parochial school system and consequently do not wish to be heavily taxed for public schools, and among Protestants in some places where Roman Catholics have opposed the development at the expense of taxpayers of adequate public school facilities. The Roman Catholic Church feels that the exclusion of religion from the public schools supported by taxation, which under the McCollum and Schempp-Murray decisions is constitutionally required, is so serious a matter that where parochial schools are provided it puts pressure upon its members to attend them.

On the other hand, from the early days of our republic the general feeling of non-Catholics has been that the State should tax all its citizens for the support of public education. If any Church wishes to provide additional schools of its own, it is entitled to do so but entirely at its own expense.

The attempt to prevent state appropriations to denominational schools goes back to James Madison in his fight against the Assessment Bill in Virginia, and his "Remonstrance." This had its repercussions in other states and doubtless influenced the broad wording of what is now the first clause of the Federal Bill of Rights. Connecticut seems to have been the first state to put into a constitution a specific provision against grants to denominational schools. Its constitution of 1818 included this important statement, repeated in letter or spirit in the constitutional or statutory requirements of nearly all the states:

. . . no law shall ever be made authorizing such [school] funds to be devoted to any other use than the encouragement and support of public or common schools among the several school societies, as justice and equity shall require.[39]

The most notable issue that arose in the matter of State aid to parochial schools in the first half-century of the republic was that in New York in the 1840's, when, under the leadership of Archbishop Hughes, the Roman Catholic Church tried to secure the legalization of the appropriation of public money for sectarian schools. The matter went so far that a Roman Catholic ticket was placed in the field in the state elections. The controversy was settled by an act of the New York State legislature, April 11, 1842, which provided that

No school shall be entitled to, or receive, any portion of the school moneys, in which the religious doctrines or tenets of any particular Christian or other religious sect shall be taught, inculcated, or practiced, or in which any book or books containing compositions favorable or prejudicial to the particular doctrines or tenets of any sect shall be used.[40]

The experience in New York was duplicated in other states and the movement to prevent State aid to parochial and other denominational schools continued vigorously through the seventies and eighties. By the close of the century few states continued to give any direct aid to private or denominational schools. (The principal exceptions were some old foundations of the academy type, which had virtually become undenominational.) The movement was stimulated by the discussions in Congress of President Grant's proposal in 1875 for an amendment to the Federal Constitution which would forbid such aid.

The fact that over the border in Canada separate schools for Roman Catholics and for Protestants and Jews are provided from public funds in most of the provinces has kept the issue much to the fore in certain Northern states with a large urban Roman Catholic population and with forceful bishops supporting the plan. One typical example may be quoted. The question was a political issue in 1933-34 in Ohio, where some Roman Catholic bishops went so far as to advise opposition to legislative candidates who did not favor State aid to parochial schools. After prolonged debate the legislature declined by a small margin, in spite of strong pressure, to "divide the fund" by granting public aid to parochial schools.[41]

In 1927 Father Richard J. Gabel, in a thorough study entitled *Public Funds for Church and Private Schools*, summed up the constitutional situation in the states as follows:

1. Thirty states with enactments against the appropriation of public money to denominational or sectarian institutions or to schools under sectarian control.
2. Nine states providing against appropriations to schools not under absolute control of the State (not including Massachusetts and North Dakota).
3. Six states with provisions against drawing on the treasury for the benefit of any religious sect, society, or theological institution.
4. Eight states with provisions against appropriations for any sectarian purpose, viz., California, Colorado, Idaho, Illinois, Mississippi, Missouri, Montana, Nevada.
5. Four states with provisions against the control of school funds by any religious sect (Ohio, Kansas, South Carolina, and Mississippi).
6. Two states forbidding the acceptance of any gift or grant for sectarian purposes (Nebraska and South Dakota).[42]

Today, after the passage of a quarter of a century and the admission of two new states to the Union, the situation has changed little if at all since this authoritative survey was made.

This is substantiated by a study issued by the United States Office of Education in 1958 under the title, "The State and Nonpublic Schools." This shows that of the 48 states then in the Union, 38 had provisions in their constitutions expressly prohibiting the state or municipalities from appropriating money or property to sectarian schools or institutions, or for the benefit of any sect or religious society. The two states that have been admitted since this study was published, Alaska and Hawaii, also have such prohibitions in their constitutions.

Of the ten states which do not have a specific prohibition in respect to sectarian schools, the following should be noted:

Arkansas has a provision in its constitution forbidding appropriations of money or property to any private school or institution, which would of course include sectarian schools.

Connecticut's constitution provides that "the school fund" shall not be "diverted to any other use than the encouragement and support of public, or common schools."

Iowa provides in its constitution that no person "shall be compelled to attend any place of worship, pay tithes, taxes, or other rates for building or repairing any church or churches, place or places of worship, or for the maintenance of any ministers, or ministry." The Supreme Court of Iowa, in the case of *Knowlton* v. *Baumhover*, interpreted this provision as prohibiting the use of public funds in support of any sectarian schools or teaching.

Maine does not appear to have any constitutional provision which would specifically bar appropriations of public funds for the support of parochial schools.

Maryland's constitution provides that no person shall be compelled to maintain any place of worship or any ministry.

New Jersey's constitution provides that no person shall be "obliged to pay tithes, taxes, or other rates for building or repairing any church or churches, place or places of worship, or for the maintenance of any minister or ministry."

North Carolina provides in its constitution that all state funds and property for education "shall be faithfully appropriated for establishing and maintaining in this State a system of free public schools, and for no other uses or purposes whatsoever."

Tennessee's constitution provides that the common school fund shall not be diverted to any other use than the support and encouragement of common schools.

Vermont's constitution provides that "no man ought to, or of right can be compelled to attend any place of worship or maintain any ministry, contrary to the dictates of his conscience."

West Virginia in its constitution forbids the levy of "any tax for the erection or repair of any house of public worship or for the support of any church or ministry."

It can be seen from this study by the United States Office of Education that all states, with the possible exception of Maine and Vermont, have provision in their constitutions which either expressly or by clear implication forbid the appropriation of public funds for the support of sectarian or parochial schools.

In view of the near universality of state constitutional provisions against direct aid to parochial schools, instances of such aid have been rare and whatever litigation there has been in the state courts on the subject has practically all concerned peripheral issues such as bus transportation, textbooks, and grants for special purposes. However, in 1961 in Vermont, perhaps the only state except Maine, which does not have a specific constitutional provision on the subject of Church-State relations in education (its constitution was last revised in 1793) the supreme court of the state declared unconstitutional a law providing for state payment of tuition for students attending parochial schools in communities which did not maintain any public schools. Although the court's decision in this case, *Swart* v. *South Burlington School District*,[43] was based exclusively on the First Amendment of the Federal Constitution (since the state constitution was silent on the subject) and the United States Supreme Court refused to review the decision,[44] it is nevertheless not binding in other states. But several years earlier, in the case of *Almond* v. *Day*, a similar result was reached by the Supreme Court of Virginia, which relied on both the Virginia and United States constitutions. Probably, therefore, should the issue arise in other states, the courts would decide the same way.

Indirect Aid to Parochial Schools—Bus Transportation

The most widespread approach to a compromise on State aid to parochial schools is the provision by direct legislative action or court decision that in about twenty states authorizes free transportation to parochial school students. Most Roman Catholics believe that, irrespective of the question of direct grants to parochial schools, there can be no valid objection to furnishing bus transportation to children attending parochial schools, since this must be considered to be exclusively a welfare service for the benefit of the children. Many Protestants, on the other hand, see a danger in such a law—an opening wedge for breaking down the traditional American separation between Church and State.

Many states have experienced the parochial bus controversy. In New York the so-called Catholic bus bill, which was a prominent issue in the 1936 campaign for the governorship because originally vetoed by Governor Herbert H. Lehman, was declared unconstitutional by the Court of Appeals in the spring of 1938 by a vote of 4 to 3. The bill required boards of education to provide transportation for students in parochial schools whenever similar transportation was provided for public school students. The majority and minority opinions in this case (*Judd* v. *Board of Education*[45]) state effectively the arguments on the constitutional question. The majority opinion said,

The argument is advanced that furnishing transportation to the pupils of private or parochial schools is not in aid or support of the schools, but rather in aid of their pupils.

This argument not only ignores the spirit, purpose and intent of the constitutional provisions, but as well their exact wording. The wording of the mandate is broad. Aid or support to the school "directly or indirectly" is proscribed. The two words must have been used with some definite intent and purpose; otherwise, why were they used at all?

Aid furnished "directly" would be that furnished in a direct line. Aid furnished "indirectly" clearly embraces any contribution to whomsoever made, circuitously, collaterally, disguised or otherwise not in a straight, open and avowed aid of the school, that may be of benefit to the institution or promotional of its interests and purposes. How could then people have expressed in the fundamental law their purpose in more apt, simple and all-embracing language?

Free transportation of pupils induces attendance at schools. The purpose of the transportation is none other than to promote the interests of the private school or religious or sectarian institution that controls and directs it.

The minority opinion took the ground that the statute is

. . . not designed to maintain the institutions themselves, that the object of the 1936 legislation was apparently to insure the attendance of the children at their respective schools for the requisite period of instruction and, perhaps, to safeguard the health of the children.

The law says to the children and parents: having chosen a proper school, you must attend regularly. The school district has been given the power to add to that; where necessary, we shall assist them in getting there.

The statute in question does not have the effect of giving public money, property or credit in aid or maintenance of religious schools. The aid is given to the pupils who are legally attending such schools, to assist them to spend the required time in attendance upon instruction.[46]

A specific proposal to permit the legislature to provide for free transportation for children to private schools was approved by the New York constitutional convention of 1938 by a large majority (134 to 9) and was further approved when the various amendments adopted were presented to the voters for ratification. The existing constitutional provision is now as follows, the last permissive clause having been added to the old regulation, which was not otherwise changed:

Neither the state nor any subdivision thereof shall use its property or credit or any public money, or authorize or permit either to be used, directly or indirectly, in aid or maintenance, other than for examination or inspection, of any school or institution of learning wholly or in part under the control or direction of any religious denomination, or in which any denominational tenet or doctrine is taught, but the legislature may provide for the transportation of children to and from any school or institution of learning.[47]

It will be noticed that this action is permissive, not mandatory; but in May, 1939, Governor Herbert H. Lehman signed a bill permitting city boards of education to provide free bus transportation for children in public, private, and parochial schools.[48]

The case of Wisconsin is particularly interesting. In November, 1946, the proposal to amend the state constitution to permit the use of public funds to provide "transportation of children to and from any parochial or private school or institution of learning" was defeated by a vote of 530,000 to 463,000 after a vigorous educational campaign on both sides. *The Christian Century* thought the result especially significant because out of a population of 3,000,000 there were about 750,000 Roman Catholics, 650,000 Lutherans, and 350,000 non-Lutheran Protestants. The Catholic group, led by the Knights of Columbus and other laymen and actively supported by the clergy through press and pulpit, took the ground that it was unjust to its pupils not to allow them to ride to their schools in buses provided in part by their parents' taxes. The Protestant group, through the state council of churches and various ministerial associations, emphasized religious liberty and Church-State separation. The Protestants asserted that if this proposed amendment referring to the aiding of pupils were adopted it would be followed in a few years, as in Maryland, with a law providing for a separate transportation system to be provided the Roman Catholic Church for its own schools—a provision which it was believed the higher Federal courts would not accept it. It is a striking fact that in Wisconsin the Lutherans, in spite of their numerous parochial schools, opposed the amendment.[49]

Fifteen years later, in 1961, the Wisconsin legislature did pass a limited bus transportation law under which children attending non-public schools would be granted free transportation to the public school in their school district, and from this point would be required to reach their non-public school on their own. However, by a vote of 4 to 2, the Supreme Court of Wisconsin in 1962 held this limited parochial bus transportation law to be in violation of the state's constitution. The majority felt that bus transportation of parochial school children even part of the way, and even to the public school where the bus in any event was going, would be a benefit to the sectarian school, since it would be relieved of a part of transportation costs which it would otherwise have to pay.[50]

Before 1947 the state courts were divided on the subject of the constitutionality of bus transportation to parochial schools out of public funds, some courts holding it constitutional and others reaching a contrary conclusion. In that year, in the famous case of *Everson* v. *Board of Education*,[51] the Supreme Court by a vote of 5 to 4 upheld a New Jersey law providing for bus transportation to parochial schools. The decision has been summarized in Chapter 5 but it is worthwhile here to set forth some extracts from both the majority opinion, written by Justice Hugo Black, and the principal minority opinion, written by Justice Wiley Rutledge. The majority opinion said,

We must consider the New Jersey statute in accordance with the . . . limitations imposed by the First Amendment. But we must not strike that State statute down if it is within the State's constitutional power even though it approaches the verge of that power. New Jersey cannot consistently with the "establishment of religion clause" of the First Amendment contribute tax-raised funds to the support of an institution which teaches the tenets and faith of any church. On the other hand, other language of the amendment commands that New Jersey cannot hamper its citizens in the free exercise of their own religion. Consequently, it cannot exclude individual Catholics, Lutherans, Mohammedans, Baptists, Jews, Methodists, Non-believers, Presbyterians, or the members of any other faith, because of their faith, or lack of it, from receiving the benefits of public welfare legislation. . . .

Measured by these standards, we cannot say that the First Amendment prohibits New Jersey from spending tax-raised funds to pay the bus fares of parochial school pupils as a part of a general program under which it pays the fares of pupils attending public or other schools. . . . That Amendment requires the state to be neutral in its relations with groups of religious believers and non-believers; it does not require the state to be their adversary. State power is no more to be used so as to handicap religions than it is to favor them.

. . . It appears that these parochial schools meet New Jersey's requirements. The State contributes no money to the schools. It does not support them. Its legislation, as applied, does no more than provide a general program to help parents get their children, regardless of their religion, safely and expeditiously to and from accredited schools.

The First Amendment has erected a wall between church and state. That wall must be kept high and impregnable. We could not approve the slightest breach. New Jersey has not breached it here.

The dissenting opinion stated,

. . . Here parents pay money to send their children to parochial schools and funds raised by taxation are used to reimburse them. This not only helps the children to get to school and their parents to send them. It aids them in a substantial way to get the very thing which they are sent to the particular school to secure, namely, religious training and teaching.

Believers of all faiths, and others who do not express their feeling toward ultimate issues of existence in any creedal form, pay the New Jersey tax. When the money so raised is used to pay for transportation to religious schools, the Catholic taxpayer to the extent of his proportionate share pays for the transportation of Lutheran, Jewish and other religiously affiliated children to receive non-Catholic religious instruction. Their parents likewise pay proportionately for the transportation of Catholic children to receive Catholic instruction. Each thus contributes to "the propagation of opinions which he disbelieves" in so far as their religions differ, as do others who accept no creed without regard to those differences. . . .

New Jersey's action therefore exactly fits the type of exaction and the kind of evil at which Madison and Jefferson struck. Under the test they framed it cannot be said that the cost of transportation is no part of the cost of education or of the religious instruction given. That it is a substantial and a necessary element is shown most plainly by the continuing and increasing demand for the state to assume it. . . .

The public function argument, by casting the issue in terms of promoting the general cause of education and the welfare of the individual, ignores the religious factor and its essential connection with the transportation, thereby leaving out the only vital element in the case. So of course do the "public welfare" and "social legislation" ideas, for they come to the same thing.

It is not because religious teaching does not promote the public or the individual's welfare, but because neither is furthered when the state promotes religious education, that the Constitution forbids it to do so. . . .

The great condition of religious liberty is that it be maintained free from sustenance, as also from other interferences, by the state. For when it comes to rest upon that secular foundation it vanishes with the resting. . . .

We have staked the very existence of our country on the faith that complete separation between the State and religion is best for the State and best for religion. . . .

The Supreme Court's decision in the New Jersey bus case created extraordinary interest and important reactions. A few examples may be cited. The New York *Times* the following day (February 11, 1947) published a two-column dispatch beginning on the front page with large headlines. Two days later Arthur Krock's column on the editorial page of the same paper was devoted entirely to the decision, pointing out particularly the danger that, unless reversed in a subsequent case, it might be a first step toward attempts to secure "more extensive support of religious education by New Jersey." In a sense, the treatment of the decision in the general press may have been one of its most significant consequences. For perhaps the first time in the nation's history, Church-State separation ceased to be taken for granted, and the general public began to think and talk about the issue. Subsequent Church-State decisions of the Supreme Court, such as the McCollum, Zorach, Regents' prayer, and Bible reading decisions, all were subject to nation-wide discussion in all media of mass communication—press, magazines, radio, and television.

The Roman Catholic press hailed the decision as an important victory for the rights of Catholic taxpayers and for the cause of religious education, although *America*, the Jesuit journal (March 5, 1949) showed that the Rutledge dissent was supported by the great majority of law reviews.

The Protestant press, led by *The Christian Century, The Churchman,* the *Methodist Southern Christian Advocate,* and various Baptist publications, was uniformly severely critical or much alarmed. The Seventh Day Adventists, a denomination which operates more than nine-hundred day schools, mostly of an elementary grade, adopted, through the executive committee of its General Conference, resolutions that show their consistent opposition to free transportation at public expense for children attending their schools. The resolution recommended that "Seventh-Day Adventists do not use busses which are operated at public expense, for the free transportation of their children to and from our schools." [52]

The bishops of the Methodist Church passed a strong resolution, which stated,

The recent decision of the Supreme Court, affirming the constitutionality of state legislation providing public funds for the transportation of children to parochial schools is, in our judgment, a departure from the American principles of the separation of church and state and carries with it a serious threat to our public educational system which is a bulwark of democracy.

We rejoice in the liberty this nation grants churches to maintain schools if they so desire, but we hold that the support from public funds of sectarian education is fraught with danger and must be resisted and ended. We shall resist all attempts of the Roman Catholic hierarchy to secure public support for such schools and other religious enterprises on the ground of the separation of the church and state because we believe that such action will create reaction here, as it has elsewhere, which may limit religious freedom. . . .[53]

Similar resolutions and statements were adopted by other major Protestant groups.[54] Out of this strong adverse reaction to the decision arose the organization Protestants and Other Americans United for the Separation of Church and State, as has already been recounted in this book.[55]

Two interesting postscripts to the Everson decision should be noted. The first occured in Pennsylvania. A Roman Catholic citizen of Kennett Square near Philadelphia, one Paul Connell, stimulated by the decision, demanded that the joint board of school directors of the Kennett school board be required under the state school code to give his daughter free bus transportation to a parochial school. The board decided that using public funds for that purpose would be contrary to the state constitution provision that "no money raised for the support of the public schools shall be used for the support of any sectarian school." [56] The Supreme Court of Pennsylvania upheld the board and a lower court.[57] Mr. Connell brought the case before the United States Supreme Court but later asked that it be dismissed.[58]

The second occurred fifteen years after the decision. Justice William O. Douglas, one of the justices who made up the majority of five in the Everson case, stated in his concurring opinion in *Engel* v. *Vitale* that he now believed he was wrong in voting to uphold the New Jersey law and should have voted to declare parochial bus transportation paid out of public funds to be unconstitutional.[59]

To the non-lawyer it might seem that the Everson decision should have settled the constitutional question and that state legislatures, if they saw fit, could thereafter freely enact transportation laws. This, however, is not the case. The fact that a state statute is held by the Supreme Court not to have violated the Federal Constitution does not preclude state courts from holding that it does violate the state constitution, even if the language of both constitutions is the same. For that reason the issue of constitutionality of bus transportation laws continued and still continues to rise in the state courts even after the Everson decision. As a matter of fact, the issue has been decided by eight state supreme courts since the Everson case, and of these, seven (Washington,[60] New Mexico,[61] Missouri,[62] Alaska,[63] Wisconsin,[64] Iowa,[65] and Oklahoma,[66]) ruled transportation laws unconstitutional.

The following extract from the opinion of the Oklahoma Supreme Court, handed down in July, 1963, is typical of the reasoning in these cases:

> The law leaves to every man the right to entertain such religious views as appeal to his individual conscience, and to provide for the religious instruction and training of his own children to the extent and in the manner he deems essential or desirable.
>
> When he chooses to seek for them educational facilities which combine secular and religious instruction, he is faced with the necessity of assuming the financial burden which that choice entails.
>
> . . . If the cost of school buses and the maintenance and operation is in aid of the public schools, then it would seem to necessarily follow that when pupils of parochial schools are transported by them such service is in aid of that school. Any such aid directly or indirectly, is expressly prohibited by that . . . provision of the constitution. It must be upheld and enforced by all courts.[67]

In addition, in one state (Oregon) a decision of the supreme court invalidating a law providing for free textbooks for parochial school use contains language indicating that the state's bus transportation law is also unconstitutional.[68] In only one state (Connecticut)[69] has a state supreme court upheld a parochial bus law after the Everson decision, although in another (Maine) the court, while holding that a city had no power to enact such legislation, stated that the state legislature could constitutionally do so.[70] It can be seen from these decisions, therefore, that the Everson decision by no means settled the issue of bus transportation, at least as far as the states are concerned.

Free Textbooks, Lunches, Etc.

Only a few states have passed laws providing free textbooks for use in parochial schools. As in the case of bus transportation, the state court decisions on the question were divided. The issue reached the United States Supreme Court in 1930 in the case of *Cochran* v. *Louisiana State Board of Education*. In that decision, which has been summarized in Chapter 5, the Court unanimously upheld such use of public funds. The question of Church-State separation was not raised in the case and the Court's opinion did not discuss or even mention it. For that reason, perhaps, the decision aroused little public interest and apparently no public controversy, even though it came but two years after the heated presidential campaign of 1928, in which the Church-State controversy played a prominent role by reason of the fact that the Democratic candidate, Alfred E. Smith, was a Roman Catholic.

Today six states have laws on their books providing for parochial school pupils to have free secular textbooks purchased with public funds—Louisiana, Mississippi, West Virginia, New Mexico, Oregon, and Rhode Island. In two, Louisiana [71] and Mississippi,[72] the state courts have upheld the laws; in two, New Mexico [73] and Oregon,[74] they have been held unconstitutional; in West Virginia and Rhode Island the issue has not yet been litigated.

The Oregon decision merits additional comment. The textbook law was defended on the ground that the books supplied were exclusively secular books, and in fact the same ones as were used in the public schools. It was therefore urged that the real beneficiaries of the law were not the parochial schools but the children, and that whatever indirect benefit accrued to the sectarian schools did not invalidate the law. At the trial of the case, the taxpayers challenging the law introduced considerable evidence and expert testimony to show that in Roman Catholic parochial schools religion is not simply another subject but the purpose and goal of all parochial school education—every subject taught there is permeated with religion. It was therefore argued that, even though the textbooks supplied out of public funds were secular, they were used for religious purposes and did in fact unconstitutionally aid the parochial schools.

With but one judge dissenting, the Supreme Court of Oregon upheld this finding and conclusion.[75] Its importance lies in the fact that if the Oregon court's finding is valid, it effectively negates the argument of many Roman Catholic spokesmen that it would be constitutional to finance out of tax-raised funds the secular subjects taught in parochial schools.

Free lunches, provided under the National School Lunch Act of 1946, and health and dental care, provided in many states to all school children, stand on a different footing. These are universally considered truly welfare benefits for the children, rather than educational aid to the schools. For this reason, while practically all major Protestant and Jewish organizations oppose bus transportation and textbook aid, they do not oppose free lunches and medical and dental services to children attending parochial schools along with those attending public schools.[76]

Federal Aid to Sectarian Schools

In the early days of the republic it was assumed that education, except for that at West Point and Annapolis, was exclusively a state matter; but in 1867, when the problem of educating the former slaves and the large number of immigrants from Europe arose, the United States Commissionership of Education was established. There was then some discussion of the possibility of Federal aid to schools in general, and to the denominational and parochial schools that were struggling courageously to meet the major educational tasks facing the nation.

The first clear-cut declaration of the Federal government against the propriety of giving financial aid to sectarian institutions was made in 1875. President Ulysses S. Grant, addressing the Army of the Tennessee, said,

. . . Encourage free schools, and resolve that not one dollar appropriated for their support shall be appropriated for the support of any sectarian schools. Resolve that neither the State nor nation, nor both combined, shall support institutions of learning other than those sufficient to afford every child growing up in the land the opportunity of a good common school education, unmixed with sectarian, pagan, or atheistical dogmas. Leave the matter of religion to the family, altar, the church, and the private school supported entirely by private contributions. Keep the church and state forever separate.[77]

It is interesting to note that the editor of the *Catholic World* which reported this address interpreted it as supporting the Roman Catholic opposition to the alleged Protestant sectarianism of the time in the public schools. He wrote,

. . . We agree with the President: 1st. No "sectarianism" in our common schools; and, therefore, not one dollar to our present system of schools, because they are sectarian. 2nd. "Not one dollar" to "Pagan" schools, in which God is ignored. 3rd. "Not one dollar" to "atheistical" schools, in which God is denied in the name of "science falsely so-called." [78]

In his message to Congress later in the year, the president reverted to the same subject, which became a matter of large public interest. The resulting debate in Congress reflects the views of the time on this Church-State issue. In accordance with this message, James G. Blaine, later Speaker of the House of

Representatives and Republican candidate for the presidency, introduced a resolution to amend the Constitution as follows:

No State shall make any laws respecting an establishment of religion or prohibiting the free exercise thereof; and no money raised by taxation in any State for the support of public schools, or derived from any public fund therefor, nor any public lands devoted thereto, shall ever be under the control of any religious sect, nor shall any money so raised or lands so devoted be divided between religious sects or denominations.[79]

In August, 1876, the resolution was passed by the House by a vote of 180 for, 7 against, and 98 not voting. In the Senate, this and similar resolutions were referred to the Judiciary Committee, which reported out a somewhat different proposed amendment reading,

No State shall make any law respecting an establishment of religion, or prohibiting the free exercise thereof; and no religious test shall ever be required as a qualification to any office or public trust under any State. No public property and no public revenue of, nor any loan of credit by or under the authority of, the United States, or any State, Territory, District, or municipal corporation, shall be appropriated to or made or used for the support of any school, educational or other institution under the control of any religious or anti-religious sect, organization, or denomination, or wherein the particular creed or tenets of any religious or anti-religious sect, organization, or denomination shall be taught. And no such particular creed or tenets shall be read or taught in any school or institution supported in whole or in part by such revenue or loan of credit; and no such appropriation or loan of credit shall be made to any religious or anti-religious sect, organization, or denomination, or to promote its interests or tenets. This article shall not be construed to prohibit the reading of the Bible in any school or institution; and it shall not have the effect to impair rights of property already vested.[80]

The final vote by the Senate on the resolution was 28 for, 16 against, and 27 absent or not voting. Since there was not a two-thirds majority in favor, the proposed amendment could not be submitted to the states.[81]

Several factors combined to bring about this result. There was a feeling that existing constitutional guarantees were adequate; that the matter, as far as not already covered, would best be left to the states; that it was unwise to raise a nation-wide religious issue, especially so soon after the divisions of the Civil War. And there was strong Roman Catholic opposition.

Another and more successful attempt over a period of years to prevent Federal funds from going to parochial or other denominational schools has been made in connection with the "enabling acts" authorizing the admission of the newer states of the West into the Union. The earlier states were admitted under the general guarantees of the Federal Constitution, but these were not considered sufficiently specific, in spite of guarantees of religious freedom in state constitutions, to cover the issue later raised in several states as to the constitutionality of efforts to secure public funds for parochial schools. Consequently Congress decided in the last quarter of the last century to go farther.

Five Northwestern states admitted in 1889—Montana, the Dakotas, Wyoming, and Washington—were required to adopt ordinances guaranteeing that public schools would be established "free from sectarian control." The same wording was later used in connection with the admission of several other Western states, generally in the form of a compact. The aim of Congress to prevent the use of public funds for sectarian purposes was made doubly clear by its restricting of the use of the township sections set apart for education not merely to "schools," as provided for in Ohio and some other states of the West early admitted to the Union, but to "common" or "public schools," and in Arizona and New Mexico (1912), to "free non-sectarian public schools." [82]

The controversy around Federal aid to sectarian schools remained more or less dormant until the conclusion of World War II. However, in 1944, just before the end of the war, Congress enacted the Servicemen's Readjustment Act, popularly called the G.I. Bill of Rights, under which every veteran who had fulfilled the minimum period of service required for eligibility was entitled to at least one year's study at any approved school or training institution of his choice in any subject for which he was fitted. The government helped meet tuition and other fees, cost of books, supplies, equipment, and other necessary expenses, as well as providing a subsistence allowance during the period. The government also helped theological students, along with other students, under the G.I. Bill and the Vocational Rehabilitation Act because of services in the war.

The rejection of many thousands of recruits because they lacked an elementary education brought to the attention of the nation the fact that at least the poorer states were unable to maintain the burden of universal education without financial assistance from the Federal government. Beginning with 1945, a number of bills were introduced to achieve this objective. The first was the Thomas-Hill bill, which would have provided Federal funds exclusively for public schools. It was for that reason vigorously opposed by the Roman Catholic Church. On the other hand, the Mead-Aiken bill, which would have included private and parochial schools in its operation, was equally vigorously opposed by the National Education Association and major Protestant groups. Neither measure was enacted.

Efforts at compromise were made during the next few years, but none succeeded. The issue flared up again in 1949 with the introduction of a bill by Congressman Graham A. Barden of North Carolina, specifically limiting Federal aid to "tax-supported grade schools and high schools which are under public supervision and control." [83] On June 23, about a month and a half after the Barden bill was introduced, Mrs. Eleanor Roosevelt, in her column "My Day" in the New York *World-Telegram*, published the following:

The controversy brought about by the request made by Francis Cardinal Spellman that Catholic schools should share in federal aid funds forces upon the citizens of the country the kind of decision that is going to be very difficult to make.

Those of us who believe in the right of any human being to belong to whatever church he sees fit, and to worship God in his own way, cannot be accused of prejudice when we do not want to see public education connected with religious control of the schools, which are paid for by taxpayers' money.

If we desire our children to go to schools of any particular kind, be it because we think they should have religious instruction or for any other reason, we are entirely free to set up those schools and to pay for them. Thus, our children would receive the kind of education we feel would best fit them for life.

Many years ago it was decided that the public schools of our country should be entirely separated from any kind of denominational control, and these are the only schools that are free, tax-supported schools. The greatest number of our children attend these schools.

It is quite possible that private schools, whether they are denominational schools —Catholic, Episcopalian, Presbyterian, Methodist, or whatever—or whether they are purely academic, may make a great contribution to the public school systems, both on the lower levels and on the higher levels.

They will be somewhat freer to develop new methods and to try experiments, and they will serve as yardsticks in the competitive area of creating better methods of imparting knowledge.

This, however, is the very reason why they should not receive Federal funds; in fact, no tax funds of any kind.

The separation of church and state is extremely important to any of us who hold to the original traditions of our nation. To change these traditions by changing our traditional attitude toward public education would be harmful, I think, to our whole attitude of tolerance in the religious area.

If we look at situations which have arisen in the past in Europe and other world areas, I think we will see the reasons why it is wise to hold to our early traditions.[84]

Two weeks later, on July 8, Mrs. Roosevelt wrote another column on the subject, in which she said,

One of my correspondents asks me if I do not realize that government tax money is already being used by many young, returned veterans for education in Roman Catholic schools and colleges and why should I object to that? The answer is that I do not have the slightest objection to that—the taxpayers' money in this instance is given to the boy or girl because of service during the war. . . .

In fact, I think there should be a great effort made to stress that education is not purely for material purposes, but is directed toward moral and spiritual aims and that religion plays a distinct part in achieving these ends.

But no school, private or public, can give any child a complete religious education. That must be done in the home, through the family and in the church. These, in cooperation with the schools, are the forces that must give our children the education that we want them to have.

But if we want our children in school to receive some particular sectarian church education, then we should pay for that education and it should not in any way lessen our interest and support of the public schools, which are attended by the vast majority of the children of our country and can be attended by all of our children if they so desire.

I do not want the public school system to be dominated by the Federal Government. That is why Federal aid should set only certain standards and not demand to control the schools of any state. But neither do I want church groups controlling the schools of our country. They must remain free.[85]

A week later she wrote another column, saying in part,

I am still getting letters from a few people who seem to think that in opposing aid from the taxpayers' money to any but public schools, I must have a particular bias against the Catholic Church. This must be because their parochial schools are more numerous than the schools of any other denomination.

I hate to continue an argument that many people think is based on prejudice, but something was written in a letter to me that seems worth mentioning.

A gentleman writes that the Barden bill was a discriminatory bill against the Negroes in the South. I have not read the bill carefully, and I have been rather careful not to say if I am for or against any particular bill or bills.[86]

It should be noted that there was only one reference in these three columns to Cardinal Spellman, and that one was entirely courteous. Nevertheless, on July 21, the latter wrote a letter to Mrs. Roosevelt of which the following represents the most important parts:

Dear Mrs. Roosevelt:

When, on June 23d in your column MY DAY, you aligned yourself with the author and other proponents of the Barden Bill and condemned me for defending Catholic children against those who would deny them their constitutional rights of equality with other American children, you could have acted only from misinformation, ignorance or prejudice, not from knowledge and understanding!

It is apparent that you did not take the time to read my address delivered at Fordham University; and, in your column of July 15th, you admitted that you did not even carefully read and acquaint yourself with the facts of the Barden Bill— the now famous, infamous bill that would unjustly discriminate against minority groups of America's children. . . .

I had intended ignoring your personal attack, but, as the days passed and in two subsequent columns you continued your anti-Catholic campaign, I became convinced that it was in the interest of all Americans and the cause of justice itself that your misstatements should be challenged in every quarter of our country where they have already spun and spread their web of prejudice. . . .

American freedom not only permits but encourages differences of opinion and I do not question your right to differ with me. But why I wonder do you repeatedly plead causes that are anti-Catholic?

Now my case is closed. This letter will be released to the public tomorrow after it has been delivered to you by special delivery today. And even though you may again use your columns to attack me and again accuse me of starting a controversy, I shall not again publicly acknowledge you.

For, whatever you may say in the future, your record of anti-Catholicism stands for all to see—a record which you yourself wrote on the pages of history which cannot be recalled—documents of discrimination unworthy of an American mother!

Sincerely yours,
FRANCIS CARDINAL SPELLMAN,
Archbishop of New York [87]

Publication of Cardinal Spellman's letter brought an immediate reaction. Overwhelmingly, the non-Catholic press and public were critical of the cardinal. The comment which received widest attention and approval was that of ex-Governor Herbert H. Lehman, who, the day after the cardinal's first statement, issued this comment:

I am deeply shocked at the attack of Cardinal Spellman on Mrs. Roosevelt. I strongly believe, as I have always believed, that in our American democracy every responsible citizen is entitled to express his or her views on public issues without being subjected to the accusation of being against any religion or any race.

The issue is not whether one agrees or disagrees with Mrs. Roosevelt on this or any other public question. The issue is whether Americans are entitled freely to express their views on public questions without being vilified or accused of religious bias.

Mrs. Roosevelt has been a public figure for twenty-five years. Her every act has been a matter of record. In that splendid record I do not know of a single act or word that would in the slightest degree indicate bias or prejudice against any religion or any race.

Her whole life has been dedicated to a constant fight for tolerance and brotherhood of men as children of one God.

She will, I am confident, retain the trust and the affection of all peoples irrespective of creed or race.[88]

Mrs. Roosevelt sent her reply to Cardinal Spellman on July 23. Extracts from the letter are the following:

Your letter of July 21st surprised me considerably.

I have never advocated the Barden Bill nor any other specific bill on education now before the Congress. I believe, however, in Federal aid to education. . . .

As we have developed in this country we have done more and more for our public schools. They are open to all children and it has been decided that there should be no particular religious beliefs taught in them. . . .

Different states, of course, have done different things as they came under majority pressure from citizens who had certain desires, but basically by and large, throughout the country, I think there is still a feeling that the public school is the school which is open to all children, and which is supported by all the people of the country and that anything that is done for the public schools should be done for them alone. . . .

Anyone who knows history, particularly the history of Europe, will, I think, recognize that the domination of education or of government by any one particular religious faith is never a happy arrangement for the people.

I have no bias against the Roman Catholic Church and I have supported Governor Smith as Governor and worked for him as a candidate for the office of President of the United States. I have supported for public office many other Roman Catholic candidates. . . .

I can assure you that I have no prejudice. I understand the beliefs of the Roman Catholic Church very well. I happen to be a Protestant and I prefer my own church, but that does not make me feel that anyone has any less right to believe as his own convictions guide him.

I have no intention of attacking you personally, nor of attacking the Roman Catholic Church, but I shall, of course, continue to stand for the things in our Government which I think are right. They may lead me to be in opposition to you and to other groups within our country, but I shall always act, as far as I am able, from real conviction and from honest belief.

If you carefully studied my record, I think you would not find it one of anti-Catholic or anti-any-religious group.

I assure you that I have no sense of being "an unworthy American mother." The final judgment, my dear Cardinal Spellman, of the worthiness of all human beings is in the hands of God.

With deepest respect, I am

> Very sincerely yours,
> ELEANOR ROOSEVELT
> (Mrs. Franklin D. Roosevelt)[89]

On August 6, 1949, the papers carried a statement by Cardinal Spellman written in a different temper from that of his letter of July 21. The essential features of this statement follow:

It is important that everyone should understand clearly what we are asking for under constitutional law, and, for what we are not asking. We are not asking for general public support of religious schools. In the State of New York, as in practically every other state, the State constitution prohibits the use of public funds for the support of sectarian schools. The Supreme Court of the United States has interpreted the Federal Constitution in the same sense.

Under the Constitution we do not ask nor can we expect public funds to pay for the construction or repair of parochial school buildings or for the support of teachers, or for other maintenance costs.

There are, however, other incidental expenses involved in education, expenses for such purposes as the transportation of children to and from school, the purchase of non-religious textbooks, and the provision of health aids. These are called "auxiliary services." The Federal-aid controversy revolves around these incidental benefits to school children, and around them alone.

Our New York State Constitution expressly allows the use of public funds for the transportation of children to any school, public or parochial. Fourteen other states follow the same non-discriminatory practice. Moreover, in some states public funds are used to provide non-religious textbooks for the children in all schools, public and parochial. In all states many communities supply public health services to pupils in all schools. The Supreme Court of the United States has upheld these practices as constitutional.

What precisely are we asking for? We believe in Federal aid for needy states and needy children. We further believe that Congress should guarantee, as it did in the School Lunch Act, that all children of whatever race, creed or color no matter what schools they attend, will share alike in the "auxiliary services" for which these Federal funds are spent in the states.

We do not think it should be left to each state to decide for itself whether or not to distribute Federal funds in a discriminatory way. And above all, we ask that Congress guarantee the use of Federal funds for health and transportation services to the 2,800,000 of America's children attending parochial schools if they guarantee Federal funds for health and transportation service to other American children attending public schools.

We are asking Congress to do no more than to continue, in its first general aid-to-education measure, the non-discriminatory policy it has followed in the School Lunch Act and other Federal laws dealing with schools and school children. We do not want Congress, for the first time, to adopt a discriminatory policy in the field of education. . . .[90]

Mrs. Roosevelt called this statement "clarifying and fair." Shortly thereafter Cardinal Spellman paid a social visit to her,[91] and this brought to an end the immediate controversy between them, at least insofar as it had become a public matter. It also brought to an end for more than a decade any major effort to obtain Federal funds for education. Political leaders of both parties recognized that the issue had become explosive and accordingly avoided it.

Before the question flared up again, Congress enacted the National Defense Education Act of 1958. This came about as a result of the Soviet government's success in orbiting a satellite in space, which aroused great concern in the United States that we might be losing the technological war. The act originally provided for grants to public schools for the purchase of mathematics, science, or foreign language equipment. On the floor of Congress an amendment was added which allowed the funds to be used also as *loans* to non-public schools for the same purpose. The latter stipulation indicates that Congress believed that direct grants as in the case of public schools would be unconstitutional, or else it sought to avoid raising the controversial question of Federal aid to parochial schools.

The candidacy of a Roman Catholic for the presidency again brought to public attention the Federal aid question. Early in his campaign Senator Kennedy expressed himself in favor of Federal aid to public education but unequivocally against Federal aid to parochial schools, which, he asserted, would be unconstitutional.[92] On February 20, 1961, a little more than a month after his inauguration, President Kennedy sent a message to Congress calling for enactment of legislation to provide Federal funds to aid the states in constructing public schools and paying teachers' salaries. The message contained the following sentence: "In accordance with the clear prohibition of the Constitution no elementary or secondary school funds are allocated for constructing church schools or paying church school teachers' salaries; and thus nonpublic school children are rightfully not counted in determining the funds each state will receive for its public schools."

Two days later the General Board of the National Council of Churches of Christ, with but one dissenting vote, issued a statement on the question of Federal aid, which concluded with the following:

We reaffirm our support of the public school system as an indispensable means of providing educational opportunity for all children; we urge provision of increased resources for the operation and improvement of the public schools; we declare our whole-hearted support of the principle of public control of public funds. THEREFORE

1. We favor the provision of federal funds for tax-supported elementary and secondary public schools under the following conditions: (a) that the funds be administered by the states with provision for report by them to the U.S. Commissioner of Education on the use of the funds; (b) that there be no discrimination among children on the basis of race, religion, class, or national origin; (c) that there be adequate safeguards against federal control of educational policy.

2. We oppose grants from federal, state, or local tax funds for non-public elementary and secondary schools.

3. We oppose the payment from public funds for tuition or "scholarships" for children to attend private or church-related elementary or secondary schools, or grants to their parents for that purpose.

4. We are opposed to "tax-credits," "tax-forgiveness," and exemption from school taxes or other taxes for parents whose children attend non-public elementary or secondary schools.

5. We favor the supplying of dental or medical services, lunches, and other distinctly welfare services to all children, whatever school they may be attending, provided such services are identifiable by recipients as public services, and the expenditures are administered by public authorities responsible to the electorate.

We are concerned to promote and safeguard the principles already expressed, and to avoid the infringement of religious liberty which arises when taxes paid under compulsion by all the people are used to aid non-public schools.[93]

Ten days passed, and on March 2, 1961, the Administrative Board of the National Catholic Welfare Conference presented its position in the following statement:

1. The question of whether or not there ought to be Federal Aid is a judgment to be based on objective, economic facts, connected with the schools of the country and consequently Catholics are free to take a position in accordance with the facts.

2. In the event that there is Federal Aid to Education we are deeply concerned that in justice Catholic school children should be given the right to participate.

3. Respecting the form of participation, we hold it to be strictly within the framework of the constitution that long-term, low-interest loans to private institutions could be part of the Federal Aid Program. It is proposed, therefore, that an effort be made to have an amendment to this effect attached to the bill.

4. In the event that a Federal Aid Program is enacted which excludes children in private schools these children will be the victims of discriminatory legislation. There will be no alternative but to oppose such discrimination.[94]

A significant change in the attitude of the Church on Federal aid to education was evident in this statement and became even clearer in later pronouncements of high Church spokesmen, particularly Cardinal Spellman, who in his statement of August 6, 1949, specifically disclaimed for the Church any demand for "public funds to pay for the construction or repair of parochial school buildings or the support of teachers, or for other maintenance costs." [95] He recognized that the Supreme Court had interpreted the Federal Constitution to prohibit the use of public funds for the support of sectarian schools. This remained the Catholic position for a decade after the exchange of letters with Mrs. Roosevelt took place. In 1959, Neil J. McCluskey, S.J., published a book entitled *Catholic Viewpoint on Education*, with a Foreword by the Right Reverend Monsignor Frederick G. Hochwalt. The fact of the Foreword is significant, for Monsignor Hochwalt, of the National Catholic Welfare Conference, has been for a long time and still is the official spokesman for the Church in testimony presented to Congress.

In this book Father McCluskey, as late as 1959 and with endorsement of Monsignor Hochwalt, echoes Cardinal Spellman's views as follows:

The Catholic laity and clergy are fully aware that direct basic support by the government to parochial schools is out of the question, for at least four reasons:

1. The U.S. Supreme Court would interpret such action as a contravention of the Federal Constitution.

2. Almost all state constitutions specifically rule out the support of sectarian schools.

3. Government support, especially federal, could readily bring such qualifications that the schools would lose their present independence.

4. Most of all, the rancor and strife set off by organized Catholic efforts to obtain such aid would poison community relations for years to come.[96]

With the adoption of the March 3, 1961, statement of the National Catholic Welfare Conference, the Church has quite clearly abandoned the moderate position maintained even as late as the publication of Father McCluskey's book. More and more one heard from the Church demands for full and equal participation by parochial and private schools in any program of Federal aid to education that Congress might enact. There were indeed reports that President Kennedy had complained to representatives of the Church about what reporters called the hardening of the Catholic line. The president was reported to be concerned that this change would be interpreted by the American public, and particularly Protestants who had long possessed reservations if not fears of the election of a Catholic to the presidency, as an effort by the Church to exploit the fact that one of its members had become president. According to the same reports, this inference was vigorously denied by the Church. Its actions, it asserted, were motivated only by the fact that since the president was pressing for enactment of general Federal aid legislation, such legislation would probably be passed, that the pattern of future Federal aid laws for many years would thereby be made, and that accordingly the Church urgently wanted the pattern so set not to be a discriminatory one.

Again the controversy on the inclusion or exclusion of church schools led to the failure to enact any measure for Federal aid to education on the elementary and secondary school levels. The controversy itself has continued. The Department of Health, Education and Welfare issued a legal memorandum to the effect that Federal aid to church grade and secondary schools, whether by way of grants or long-term low-interest loans, would be unconstitutional.[97] The National Catholic Welfare Conference issued a legal memorandum of its own, taking a contrary position and asserting that it would be constitutional for the Federal government to finance the secular subjects taught in parochial schools.[98] All that was needed, the memorandum asserted, was to apply "the art of cost accounting" to draw a dividing line between costs attributable to secular aspects of education and those attributable to religious aspects.[99]

In reply non-Catholics pointed out that this assertion rests on a premise that has been uniformly and consistently denied by Catholic educators, theologians, and philosophers, i.e., that the secular can be divided from the sacred and that the Catholic parochial school is nothing but a public school with religion added as a supplementary subject. If this were so, there would be no reason for parochial schools, since the religious instruction could easily be provided after regular public school hours.

It was further pointed out that in his authoritative book published in 1958, *Parochial Schools: A Sociological Study*, the Reverend Joseph H. Fichter, S.J., states,

> It is a commonplace observation that in the parochial school religion permeates the whole curriculum and is not confined to a single half-hour period of the day. Even arithmetic can be used as an instrument of pious thoughts, as in the case of the teacher who gave this problem to her class: "If it takes forty thousand priests and a hundred forty thousand sisters to care for forty million Catholics in the United States, how many more priests and sisters will be needed to convert and care for the hundred million non-Catholics in the United States?"[100]

In November, 1961, the Supreme Court of Oregon, in declaring unconstitutional a state law providing free use of public school textbooks in parochial schools, had upheld the trial court's finding that "the purpose of the Catholic Church in operating schools under its supervision is to permeate the entire education process with the precepts of the Catholic religion."[101] This ruling had been based upon extensive trial testimony by expert witnesses and presentation of authoritative writings from Catholic sources, including the definitive encyclical of Pius XI, *The Christian Education of Youth*, in which the pope stated that "It is necessary not only that religious instruction be given to the young at certain fixed times, but also that every other subject taught be permeated with Christian piety."

On the basis of this encyclical, the standard Catholic text on education, Redden and Ryan's *A Catholic Philosophy of Education*, states that "the only school approved by the Church is one wherein Catholics are free to follow their own plan of teaching, and where religious instruction is given in accordance with the legitimate demands of parents, and where the Catholic religion permeates the entire atmosphere, comprising, in truth and fact, the 'core curriculum' around which revolve all secular subjects."[102] In the Catholic parochial school religion is intimately correlated, articulated, integrated in every secular subject.[103]

In May, 1963, Senator Abraham Ribicoff of Connecticut, former Secretary of Health, Education and Welfare, sought to achieve a compromise which, he hoped, would end what he called the "religious controversy" that had for so long blocked any Federal aid legislation.[104] He proposed a six-point program for financial assistance of private and parochial schools, as follows:

1. Permit income tax deductions of up to $1,500 per college student and $100 per student for private school expenses.
2. Public financing of "shared-time" arrangements.
3. Aid for instruction in certain areas, such as mathematics, science and foreign languages, and possibly for classroom construction.
4. Broadening of federal assistance in teacher training programs and student scholarships.
5. Increase in programs of direct benefit to the child, such as free school lunches and bus transportation.
6. More aid to all types of higher education.[105]

Some, including President Kennedy and his advisers, were of the opinion that a distinction could be made between higher and lower education, and that loans or perhaps even special-purpose grants might be made to Church-related colleges and universities though they could not perhaps constitutionally be made to sectarian elementary and secondary schools. Many Protestant and Jewish organizations disagree and oppose Federal aid to Church-related educational institutions at all levels.

Congress, under the leadership of Presidents Kennedy and Johnson, accepted the distinction between higher and lower educational institutions, and toward the end of 1963 enacted the Higher Education Facilities Act of 1963. This is probably the first law enacted by Congress granting direct financial aid for the construction of buildings at sectarian colleges. The law envisaged a five-year program with the funds allotted without distinction to public and private, secular and sectarian, institutions.

There was considerable opposition within and without Congress on the ground that inclusion of sectarian institutions rendered the bill unconstitutional. To meet this challenge Congress provided that the funds were not to be used for general construction but only for structures or portions thereof especially designed for instruction or research in the natural or physical sciences, mathematics, modern foreign languages, or engineering, or for use as a library. It also expressly forbade the use of any part of the funds for the construction of any facility for sectarian instruction or religious worship or of any facility used or to be used primarily for any part of the program of a school or department of divinity.

There were many who were not convinced that these restrictions were sufficient to make the measure constitutional. They believed that as far as the First Amendment's provision for Church-State separation was concerned there was no difference between colleges and universities on the one hand and elementary and secondary schools on the other. Nor did they believe that unconstitutionality could be avoided by earmarking the Federal funds for certain presumably "secular" facilities at a sectarian institution, particularly since, after twenty years, the restrictions would lapse by the express terms of the law, and the facilities could then legally be used for any purpose.

For these reasons a move was made to amend the bill so as to provide that its constitutionality could be challenged by a taxpayer's suit in the Federal courts. This proposal, in the form of an amendment by Senator Sam Ervin of North Carolina, was adopted by the Senate, but the House refused to accept it. The opposition of the House (and of the organs of the Roman Catholic Church) against a provision for judicial review was such, that it quickly became clear that insistence upon such a provision would mean no College Aid Law at all. Accordingly, the Senate yielded and the law was enacted without any specific provision for a court test of its constitutionality.

Despite the deletion of the Ervin Amendment, it is probable that sooner or later the Supreme Court will pass upon the constitutionality of Federal aid to sectarian colleges. The nature of the American political system is such that ultimately all strongly contested constitutional issues find their resolution at the bar of the Supreme Court.

Chapter 17

ADJUSTMENTS IN THE SOCIAL-LEGISLATIVE FIELD

The National Activities of the Churches

The major instrumentality of the Protestant churches for social and legislative activities on the national scene has been the Federal Council of Churches of Christ and its successor, the National Council of Churches of Christ in the United States of America. The Federal Council, inheriting the social reform attitude of New England Protestantism, was created in 1908 by the official action of over a score of national denominations.[1] One of its major purposes, as set forth in its *Biennial Report* of 1946, is to be "an instrument for bearing a combined witness to the principles, derived from our Christian faith, which must be applied in the social, political and international life of the world."[2]

Illustrative of the Federal Council's concern in these areas are the resolutions adopted in 1937, which included one urging the ratification of the National Child Labor Amendment; one urging "a modification of the status of the Army and Navy chaplains as will make clear that they are a part of the regular ministry of the Churches rather than of the armed forces of the Nation";[3] an "appeal to church members generally to support all sound and effective measures for slum clearance and the rehousing of low-income wage-earners, and without passing judgment on any particular legislative proposals, approve the general principle of assistance by federal, state and local government . . .";[4] a plea that "any program of war-time conscription should be put into force only by Act of Congress with reference to a specific emergency . . ."; a demand that "whenever life is subjected to conscription, material resources should be conscripted with equal thoroughness and vigor";[5] and an expression of support of "the government of the United States in its protest over the bombing of non-combatants in China and its collaboration with the Advisory Committee of the League of Nations on the Far Eastern Situation."[6]

In November, 1950, the Federal Council merged with the Foreign Missions Conference of North America, the Home Missions Council of North America, the International Council of Religious Education, the Missionary Education Movement in the U.S. and Canada, the National Protestant Council on Higher

Education, the United Council of Church Women, and the United Stewardship Council to form the National Council of Churches of Christ.[7] Some thirty-three denominations embracing close to forty million church members are affiliated with the National Council. The Council functions through four main divisions: Christian Education, Christian Life and Work, Home Missions, and Foreign Missions. Its activities in the social-legislative field are carried on through the Division of Christian Life and Work, which includes departments devoted to international affairs, pastoral services, racial and cultural relations, social welfare, worship and the arts, church and economic life, and religious liberty.[8] Its vigorous participation in the Negro's struggle for equality, which has been recounted in a previous chapter,[9] shows clearly that the National Council is carrying on fully the activities begun by the Federal Council in the arena of social and legislative problems.

As the National Council of Churches is the major instrumentality of American Protestantism for the expression of its concern in the social and legislative field, so the National Catholic Welfare Conference is the major outlet for Roman Catholic activities in that field. The Conference[10] grew out of the National Catholic War Council, formed in 1917 under the leadership of Cardinal Gibbons to channel Roman Catholic efforts in the First World War. At the conclusion of the war the hierarchy, in response to a letter by Pope Benedict XV recommending that the American hierarchy join him in working for the cause of peace and social justice, decided to form the National Catholic Welfare Council as a continuation in times of peace of the War Council. The plan formulated was that all the bishops in the United States should constitute the Council, but that its operating agency should be the Administrative Committee, consisting of all American cardinals and a number of bishops, each of whom heads a specific department.

As a national organization representing the combined thinking of the bishops, it was feared by some that it would begin to dictate Church policy or stand as a sort of "super holding corporation" over the dioceses of the country. If this happened, the Council would certainly be a threat to the autonomy of each diocese. The situation was clarified in 1922 when the Holy See asked the bishops to explain the organization. Two points were permanently clarified. First, the Council is a voluntary organization, depending for membership on the free choice of each bishop; second, it possesses no ecclesiastical jurisdiction or compulsory authority. Whatever authority it has is that granted to it by the consent of the bishops, and any bishop may choose to align himself with it or not. To make the nature of the body better understood, at the request of the Holy See its name was changed from Council to Conference, since the term "Council" implied legislative power. From 1923 on it has been called the National Catholic Welfare Conference.

When one studies the work of the National Catholic Welfare Conference and the National Council of Churches in the social welfare field several differences stand out:

1. The Roman Catholic Church, through the fact that its bishops, who have all come up through the priesthood, have mostly had parish experience among the lower economic and social groups in our large cities, speaks with an authority on social reform which is in some ways more impressive than that of most of their Protestant brethren, who have less generally had this experience.

2. The Roman Catholic leaders are more aggressive in their opposition to Communism. Both Roman Catholic and Protestant leaders are opposed to Communism and Fascism, but most Protestant leaders, at least during the World War II period, were inclined to think the danger of Fascism actually greater in the United States than that of Communism, whereas the Roman Catholics have consistently taken the opposite point of view, though equally opposed to a Nazi victory. The Protestant attack on Communism is generally less direct, being largely concerned with removing the social conditions which produce Communism and upholding the Christian ideal.

3. The pacifist position has been much less noticeable in Roman Catholic circles, where supreme emphasis is laid on the importance of maintaining law and order, and on respect for authority and government. For similar reasons the Roman Catholics put less specific emphasis on freedom of speech and press.

4. The Roman Catholic Church has always been opposed to prohibition, which was at one time supported by the Federal Council, but both groups are equally interested in temperance.

5. The Roman Catholics do not carry the emphasis on the separation of Church and State as far as Protestants. For example, they favor direct financial aid from the State for education under religious auspices, a policy which Protestants believe fraught with serious danger to religious freedom.

6. The Roman Catholic attitudes almost always go back for their inspiration to the great encyclical letters of the popes, particularly the *Rerum Novarum* of Leo XIII, the *Quadragesimo Anno* of Pius XI, and perhaps above all the *Mater et Magistra* and *Pacem in Terris* of John XXIII.

7. The Roman Catholics have been more outspoken in integrating their social program with the definitely doctrinal and religious teachings of the Church.

The counterpart within American Jewry of the National Council of Churches and the National Catholic Welfare Conference is the Synagogue Council of America, whose structure has already been outlined in a previous chapter.[11] Recently the Synagogue Council has become increasingly active in the struggle against racial discrimination and segregation, but in the main its major concern has been in the area of Church-State relationships and interfaith activities.[12]

Jewish expressions on matters of social welfare and justice have come primarily from the six constituents of the Synagogue Council rather than from the Council itself, perhaps because the Council may not speak except with the unanimous agreement of its constituents.

Among these it was the Reform branch, particularly the Central Conference of American Rabbis, which was first in the field of struggling for social justice. In this respect, perhaps no person was more influential than the Reform rabbi Stephen S. Wise. American Reform Jewry was the first to establish a Joint Committee on Social Action.[13] It was soon followed, however, by the formation of a similar Joint Committee within Conservative Jewry.[14] Today there is practically no difference between the positions taken by Reform and Conservatism on questions of social welfare and justice. Moreover, these positions are generally in advance of the stands token by either Protestantism or Roman Catholicism. It is unlikely, for example, that any major Protestant or Roman Catholic clerical organization would have adopted the 1934 Pronouncement of the Rabbinical Assembly of America on Social Justice,[15] which includes the following section on "The Social Use of Wealth":

When Judaism teaches the divine creation of the world, it points explicitly and implicitly to the attitude that God intended the world's resources to be used in the interest of all Mankind.

This attitude is affirmed again and again throughout Jewish tradition. The natural resources of the world are a divine gift to Mankind. Each generation inherits vast stores of wealth which all society has slowly accumulated. No single individual contributes to the sum of the world's goods more than an infinitesimal share. From all these considerations it follows that the wealth of the world should be used socially. Nor has any individual the right to own without social responsibility what all have created and what all must use. Such concentration of wealth is an abuse of the right to private property. It is the equivalent of an unjustifiable expropriation of the great masses of Mankind.

Wherefore, we call upon the State to use its power of taxation to correct this gross inequity in the distribution of wealth. We ask for sharply increased taxes on land values, incomes, gifts, inheritances, corporation surpluses, and capital levies which shall use the power of taxation to redistribute the social resources of our society.

Although we regard all private ownership of natural resources and the machinery of large scale production as involving injustice, we recognize the impracticability of an immediate transfer of all capital from private to public ownership. But there are some social enterprises that are so completely essential to all economic activity that society cannot be content with efforts to regulate them. It must actually own them. We call for their socialization. We call therefore for public ownership of the following:

(a) Instruments of Banking and Credit.
(b) The Transportation and Communication Systems.
(c) Sources of Power such as Water—Coal—Oil—Gas and Electricity.

Illustrative, too, are the numerous resolutions adopted by Reform and Conservative bodies against censorship, loyalty probes and oaths, the House Committee on Un-American Activities, capital punishment, and in favor of academic freedom, Federal aid to public education, social welfare legislation, and the cessation of testing of atomic weapons. Orthodox Jewry has been concerned in the main with matters of religious education and practices and has taken comparatively little action in the field of social welfare legislation. There are, however, strong indications that its activities in the field will increase, as is evidenced by its active participation in the race relations problem.[16]

Marriage

In the fields of marriage, divorce, and related problems the primary concern of the Church is the protection of the family—the social basis of our civilization, and an institution which owes much to the Jewish-Christian tradition. The safeguarding of the marriage tie and the protection of children are matters of supreme concern to all the religious forces of the country. The Roman Catholic Church is strongly opposed to artificial birth control, public sex education, artificial insemination, mixed marriages (except under rigid Catholic conditions), divorce (as distinct from annulment), sterilization, therapeutic abortion, euthanasia, and cremation. These are in its judgment, matters on which the Church alone should decide, and it has decided against them.

Marriage was never recognized as a strictly religious institution prior to the time that the Church exerted such profound influence on all social customs in the Middle Ages. Professor Edward Westermarck, in his standard history of the subject, states,

The legal importance which has been attached to the religious ceremony in Christian countries has no counterpart in either Jewish or Muhammadan law. Although the former regards marriage as a divine institution, the omission of the benediction would not invalidate a marriage. The priestly benediction is mentioned neither in the Bible nor in the Talmud; and the regular presence of a Rabbi at a wedding is not earlier than the fourteenth century. Nor does Muhammadan law require religious rites for the contraction of a valid marriage.[17]

At least since the Council of Trent in 1563 it has been the theory of the Roman Catholic Church that marriage between Christians is a sacrament over which the Church has entire control and the State has no rightful jurisdiction.

The Council felt it necessary to try to enforce this view because of the many abuses which had arisen in clandestine and irregular marriages. One of its decisions was that a Catholic could contract a valid marriage only in the presence of a friend and two witnesses. This law was not strictly enforced in the United States until after 1908, when this country, as far as Catholics were concerned, was definitely placed under the common law of the Church. The action affected the validity of mixed marriages, as theretofore the Church had recognized many marriages contracted by a Protestant minister or a civil magistrate.[18]

The Protestant Reformation created a profound change in the status of marriage. Luther defended the legitimacy of civil marriage and even went so far as to say, "Since weddings and matrimony are a temporal business it becomes us clerks and servants of the Church to order or rule nothing therein, but to leave to each city and state its own usages and customs in this regard." [19]

This extreme view of Luther was not accepted in practice, but his assertion that marriage was essentially a civil institution and that primary responsibility for its regulation rested with the civil authorities was ultimately to become accepted in all countries where Church and State were separated.

John Calvin, whose influence on America was far greater than that of Luther, though believing that marriage was a divine plan for human good, also accepted the view that the State had the right to determine the laws governing it. He repudiated the sacramental theory of marriage and suggested that regulation of marriage should be transferred to the civil courts. These Protestant ideas, and especially that marriage was a civil contract, were adopted by Puritan New England generally. Since then, the civil-contract conception of marriage has prevailed in the United States, and matrimonial jurisdiction has in the last resort been within the domain of the State. Marriage is therefore from a civil and legal standpoint considered not a sacrament but a contract. Consequently a civil marriage is entirely valid and legitimate in all our states except perhaps in West Virginia, where a religious ceremony seems still to be required.[20] (Maryland had a similar law requiring all marriages to be solemnized by a clergyman, but it was repealed in March, 1963.)

The American law of marriage thus embodies basically Protestant concepts. Under Roman Catholic doctrine, however, marriage between baptized persons remains a sacrament. It is therefore the position of the Roman Catholic Church that it must control virtually everything having to do with the marriage of its members. Its law on this matter is specific:

The Church claims full, independent and exclusive power over the marriage of all baptized persons—Catholics, heretics, schismatics. . . . That power is exclusive. . . . It includes the legislative, judicial, and coercive power; that is, the power of establishing impediments both diriment and impedient, of deciding all matrimonial causes, of constraining married persons to comply with their obligations, etc.[21]

It is in the matter of mixed marriage that these differences between Roman Catholic and Protestant-civil philosophies become most clear. Technically, a mixed marriage—that is, what the Catholic Church calls *matrimonia mixta*—is generally a marriage between a Catholic and a non-Catholic. In 1791 the first National Synod of the Roman Catholic Church in the United States recognized the "unavoidability of mixed-marriages" but took strong steps to make them as few as possible and to protect Catholic interests.[22] The Church, anxious to do everything in its power to encourage unity in the family and to protect what it believes to be the interests of the children, discourages such marriages always and everywhere, permitting them only under certain very definite conditions.[23] Under all normal circumstances, to make such a marriage valid a priest of the Church must officiate, the Catholic party must be considered in no danger of being converted to Protestantism and must undertake to strive to convert the non-Catholic party to Catholicism, and both parties must agree that all children are to be brought up in the Catholic Church.[24] The promises required of the non-Catholic party to a permitted mixed marriage, to be made in the presence of two witnesses, are these:

I, the undersigned, not a member of the Catholic Church, wishing to contract marriage with N. N., a member of the Catholic Church, intend to do so with the understanding that the marriage tie cannot be dissolved, except by death, and promise her on my word of honor, that she shall enjoy the free exercise of her Catholic religion, and that all the children of either sex, born of this marriage, shall be baptized and educated in the faith and according to the teaching of the Roman Catholic Church. I further promise that no marriage ceremony other than that performed by the Catholic priest shall take place.[25]

Protestants have often expressed indignant opposition to this procedure. An example of this attitude in a conservative Church was the resolution passed by the Protestant Episcopal Triennial Convention in San Francisco in October, 1949, which said, "We assert that in no circumstances should a member of this church give any understanding, as a condition of marriage, that the children should be brought up in the practice of another communion."[26] The Federal Council of Churches, in a statement issued in 1932, took equally strong exception to the requirement that the Roman Catholic partner undertake to convert the other. "If either partner," the statement, "enters upon the union as a propagandist, determined through the intimacies of marriage to subvert the religious faith of the other, disaster is imminent."[27]

There has been recognition within American Catholicism that the Church's position on mixed marriages has alienated many non-Catholics who are otherwise friendly to the Church. In fact, there were reports that one of the matters to be considered by the Vatican Council convened by Pope John XXIII and continued by Paul VI was the possible modification of the canon law on mixed marriages so as to make it less objectionable to non-Catholics. However, so far, the present rules are still in full force and effect.

There have been many lawsuits in which the courts have been asked to enforce agreements made as part of a mixed marriage to raise the offspring in the Roman Catholic faith. The cases usually arise when the father is Roman Catholic and the mother is non-Catholic. When a marriage breaks up, custody of the children is most often given by the courts to the mother, whereupon the father may seek to compel her to raise them as Roman Catholics. With rare exceptions the courts in this country have refused to enforce these agreements and have left it to the mother to decide for herself in what faith she would raise the children.[28]

Divorce and Annulment

The churches are also deeply concerned to reduce the divorce evil, which has reached alarming proportions because of what many believe to be the frivolous grounds on which some states permit the dissolution of the marriage tie. The laws regarding divorce vary from state to state. Generally, divorces are granted for adultery, desertion, habitual drunkenness, conviction for felony, and extreme cruelty.[29] It is clear that the varied laws cause great difficulties for most of the churches, which frequently wish to enforce their own standards of the marital relation. These standards, except for annulments, are likely to be stricter than those of the states.

Separation laws also differ. They involve the cessation of conjugal relations by mutual consent or by a judicial decree and do not permit remarriage while the condition continues. The most common grounds are extreme cruelty, adultery, desertion, conviction for felony, habitual drunkenness, and non-support by the husband. This marital status does not, however, involve as serious family and social dislocations as does divorce.

In 1946 the Federal Council of Churches, on the advice of its Committee on Marriage and the Home, issued a statement, "Most Divorces Could Be Prevented," [30] which included some striking figures based on census reports. These showed that the divorce rate was one to nine marriages just before World War I, one to six before World War II, and one to three in 1945, after World War II. Further, in 1946 in some communities the divorces equaled the marriages. There are also thousands of broken homes due to desertion, often referred to as the "poor man's divorce." Desertion is a legal ground for divorce in all states except three, but thousands among the poor end their marriage by desertion without obtaining any legal sanction. This situation is due partly to the expense of proceedings for divorce, partly to its prohibition by the Roman Catholic Church, and partly to fear of the courts that keeps certain groups, especially among the more recent immigrants, from applying to them.[31] It is commonly recognized that the number of divorces in our country is actually in excess of the number reported from all other Christian countries combined.[32] On the other hand, illicit connections among married people are probably much less common than in most other countries.

Protestants, Roman Catholics, and Jews are agreed that the widespread prevalence of divorce in the United States represents a grave problem. They agree too that the state of divorce laws and civil divorce procedures is shocking and deplorable. They agree further that the situation cries desperately for remedial action. But at this point their agreement ends. There is a wide difference among them, principally between the Catholics and non-Catholics, as to the cause of the evil and the nature of the appropriate remedial action.

The situation in New York dramatically illustrates the problem and the division. The law of the state permits divorce on only one ground, adultery. Yet it is well known (and has been substantiated by an investigation conducted in New York City in 1948) that divorce can easily be obtained in New York if both parties are willing and are prepared to commit perjury or to participate in collusion. The effect, therefore, is that, for all practical purposes, divorce is obtainable in New York on no ground at all other than mutual consent; the only price the parties need pay (besides counsel and court fees) is a lowering of their standards of honesty and truthfulness.

To many non-Catholics the solution must include (although, of course, not be limited to) recognizing reality by amending the divorce laws to allow other grounds for divorce, such as desertion, cruelty, etc. To the Catholic Church, however, the obvious answer is the reverse: not to liberalize divorce laws and procedures but to tighten and strengthen them. So determined is the opposition of the Church to liberalized divorce, and so strong is its influence in New York, that there is little chance that the New York divorce statute will be liberalized in the immediate future. Indeed, it is difficult to find a legislator who is willing to introduce a bill for liberalized divorce.

The Roman Catholic Church in New York opposes even legislative inquiries and studies of the divorce laws and their operation, lest such studies lead to liberalizing legislation.[33] For years efforts have been made in the New York State legislature to establish study commissions. In 1955 a rural district Republican Assemblywoman, Janet Hill Gordon, who had long been introducing such bills without success, was joined by a rural district Republican State Senator, Dutton S. Peterson (he was also a Methodist clergyman), in sponsoring a bill to establish a temporary state commission to study New York's marriage and divorce laws. The measure was warmly supported by the (Protestant) State Council of Churches and the (Jewish) New York Board of Rabbis. It was opposed by the State Roman Catholic Welfare Committee, whose representatives characterized the measure as the "entering wedge of a drive for liberalization of the law." The latter urged instead the enactment of measures aimed at the "preservation of the marital relationship and the family unit," as for example by establishing mandatory conciliation facilities for divorce applicants and restricting actions for annulment.[34] Neither the Gordon-Peterson measure nor the Catholic Church-sponsored measure succeeded of passage.

The question of divorce and the Roman Catholic Church has been somewhat complicated by an address made by Pope Pius XII on November 6, 1949, to the central committee of the Union of Catholic Italian Lawyers. He warned Catholic jurists throughout the world against granting divorces when a marriage is valid. "A Catholic judge cannot, except for very grave reasons, pass a sentence of civil divorce (wherever divorce is in effect) for a marriage which is valid before God and the Church." This remark was based on the principle that "Under no circumstances can a judge acknowledge and approve an unjust law (which would not in any case be valid before God)."[35]

The warning was evidently written with conditions in eastern Europe and in Italy especially in mind, but in the wording of it as given out by the Vatican there was nothing which would exclude Catholic judges in the United States from being expected to follow the "fundamental norms" expressed. There is nothing new in the declaration as far as Catholic theory is concerned.[36] Nevertheless, it is well known that hundreds of Catholic civil court judges in the United States continue to issue divorces even to Catholics.

Birth Control Legislation

The problem of birth control is one over which the State and the Church, especially the Roman Catholic Church, come into occasional conflict. Many of our states have tried to legislate in one way or another for or against birth control. Some have followed the lead of New York, which in an 1869 law designed to prevent obscenity specifically banned the giving of contraceptive information and material. At present, however, there are only two states, Massachusetts and Connecticut, with statutes so worded as to restrict even physicians of standing from giving what they believe to be necessary information on birth control. Four others, Mississippi, Missouri, Pennsylvania, and Washington, have statutes which if literally construed might prevent even the prescription of contraceptives by physicians.[37] About 40 per cent of the states have left the matter alone.

Furthermore, the United States Congress, in passing the so-called Comstock law in 1873, forbade the dissemination by mail of contraceptive knowledge.[38] A much criticized feature of this Federal law is that it makes no distinction between information designed for scientific purposes and that intended merely to satisfy lewd curiosity.[39] This is an evidence of the unwisdom of trying to regulate the dissemination of scientific knowledge under an obscenity statute. A case which attracted much attention to the birth control issue was the jailing of William Sanger in 1915 for distributing through the mails copies of pamphlets on the subject written by his wife, Mrs. Margaret Sanger, the founder of the modern birth control movement.[40]

The position of the opponents of birth control, as authoritatively expressed by Roman Catholics, is clear and specific. They believe positively that it is the duty of Christians to "multiply and replenish the earth," and negatively that to interfere with the sacred processes of nature is "sinful." They consider that voluntary abstinence is the only legitimate method of controlling parenthood. They have the authority of the papacy behind them, as expressed in various official utterances dating back to 1851. With these and similar statements of Rome in mind, the *New Catholic Dictionary* states that the Church "does condemn each deliberate act of birth control as intrinsically evil," because it defeats the primary purpose of the marriage relation. The Catholic doctrine that birth control is essentially wrong is not a mere disciplinary measure, like the law of clerical celibacy, which can be abrogated or modified by the Church. "It is a definition of the law of God, which no power, not even the Church itself, can abrogate or contravene. . . ." [41]

In the past the Roman Catholic Church has attempted to prevent the holding of public meetings called for the discussion of birth control. A particularly serious case occurred in Holyoke, Massachusetts, in 1940. Here the First Congregational Church, by action of its standing committee and with the approval of its pastor, complied with the request of the Massachusetts Mothers Health Council to permit the use of the church for a meeting to be addressed by Mrs. Sanger on behalf of "fundamental civil liberties in the matter of birth control." In the request for the use of the church the Council had called attention to the fact that Massachusetts was one of only two states in the Union where the law forbade doctors to provide and married persons to receive contraceptive information and care. It added,

. . . The outlawing of responsible medicine from the state has resulted in the growth of an enormous commercial and bootleg traffic in contraceptives which can be sold indiscriminately through legal subterfuges. The legalizing of contraceptive medical care would be a direct step toward sane legal, medical and social control of birth control knowledge.[42]

The purpose of the meeting was to present an initiative petition, in behalf of a modification of the law, signed by the dean of the Harvard Medical School, the president of the Massachusetts Institute of Technology, the director of the Massachusetts General Hospital, the president of the American Unitarian Association, and other responsible persons. Two weeks after the standing committee of the church gave permission for its use for this meeting, the Right Reverend Monsignor John F. Fagan, ranking leader of Roman Catholicism in Holyoke, issued a statement which was read at masses and, as reported in the local papers, said,

> Those who are sponsoring this lecture are engaged in a work that is unpatriotic and a disgrace to a Christian community, and for that we condemn them without hesitation. Catholics, of course, will be guided by the mind of Christ and His Church, and will actively oppose any attempt to label this locality as a center of such immoral doctrine.[43]

Holyoke was now seething. Business and professional men favoring the petition feared a boycott, and there may have been threats of boycott by irresponsible persons. As a result, some members of the First Congregational Church became anxious. Seven of the twenty members of the standing committee, at a specially called meeting, and by a vote of 5 to 2, which was not a quorum, asserted that they felt they must assume power to rescind the permission granted. This action was due to the emergency created by Roman Catholic opposition, the interests of community harmony, and concern for the economic well-being of members of the church congregation. Consequently, the Mothers Health Council rented the Turnverein Hall, securing receipt for payment, but on the afternoon of the day the meeting was to take place the permission was withdrawn. Later the same day the Textile Workers Union granted the use of its headquarters.

In spite of normal good feeling between Protestants and Catholics in the community, there was much friction over this issue. The mayor stated that civil liberty gave any group the right to hold a meeting in Holyoke; if any group withdrew permission for the use of its hall, that was its own concern. The ranking Catholic priest stated that since birth control was morally wrong, the proposed law was morally wrong, and therefore Catholics were bound to oppose it vigorously. He denied that those responsible for preventing the meeting planned an economic boycott but acknowledged that when people become aroused such things might happen.

The issue became a particularly important one because the First Congregational Church was a member of the General Council of Congregational Christian Churches, which in 1931 endorsed the majority report of the Committee on Marriage and the Home of the Federal Council. In its endorsement the General Council held that the use of birth control under the guidance of the Christian conscience and the direction of the medical profession is both moral and right. The report stated that a Church "should not seek to prohibit physicians from imparting such information to those who in the judgment of the medical profession are entitled to receive it." [44]

Another incident occurred the following year (1941) in Louisville, Kentucky. There the well-known newspaper, the *Courier-Journal*, carried advertisements of the National Committee for Planned Parenthood and the Birth Control Federation of America. Not only was an attempt made to indict the newspaper for its action, but the archbishop made an attack on it which was read in all the Roman Catholic churches of the archdiocese. The *Courier-Journal* defended editorially its right to disagree with the Church and its archbishop, stating that "It is no more wicked for a newspaper to disagree with an Archbishop than to disagree with the President of the United States." The threats against the paper because of printing an advertisement in behalf of the Birth Control Federation included a boycott by eighty-five Roman Catholics of New Haven, Kentucky, who cancelled their subscriptions to the paper. The editor, however, stated that the incident had had no noticeable effect on the *Courier-Journal's* circulation.[45]

The question of birth control therapy in municipal and state hospitals is another matter that has aroused considerable controversy and ill feeling between the Roman Catholic Church and the non-Catholic community. New York City presents an illustrative example.[46] For many years physicians practicing at the municipal hospitals refrained from prescribing or advising patients to use contraceptive devices or medicines although there was no official regulation prohibiting such prescription or advice. The matter came to a head when, early in 1958, the director of obstetrics at one of the city hospitals tested official policy in a carefully selected case. He prescribed a contraceptive device for a Protestant woman seriously ill with diabetes who would be in danger of death in the event of a pregnancy. Dr. Morris A. Jacobs, the commissioner of hospitals, refused to allow the prescription to be filled.

When this action became public, strong protest came from the Protestant Council of New York, along with other groups such as the New York Board of Rabbis, the American Jewish Congress, the United Lutheran Church, the Presbytery of New York, and the National Congregational Church Association. The statement of the Protestant Council, presenting as it does the present view of the Protestant Church on the subject of artificial birth control, is set forth here in full:

There is no moral reason why a Protestant patient should be denied accepted birth-control therapy by the City Commissioner of Hospitals.

Christian morality is finally dependent upon Christian compassion. Morality, although always demanding discipline and sacrifice, is nevertheless responsive to individual opportunity and need. The case at Kings County Hospital must be seen in that perspective.

God has established and sanctified marriage for the propagation, welfare and happiness of mankind. He has, through the Bible and through the marriage vows, instructed those who enter into this relation to cherish a mutual esteem and love and live together as heirs of the grace of life.

Parenthood is, therefore, one of the major purposes of marriage. With this privilege, however, come tremendous responsibilities, particularly in the kind of world in which we live. The welfare and happiness of parents and each child are extremely important. Prayer, study and judgment must be used in planning the number and spacing of children. It is the duty of responsible parents to use all truth from God revealed through the church, minister, doctor, researcher, marriage counselor and the Holy Spirit speaking directly to their conscience in planning and producing their family in order to fulfill God's highest expectations of them as parents.

The conjugal act itself contributes important spiritual benefits to a happy marriage. Failure to recognize the need of sex relations in married life, separate from the intention for pregnancy, is a serious error in understanding the nature of man created by God to be bound together, wife and husband, in the spiritual union that God has made possible through the conjugal act. Parents who fail to recognize this fact often produce children by accident and bring new life into the world that they themselves do not want and at times bring economic hardship, serious health complications to the wife, and in instances serious burdens upon government agencies and society in general.

The responsible use of contraceptive devices is, therefore, approved by most Christian leaders.

On the other hand, Roman Catholic organizations quickly came to the defense of Dr. Jacobs' ruling. A statement by the chancery office of the New York archdiocese quoted Pope Pius XII as authority for the principle that any attempt, through contraception, to hinder the natural results of the conjugal act was immoral. Support for the ruling came also from the Guild of Catholic Physicians, the National Council of Catholic Men, the National Council of Catholic Women, the National Council of Catholic Nurses, and the Knights of Columbus.

The Board of Hospitals eventually reversed Dr. Jacobs' ban on contraceptive therapy and ruled that such measures are proper medical practice when a patient's health or life may be otherwise jeopardized; that municipal hospitals should provide such therapy where warranted in a physician's judgment and acceptable to the patient; but that hospital personnel who have religious or moral objections should be excused from participating in contraceptive procedures.

Thus ended this incident. Similar incidents have since occurred in other cities, including Chicago and Washington, D.C. The controversy has been complicated and broadened by the introduction of the question whether governmental social welfare workers should or may advise birth control to clients receiving relief payments.

Efforts to effect repeal of the Massachusetts and Connecticut anti-birth control laws have uniformly failed because of Roman Catholic opposition. For example, in Massachusetts, after a vigorous campaign in the fall of 1942 the question whether the state law should be modified to permit physicians to give advice on contraceptives and contraceptive supplies to married persons for health reasons was voted down by referendum. Cardinal O'Connell condemned the proposal. The Roman Catholic bishop of western Massachusetts ran a half-page advertisement in the *Springfield Republican*, in which he said, "The same dilemma faces mankind today that faced the human race at the dawn of its existence—either increase and multiply or decrease and disappear from the earth." Posters were placed in the vestibules of churches urging the faithful to vote "No," and from the pulpit priests asked their parishioners to take this stand. From the Roman Catholic standpoint it was a crusade to prevent what they believed to be a sin.[47]

Many representative Protestant organizations and many religious leaders favored the proposed change. Among its supporters were the Massachusetts Council of Churches, the Department of Social Welfare of the Episcopal Church, the Boston Y.W.C.A., and the Department of Social Service of the Episcopal Diocese of Massachusetts. They desired the change in the interest of maternal and child health and of medical freedom. They also emphasized that such a law would strike a blow at the serious situation evident in the hundreds of thousands of illegal abortions performed annually in the United States. Similar attempts since then to secure a change in the Massachusetts law have failed—specifically another referendum, in 1948, which also lost by a 7 to 5 ratio.

The Connecticut situation is equally serious. On the one hand, the hierarchy is opposed to any modification of the state statute on birth control. This reads, "Every person who shall use any drug, medicine, article or instrument for the purpose of preventing conception shall be fined not less than fifty dollars or imprisoned not less than sixty days nor more than one year, or be both fined and imprisoned." [48]

Opposed to the Roman Catholic group and some of their sympathizers in other churches have been strong forces led by the Reverend Dr. Robbins W. Barstow, recently president both of the Hartford Seminary Foundation and of the Connecticut Birth Control League. They have sought an amendment to the birth control law that would permit licensed physicians legally to give supervision or advice to any patient "when in such a physician's opinion pregnancy is detrimental to the health of such mother or child." The discussion has been vigorous and at times bitter.

The constitutionality of anti-birth control laws has not as yet been decided by the United States Supreme Court. On two occasions, the first in 1943 [49] and the second in 1961,[50] the Court was faced with appeals challenging the Connecticut law, but in each instance the appeal was dismissed for technical reasons. However, at the present time a test suit is again on the way up,[51] and it is probable that the Court will finally decide the constitutionality of anti-birth control laws.

Closely related to the giving of birth control information, as far as Roman Catholic opposition is concerned, is the whole question of sex education. The Church takes the ground that this is a matter entirely for the Church and home, not for the state and its public schools. A serious issue arose in New York State in the summer of 1949.[52] The New York State Catholic Welfare Committee opposed the state health commissioner and the state department of education in the showing in schools of two films entitled *Human Growth* and *Human Reproduction*. With reference to the former the health department said, "It is quite impossible to modify our health education efforts, which are based upon modern knowledge of medicine and science, to fit every religious tenet in the field of health."

The secretary of the committee, Mr. Charles J. Tobin, stated that the state was within its rights in disseminating scientific and medical information to parents to promote the well-being of the community, but he added that parents should "resist the state and its agencies when an attempt is made to usurp parental rights or to invade the sanctity of the home by disseminating sex knowledge, without morality, to their children in the school." [53]

This is one example of the difficulties that have arisen in many communities between Church and State in the matter of sex education. Another took place in Levittown, New York. There the election in 1956 of a new public school board, a majority of whose members were Catholic, resulted in the immediate cancellation of the exhibition of a film on menstruation for the girl students.[54] In these and similar cases the Catholic Church does not dispute the desirability and even necessity of proper sex education for the young. It takes the position, however, that this is the exclusive and sacred responsibility of the family, aided by the family's spiritual advisers, and may not be conducted in public schools.[55]

In this respect the stand of the Catholic Church must be distinguished from that of the Christian Science Church. Christian Scientists object to the compulsory participation of their children in the public schools in instruction on the germ theory of disease, a theory inconsistent with Christian Science teachings. They do not, however, object to the inclusion of such teaching in the public school curriculum so long as their children are excused from participating. (On the other hand, it must be pointed out that the Christian Science Church vigorously opposes fluoridation of municipal water supplies even though the majority of the residents are not Christian Scientists and have no conscientious objections to drinking fluoridated water.)

Also related to the question of birth control is that of therapeutic abortion, i.e., abortion deemed necessary to save the mother's life or protect her from grave illness. The official position of Roman Catholicism was stated in 1930 by Pius XI in his encyclical letter *Casti Connubii*:

> However much we may pity the mother whose health and even life is gravely imperiled in the performance of the duty allotted to her by nature, nevertheless what could ever be sufficient reason for excusing in any way the direct murder of the innocent? This is precisely what we are dealing with here. Whether inflicted upon mother or upon the child, it is against the precept of God and the law of nature: "Thou shalt not kill." The life of each is equally sacred, and no one has the power, not even the public authority, to destroy it.[56]

Notwithstanding the assertion that "not even the public authority" may permit a therapeutic abortion and that it is against "the law of nature" and hence an obligation binding on non-Catholics as well as Catholics, the Church has made no effort thus far to obtain enactment of laws prohibiting therapeutic abortion. Possibly the Church recognizes that its position is so unacceptable to the American people generally that an effort to translate it into law would not only be futile but alienate many non-Catholics. Or it may be—and this is probably the reason the Church would give—that with the advance of medical science the problem of therapeutic abortion is more theoretic than real. Medicine has progressed to the point that a physician is rarely faced with the terrible dilemma of choosing between the life of the mother and the life of the child. Moreover, as is also frequently urged in defense of the Catholic position, in those rare cases where an abortion is indicated, the situation is almost always such as would justify an indirect abortion, that is, one having the direct purpose of removing a diseased condition in the mother even though this removal indirectly causes the death of the fetus, and such an operation is permissible under Catholic canon law.

Adoptions

Adoption of children across religious lines has also been a Church-State issue which in recent years has caused increasing interreligious misunderstanding and often bitterness. Ever since the leading Massachusetts case of *Purinton* v. *Jamrock*,[57] decided in 1907, it has been the general rule that the test which a court should apply in passing upon a petition of a couple to adopt a child is whether the adoption would serve the best interests of the child. The fact that the child was born into a faith different from that of the adopting couple, the court held, may be considered, but it does not constitute an absolute bar if the child's welfare will be benefited by the adoption. Many states have passed laws stating that "whenever practicable" or "whenever possible" a child should be placed for adoption with a family of the same faith, but the courts in these states have interpreted the laws as being consistent with the principle of *Purinton* v. *Jamrock*, that is, that religious difference does not constitute an absolute bar to adoption.[58]

This, in any event, is how the supreme judicial court of Massachusetts interpreted the statute in 1952 when, in the Gally case, it approved the adoption by a Protestant couple of a child born to Roman Catholic parents. The decision was bitterly criticized in the editorial columns of the Boston *Pilot*, official organ of the Roman Catholic archdiocese, which called it a "supreme tragedy" and a "victory for the current secularist philosophy, which considers religion, any religion, of secondary or minor importance and the material advantages of life as of prevailing consequence." [59]

Two years later the Goldman case came before the court. It involved illegitimate twins, born to Pearl L. Dome, a divorced Roman Catholic woman, in 1951. The natural father was also Roman Catholic. Two weeks after the birth of the children a Jewish couple, Reuben and Sylvia Goldman of Marblehead, took them for adoption. Pearl Dome consented in writing and was agreeable to their being raised in the Jewish faith. But at the adoption hearing Judge John V. Phelan found that, although the Goldmans were otherwise suitable adopters, many nearby Catholic couples had applications for similar children on file with the Catholic Charities Bureau. He ruled therefore that, even though these Catholic couples had never sought to adopt the Dome twins and had not in fact ever seen them, nevertheless it appeared "practicable" to give the twins to a Catholic couple. He accordingly denied the Goldmans' petition. The supreme judicial court affirmed the decision, in effect thereby overruling the Gally decision, and the State Department of Public Welfare started proceedings to take the twins from the Goldmans and place them in a Catholic institution. The Goldmans thereupon abandoned their home and business, a clothing store in Boston, and departed with the twins to establish a new home in another state.[60]

Shortly after the Goldman case came the even more publicized "Hildy" case. Hildy was born in February, 1951, to a Catholic student nurse, said to have been unmarried. Records indicate that the court had ascertained that the father of the child, an intern, was a Protestant. With the oral consent of the young mother, Hildy was placed by her physician with a Jewish couple, Mr. and Mrs. Melvin Ellis of Boston. When Hildy was five weeks old, the natural mother, who later married Mr. McCoy, claimed that she had learned for the first time that the adoptive parents were not Catholics and that both had been divorced previously. With the vigorous co-operation of the Roman Catholic Church, she began proceedings for Hildy's return. There followed a long battle in the courts, climaxed in February, 1955, when the supreme judicial court, following the Goldman decision, ruled in favor of Marjorie McCoy. Like the Goldmans, the Ellises, defying the court, fled Massachusetts with Hildy. In 1957 they were discovered living in Florida, and the Massachusetts authorities sought to extradite them for trial on kidnapping charges, but Governor Leroy Collins of Florida refused the extradition request. Periodic feature stories through the years since then have portrayed Hildy's apparent happiness with her adoptive parents.[61]

Most state courts have refused to follow the lead of Massachusetts in interpreting their "when practicable" statutes as in effect barring all interreligious adoptions. More typical of their approach to the problem is a case decided in the courts of Pennsylvania in 1954. The crazed neighbor of a young couple in Michigan entered their house and shot them both. The husband had been a Catholic, the wife a Protestant. They had one young child whom they had agreed to rear in the Catholic faith and accordingly had had him baptized as a Catholic. On the death of the couple, the child's (Protestant) maternal aunt came from Pennsylvania, took him, and brought him back with her with the intent to adopt him. The child's (Catholic) paternal grandparents followed her to Pennsylvania and, with the support and backing of the Roman Catholic Church, brought legal proceedings to recover the child for adoption by them. The Pennsylvania courts ruled in favor of the aunt and her husband on the ground that the welfare of the child dictated that he be brought up away from the scene of the tragedy and by a couple whose age relationship to him was more nearly that of the normal age relationship between parents and children. While the religious factor, the court said, is important and must be given consideration, it may not be allowed to override the demands of the child's welfare.[62]

The position of the Roman Catholic Church against interreligious adoptions is quite logical and understandable in the light of its dogmatic concepts and philosophical principles. Those particularly relevant here are that (1) religion is a matter of status and not of election; (2) Catholic baptism is immutable and accordingly there is no exit from the Catholic faith; (3) eternal salvation is more important than temporal happiness, and if a choice must be made the first must always be chosen above the second; (4) Catholicism is the one and only true faith, and membership therein is the surest if not the only certain road to eternal salvation; (5) voluntariness is not the ultimate test nor basic requirement in religion, and therefore the wishes of a Catholic mother that her child be adopted by a couple of a non-Catholic faith need not be honored (". . . no one," said a Catholic judge in a Massachusetts custody case, "not even the parents have the right to deny an immature child who has been baptized a Roman Catholic the privilege of being reared in Catholicity"); (6) the Church has a legitimate and legally recognizable interest in the faith of its members and has the right to call upon the state to use its machinery to protect that interest and preserve the sovereignty of the Church over its members.[63]

None of these concepts or principles is acceptable to Protestantism,[64] and it was therefore no more than to be expected that the Catholic position was strenuously contested by Protestants. In the Hildy case the Massachusetts Council of Churches urged the Florida governor to base his decision in the extradition primarily on the welfare of the child. Methodist Bishop John Wesley Lord of Boston asserted that superior to the Massachusetts law was "moral judgment (which) must always be the last judge in any matter." "It is," he continued, "moral judgment that, for the welfare and good of this six-year-old adopted daughter, the law be superseded by the divine law of love. . . . This devout Jewish couple, at sacrifice of earthly possessions and with a devotion none can deny, wishes to continue to rear the child in a home in which love and devotion are the paramount factors. No law of the land can supersede moral law." Similarly, in Missouri, the local chapter of Protestants and Other Americans United for Separation of Church and State joined with the local chapter of the American Civil Liberties Union and the local chapter of the American Jewish Congress to oppose a bill that sought to add a "religious protection" clause to the state's adoption law.[65]

Many legal scholars believe that when a court refuses to permit an adoption for the sole reason of differences in religion it is violating the constitutional guarantee of freedom of religion and Church-State separation.[66] The United States Supreme Court, although it refused to review the Goldman decision, has never specifically passed upon the issue. Probably, however, sooner or later it will be required to decide this troublesome constitutional question and hopefully thereby ease some of the interreligious bitterness that the question has engendered.

Justice and the Courts

Except for slavery (including the evils that live after it—segregation and discrimination) perhaps the greatest moral issue that has confronted American Christianity has been that of justice. The Churches have been all too slow to recognize their responsibility for high ideals of public justice. There may have been truth in the statement of Professor John R. Commons that Christianity was strong in promoting charity but weak in promoting justice.[67] There can, however, be no question that the emphasis on justice, for which the Jewish prophets of old stood supremely, has been reawakened lately among the forward-looking Protestant, Catholic, and Jewish leaders alike. Only with the rise of the present century has this matter been uppermost in the minds of many Church leaders. It has shown itself in the opposition of the Church in the North and the South to the infamous practice of lynching; the obtaining of rights for conscientious objectors to military training in peacetime and military service in wartime; and the procuring of a fair hearing for radicals on trial when public opinion was inflamed and there was fear that justice might not be assured. Cases of the latter sort have been increasingly conspicuous in recent years and have caused considerable friction between the more radical social reform groups in the Church and the State authorities.

The Scottsboro case (1931 on) against nine Negro boys in Alabama for alleged rape of a white woman was one in which many churches were gravely concerned. Believing that race prejudice interfered with a fair trial for the accused Negro youths, they supported various agencies which secured new trials in the state as well as effective appeals to the Supreme Court of the United States.[68]

In both the Sacco-Vanzetti case in Massachusetts (1920-27) and the Mooney bomb killings in California in the Preparedness Day parade in 1916, large groups in the churches supported radical organizations in demanding gubernatorial reprieves or pardons on the ground that conservative courts had been unduly influenced by prejudice against the political and social views and affiliations of the persons accused. The Sacco-Vanzetti case attracted worldwide attention. There was more questioning of the decision than in any case involving personal guilt or innocence before an American tribunal perhaps in our entire history. The churches as a whole did not commit themselves further than to urge the governor of Massachusetts to commute the sentence to life imprisonment or to stay execution pending the hearing of additional evidence. The Federal Council of Churches took no definite action, but its general secretary, the executive secretary of its Commission on the Church and Social Service, and some other representative Church officials, telegraphed the governor as follows:

We, the undersigned national church officials, acting, however, in our personal capacities, are impelled to say that, in view of the present uncertainty among conservative as well as radical citizens as to the guilt of Sacco and Vanzetti, we think it would be against humanity and public policy and would shock the moral sense of the nation to allow their execution tonight.

We therefore urge you to stay execution long enough to allow consideration of all pertinent evidence. If the certainty of guilt does not become reasonably conclusive in the public mind, we strongly recommend commutation of sentence.[69]

In the early fifties of this century many Protestant and Jewish clergymen joined in appeals for clemency to Julius and Ethel Rosenberg, who had been convicted of espionage and had been sentenced to death. (There do not appear to have been any Roman Catholic priests joining in the pleas, but there were wide-spread and apparently well-founded reports in 1953 that Pope Pius XII had intervened with President Eisenhower in an effort to gain clemency for the Rosenbergs.) Unlike the Mooney, Scottsboro, and Sacco-Vanzetti cases, the appeals were not in the main based upon an assertion of the innocence of the defendants or the lack of a fair trial—although many clergyman believed that the Rosenbergs' guilt had not been established beyond a reasonable doubt—but rather on considerations of mercy. The appeals, however, proved fruitless and both Rosenbergs were executed by electrocution in June, 1953.

These are typical of the more important cases where many Church leaders have been duly concerned to try to see that justice was done.

Prison Reform and Chaplains

Prison reform in its early days owed much to the Quakers. In Penn's "Great Law" or charter of 1682 the position was taken that all prisons should be workhouses. The state of Pennsylvania provided in its constitution in 1770 that the legislature should proceed "as soon as might be, to the reform of the penal laws, and invent punishments less sanguinary and better proportioned to the various degrees of criminality."[70] Here, as so often, a religious motive led to reforms in administration. Furthermore, the reforms which followed in Pennsylvania and New York had a potent effect on legislation and practice in England in the third decade of the last century.[71]

Since the founding of the national and state governments our churches have become especially concerned with these problems. Alexis Charles de Tocqueville, who visited the United States in 1831 and was much interested in prisons, pointed out that prison reform in America originated with religious concern for the criminal. He noted that the heads of many of the best penal institutions, reform schools, and asylums were former Protestant ministers.[72] From that day to this, ministers of religion have been active in the cause of prison reform.

A criticism frequently leveled against the Church is that most of the prisoners in the United States are said to be members of various religious denominations. This matter has been carefully studied by several people, perhaps the most important study having been made by two Catholic priests long connected with the Illinois State Penitentiary. It shows that an investigation of some forty-five prisons made about 1925 indicated 86.95[73] per cent of prisoners reporting some religious affiliation and only 13.05 per cent no religious affiliation. These facts, taken by themselves, were somewhat alarming in connection with one of the main claims of the churches to exemption from taxation, namely, that they save the State enormous sums of money through the development of character and consequently the prevention of crime. It was found, however, that in a very large percentage of cases registrants on entering prison, thinking that they are expected to report some religious affiliation, give a label which often meant little more than the recollection of a family tradition or a hypothetical preference for a Church with which the prisoner had had some brief association. Evidence of this conclusion was that among the Catholics enrolled in the Illinois State Penitentiary 80 per cent had not made their Easter communion, which is considered the minimum test of a practicing Catholic, and not 4 per cent had followed their religion "to the average extent of Catholic practice."[74]

John Edgar Hoover, director of the Federal Bureau of Investigation and a man whom most Americans would probably consider the best-qualified person in the country to speak with authority on the problem of crime and its prevention, is strongly of the opinion that religious affiliation, training, and practice constitute the most important single factor in crime prevention.[75]

As a result of the convictions expressed by Mr. Hoover and apparently shared in general by his colleagues, the Department of Justice provides both Catholic and Protestant chaplains to all Federal penitentiaries and reformatories. In each of the smaller institutions there is at least one chaplain. Jewish chaplaincy services are provided on a part-time basis.

The Church in this country, both Protestant and Catholic, has always taken a special interest in prison chaplaincies. It was mainly under Church leadership, or under that of persons motivated by strong Christian convictions, that the theory of the prison primarily as a place of punishment was broken down and the ideas of reformation of the individual and of the protection of society were substituted. The Pennsylvania Prison Society, early inspired by the Quakers, is a good example of this change. Also, throughout the first half of the nineteenth century it was the Church that was mainly responsible for developing various welfare services in penal institutions, as well as the first organizations to help discharged inmates. From an early date the Church supplied prison chaplaincies at its own expense, though increasingly the financial burden was assumed by the state or the municipality.[76]

In a few cases special Protestant and Roman Catholic chapels are on the grounds of an institution, but more commonly, and more appropriately when they are for the special use of one religious group, they are on privately owned adjoining property. The erection, with the aid of the labor of about two hundred convicts over a period of three years, of the "Chapel of the Good Thief" on state property at the Clinton State Prison, Dannemora, New York, was opposed as unconstitutional by the New York League for the Separation of Church and State in 1940, but without success. On the other hand, in 1946 the Supreme Court of Virginia ruled it an unconstitutional abridgment of freedom of religion to compel either adult criminals or juvenile delinquents to attend chapel or participate in any religious exercise or training.

In that case, *Jones* v. *Commonwealth*,[77] the Supreme Court of Virginia reversed the decision of a lower court that fined certain boys for disorderly conduct and ordered them to attend church and Sunday school each Sunday for

a year. These paragraphs from the opinion of the higher court are significant:

Nothing is more clearly set forth or more plainly expressed than the determination of our forefathers to establish and perpetuate in the several states of the Union complete religious liberty. No state has more jealously guarded and preserved the questions of religious belief and religious worship as questions between each individual man and his Maker than Virginia. . . .

Thus, in these statutes and constitutional provisions are contained the fundamental principle of the separation of church and state. There is preserved and assured to each individual the right to determine for himself all questions which relate to his relation with the Creator of the Universe. No civil authority has the right to require anyone to accept or reject any religious belief or to contribute any support thereto. The growth of religion is not made dependent on force or alliance with the state. Its support is left to moral and spiritual forces.

For the foregoing reasons we are of the opinion to reverse and annul each of the judgments complained of and to dismiss the proceedings against each of the defendants.[78]

An increasingly serious problem involving prison life and Church-State relations has arisen in recent years. It concerns the Black Muslims,[79] a group of Negroes who believe in the supremacy of the black race and hatred for whites. They also profess to adhere to the faith of Islam, although they are not accepted by the recognized Mohammedan Churches. In many cases Black Muslim prisoners have complained that they are not permitted to practice their faith in prisons, are deprived of opportunity to read the Koran, and are otherwise discriminated against because of their beliefs. A number of these complaints have been taken to the courts. The legal issues in them are twofold: first, are the Black Muslims really a religious group, and second, if they are, to what extent is the constitutional guarantee of religious freedom applicable within a prison community? These issues have not yet been definitively decided by the Supreme Court, but in most cases prison wardens have been making every effort to accommodate the Black Muslims in their beliefs as far as they can without unduly interfering with prison discipline.

Military Chaplaincies

The government's attitude toward religion and religious denominations as shown in the army and navy is, speaking generally, characteristic of the fundamental American position. It is sympathetic with the cause of religion, appreciates its significance in individual and national life, and encourages provisions for worship in all branches of military service, while at the same time retaining an impartial attitude toward the various denominations. An individual's religious creed is not considered in matters of enlistment and promotion. The only recognition of creedal differences is the attempt to distribute chaplaincies fairly and the custom, for the guidance of chaplains, of having the identification tag worn by a soldier or sailor show whether he is Catholic, Jewish, or Protestant, and the indication of this fact on admission blanks to army hospitals.

The chaplaincies of Congress and of the army and navy and other military forces are frequently the object of attack on the ground that they lead to confusion between the ideals of the Church and the State and are dangerous to religious freedom. Chaplaincies under the army and navy have also been attacked from a very different angle—that of the more extreme Church pacifists, and by some who think that they should be supported by the churches and carry no military rank. That many thoughtful religiously motivated persons are troubled by the question is indicated by the following extract from the overall statement on Church and State adopted by the General Assembly of the United Presbyterian Church in May, 1963:

The Special Committee on Church and State *recommends* that:

1. Ministerial candidates and ordained clergymen, like other Americans, claim exemption from military service only on grounds of conscientious objection, and that the historical support our Church has given to conscientious objectors be reaffirmed.

2. The Church recognizes that the continuation of the present practice whereby its ministers serve as military chaplains, paid by the state, raise serious questions in the light of separation of church and state, and that its policies in this connection be thoroughly re-examined. For the time being, ministers of the United Presbyterian Church should continue to be enlisted for service as chaplains, according to the standards which are now followed, or those which may subsequently be

adopted, conformably to the requirements of the military and the will of the church.

3. In all conversations with the leaders of the nation's military establishment the representatives of the church continue to insist on the religious function of the chaplaincy as over against all other interpretations, and that additional duties not be assigned chaplains lest the ministerial nature of the office be weakened.

4. Since the chaplaincy is rated as special staff in the military structure, the church, for the protection of the ministry of the Word and sacraments, insist on the restrictions of the oversight of the chaplaincy to the proper superiors in the chaplain corps.[80]

Similar uneasiness on the question of military chaplains has been expressed in the editorial columns of *The Christian Century* and in other Protestant sources. Nevertheless, it is undoubtedly true that the overwhelming majority of the American people are satisfied with the chaplaincy system in the military forces and do not seriously doubt either its constitutionality or its wisdom.

The chaplaincy had its inception during the Revolutionary War when the Continental Congress in 1775 provided for the pay of chaplains and the following year specifically authorized the appointment of ministers of the gospel as chaplains. General Washington issued an order carrying out the purpose of the Congress, generally considered a milestone in the history of our army chaplaincies. In 1791, two years after the organization of the American army, the office of chaplain received actual recognition as an integral part of the armed forces.[81] There was then only one chaplain, but the number was increased from time to time, though the chaplaincy was also discontinued during various periods. Not until Samuel L. Southard became secretary of the navy in 1823 was a definite rule passed requiring chaplains to be accredited ordained ministers, holding a definite relation to some ecclesiastical body—a plan formally followed by the army in 1861-62.

In 1838, when the office was placed on a fairly firm basis, the number of chaplains was increased to twenty, and the system of post chaplains was adopted. The selection in each case was left to the army post council of administration subject to the approval of the secretary of war.[82]

In 1854 an attempt was made to eliminate all chaplaincies. Since the principal attack was directed against Congressional chaplaincies,[83] it will be discussed more fully, shortly when we deal with that subject. Here it is sufficient to note that memorialists to Congress laid emphasis not only on the first clause of the Bill of Rights but on Article VI of the Constitution to the effect that "no religious test shall ever be required as a qualification to any office or public trust under the United States." But Congress was not impressed. The report of the Committee on the Judiciary of the House brought out the fact that the context clearly showed this reference to be "to a class of persons entirely distinct from chaplains."

The first Roman Catholic priest for army service was appointed in 1846 by President Polk during the Mexican War. Only three Catholics had been named up to 1856.[84] Since then Catholic representation in the chaplaincy has steadily increased. In the Civil War there were in all about one hundred Catholic priests, mostly serving at first with state militia, but later regularly commissioned by the Federal government. In the Spanish War there were fifteen regularly appointed, in addition to many more with militia regiments. In World War I there were several hundred. Before the outbreak of World War II there were thirty-one regular Catholic chaplains in the army, nineteen in the navy, and many more in the National Guard and on the reserve list.[85]

Jewish chaplains were first authorized during the Civil War. In December, 1861, President Lincoln wrote to Dr. A. Fischel, who was especially interested in providing for the religious needs of Jewish soldiers,

I find that there are several particulars in which the present law in regard to Chaplains is supposed to be deficient, all of which I now desire presenting to the appropriate Committee of Congress. I shall try to have a new law broad enough to cover what is desired by you in behalf of the Israelites.[86]

At this time the act of July 22, 1861, was in force, providing for the appointment of chaplains but stating that "The chaplain so appointed must be a regular ordained minister of a Christian denomination." As a result of the president's bringing this matter to the attention of Congress the law was amended by an act passed July 17, 1862, which removed the requirement that chaplains must be Christians. The new act stated merely

That no person shall be appointed a chaplain in the United States army who is not a regularly ordained minister of some religious denomination, and who does not present testimonials of his good standing as such minister, with a recommendation for his appointment as an army chaplain from some authorized ecclesiastical body, or not less than five accredited ministers belonging to said denomination.[87]

The percentage of chaplains among the different faiths has changed from time to time with estimates of the percentages of the different groups in the service. The Roman Catholic percentage has been a matter of special interest. In World War I it was 37.5; in World War II, 21; and on May 1, 1945, it was established by the secretary of war as 30.46.

All the governmental military academies require the students to participate in religious exercises. Regulations for the U.S. Corps of Cadets, 1947, state, "Attendance at chapel is part of a cadet's training; no cadet will be exempted. Each cadet will receive religious training in one of the three particular faiths: Protestant, Catholic or Jewish." [88]

At the Naval Academy the regulations read, "All Midshipmen, except those on authorized outside church parties, shall attend Sunday services in the chapel." [89] Midshipmen may on their request attend services at the churches in Annapolis, where there are a Roman Catholic church, a Jewish synagogue, and various Protestant churches; but most of them attend the Academy chapel, where the services are non-sectarian but follow in an abbreviated form the order of morning prayer of the Episcopal Church.

Military Exemptions and Conscientious Objectors [90]

Closely related to the question of military chaplaincies is the matter of military exemptions. Congress has for many years exempted from military service both clergymen and divinity students. There has been considerable litigation in the application of this exemption, particularly in reference to the Jehovah's Witnesses sect, in which every believing member is considered a minister. Congress has also provided by statute for the exemption from combat service of persons with religious scruples against bearing arms, and while this statute has precedents going back in this country to colonial times, the question of conscientious objections has always proved a difficult one.

The Friends have always taken strong ground against war and war preparations. Like the Mennonites, they have made pacifism a dogma, to which they have generally stood true. In many ways the hardest strain to which their pacifist views have put them in America was in the seventeenth century when they dominated the Pennsylvania Assembly and the colony was threatened by Indians on its western border. The question was how they could protect the colony and at the same time vote conscientiously and consistently on appropriations to be used for military purposes. Benjamin Franklin tells us that the difficulty was usually met by making the appropriation "for the King's use," without further specification.[91] The Friends have commonly been exempted by public authority from all forms of military service, an exception based directly on respect for their religious convictions.

Similarly, in 1749, Parliament excused the Germans of Pennsylvania from service in the Indian wars on the ground of their conscientious scruples. This exemption covered such groups as the Mennonites, Dunkers, and Schwenkfelders, as well as a considerable number of members of the Reformed Church.[92] Since one-third of the population of Pennsylvania at the time of the American Revolution was German, the exemption involved a good many citizens.[93]

When the national government was formed, Madison proposed during the discussion of the Second Amendment of the Bill of Rights that "No person religiously scrupulous shall be compelled to bear arms." This proposal did not commend itself to the majority, but some of the state constitutions were drafted to incorporate the same idea. For instance, the New York constitution, adopted in 1821, in providing for citizens serving in the militia, stated, "But all such inhabitants of this State, of any religious denomination whatever, as from scruples of conscience may be averse to bearing arms, shall be excused therefrom by paying to the State an equivalent in money. . . ." [94]

In the Civil War the draft laws in the North[95] permitted exemption when a substitute was paid for and in both North and South [96] provided that men who were conscientiously opposed to bearing arms might serve in some other capacity. After the Civil War conscription was not again considered necessary until American entry into World War I in 1917. Then Congress exempted "the members of any well-recognized religious sect or organization whose existing creed or principles forbid its members to participate in war in any form, but no person shall be exempted from service in any capacities that the President shall declare to be non-combatant." [97] This clause was liberally interpreted, but those who refused such noncombatant service were court-martialed. Four hundred and fifty men were imprisoned, mainly members of religious groups which felt it wrong to advance any war even indirectly.[98] Some persons, including Judge J. F. Rutherford, the leader of Jehovah's Witnesses, also served terms in prison under the Espionage Act for circulating anti-war literature.

In 1940 the law was changed to remove the requirement that a conscientious objector to be exempt from combat service must belong to some recognized religious sect or organization. The Selective Service Act of that year liberalized the requirements for exemption to include anyone who by "reason of religious training and belief" possessed conscientious scruples against "participation in war in any form," thus making it unnecessary to prove membership in a particular pacifist denomination.

A number of cases have reached the Supreme Court involving conscientious objectors, and all have given the churches serious concern. In the first, *United States* v. *Schwimmer*, the Court decided in 1929 that an applicant for naturalization, a Hungarian woman forty-nine years of age and of the highest character, could not be admitted to naturalization because of her uncompromising pacifist views. The second, *United States* v. *Macintosh* (see Chapter 5) reached a similar conclusion in the case of a member of the Yale faculty who, though not a pacifist, would not give a definite pledge in advance to fight in any war in which the country should engage but claimed the right to decide whether the particular war was moral and righteous. However, in 1946 the Supreme Court in the case of *Girouard* v. *United States* (see Chapter 5) overruled the Macintosh decision and held that Congress had not intended to bar conscientious objectors from the privilege of naturalization, and several years later Congress amended the naturalization law to make this clear.

Other cases in which the question of the consequences of conscientious objection was decided by the Supreme Court include *Hamilton* v. *Regents of the University of California* (see Chapter 5), in which the Court held that conscientious scruples did not excuse students at a state university from participating in required military training, and *In re Summers* (see Chapter 5), in which it held that a state could constitutionally bar a pacifist from the privilege of practicing law.

While the law no longer requires that a conscientious objector belong to any particular religious group in order to qualify for exemption, it does require that he believe in a Supreme Being and that his objection to military service be based on his belief that such service would violate his superior duty to the Supreme Being. After the decision in *Torcaso* v. *Watkins* (see Chapter 5) invalidating religious oaths for office, the constitutionality of this requirement was challenged in several Federal courts by conscientious objectors who could not truthfully say that they believe in God or a Supreme Being. The Supreme Court has not yet passed upon the question and the lower Federal courts have come to different and opposite conclusions. It cannot therefore be said at the present time whether or not the requirement of belief in God as a prerequisite to exemption from military service as a conscientious objector is constitutional. It can, however, be predicted that the Supreme Court will decide the issue before very long.

Aside from the question of individual conscientious objection is the more general one of opposition to war as an instrument of national policy. Of the three major faiths, Protestantism has been the most vocal and active in support of peace movements. The Church Peace Union and a number of similar organizations were organized under Protestant sponsorship to promote the cause of world peace. In 1934 a questionnaire sent to some 100,000 Protestant clergymen, and returned by about one-fifth of the recipients, revealed that two-thirds of those who answered believed that the churches should not sanction or support any future war; about the same number stated that as individuals they would not participate in or sanction any future war. Only one-third felt that there was a sufficient moral distinction between "aggressive" and "defensive" wars to justify sanction or support of the latter.[99]

The spread of Nazi domination over Europe and the outbreak of World War II effected a substantial change in Protestantism on the issue of war and peace. Yet, up to the day of Pearl Harbor *The Christian Century*, the nation's leading Protestant publication, vigorously opposed American entry into the war or even the rendering of such aid to Great Britain as carried with it the risk of American involvement. The American Protestant clergy was divided on the issue. A strong minority favored all-out intervention on the side of Great Britain (*Christianity and Crisis* was launched under the editorship of Reinhold Niebuhr as an organ for the views of this segment of Protestantism). The majority of Protestant clergymen were probably in the center, favoring material aid to Britain but shunning direct involvement in the war.

Pearl Harbor effectively stilled Protestant opposition to war and to the particular war in which America was engaged. In 1940 the Methodist General Conference asserted unequivocally and unqualifiedly that "the Methodist Church . . . will not officially enforce, support or participate in war." [100] Four years later it adopted a resolution which "in Christ's name" invoked "the blessing of God upon the men in the armed forces," prayed "for victory," and declared that it is "well within the Christian position" to assert "the necessity of the use of military force to resist an aggression which would overthrow every right which is held sacred by civilized men." Yet it is significant that the clergy in the Conference were almost exactly divided on the resolution, which carried only because of the 2-1 vote in its favor on the part of the laity in the Conference. (The resolution was bitterly denounced by *The Christian Century*.[101])

The return of peace revived the strong pro-pacifism of American Protestantism. Today the Protestant clergy is again taking the lead in the call for the complete and total abolition of war. Even proportionately, more Protestant clergymen signed the Stockholm Peace Petition than clergymen of any other faith. Opposition to American involvement in the Korean conflict was stronger within the Protestant clergy. Also strongest is Protestant opposition to the manufacture and testing of atomic and nuclear weapons.

Roman Catholicism does not have this firm feeling of opposition to war. Until recently the Church in this country has on the whole been quite unsympathetic both to pacifism in general and to peaceful coexistence with Soviet Russia in particular. However, the epoch-making encyclical of John XXIII, *Pacem in Terris*, which condemned international war and called for peaceful resolution of our differences even with Communist states, may well have marked the beginning of a change in the attitude of the Church in America on that subject. This is rendered more probable by reason of the early statements by Pope Paul VI, which indicate an agreement with the policy of his predecessor and an intention to carry it forward.

While American Judaism has also not participated actively in pro-pacifist activities, other than in vigorous opposition to nuclear arms testing, it does possess a small pacifist group. Known as the Jewish Peace Fellowship, it was organized in 1941 to unite those who believe that Jewish ideas and experience provide inspiration for a pacifist philosophy of life and to establish the right of Jews to be recognized as conscientious objectors.[102]

Potential points of conflict between Church and State over questions of war and preparation for war are many and serious. A consideration of the fundamental factors in the situation will show that this clash is almost inevitable. The State's first duty is to protect itself and its citizens. If these are attacked, or are in immediate and critical danger of being attacked, national defense seems to it paramount. But to the Church national defense is very largely a matter of morale and ideals, and anything which weakens these or puts them in second place seems fraught with danger. It consequently, and rightly, is concerned primarily with things moral and spiritual, and knows the demoralization that inevitably follows in their fields in the wake of war. It therefore insists that war should not be waged except in clear cases of national defense, the preservation of civilization, or the rescue of an oppressed people, and even then only when earnest and persistent efforts at peaceful settlement have failed. Because it knows how difficult it is to reason objectively and dispassionately about such matters, it is inclined to question the motives and objectives of any war in which its people are asked to take part unless the enemy is at the gates or pressing toward them. Consequently, the problems of war almost inevitably raise fundamental issues in which the State as the guardian of political and social security and the Church as the guardian of conscience and spiritual idealism come into occasional conflict.

Congressional Chaplaincies

The origin of Congressional chaplaincies has been dealt with in an earlier historical section.[103] Here it may be enough merely to call attention to the fact that the chaplains of the United States Senate and House of Representatives are chosen by these bodies respectively and receive annual stipends for their services. They offer prayer at the beginning of every session—other than adjournments—of both houses of Congress, as well as on other official occasions of importance, and are frequently called upon to conduct the funerals of members and to perform other pastoral duties. Their prayers are printed in the *Congressional Record,* and occasionally Congress has ordered volumes of them published.

The chaplains have almost invariably been Protestant ministers. An exception was the choice by the Senate of the Reverend Charles Constantine Pise,[104] a Roman Catholic who was elected chaplain in 1832.[105] He was a native of Maryland, educated at Georgetown College in the District of Columbia and at the College of the Propaganda in Rome and at the time of his election was connected with St. Patrick's Church in Washington. He was a distinguished Latinist, an author of some note, and a warm personal friend of Henry Clay, who nominated him for the Senate chaplaincy and later had him offered a chair in Transylvania University. There was opposition to his election to the chaplaincy on the old ground of his "double allegiance," but his reply to this was in an address delivered in Annapolis on July 4, 1833, in which he said,

I acknowledge no allegiance to the Pope's temporal power—I am no subject of his dominions—I have sworn no fealty to his throne—but I am, as all American Catholics glory to be, independent of all foreign temporal authority—devoted to freedom, to unqualified toleration, to republican institutions. America is our country; her laws are our safeguard; her Constitution our Magna Charta; her tribunals our appeal; her Chief Magistrate our national head—to all which we are subject and obedient, in accordance with the injunction of religion, which commands us to give honor where honor is due—to be subject to the powers that are—and to give unto Caesar the things that are Caesar's.[106]

In the middle of the last century an early experiment was renewed of having two chaplains, one elected by the Senate and one by the House, "to officiate alternately," during the session of Congress.[107] In this and later session the question of Congressional chaplaincies was much discussed. There was then, as at other times, opposition to the office on the part of persons who were inspired by very different motives but united in opposing government chaplaincies as breaking down the line of demarcation between Church and State.

Typical was the petition submitted in 1855 by certain Baptists of Henderson County, Tennessee, of which the following is an extract:

We cannot perceive why clergymen should be sustained by Government in either House of Congress, at our military and naval stations, on board our vessels of war, and in each regiment of our army, any more than in each township, parish, district, or village throughout the land; and to sanction the former could not be regarded otherwise than as an assent to the extension of the same system that would place us upon a level with the priest-ridden despotisms of the Old World. Our members of Congress, military and naval officers, soldiery and seamen, are, or should be, paid a just compensation for their services, and be left, like all other citizens, to support any clergymen, or none, as their consciences may direct them, without legal agency or coercion. Neither Christianity nor the genius of our institutions contemplates any aristocracy predicated upon the clerical profession, and no special provision therefore is necessary by the Government to admit clergymen to our Army and Navy, as they may enlist like other men, and labor like Jesus himself and his apostles among the poor fishermen on the sea-side. If it be objected that few clergymen would serve among the troops and marines upon such terms, we can only say that, if actuated by correct religious motives, no minister would wait for Government gold to lead him to his labors of love among them, and that none but hypocrites would be debarred by the want of it. We think the Government should not evince more religious zeal than professed ministers of the gospel themselves by bribing them to perform religious services. If the clergymen in the Army and Navy look for other compensation than the voluntary contribution of those among whom they labor, the various religious societies of the country might be more appropriately appealed to, as their funds are voluntarily contributed for such purposes; while those of the Government are taken for national purposes, by authority of law, equally from all classes of citizens of whatever sects, and whether professors or non-professors of religion.[108]

The petitions and remonstrances were considered by the judiciary committees of both houses of Congress, and both rejected them and upheld the institution of governmental chaplaincies. Thus the report of the Committee on the Judiciary of the House of Representatives in 1854 regarding a memorial of citizens from several states "praying that the office of chaplain in the army, navy, at West Point, and Indian stations, and in both houses of Congress be abolished" closes with the following statement:

While your committee believe that neither Congress nor the army or navy should be deprived of the service of chaplains, they freely concede that the ecclesiastical and civil powers have been, and should continue to be, entirely divorced from each other. But we beg leave to rescue ourselves from the imputation of asserting that religion is not needed to the safety of civil society. It must be considered as the foundation on which the whole structure rests. Laws will not have permanence or power without the sanction of religious sentiment—without a firm belief that there is a Power above us that will reward our virtues and punish our vices. In this age there can be no substitute for Christianity; that, in its general principles, is the great conservative element on which we must rely for the purity and permanence of free institutions. That was the religion of the founders of the republic, and they expected it to remain the religion of their descendants. There is a great and very prevalent error on this subject in the opinion that those who organized this government did not legislate on religion. They did legislate on it by making it free to all, "to the Jew and the Greek, to the learned and unlearned." The error has risen from the belief that there is no legislation unless in permissive or restricting enactments. But making a thing free is as truly a part of legislation as confining it by limitations; and what the government has made free, it is bound to keep free.[109]

These and other reports and actions, which it is not necessary to quote further, resulted in the continuance of the chaplaincies. But in the years immediately preceding the Civil War the chaplains were occasionally involved in political discussions, slavery and anti-slavery men advocating their respective convictions. The desire to advance personal friends, and even denominational interests, was not lacking. The situation reached such a point that during the Civil War a Senator offered the following resolution:

Resolved, That the Chaplain of the Senate be respectfully requested hereafter to pray to and supplicate Almighty God in our behalf, and not to lecture Him, inform Him what to do, or state to Him, under pretense of prayer, his (the said Chaplain's) opinion in reference to His duty as the Almighty; and that the said Chaplain be further requested, as aforesaid, not, under the form of prayer, to lecture the Senate in relation to questions before the body.[110]

In the Reconstruction period too there were untoward incidents, as when the chaplain of Congress between 1865 and 1867 is said to have prayed frequently that President Andrew Johnson "might be humbled and cast down" and his own "party might be covered with glory." [111] But in general during the past half-century or more the chaplaincies have been filled without any division on political or denominational grounds, though it has been customary to continue to have Protestants, who are always in a large majority in both houses.

Following the example of Congress, the major political parties always arrange to have each session of their national conventions opened with a prayer by some prominent clergymen. They generally have this function divided among Protestant, Roman Catholic, Jewish, and (in the 1960 conventions) Greek Orthodox clergymen. Probably this custom is dictated partly by religious motives, and even more by the favorable impression that the maintaining of the tradition is supposed to create in the electorate.

Notwithstanding the uniform rejection by Congress of objections to governmental chaplaincies, the constitutional issue is by no means free from doubt. James Madison, who was father of both the Constitution and the First Amendment, had this to say in his *Detached Memoranda*, written after he retired from the presidency:

Is the appointment of Chaplains to the two Houses of Congress consistent with the Constitution, and with the pure principle of religious freedom?

In strictness the answer on both points must be in the negative. The Constitution of the United States forbids everything like an establishment of a national religion. The law appointing Chaplains establishes a religious worship for the national representatives, to be performed by Ministers of religion, elected by a majority of them; and these are to be paid out of the national taxes. Does not this involve the principle of a national establishment, applicable to a provision for a religious worship for the Constituent as well as of the representative Body, approved by the majority, and conducted by Ministers of religion paid by the entire nation.

The establishment of the Chaplainship to Congress is a palpable violation of equal rights, as well as of Constitutional principles: The tenets of the chaplains elected [by the majority] shut the door of worship against the members whose creeds and consciences forbid a participation in that of the majority. To say nothing of other sects, this is the case with that of Roman Catholics and Quakers who have always had members in one or both of the Legislative branches. Could a Catholic clergyman ever hope to be appointed a Chaplain? To say that his religious principles are obnoxious or that his sect is small, is to lift the evil at once and exhibit in its naked deformity the doctrine that religious truth is to be tested by numbers, or that the major sects have a right to govern the minor.[112]

It is not likely that the constitutional issue will be passed upon by the Supreme Court. The reason is technical; the Court has ruled that it will not undertake to pass upon an allegedly unconstitutional expenditure of Federal funds in a suit brought by an ordinary taxpayer who has no legal interest in the controversy other than the fact that he pays taxes just as every other American does. In 1928, in the case of *Eliott* v. *White*,[113] a Federal court dismissed for that reason a suit brought by a taxpayer challenging the constitutionality of governmental payment of salaries to Congressional and military chaplains, and the issue thus did not reach the Supreme Court.

In the absence of a definite decision by the Supreme Court, it is certain that the institution of governmental chaplaincies will not be disturbed, for it is undoubtedly a tradition that commends itself to the great majority of Americans, although there are some who believe it would be wiser if the chaplains in Congress were paid out of the voluntary contributions of the members of Congress and the military chaplains by the various churches.

Religious Oaths for Public Office

The question of the required taking of oaths by government officials, jurors, court witnesses, and certain other persons has occasionally caused trouble between Church and State. The Constitution of the United States merely provides that Federal and state officeholders, including legislators and judges, shall "be bound by Oath or Affirmation, to support this Constitution. . . ."[114] The words "or Affirmation" were added to meet possible religious scruples of Quakers, Mennonites, and others who objected to oaths on the ground that they were unnecessary—a Christian man was under obligation to speak the truth on all occasions.[115] But before we consider the constitutional provision, something should be said about the history of religious oaths for office in the home country of England. For, as the Supreme Court said in the Everson case, the religious clause in the First Amendment "reflected in the minds of early Americans a vivid mental picture of conditions and practices which they fervently wished to stamp out in order to preserve liberty for themselves and their posterity." [116]

The Act of Supremacy, 1558, required of all holders of office in Church and

State an oath accepting the queen as supreme governor of all things ecclesiastical and temporal.[117] This oath was extended in 1562 to teachers, lawyers, officers of the courts, sheriffs, and members of the House of Commons. By the Presentation of Benefices Act of 1605, "popish recusants," convicted under one of the uniformity or supremacy acts, were denied access to the courts and "utterly disabled to exercise any public office or charge in the commonwealth."

Under Charles II a sacramental test "according to the rites of the church of England" was imposed on all officers of municipal corporations. By the Corporations Act of 1661 and by the Test Act of 1672 all officeholders, civil and military, were required to take the sacrament and make a declaration against the Catholic doctrine of transubstantiation. A stricter test was imposed on all members of both houses of Parliament, but annual indemnity bills and the practice of taking the sacrament once a year gave non-Catholic dissenters *de facto* immunity from these penalties.

The relationship between the "test oath" and the Establishment in England was summarized approvingly by Blackstone in his *Commentaries*:

In order the better to secure the established church against perils from non-conformists of all denominations, infidels, Turks, Jews, heretics, papists, and sectaries, there are, however, two bulwarks erected; called the corporation and test acts: by the former of which no person can be legally elected to any office relating to the government of any city or corporation, unless within a twelve-month before he has received the sacrament of the Lord's supper according to the rites of the church of England; and he is also enjoined to take the oaths of allegiance and supremacy at the same time that he takes the oath of office; or, in default of either of these requisites, such election shall be void. The other, called the test act, directs all officers, civil and military, to take the oaths and make the declaration against transubstantiation in any of the king's courts at Westminster, or at the quarter sessions, within six calendar months after their admission; and also within the same time to receive the sacrament of the Lord's supper according to the usage of the church of England, in some public church, immediately after divine service and sermon, and to deliver into court a certificate thereof signed by the minister and church-warden, and also to prove the same by two credible witnesses, upon forfeiture of £500 and disability to hold the said office. And of much the same nature with these is the statute 7 Jac. 1. c.2, which permits no person to be naturalized or restored in blood but such as undergo a like test: which test having been removed in 1753, in favor of the Jews, was the next session of parliament restored again with some precipitation.[118]

With special reference to those remarks of Blackstone, Joseph Story subsequently acclaimed the Constitution's ban on religious tests:

. . . Let it be remembered, that at the very moment when the learned commentator was penning these cold remarks, the laws of England merely tolerated

Protestant dissenters in their public worship upon certain conditions, at once irritating and degrading; that the Test and Corporation Acts excluded them from public and corporate offices, both of trust and profit; that the learned commentator avows that the object of the Test and Corporation Acts was to exclude them from office, in common with Turks, Jews, heretics, papists and other sectaries; that to deny the Trinity, however conscientiously disbelieved, was a public offense, punishable by fine and imprisonment; and that, in the rear of all these disabilities and grievances, came the long list of acts against papists, by which they were reduced to a state of political and religious slavery, and cut off from some of the dearest privileges of mankind.

It was under a solemn consciousness of the dangers from ecclesiastical ambition, the bigotry of spiritual pride, and the intolerance of sects, thus exemplified in our domestic as well as in foreign annals, that it was deemed advisable to exclude from the national government all power to act upon the subject.[119]

Many of the American colonies had like restrictions on eligibility for public office, with variation from place to place depending on which sect was established. But in the Bill for Establishing Religious Freedom Thomas Jefferson and James Madison sought to do away with this form of repression. The bill was particularly concerned with two forms of establishments: (1) taxation of citizens to support the established church and (2) disqualification for public office based on religious beliefs. We repeat here the relevant portions directed against disqualification. In pertinent part the preamble of the bill read,

That our civil rights have no dependence on our religious opinions, any more than on our opinions in physics or geometry; that therefore the prescribing of any citizen as unworthy of public confidence by laying upon him an incapacity of being called to offices of trust and emolument, unless he profess or renounce this or that religious opinion, is depriving him injuriously of those privileges and advantages to which in common with his fellow citizens he has a natural right; that it tends only to corrupt the principle of that religion it is meant to encourage by bribing with a monopoly of worldly honors and emoluments, those who will externally profess and conform to it.[120]

The operative section of the act provided that

. . . no man . . . shall be enforced, restrained, molested, or burthened in his body or goods, nor shall otherwise suffer on account of his religious opinions or belief; but that all men shall be free to profess, and by argument to maintain, their opinions in matters of religion, and that the same shall in no wise diminish, enlarge or affect their civil capacities.[121]

While the bill was being pressed in Virginia, Joseph Hawley in Massachusetts, though a member of the established Congregational Church, refused to take his place in the legislature in protest against the test oath. He wrote, "Did our Father Confessors imagine that a man who had not so much fear of God, as to restrain him from acting dishonestly and knavishly in the trust of a Senator or representative would hesitate a moment to subscribe to that declaration?" [122]

At the Constitutional Convention, discussion of religious disqualification was in terms of the proposal that was enacted as Article VI, clause 3, prohibiting a religious test for public office "under the United States." This proposal was presented by Charles Pinckney who told the convention that it was "a provision the world will expect from you in the establishment of a System founded on Republican Principles and in an age so liberal and enlightened as the present." [123] Although Sherman of Connecticut thought the prohibition was unnecessary since no one would seek to impose a test,[124] the proposal was adopted unanimously.[125]

The ban on religious tests won wide, although not unanimous, approval in the ratification conventions of the states. The expressions in support are further evidence of the intimate relationship between these tests and religious liberty.

Edmund Randolph, addressing the Virginia convention, stated that although he had once thought that freedom of religion was endangered by the Federal Constitution, his opinion was changed by Article VI. He explained that while public officers would be required to take an oath that they would support the Constitution, yet they were not bound to support one mode of worship or to adhere to one particular sect. A man of abilities and character of any sect whatever could be admitted to any office or public trust under the United States. Because of the many sects that were and might be in Congress, he felt that Congress would always support religious freedom.[126]

Oliver Ellsworth, later chief justice of the United States Supreme Court, published simultaneously in the *Connecticut Courant* at Hartford and the *American Mercury* at Litchfield a series of anonymous letters on the proposed Federal Constitution, signed "A Landholder." The seventh of the series dealt with the religious-test clause. He explained that its sole purpose and effect was to exclude persecution and to provide religious liberty, a right of human nature which few other people in the world shared.[127] He agreed with Randolph that a test in favor of any one denomination of Christians would be absurd in the United States. "If it were in favor of either congregationalists, presbyterians, episcopalians, baptists, or quakers, it would incapacitate more than three-quarters of the American citizens for any public office; and thus degrade them from the rank of free men. . . ." [128]

Ellsworth pointed out that if any test oath were to be imposed, the least exceptionable would be one requiring all persons appointed to office to declare, at the time of their admission, their belief in the being of a God, and in the divine authority of the Scriptures. In favor of such a test, he explained, it might be said that one who believed these great truths would not be so likely to violate his obligations to his country as one who disbelieved them. However, he rejected this argument. The making of a declaration of such a belief, he said, would be no security at all. For an unprincipled man who neither believed the word nor the being of God and was governed merely by selfish motives would easily make a public declaration of his belief in the creed which the law prescribed and excuse himself by calling it a mere formality.

Test oaths, he continued, would bar from public office honest men, men of principle, who would rather suffer an injury than act contrary to their consciences. It is within the authority of the people to choose their officers, he stated, and if they wished to insure that those appointed to public offices would be sincere friends of religion, they should take care to choose such persons and not rely upon such "cob-web barriers as test-laws are." Connecticut, he said, had never thought it expedient to adopt a test law, yet religion and morality were as extensive in that state as in England, where "every person who holds a public office must either be a saint by law or a hypocrite by practice." [129]

In Massachusetts, the Baptist Isaac Backus defended the prohibition of test oaths on the ground that "nothing is more evident, both in reason and the Holy Scriptures, than that religion is ever a matter between God and the individuals." [130] Even a fellow delegate who was a minister in the established Congregational Church agreed with the ban on the ground that "God alone is the God of a conscience, and, consequently, attempts to erect human tribunals for the conscience of men, are improper encroachments upon the prerogatives of God." [131]

There was considerable debate on Article VI at the North Carolina convention. James Iredell, later a justice of the Supreme Court, vigorously approved, saying,

> Yet it is notorious that dissenters qualify themselves for offices in this manner, though they never conform to the Church on any other occasion; and men of no religion at all have no scruple to make use of this qualification. It never was known that a man who had no principles of religion at all hesitated to perform any rite when it was convenient for his private interest. No test can bind such a one. I am therefore clearly of the opinion that such a discrimination would neither be effectual for its own purposes, nor, if it could, ought it by any means to be made. . . . But it is objected that the people of America may, perhaps, choose representatives who have no religion at all, and that pagans and Mahometans may be admitted into offices. But how is it possible to exclude any set of men, without taking away that principle of religious freedom which we ourselves so warmly contend for? [132]

Governor Johnston agreed with Iredell. He granted that Jews and pagans might be elected but deemed this an insufficient objection. If, he said, "persons of such description should, notwithstanding their religion, acquire the confidence and esteem of the people of America by their good conduct and practice of virtue," it was proper that they should be permitted to serve—though he thought it was not very probable that this would happen. Johnston thought it would have been dangerous if Congress could intermeddle with the subject of religion.[133]

One delegate, however, contended that "in a political view, these gentlemen who formed this Constitution should not have given this invitation to Jews and heathens."[134]

But another responded, "It is feared that persons of bad principles, deists, atheists, etc. may come into this country; and there is nothing to restrain them from being eligible to offices. . . . But in this case as there is not a religious test required, it leaves religion on the solid foundation of its own inherent validity, without any connection with temporal authority; and no kind of oppression can take place."[135]

The ban on religious tests aroused opposition among some religionists. When the issue was raised in the Maryland legislature, Luther Martin related,

The part of the system which provides that no religious test shall ever be required as a qualification to any office or public trust under the United States was adopted by a great majority of the Convention and without much debate; however, there were some members so unfashionable as to think that a belief in the existence of a Deity, and of a state of future rewards and punishments would be some security for the good conduct of our rulers, and that, in a Christian Country, it would be at least decent to hold out some distinction between the professors of Christianity and downright infidelity or paganism.[136]

The arguments presented in the state legislatures and ratifying conventions for and against the ban on religious tests for office in Article VI may be summarized as follows:

One group felt that history showed the grave danger of religious tests leading to persecution; that the Federal government should have no right to interfere with the states in this matter; that Christ never called for support for his religion by worldly authority; that the people of this country might be relied upon not to entrust government to irreligious people; that the only way to produce national political unity was to leave religion "free and unshackled"; that permitting a variety of sects encouraged religious freedom and prevented any State Church; that to require a religious test would exclude some well-qualified citizens from holding office; that likewise such a test would not prevent some unscrupulous men from entering public life; that St. Peter's statement that "God is no respecter of persons" is applicable in this case; that religion is exclusively a matter between God and the individual and not subject in any way to State approval; that the high state of intelligence and liberty in the country made further guarantees of religious liberty unnecessary, especially as the Constitution gave no power to Congress to intervene in religious matters.

A second group was represented by those who feared that they might be deprived under the Constitution of the privilege of worshiping God according to their consciences; that the treaty-making power of the Senate might result in a treaty or treaties making the Roman Catholic religion compulsory; that the pope might be elected president; that "Popish priests" might not be excluded from office holding; that unbelievers or Mohammedans might be elected to office; that the oath of office might be sworn merely by Jupiter or by Minerva; and that as the Constitution did not guarantee that officeholders be men believing in God or in Christ, it was dangerous.

The inclusion of Article VI into the Constitution settled the issue as far as service in the Federal government was concerned, but the issue remained in the case of state or municipal officials. We have seen that for many years after the Federal Constitution was adopted, some states continued their disqualification of non-Christians for public office. By their own actions the states removed these disqualifications as against Jews and members of other theistic religions. Nevertheless, a few states (Arkansas, Maryland, Pennsylvania and Tennessee) continued in their constitutions provisions requiring all public officers to take an oath or make a declaration that they believe in the existence of God.

As we have seen in Chapter 5, the Supreme Court ruled these requirements unconstitutional in the case of *Torcaso* v. *Watkins*. It can therefore be said definitely that today neither the Federal government nor any state, city or other governmental authority can impose any religious test for public service, whether by election or appointment. This does not mean that governments may not impose certain reasonable and necessary duties upon public officials the performance of which might be inconsistent with the commands of their religion. Thus, for example, a state constitutional provision making the governor commander of the state militia would not be unconstitutional on the ground that it imposes a religious qualification which many conscientious Quakers might feel they could not meet. The test is whether the duties imposed are secular; if they are, the fact that their imposition may make it impossible for members of some religious groups to accept the office does not forbid the government from imposing the duties. If, however, the duties are religious in nature, then it would seem that Article VI of the Federal Constitution and the principle of *Torcaso* v. *Watkins* would be violated. It is for that reason that there is ground to believe that the requirement in the governmental service academies that cadets attend chapel may well be unconstitutional.

Even though a political party's refusal to nominate a person for a particular elective office, from President down, because he is a member of a minority or unpopular religious group would not technically violate either Article VI or the rule of *Torcaso* v. *Watkins*, nevertheless it may be suggested that it would violate their spirit and intent. And so too, it may be added, would a citizen's refusal to vote for an otherwise qualified candidate because of his religious beliefs or associations.

Religious Tests for Court Witnesses

Article VI of the United States Constitution does not expressly forbid the imposition of a religious oath upon witnesses testifying in a Federal court. Nor does the Torcaso decision deal specifically with the problem.

The Quakers had early taken a stand against oaths, and in 1702 when they controlled the Pennsylvania Assembly they enacted a measure to the effect that

Every one of whatever religious views he might be, who could not conscientiously make an Oath in the form and manner that was done in Britain, should have liberty to make his affirmation in the Quaker manner, that is to say, when any one is by law called upon to assume any office or testify in any matter, that shall not be demanded as in the presence of Almighty God, according to the teachings of the Holy Evangelists, and by kissing the Bible, but only by a "yea," or a little inclination of the head.[137]

Although the Privy Council of England disallowed this act, it was revived in 1714 and three years later secured the approval of the Council.

Some colonies and early states did not have such broad provisions, and as a result Jews were at times refused as witnesses. For example, the New York Assembly in 1737 decided "that it was the opinion of the house that none of the Jewish profession could be admitted as evidence in the controversy now depending."[138] The English common law took the position that no one but a believer in God and in a future state of rewards and punishments was eligible as a witness or juryman. Since the oath was commonly taken on the Bible—which included the New Testament—the conscientious Jew was in effect disqualified. In some places the privilege of serving as a witness or on a jury was expressly restricted to Christians, and this was the early American interpretation of the common law.[139]

In 1828 the Supreme Court of Connecticut ruled that disbelievers in accountability to God or in an afterlife were not competent witnesses. It even went so far as to throw out testimony in the lower court by a Universalist.[140] In 1830, however, a compromise bill passed the state legislature permitting Universalists to testify, but the line was still drawn at unbelievers. This was a period when in New York, Connecticut, and other states religious tests were under fire from the Democrats, who in New York even tried to exclude clergymen from the public schools and to have the chaplaincy of the state legislature abolished.[141]

The general situation in this country is that in all court proceedings witnesses may give testimony only after they have qualified themselves by taking an oath in the usual form ending with "So help me God," or by making an affirmation without that phrase. The provisions for witnesses generally apply also to jurors. According to a study made in 1939, five states and the District of Columbia still follow the ancient rule of the common law by excluding from testifying those who profess disbelief in God, while in some states where such persons are permitted to take the stand as witnesses their testimony is subject to attack on the ground that their credibility is open to question because of their want of faith in a deity. The states which exclude non-believers in the way indicated are Arkansas and Maryland, by their constitutions, and New Hampshire, New Jersey, and South Carolina, by law. In addition, there are about a dozen states which permit their impeachment—that is, they may be legally attacked as not deserving credence because of their irreligion, thus providing ground for prejudice against them. The remaining states admit non-believers as witnesses and either forbid their impeachment on religious grounds, or have no ruling on the subject, or deny the right of counsel to cross-examine them on their lack of religious belief.[142]

The constitutionality of excluding non-believers as witnesses in judical proceedings has never been squarely decided by the Supreme Court. In 1900, in the case of *Li Sing* v. *United States*, it did uphold a Federal statute requiring that the testimony of Chinese, in certain cases, be corroborated by that of white men, because of the "loose notions entertained by [Chinese] witnesses of the obligation of an oath." It is highly improbable that this decision would be followed by the Supreme Court today. In fact, in view of the Court's unanimous 1961 decision in the case of *Torcaso* v. *Watkins* holding unconstitutional all Federal or state requirements of a belief in God as a prerequisite to the right to hold public office, the Court would probably likewise hold unconstitutional any remaining Federal or state statutes which disqualify atheists or other non-believers as witnesses in legal proceedings, and perhaps even forbid the impeachment of the credibility of a witness on that ground.

Blasphemy Laws

Blasphemy, the showing of disrespect to God or to persons, writings, or things considered holy, has been judged a serious offense by Jewish, ecclesiastical, and English common law. Many statutes have been passed in this country against it, on the ground that it is so offensive to most respectable citizens that it is likely to disturb communal peace. As was stated in a case before the Massachusetts Supreme Court, such laws have not been "to prevent or restrain the formation of any opinions or the profession of any religious sentiments whatever, but to restrain and punish acts which have a tendency to disturb the public peace." The State does not forbid the serious discussion of opinions on religious or other subjects, but it claims the right to stop clearly malicious attacks in public on belief in God, or the Christian religion,[143] or any spiritual faith.

Prosecutions for blasphemy occurred frequently during the first third of the nineteenth century. They were based on old colonial statutes which had not been abolished by the American states, or upon the provisions of the common law. Two cases were especially famous.

The first, *People* v. *Ruggles*,[144] was decided in 1811. Ruggles was convicted and sentenced to three months in prison and payment of a fine of $500 for, in the words of the indictment, "wickedly, maliciously, and blasphemously uttering and with a loud voice publishing in the presence of divers Christian people, of and concerning the Christian religion and of and concerning Jesus Christ the false . . . blasphemous words: 'Jesus Christ was a bastard and his mother must be a whore!'" In affirming the conviction, Chancellor Kent said,

The reviling is still an offense because it tends to corrupt the morals of the people, and to destroy good order. Such offenses have always been considered independent of any religious establishment or the rights of the church. They are treated as affecting the essential interests of civil society. . . . There is nothing in our manners or institutions which has prevented the application or necessity of this part of the common law. . . . The people of this State, in common with the people of this country, profess the general doctrines of Christianity . . . and to scandalize the author of these doctrines is not only in a religious point of view, extremely impious, but even in respect of the obligations due to society, in gross violation of decency and good order. . . .

The free, equal, and undisturbed enjoyment of religious opinion, whatever it may be, and free and decent discussion on any religious subject, is granted and secured; but to revile with malicious and blasphemous contempt . . . is an abuse of that right. . . . Though the constitution has disregarded religious establishments, it does not forbid judicial cognizance of those offences against religion and morality, which have no reference to any such establishment. . . . This constitutional declaration, noble and magnanimous as it is, never meant to withdraw religion in general and with it the best sanctions of moral and social obligations from all consideration and notice of the law. . . . The proviso guards the article from such dangerous latitude of construction when it decrees "that the liberty of conscience hereby granted shall not be construed as to excuse acts of licentiousness, or to justify practices inconsistent with the peace and safety of the State." It was all that reasonable minds could require. . . .[145]

Probably the last of the American trials for blasphemy resulting in imprisonment for a considerable period took place in Boston in 1838 when one Reverend Abner Kneeland, a former minister and social radical, was indicted because of an article in *The Investigator*, a free-thought magazine of which he was editor. His conviction, in his opinion, was due to the following sentence for which he was held responsible: "Universalists believe in a god which I do not; but believe that their god, with all his moral attributes (aside from nature itself) is nothing more than a chimera of their own imagination."[146]

After many retrials and appeals Kneeland was sentenced to sixty days in the Suffolk County jail.[147] This is believed to have been the last conviction for blasphemy in Massachusetts.

A prosecution reaching a different conclusion from that in the Ruggles and Kneeland cases occurred in 1894. In that year, at the instigation of a Methodist clergyman, one C. M. Moore was indicted on a charge of blasphemy for saying,

When I say that Jesus Christ was a man exactly like I am, and had a human father and mother like I had, some of the pious call it blasphemy. When they say that Jesus Christ was born as the result of a sort of Breckinridge-Pollard hyphenation between God and a Jewish woman, I call it blasphemy, so you see there is a stand-off.[148]

In dismissing the indictment the Kentucky court said,

In this country, where the divorce between church and state is complete and final, we should examine with care and accept with caution any law framed and intended for a country where church and state are one. The difficulties in reconciling religious freedom with the right to punish for an offense against any given religion are manifest. From the opinion given in *The People* v. *Ruggles* we may deduce as conclusions of the court that the people generally in this country are Christians; that Christianity is engraved upon the morality of the country; . . . that to revile the Christian religion is an offense, but that to revile other religions is not an offense punishable by law. . . .

Under this Constitution no form of religion can claim to be under the special guardianship of the law. The common law of England, whence our law of blasphemy is derived, did have a certain religion under its guardianship, and this religion was part of the law. . . . The essence of the law against blasphemy was that the offense, like apostasy and heresy, was against religion, and it was to uphold the established church, and not in any sense to maintain good order. . . .

Blasphemy is a crime growing from the same parent stem as apostasy and heresy. It is one of a class of offenses designed for the same general purpose, the fostering and protecting of a religion accepted by the state as the true religion, whose precepts and tenets it was thought all good subjects should observe. In the code of laws of a country enjoying absolute religious freedom, there is no place for the common law crime of blasphemy.[149]

A case which received much attention in the press was one in Arkansas in 1928, when the president of the American Association for the Advancement of Atheism, who had gone to Arkansas to oppose a referendum on the anti-evolution law and was distributing atheistic literature on the Bible and evolution, was prosecuted for "ridiculing the Christian religion." He was not permitted to testify in his own defense and was sentenced to a fine and imprisonment, but the case was dismissed when appealed to a higher court.[150]

The United States Supreme Court has never had occasion to pass on the constitutionality of blasphemy laws. In view of its decision in *Cantwell* v. *Connecticut* and in *The Miracle* case, *Burstyn* v. *Wilson* (see Chapter 5), there may be some doubt whether it would uphold such laws. On the other hand, the Court's decision in *Chaplinsky* v. *New Hampshire* (see Chapter 5) indicates that where blasphemous expressions do in fact provoke a breach of the peace, a conviction on that ground, rather than for blasphemy itself, might be upheld.

Sunday Observance Laws

It is well known that Sunday was very strictly observed under the laws of Puritan New England, and observed, though less strictly, in the other colonies. The middle colonies, where Presbyterianism and the Dutch Reformed Church were strong, were midway between New England and the Anglican South in this matter. That the leaders of the young nation believed in Sunday as a day of rest is shown by the fact that the Constitution omits the day—"Sundays excepted"—from the ten days within which the president may exercise his veto over acts of Congress.[151]

The first national issue on the matter of Sunday observance came in the second decade of the nineteenth century. By a law passed in 1810 the postmaster general felt that he was bound to compel deputy postmasters at places where mail arrived on Sunday to keep the office open for some time on that day, generally the hour following public worship, or early in the morning. At the following session of Congress there were protests against this practice. Remonstrances were presented in 1812, 1815, and 1817; nevertheless, a law was passed in 1825 requiring that post offices at which mail arrived on Sunday should be kept open during the whole of that day. This greatly stirred the religious forces of the country, and in 1829-30 the discussion in Congress over the Sunday mail question attracted much national attention, which we have considered earlier in this book.[152]

In 1828 a general union for the observance of the Sabbath had been organized in New York, and in 1844 a National Sabbath Convention was held in Baltimore, attended by seventeen hundred delegates from eleven states.[153] These and similar efforts were due largely to conservative Protestants' alarm over the large immigration from Europe of a population accustomed to what is generally called the Continental Sunday. Other factors contributed, such as the development of railroads, with Sunday railroad schedules; the growth of Sunday newspapers; and certain forms of Sunday entertainments. But the immigration situation, especially in the large cities of the East, was uppermost in the minds of those who called the National Sabbath Convention.

It must not be thought, however, that they represented all the intelligent public opinion of religious people in the country. Many persons sympathetic with the Christian traditions of the nation believed that Sunday legislation, especially in any rigid form, was contrary to the fundamental principles of Church and State separation on which the nation was founded. They felt that Sunday observance was an individual matter, not one for municipalities, state legislatures, and Congress to deal with. One such person was Alexander Campbell, co-founder with his father of the Disciples of Christ. He took the ground that Sunday laws were unscriptural and unchristian, that there was not a precept in the New Testament to compel any man by civil law to regard the day, and that to try to command those who did not believe in the Christian religion to observe it is "anti-evangelical or contrary to the gospel."

A remarkable expression of this view was made by William Lloyd Garrison. It was in the form of an appeal in 1848 for an American Anti-Sunday Law Convention. A direct reaction to the National Sabbath Convention of 1844 and the work of the American and Foreign Sabbath Union, it includes the following representative paragraphs:

Within the last five years a religious combination has been formed in this land, styling itself "The American and Foreign Sabbath Union," whose specific object it is to impose the Sabbatical yoke yet more heavily on the necks of the American people. In a recent appeal made for pecuniary assistance by the executive committee of the Union, it is stated that "the Secretary has visited twenty of the United States, and traveled more than thirty thousand miles, addressing public bodies of all descriptions, and presenting reasons why, as a nation, we should keep the Sabbath,—all secular business, traveling, and amusement to be confined to six days in a week,—and all people assemble on the Sabbath, and worship God." A "permanent Sabbath document" has been prepared by the Secretary; and "what has already been done will put a copy of this document into more than three hundred thousand families." Still greater efforts are to be made by the "Union" for the furtherance of its object.

That this combination is animated by the spirit of religious bigotry and ecclesiastical tyranny—the spirit which banished the Baptists from Massachusetts, and subjected the Quakers to imprisonment and death, in the early settlement of this country—admits of little doubt. It is managed and sustained by those who have secured the enactment of the penal laws against Sabbath-breaking (all that the spirit of the times will allow), and whose disposition it manifestly is, if they can increase their power, to obtain the passage of yet more stringent laws against those who do not "esteem one day above another," but esteem "every day"—who are not willing that any man shall judge them "in respect of a holy day, or of the new moon, or of the Sabbath"—and who mean to "stand fast in the liberty wherewith Christ hath made them free, and not to be entangled again with the yoke of bondage." Its supporters do not rely solely upon reason, argument, persuasion, but also upon brute force—upon penal law; and thus in seeking to crush by violence the rights of conscience, and religious liberty and equality, their real spirit is revealed as at war with the genius of republicanism and the spirit of Christianity.[154]

From the time of this controversy the "Sunday question" became prominent, especially in states with a large Roman Catholic urban population, which wished to have the laws relaxed, and a well-organized Protestant group, generally led by Presbyterians, Methodists, and Baptists, which was determined not to permit any change that would bring in the wide-open "Continental Sunday." The fight has been long and stubborn, although, as will be indicated shortly, there has in recent years been a remarkable change of position in respect to Sunday laws on the part of the Roman Catholic Church in this country. Before the change is recounted and the constitutional issue considered, something should be said of the history of Sunday observance laws.

All Sunday laws go back to the Fourth Commandment. However, the Sabbath of that Commandment and of the Bible generally was not the first but the seventh day of the week. The Sabbath is still the seventh day of the week, even in the New Testament, and for that reason some Christian sects (notably the Seventh Day Adventists and the Seventh Day Baptists) observe the Sabbath on Saturday. The early Christian Church fathers, in pursuance of the policy initiated by Paul, changed the Sabbath to Sunday, the day on which, according to the New Testament, Jesus rose from the dead.

The first known compulsory Sunday law was promulgated by Emperor Constantine as part of his program to unify the Roman Empire.[155] One American court summarized the history of Sunday laws as follows: "All Sunday legislation is the product of pagan Rome; the Saxon laws were the product of the Middle Age legislation of the Holy Roman Empire. The English laws are the expansion of the Saxon, and the American are the transcript of the English." [156]

Sunday laws are thus historically the product of a union of Church and State which the American colonists brought here from the Old World. The first prosecution for violation of a Sunday law in New York of which we have a record occurred in 1655, while the colony was still under Dutch rule. Abraham de Lucena, a Jewish merchant, was charged with violating the law by keeping his store open during the Sunday sermon.[157] (We have no record of the disposition of this case.)

When the colonies became states they uniformly carried over the colonial Sunday laws. At the beginning of the Revolutionary period the Sunday law in force in many of the British-American colonies was a late seventeenth-century law (Charles II), which read,

> For the better observation and keeping holy the Lord's day, commonly called Sunday, bee it enacted . . . that all the lawes enacted and in force concerning the observation of the Lords day and repaireing to the church thereon be carefully putt in execution. And that all and every person and persons whatsoever shall on every Lords day apply themselves to the observation of the same by exerciseing themselves thereon in the dutyes of piety and true religion publiquely and privately and that noe tradesman, artificer workeman labourer or other person whatsoever shall doe or exercise any worldly labour, business or worke of their ordinary callings upon the Lords day or any part thereof (workes of necessity and charity onely excepted) and that every person being of the age of fourteene yeares or upwards offending in the premisses shall for every such offence forfeit the summe of five shillings, and that noe person or persons what soever shall publickly cry shew forth or expose to sale any wares merchandizes, fruit, herbs goods or chattels whatsoever upon the Lords day.[158]

Sunday observance laws, like most other police regulations in the United States, are both state statutes and municipal ordinances. The statutes frequently give local communities the right within certain limits to determine their own regulations. These have varied according to the times, the size and character of communities, and the historic traditions. In New England and in parts of the Middle Atlantic states the tradition of the Puritan Sabbath was particularly strong. There, and in the Western Reserve (Ohio) and other parts of the Middle West settled by people inheriting their colonial traditions, Sunday was until lately considered a day in which everything was subservient to worship. Even the largest Eastern cities, such as New York and Philadelphia, had as late as 1825 regulations which permitted churches to place chains across the streets in front of their buildings to prevent traffic from passing during Sunday service hours.[159] But in the early days of the Western frontier there was relatively little observance of Sunday.

Among Protestants, leadership in the enforcement of Sunday laws has long been taken by the Lord's Day Alliance. This interdenominational organization, founded in 1888, with the major object of the protection of the Christian Sabbath, has had a large following among the same Protestant groups which formed the background of the prohibition movement. It works locally through its own agents and branches, and through ministerial associations and church federations. Its purpose is "to uphold and defend the sanctity of the Lord's Day and the rights of the civil institution of Sunday." [160] As to the first of these objectives, it claims to defeat annually many commercial Sunday bills in the state legislatures.[161] A slogan of the Alliance is "As goes the Sabbath in the United States, so will go this Republic." Some of its work, especially in protecting the rights of workers to one day's rest in seven, is admirable; much of it in the field of restricting Sunday recreations is inclined to be puritanical. An important achievement for which it was largely responsible was the closing on Sunday about forty years ago of all first- and second-class post offices as far as public service was concerned. This regulation, still in force, gives much-needed rest to more than 300,000 postal employees.

Notwithstanding the strong opposition of the Lord's Day Alliance, it has been recognized universally even by those favoring Sunday laws that the strict colonial statutes must be modified to meet contemporary conditions. This was dramatically illustrated in North Dakota in 1917. Up to that year there were all sorts of Sunday laws on the statute books which were not observed and were unenforceable. There was, for instance, a law prohibiting the sale of groceries on Sunday, so severe in its character that it was illegal to sell milk even for babies' use. Baseball was prohibited. Farmers could not thresh in their fields on Sunday. It was unlawful to send a telegram. Bootblacks could not practice their trade, nor could newspaper boys. It was unlawful for taxicabs to operate, and so on.

In 1917 William Langer, later United States Senator, became attorney general. He made up his mind that the best way to repeal the obsolete laws was to have them enforced; that only in this way could respect for law and order be obtained and legislation secured that would be suited to the needs of the state. Thereupon, with the assistance of the fifty-three sheriffs and the same number of state attorneys and their deputies and various persons in the office of the attorney general, he proceeded to enforce all the Sunday laws on the statute books, with the single exception of permitting power companies to continue to furnish light and heat. He had taken an oath to enforce all the laws of the commonwealth, he said, and he had no authority to decide which laws should not be enforced. He was no opponent of religion but was in fact a church attendant. It was, however, his conviction "that under the American plan of government the State cannot rightfully be called upon to enforce the teachings of the church." [162]

Within three weeks the attitude of the people all over the state was reversed. The legislature being in session, old laws were repealed and new ones enacted legalizing some of the prohibited activities and modifying the laws regarding others. The state also adopted the initiative, referendum, and recall plan, which provided for legislation by referendum on a petition signed by ten thousand qualified citizens. Through this means new laws regarding Sunday afternoon theaters, baseball, etc., were duly adopted. The most interesting feature of the experience, according to Senator Langer, was that "As a result of this enforcement of the Sunday laws, . . . people became law-conscious. Overnight the citizens insisted that all the laws be enforced or repealed." [163]

The two groups which are put in the most difficult position with reference to Sunday laws are the Jews and the Seventh Day Adventists. There is of course no legal objection to both these groups' observing Saturday, the old Jewish Sabbath, in place of Sunday, but schedules of industrial and commercial work sometimes make this difficult or create financial handicaps. Furthermore, it is natural that men who have observed Saturday should feel they are exempt from observing Sunday, except as they should do nothing to cause disturbance of public worship on this day more or less observed by the majority of our citizens. In 1939 there was an interesting case in Arkansas, which in 1888 adopted laws exempting those who observed Saturday for religious reasons from some of the Sunday law provisions, such citizens being for instance permitted to work on Sunday but not to engage in business. A deacon in the Little Rock Seventh Day Adventist Church, who conducted a barber shop in a theater building, was arrested for operating on Sunday. He was convicted in spite of the fact that no attempt was made to close the theater on Sunday or to interfere with other stores. The circuit criminal court ruled that he might cut his own hair or shave himself on Sunday but that if his service was for pay he was guilty of doing commercial business on Sunday and was therefore a "Sabbath breaker." [164] An appeal was not perfected for technical reasons, but the prosecuting attorneys agreed not to molest the barber in the future.

In recent years the leadership in the struggle to enforce Sunday laws and to defeat liberalizing amendments has been taken from the Lord's Day Alliance by two groups which had not previously manifested interest in such legislation. One of these is the commercial class represented by owners of stores within cities selling household furnishings, variety items, furniture, and similar merchandise generally sold in department stores. This class has been recently faced with competition from a new phenomenon in American society, the highway discount house, which sells the same items at substantially lower prices than do the regular city stores. Moreover, the highway discount houses do a substantial amount of business on weekends, and Sunday has become a particularly profitable day for them. Business associations representing city stores have discovered the Sunday laws and have been using them as a means to meet the new competition. These associations have been spending large amounts of money in campaigns for stricter enforcement of Sunday laws and the enactment of new ones. Conversely, associations representing discount houses have been spending similarly large amounts in fighting for the repeal of Sunday laws and in financing litigation challenging their constitutionality. It is significant that in two of the four cases in which the Supreme Court in 1961 upheld the constitutionality of Sunday laws the defendants were owners of highway discount houses.[165]

A second and more surprising entrant in the campaign for Sunday law enforcement has been the Roman Catholic Church. This is surprising because, as has been indicated, nothing in Catholic dogma requires strict Sunday observance of the type prescribed by American Sunday laws. Yet the determination with which the Church, at least in some states, now opposes liberalization of Sunday laws can be seen from events which recently occurred in Massachusetts.[166] One of the cases decided by the Supreme Court came from that state, and the Court's decision upholding the law even against Orthodox Jewish storekeepers who kept their businesses closed on Saturday led to the appointment by the governor of Massachusetts of a citizens' committee to study the operation of the state's Sunday law and make recommendations for its improvement. The committee, headed by Professor Arthur E. Sutherland of Harvard Law School, was almost evenly divided on whether to recommend amendment of the law to exempt conscientious Sabbatarians—nine favored such an amendment and eleven opposed it. Nevertheless, the arguments set forth in the minority report (written by Professor Sutherland) were so cogent that the demand for an exemption law became stronger as a result of the report.

Professor Sutherland himself drafted the proposed amendment. It was patterned after a recently enacted exemption to the Vermont Sunday law and was quite broad in its scope, exempting from the statute "any person who pursuant to his conscientious religious requirements" refrains from secular activities for twenty-four consecutive hours each week. This and other, somewhat narrower, proposals were introduced in the Massachusetts legislature during the 1962 session.

A rather more modest exemption proposal passed the Senate by a vote of 21 to 14 early in June, 1962. A few days later *The Pilot*, official organ of the Roman Catholic archdiocese of Boston, published an editorial entitled "Assault on Sunday." (The editor of *The Pilot* is Monsignor Francis J. Lally, a vigorous and articulate member of the majority on the governor's committee.) The editorial opened with the statement that "The Massachusetts Senate, in a shocking assault on the day of rest statute, voted this week to except Sabbatarians from the requirements of the Sunday law. In simplest terms the Senators responded to pressures that will destroy the Sunday observance in favor of those—principally Jews and Adventists—who worship on Saturday." The editorial went on to say, "We will leave it to others to say how a carefully organized minority has done its work to destroy Sunday; we only point out that this bill is both unjust and offensive. . . . It is bad legislation, passed under pressure."

The Pilot printed the names "of those Senators who so unwisely" voted for the exemption and expressed "the hope" that they would "reconsider." *The Pilot's* hope was realized. The Senate immediately reconsidered the measure and, with only seven of the original twenty-one standing firm, defeated it. Paradoxically, the Massachusetts legislature did enact more than forty liberalizing changes in the law for the benefit of real estate concerns, gift shops, antique dealers, and recreational enterprises.

One interesting note in this incident was the action of Senator George A. Sullivan, a Catholic, who not only stood firm on the reconsideration vote but wrote a letter to *The Pilot* in which he charged that the paper's editorial "was deliberately designed to exert the highest form of pressure" on the senators to change their votes. "I cannot," he continued, "for political expediency disregard my Catholic teachings in matters of charity, justice, and the dignity of human beings. To ignore my conscience and our Constitution by voting on secular matters in accordance with the dictates of the Catholic press would be a breach of trust placed in me as a legislator."

It is probable that others besides Senator Sullivan reacted adversely to the action of *The Pilot*. This, at least, would seem to be the most reasonable explanation for the complete reversal of position on its part a year and a half later. In January, 1964, a bill was introduced in the Massachusetts legislature very similar to the one so vigorously opposed in 1962 by *The Pilot*. In its issues of February 29, 1964, *The Pilot* published the following editorial comment on the bill:

Law and Goodwill

The General Court now has under discussion an amendment to the Day of Rest law that seems to us both intelligent and helpful. Although the body of the law is of recent origin, it was always understood that exceptions could be made when the occasion required, just so long as they did not conflict with the general purpose of the law which was to protect the nature of the day itself. We feel that the proposed amendment relieves a burden on a minority portion of the community while respecting the rights of the majority.

To be sure, the wording of the new amendment had to be precise so that unscrupulous elements would not use it to make Sunday a business-as-usual day and thus thwart the purpose of the Day of Rest statute. Arrived at through the co-operation of the Orthodox Jewish community especially, the proposal is a modest one that provides relief for the Sabbatarian without distressing the rest of the citizenry. We are of the opinion that the passage of this particular piece of legislation will rein-force good will by dealing satisfactorily with the legitimate demands of all. It deserves the support of conscientious legislators.

In view of this endorsement by the official organ of the Boston Archdiocese it is hardly surprising that the measure passed the Massachusetts legislature in a voice vote.

The constitutional justification for Sunday laws was first expressed by the United States Supreme Court in 1885 in an opinion by Justice Stephen J. Field: "Laws setting aside Sunday as a day of rest, are upheld not from any right of government to legislate for the promotion of religious observance, but from its right to protect all persons from the physical and moral debasement, which comes from uninterrupted labor." [167] In the Sunday law cases of 1961 (sum-marized in Chapter 5), the Court, with only Justice William O. Douglas dis-senting on this point, adopted this reasoning in upholding the Sunday laws of Massachusetts, Pennsylvania, and Maryland. The majority opinion recognized that Sunday laws in their origin were religious laws aimed at compelling adherence to the Christian Sabbath, but it held that through the passage of time they have become today secular or welfare laws whose purpose is to assure a uniform day of rest and relaxation. In the same cases the Court also held—although on this point Justices William J. Brennan and Potter Stewart joined Justice Douglas in dissent—that the laws were constitutional even when enforced against persons who conscientiously observe a day other than Sunday as their religious day of rest. The Court said that while fairness might indicate that Sunday laws should have an exemption for such persons, the absence of an exemption does not make the law unconstitutional. (Some fifteen states have statutory exemptions broad enough to permit conscientious Jews, Seventh Day Adventists and Seventh Day Baptists to keep their stores open for business on Sundays.) [168]

In 1963 the Court did hand down a decision favorable to Sabbatarians. In *Sherbert* v. *Verner* (summarized in Chapter 5), with but two justices dissent-ing, the Court held that a Seventh Day Adventist who for reasons of conscience refused to work on Saturdays could not constitutionally be denied unemploy-ment insurance benefits.

There occasionally arises a question regarding the observance in the schools of Moslem holy days by Mohammedans. Their number in this country is very small, but they have erected several places of worship and are active among some groups. The question of their pupils in public schools came before the courts in 1947 when Mohammedan parents asked the Federal district court in Pittsburgh for an injunction that would permit their four sons to stay out of school on Friday on the ground that it was a sacred day of their faith and that they would like to give the children home instruction that day in the Koran and teach them Moorish-American prayers. The injunction they sought would have restrained the school district from requiring attendance of the children on Friday. However, the court denied the application, and the parents were later prosecuted under the state's compulsory school attendance law for keeping their children out of school on Friday. The superior court in Pittsburgh upheld the prosecution and ruled that the parents' religious liberty was not thereby unconstitutionally violated.[169]

Government Observance of Religious Days and Occasions

In addition to government recognition and regulation discussed in the previous section, the calendar has caused some difficulties with the churches. A new problem has arisen within recent years which may cause further difficulties. It has to do with the advocacy by certain progressive groups of a new world calendar to be substituted for the Gregorian calendar, so long in use. The purpose is to provide a new time system which would be uniform and perpetually the same, regulated astronomically, retaining the present twelve months, with each month containing twenty-six working days plus Sundays, and dates agreeing from year to year.

Some religious bodies, specifically Jews and Seventh Day Adventists, are strongly opposed to the plan; and the Religious Liberty Association, which is the agency of the Seventh Day Adventists, sent out a circular in the summer of 1949 protesting against it, as follows:

The ugly and dangerous feature of the World Calendar plan is that it leaves the last day of each year, and the day following the last of June in each leap year, unnamed and undated days. These days would not be included in the count of the days of the week; therefore, they could completely disrupt the historic week and set the sacred days of the week to wandering through the new synthetic week of the so-called World Calendar.

A similar proposal involving this so-called "blank-day" type of calendar revision has been proposed to Congress more than once. The fact that it involves serious change causes opposition. On the other hand, the plan has been approved by the Universal Christian Council, the Methodist Church Council of Bishops, and other religious groups, as well as by many scientific and business organizations.

Observance of Christmas in the public schools has been discussed in a previous chapter. Observance of Good Friday also occasionally raises Church-State questions. Good Friday was recognized on April 2, 1790, by the Federal House of Representatives, which adjourned out of respect for the day. It is now a legal holiday in a number of states. Bills to make it a national holiday have been introduced in Congress for a number of years, but as yet none has been passed. That observance of Good Friday may sometimes cause interreligious friction and misunderstanding is evidenced by an incident that occurred in New York City in 1952.

In that year the Anchor Club, consisting of members of the Knights of Columbus who are employed as city firemen, undertook to achieve a more reverent observance of Good Friday. Shortly before the holiday, merchants in a section of the Bronx, most of whom were Jewish, were visited by representatives of the organization and requested to close their stores for three hours on Good Friday. Those who consented were given a printed card for window display reading, "We will close from 12 noon to 3:00 P.M., April 11, 1952, in observance of the death of Christ." Shopkeepers, including Jews, who did not consent were threatened with loss of trade. However, after representations were made by Jewish groups to the Church authorities, the chancery office issued a statement saying that it did not approve the campaign to persuade Jewish merchants to post the placards and close their stores on Good Friday and that if approval had been sought it would not have been granted.[170]

Thanksgiving Day, to which little objection is made except by militant atheists, is observed throughout the country. Catholics are profound believers in thanksgiving and in the spirit which the day is designed to inculcate, but its identification with a Puritan custom and the fact that its observance is proposed by the State rather than the Church made them slow in giving it ecclesiastical recognition. The *Catholic Encyclopedia* says, "Catholic recognition of the day by special religious features has only been of comparatively recent date and not as yet of official general custom." [171]

President Franklin D. Roosevelt's decision to set the day a week earlier in 1939-41 caused the Federal government and many of the states to depart from the tradition of several decades in observing the last Thursday in November, which Lincoln had set apart in 1864, during the Civil War. Resentment at the change was widespread, partly because it was a departure from custom taken without any broad consultation, partly because it resulted in much confusion, and partly because it was dictated by certain commercial interests who thought that a longer interval between this observance and the Christmas holiday season would bring larger sales. Consequently the president announced in the fall of 1941 that he planned to return in 1942 to the recognition of the historic day; but on December 26, 1941, Congress directed the president to fix the fourth Thursday in November for the usual Thanksgiving Day. Eight states in the South and West, however, continue to observe the last Thursday by proclamation of their governors.

In addition to the national holiday of Thanksgiving there have been numerous other instances of Federal action to set aside a particular day for thanksgiving or prayer and fasting. The Continental Congress appointed July 12, 1775, as a day of prayer and fasting for the united colonies, but the first actual day of thanksgiving of the newly organized United States was held on December 18, 1777. It was appointed in connection with great civic and political events, following the Declaration of Independence. The proclamations issued by the Continental Congress on these and other occasions have already been referred to, as well as proclamations on national days of prayer and thanksgiving issued under Washington, Adams, and Madison.[172] But Jefferson, as we have seen, objected to the practice on constitutional grounds. Here we are concerned with later developments.[173]

The period of the War of 1812 continued the American tradition of days of prayer and thanksgiving. At its outset Congress passed resolutions, to which President Madison yielded, as he did again at the close of the war.[174] These proclamations during the War of 1812 were not seriously opposed, but Congress did not try to deal with the fast-day matter for sixteen years after 1815. Then the question arose in connection with a desire to request President Andrew Jackson to proclaim a fast day because of the threat of the Asiatic cholera, the first case of which appeared in this country in New York in 1832. Senator Henry Clay proposed a resolution to appoint a joint committee of Congress to request the president to recommend a day of "public humiliation, prayer and fasting to be observed by the people of the United States with religious solemnity" so that the Asiatic scourge might be averted or its severity mitigated.[175]

The known antipathy between Clay and President Jackson made this a matter of political contention. It was complicated by the fact that only a few days before President Jackson had addressed a letter to the General Synod of the Dutch Reformed Church, declining to issue a national fast-day proclamation because he believed it would be unconstitutional; the existence of his letter was probably known to Clay. Jackson wrote,

Whilst I concur with the Synod in the efficacy of prayer, and in the hope that our country may be preserved from the attacks of pestilence "and that the judgments now abroad in the earth may be sanctified to the nations," I am constrained to decline the designation of any period or mode as proper for the public manifestation of this reliance. I could not do otherwise without transcending the limits prescribed by the Constitution for the President; and without feeling that I might in some degree disturb the security which religion now enjoys in this country in its complete separation from the political concerns of the General Government. It is the province of the Pulpits and not the State Tribunals to recommend the time and mode by which the people may best attest their reliance on the protecting arm of the Almighty in times of great public distress; whether the apprehension that the Cholera may visit our land furnishes a proper occasion for this solemn notice, I must, therefore, leave to their consideration.[176]

In presenting his resolution Senator Clay stated,

I am a member of no religious sect. I am not a professor of religion. I regret that I am not. I wish that I was and I trust I shall be. But I have, and always have had, a profound respect for Christianity, the religion of my father, and for its rites, its usages, and its observance. Among these, that which is proposed in the resolution before you has always commanded the respect of the good and devout; and I hope it will obtain the concurrence of the Senate.[177]

The proposal passed the Senate by a vote of 30 to 13 with a good deal of Democratic opposition, though Senator Littleton Tazewell, a Democrat from Virginia, stated that in his opinion Congress had "no more power to recommend by joint resolution than to enact by law any matter or thing concerning any religious matter or right whatsoever." [178] The whole question now became a national issue. Congress debated the pros and cons. The supporters quoted precedents and called attention to the fact that there was nothing compulsory about the proposed observance of the day and that it was entirely undenominational and appropriate. They felt that opposition to the resolution was "a horrid mockery of Almighty God."

The opponents thought it was a matter for the churches, not for the government, and more especially not for the Federal government. They saw no warrant in the Constitution for such a proclamation. One member from Alabama said,

It is incumbent on us to follow out the principles of the Constitution by keeping religious and political affairs entirely distinct and separate from each other and to put the seal of reprobation on the first attempt to prostitute our holy religion to purposes such as he would not mention.[179]

Gulian C. Verplanck of New York said,

Whenever Congress or any other political body in this country meddles in affairs of religion, they must run counter more or less to the spirit of our free institutions securing equal religious rights—offend the conscience or wound the feelings of some or other of our citizens. Many look with dislike, as their ancestors did with honor, upon all days or times of formal and stated supplication. . . . You cannot make religion a party and an actor in the halls of human legislation without infinite and incalculable evil—evil to religion, evil to the State. You inflame the rancor of party politics by adding to it the fervor of religious zeal or that of sectarian fanaticism. Or else you do worse—you pollute and degrade religion by making her the handmaid of human power or the partisan of personal ambition.[180]

He ended with the words "Let us leave prayer and humiliation to be prompted by the devotion of the heart and not the bidding of the State."[181] Finally, the motion to report an amendment for a national fast day by Congressional action alone, not by reference to the president, was adopted by a vote of 86 to 70, but Congress adjourned without taking further action.

Later presidents did not share Jackson's views on the propriety of governmental proclamations of days of thanksgiving, prayer, or fasting. For example, when in 1849, sixteen years after the first appearance of cholera, a second serious outbreak occurred, President Zachary Taylor had no reluctance to set aside the first Friday in August as a day of special prayer, to order the suspension of all public business for that day, and to recommend to persons of all religious denominations "to abstain as far as practicable from secular occupations and to assemble in their respective places of public worship, to acknowledge the Infinite Goodness which has watched over our existence as a nation, and so long crowned us with manifold blessings, and to implore the Almighty in His own good time to stay the destroying hand which is now lifted up against us. . . ."[182]

During the Civil War crisis President Lincoln issued several executive orders and proclamations regarding prayer as well as setting aside the last Thursday in November for a day of official Thanksgiving.[183] Other presidents, particularly during times of national mourning[184]—as on the deaths of Presidents Garfield and McKinley—or crisis—as during World War II—issued proclamations setting aside particular days for prayer, and on occasion even formulating and reciting a particular prayer.[185]

Freedom and Censorship

For the purpose of our discussion, censorship may be divided into political censorship and moral (including religious) censorship. Political censorship does not concern us primarily in this book, though there have been some Church-State conflicts. For instance, a good many clergymen—especially Anglicans—got into trouble with the State in the middle colonies and New England because of their Tory sympathies and writings during the Revolution.[186] Some were imprisoned; others were tarred and feathered or suffered other indignities; others were forbidden by public authority to preach in their churches; others found the printing press and the public journals closed to them; and many found it necessary or advisable to flee, mostly to Nova Scotia. When the republic was established many of the new states passed laws banishing those who refused to sign the oath of allegiance.

An attempt to enforce similar oaths against clergymen because of their political opinions, as shown in press and pulpit, was also occasionally made by the Federal government in Southern states under its jurisdiction during and after the Civil War. Somewhat similar difficulties involving Roman Catholic priests and their institutions and publications occurred during the Nativist agitations, whose extremes have disgraced our national life from time to time but especially in the second third of the nineteenth century.[187]

In the main, political censorship has created Church-State problems in cases where clergymen, in pursuance of what they deemed to be their religious mission, expressed orally or in writing their opposition to American participation in war in general or in a particular war. For example, during World War I a prominent Episcopal clergyman wrote a pamphlet vigorously opposing American participation. In it he said, "Our entry into it was determined by the certainty that if the allies did not win, J. P. Morgan's loans to the allies would be repudiated, and those American investors who bet on his promises would be hooked." While the clergyman was not himself prosecuted for publishing the pamphlet, three Socialists who distributed it were, and their conviction was upheld by the Supreme Court.[188] Similarly, in 1949 a divinity student was prosecuted and convicted for urging his friends not to register with the draft boards as required by law. Jehovah's Witnesses have also on occasion been involved with political censorship, particularly in connection with their refusal to salute the flag. One of these cases was *Taylor* v. *Mississippi* (see Chapter 5), in which the Supreme Court upset the conviction of a number of Witnesses for counseling others not to salute the flag.

On the whole, Protestant and Jewish religious leaders and organizations have combated political censorship. They frequently find themselves in disagreement with the positions taken by many responsible "patriotic" organizations, such as the American Legion and the Daughters of the American Revolution, which are all too likely to oppose freedom of speech. Roman Catholic Church leaders, on the other hand, have on the whole been sympathetic to the objectives of political censorship. This difference in attitude stems from the fact that, unlike their non-Catholic brethren, they deem the danger of Communism to be more serious and imminent than the possible loss or erosion of constitutional liberties through the action of our own government.

In moral censorship the line of demarcation between the responsibilities of the State and the Church is difficult to define, for in many cases both are directly concerned. The Church rightly believes that anything which affects the moral standards of youth, whether it be the legalizing of gambling, or objectionable tendencies in the theater and motion pictures, the radio, television, books, magazine and newspaper advertising, or attire, is a matter of grave concern. As an example, a Roman Catholic Congregation of the Holy Office issued in 1927 an instruction to all bishops of the Church on the vital importance of Catholics' observing decent standards in books, motion pictures, and plays.[189] It has also spoken out sharply about women's clothes.

Moral (and religious) censorship has operated upon all media of mass communication—the press, books and periodicals, plays and motion pictures, radio and television. In respect to the press, the question of the occasional boycotting by the Roman Catholic Church of newspapers that oppose its views on such matters as birth control, or the inspection of Catholic institutions when the Church does not deem such inspection proper, is a serious one, especially when it affects business houses advertising in those publications. A widely publicized case in Washington arose in 1913 because a newspaper tried to investigate conditions in a Catholic home for wayward girls. Commenting on this incident, a Jesuit contributor to *America* under date of February 11, 1928, declared frankly that a magazine or newspaper should be attacked through its business office rather than through its editorial department, and that an attempt should be made to bring pressure to bear through canceling subscriptions, advertising, etc.[190]

A more recent instance of the apparent power of the Roman Catholic Church in controlling advertising not acceptable to its views, and of the tendency of the press to yield to its influence, occurred in New York. According to the Beacon Press of Boston, the New York *Times* apparently accepted an advertisement of the book by Paul Blanshard on *American Freedom and Catholic Power*. This, howover, was declined for printing at the last moment on the ground that it contained an intolerant attack on the Church and its clergy, especially in a controversial chapter on "Sex, Birth Control and Eugenics." The New York *Herald Tribune* published the advertisement, as did other newspapers.[191] Blanshard's later books do not appear to have been subjected to newspaper censorship of advertisements, at least not to the extent of *American Freedom and Catholic Power*.

The boycott has more often been used by religious groups against plays and motion pictures, but occasionally it is directed against books, and increasingly so in recent years. Christian Scientists have tried to prevent the sale of biographies of Mrs. Eddy which they disapproved; Protestant fundamentalists have tried to prevent the distribution of liberal theological books; Roman Catholics have used their influence in extreme ways to keep from publication, notices and advertisements unacceptable to them. Occasionally a boycott fails, like that by the Roman Catholic Church in 1938 against the *Woman's Home Companion* and related publications because of an editorial favorable to birth control.

According to canon 1386, the local bishop of the Roman Catholic Church has large authority in the matter of censorship, and no publication by a priest or member of a religious order should appear without his permission even on a secular subject. That is why students become so accustomed to the *nihil obstat* of the censor and the *imprimatur* of the bishop or archbishop on an early page in Catholic books. The censorship applies especially, but not exclusively, to books dealing with theological, ecclesiastical, and ethical matters. Ethical subjects as treated by non-Catholics are the special concern of the National Office for Decent Literature. The Legion of Decency, working in the field of motion picture censorship, it at least as much interested in points of dogma as in matters of life. Consequently non-Catholics sometimes think it goes to an extreme. It seems to them at times to approach the attitude of the historic *Index* of the Church. This, through the Holy Office, still continues on its list some great works of literature, history, and philosophy, including Hugo's *Les Miserables,* Kant's *Critique of Pure Reason*, Gibbon's *Decline and Fall of the Roman Empire*, Taine's *History of English Literature*, and Bergson's *Creative Evolution.*

The threat of a Church boycott is serious. A form of expressing disapproval of the editorial or business policy of a newspaper, but one which is apparently not generally subject to legal redress, is that taken by some religious groups in large cities, to try to control policy through the business department of the paper. It includes such methods as writing to the editor to inform him that the periodical will not be purchased again unless the policy changes, securing pledges from friends to do the same, and, even more alarming, notifying merchants that the writer will not buy goods at stores that continue to advertise in it while the policy objected to continues.

The methods recommended to Roman Catholics for such a boycott, often at the instigation of a Catholic Truth Society, were stated, in an article to which reference has been made, in the representative Jesuit magazine *America*, in its issue of February 11, 1928, where they may be carefully studied. This is probably the frankest statement that has been made, but there may well have been cases in which Protestant and Jewish groups have adopted similar procedures. Pressure of the Roman Catholic Church on certain New York newspapers was publicly denounced some years ago by Heywood Broun, the well-known journalist (who before his death entered the Roman Catholic Church) as a real threat to free speech and the independence of the press.

Censorship, as distinguished from boycott, has been authoritatively defined in the *Encyclopedia of the Social Sciences* as the policy of restricting the public expression of ideas, opinions, conceptions, and impulses which have or are believed to have the capacity to undermine the governing authority or the social and moral order which that authority considers itself bound to protect.[192]

Censorship in past centuries, both in the Roman Catholic Church and in the Protestant churches, presents many pathetic errors of judgment, especially where unorthodox views are concerned. It has often been said that the foundation of a very good library would be provided by the list of books forbidden by the Roman *Index librorum prohibitorum* during the past four centuries, since the Lateran Council of 1515 formulated the decree *De Impressione librorum.* This required, under the most severe penalties, approval by the proper ecclesiastical authority of any work prior to publication. But the Protestant civil authorities in Geneva in Calvin's day, in London during the Commonwealth, and in the Boston of Cotton Mather were scarcely less open to criticism. Even since the United States came into existence as a republic, with freedom of the press guaranteed under the Bill of Rights, we have not always been in a position to cast the eye of scorn on others.

The beginnings of censorship in the British-American colonies may be found in New England, involving conflicts between the established Congregational clergy and the State, on the one hand, and various heretical groups charged with lack of concern for the moral law—particularly Antinomianism—on the other. The banishment of Anne Hutchinson because of her commitment to the "covenant of grace" [193] was an illustration, but in its spirit of persecution and its banning of books and sermons of various Quakers, Baptists, and Antinomians generally, New Engand was merely reproducing the contemporary attitude in old England toward the controversy that was afflicting Massachusetts and Rhode Island. For instance, in August, 1644, the Westminster Assembly of Divines, summoned by Parliament and representing the Puritan conscience, sent a delegation to the Commons against the enormities of which Anabaptists, Antinomians, and other heretical groups were considered guilty. As a result, the Commons passed this resolution regarding Roger Williams' *Bloudy Tenent of Persecution,* just published in England by the leading apostle of toleration in New England: "Ordered, That Mr. White do give Order for the publick Burning of one Williams his Books, intituled Ec. concerning the Tolerating of all Sorts of Religion." The speaker thereupon announced that this order had been referred to a committee, "to consider of remedying and preventing the Mischiefs that arise from the spreading of dangerous Opinions of Antinomianism and Anabaptism." [194]

Within six years the precedent established in England by the burning of Roger Williams' great book was followed in New England. The General Court of the Massachusetts Bay colony also believed it its duty to enter vigorously the field of theological censorship. At its session in October, 1650, it passed an order to burn a book by William Pynchon, founder of Springfield, Massachusetts, entitled *The Meritorious Price of our Redemption . . . clearing it from some Errors,* a book which advocated liberal and at the same time heretical views of the atonement.[195]

Immediately after the Revolution, and owing partly to French influence, there was some relaxation of moral standards, but the Great Revival of 1797 to 1805 brought new concern for personal and social morality. Such organizations as the Society for the Suppression of Vice, organized in New York in 1802, the Society for the Reformation of Morals (1813), the American Tract Society (1825)— which absorbed more than forty groups that were printing and distributing leaflets and pamphlets on temperance, purity, the evils of gambling, Sabbath observance, religion, etc.—and the New York Moral Society (1834) were typical. Almost all were puritanical in their views and inclined to be prudish and critical of those who differed from them, though doing much to uphold high moral ideals of personal life. They succeeded in getting various state legislatures to adopt laws against obscene publications and exhibitions. In this activity Vermont led the way in 1812, followed by Connecticut in 1834 and Massachusetts in 1835.[196]

An early case in our national history of censorship of alleged immoral literature had to do with *McDowall's Journal.* The incident is of special interest in our study because it was a young reforming Presbyterian clergyman, John Robert McDowall, who was accused by the grand jury in New York of publishing articles on prostitution that were "injurious to morals." The young man, in an apparently sincere effort to show the evils of commercialized vice in the metropolis in 1834—more than fifty years before the Reverend Dr. Parkhurst's activities—decided to get to know the prostitute class and publish their stories. His motive, evidently religious, resulted in his establishing a short-lived home for wayward girls. His monthly magazine, which lasted for a year or more, was his medium for making his disclosures known, and it gave New York a bad reputation. A contemporary newspaper says that the magazine was presented by the grand jury "as a nuisance which calls loudly for the interference of the civil authorities. Under the pretext of cautioning the young of both sexes against the temptations of criminal intercourse, it presents such odious and revolting details as are offensive to taste, injurious to morals, and degrading to the character of our city." [197] Nothing was finally done to the editor, but his magazine was soon discontinued.

Among the criminal statutes of Massachusetts is a law against the sale of "a book which is obscene, indecent, impure, or manifestly tends to corrupt the morals of youth." A phrase often found in statutes of other states covering this same matter is that books are unlawful if they are "lewd, lascivious and filthy." [198] Periodical literature is frequently covered as well as books, and sometimes the statutes are broad enough to cover pornographic representations in all forms— books, magazines, articles, pictures, and advertisements which make an appeal to the passions, especially of youth. Certain cheap illustrated magazines with lurid accounts of crime, prostitution, and illicit love affairs, which are all too often prominently exhibited on newsstands, are the frequent objects of concern of local federations of churches and other religious groups.

The Federal government's first real attempt to meet the problem was the Tariff Act of 1842 prohibiting the admission of obscene books through the customhouse, a provision which has been included in all succeeding tariff acts. This was the precursor of similar acts controlling the actions of the Post Office Department. They began effectively with the act of 1873 authorizing the department to refuse to transmit "obscene" matter through the mail. Another act was passed in 1909 and amended two years later, declaring unmailable "every obscene, lewd, or lascivious, and every filthy book, pamphlet, picture, paper, letter, writing, print, or other publication of an indecent character," including advertisements of any medicine or device "for preventing conception or producing abortion, or for any indecent or immoral purpose." [199] Under these and similar Federal laws well-known books were banned, including Tolstoi's *Kreutzer Sonata* (1890), pamphlets by Mrs. Sanger on birth control (1915), James Joyce's *Ulysses*, and Boccaccio's *Decameron* (1922). Even Emanuel Swedenborg's *Amor Conjugalis* and Rousseau's *Confessions* have been banned—the first by the post office, the second by the United States customs office.[200]

Perhaps the best known of the quasi-public organizations that have dealt with the problem is the New York Society for the Supression of Vice, established in 1873 and nationally known because of the vigorous, sincere, but not always wise activity of its leader, Anthony Comstock. It has worked in close cooperation with certain Protestant churches, and under the act of the New York legislature establishing it, its agents were given the rights of search, seizure, and arrest. Within a few years similar societies with strong Church support were organized in other states, of which the New England Watch and Ward Society, founded in 1878 as the New England Society for the Suppression of Vice, has been the most prominent. The 1929 attempt to clean up Boston, led by this society, resulted in the forbidding of the sale of some sixty-eight books, among them books by H. G. Wells, Sinclair Lewis, Upton Sinclair, and other equally well-known writers.[201]

A case which involves these two aspects of censorship, Federal and local (through the society last named), is particularly illuminating. In 1926 the April number of *The American Mercury* was not permitted to be sold in Boston because it contained an article entitled "Hatrack," a chapter from *Up From Methodism*. The article, by a member of the well-known Methodist Asbury family, was an attack on revivalist meetings in a small town in Missouri. "Hatrack" was a household drudge who occasionally yielded to immorality, but on Sundays she would go to church to "Offer her soul to the Lord." Since the respectable citizens of the town shunned her, she "went to the Devil." The suppression of the article in Boston was believed due to the fact that the *Mercury* had previously published an article against the local Watch and Ward Society entitled "Keeping the Puritans Pure." After this second suppression, the editor of the *Mercury*, Henry L. Mencken, went to Boston and personally sold copies in defiance of the law. He was brought before a judge, who acquitted him, though later the same week a newsdealer who had sold the *Mercury* was found guilty in a Cambridge court. Mr. Mencken applied for an injunction to prevent further interference with the regular sale of his magazine. The injunction was granted in the Federal court, and the judge, referring to the Watch and Ward Society, said,

> The defendant Chase and the society of which he is secretary scrutinize publications of various kinds, including books and magazines. If they believe that a book or article violates the law, they inform the large distributors of their opinion, with the intimation, express or implied, that if the book or magazine be sold or distributed prosecution will follow. Where the warning is ignored, it is their custom to institute prosecutions. . . .
>
> They secure their influence, not by voluntary acquiescence in their opinions by the trade in question, but by the coercion and intimidation of that trade through the fear of prosecution if the defendants' views are disregarded. . . .
>
> In my judgment this is clearly illegal. The defendants have the right of every citizen to come to the courts with complaints of crime; but they have no right to impose their opinions on the book and magazine trade by threats of prosecution if their views are not accepted. . . .[202]

In recent years, leadership in the attack upon immoral and obscene literature has passed from the Protestant churches to the Roman Catholic Church. The Church operates through the National Office for Decent Literature (organized in 1938 by the Catholic bishops in the United States under the title National Organization for Decent Literature) in much the same way as the Protestant churches acted through the Society for Suppression of Vice and the Watch and Ward Society. The activities of the N.O.D.L. have resulted in the banning of such well-known books as Erskine Caldwell's *God's Little Acre*, James T. Farrell's *A World I Never Made*, Hemingway's *To Have and Have Not*, Huxley's *Antic Hay*, Christopher Isherwood's *The World in the Evening*, D. H. Lawrence's *Women in Love*, Richard Wright's *Native Son*, and Émile Zola's *Nana*.[203]

It should also be noted that, among the religious groups, American Jewry is least sympathetic to censorship on any ground. While the rabbis of course do not favor immoral or obscene books, they are more inclined than their Christian colleagues to rely upon the good judgment of the individual readers rather than upon governmental compulsion through censorship.

It was not until 1957 that the Supreme Court definitively decided in favor of the constitutionality of anti-obscenity laws. In two cases (*Roth* v. *United States* [204] and *Alberts* v. *State of California* [205]), it upheld a Federal and a state statute forbidding respectively the mailing or selling of "every obscene, lewd, lascivious or filthy book." Speaking for the majority of the Court, Justice Brennan said that obscene material is not within the protection of the freedom of speech and press guarantees of the First Amendment since it is "utterly without redeeming social importance." In order to determine whether a publication is obscene, the Court accepted the test "whether to the average person, applying contemporary community standards, the dominant theme of the material taken as a whole appeals to prurient interest." [206]

Following these decisions, laws have been enacted in some states, such as Massachusetts, setting up official advisory committees on obscenity, presumably on the theory that they will reflect "contemporary community standards." The Church-State question is directly involved because some of these laws specifically provide that clergymen of the three major faiths shall be members of the committees. Whether this stipulation does not constitute a violation of the First Amendment's prohibition of laws respecting an establishment of religion may yet have to be decided by the Supreme Court.

Censorship of the theater in this country also goes back to Puritan days. It was in the field of sex and "deportment" that the Puritan was especially insistent that nothing should be permitted which would tend to break down the strict inherited standards of Christian conduct. For example, stage performances, thought inimical to morality, were banned in Boston in 1750, largely through the influence of the clergy, and in Rhode Island in 1762. The effect of the theater for good or ill has long been argued, but the Puritans were inclined to see only its black side. They were well aware that even England as late as 1737 had thought it advisable to pass a licensing act restricting the number of theaters and requiring a license from the lord chamberlain as an indispensable preliminary to any stage presentation, thus attempting to secure an effective censorship of political opinion and morals.

The Puritans also tried to ban all but the most simple country dancing, horse racing, tavern sports, and many other forms of amusement, including harmless Sunday recreations which were openly practiced by Southern society. They feared the effect on moral standards of such activities, especially the theater— "the Devil's Church." The smaller Protestant sects, such as those which overran Pennsylvania in the eighteenth century, were equally concerned about them. The Quakers particularly disapproved. In 1760 a law was adopted to suppress theaters in Pennsylvania,[207] but it was not long effective, especially in Philadelphia. In fact, the first drama written by an American and produced professionally was staged in Philadelphia in 1767.

In time the theaters became respectable, but during the latter part of the nineteenth century the question of indecency and immorality on the stage grew increasingly prominent, and various Church groups made protests. Even as late as 1930 Bishop Manning of the Episcopal Church issued a statement to the effect that most Broadway plays were "unfit." The veteran theater manager William A. Brady agreed with him, and the editor of the *Catholic World*, the Reverend James M. Gillis, condemned theatrical realism as "a hypocritical excuse for introducing lewdness." [208]

On the whole, however, there has been comparatively little effort on the part of government to censor the theater. The reason is that unlike radio, television, and motion pictures, which are witnessed by millions of Americans in all age groups, theaters are generally located only in metropolitan areas and are visited by mature audiences. Occasionally an act of governmental censorship still occurs, as in New York City in 1963, when the city commissioner of licenses invoked an old and unenforced state law forbidding the stage presentation of the deity of any recognized faith to cause the removal from a presentation called *The Establishment* of a skit which offensively satirized the crucifixion of Jesus.

As in the case of book censorship, the Protestants preceded the Roman Catholics in seeking censorship of motion pictures. A characteristic utterance was that of the Presbyterians (Northern), who in 1921 adopted this resolution:

> Deploring the menace of moving picture shows to young people because of films that suggest crime, immorality, etc., we condemn the use of such films and those that make light of the marriage relation. We urge our people to cooperate with the widespread movement for better motion pictures. Since some of those engaged in the business are not amenable to the appeal for clean movies, we urge a nation-wide campaign for legal censorship by the Federal Government.[209]

The following year the General Assembly instructed its Board of Temperance and Moral Welfare

> (1) To inaugurate a movement which will seek to unite all the moral agencies of America in a concerted request of Congress that such legislation be enacted as will make mandatory, production of pictures in accordance with certain well-defined moral standards, this legislation to be applied at the point of production; that is, before the picture is made.
> (2) To lend the aid of the Board whenever possible to the moral forces of such states and communities as are endeavoring to secure some form of regulation of the Movies. . . .[210]

It was not long, however, before in this field of censorship too, the lead was taken by Catholics. The Production Code, promulgated in 1930 by the Motion Picture Producers and Distributors of America, is believed to have been prepared by Martin Quigley, author of *Decency in Motion Pictures*, and the

Reverend Daniel A. Lord, S.J. Its major principle was thus expressed: "No picture is to be produced which will lower the moral standards of those who see it. The sympathy of the audience must never be thrown to the side of crime, wrongdoing, evil or sin." [211]

Among the specific regulations were those requiring that the sanctity of marriage and the home must be upheld, religious faiths must not be ridiculed, ministers of religion must not be used as comic characters or as villains, and forms of gross immorality must not be permitted. Many things relating to religion have been deleted from films by this board or by various state boards, such as, from Potemkin's picture, Lenin's tomb bearing the inscription "Religion is the opiate of the people"; from *Joan of Arc*, her words at the stake, "Oh, God, why hast thou forsaken me?"; and others, some of which as statements of historic fact seem legitimate.

The 1934 edition of the code contained under Section VIII, "Religion," the following:

1. No film or episode may throw ridicule on any religious faith.

2. Ministers of religion in their character as ministers of religion should not be used as comic characters or as villains.

3. Ceremonies of any definite religion should be carefully and respectfully handled.[212]

The concern of the Roman Catholic Church about the character of motion pictures because of their influence on the moral standards and ideals of youth led to the establishment of the National Legion of Decency in the fall of 1933, when the bishops united in a planned crusade for purifying the movies. The Legion expressed its objective in the following way:

To secure a screen conforming to the accepted and God-given morality upon which our homes and civilization are builded. We would stamp out films which present false moral standards. We would revitalize on the screen the ideals of natural and Christian rectitude. We have taken the field against the motion picture which is immoral in theme or indecent in treatment. By time-tested standards of morality, adultery is wrong; murder is wrong; stealing is wrong; lying is wrong; honor is due to father and mother. These norms of human conduct spring from a code of right and wrong written by God Himself upon the tablets of men's hearts.[213]

The Legion urges producers to exercise a self-control responsive to an aroused public opinion. Its principal aim is "to discourage the production and patronizing of films which present false moral standards, which, in turn, lower traditional morality." [214] It seeks to create wholesome moral standards and a determination by the laity to have nothing to do with anything that is vile or indecent in public entertainment. The pledge of the Legion, which has been signed by millions of American Catholics, is distributed once a year by pastors in accordance with Pope Pius XI's encyclical letter on motion pictures. It reads as follows:

> In the name of the Father and of the Son and of the Holy Ghost. Amen. I condemn indecent and immoral motion pictures, and those which glorify crime or criminals.
>
> I promise to do all that I can to strengthen public opinion against the production of indecent and immoral films, and to unite with all who protest against them.
>
> I acknowledge my obligation to form a right conscience about pictures that are dangerous to my moral life. As a member of the Legion of Decency, I pledge myself to remain away from them. I promise, further, to stay away altogether from places of amusement which show them as a matter of policy.
>
> Name..
> Parish...   Diocese............................[215]

The Legion of Decency publishes reviews of films. In 1936, after but three years of existence, it reviewed 1,271 motion pictures. Of these 780 were rated as not objectionable for general participation; 380 others, not objectionable for adults; 98, objectionable in part; and 13, condemned.

Censorship of motion pictures is not limited to those deemed immoral. Occasionally it is applied on political grounds, on other occasions on religious and theological grounds, and sometimes, as in the case of *The Miracle*, on grounds asserted to be both moral and religious. Illustrative of the first type was a case of conflict over European political ideologies which occurred in 1939, in connection with the film *Blockade*—an attempt to depict the bombardment of Spanish towns by General Franco's forces. This film created great offense in Roman Catholic circles, inasmuch as the Church was on the whole strongly behind Franco, opposing the Loyalists on the ground that they were anti-Church and communistic. The film was consequently banned under Roman Catholic pressure in many cities, sometimes by the distributors and sometimes by the police. For instance, it was entirely banned from Somerville, Massachusetts, and from the second running in Providence, Rhode Island. In Boston the City Council, with a Roman Catholic majority, adopted a resolution against the film, but the mayor refused to ban the picture.

A somewhat similar case occurred the same year when an anti-Nazi film depicting the tragedy of a Jewish family was protested in many cities but in most cases released. In Boston it was banned on Sunday but permitted during the week.[216]

An instance of censorship involving religious issues took place in 1928 when the Lutheran Church brought to this country a motion picture of the history of the Reformation under the title *Freedom*. A statement covering this incident, as prepared by the Associated Church Press, thus describes it:

The New York State Board of Censorship demanded the elimination of sub-titles and scenes which presented the story of Reformation "protest" against Roman Catholic practices of the day, such as the sale of indulgences, heresy, the Roman court of inquisition, Papal doctrines, and so on. The Board wrote: "The reasons for the above eliminations are: 'sacrilegious,' 'tend to incite to crime,' and 'inhuman.'" The deletions would have cut the historic heart out of the film. The Lutherans put on a nation-wide campaign which resulted in the sending of more than 40,000 letters to the censorship board. This brought the withdrawal of the original demands for deletions and the release of the film.[217]

A somewhat similar instance occurred in the fifties in connection with the motion picture *Martin Luther*, a vivid and dramatic portrayal of the life and teachings of the great reformer.[218] However, the most noted case involving censorship on religious ground was that of *The Miracle*.[219]

This was a forty-minute Italian-language film relating the tale of a simple peasant girl who is seduced by a bearded stranger she imagines to be St. Joseph and who later gives birth at the foot of the altar in a church to a baby she believes to have been divinely conceived. The film had been publicly exhibited in Rome under a permit issued by the government censor and had run into no trouble there. It passed without objection by the United States customs authorities when it was brought into this country. In March, 1949, and again in November, 1950 (when English subtitles were added), it was licensed for exhibition in New York by the Motion Picture Division of the state's Department of Education, the official censor. It opened a month later in a small theater in New York City.

No sooner did the picture open than the Legion of Decency prepared a report condemning it and instructing Roman Catholics to refrain from seeing it. Shortly thereafter the city's commissioner of licenses, a devout Catholic and former state commander of the Catholic War Veterans, informed the theater management that he found the picture "officially and personally to be a blasphemous affront to a great many of the citizens of our City." He warned that unless the film were withdrawn he would revoke the theater's license to operate. This warning, however, proved ineffective since a New York judge ruled that the commissioner's power to license theaters did not empower him to revoke licenses because of the content of the films shown there.

About a week later, on the first Sunday in 1951, a statement by Cardinal Spellman was read at all the masses in St. Patrick's Cathedral in New York City. In it he called for a boycott both of the film and of any theater exhibiting it.

In addition he criticized the Motion Picture Division for approving the picture, declaring that its members should be "censured" for offending and insulting "millions of people."

That afternoon pickets representing the Catholic War Veterans and other Catholic organizations appeared before the theater with signs urging the public not to enter the theater. The next step was the appointment by the state Department of Education of a committee of three prominent citizens—a Prottestant, a Catholic, and a Jew—to review the picture and make recommendations. The committee reported that the picture was sacrilegious and recommended that its license be revoked on that ground. The department followed the recommendation, and the producer of the film appealed, first—unsuccessfully—to the New York courts [220] and then—successfully—to the United States Supreme Court. The decision—*Burstyn* v. *Wilson*—has been summarized in Chapter 5. Here it need only be added that after the decision the film returned to the theater and was exhibited thereafter without incident.

One footnote should be added to this case. The Supreme Court's opinion was based on the holding that motion pictures were a form of expression which, like speech and the press, are protected by the First Amendment. Under this amendment, the Court had ruled in the past, neither the Federal government nor the states could censor books although it could, of course, punish the publisher after publication, if in fact a book was obscene. It was not clear from the decision in *Burstyn* v. *Wilson* whether motion pictures enjoyed the same immunity. The situation was clarified in 1961 when the Court, in the case of *Times Film Company* v. *City of Chicago*,[221] ruled that motion pictures were in a different category and could constitutionally be censored in advance of exhibition. This does not mean that the censor may act unreasonably or arbitrarily; his action is always subject to review by the courts, which can nullify it if they find that there is no legal basis for his determination that a particular motion picture is obscene.

Major Church-State problems have not yet arisen in the field of radio and television broadcasting. The right of atheists to have free broadcasting time was upheld in principle by the Federal Communications Commission in July, 1946. It stated that "freedom of religious belief necessarily carries with it freedom to disbelieve," and that "if freedom of speech is to have meaning . . . it must be extended as readily to ideas which we disapprove or abhor as to ideas which we approve." The opinion continues,

It is true that in this country on overwhelming majority of the people profess a belief in the existence of a Divine being. But the conception of the nature of the Divine Being is as varied as religious denominations and sects and even differs with the individuals belonging to the same denomination or sect.

So diverse are these conceptions that it may be fairly said, even as to professed believers, that the God of one man does not exist for another. And so strongly may one believe in his own particular conception of God that he may easily be led to say: "Only my God exists, and therefore he who denies my God is an atheist, irrespective of his professed belief in a God." [222]

This right of an atheist to express his views over the radio was first availed of in November, 1946, by Robert Harold Scott, who spoke over station KQW in San Jose, California. Strong protests were voiced by the California State Council of the Knights of Columbus and other groups. The Scott question was appealed to the Federal Communications Commission in an attempt to secure the revocation of the licenses of radio stations KPO, and PFRC for refusing to grant permission to allow Mr. Scott to give atheistic addresses over the air. The broadcasting companies took the ground that such talks would not be in the public interest, that they had acted within their legal rights, and that this was not a case of "a controversial public issue" on which both sides should be heard. The petitioner, on the other hand, stated, "I respect every man's right to have and to express any religious belief whatsoever. But I abhor and denounce those who, while asserting this right, seek in one way or another, to prevent others from expressing contrary views."

The Commission recognized the case as important, but it did not feel warranted on the basis of this single complaint "in selecting these stations as the subject of a hearing looking toward termination of their licenses, when there was no urgent ground for selecting them rather than many other stations." It accordingly denied the petition. [223]

Another incident involving freedom of religious expression over the air occurred in April, 1949, in Lawrence, Massachusetts. There Station WLAW refused to accept an Easter sermon by a Universalist minister, Reverend Kenneth Patton, in which he denied the divinity of Jesus Christ. The ban was not due to any protest by official Protestant or Catholic organizations, though certain clergymen consulted felt that it should not be broadcast, doubtless because of its unorthodox character. The incident is particularly interesting because it brought out the following official reply from the Federal Communications Commission to an inquiry on the subject:

The Commission has always regarded the broadcast of religious programs as part of a diversified service as being in the public interest. But, as you may know, under the Communications Act of 1934, as amended, the selection and presentation of program material rests in the discretion of the individual station licensee, subject only to his general obligation to operate his station in the public interest. The Commission has no authority to interfere with the management of the station in the exercise of that discretion and has, therefore, promulgated no rules with respect to the making of judgments as to particular programs in the course of day-to-day operations of broadcasting stations. Such decisions rest with the radio station management. As you can readily appreciate, the Commission cannot advise radio stations with respect to the propriety of broadcasting individual programs. This is a judgment which the licensee must make initially in the light of all the facts and circumstances, which he is in the best position to ascertain.[224]

The banned sermon was thereafter published in *Zion's Herald*, a well-known independent journal of the Methodist Church, which had protested, in the interest of freedom of speech and the right of expression of minority religious opinion, to its being kept off the radio.

In closing this section on censorship, attention should be called to several Supreme Court cases involving censorship of the writings and oral statements of the Jehovah's Witnesses. These decisions have been summarized earlier in this volume, in Chapter 5. It is appropriate here to set forth an extract, quoted by Justice Robert H. Jackson in one of these cases,[225] from the book *Religion* by Judge J. H. Rutherford, who succeeded Pastor Charles Russell as president of the organization in 1916 and served until his death in 1942.

God's faithful servants go from house to house to bring the message of the kingdom to those who reside there, omitting none, not even the houses of the Roman Catholic Hierarchy, and there they give witness to the kingdom because they are commanded by the Most High to do so. "They shall enter in at the windows like a thief." They do not loot nor break into the houses, but they set up their phonographs before the doors and windows and send the message of the kingdom right into the houses into the ears of those who might wish to hear; and while those desiring to hear are hearing, some of the "sourpusses" are compelled to hear. Locusts invade the homes of the people and even eat the varnish off the wood and eat the wood to some extent. Likewise God's faithful witnesses, likened unto locusts, get the kingdom message right into the house, including candles and "holy water," remove the superstition from the minds of the people, and show them that the doctrines that have been taught to them are wood, hay and stubble, destructible by fire, and they cannot withstand the heat. The people are enabled to learn that "purgatory" is a bogeyman, set up by the agents of Satan to frighten the people into the religious organizations, where they may be fleeced of their hard-earned money. Thus the kingdom message plagues the religionists, and the clergy find that they are unable to prevent it. Therefore, as described by the prophet, the message comes to them like a thief that enters in at the windows, and this message is a warning to those who are on the inside that Jesus Christ has come, and they remember his warning words, to wit: "Behold, I come as a thief." (Revelation 16:15.) The day of Armageddon is very close, and that day comes upon the world in general like a thief in the night.[226]

It is worth recording that although the Roman Catholic Church has been

the special target of Jehovah's Witnesses, *America*, one of the most respected
of Catholic journals, supported the Supreme Court's decisions in these cases. It
said,

Freedom of speech might almost be defined as freedom to disagree with the
majority. . . . It is the small, discordant groups who need protection. . . . So
long as a small and very unpopular minority can engage the attention and win
the protection of the Supreme Court, at a time, too, when the national danger
has darkened counsel in many minds, we have reason to trust in the staying power
of our democratic principles and regime.[227]

Finally, lest the reader assume that only Jehovah's Witnesses enjoy the
Supreme Court's protection from censorship in their aggressive and, to many,
offensive missionary activities, his attention is called to the case of *Kunz* v.
New York, summarized in Chapter 5. This and other decisions show that while
it is usually the extremist's activities which become publicized and reach the
Supreme Court, the First Amendment's guarantee of the free exercise of religion protects all Americans.

Chapter 18

THE LEGAL BASIS OF CHURCH RIGHTS

We pass now from public educational and social-legislative activities in which the Church has been concerned to a consideration of the major questions in the fields of Church property and clergy rights, with the resulting legal situation. It will be noticed as we proceed that though constitutions, statutes, and court decisions have on the whole tried to be scrupulously fair and impartial in dealing with all religious bodies, and that although the State has not recognized any specific form of religion, it has nevertheless been favorable to all agencies which promote the religious spirit and which remain loyal to the government. In other words, it has shown by its public actions that it considers religion a matter of great public importance. The recognition of this American attitude has been noted by all qualified foreigners who have visited this country or who have studied carefully its government and history.

A striking statement of this impression is found in the writings of Luigi Luzzatti, former premier of Italy and a careful student of Church-State problems. Writing in 1908, he said that "the character of politico-ecclesiastical legislation in the United States is one of religious freedom in *favor of* the churches and not *against* them." [1] Since that was written our Supreme Court has interpreted the First Amendment as imposing upon government a neutrality not only as between competing religious faiths but also as between religion and non-religion. Nevertheless, the statement remains basically true. This neutrality, the Court has repeatedly emphasized, is based not (as in some countries) upon hostility to religion but upon friendliness to it, a friendliness which reflects the almost universal feeling of the American public and its governmental agencies toward religion.

Church-State separation in the United States has historically very little European secularism about it. Not only are churches, and the necessary buildings and grounds immediately surrounding them, generally exempt from taxation, but they receive certain other favors—for example, in zoning regulations. Here, under state laws, certain types of business which might be demoralizing or annoying to worshipers, such as liquor saloons, theaters, garages, are generally excluded within specified distance of churches, or permitted only with church approval. Many other evidences of consideration shown to churches and their ministers as important factors in social welfare could be cited to show the high esteem this nation has for religion and religious institutions, as esteem probably unequaled anywhere else in the world.

The Civil Courts and Religious Freedom

The American courts have nothing to do with religion, as distinguished from the property of religious organizations, other than (1) acting as arbiters in disputes between different Church groups or between a church and some outside person, organization, or public authority and (2) acting as arbiters when acts of a religious group are considered to contravene flagrantly our accepted moral standards or when they appear dangerous to the public welfare. Cases in the second group are relatively infrequent, but they are of such fundamental importance that they are here dealt with first.

The most authoritative statement of religious freedom as viewed by our courts comes from the Supreme Court of the United States. In 1871 it stated,

In this country the full and free right to entertain any religious belief, to practise any religious principle, and to teach any religious doctrine which does not violate the laws of morality and property, and which does not infringe personal rights, is conceded to all. The law knows no heresy, and is committed to the support of no dogma, the establishment of no sect.[2]

The State takes the ground that all religions are permissible under two provisos, namely, that they do not advocate and/or indulge in polygamy or some other practice that is entirely inconsistent with the ethical code derived by English-speaking people from their Jewish-Christian ethical background, and that they do not unduly disturb the public peace or otherwise threaten the welfare of the State. The most famous group of cases involving both of these considerations was that of the Mormons, which came to a head in the issue of polygamy. The Supreme Court decided that polygamy might not be practiced under the laws of the United States because it was both "in violation of social duties"—that is, ethics—and "subversive of good order"—that is, public welfare. The constitutional issues involved in Mormon polygamy have been described at length elsewhere in this volume.[3] Here we will deal with a number of other instances in which the free exercise of religion may conflict with public morality, safety, health, or welfare.

One example of conflict is found in instances where the government's need to protect the people from fraud clashes with a claim to the free exercise of religion. The most important case, *United States* v. *Ballard*,[4] has been summarized in Chapter 5. It is useful here to set forth the specific allegedly fraudulent representations made under the guise of religion by the defendants and their groups known as the "I Am" movement. The indictment against them read in part,

That Guy W. Ballard, now deceased, alias Saint Germain, Jesus, George Washington, and Godfrey Ray King, had been selected and thereby designated by the alleged "ascertained masters," Saint Germain, as a divine messenger; and that the words of "ascended masters" and the words of the alleged divine entity, Saint Germain, would be transmitted to mankind through the medium of the said Guy W. Ballard;

That Guy W. Ballard, during his lifetime, and Edna W. Ballard, and Donald Ballard, by reason of their alleged high spiritual attainments and righteous conduct, had been selected as divine messengers through which the words of the alleged "ascended masters," including the alleged Saint Germain, would be communicated to mankind under the teachings commonly known as the "I Am" movement;

That Guy W. Ballard, during his lifetime, and Edna W. Ballard, and Donald Ballard, had, by reason of supernatural attainments, the power to heal persons of ailments and diseases and to make well, persons afflicted with any diseases, injuries or ailments, and did falsely represent to persons intended to be defrauded that the three designated persons had the ability and power to cure persons of those diseases normally classified as curable and also of diseases which are ordinarily classified by the medical profession as being incurable diseases; and did further represent that the three designated persons had in fact cured either by the activity of one, either, or all of said persons, hundreds of persons afflicted with diseases and ailments.[5]

The decision in this case shows the extreme reluctance of our courts to interfere with the inviolability of religious convictions. The majority of the Supreme Court refused to permit the jury to determine whether the representations made by the Ballards were true or false. If a jury in a secular court were allowed to pass upon the truth of these apparently extreme assertions, it could also pass upon assertions which are part of more conventional and orthodox faiths, and jury trials might well become heresy trials. The majority opinion written by Justice Douglas speaks quite forcefully on this point:

Freedom of thought, which includes freedom of religious belief, is basic in a society of free men. It embraces the right to maintain theories of life and of death and of the hereafter which are rank heresy to followers of the orthodox faiths. Heresy trials are foreign to our Constitution. Men may believe what they cannot prove. They may not be put to the proof of their religious doctrines or beliefs. Religious experiences which are as real as life to some may be incomprehensible to others. Yet the fact that they may be beyond the ken of mortals does not mean that they can be made suspect before the law. Many take their gospel from the New Testament. But it would hardly be supposed that they could be tried before a jury charged with the duty of determining whether those teachings contained false representations. The miracles of the New Testament, the Divinity of Christ, life after death, the power of prayer are deep in the religious convictions of many. If one could be sent to jail because a jury in a hostile environment found those teachings false, little indeed would be left of religious freedom. The Fathers of the Constitution were not unaware of the varied and extreme views of religious sects, of the violence of disagreement among them, and of the lack of any one religious creed on which all men would agree. They fashioned a charter of government which envisaged the widest possible toleration of conflicting views. Man's relation to his God was made no concern of the state. He was granted the right to worship as he pleased and to answer to no man for the verity of his religious views. The religious views espoused by respondents might seem incredible, if not preposterous, to most people. But if those doctrines are subject to trial before a jury charged with finding their truth or falsity, then the same can be done with the religious beliefs of any sect. When the triers of fact undertake that task, they enter a forbidden domain. The First Amendment does not select any one group or any one type of religion for preferred treatment. It puts them all in that position.[6]

The majority of the Court held that it was proper for the jury to decide whether the Ballards acted in good faith, that is, whether they themselves believed in the truth of what they represented. If the jury were to find that in fact they themselves never believed the statements they made, then they could be convicted of having committed fraud in obtaining contributions of money on the basis of these statements. Even this was not acceptable to Justice Jackson, who, in dissenting, said, "I would dismiss the indictment and have done with this business of judicially examining other people's faith."

The question of the constitutionality of requiring licenses for the collection of funds in the name of religion or for the sale of religious literature, in order to protect the people from fraud, was involved in the Jehovah's Witness case of *Cantwell* v. *Connecticut*,[7] summarized in Chapter 5, to which the reader is referred. That case, as well as a number of other Jehovah's Witnesses cases (e.g., *Chaplinsky* v. *New Hampshire*[8]) as well as some non-Jehovah's Witnesses cases (e.g., *Kunz* v. *New York*[9]) also raised the question arising out of the conflict between the free exercise of religion and the need of the government to preserve the public peace and prevent disorder. In these and many similar cases in Federal and state courts, an effort has generally been manifested to preserve the rights of individual conscience to the fullest extent consistent with public order.

In a civilized society it is the duty of government to protect not only the public morals (Mormon cases), the public's property (Ballard and Cantwell cases), and the public peace and order (Jehovah's Witnesses and Kunz cases), but also the public health. Here, too, this duty sometimes clashes with some group's or individual's claim to the free exercise of religion. The most frequent instances concern Christian Scientists and other less well-known believers in faith healing. Here, too, the state governments have shown on the whole a sincere desire to avoid as much as possible infringing upon the religious conscience of Americans without endangering the public health. For example, some states exempt faith healers from the requirement of obtaining a medical license imposed upon physicians generally, and the children of Christian Scientists are excused from participating in public school courses teaching the germ theory of disease.

Nevertheless, where there is a serious danger to the public health, the courts have uniformly ruled that the individual conscience must yield. The first and most important Supreme Court case establishing this principle was *Jacobson* v. *Massachusetts* [10] (see Chapter 5). While in that case the defendant's refusal to allow himself to be vaccinated, as required by the municipal authorities to avert a threatened epidemic, was not motivated by religious considerations, the Court has since then often made it clear that the decision would not have been different even if it had been.

Another illustration involves the fluoridation of the water supply, recommended by many dental experts as a means to lessen dental cavities of children. Drinking fluoridated water violates the religious conscience of Christian Scientists, and in a number of states they brought suit to enjoin the municipal authorities from fluoridating a city's water supply. In all cases they have been unsuccessful, and although they have appealed to the United States Supreme Court, that tribunal has refused to overrule the state courts on this issue.[11]

When the life or health of children is endangered the courts are far less reluctant than otherwise to set aside religious convictions. Blood transfusions for children of Jehovah's Witnesses offer a dramatic illustration. According to the beliefs of that sect blood transfusions violate the Biblical prohibition against the drinking of blood. Often the members of the sect have refused to allow blood transfusions for their ill or injured children even where physicians have warned that the child's life could not be saved in any other way. In this situation, if the matter is brought to the attention of the state or municipal health or welfare authorities, they usually obtain an order from a judge authorizing them to give the transfusion notwithstanding the parents' refusal to consent. The state courts have uniformly upheld these orders on the ground that whatever constitutional right an adult may have to make a martyr of himself in the cause of religion, he has no right to sacrifice his children, no matter how strong his religious commitment may be. Here, too, the United States Supreme Court has refused to overrule the state courts' holdings.[12]

It is by no means certain that even in respect to adults there is a constitutional right to sacrifice or even unduly endanger one's life in the name of religion. In upholding the law against polygamy, the Supreme Court said that the First Amendment would not protect a widow's right to throw herself on the funeral pyre of her husband.[13] The great value our society puts on human life would empower the State to forbid and forcibly prevent such a practice. For that reason the Supreme Court has refused to declare unconstitutional laws enacted in some Southern states forbidding the practice of religious snake-handling, under which persons deliberately handle deadly snakes in the belief that their faith will prevent their being harmed by them.[14]

Another instance in which the Supreme Court has held that the health and welfare of children may be protected by the government notwithstanding the religious objections of the parents in the case of *Prince* v. *Massachusetts* [15] (see Chapter 5). The fact that the defendant, a Jehovah's Witness, and her young niece, of whom she had legal custody, believed it to be their religious duty to sell the publications of the sect did not exempt them, the Court held, from the operation of the state's anti-child labor law. The opinion of the Court included the following significant statement:

> The right to practice religion freely does not include liberty to expose the community or the child to communicable disease or the latter to ill health or death. . . . Parents may be free to become martyrs themselves. But it does not follow that they are free, in identical circumstances, to make martyrs of their children before they have reached the age of full and legal discretion when they can make that choice for themselves.

Our society is concerned not only with children but also with animals. The many animal conservation laws and societies for the prevention of cruelty to animals are evidence of this feeling. It occasionally happens that here too a conflict with religious conscience arises. A recent example is humane slaughter legislation. In 1958 Congress passed a law—and since then a number of state legislatures have passed laws—requiring that packing houses engaged in slaughtering animals for food shall employ specified humane methods in this process. The Orthodox Jewish faith requires that animals be slaughtered in a particular manner prescribed in the Talmud, and many adherents of that faith felt that these laws would make it ritually impossible for them to eat meat. However, the matter was satisfactorily settled when at the hearings before the Congressional committees it was shown that the method prescribed by the Talmud complies with the strictest standards of humaneness and causes the instantaneous death of the animal with no significant pain. On the basis of this scientific and undisputed testimony, the bill was amended to include this method of slaughtering as one of the acceptable procedures.[16] Similar provisions have since then been included in the various state laws.[17]

In recent years conflict between the needs of the community and the unrestricted exercise of religion has centered around the question of zoning laws and ordinances. Often, in order to insure that particular areas of a community or, on occasion, the entire community will be maintained exclusively for residences, zoning ordinances have been passed forbidding the erection of any non-residential structures in these areas. Ordinarily, the constitutionality of the ordinances is not seriously questioned, but where they are enforced against a religious group seeking to build a church or religious school in the restricted area, questions of religious freedom arise. The matter has come to the courts in a number of states, and in most cases the courts have held in favor of the religious groups, although not always on the ground of religious freedom.[18] In a few states a contrary result has been reached by the courts, and in two instances, one in California and the other in Wisconsin, these decisions have been appealed to the United States Supreme Court. In both cases the Supreme Court has refused to reverse the state courts or set aside the restrictive ordinances, although in neither case did it write an opinion setting forth its reasons for its determination.[19] Probably before long the question will again come to the Supreme Court, at which time, it may be hoped, a complete discussion of the issues will be forthcoming.

The Civil Courts and Church Disputes

We are to deal here with the decisions by civil courts in matters affecting religious organizations. There are many questions involved, in view of the fact that under the American system the churches, though not *of* the State, are *in* it. For instance, to what extent should religious bodies take to the courts disputes regarding the administration of church property, discipline, or breach of trust? Or, in rival claims of two parties in a church dispute over control of church property, what principles shall settle the decision? In general, the civil courts have recognized the authority of ecclesiastical courts in such cases when it is shown that they have had competent jurisdiction and that procedure has been regular. This attitude was clearly laid down in a case before the Supreme Court of Illinois in 1863. The court stated that

In all matters of religious faith and practice, the ecclesiastical courts, provided they have obtained jurisdiction, are as entirely independent of the civil tribunals as the latter are of the former upon all questions relating to property interests.[20]

But there are times when one of the parties in a church dispute is dissatisfied with the ecclesiastical decision and strives for redress in the civil courts.

The law never loses sight of the distinction between the church as a religious group devoted to worship, preaching, missionary service, education, and the promotion of social welfare and the church as a business corporation owning real estate, making contracts, and so on. The two functions may be performed by the same individuals, but only when they act in different capacities. The former is a matter in which the State has no direct legal concern, while in the latter the activities of the church are subject in general to the same laws as are those of secular corporations.

It will be seen that cases involving religious beliefs alone, as distinct from the questionable actions which sometimes result from them, almost never appear before the courts, except as they are involved in disputes regarding the ownership of property held in trust or the qualifications of certain persons to act in certain cases. The courts have fairly consistently adopted the views of the fathers of the Constitution and its leading interpreters as to the full right of religious bodies to determine their own creeds and their own forms of organization, as long as these do not run counter to the law of the land and do not result in actions detrimental to the State.

This theory has good New Testament sanction. The Roman deputy Gallio seems to have been one who early saw the distinction between the responsibilities of the State and those of the Church as far as civil courts are concerned. There is an interesting passage on the insurrection against Paul when Gallio was the deputy of Achaia. According to the account in Acts 18, a Jewish group tried to bring Paul before the judicial authorities because his preaching seemed to be contrary to Jewish belief. What happened is clearly brought out in the Revised Standard Version of the New Testament, verses 14, 15, and 16:

> But when Paul was about to open his mouth, Gallio said to the Jews, "If it were a matter of wrongdoing or vicious crime, I should have reason to bear with you, O Jews; but since it is a matter of questions about words and names and your own law, see to it yourselves; I refuse to be a judge of these things."
> And he drove them from the tribunal.

This newer translation has been quoted because it brings out the distinction between the two types of cases more clearly than the old King James Version. In other words, if Paul's teaching had resulted in deeds that were contrary to public order or public morality, the civil court could take jurisdiction, but as it had to do only with a matter of beliefs the court would have none of it. This is an anticipation of the Jeffersonian teaching.

An early case of importance, generally referred to as the Dedham case, was decided by the Supreme Court of Massachusetts in 1820. It concerns the old-time union between a Congregational church and its Congregational society, the former having to do with the spiritual concerns of the parish and the latter with the secular. The distinction still holds in many religious bodies. In general, the object of the church is the worship of God, while the object of the society is the control of church property. The church is subject to spiritual control, the society to the temporal powers. The courts in general deal with the society, which may be considered the body of the church, not with the church itself, which is its soul.[21]

To understand the significance of this case, which resulted in the Congregationalists' losing to the Unitarians some eighty-one seceded churches,[22] we must remember that the Trinitarians—that is, the old-time Congregationalists—maintained that church property belonged to church members collectively, whereas the Unitarians held that it belonged to the parish society, basing their claim largely on the clause of the state constitution which recognized "towns, parishes, precincts, and other bodies politic or religious societies" as being on the same plane.[23]

The case came before the courts in 1818. A majority of the church members were evangelical (that is, old-time Congregationalists) while the society (that is, the legal voters of the first parish in Dedham) were preponderantly Unitarian. The latter took the initiative in calling a minister in spite of the protests of two-thirds of the church. They also invited a council of Unitarians to ordain him.[24] A serious legal question was consequently involved as to which faction of the Dedham church was entitled to use the meetinghouse and property of the society. The supreme court of the state decided in 1820 that a church has no legal existence save in "connection with some regularly constituted society," and that in case of any division in a church only the faction recognized by the society has the right to the name and use of the property.[25] The wording of the court's decision was that "whatever the usage in settling a minister, the Bill of Rights of 1780 secures to towns, not to the churches, the right to elect the minister in last resort"[26]—a good example of the old-time connection between Church and State in Massachusetts. The court based its decision on the ground that the property was held by the church merely as a trustee for the town or parish, and that therefore "If the church seceded from the parish it could not take the property with it."[27]

As a result 3,900 members of Massachusetts Congregational churches withdrew, leaving property valued at over $600,000 to the use of 1,282 Unitarian members who remained.[28] Other churches, in addition to the eighty-one directly affected, withdrew voluntarily. When the church was finally disestablished by action of the voters ratifying a constitutional amendment in 1833, it kept the property then in its possession.

Another famous civil court case involving churches was the Girard will case in 1844, summarized in Chapter 5. Few cases ever came to the United States Supreme Court in which the question of religion was as prominent as in this one. Here the court, rejecting the argument advanced on behalf of the contesting heirs, unanimously upheld the will of Stephen Girard making a bequest of several million dollars to the city of Philadelphia for the benefit of poor white orphans, subject to the condition that

No ecclesiastic, missionary or minister of any sect whatsoever, shall ever hold or exercise any duty whatsoever in the said college; nor shall any such person ever be admitted for any purposes, or as a visitor, within the premises appropriated to the purposes of the said college. . . . I desire to keep the tender minds of orphans . . . free from the excitements which clashing doctrines and sectarian controversy are so apt to produce.[29]

Daniel Webster, who had just retired as secretary of state, was one of the counsel who was trying to break the will, laying emphasis on the fact that since the proposed foundation was apparently opposed to Christianity it was against public policy. His argument, it must be confessed, was rather emotional, and it was commonly believed and stated in the press at the time that its tone had been at least partly determined by his desire to secure the support of the clergy, and of the most religious lay elements, in his candidacy for the presidency. Joseph Story, who was a justice at the time, and who handed down the opinion, has left us a most interesting contemporary account of the discussion, indicating how difficult it is for a court at times to keep entirely out of theological arguments. In a letter to his wife he said,

The curious part of the case is that the whole discussion has assumed a semi-theological character. Mr. Girard excluded ministers of all sects from being admitted into his college as instructors or visitors; but he required the scholars to be taught the love of truth, morality, and benevolence to their fellow-men. Mr. Jones and Mr. Webster contended that these restrictions were anti-Christian, and illegal, Mr. Binney and Mr. Sergeant contended that they were valid, and Christian, founded upon the great difficulty of making ministers cease to be controversialists, and forbearing to teach the doctrines of their sect. I was not a little amused with the manner in which, on each side, the language of the Scriptures and the doctrines of Christianity were brought in to point the argument; and to find the Court engaged in hearing homilies of faith and exposition of Christianity, with almost the formality of lectures from the pulpit.[30]

As is well known, Girard College has had a most useful career. The terms of the will have been strictly adhered to, and no clergymen are ever admitted to the grounds. The spirit of the place, however, is definitely Christian, and representative laymen are constantly invited to give religious addresses to the students.

Another case of very great importance in the history of religious bodies in the United States is that of *Watson* v. *Jones*,[31] decided by the United States Supreme Court in 1872. The decision, which has been summarized in Chapter 5, grew out of a split within the Presbyterian Church on the issue of slavery. The Court held that the Northern party in the local Louisville church, because of its recognition by the General Assembly, the highest official body within the Presbyterian Church, was entitled to possession of the Louisville church buildings and property. The Court laid down the following important principle:

If questions of property rights or of discipline, or of faith, or ecclesiastical rule, custom, or law have been decided by the highest church judicatory to which the particular congregation is subject, and to which the matter has been carried, the legal tribunals must accept such decision as final and as binding on them in their application to the case before them.[32]

The decision in *Watson* v. *Jones* has been criticized by some on the ground that it leaves individual members of a church with practically no legal protection against even tyrannical and unjust treatment by higher Church authorities. For example, Carl Zollmann, whose *American Church Law* has long been deemed an authoritative text on the subject, says that "To afford to individual members of a church no protection whatever against usurpation on the part of those in power is not only a travesty on justice but a blow in the face of the doctrine of religious liberty."[33] He recognizes that the decision saves the civil courts from a great amount of litigation, even though no ecclesiastical cases reach them except those which involve property or civil rights, but feels that often it denies justice, and that it concedes too great jurisdiction to Church tribunals.

A case dramatically supporting Zollmann's views occurred in Michigan about a century ago. In 1856 it was decided to build a new Roman Catholic chapel, known as St. Augustine's, in Kalamazoo. The priest involved was Father Lebel, the diocesan, Bishop Lefevre. As the subscriptions for erecting the building were inadequate, Father Lebel borrowed money from a prominent local Catholic layman, Patrick Bunbury. A man of excellent reputation, Bunbury first gave his notes for various sums and finally mortgaged his farm, the major part of his property, to secure the creditors. This he did because of his devotion to the Church and because of assurance that he would be promptly repaid. The title to the land and church building, in accordance with Catholic practice, was in the hands of Bishop Lefevre, who died in 1869, Bishop Borgess taking his place.

Bunbury, who badly needed the money he had loaned—about $10,000—applied to the new bishop for repayment. The bishop, informed by the priest about the circumstances which had led to the original loan, assured Bunbury that a mortgage would be executed on the valuable property of the church to protect his loan adequately. But the priest died, and there were many difficulties involved, including allegations that the money had not been applied to the purpose for which it was intended. The facts are not all clear, but the bishop declined to admit the claim, so that Bunbury, who feared the loss of his farm by foreclosure, brought suit against him to recover the money. This seems to have brought about the bitter opposition of the bishop, who in 1872 when visiting the church refused communion to Bunbury, kneeling at the altar rail, and in the presence of the congregation read the sentence of excommunication against him. Bunbury, a loyal Catholic, was greatly distressed by this action, which he thought to be due entirely to his having attempted to sue a bishop of the Church.

Since he was seventy years of age, and shocked by the excommunication which cut him off from the privileges of the Church, he yielded and discontinued the lawsuit. He preferred to lose his money than to lose his standing in the Church; but the painful experience caused him anxiety and anguish and is believed to have hastened his death. The incident created much unfavorable comment, as a result of which a bill designed among other purposes to limit the power of bishops in the matter of excommunication was introduced into the Michigan legislature. It was advocated by a local paper and was actually desired by some of the leading Catholics of the diocese, who felt that an honored man had been outrageously treated and that there should be some public protection against such procedure in the future. This bill passed in spite of the opposition of the bishop and a very active local priest.[34] Since then it has been modified to limit its applicability to cases where a person is excommunicated or threatened with excommunication in order to influence his vote in a public election.

Two other cases might be mentioned in this connection. The first arose in 1822 when a Roman Catholic priest, Father Gabriel Richard, was imprisoned through the efforts of one of his parishioners who had obtained a divorce in a civil court and remarried. The priest had declared him excommunicated, and the man sued for damages to his reputation and business, securing a judgment of $1,116. Father Richard refused to pay this amount and was put in prison until he secured a bondsman. The judgment was eventually reversed.[35]

The second, the case of Bishop William Hickey of Rhode Island, also shows that the Roman Catholic Church is prepared to go to the legal limit to support a bishop against any appeal to the civil courts from his authority. The difficulty arose in the period from 1922 to 1927, when a group of French Canadian Catholics in Providence opposed the Americanization policy of the Church and demanded French-speaking parishes and clergy. The leaders of the movement were excommunicated, but before this action became public, they carried the case to the courts, to the embarrassment of the diocesan authorities. The bishop, as head of the parish corporation, was summoned to render an account of moneys devoted to other than purely parish expenditures. He took the position that this was a matter of Church discipline and not a case for the courts. His plea was denied, but the court decided that the corporation could use its revenues to support Catholic institutions other than those of the parish church.[36]

These cases support the claim of Zollmann that *Watson* v. *Jones* was improvidently decided, and that it would be more consistent with justice and fairness to allow parishioners freely to appeal to the civil courts when they deem themselves wronged by ecclesiastical authorities.

On the other hand, if a civil court were to have the authority to overrule a decision on religious dogma or doctrine made by an authorized body in a particular Church, the civil courts would themselves become ecclesiastical courts. Let us consider a specific case, which, though extreme, nevertheless illustrates what could well happen if the decision in *Watson* v. *Jones* were not followed. A few years ago a Roman Catholic priest in Boston by the name of Leonard Feeney asserted that the dogma "outside the Church there is no salvation" was not being properly interpreted by the local Roman Catholic authorities. Its true meaning, he felt, was the literal one, that is, that no one who has not been actually baptized as a Roman Catholic can ever be saved or enter heaven. With his followers he formed a small group called "Slaves of the Immaculate Conception." Archbishop (later Cardinal) Richard Cushing ordered him to desist and to disband his group. Feeney, however, appealed to the Holy See and, even though it upheld Archbishop Cushing's ruling, persisted. Finally he was unfrocked and ousted from the Church.[37]

The matter ended there, but suppose he had appealed to the civil courts asserting that both the archbishop and the pope himself were in error in interpreting Roman Catholic dogma and that his own interpretation was the correct one? If the rule of *Watson* v. *Jones* were not followed, the civil judge, and perhaps a jury, could decide in his favor and thus overrule the pope on what is true Roman Catholic doctrine. Certainly such a result would not be consistent with religious liberty. For this reason most authorities disagree with Zollmann and are of the opinion that the interests of religious liberty and the separation of Church and State are best served if the principle announced in *Watson* v. *Jones* is strictly adhered to.

That, in any event, is what the Supreme Court held in 1952 in the Russian

Orthodox Church case, *Kedroff* v. *St. Nicholas Cathedral*,[38] summarized in Chapter 5. There the Court held that under the First Amendment's guarantee of religious liberty and the separation of Church and State neither the legislature nor the courts of New York could overrule the determination of the Moscow Patriarchate as to who is the true representative of the Church in the United States and as such entitled to possession of St. Nicholas Cathedral and other Church property. Speaking of *Watson* v. *Jones*, the Court said,

> The opinion radiates . . . a spirit of freedom of religious organizations, an independence from secular control or manipulation, in short power to decide for themselves, free from state interference, matters of church government as well as those of faith and doctrine. Freedom to select the clergy, where no improper methods of choice are proven, we think, must now be said to have federal constitutional protection as a part of the free exercise of religion against state interference.[39]

The Court concluded its opinion with:

> Ours is a government which by the "law of its being" allows no statute, state or national, that prohibits the free exercise of religion. There are occasions when civil courts must draw lines between the responsibilities of church and state for the disposition or use of property. Even in those cases when the property right follows as an incident from decisions of the church custom or law on ecclesiastical issues, the church rule controls. This under our Constitution necessarily follows in order that there may be free exercise of religion.[40]

THE MELISH CASE [41]

Another contemporary case in which the civil courts were involved in church disputes was the nationally publicized controversy between the Episcopal Holy Trinity Church, Brooklyn, New York, its rector, the Reverend John Howard Melish, D.D., a much honored citizen, and the congregation, on one hand, and the vestry, aided by the bishop and the standing committee of the diocese, on the other. The case arose mainly over the activities of the rector's son in various movements that were considered by the vestry to have a left-wing tendency and the father's unwillingness to dismiss him from his position of assistant rector, as directed by the bishop. The matter was long merely a church issue between the Bishop of Long Island, the vestry, and the rector and congregation of Holy Trinity. It had from the beginning significance in the field of the relation of the Church to social questions, and also involved a minister's freedom of conscience. It became an important Church-State issue when the vestry brought the case before the civil courts in the hope of securing a decision that the bishop acted within his legal rights in finally ordering the rector and his son to vacate their offices in the parish.

The case, a complicated one, revealed the following facts. In 1904 the Reverend John Howard Melish of Christ Church, Cincinnati, who had made a reputation both as a parish minister and as a civic reformer, accepted the call to the rectorship of Holy Trinity. He came with the understanding that a free pew system would be established and that as rector he would be expected to play the major part in determining matters of parish policy. During the next thirty-five years Dr. Melish associated himself with many liberal and some rather radical movements and organizations without serious friction with the vestry, whose members were always elected by the congregation on nomination of the rector and the members of the vestry then in office. Among these associations and causes were the Central Labor Union of Brooklyn; the case of the Reverend Algernon Crapsey, accused of unorthodox views on the Virgin Birth; the cause of the Socialist bishop, Frank Spalding of Utah (although Dr. Melish was never himself a Socialist); support of the workers in the steel strike; the Fusion movement, designed to rid New York City of Tammany Hall domination; and defense of his assistant, the Reverend Bradford Young, even though the latter became a Socialist. By many similar affiliations and acts Dr. Melish took the position that the rector was justified as a Christian minister in aiding social betterment causes, even when they were unpopular. He made his parish, in a neighborhood that used to be aristocratic but was lately going downhill economically and socially, into an effective institutional church grappling with new local problems.

During much of this third of a century of his spiritual rectorship and his Christian social welfare work, he was recognized by the Episcopal Church by appointment as secretary of the Joint Commission on Social Service of the General Convention, to which he was on four occasions elected a deputy from Long Island, and in other ways.

In 1939 Reverend William Howard Melish, a graduate of Harvard and Episcopal Theological School, Cambridge, who had studied in England and at the time was associate minister of Christ Church, Cincinnati, where he had made an excellent reputation, received a call as assistant to his father. A contract was entered into that he should have the right of succession upon his father's retirement or death. Mr. Melish soon became active in the work of the diocese, serving as chairman of the Diocesan Department of Christian Social Relations.

In 1942 the Right Reverend James Pernette De Wolfe, dean of the Cathedral of St. John the Divine, was consecrated Bishop of Long Island. Bishop De Wolfe was known as a man of ability and consecration, very conservative in his political and social outlook, and an Anglo-Catholic in churchmanship. He was not sympathetic with the rector of Holy Trinity in his emphasis on social democracy, interdenominational toleration, and a liberal approach to theological problems.

In June, 1946, the assistant minister was elected chairman of the National Council of American-Soviet Friendship. From this time on his outside activities in various organizations were considered by some of the parish to be radical and inclined to favor the Soviets in discussions with the United States. Friction began in the parish.

In 1947 the question of the extent of these outside activities of the assistant minister was brought up for formal discussion at a vestry meeting. The assistant minister presented his side of the case, denying that he was or had been a Communist, and stating that his activities were part of his work as a Christian minister and in no way interfered with the life of the parish.

At a vestry meeting on May 17, 1948, resolutions were formally adopted asking the assistant to resign, and calling on the rector, to whom the assistant minister is canonically responsible, to bring about his resignation. When the two clergymen were unwilling to comply with these resolutions, the matter was referred, by a vote of 7 to 2, with two members absent, to the bishop and the standing committee.

In 1948 Dr. Melish and his son identified themselves actively with Henry Wallace's Progressive party, primarily because they thought it the best way to prevent war with Russia.

During the same year Dr. Melish welcomed an old acquaintance, the Very Reverend Hewlett Johnson of Canterbury, known as "the red Dean," to the pulpit of Holy Trinity.

These various events stirred the bishop and the conservative vestry, and it was evident that things were moving to a crisis.

In December, 1948, the Bishop of Long Island, accompanied by his chancellor, an able and very conservative lawyer, Colonel Jackson Dyckman, made a formal visitation of the parish, as was his right, and met with the rector and the eleven vestrymen. The assistant minister, the accused party, was not invited. The delegation made no statement but listened to the prepared statements of vestry and rector.

Following this visitation, the bishop and chancellor consulted with the standing committee of the diocese, which passed a resolution recommending that both ministers resign their positions. This they declined to do.

The vestry, having been unable to persuade the rector to have his son resign, voted unanimously to send a letter to the members of the parish to find out the extent of the dissension that existed because of the assistant minister's outside activities. The letter was sent out under date of December 15, being officially authorized by all members of the vestry, although the rector stated that it should not be considered as an official act of the vestry, but as a personal act of its members. He added that he approved his son's activities. The letter of inquiry showed that 53 per cent believed that the outside activities of the assistant were detrimental to the parish, 47 per cent felt they were not. Many persons, both liberals and conservatives, disagreed with the wisdom of some of Mr. Melish's public commitments but supported his right as a clergyman to express his reasoned convictions.

In January, 1949, by a vote of 9 to 2 the vestry petitioned the bishop to dissolve the pastoral relation between the rector and the parish, this being in their judgment the only way they could get rid of his assistant, who was canonically subject to the rector.

It should be remembered that at Holy Trinity it had been the tradition for the rector and vestry to nominate candidates for vacancies in the vestry, which in spite of the liberalism of the rector and of the inherited traditions of the parish had been made up for the most part of lawyers and businessmen who looked after the financial and real estate interests of the parish, the spiritual interests and policy being mainly determined by the rector.

In January, 1949, immediately after the vestry's action, "The Committee to Retain the Rector" was formed and 321 signatures were secured to a statement of "utmost affection for Dr. Melish" and opposition to the attitude of the vestry. This new action represented the views of about 70 per cent of the legal membership of the parish. It was transmitted to the vestry and the bishop with the hope expressed that diocesan action might be deferred until the parish meeting.

On March 2, 1949, a message was received by the rector from the bishop containing the bishop's "judgment" that as Dr. Melish was unwilling to abide by the decision of the bishop and standing committee, the pastoral relationship be dissolved by April 4, two weeks before the stated annual meeting of the parish. This judgment was accompanied by a memorandum and a report of the standing committee which sustained the charge that there was serious "dissension" in the parish because the rector would not remove his son as assistant rector in spite of the latter's "detrimental outside activities."

On March 7, 1949, a parish meeting was called to consider the removal of the nine vestrymen who had voted for Dr. Melish's removal. Three hundred and fifty parishioners attended, and the vote for removal of the vestrymen was 261 for, 27 against.

On March 13, 1949, a meeting was called to fill the vacancies in the vestry, since under the Religious Corporations Act of the state of New York this is necessary when no vestry quorum exists. Anticipating this action, the deposed vestrymen filed papers in court for a restraining order to prevent the holding of a special election and asked that they be reinstated. The judge issued a temporary injunction holding everything in status quo pending court action.

On April 16, 1949, Justice Meir Steinbrink of the New York Supreme

Court held a formal trial. The vestry through their counsel laid emphasis on the "dissension" in the parish. They asked the court to declare the special meeting illegal, to forbid a new election, to sustain them in the exercise of their offices, and to enforce the bishop's judgment. The counsel for the bishop and standing committee took a similar stand, declaring that a vestry was the corporate body in an Episcopal church, and alone entitled to act in such matters.

The judge decided in favor of the bishop, the standing committee, and the vestry, taking the ground that under the canons they had acted legally; that the meeting called to remove the nine vestrymen had been illegally called; that the "dissension" in the parish and the refusal to obey the order of the bishop and standing committee were serious matters; and that their order removing the rector as of April 4 stood. He further issued a permanent injunction restraining the defendants from interfering with the vestry. The judge's ruling was based upon the decision in *Watson* v. *Jones*; since the bishop was the highest ecclesiastical judicatory under Protestant Episcopal canon law, his removal of Dr. Melish could not be interfered with by the civil courts.

The decision was appealed to the state's highest court, which affirmed it. A petition was then filed with the United States Supreme Court asking it to review the decision. In support of the petition a brief as "friend of the court" was filed by 2,576 Protestant clergymen of all denominations and from all states, including a large number of bishops, faculty members of divinity schools, and prominent Church leaders. However, the Supreme Court, without giving any reasons, refused to review the decision of the New York court, thus upholding the bishop's action but leaving the entire situation in a rather unsatisfactory state. This affair dragged on for about a decade when it came to an end by reason of the fact that the social, racial, and religious complexion of the neighborhood changed so radically that the Holy Trinity Church was closed down entirely.

OTHER CASES OF CHURCH DISPUTES

It was the same principle of *Watson* v. *Jones*—that the courts will not intervene in the internal affairs of religious organizations or undertake to decide questions of ecclesiastical law, organization, or discipline—that led the courts in 1957 to refuse to interfere with the union of the General Council of the Congregational Christian Churches and the Evangelical and Reformed Church even though this was an unprecedented joinder, at least in the United States, of churches with differing forms of Church government—Congregational and modified Presbyterian—and with different historical backgrounds.

To complete this section, reference ought also to be made to a class of instances in which American Jews, like Protestants and Roman Catholics, have sought to invoke the State's judicial machinery to decide internal disputes regarding doctrine and practice. The rules of Orthodox Judaism require that in synagogues men and women sit in different sections during services, with a curtain or other partition separating the two sections. Reform and Conservative Jewry follow the custom, familiar to most Americans, of having the family, or at least the adult members, sit together. In many communities the younger generation of Orthodox Jews have, upon acquiring a majority of the membership in an Orthodox congregation, passed resolutions for the introduction of mixed seating. In a number of instances the older members have gone to court for an injunction against this change on the ground that it would violate the doctrines of Orthodox Judaism.

While in a few cases courts have issued such an injunction, in the better-considered cases the courts have refused to do so and have followed the rule that in independent or non-hierarchical churches, such as Jewish congregations (and Baptist, Quaker, Unitarian, and other churches in Protestantism), a majority of the membership is the highest ecclesiastical authority and its determination may not be overruled by a civil court. The following short decision of the Supreme Judicial Court of Massachusetts, issued in May, 1962, in the case of *Solomon* v. *Congregation Tiffereth Israel*, is typical of these rulings:

> The plaintiffs, members of the defendant synagogue, "an orthodox Jewish Congregation," bring this bill in equity against the synagogue and its officers. They allege that "in violation of the Mosaic law" the members have "voted to introduce mixed seating within the synagogue." They allege that this action "will deprive the plaintiffs and the adhering members of the congregation of their property rights in the Synagogue as adhering orthodox members of the congregation, as it was originally organized," and pray that mixed seating be enjoined. The defendants filed a "plea to the jurisdiction" on the ground that the questions raised are exclusively ecclesiastical. The "plea" was sustained by an interlocutory decree. A final decree was entered dismissing the bill, and the plaintiffs appealed. . . . It is not the province of civil courts to enter the domain of religious denominations for the purpose of deciding controversies touching matters exclusively ecclesiastical. There was no error.

Incorporation and Tenure of Church Property

In general, churches today are not incorporated by special act of the legislature but under general laws which have to do with various charitable, literary, and religious corporations.[42] This also applies to Churches as denominations.

Such corporations are constituted in different ways in different states. Indeed, the same state frequently provides for several methods acceptable to different ecclesiastical organizations. For instance, provision is often made for vestries in the Episcopal Church; for the corporation sole in the Roman Catholic Church; for the presiding elder and a majority of the district stewards in the Methodist Church; or for trustees (as distinct from deacons, who look after spiritual concerns) in many independently organized churches. These are the boards and officers competent to transact financial affairs with whom the law deals.

The State deals with such an incorporated religious body only in temporal concerns. Certain features are generally recognized, such as that each church or religious organization must be known to the law as a body corporate; that the lay element must at least be represented on it when it is not a corporation sole; and that the incorporated body is restricted in its annual income from real and personal property, and in the total of its property exempt from taxation. The State also restricts in various ways the activities of churches—that is, local religious corporations—with a view to keeping them strictly within their religious, moral, philanthropic, and educational fields, and sometimes preventing their competition, as exempt from taxation, with ordinary business interests.

The question of the tenure of church property often involves difficult ecclesiastical questions into which the courts enter reluctantly. The matter is specially complicated in relations with the Roman Catholic Church, which does not favor the ordinary American custom of tenure of property by lay trustees, preferring to have it vest in the hierarchy. This difference between the American custom and the tradition of the Church—and both have been somewhat modified to meet the situation in America—sometimes resulted, especially in early days, in disputes between the ecclesiastical authorities on the one hand, who wished to observe strictly the canon law, and lay trustees on the other, ending in appeals by the trustees to the courts.

Zollmann thus summarizes the general situation in the United States:

> It is now apparent that there are three forms of church corporations in full bloom in the states of the Union. Of these the corporation sole serves the necessities of those churches who believe in vesting their bishops or similar dignitaries with large discretion in matters of property. The trustee corporation is adapted to the needs of those churches who are somewhat more democratic without being congregational, while the membership corporation represents the triumph of democratic government in church affairs and fills the wants of those churches which vest the complete control of church property directly in the congregations.[43]

With this general status of church incorporation in mind we must now consider historically one important phase of it which required two generations

of tact and trial and error by both Church and State before a mutually satisfactory and workable adjustment was reached.

The early incorporation laws of New York and other states requiring lay
trustee boards, or boards on which the laity were at least represented, caused
special problems in the Roman Catholic Church. There was a very difficult
adjustment to be made—that between the ecclesiastical control plan common
in the Roman Catholic Church in Europe, and contemplated by the canon
law, and the American lay trustee system. We have already traced the attempts
to introduce the latter and have seen the opposition of the hierarchy to it, and
its determination, backed by Rome, to change to some form of ecclesiastical
control of church property more in keeping with the European tradition of
the Church.[44] We are now to see the virtual accomplishment of this purpose,
at least in principle, in the changes adopted during the nineteenth century.

Bishop John England of Charleston favored a full trial of the trustee system
with some controls that he thought would prevent abuses, but the decision of
the 1829 Provincial Council practically recommended that all churches built
thereafter should wherever possible be deeded to the bishop.[45] At the Second
Provincial Council (1833) a decree was for the first time promulgated in
America giving a Catholic prelate, the Archbishop of Baltimore, the powers of
a corporation sole.

A leading authority on the history of incorporation of Catholic Church property in the United States, discussing this action, says,

> The obvious advantages of the corporation sole for the Catholic Church, in the
> light of the troubles of the preceding half century, were very great. On the one
> hand the delicate problem of the transmission of diocesan property, when held in
> absolute fee simple title by the bishop, was eliminated. On the other, episcopal
> jurisdiction, the corner-stone of Catholic discipline, was safeguarded by the civil
> law.[46]

But lay trusteeship died hard. In the First Plenary Council of Baltimore
(1852), the hierarchy, with the difficult situation in mind, decreed,

> We warn priests who administer churches, the title to which has been given
> to the bishop, not to constitute lay-trustees without episcopal sanction, or permit
> them to be elected by the faithful, lest an impediment arise to their free
> administration.[47]

It became increasingly evident that no plan would satisfy both Catholic
tradition and American requirements except some form of incorporation and
trusteeship giving large powers to the hierarchy in the holding of Church
property. There now developed to meet this situation a variation of the corporation sole plan known as "the corporation aggregate." This plan, first adopted

by the New York legislature in 1863 but since then followed in many other states, "implies that the church members as a whole are the incorporators, as distinct from the trustees, and the latter fill the role of business managers of the corporation," [48] the officers being like the directors of a banking establishment. The bishop, the vicar general, and the pastor are the ex-officio members, and they appoint two additional lay members. Furthermore, the laws of the state provide that no acts of trustees are valid without the consent of the bishop or archbishop. Thus we have in essence the *fabrique* system of Europe, in which proprietary rights cannot be claimed in opposition to ecclesiastical authority.

From the Church standpoint, the situation in the country at large regarding incorporation and trusteeship was not yet satisfactory in spite of the wide influence of the New York incorporation law and the previous actions of the various councils of Baltimore. Finding that the principles of the canon law were still not generally recognized and that the Church could not always enforce its claims, the Second Plenary Council (1870) found it necessary to assert that

In order to obtain protection from the improper interference of lay tribunals, which in practice scarcely acknowledge the ecclesiastical laws, nothing now remains to the bishops for carrying out ecclesiastical decrees but to claim for themselves the fullest administration of property before the civil power. As, however, church regulations are not acknowledged as yet in some States, it is our duty to see that in those places where no provision has been made by the civil law, the impediments to the liberty of the Church and to the security of ecclesiastical property be removed or diminished.[49]

The Third Plenary Council (1884) further considered the same matter:

On account of the grave dangers to which temporal goods are often exposed when bishops are not allowed to control them according to the prescriptions of the Church, it is much to be regretted that in many parts of the United States the civil laws concerning the possession and administration of temporal goods rest upon principles which the Church cannot admit without departing from the rule which she has always held from the time when she first became free to put her religious principles into practice.[50]

To obviate these difficulties the Church at this council again favored some system by which ecclesiastical property is held in the name of the archbishop or bishop, acting as corporation sole or as a trustee or in fee simple in his own name. It did, however, provide in certain cases for trustees—generally (as in New York) the ordinary, vicar general, rector, and two laymen approved by the bishop—but in such a way as to give the bishop final authority in case of any dispute.[51]

The problems regarding church tenure and the opposition of the hierarchy to appeals in such matters to the civil courts led to a pronouncement by the

Holy See in 1911 in an attempt to settle the controversy. It adopted "the corporation aggregate," composed of the bishop, vicar general, and pastor, as the preferable form for holding parish property, but also recognized the bishop as corporation sole, acting after due consultation with others concerned, as a legitimate method of administration.

A few of the older parishes and a considerable number of charitable institutions are still under lay trustees working in close co-operation with a bishop, but new incorporations of parishes are under one of the three methods authorized in 1884 or 1911. The ownership or control of educational institutions is frequently in the name of a religious society, order, or congregation. A few, like the University of Notre Dame, have an associated board of lay trustees which administers the finances.

It will be seen that there have been not only differences of opinion within the Church between ecclesiastical authority and democratic-minded lay Catholic churchmen, but occasionally, albeit decreasingly, actual conflict between the Church and local trustees. As some states require for incorporation a group of five or more responsible residents and do not recognize the exact forms favored by the Vatican, and as the Catholic layman in America is often inclined to favor the American practice of effective non-clerical representation on trustee boards and is entirely willing to refer decisions in disputed matters to the civil courts, the question is one which may still cause friction between Church and State.

The question of Federal incorporation of church property early came before Congress, which in 1811 passed a bill to incorporate an Episcopal church in Alexandria, then in the District of Columbia. In February, 1811, President James Madison, always a strong supporter of the complete separation of Church and State, vetoed the measure on the ground that

The bill exceeds the rightful authority to which governments are limited by the essential distinction between civil and religious functions, and violates in particular the article of the Constitution of the United States which declares that "Congress shall make no law respecting a religious establishment." The bill enacts into and establishes by law sundry rules and proceedings relative purely to the organization and policy of the church incorporated, and comprehending even the election and removal of the minister of the same, so that no change could be made therein by the particular society or by the general church of which it is a member, and whose authority it recognizes. This particular church, therefore, would so far be a religious establishment by law, a legal force and sanction being given to certain articles in its constitution and administration.[52]

This message created a precedent which has been generally followed by Congress, although there have been occasional deviations, as, for example, in the chartering of a corporation, composed of nuns, to operate the Providence Hospital (see *Bradfield* v. *Roberts* in Chapter 5), the incorporation of American University, a Methodist college, in 1893,[53] and the incorporation of the Convention of the Protestant Episcopal Diocese of Washington in 1896.[54]

Tax Exemption for Churches

There is a fairly general agreement in the United States—outside of perhaps a few radical groups—that the property of incorporated educational institutions not conducted for private gain should be exempt from taxation. The same principle is applied by most Americans to churches, to church schools, and to certain other forms of church property, such as burial grounds. According to a 1937 study, such exemption from taxation is required by about one-third of our state constitutions and authorized by another third, while the remainder—mostly constitutions adopted in the early years when exemption was taken for granted—make no specific mention of the subject. The exemption does not generally include property held for investment purposes.

The exemption from taxation of churches, and of the land immediately about them used for church purposes, is based on a European tradition going back to the fourth century, when the Emperor Constantine the Great, after his conversion, gave the Church this privilege.

The grounds on which exemptions are based have been well stated in a decision of the Nebraska Supreme Court in 1890:

Exemptions are granted on the hypothesis that the association or organization is of benefit to society, that it promotes the social and moral welfare, and, to some extent, is bearing burdens that would otherwise be imposed upon the public to be met by general taxation.

The particular institution concerned in this case was the Y.M.C.A. of Omaha, but the same reasoning has often been applied in cases involving churches.

The exemption of church property was so generally recognized in the early days of the republic that in some states no special exemption laws were passed until near the middle of the nineteenth century. Massachusetts did not have such a law until 1837, or New Hampshire until 1842. Then it seemed best to stabilize custom by legislation. Constitutional provisions followed in many of the states, and now churches are everywhere exempted either by constitutions or by statutes.[55]

The general principle of exemption of religious property from taxation [56] is opposed by many individuals and groups on the ground that it is an indirect subsidy to religion, that even this form of aid by the State is a dangerous precedent, and that the Church would be in a stronger moral position if it gave up every form of special privilege. These opponents of exemption feel that it is inconsistent with the separation of Church and State. They acknowledge that it was justifiable in the colonies when there was an Established Church, but not today under our Federal and state constitutions. They regard it as an inheritance from colonial times without adequate present-day justification and believe that the State should be allowed to tax religious institutions, if not churches themselves, with a view to increasing revenue. The most important utterance by a representative public officer raising the question of possible changes in policy in this matter was by President Grant, in his seventh message to Congress. "I would suggest," he said, "the taxation of all property equally, whether church or corporation, exempting only the last resting place of the dead, and possibly, with proper restrictions, church edifices." [57] This view has a good deal of support from some secular organizations and from a few Church leaders. It has never gained large public support and is denounced with vigor by the authorities of the Roman Catholic Church.

Among the Church representatives who have officially questioned the wisdom of tax exemption may be mentioned the Evangelical Lutheran Church South Minnesota District, representing some 140,000 members. In 1947 it authorized the study of a recommendation by a committee of its pastoral conference which declared that "developments throughout the world have made it imperative that the Christian religion, and all religions, make themselves completely free of all obligations of debt, except that of service, to any state or government." The resolution referred to the then recent decision of the Supreme Court declaring constitutional the free school bus law of New Jersey permitting the public school buses to carry pupils of parochial schools, which "made it incumbent upon the Protestant church to examine its own position over against the State." [58]

The question of taxing Church property has been brought to the attention of the religious public from time to time by The Christian Century. For example, on April 9, 1947, it published a forceful editorial entitled "Churches Should Pay Taxes." This is a position which its former editor, Dr. Charles Clayton Morrison, long advocated, though receiving little Church support. He made a distinction between such "eleemosynary" institutions as hospitals, which, he thought, might still be exempted, and church buildings and their schools, whose taxation he advocated, believing that they should not receive this form of indirect subsidy from the State. Later Dr. Morrison debated the matter in Look magazine with Joseph V. McKee, then counsel for the Roman Catholic diocese of New York. The latter took the ground that the amount of Church property exempt from taxation was only a slight fraction of total exemptions, and that the United States "has long recognized the need to encourage, not handicap, those instrumentalities which foster and inculcate the principles of mercy, religion and charity," and which through their ethical teachings are a great public asset "in the field of public order." [59]

The position taken by Dr. Morrison has continued to be expressed in the editorial pages of *The Christian Century* up to the present time. It has been echoed by some other influential religious leaders, almost entirely Protestant. For example, the Reverend Dr. Eugene Carson Blake, chief executive officer of the United Presbyterian Church and a former president of the National Council of Churches, urged in the August 3, 1959, issue of *Christianity Today* that churches pay some taxes on their real estate. Dr. Edwin T. Dahlberg, then president of the National Council of Churches, supported Dr. Blake's recommendation that churches start to pay 1 per cent of the amount they would pay if their property were assessed, increasing this contribution by 1 per cent a year to a ceiling of 10 per cent.

Advocates of the status quo point out that the State loses less than it gains by the exemptions, in that churches, parochial schools, and other Church institutions save the State much money in educating youth under inspiring ethical and religious auspices; and that these institutions contribute enormously to the moral standards of the community, thereby ultimately relieving the State treasury of excessive contributions to reformatory and penal institutions. They call special attention to the fact that the total amount of taxes actually lost is relatively small. For instance, in the well-known case of Trinity Churchyard in New York, the exemption is made up by the increased value of adjoining real estate dut to the large open space.

It is also appropriate to quote here the section on tax exemption in the report "Relations Between Church and State" adopted by the 175th General Assembly of the United Presbyterian Church in May, 1963:

The Special Committee on Church and State recommends that:

1. The United Presbyterians study the nature of our Church's involvement in economic activity and seek ways by which it can begin the process of extricating itself from the position of being obligated, or seeming to be obligated, to the state by virtue of special tax privileges extended to it.

2. The United Presbyterian Church carefully examine its national and local related business enterprises to assure itself that under present tax laws these enterprises are not unfairly competitive with secular businesses operating in the same fields. To this end the Committee suggests that the General Assembly authorize the Stated Clerk to canvass the boards, agencies, institutions, and judicatories to determine the extent of their economic involvement subject to tax exemption and to report to the General Council of the United Presbyterian Church, which is to report to a future General Assembly.

3. The United Presbyterian Church begin efforts to obtain repeal of the section of the Internal Revenue Code that allows "churches and church organiza-

tions" exemption from the corporate income tax on profits from businesses un-related, or only remotely related, to the purpose or activity of the church or church organization.

4. The local churches take the initiative in making contributions to local communities, in lieu of taxes, in recognition of police, fire, and other services provided by local government. This consideration commends itself especially to well-established and financially stable churches and particularly to those in communities where tax problems are developing due, in part, to the increase in exempted properties for all purposes—educational, governmental, charitable, and religious.

5. The state expect no *quid pro quo* from the church in recognition of exemption granted by the state; and that the church expect no *quid pro quo* from the state, as though the state owed the church some kind of special consideration in response to voluntary contributions in lieu of taxes.

On the other hand, President Charles W. Eliot of Harvard University, in a public address in 1906, thus defended the general form of exemption of taxation of church, philanthropic, and educational property:

We have learned that reservations from taxation are not burdensome, wasteful things, but, on the contrary, that they are highly profitable and precious things; and that the question really is not how few reservations a community can get along with, but how many they can indulge in. The long and the short of it is, gentlemen, that the things which make it worth while to live in Massachusetts,—to live anywhere in the civilized world,—the precisely the things which are not taxed; the things exempted are the things which are in the highest degree profitable to the community, the colleges, museums, churches, schools, hospitals, courts, libraries, gardens, commons, parks. Let nobody persuade you for a moment that these invaluable reservations from taxation are a burden on the public; they are what makes the common life worth living.[60]

That this exemption is an indirect form of subsidy cannot be denied, but to many it seems a far wiser one than direct financial grants. It has a long history and many sound reasons of public policy to support it.

Dr. John C. Bennett, dean of Union Theological Seminary, has suggested that tax exemption, which he calls "the most remarkable of all forms of aid to all religious bodies," is "good for the State perhaps more than for the Church," for it signalizes the high place given to religion in our democratic society.[61]

Another defense of tax exemption was asserted in the May-June, 1962, issue of *Religious Liberty* in an article by Professor Daniel Walthar on "Tax Exemption and the Church." The author, after writing about possible abuses of tax exemption by the churches, concludes,

Church property *per se* must remain tax free. To lay a tax on churches would enhance the power of the State; it would enable the State to control the churches and would certainly be contrary to the basic principle of church-state separation.

The State that has ever-increasing need of financial resources might jeopardize the church's ability to operate as an effective agency. Moreover, church taxation would enable only wealthy churches to subsist.

There was much legitimate criticism in early days when exemptions were made by private bills passed by the legislature, but now the general custom is to have all exemption provisions brought into a general law such as was enacted in New York. This state in 1901 amended its constitution so that the legislature could no longer continue its former practice of passing private or local bills granting to private corporations exemptions from taxation on real or personal property.[62]

The question of tax exemption for religious institutions has been somewhat acute in several places during recent years. The commissioners of the District of Columbia, wishing to increase the revenue in 1940, began the process of placing on the tax rolls property belonging to churches which in their judgment was not definitely used for church purposes. They decided to remove the exemption on certain buildings (not churches) and on what was believed to be "excess" land belonging to religious, educational, and charitable institutions which were otherwise tax exempt. Within a few months, as a result of the report of a committee of District officials, some $2,000,000 of church property was made taxable, including property of thirteen Roman Catholic religious orders, the American University (Methodist), and some of the grounds adjoining Washington Cathedral (Episcopal).[63]

In the case of the cathedral, the action removed the exemption from twenty-two acres, or about one-third of the cathedral close. The Real Estate Tax Exemption Board stated in its findings that the cathedral itself was properly exempt as church property, but that "the right of exemption does not carry with it the privilege of having church acreage of land adjacent thereto exempt from taxes."[64] If this decision had held, the cathedral would have been obliged to pay an additional tax of about $10,000 a year. The commissioners stated that "their action must be more or less arbitrary in determining what is 'excess' land holdings since the exact standards are lacking."[65]

Although many religious leaders felt that there was a good deal to be said in favor of taxing grounds about religious institutions that are not generally available for public use or essential for an institution's religious work, others believed the commissioners had gone too far. Representative John F. Hunter of Ohio and Senator Patrick McCarran of Nevada therefore introduced legislation in Congress to relieve churches from property taxation.

An able report describing and supporting the measure was presented to the House by the Committee on the District of Columbia. It called attention to the fact that only those private institutions were exempt which were non-profit.

In consequence, the bill was passed by Congress on the consent calendar and signed by the president in December, 1942. This virtually re-established tax exemption of church properties on the basis which had existed before January 1, 1941, when the campaign of the commissioners to secure new revenue resulted in assessment of the taxes mentioned above.

Because the attempts of the commissioners to collect taxes from religious institutions during 1941 and 1942 were among the most serious made in any American community in modern times, the fact that they were overruled by Congress is highly significant. In this connection, it is worthy of record that the vote on the bill in the Senate and House was on the general consent calendar, implying no serious objection.

On the other hand, it should be noted that in recent years tax exemption has become an increasingly difficult problem for public taxing authorities and for the general public as well. To what many feel is an alarming extent, formerly taxable property and income is being transferred to tax exempt funds, foundations, and institutions, so that other citizens and property are required to carry an ever-increasing portion of the total tax burden. Where the non-profit organization employs its resources for such social welfare services as hospitals, old-age homes, etc., there is reasonable justification for the tax exemption in that if the private organization did not supply the services the government would have to do it, so that to that extent the taxpayer is relieved of what would otherwise be a larger tax burden. In the case of churches, however, this justification is not applicable, for the Constitution forbids the government from setting up churches even should private contributions for that purpose fail.

In this respect, the zoning question, which has been discussed earlier in this chapter, becomes complicated. In quite a number of cases, community ordinances restricting the acquisition of real estate by churches have been motivated in substantial part by the fact that the consequences of such acquisition would be the narrowing of the taxable base, and thus an increased tax burden for other taxpayers. Moreover, the situation is aggravated because the erection of a church or church school has the effect of requiring additional and costly governmental services, such as added police, fire, and safety protection.[66]

On the whole it cannot be said that the question of either the wisdom or the morality of tax exemption for churches is entirely one-sided. Yet it can hardly be doubted that the overwhelming majority of Americans favor the principle of tax exemption for religious groups along with charitable and educational organizations.

The United States Supreme Court has not written a definitive decision on the question of the constitutionality under the First Amendment of tax exemption for churches. On two occasions in recent years, however, it has refused to review state laws granting such exemption. One of these arose in California, where for many years the practice had been to grant exemption from taxation to private educational institutions on the college or university level but not on the primary or secondary school level, a distinction not followed in any other state. Since 90 per cent of children who attend non-public elementary and secondary schools are Roman Catholic, the effect of this distinction appeared to most persons in California to be discriminatory. In any event, after a protracted and bitter campaign, in which there were charges on the one hand of Catholic pressure and power politics and on the other of anti-Catholic bigotry, in 1952 the people of California adopted an amendment removing the distinction and making church schools below the college level likewise exempt from taxation.[67] The constitutionality of this change was challenged in the state courts on the ground that it violated the principle of Church-State separation. The California Supreme Court, however, ruled in favor of the constitutionality of the new provision,[68] and the United States Supreme Court, without writing any opinion, dismissed an appeal from the ruling.[69]

Six years later, in 1962, the Supreme Court again refused to review a state court decision upholding tax exemption for churches. This involved a suit by a financial corporation owning taxable real estate in Cranston, Rhode Island. It brought suit in the state courts, asserting that the exemption from taxation enjoyed by property owned by churches was unconstitutional and if this property were added to the tax rolls its own tax burden would be reduced. The Rhode Island courts upheld the constitutionality of the exemption and dismissed the corporation's suit.[70] A petition to the United States Supreme Court to review that decision was denied without opinion,[71] and in the light of this action and its action in the California case it is safe to assume that the Supreme Court will not in the immediate future declare unconstitutional tax exemption of churches and religious organizations.

This section on tax exemption may be well concluded with a quotation from the recently published book *Religion, the Courts, and Public Policy* by Robert F. Drinan, S.J. While Father Drinan, dean of the Jesuit Boston College Law School, writes from a (liberal) Catholic viewpoint, it is certain that many thoughtful non-Catholics would agree with his views on this and other questions. Indeed, on some matters it is quite possible that Father Drinan's views would be accepted more hospitably among non-Catholics than among the more conservative elements within the Roman Catholic church. Father Drinan writes (pp. 9, 10),

No entirely satisfactory rationale for tax exemption has ever been stated in any American judicial decision. It may be that the only possible ultimate justification is a public policy consciously encouraging religion as a valuable aid to good citizenship. Courts and commentators quite understandably are reluctant to reach such ultimates and, if they must give a plausible reason for tax immunity for religious bodies, tend to urge one of the three following justifications:

1. Tax exemption for churches and related institutions has always existed in American law; in fact, it can be traced back to Constantine or even to the Talmud, according to which rabbis were given certain tax exemptions.

2. Churches, by means of the educational programs which they sponsor, participate in the work of the state and thereby relieve it of some of its burdens.

3. No court decision in American jurisprudence has ever ruled that tax exemption to religious groups is a discrimination against nonbelievers.

However popular and widely accepted these reasons may be, the fact is that American courts have never carefully scrutinized the implications of the complex structure of tax-exemption benefits upon religious bodies in America. The American judiciary has not even raised the hard questions, much less resolved them. The extent of the benefits granted to religion by tax exemption are almost beyond calculation; some indication of the amount of direct subsidy available to churches can be seen in the exemption of church-operated cemeteries, the revenues from which not infrequently supply one of the main sources of financing for many parishes. If the trend toward the establishment of an absolute separation of church and state is to continue, it would seem logical to predict that the constitutionality of tax exemption may be challenged. By an inexplicable paradox, however, such does not appear to be the case. Except for the voices of some extremists and the urgings of some sincerely troubled religionists, tax exemption for religious purposes seems today to be as securely guaranteed as at any time in American history.

The Exemption and Special Privileges of Clergymen

Earlier we have considered certain legal restrictions on the political office holding of clergymen which have existed from time to time in certain states. Here we are concerned merely with special privileges which ministers of religion as such enjoy. Since there is no Established Church in the United States, all the special privileges of Anglican (Episcopal) clergymen in England have been discontinued. The only survivals apply to all ministers of religion alike, whether Jew, Catholic, Protestant, or other. And these, though important, are relatively few. For instance, it takes a chapter of some twenty-four pages of Blackstone's *Commentaries on the Laws of England,* originally published 1765-69, to enumerate the special rights "Of the Clergy," and a study of these shows the clear-cut line of differentiation between the "two kinds" of people in England— the clergy and the laity.[72] There is, of course, no such general distinction recognized by the State here. Similarly, the right of excommunication is in this country an ecclesiastical matter without any effect on the civil rights of the excommunicated. A person may be prevented by it from participating in the sacraments or in public worship and may be denied participation in formal, legal acts of the Church, but it cannot deprive him of the right of political suffrage or of holding public office.

But ministers of religion, just because they are the servants of religious bodies devoting their time to the conduct of worship and works of education and mercy, are granted certain exemptions by the State. For instance, they are exempted from state or local poll taxes in most of the Southern states which still impose such taxes.[73] In New York State a clergyman of any denomination engaged in work assigned by his church enjoys (as does his widow during her lifetime) a partial exemption on his real property to the extent of diminishing the assessed taxable valuation of the property by $1,500.[74]

Furthermore, rectories, manses, and other residences of clergymen when attached to parishes or incorporated educational institutions are generally exempt from taxation. There are also a few states, such as Louisiana, where certain tax exemptions are accorded personally to ministers in good and regular standing. With these exceptions, however, clergymen as such are generally not exempt from taxation. The law of New Hampshire, as passed in 1816, may be considered typical of practice under the republic:

That the real and personal estates of all ordained ministers of the gospel of every denomination, within this State, shall hereafter be assessed and taxed in the same way and manner as other estates are now, or hereafter may by law be taxed; any law, usage or custom to the contrary notwithstanding.[75]

Several state constitutions, such as those of Florida, Kansas, Oregon, and Tennessee, exempt citizens from militia duty on account of religious duties on such conditions as the legislature may decide,[76] and the United States Supreme Court upheld in World War I the selective draft law which exempted clergymen, theological students, and the adherents of sects which consider the bearing of arms to be sinful.[77] In World War II they were also specifically exempted.[78]

Ministers as such are generally exempt from jury duty, presumably on the ground that jury service might interfere, as in the case of physicians, with their important regular responsibilities and duties. New York State is typical, where the list of exemptions for "service as a trial juror" begins with "A clergyman or minister of religion officiating as such and not following any other calling." [79]

In the absence of a specific statutory exemption, clergymen must serve as jurors equally with other citizens. Moreover, in 1963 the Supreme Court of Minnesota, in the case of In re Jenison, ruled that a woman who believed that she would be violating the mandate of Jesus, "Judge not, so you will not be judged," if she served as a juror could nevertheless be punished for contempt of court if she refused to serve, and that her religious beliefs must yield to her obligations as a citizen. However, the United States Supreme Court ordered reconsideration of the decision by the Minnesota Supreme Court, and the latter, on reconsideration, changed its decision and exonerated this conscientious woman.

Mention should also be made of an indirect quasi-public survival of the early favored status of clergymen. In some parts of the country ordained ministers who are engaged exclusively in religious work, as well as sisters of charity and certain other groups, are entitled to secure an annual clergy fare certificate which permits the purchase of transportation on ordinary trains at considerable reductions. These certificates are of course not issued by the state but by the clergy bureaus of railroad passenger associations in various sections of the country. Their legal authorization, however, goes back to the Interstate Commerce Act of 1887, which in trying to eliminate the abuses of the free-pass system on railroads especially exempted the clergy from its prohibitions.[80]

The Seal of the Confessional

The question of the sacredness of confessions made to a priest has frequently been a matter of judicial consideration. In general, what is called the "seal of the confessional" has been recognized by the civil courts, though by the old common law confessions were not considered privileged. New York is said to have been the first of all English-speaking states from the time of the Reformation to protect by its courts and laws the secrecy and sanctity of auricular confession.[81] The decision was made in June, 1813, by De Witt Clinton, then presiding in the mayor's court in New York City. It was judicially determined that auricular confession, being a recognized part of Church discipline, protects a priest from being compelled in a court of law to testify as to statements made to him in the confessional. Many states, following this decision, specifically protect a priest against the necessity of disclosing confessions made to him in confidence and in his professional capacity. In some states a characteristic provision is that found in an Arkansas statute:

No minister of the gospel or priest of any denomination shall be compelled to testify in relation to any confession made to him in his professional character, in the course of discipline by the rules or practice of such denomination.[82]

In other states, such as Michigan and New York, the provision goes even farther and substitutes the word "allowed" for "compelled," which means that even if the clergyman were willing to testify concerning the confession made to him and none of the attorneys objected to the testimony, the court would still have to forbid him to do so.

There are states with no specific legislation, but attempts are extremely rare where any responsible court tries to compel a priest to disclose knowledge gained through the confessional. Perhaps the most interesting case that has come before the courts was in Richmond, Virginia, in 1855, when the vicar general, the Very Reverend John Teeling, D.D., was summoned to testify against a man who had fatally wounded his wife. The vicar general had taken her confession as she was dying and was ordered to reveal it. He replied, "Any statement made in her sacramental confession whether inculpatory or exculpatory of the prisoner, I am not at liberty to reveal." [83] The presiding judge of the circuit court then gave a decision in which he said,

I regard any infringement upon the tenets of any denomination as a violation of the fundamental law, which guarantees perfect freedom to all classes in the exercise of their religion. To encroach upon the confessional, which is well understood to be a fundamental tenet in the Catholic church, would be to ignore the Bill of Rights, so far as it is applicable to that Church. In view of these circumstances, as well as of other considerations connected with the subject, I feel no hesitation in ruling that a priest enjoys a privilege of exemption from revealing what is communicated to him in the confessional.[84]

The records of the court were lost in the Civil War, and little information is available about either the defendant or the priest. Hence, it cannot be said what the ultimate outcome of the trial was or whether the defendant was convicted and executed. It should be noted that the priest refused to testify even if the testimony would have been "exculpatory of the prisoner." In thise circumstances it can hardly be said that the moral issue was clearly in favor of upholding the execution of a man for a crime he never committed. Nevertheless, there is no exception made in the law in respect to exculpatory confessions, and in general the courts hold that the confidence which was recognized by the English common law as existing between lawyer and client should also exist between physician and patient and between priest as confessor and his parishioner or other penitent. This applies not only to the Roman Catholic Church with its regular confessional but to similar confidence between non-Catholic clergymen, when acting as such, and their parishioners.

Bequests to Churches and for Masses

In England centuries ago statutes were adopted to prevent ecclesiastical abuses in respect to land, especially the undue growth of large landed estates in the control of monasteries and other religious houses. Statutes of mortmain severely restricted such ecclesiastical alienation. We have, for instance, the Statute *de Religioso*, enacted in 1279 during the reign of Edward I; the Act of 1391, which forbade alienation to any ecclesiastical corporation, except under a royal license; and the Act of 1736 which declared wills for charitable purposes void except under certain conditions.

These ancient statutes have retained their influence in this country,[85] and some states still have on their books laws limiting, either by value or by acreage, the amount of real estate a church may own.[86]

In general, mortmain provisions, when they exist, apply only to the churches, that is, to religious corporations whose members meet regularly for worship in some definite place, and are not extended to such related church organizations as church colleges, missionary societies, publishing firms, synods, etc.[87]

A matter involving bequests where Church and State occasionally meet has to do with the requirement of certain formalities to validate the transfer of property on the part of persons at the point of death by gift or bequest for charitable or religious uses. To prevent the undue influence of priests on persons near death, some states have adopted detailed legislation invalidating bequests to religious or philanthropic institutions made under these conditions. The code of the District of Columbia may be taken as characteristic.

Section 1635. *Bequests for Religious Purposes.*—No devise or bequest of lands, or goods, or chattels to any minister, public teacher, or preacher of the gospel, as such, or to any religious sect, order or denomination, or to or for the support, use, or benefit of or in trust for any minister, public teacher, or preacher of the gospel, as such, or any religious sect, order, or denomination, shall be valid, unless the same shall be made at least one calendar month before death of the testator.[88]

In general, the Protestant Churches believe that such a law is wise. The Roman Catholic Church is not disposed to favor it.

A special type of bequest occasionally involving Church and State in some difficulty is that of masses for the dead. Prior to the Reformation, when England acknowledged the authority of the papacy and the Roman Catholic Church, such bequests were frequent. But after the Protestants gained control of the Church and the government, a distinction was soon recognized by the courts between "pious" or "religious" bequests, for various Anglican Church purposes, and "superstitious" uses in connection with the Roman Church or other religious organizations. One of the principal purposes of this distinction was to prevent large alienation of land to support activities of the Church of Rome.

The old distinction lost all meaning under Federal and state constitutions ruling out all forms of establishment. The American courts, in view of the first part of the first section of the Bill of Rights, cannot decide which form of religion is the true religion and what forms are untrue; consequently the English doctrine of superstitious uses, which ruled out among other things bequests to maintain masses for the dead, is not and cannot be recognized in the United States.[89] In this country such bequests are occasionally disallowed by the courts because they do not comply with certain statutory requirements as to wills (that no such bequest is valid, for example, if made within a month or some other specified time before death) or for other reasons, but they are never denied on the ground that they represent superstitious uses.

The Supreme Court of Alabama held a bequest to a given church to be used for solemn masses for the repose of the soul of the testator invalid because, among other reasons, it was not a bequest to a church for its general purposes, and it did not create a charitable trust or a valid private trust. The second reason was interesting: the court's holding that a bequest for the benefit of a man's own soul was not a public charity.[90] But most American courts reach the opposite conclusion when all the legal formalities for making a will have been met, and especially when others besides the testator are included in the proposed benefits. Typical is the statement of the Supreme Court of Pennsylvania, which is quoted both because it represents the prevailing attitude of our courts and because it gives the Roman Catholic *raison d'être* of masses for the dead:

According to the Roman Catholic system of faith there exists an intermediate state of the soul, after death and before final judgment, during which guilt incurred during life and unatoned for must be expiated, and the temporary punishments to which the soul of the penitent are thus subjected may be mitigated or arrested through the efficacy of the Masses for the departed. It cannot be doubted that, in obeying the injunction of the testator, intercession would be specially invoked in behalf of the testator alone. The service is just the same in kind whether it be designed to promote the spiritual welfare of one or many. Prayer for the conversion of a single impenitent is as purely a religious act as a petition for the salvation of thousands. The services intended to be performed in carrying out the trust created by the testator's will, as well as the objects designed to be attained, are all essentially religious in their character.[91]

Chapter 19

THE STATUS OF RELIGION AND CHRISTIANITY

Definition of Religion and Christianity

In this penultimate chapter we consider the status of religion in general and of Christianity in particular in our constitutional democratic society as reflected primarily in official governmental documents, acts of Congress, state constitutions, and court decisions. Before we do so, however, it will be helpful to see how the term "religion" has been defined by American courts.

What has long been considered the classic definition was stated by the United States Supreme Court in 1890 in the case of *Davis* v. *Beason* (see Chapter 5). In that case the Court said,

The term "religion" has reference to one's views of his relations to his Creator, and to the obligations they impose of reverence for his being and character, and of obedience to his will. It is often confounded with the cultus or form of worship of a particular sect, but is distinguishable from the latter. . . . With man's relations to his Maker and the obligations he may think they impose, and the manner in which an expression shall be made by him of his belief on those subjects, no interference can be permitted, provided always the laws of society, designed to secure its peace and prosperity, and the morals of its people are not interfered with.

Almost a century earlier, in 1803, the New Hampshire Supreme Court defined religion as follows:

Religion is that sense of Deity, that reverence for the Creator, which is implanted in the minds of rational beings. It is seated in the heart and is conversant with the inward principles and temper of the mind. It must be the result of personal conviction. It is a concern between every man and his Maker. Public instruction in religion and morality, within the meaning of our constitution and laws, is to every purpose a civil and not a spiritual institution.[1]

Of course, the concluding statement in this paragraph, that public instruction in religion is a civil and not a spiritual institution, is no longer valid in view of the United States Supreme Court decisions in the released-time and Bible reading cases. Our interest here, however, is with the definition of religion rather than with responsibility for religious education.

The use of the terms "Creator," "Maker," and "Deity" in these definitions, particularly with the capitalization of the initial letters, indicates quite clearly that they contemplate belief in God as an indispensable element in religion. It is quite probable that this was the unanimous assumption among both Federal and state courts during the nineteenth century and the first half of the twentieth. Most courts, like most Americans generally, would probably have been shocked at the suggestion that there could be religion without God. Nevertheless, it was true then as it is today that there are well-recognized religions which are not founded upon a belief in the existence of God or other supernatural deity who created and controls the world. One of these is the Buddhist religion, with over 150 million adherents throughout the world, including the United States; indeed, in one of the states, Hawaii, it is probably the major faith, if Protestantism and Roman Catholicism are deemed different faiths.

This fact—that religion does not necessarily encompass belief in the existence of God—was pointed out by the Supreme Court in the Maryland notary public case, *Torcaso* v. *Watkins* (see Chapter 5). The Court also referred to other non-theistic religions, such as Taoism, Confucianism, and Ethical Culture. Reference to Ethical Culture as a religion should not be surprising (although the Court's reference to "Secular Humanism" as a religion is surprising and would probably not be accepted by most students of religion). Ethical Culture has long been listed as a religion with the recognized religions in the *Yearbook of American Churches*,[2] published by the National Council of Churches, and in the *World Almanac*.[3] Its leaders are generally recognized as clergymen, legally empowered, like other clergymen, to solemnize marriages. Even before *Torcaso* v. *Watkins* the Federal Circuit Court of Appeals for the District of Columbia unanimously held that the Ethical Culture Society is a religious society, entitled equally with other religious societies to tax exemption,[4] and a similar ruling was made about the same time by a California court.[5]

Not only the tax laws but many other laws, Federal and state, make special provisions regarding religion and religious organizations. The First Amendment to the United States Constitution itself forbids any law prohibiting the free exercise of religion. The legal definition of religion is therefore a matter not merely of academic interest but of major practical importance. The definition of Christianity is today of considerably less practical importance, although even now a court is occasionally called upon to interpret wills or deeds which use the word "Christianity" or "Christian."

Among the more interesting court definitions of Christianity, in order of date, are the following:

New York, 1811: Christianity is the religion that is revealed and taught in the Bible.[6]

New Hampshire, 1868: Christianity is the religion of those who believe that Jesus Christ is the true Messiah and Savior of men, and who receive the Holy Scriptures of the Old and New Testaments as the Word of God. The grand subdivisions among Christians are, first, the Greek or Eastern Church; second, the Roman Catholics, who acknowledge the authority of the pope; third, the Protestant or Reformed Churches, or sects who reject the authority of the pope.[7]

In this same opinion the court turns to *The Encyclopaedia of Religious Knowledge* and quotes with approval its statement that the term "Christian,"

... when used in its more strict scriptural and theological sense, denotes one who really believes the Gospel, imbibes the spirit, is influenced by the grace and obedient to the will of Christ, and this it called the "sacred and proper" use of the word. It mentions another use of the word, which it calls the "political or conventional" use, which denotes one who assents to the doctrines of the religion of Christ, and who, being born of Christian parents or in a Christian country, does not profess any other religion or belong to any other of the divisions of men, such as Jews, Mohammedans, deists, pagans, and atheists; or, as is said in another part of the article, Christians may be considered as "nominal and real."

New Jersey, 1935: A "Christian" is one who believes or professes or is assumed to believe in Jesus Christ, and the truth as taught by him.[8]

Reference to God and Christianity in Constitutions and Court Opinions

The Declaration of Independence refers to "nature's God," man's "Creator," "the Supreme Judge of the world," and "Divine Providence." The Federal Constitution, drafted eleven years later, does not contain any invocation or even reference to God. On the other hand, reference to God in state constitutions are quite common. In fact, all state constitutions except those of New Hampshire, Oregon, Tennessee, Virginia, and West Virginia contain a preamble expressing reverence of or gratitude to God, referring to Him generally as "Almighty God," and sometimes as "God," "the Supreme Being," "the Sovereign Ruler of Nations," or "the Supreme Ruler of the Universe."[9]

Formerly, references to Christianity were likewise common in state constitutions. Virginia, in adopting its Bill of Rights as the beginning of its constitution of 1776, stated, after declaring for entire religious freedom, "that it is the mutual duty of all to practise Christian forbearance, love, and charity towards each other."[10]

South Carolina in its second constitution, that of 1778, stated, "the Christian Protestant religion shall be deemed, and is hereby constituted and declared to be, the established religion of this state."[11]

Maryland by its constitution of 1776 provided that "all persons, professing the Christian religion, are equally entitled to protection in their religious liberty" and authorized the legislature to "lay a general and equal tax, for the support of the Christian religion." [12]

New Jersey by its constitution of 1776, and some other states, required "a belief in the faith of any Protestant sect" for membership in the legislature.[13]

Pennsylvania by its constitution of the same year limited the right to sit in the legislature to professing Christians—understood as being those who could subscribe to this declaration: "I do believe in one God, the creator and governor of the universe, the rewarder of the good and the punisher of the wicked. And I do acknowledge the Scriptures of the Old and New Testament to be given by Divine inspiration." [14]

Connecticut and Massachusetts continued a legal tie with Puritan Christianity as embodied in the Congregational churches until 1817 and 1833 respectively.[15]

New Hampshire's constitution of 1784, inheriting the early (1680) charter provision that the council should take care to discountenance vice and encourage virtue, "that by such examples yᵉ infidel may be invited & desire to partake of yᵉ Christian religion . . . ," guaranteed to "every denomination of christians demeaning themselves quietly, and as good subjects of the state, . . . the equal protection of the law" and limited membership in the state Senate and House to those "of the protestant religion." [16]

The only specific reference to a "Christian Nation" or a "Christian State" in any American constitution of the past hundred years is in that of North Carolina as adopted in 1868. It has to do with public charities, and reads,

Beneficent provision for the poor, the unfortunate, and orphan being one of the first duties of a civilized and Christian State, the general assembly shall, at its first session, appoint and define the duties of a board of public charities, to whom shall be intrusted the supervision of all charitable and penal State institutions, and who shall annually report to the governor upon their condition, with suggestions for their improvement.[17]

Now let us consider some of the more important decisions of the Supreme Court and other courts dealing with matters involving the Church, the Christian religion, and Christian moral standards.

The Supreme Court in an 1844 decision of *Vidal* v. *Girard's Executors*, to which we have previously referred,[18] stated that Christianity is part of our common law in "this qualified sense, that its divine origin and truth are admitted, and therefore it is not to be maliciously and openly reviled and blasphemed against, to the annoyance of believers or the injury of the public.[19]

The same idea is at least implied in the decision of 1889 by the same court in one of the Mormon Church cases, in which the practice of polygamy was outlawed. The court said,

The organization of a community for the spread and practice of polygamy is, in a measure, a return to barbarism. It is contrary to the spirit of Christianity and of the civilization which Christianity has produced in the Western World.[20]

One of the most authoritative statements of the fundamental importance of religion in general and of Christianity in particular to the American State is that given in the opinion of the United States Supreme Court in the case of the *Church of the Holy Trinity* v. *United States* (see Chapter 5). The following quotation gives those portions of the opinion most pertinent to our subject:

. . . No purpose of action against religion can be imputed to any legislation, state or national, because this is a religious people. This is historically true. From the discovery of this continent to the present hour, there is a single voice making this affirmation.[21]

There follows a long enumeration of quotations from colonial grants, charters, and state constitutions, and the opinion continues,

If we pass beyond these matters to a view of American life as expressed by its laws, its business, its customs and its society, we find everywhere a clear recognition of the same truth. Among other matters we note the following: The form of oath universally prevailing, concluding with an appeal to the Almighty; the custom of opening sessions of all deliberative bodies and most conventions with prayer; the prefatory words of all wills, "In the name of God, amen"; the laws respecting the observance of the Sabbath, with the general cessation of all secular business, and the closing of courts, legislatures, and other similar public assemblies on that day; the churches and church organizations which abound in every city, town and hamlet; the multitude of charitable organizations existing everywhere under Christian auspices; the gigantic missionary associations, with general support, and aiming to establish Christian missions in every quarter of the globe. These, and many other matters which might be noticed, add a volume of unofficial declarations to the mass of organic utterances that this is a Christian nation. In the face of all these, shall it be believed that a Congress of the United States intended to make it a misdemeanor for a church of this country to contract for the services of a Christian minister residing in another nation?[22]

This decision was referred to with approval by the Supreme Court as late as 1930. Then in the Macintosh case it was stated, "We are a Christian people, according to one another the equal right of religious freedom, and acknowledging with reverence the duty of obedience to the will of God." [23]

The assertion made by the Supreme Court in *Vidal* v. *Girard's Executors* that Christianity is part of the common law or of the law of the land had earlier been made by the Supreme Court of Pennsylvania when it stated that "Christianity, general Christianity, is, and always has been a part of the common law of Pennsylvania." [24] This principle, however, was vigorously contested by Jefferson.[25] It was also challenged by the Supreme Court of Ohio in 1857 in a decision in which it said,

The assertion that Christianity is a part of the common law of the country, lying behind and above the constitutions, can hardly be a serious one. If Christianity is a law of the state, it must have a sanction. Adequate penalties must be provided to enforce obedience to its requirements and its precepts. The only foundation for the proposition that Christianity is a part of the law of the country is the fact that it is a Christian country, and that its constitution and laws are made by a Christian people.[26]

Five years later, in 1860, the North Carolina Supreme Court, perhaps trying to find a middle ground between these two opposing viewpoints, said, "Ours is a Christian country, but Christianity is not established by law, and the genius of our institution requires that the church and state should be kept separate." [27]

The United States Supreme Court's quotation in 1930 of the statement in the Holy Trinity Church case that "We are a Christian people" appears to be the last time the Court made such a reference. In the 1952 decision of *Zorach* v. *Clauson* [28] the Court significantly said only that "We are a religious people whose institutions presuppose a Supreme Being."

The next words spoken by the Supreme Court on this specific question were contained in a footnote in the majority opinion in *Engel* v. *Vitale* [29] in 1962:

There is of course nothing in the decision reached here that is inconsistent with the fact that school children and others are officially encouraged to express love for our country by reciting historical documents such as the Declaration of Independence which contain references to the Deity or by singing officially espoused anthems which include the composer's professions of faith in a Supreme Being, or with the fact that there are many manifestations in our public life of belief in God. Such patriotic or ceremonial occasions bear no true resemblance to the unquestioned religious exercise that the State of New York has sponsored in this instance.

The last statement up to the present time made by the Supreme Court on the matter we are considering appeared in the 1963 Bible reading case, *Abington School District* v. *Schempp* (See Chapter 5) in the following words:

It is true that religion has been closely identified with our history and government. As we said in *Engel* v. *Vitale,* "The history of man is inseparable from the history of religion. And . . . since the beginning of that history many people have devoutly believed that 'More things are wrought by prayer than this world dreams of.' " In *Zorach* v. *Clauson,* we gave specific recognition to the proposition that "[w]e are a religious people whose institutions presuppose a Supreme Being." The fact that the Founding Fathers believed devotedly that there was a God and that the unalienable rights of man were rooted in Him is clearly evidenced in their writings, from the Mayflower Compact to the Constitution itself. This background is evidenced today in our public life through the continuance in our oaths of office from the Presidency to the Alderman of the final supplication, "So help me God." Likewise each House of the Congress provides through its Chaplain an opening prayer, and the sessions of this Court are declared open by the crier in a short ceremony, the final phrase of which invokes the grace of God. Again, there are such manifestations in our military forces, where those of our citizens who are under the restrictions of military service wish to engage in voluntary worship. Indeed, only last year an official survey of the country indicated that 64% of our people have church membership, Bureau of Census, U.S. Department of Commerce, Statistical Abstract of the United States, 48 (83d ed. 1962), while less than 3% profess no religion whatever. It can be truly said, therefore, that today, as in the beginning, our national life reflects a religious people who, in the words of Madison, are "earnestly praying, as . . . in duty bound, that the Supreme Law-giver of the Universe . . . guide them into every measure which may be worthy of his . . . blessing . . ." Memorial and Remonstrance Against Religious Assessments.

This not to say, however, that religion has been so identified with our history and government that religious freedom is not likewise as strongly imbedded in our public and private life. Nothing but the most telling of personal experiences in religious persecution suffered by our forebears could have planted our belief in liberty of religious opinion any more deeply in our heritage. It is true that this liberty frequently was not realized by the colonists, but this is readily accountable to their close ties to the Mother Country. However, the views of Madison and Jefferson, preceded by Roger Williams, came to be incorporated not only in the Federal Constitution but likewise in those of most of our States. This freedom to worship was indispensable in a country whose people came from the four quarters of the earth and brought with them a diversity of religious opinion. Today authorities list 83 separate religious bodies, each with memberships exceeding 50,000, existing among our people, as well as innumerable smaller groups.

Proposals to Amend the Constitution

As we have noted, the Constitution drafted in Philadelphia in 1787 omitted any direct recognition of God or of the Christian religion. Regret at this omission was expressed in at least five of the state conventions called to ratify the document. Two small Presbyterian bodies, the Associated Church and the Reformed Presbyterian Church, decided to abstain from voting at elections until the Constitution of the United States was so amended as to acknowledge God's sovereignty and the subservience of the State to Christ's kingdom. Since then there have been many efforts to rectify the omission.[30]

A proposal for a constitutional amendment recognizing God gained national recognition in the sixties, seventies, and eighties of the nineteenth century. The National Reform Association, which sponsored the movement, was founded in 1863. It published in Philadelphia a journal entitled *The Christian Statesman* and held several national conventions. One of its major purposes was to secure such an amendment to the Constitution of the United States as would declare the nation's allegiance to Jesus Christ, and its acceptance of the morals of the Christian religion, and to indicate that this is a Christian nation and place all the Christian laws, institutions, and usages of our government on an undeniable legal basis in the fundamental law of the land.[31]

The movement was particularly strong among the Presbyterians in Pennsylvania, and more especially among the various Reformed churches, but there were some twenty auxiliary groups in different parts of the country all working toward the same end—"to put God in the Constitution," according to the covenant adopted by the Synod of the Reformed Presbyterian Church. Those accepting it were pledged to work for "a constitutional recognition of God as the source of all power, of Jesus Christ as the ruler of nations, of the Holy Scriptures as the supreme rule, and of the true Christian religion.[32] They even went on record as opposing taking part in elections, or accepting national or state offices, until such constiutional changes could be secured. They laid emphasis on "dissent from all immoral civil institutions,"[33] while allowing each individual to decide to what extent this might apply.

A somewhat similar proposal was unsuccessfully introduced in the Senate of the United States in May, 1888, by Senator Henry William Blair of New Hampshire. It was known as the Religious Education Amendment. Section 2 reads as follows:

Each state in this union shall establish and maintain a system of free public schools, adequate for the education of all the children therein, between the ages of six and sixteen years inclusive, in the common branches of knowledge and in virtue, morality, and the principles of the Christian religion.[34]

The proposal for the "Religious Amendment" sanctioned by the National Reform Association was taken so seriously in 1874 as to be carefully considered in Congress, which approved the following report by the Committee on the Judiciary:

That, upon examination even of the meager debates by the fathers of the Republic in the convention which framed the Constitution, they [the committee] find that the subject of this memorial was most fully and carefully considered, and then, in that convention, decided, after grave deliberation, to which the subject was entitled, that, as this country, the foundation of whose government they were then laying, was to be the home of the oppressed of all nations of the earth, whether Christian or pagan, and in full realization of the dangers which the union between church and state had imposed upon so many nations of the Old World, with great unanimity that it was inexpedient to put anything into the Constitution or frame of government which might be construed to be a reference to any religious creed or doctrine.

And they further find that this decision was accepted by our Christian fathers with such great unanimity that in the amendments which were afterward proposed in order to make the Constitution most acceptable to the nation, none has ever been proposed to the States by which this wise determination of the fathers has been attempted to be changed. Wherefore, your committee report that it is inexpedient to legislate upon the subject of the above memorial, and ask that they be discharged from the further consideration thereof, and that this report, together with the petition, be laid upon the table.[35]

Since then similar proposals to amend the Constitution have often been made. At present, the leading organization pressing for such a proposal is the Christian Amendment Movement. At the request of this organization Senator Ralph Flanders of Vermont in June, 1953, introduced the following Joint Resolution to amend the Constitution:

"Section 1. This Nation devoutly recognizes the authority and law of Jesus Christ, Saviour and Ruler of Nations through whom are bestowed the blessings of Almighty God.

"Sec. 2. This amendment shall not be interpreted so as to result in the establishment of any particular ecclesiastical organization, or in the abridgement of the rights of religious freedom, or freedom of speech and press, or of peaceful assemblage.

"Sec. 3. Congress shall have power, in such cases as it may deem proper, to provide a suitable oath or affirmation for citizens whose religious scruples prevent them from giving unqualified allegiance to the Constitution as herein amended." [36]

Public hearings on this proposal were held by the Senate Committee on the Judiciary in May, 1954.[73] The committee did not report the resolution out, nor apparently take any other action with respect to it. Nevertheless, since then the proposal has from time to time been re-introduced into Congress, the latest occasion being in June, 1959, when it was introduced by Representative Denver Hargis of Kansas and Representative Eugene Siler of Kentucky.[38] There have been no public hearings called on these resolutions and at the present time there appears to be no likelihood that the proposal will even be put to a vote in either house of Congress, much less adopted.

The National Motto—"In God We Trust"

We have dealt in previous chapters with the religious situation at the time of the founding of the republic and seen the recognition of religion by the official representatives of the American people at that time. We have also dealt with the various sanctions of religion today, such as government chaplaincies, exemption of church property from taxation, etc. Here we wish merely to call attention to a few rather striking more recent government actions indicating the dependence of the nation on religion.

During the Civil War the government received so many suggestions for the broader recognition of religion that the secretary of the treasury, Salmon P. Chase, stimulated by letters urging action, wrote under date of November 30, 1861, to the director of the mint at Philadelphia, requesting that some "device be prepared without delay with a motto expressing in a few words the recognition of the trust of our people in God." [39] Several suggestions were made. The patterns for the half dollar and half eagle submitted in 1862 showed "God our Trust," while a pattern for a two-cent piece the following year had a bust of Washington and the legend "God and our Country." [40]

The same year (1862) the proposal that the name of the deity should be placed on the coins of the United States was made in a sermon by the Reverend Henry Augustus Boardman of Philadelphia. "The coinage of the United States is without a God" [41] was his summons to action.

In 1864 the present motto "In God We Trust" appeared for the first time on American coins—the two-cent piece issued April 22—but the motto did not receive formal Congressional sanction until the following year.[42] By act of Congress March 3, 1865, the director of the mint, with the approval of the secretary of the treasury, was authorized to add the words upon all the gold and silver coins of the United States thereafter issued and susceptible of such addition. Here is the essential portion of this act of Congress:

And be it further enacted, That, in addition to the devices and legends upon the gold, silver, and other coins of the United States, it shall be lawful for the director of the mint, with the approval of the Secretary of the Treasury, to cause the motto "In God we trust" to be placed upon such coins hereafter to be issued as shall admit of such legend thereon.[43]

It is interesting to know that this familiar motto on our coins was the direct result of the crisis through which the country was passing during the Civil War, and was an evidence of the feeling that the nation needed to cultivate the spirit of religion.

In 1907, in the administration of President Theodore Roosevelt, the motto was removed in connection with some new coins designed by Augustus Saint-

Gaudens. The president had been much thrilled by his inauguration medal in 1905 and secured the consent of the secretary of the treasury to have the same sculptor design some gold coins imitating the spirit of the ancient Greek coinage with its sharp relief. When the designs, somewhat modified, were approved, they did not contain the familiar "In God We Trust," and there was much discussion of the omission and some unfavorable comment, especially among Church groups. In November, 1907, the president wrote a letter to a clergyman who objected to the omission. In it he stated that there was "no legal warrant for putting the motto on the coins." This, as we know, was a mistake, since it had been authorized by Congress, though the authorization was not made mandatory. He continued,

My own feeling in the matter is due to my very firm conviction that to put such a motto on coins, or to use it in any kindred matter, not only does no good but does positive harm, and is in effect irreverence which comes dangerously close to sacrilege. A beautiful and solemn sentence such as the one in question should be treated and uttered only with that fine reverence which necessarily implies a certain exaltation of spirit. Any use which tends to cheapen it, and above all, any use which tends to secure its being treated in a spirit of levity, is from every standpoint profoundly to be regretted. It is a motto which it is indeed well to have inscribed on our great national monuments, in our temples of justice, in our legislative halls, and in buildings such as those at West Point and Annapolis—in short wherever it will tend to arouse and inspire a lofty emotion in those who look thereon. But it seems to me eminently unwise to cheapen such a motto by use on coins, just as it would be to cheapen it by use on postage stamps, or in advertisements.

As regards its use on the coinage we have actual experience by which to go. In all my life I have never heard any human being speak reverently of this motto on the coins or show any sign of its having appealed to any high emotion in him. But I have literally hundreds of times heard it used as an occasion of, and incitement to, the sneering ridicule which it is above all things undesirable that so beautiful and exalted a phrase should excite. For example, throughout the long contest, extending over several decades, on the free coinage question, the existence of this motto on the coins was a constant source of jest and ridicule; and this was unavoidable. Every one must remember the innumerable cartoons and articles based on phrases like "In God We Trust for the other eight cents"; "In God we trust for the short weight"; "In God we trust for the thirty-seven cents we do not pay"; and so forth, and so forth. Surely I am well within bounds when I say that a use of the phrase which invites constant levity of this type is most undesirable. If congress alters the law and directs me to replace on the coins the sentence in question the direction will be immediately put into effect; but I very earnestly trust that the religious sentiment of the country, the spirit of reverence in the country, will prevent any such action being taken.[44]

The matter inevitably came before Congress, and on May 18, 1908, an act was passed for the restoration of the motto. The essential part of the act reads as follows:

That the motto "In God we trust," heretofore inscribed on certain denominations of the gold and silver coins of the United States of America, shall hereafter be inscribed upon all such gold and silver coins of said denominations as heretofore.[45]

Since this act was duly approved by the president, it became a mandatory law instead of merely permissive action, as in the earlier case.

In 1955 Congress extended the act by requiring the phrase to appear not only on all coins but on all paper money thereafter minted or printed.[46] The next year, 1956, Congress enacted a law making the phrase "In God We Trust" officially the national motto.[47]

The motto "In God We Trust" has also appeared on postage stamps. Particularly significant was the 1928 two-cent Valley Forge stamp, issued to commemorate the 150th anniversary of Washington's encampment at that place, which contains the well-known vignette of Washington kneeling in prayer in the critical days during the winter of 1777-78.

God in the Pledge of Allegiance [48] and the Capitol Prayer Room [49]

While he was president of the United States, Dwight D. Eisenhower worshiped at the New York Avenue Presbyterian Church in Washington, D.C. One Sunday in February, 1954, he heard the pastor of the church, the Reverend George M. Docherty, deliver a sermon in which he spoke about the pledge of allegiance to the American flag as follows:

There is something not in the pledge, something that is a characteristic and definitive factor in the American way of life.

Indeed, apart from the mention of the phrase "the United States of America," it could be the pledge of any republic. In fact, I could hear little Muscovites repeat a similar pledge to their hammer-and-sickle flag in Moscow. Russia is also a republic that claims to have overthrown the tyranny of kingship. Russia also claims to be indivisible.

Three days later, Senator Homer Ferguson of Michigan introduced a resolution in the Senate to change the pledge of allegiance so as to add the words, "under God." The pledge would then read: "I pledge allegiance to the flag of the United States of America and to the Republic for which it stands, one nation under God, indivisible with liberty and justice for all."

Hearings were held on the proposal and the appropriate committee quickly reported the bill favorably. The Senate speedily adopted the measure without a dissenting vote and sent it to the House of Representatives, which also unanimously approved it and sent it on to the president for his signature. In May, 1954, just about three months after the sermon of the Reverend Mr. Docherty, it became the law of the land. Actually, the report of the committee consisted of no more than a statement by Senator Ferguson, in which he incuded the above quotation from the sermon and answered a claim that the change might be unconstitutional in the following words:

Adoption of the resolution would in no way run contrary to the provisions of the first amendment to the Constitution. This is not an act establishing a religion. A distinction exists between the Church as an institution and a belief in the sovereignty of God. The phrase "under God" recognizes only the guidance of God in our national affairs, it does nothing to establish a religion. Neither will this resolution violate the right of any person to disbelieve in God or reject the existence of God. The recognition of God in the pledge of allegiance to the flag of our nation does not compel any individual to make a positive affirmation in the existence of God in whom one does not believe.

Almost simultaneously with the passage of the resolution, both houses passed another resolution directing the Capitol architect to make available "a room, with facilities for prayer and meditation, for the use of members of the Senate and House of Representatives. The architect shall maintain the prayer room [the resolution continued] for individual use rather than assemblies and he shall provide appropriate symbols of religious unity and freedom of worship."

Pursuant to this resolution a non-denominational room for prayer and meditation was constructed off the rotunda of the Capitol. Decorated in blue, it has a white oak altar with an open Bible, and candelabra, ten seats, and two kneeling benches. A stained-glass window depicts Washington at prayer, while panels show the obverse and reverse of the Great Seal. Also depicted are a candle and an open book, with a sentence from the 119th Psalm: "Thy word is a lamp unto my feet and a light unto my path."

Religion and the Census

When the Bureau of the Census was made a permanent organization in 1902, it was required to collect decennial statistics on religious bodies. These statistics were given in the *Census of Religious Bodies* in 1906, 1916, and 1926, and in the similar but delayed census of 1936, published in 1941—the delay being due mainly to the fact that as an economy measure no provision was originally made by Congress for this special census. No official census appeared in the decade of the forties owing to Congressional failure to provide adequate funds.

The entire separation in time of publication and material of the religious census from the regular census of population, occupation, wealth, etc., although it had disadvantages from the standpoint of comparative statistics, seemed to meet general approval and to be in keeping with the best American tradition, for it tended to emphasize the separation of matters political and religious.

The material for the 1936 census was based on a series of bulletins regarding each religious body. Each is headed "Unitarians," or whatever the religious body may be, followed by the subtitle "Statistics, Denominational History, Doctrine, and Organization." The bulletin of each denomination is preceded by the same general introduction. It calls attention to the fact that it is "a census of the religious organizations in the United States rather than of individuals classified according to denominational affiliations." [50] The Bureau of the Census secured information from each church, congregation, or other local organization of each religious body, the material being obtained in most cases with the co-operation of the denominational headquarters. The data for each denomination are contained in the following tables:

Table 1. Summary of statistics for churches in urban and rural territory, membership by sex, and Sunday schools, by States, 1936.

Table 2. Comparative summary, 1906 to 1936.

Table 3. Number and membership of churches in urban and rural territory, membership by sex, and Sunday schools, by States, 1936.

Table 4. Number and membership of churches, 1906 to 1936, and membership by age in 1936, by States.

Table 5. Value of churches and parsonages and amount of church debt by States, 1936.

Table 6. Church expenditures by States, 1936.

At the close of each bulletin is a summary of "History, Doctrine, and Organization," including also a section on "Work," all prepared in co-operation with the denomination referred to.

The significant thing from the point of view of this study is that the government of the United States has considered it a matter of importance to provide full information on the churches, their condition, and their work. This material is of value to the churches themselves and to the general public.

The 1936 religious census was immediately attacked because it showed a decrease in the number of local churches reporting from that in the previous census. The difference appeared mainly among Southern Baptists and the denomination known as Methodist Episcopal Church, South, which together, according to the official figures, showed some 24,000 fewer churches than in 1926. Investigation proved that this situation resulted mostly from the fact that the statistics were colleced from the ministers of churches rather than from denominational headquarters or personal enumeration, and in many cases, especially in rural districts, the ministers proved non-co-operative, fearing that the taking of the census might be used in some way to apply State pressure on the churches. This attitude, in turn, was due to the fact that the Bureau of the Census adopted a uniform procedure of citing on all schedules sent out the legal authority for its investigation. The statement on the 1936 census schedule closed with the words

The information to be used as a basis of religious statistics is collected by the Census Bureau under authority of Acts of Congress approved June 7, 1906, and June 18, 1929. These Acts make it the duty of every person in charge of any religious body to answer all questions on the printed schedule, applicable to the religious body, church, or organization, and upon refusal or neglect to comply, such person is subject to a fine not exceeding $500 or to imprisonment not exceeding 60 days, or both; and if any such person willfully gives false answers, he is subject to a fine not exceeding $10,000 or to imprisonment not exceeding one year, or both.[51]

It was shown that hundreds of ministers, noting the penalties for refusing to comply with the government request, felt that legal measures to gather statistics were unwarranted interference by the State in Church affairs and might lead to serious consequences.

Most religious bodies have welcomed the securing by the government of statistics regarding the Churches and their membership six years after the regular population statistics. There continues to be, however, occasional opposition by some denominations which feel that the taking of a religious census paid for by the government is inconsistent with the idea of separation between Church and State. As late as the fall of 1938 the Alabama Baptist State Convention—the largest single religious body in the state—adopted resolutions calling on its ministers to decline to co-operate in the program of the Federal census of religious bodies because of their conviction that such a census is an opening wedge to government interference in Church affairs.[52]

Nearly a decade later, when another proposed religious census was under consideration, Congress passed a law directing that the Bureau of the Census shall not require a religious body to report its statistics if its "doctrine" prohibits the disclosure of the information. But in spite of this, opposition by some religious groups, on the ground of wishing to apply rigidly the Church-State separation idea and for other reasons, as well as Congressional economy, led to the omission of the proposed 1946 census of religious bodies.[53] Nor was any census of religious bodies undertaken in 1956.

In 1940 some groups sought to have some religious questions, such as one regarding belief in God, included in the regular decennial census of 1940, but the Bureau of the Census rejected the proposal,[54] as it did again in 1950. (It is interesting to note at this point that when the first Federal census of 1790 was being considered, Madison expressed reservations regarding the propriety of including in it a category of "the learned professions." "As to those who are employed in teaching and inculcating the duties of religion," he said, "there may be some indelicacy in singling them out, as the General Government is proscribed from interfering, in any manner whatever, in matters respecting religion; and it may be thought to do this, in ascertaining who are, and who are not ministers of the Gospel." [55])

However, in April, 1956, concurrent with the omission of the census of religious bodies, the Bureau of the Census issued a brief public statement to the effect that a question about religious affiliation was "under consideration" for inclusion in the coming 1960 decennial census.[56] There was not then or later any definite decision as the form of the question, but tentative agreement was reached within the Bureau that it was to be "What is your religion?" and that answers were to be channeled into five categories: (1) Catholic, (2) Jewish, (3) Protestant, (4) all others, and (5) none. For a time consideration was given to making the answer to this question, as distinguished from all other questions, voluntary, but this was discarded as impractical.

For about a year there was no significant reaction to the announcement, but in July, 1957, Rabbi Dr. Israel Goldstein, president of the American Jewish Congress, wrote a letter which was published in the New York *Times* expressing strong opposition to the proposal. The letter aroused considerable comment and was reprinted in a number of major newspapers of the country, including the Washington *Post*, the *Christian Science Monitor*, the St. Louis *Post-Dispatch* and the Chicago *Sun-Times*. The issue became a subject of discussion in the editorial columns of the newspapers and magazines. Support of Dr. Goldstein's position came from the Washington *Post*, the St. Louis *Post-Dispatch*, the Indianapolis *News*, the Detroit *News*, *The Christian Century*, and the liberal Catholic weekly *The Commonweal*. Opposition to Dr. Goldstein and support of the proposal to include the question was expressed by the editors of the San Francisco *Chronicle*, the Cincinnati *Enquirer*, the Dallas *News*, and the Jesuit weekly *America*.

National organizations, too, began to take sides. Favoring inclusion of the question were two main groups: Christian Church groups and demographers. The former desired the information which the census would elicit to aid them in Church planning and recruitment. Support of the proposal was expressed by the Association of Council Secretaries (Protestant) and a number of Roman Catholic organizations and publications. The demographers favored the proposal because it would assist them in their study of contemporary American society.

Formal opposition to the inclusion was expressed by the American Civil Liberties Union; the General Conference of the Seventh Day Adventists; the

American Baptist Convention; the Baptists Joint Committee on Public Affairs; the International Religious Liberty Association, and a number of Jewish groups including, besides the American Jewish Congress, the National Community Relations Advisory Council and the Synagogue Council of America.

Among the arguments presented in favor of including the question were the following:

1. It would help church groups in planning and recruitment.

2. It would help demographers.

3. The Supreme Court in the Zorach case said that "we are a religious people." Therefore, there was no reason why information helpful to religion should not be procured by the government for use by religious groups.

4. Canada includes a question on religion in its census with no ill effects.

5. A trial run had been conducted by the Federal government early in 1957 in four Wisconsin counties and, according to the Census Bureau, "very few persons" objected to the inclusion of the question or refused to answer it.

Among the arguments against inclusion were the following:

1. It would violate the constitutional guarantee of freedom of religion. Refusal to answer the census taker constitutes a Federal crime punishable by imprisonment.

2. It was alien to American tradition and concepts to divide the American people into categories of religious and non-religious or to subdivide the religious classification into sects and denominations.

3. It violated the principle of separation of Church and State since it employed a governmental instrumentality to further Church purposes.

4. It was an unwarranted infringement upon the privacy of Americans.

5. It would create a dangerous precedent which might well lead to further encroachments.

6. It would constitute a radical departure from long-established traditions. For 170 years the Federal government had refused, notwithstanding frequent pressure, to include questions on religious beliefs or affiliations in the census questions asked of individual citizens.

7. The Canadian precedent was not one to be followed, since in Canada there was no separation of Church and State and persons were divided according to their religion.

The controversy continued until December 12, 1957, when the Bureau of the Census issued a public statement announcing that it had decided not to include the question. The full statement is worth quoting:

The 1960 Census of Population will not include an inquiry on religion. This decision was announced today by Director Robert W. Burgess of the Bureau of the Census, Department of Commerce.

The primary reason for this decision, Dr. Burgess said, was recognition that at this time a considerable number of persons would be reluctant to answer such a question in the Census where a reply is mandatory. Under the circumstances it was not believed that the value of the statistics based on this question would be great enough to justify overriding such an attitude. Cost factors also were a consideration.

Director Burgess called attention to the fact that the decision does not deal with the question of inclusion of an inquiry on religion, on perhaps a modified basis, in later censuses nor with the publication of information based on an inquiry on religion asked of a national sample of individuals on a voluntary basis. As a matter of fact, a survey of this type was carried out in March, 1957, covering a nation-wide sample of about 35,000 households. The results of this survey are now being prepared for publication.

Thus ended the controversy, probably to be renewed when preparations are begun for the 1970 decennial census.

General Conclusions on the Legal Status of Religion

The general conclusions that we have reached regarding the legal status of religion in the United States may be summed up in four statements.

1. No church or religious body has any prior standing over other churches or religious bodies in the United States. All have in the eyes of the law precisely the same status as long as their members are law-abiding citizens. In other words, all churches as such have constitutionally and legally complete religious equality in the United States.

2. The result of the Federal and state guarantees of religious freedom is to make institutionalized religion a purely voluntary matter. Any church becomes from the point of view of the State what John Locke called it when he wrote his *Letter Concerning Toleration* in 1685, "a voluntary society of men, joining themselves together of their own accord in order to the public worshiping of God." [57] This involves private support without any government subsidy and does not prevent any church from adopting its own definition.

3. Religion is respected by the State and encouraged in various ways, such as through exemption of church property from taxation, government chaplaincies, and references to God. Along with our legal separation of Church and State so that their union in this country is unthinkable, we have a friendly fellowship between them. The fact that our presidents have been almost all affiliated with some church and fairly regular in attendance at public worship, while at the same time expressing in their public utterances, from the time of Washington down, sympathetic interest in the work of all our great national religious groups, is highly significant. Such a situation as existed in France in the days of the pre-World War II republic, when it was rare to have a president

or prime minister a "practising" Christian, or even one who identified himself with the cause of religion, is almost unthinkable here.

In other words, the American people, through their laws, their chaplaincies, their setting apart of Thanksgiving Day, and in other ways recognize the importance of belief in God as Father of all mankind.

4. The religious ethical ideal in its elementary form, as expressed for instance in the Golden Rule, the summary of the law, and the underlying principles of the Sermon on the Mount, has been so incorporated in the fundamental documents of the American government as to deserve the continued respect it has almost invariably received from public officials, lawmakers and courts.

Chapter 20

THE GENERAL CONCLUSIONS OF THIS BOOK

Looking back on the history of Church-State separation and religious freedom in this country, and considering their contemporary status, we feel that certain definite conclusions stand out as having special significance:

That problems of necessary adjustment between Church and State in the United States have been and are much more frequent than is generally realized even by the better-informed public.

That though religious factors in colonial history have been fully recognized by most historians, those in national history, which have been less marked but considerable, have been given inadequate attention, Church-State contacts in co-operation having been many, and in debate or conflict not infrequent.

That the founders of our government and those who succeeded them in state constitutional conventions and in Congress and legislatures have generally by their attitude on public questions shown both a deep respect for religion and a determination to uphold Church-State separation and its closely related religious freedom.

That the president, the secretary of state, and other high officers of the Federal government, when confronted with new and difficult problems affecting religious freedom and the separation of Church and State, have almost always acted in accordance with the letter and spirit of the religious-freedom guarantees of the Constitution.

That our Federal judiciary and higher state courts have rendered a service of inestimable significance to this country in supporting religious freedom, and that their independence, under fearless and open-minded judges well versed in the law, should be maintained at all hazards.

That constitutional religious freedom and actual separation of Church and State in this country are historically the result mainly of two factors working in a new country: the convictions and interests of non-conformist religious groups, among which the Baptists and Quakers were prominent; and the conclusions, based on a study of history, political philosophy, and the practical needs of a situation involving many divergent religious sects, reached by certain broad-minded statesmen, particularly in Virginia.

That American religious freedom had its inspiration primarily in two sets of ideals which were not unrelated—those of the natural law and of Christianity.

That the constitutional provisions for Church and State separation, especially since the Supreme Court has interpreted the Fourteenth Amendment as applying to the protection of religious freedom in the various states, have been a highly important, significant, and successful contribution of the United States to political thought.

That only one additional amendment in the field seems worthy at present of serious consideration, namely, one already embodied in many state constitutions, in the statutes of most states, and in the interpretations of the Supreme Court, to forbid the grant of public funds to denominational institutions or agencies.

That though religious freedom in this country owes much to the Ordinance of 1787, the Federal Constitution with its Bill of Rights, and (indirectly) the Fourteenth Amendment, many of the important battles have been fought out and won in the states: the successful contest of Jefferson, Madison, and Mason in the epoch-making debates in Virginia; the struggle of Roman Catholics for the protection of their rights in New York; the battle for Jewish enfranchisement, due largely to a single Protestant legislator, Thomas Kennedy, in Maryland; and the struggle between the state and the standing order in Connecticut, which was won through the co-operation of the Jeffersonians and a fairly well-knit phalanx of non-Congregationalists.

That the most difficult adjustments have been and are matters of state rather than of Federal jurisdiction, since they are in the fields of education and of the marriage tie, in which the churches are deeply interested, and where the states, rather than the Federal government, are in legal control.

That there has been on the whole a fairly steady increase in religious freedom both in state statutes and in their observance.

That the Church has rendered the nation important public service not only in the fields of morals and religion but in many large matters of social welfare, such as the abolition of slavery, the education of the West, and the bringing about of greater consideration for racial minorities.

That democracy cannot well exist without religion.

That religious freedom carries with it high responsibilities.

That religious freedom is one of our most precious heritages from the past, and that it is intimately related to the other freedoms of the Bill of Rights.

That our citizenship should be alert to prevent any attempts on the part of any religious body to secure special favors from the State, because the maintenance of Church-State separation, without any loss of mutual sympathy or interest, is fundamental if our form of democratic government is to be preserved, and is also to the advantage of the churches.

That our churches should interest themselves vitally in social welfare, and should always uphold the highest standards of citizenship, but that they should as a general rule abstain from party politics, and should take an active, assertive part in political matters only when great moral issues, such as slavery, child labor, civil corruption, or civil rights, are concerned, and that even then they should generally emphasize the fundamental principles involved rather than the details of legislation or action.

That it is a matter of vital importance that our Federal Constitution, with its Bill of Rights and other amendments, should be held in the highest honor and its provisions scrupulously observed, because they control in the Federal field in religious-freedom issues and set standards which the states must observe.

NOTES

Chapter 1

1. For the Old World background, see: M. Searle Bates, *Religious Liberty: An Inquiry;* Luigi Luzzatti, *God in Freedom;* Francesco Ruffini, *Religious Liberty;* Luigi Sturzo, *Church and State;* Roland H. Bainton, "The Struggle for Religious Liberty," *Church History,* Vol. X, No. 2.
2. See Merle Curti, "The Great Mr. Locke," *Huntington Library Bulletin* (Apr., 1937) No. XI, pp. 107-151.
3. See particularly John Locke, *Letter Concerning Toleration.*
4. Charles M. Andrews, *The Colonial Period in American History: The Settlements,* I, 372.
5. "The Mayflower Compact," in Henry Steele Commager, ed., *Documents of American History,* I, 15-16.
6. Professor Evarts Greene, in William A. Brown, *Church and State in Contemporary America,* Appendix I, pp. 304, 305.
7. Sanford H. Cobb, *The Rise of Religious Liberty in America,* pp. 133 ff.
8. William Warren Sweet, *Religion in Colonial America,* p. 88.
9. Brown, *op. cit.,* Appendix I, p. 304.
10. *Ibid.,* p. 306. The Carolinas, originally under a group of proprietors, sold all but a small part of their land to the king in 1729.
11. See Cobb, *op. cit.,* pp. 301-418, 440-453.
12. Conrad H. Moehlman, *School and Church,* p. 26.
13. Cobb, *op. cit.,* p. 449.
14. Frederick G. Livingood, *Eighteenth Century Reformed Church Schools,* pp. 11, 12.
15. Letter from Professor W. W. Sweet, May 28, 1949. Cf. Evarts B. Greene, *Religion and the State in America,* pp. 56-60.
16. Charles Francis Adams, ed., *Antinomianism in the Colony of Massachusetts Bay, 1636-38;* "Hutchinson, Anne," *Dictionary of American Biography,* Vol. IX; Winthrop, *A Short Story,* as reprinted in Adams, *op. cit.*
17. Paul Wakeman Coons, *Achievement of Religious Liberty in Connecticut.*
18. Vernon Louis Parrington, *Main Currents in American Thought,* I, 59.
19. Wm. H. Browne, *George Calvert and Cecilius Calvert,* p. 38.
20. *Ibid.,* p. 102.
21. Cf. Wm. T. Russell, *Land of Sanctuary,* pp. 57-59.
22. *The Calvert Papers, Number One,* in Maryland Historical Society *Publication,* No. 28, p. 132; cf. Browne, *op. cit.,* pp. 46-47.
23. William Warren Sweet, *The Story of Religion in America,* p. 117.
24. Cf. "Religious Freedom," *Encyclopedia of the Social Sciences.*
25. Justin Winsor, *Narrative and Critical History of America,* III, 534. Petri in *Church and State in Early Maryland,* p. 30, gives 6 Protestants, 8 Catholics, and 2 uncertain.
26. Commager, *op. cit.,* I, No. 22 pp.

31-32, quoting W. H. Browne, ed., *Archives of Maryland*, I, 244 ff.

27. Cf. Ruffini, *op. cit.*, p. 274.

28. Browne, *George Calvert and Cecilius Calvert*, p. 124.

29. Narragansett Club *Publications*, VI, 356.

30. Emily Easton, *Roger Williams*, pp. 168, 169, quoting, with modern spelling, *Records of the Governor and Company of Massachusetts Bay*, I, 160-163.

31. "Roger Williams," *Dictionary of American Biography*, XX, 287, 288.

32. Roger Williams, *The Bloudy Tenent of Persecution for cause of Conscience, discussed, in A Conference betweene Truth and Peace*, *Preface*, in Narragansett Club *Publications*, 1st ser., III, 3, 4.

33. *Letters of Roger Williams, 1632-1682*, in Narragansett Club *Publications*, 1st ser., VI, 278-279.

34. *Bloudy Tenent*, quoted in *ibid.*, I, 71.

35. Georg Jellinek, *The Declaration of the Rights of Man and of Citizens*, p. 77.

36. Thomas W. Bicknell, *The Story of Dr. John Clarke* (2d ed., 1915), p. 77.

37. John Clarke, *Ill Newes From New-England*, sig. A2.

38. *Ibid.*, p. 36.

39. *Ibid.*, p. 62.

40. *Ibid.*, p. 66.

41. *Ibid.*, p. 69.

42. *Ibid.*, p. 72.

43. Appleton's *Cyclopedia of American Biography*, I, 634, quoting *Records of the Colony of Rhode Island and Providence Plantations*, I, 485-491.

44. Leon Whipple, *Our Ancient Liberties*, pp. 65, 66.

45. Bicknell, *op. cit.*, title page.

46. Benjamin P. Poore, comp., *Federal and State Constitutions, Colonial Charters, and Other Organic Laws of the United States*, II, 1594. It will be noticed that this provision is more liberal than Oglethorpe's charter for Georgia a half-century later (1732), which merely provided that "there shall be a liberty of conscience allowed in the worship of God, to all persons inhabiting . . . and that all such persons, except papist, shall have a free exercise of religion." *Ibid.*, I, 375.

47. See "Charter of Privileges," *Dictionary of American History*, I, 346.

48. *Charter to William Penn, and Laws of the Province of Pennsylvania, Passed between the Years 1682 and 1700* (Harrisburg, 1870), pp. 107-108.

49. Albert Barnes, "Introductory Essay on the Life and Times of the Author," in *Sermons on Important Subjects by the Reverend Samuel Davies*, I, xxxiii.

50. Jacob Harris Patton, *The Triumph of the Presbytery of Hanover; or, Separation of Church and State in Virginia*. pp. 16-18.

51. *Ibid.*, pp. 16-18.

52. *Ibid.*, p. 22.

53. Sweet, *The Story of Religion in America*, p. 3.

54. *Ibid.*, p. 95.

55. Cited by Ruffini, *op. cit.*, p. 199.

56. See W. W. Sweet, "Church Membership," *Dictionary of American History*.

57. Harold E. Davis, "Religion, American," in *ibid*.

58. Colin Brummitt Goodycoontz, *Home Missions on the American Frontier*, p. 74.

59. Cobb, *op. cit.*, p. 485.

60. Cf. remarks of Luther A. Weigle, *American Idealism*, p. 115.

61. Wesley M. Gewehr, *The Great Awakening in Virginia*, esp. Chap. VIII.

62. See Philip A. Roth, *Masonry in the Formation of Our Government*.

63. *Negro Year Book* (1937-38), p. 562.

64. See Louis B. Wright, *Religion and Empire, passim,* esp. pp. vi, 34, 114.

65. Ruffini, *op. cit.,* p. 289.

Chapter 2

1. *Pennsylvania Packet,* Oct. 31, 1774, quoted by Ray Allen Billington, *The Protestant Crusade,* p. 17.
2. *Writings of Samuel Adam,* III, 213.
3. Peter Guilday, *The Life and Times of John Carroll,* p. 76.
4. *Journal of the Continental Congress,* I, 34-35; quoted in *ibid.*
5. *Journal of the Continental Congress* (Ford ed.), I, 72.
6. *Ibid.,* p. 83.
7. *Ibid.,* p. 117.
8. See Leo Pfeffer, *Church, State and Freedom,* pp. 133-159; James Milton O'Neill, *Religion and Education Under the Constitution.*
9. Cf. G. Adolf Koch, *Republican Religion, the American Revolution and the Cult of Reason,* p. 24.
10. *Prospect,* Aug. 18, 1804, p. 296, quoted in *ibid.,* p. 110.
11. See Elihu Palmer, *Posthumous Pieces,* pp. 10-11, quoted by Koch, *op. cit.,* p. 79.
12. B. F. Morris, *Christian Life and Character of the Civil Institutions of the United States,* pp. 448-449.
13. "American Army Chaplaincy—A Brief History," prepared in the Office of the Chief of Chaplains (1946), p. 6.
14. *Writings of Washington* (Sparks ed.), XII, 401, citing *Orderly Book;* cf. also the orders of Aug. 3, 1776, in *ibid.,* IV, 28 n.
15. "Immigration," *Dictionary of American History,* III, 74.
16. Carl Zollmann, *American Church Law,* p. 4.
17. This subject is treated more fully in Chapter 3.
18. For this and other quotations in this paragraph see Richard Hildreth, *History of the United States of America,* III, 346-347.
19. See *American Museum* (Dec., 1790), VIII, 254.
20. Alice M. Baldwin, *The New England Clergy and the American Revolution,* pp. 183 ff.
21. William Warren Sweet, *The Story of Religion in America,* p. 250; Charles A. and Mary R. Beard, *The Rise of American Civilization,* I, 259.
22. See discussion of Isaac Backus in this chapter and of the Baptists of Virginia in Chapter 3.
23. Charles Mamapoteng, "The New England Anglican Clergy in the American Revolution," *Historical Magazine of the Protestant Episcopal Church,* Dec., 1940, p. 269.
24. Sweet, *op. cit.,* p. 264.
25. Guilday, *op. cit.,* pp. 77 ff.
26. *Universal Jewish Encyclopedia,* X, 350.
27. Joel Barlow, *The Columbiad,* I, 39, quoted in Merle Curti, *The Growth of American Thought,* p. 174.
28. The Franklin Institute, *Benjamin Franklin on Religion,* p. 14.
29. Luther S. Livingston, *Benjamin Franklin's Parable Against Persecution.*
30. *Works of Benjamin Franklin* (Sparks ed.), VIII, 505-506; in Bigelow ed., VII, 139, 140.
31. See *Dictionary of American Biography,* Vol. XX, and Varnum L. Collins, *President Witherspoon.*
32. Cf. George Bancroft, *History of the United States,* V, 125.
33. *Works of John Witherspoon, D.D.* (1777), IX, 202-203.
34. Kate Mason Rowland, *The Life of George Mason,* I, 435.

35. Allan Nevins, *American States during and after the Revolution*, p. 432. See also William C. Rives, *History of the Life and Times of James Madison*, I, 142 n.

36. *Letters and Other Writings of James Madison*, I, 24 n.

37. Rives, *op. cit.*, I, 142, 143 n.

38. Rowland, *op. cit.*, I, 441.

39. William Waller Hening, *Statutes at Large; being a Collection of all the Laws of Virginia, from the First Session of the Legislature, in the year 1619*, IX, 164-166.

40. W. B. Sprague, *Annals of the American Pulpit*, VI, 56.

41. *Dictionary of American Biography*, I, 468.

42. Cf. Richard J. Purcell, *Connecticut in Transition, 1755-1818*, p. 69 and *passim*.

43. Isaac Backus, *A History of New England with Particular Reference to the Denomination of Christians Called Baptists* (2d ed.), II, 202; See also Alvah Hovey, *A Memoir of the Life and Times of Isaac Backus*, pp. 203-215, 349-351; *Works of John Adams*, II, 397-399.

44. Backus, *op. cit.*, II, 335.

45. *Debates, Resolutions and other Proceedings of the Convention of the Commonwealth of Massachusetts*, p. 182.

46. Rowland, *op. cit.*, II, p. 89.

47. This case is discussed more fully in Chapter 3.

48. For influence of Davies on Henry, see William Wirt Henry, *Patrick Henry, Life, Correspondence and Speeches*.

49. *Ibid.*, I, 317-318.

50. Rowland, *op. cit.*, p. 89.

51. Henry, W. W., *op. cit.*, I, 430, 431.

52. Jonathan Elliot, *The Debates in the Several State Conventions, on the Adoption of the Federal Constitution*, III, 317-318.

53. N.H. State Papers Series, Nathaniel Bouton, ed., *Miscellaneous Documents and Records Relating to New Hampshire*, X, 18, quoting the *Journal* of the convention.

54. *Ibid.*, p. 17.

55. *Ibid.*, p. 18.

56. See discussion in Chapter 4.

57. Joseph Gales, *Debates and Proceedings in the Congress of the United States* (Washington, Gales & Seaton, 1934), I, 759.

58. Daniel Edwin Wheeler, ed., *Life and Writings of Thomas Paine*, II, 93.

59. Moncure Daniel Conway, ed., *Writings of Thomas Paine*, I, 108-109.

60. *Ibid.*, II, 325-328.

61. *Ibid.*

62. *Ibid.*

63. Frank Smith, *Thomas Paine, Liberator*, p. 2.

64. For a favorable interpretation of Paine, including the statement that he was "a deeply religious man himself, a believer in God and immortality . . . ," see Van Wyck Brooks, *The World of Washington Irving*, p. 74; see also W. E. Woodward *Tom Paine, America's Godfather, 1737-1809*.

65. Guilday, *op. cit.*, p. 201.

66. *Ibid.*, p. 326.

67. *Studies in American Church History* (1922), I, 9, 10.

68. Baltimore Cathedral Archives, quoted by Guilday, *op. cit.*, p. 220.

69. Guilday, *op. cit.*, p. 375.

70. *Ibid.*, p. 113.

71. Edward F. Humphrey, *Nationalism and Religion in America*, p. 403.

72. Irwin Edman and Herbert W. Schneider, *Fountainheads of Freedom—The Growth of the Democratic Idea*, pp. 454-456.

73. *Writings of Thomas Jefferson* (Monticello ed.), XVI, 281-282.

74. *Writings of Jefferson* (Ford ed.), VIII, 344.

75. *Writings of Thomas Jefferson* (Monticello ed.), XV, 134-135.

76. Philip Alexander Bruce, *The His-*

tory of the University of Virginia,
II, 362-363.

77. *Ibid.,* p. 365.
78. *Ibid.,* pp. 366, 369.
79. *Ibid.,* pp. 367-369.
80. Conrad H. Moehlman, *School and Church,* p. 90, citing H. R. Washington, *Works of Thomas Jefferson,* VI, 389, VII, 267.
81. *Ibid.,* citing Roy J. Honeywell, *The Educational Work of Thomas Jefferson,* p. 256.
82. See, generally, Robert M. Healey, *Jefferson on Religion in Public Education.*
83. See Appendix to Jefferson's *Reports of Cases Determined in the General Court from 1730 to 1740; and from 1768 to 1772.*
84. Quoted by Morris, *op. cit.,* p. 35.
85. Gaillard Hunt, "James Madison and Religious Liberty," Amer. Hist. Assn. *Annual Report* (1901), I, 167.
86. James Madison, *A Memorial and Remonstrance,* set forth in Chapter 3. *See also,* Bernard Smith,

ed., *The Democratic Spirit,* pp. 104-110.
87. Irving Brant, *James Madison the Nationalist* (Vol. II of life), p. 353.
88. Elizabeth Fleet, "Madison's 'Detached Memoranda,'" in *William and Mary Quarterly,* Oct., 1946.
89. Joseph Gales, Sr., *Debates and Proceedings of the Congress of the United States,* I, 1106-1108.
90. Fleet, *op. cit.*
91. J. D. Richardson, ed., *Messages and Papers of the Presidents, 1789-1907,* I, 489, 490.
92. William A. Blakely, *American State Papers on Freedom in Religion,* pp. 592, 593.
93. Hunt, *op. cit.,* p. 170.
94. Andrew J. Bethea, *Contribution of Charles Pinckney to the Formation of the American Union.*
95. *Sprague,* op. cit., VI, 174-186.
96. Purcell, *op. cit.,* p. 76.
97. "Virginia Chronicle," *Works,* p. 118, quoted by Wesley M. Gewehr, *The Great Awakening in Virginia,* pp. 190, 191.

Chapter 3

1. Georg Jellinek, *The Declaration of the Rights of Man and of Citizens,* p. 48.
2. *Ibid.,* p. 53.
3. See, generally, H. J. Eckenrode, *Separation of Church and State in Virginia;* Charles F. James, *Struggle for Religious Liberty in Virginia;* S. H. Cobb, *The Rise of Religious Liberty in America,* pp. 74-115; Elizabeth Fleet, "Madison's 'Detached Memoranda,'" in *William and Mary Quarterly,* Oct., 1946.
4. Eckenrode, *op. cit.,* p. 22.
5. *Ibid.,* pp. 27, 28.
6. James, *op. cit.,* p. 32.
7. A. H. Newman, *History of the Baptist Churches in the United States,* p. 367; Eckenrode, *op. cit.,* pp. 12 ff.

8. James, *op. cit.,* p. 52.
9. Eckenrode, *op. cit.,* p. 38.
10. *Journals of the House of Burgesses* (Virginia State Library) 1773-76, p. 92, quoted by Eckenrode, *op. cit.,* p. 39.
11. Newman, *op. cit.,* p. 367.
12. *Ibid.,* p. 368.
13. *Ibid.,* p. 370.
14. *Ibid.,* p. 371.
15. *Ibid.*
16. Eckenrode, *op. cit.,* p. 119.
17. Henry Steele Commager, ed., *Documents of American History,* I, 124, 125; *American State Papers on Freedom in Religion,* pp. 103-105.
18. See sketch of Mason in Chapter 2.
19. Irving Brant, *James Madison,* I, 245.
20. Jacob Harris Patton, *The Triumph*

of the Presbytery of Hanover; or, Separation of Church and State in Virginia, p. 35.

21. Ibid., p. 36.

22. Kate Mason Rowland, The Life of George Mason, I, 243.

23. Patton, op. cit., p. 40.

24. Eckenrode, op. cit., pp. 83, 84.

25. Rowland, op. cit., II, 72-73.

26. See James, op. cit., p. 140.

27. See Eckenrode, op. cit., Chap. V.

28. David Wuntch, Epoch-Making Liberty Documents, pp. 103, 104. This is also found in Commager, op. cit., I, 125, 126.

29. Ibid.

30. Writings of Jefferson (Ford ed.), I, 62.

31. William Waller Hening, Statutes at Large . . . , XII, 84.

32. Wesley M. Gewehr, The Great Awakening in Virginia, p. 125; Robert B. Howison, History of Virginia, passim.

33. Stephen Beauregard Weeks, Church and State in North Carolina, p. 213. This is in the Eleventh Series of Johns Hopkins University Studies in Historical and Political Science.

34. Ibid., p. 247.

35. Francis Newton Thorpe, The Federal and State Constitutions, Colonial Charters, and other Organic Laws of the States, Territories, and Colonies Now or Heretofore Forming the United States of America, V, 2788.

36. Ibid., p. 2793.

37. Ibid., p. 2799.

38. Ibid., p. 38. This disqualification has been rendered unconstitutional by the decision of the United States Supreme Court in Torcaso v. Watkins, discussed in Chapter 5.

39. Jared Sparks, The Life of Gouverneur Morris, I, 124; cf. "Rise of Religious Liberty in the United States," Catholic World, XXIII (1876), 734, quoted in Patrick J. Dignan, History of the Legal Incorporation of Catholic Church Property in the United States (1784-1932), p. 26.

40. Thorpe, op. cit., V, 2636, 2637.

41. Ibid., p. 2637.

42. Ibid., p. 2636.

43. Peter Guilday, Life and Times of John Carroll, p. 770. Cf. Dignan, op. cit., p. 28.

44. Thorpe, op. cit., V, 2648, 2653.

45. Quotation from Ebenezer Frothingham, A Key to Unlock the Door.

46. Richard J. Purcell, Connecticut in Transition, 1775-1818, p. 191.

47. Ibid., p. 310.

48. Cf ibid., p. 326.

49. Ibid., p. 331.

50. Allan Nevins, The American States during and after the Revolution, p. 405.

51. Purcell, op. cit., p. 40.

52. Acts and Laws of the State of Connecticut (1784 ed.), pp. 403, 404; quoted in M. Louise Greene, The Development of Religious Liberty in Connecticut, p. 372.

53. Nevins, op. cit., p. 426.

54. Purcell, op. cit., pp. 384, 385.

55. Ibid., p. 385.

56. Ibid., p. 401 (art. 7). Thorpe, op. cit., I, 544, 545.

57. Joseph Francis Thorning, S.J., Religious Liberty in Transition, p. 26.

58. J. E. A. Smith, History of Pittsfield, Massachusetts, 1734-1800, pp. 366-368, quoted by Alice M. Baldwin, The New England Clergy and the American Revolution, p. 144.

59. Jacob C. Meyer, Church and State in Massachusetts from 1740 to 1833, pp. 234-235.

60. Ibid.

61. Ibid.

62. Ibid., pp. 197, 198, based on Journal of the Convention, pp. 613, 614.

63. Ibid., pp. 219, 220.

64. Proceedings of Convention of 1820, p. 667. Cf. B. P. Poore,

Federal and State Constitutions, I, 975, quoted in Thorning, *op. cit.,* pp. 90, 91.

65. For the history of a typical state constitutional provision guaranteeing religious liberty, see *Tudor* v. *Board of Education of Rutherford,* 14 N.J. 31 (1953).
66. Thorpe, *op. cit.,* IV, 2454.
67. *Ibid.,* pp. 2492, 2494.
68. *New Hampshire Manual* (1937), pp. 9, 10.
69. *Ibid.,* p. 10.
70. *Ibid.*
71. Thorpe, *op. cit.,* VI, 3255-3257.
72. *Ibid.*
73. *Ibid.,* p. 3264.
74. *Ibid.,* V, 2597, 2598.

75. *Ibid.,* p. 2599, Art. I, 4.
76. *Ibid.,* I, 567, 568, quoting Art. 29.
77. *Ibid.,* p. 566.
78. *Ibid.,* p. 568; cf. pp. 582, 601.
79. *Ibid.,* V, 3082.
80. *Ibid.,* p. 3085.
81. *Ibid.,* p. 3096.
82. *Ibid.,* p. 3100.
83. See *Torcaso* v. *Watkins,* discussed in Chapter 5.
84. Thorpe, *op. cit.,* II, 784.
85. *Ibid.,* pp. 800, 801.
86. *Ibid.,* VI, 3740.
87. *Ibid.,* p. 3767.
88. *Ibid.,* pp. 3212, 3213.
89. *Ibid.,* pp. 3222, 3223.
90. Based on Cobb, *op. cit.,* p. 507, supplemented from other sources.

Chapter 4

1. *Journal of the Continental Congress,* I, 26.
2. *Ibid.,* I, 26 n.
3. *Ibid.,* cf. references in Edward Frank Humphrey, *Nationalism and Religion in America, 1774-1789.*
4. Charles Francis Adams, *Familiar Letters of John Adams and his Wife, Abigail Adams, during the Revolution,* p. 320.
5. *Ibid.*
6. "Duché, Jacob," Appleton's *Cyclopedia of American Biography,* II, 241.
7. W. DeLoss Love, Jr., *The Fast and Thanksgiving Days of New England,* pp. 339, 340.
8. Adams, *op. cit.,* p. 66.
9. Love, *op. cit.,* pp. 400, 401.
10. *Ibid.*
11. Max Farrand, *Records of the Federal Convention of 1787,* I, 450-452; cf. *Madison Papers,* pp. 984-986.
12. *Ibid.*
13. Donald H. Magridge, unpublished memorandum on matters of religious concern in the Constitution and Bill of Rights.
14. George Bancroft, *History of the*

United States, VII, 159.
15. *Journal of the Continental Congress,* I, 108-109.
16. *Ibid.,* p. 112.
17. Peter Guilday, *The Life and Times of John Carroll,* I, 97.
18. Ray Allen Billington, "American Catholicism and the Church-State Issue," *Christendom,* V, 3 (1940), quoted in James M. O'Neill, *Religion and Education Under the Constitution,* p. 33.
19. David Wuntch, *Epoch-Making Liberty Documents,* p. 110. Cf. Humphrey, *op. cit.,* p. 438.
20. Wuntch, *op. cit.,* p. 111.
21. *Journal of the American Congress, 1774-1788* (Washington, 1823), II, 261-262.
22. For full account, see Robert R. Dearden, Jr., and Douglas S. Watson, *The Bible of the Revolution,* pp. 16-22.
23. The resolution is printed after the title page in the Bible itself.
24. William M. Malloy, *Treaties, Conventions, etc.,* p. 1235, quoted by Carl Zollmann, *American Church Law,* p. 12, n. 44.
25. Malloy, *op. cit.,* II, 1480, quoted

in Zollmann, *op. cit.*, p. 13, n. 44. This provision was repeated in Article 9 of the treaty of 1799, ratified in 1800 (Malloy, II, 1490).

26. Humphrey, *op. cit.*, pp. 430, 431, quoting *Diplomatic Correspondence of the American Revolution*, IV, 158-159. See also a translation in Jules A. Baisnée, *France and the Establishment of the American Catholic Hierarchy*, pp. 49, 50.

27. *Ibid.*

28. Baisnée, *op. cit.*, pp. 50, 51.

29. Humphrey, *op. cit.*, p. 432, quoting *Secret Journal of the Acts and Proceedings of Congress*, III, 493.

30. Humphrey, *op. cit.*, p. 407.

31. Cf. *ibid.*, Chap. 14, "Continental Congress and Religion," esp. p. 408.

32. *Journal of the First Session of the Senate of the United States of America* (Washington, Gales & Seaton, 1820); *Senate Journal*, under April 27 and April 30, 1789.

33. *Daily Advertiser*, May 1, 1789.

34. *Annals of Congress*, Sept. 25, 1789.

35. Charles Warren, *Odd Byways in American History*, p. 222.

36. *Writings of Washington* (Sparks ed.), XII, 119-120.

37. *Yale University Library Gazette*, XIII, No. 3 (Jan., 1939).

38. See *Works of John Adams*, IX, 169-170.

39. See Jefferson's note to Attorney General Levi Lincoln in *Writings of Thomas Jefferson* (Monticello ed.), X, 305.

40. *Writings of Thomas Jefferson*, XI, 428-430.

41. Love, *op. cit.*, p. 392.

42. *Letters and Other Writings of James Madison*, III, 274-275.

43. *Ibid.*

44. Isaac Amada Cornelison, *The Relation of Religion to Civil Government in the United States*, p. 163.

45. Malloy, *op. cit.*, II, 1791.

46. *Washington City and Capital* (1937), p. 195.

47. *Ibid.*, p. 211; William P. and Julia Cutler, *Life, Journals and Correspondence of Rev. Manasseh Cutler, LL.D.*, II, 58, 59.

48. Art. VI, last clause.

49. First Amendment.

50. Art. I, Sec. 7.

51. Following Art. VII.

52. Art. VI, last clause.

53. *President Dwight's Decisions of Questions discussed by the Senior Class in Yale College in 1813 and 1814*, p. 111.

54. Jonathan Elliot, *The Debates in the Several State Conventions, . . .* (2d ed.), I, 277.

55. See Sister M. Augustina, *American Opinion of Roman Catholicism in the Eighteenth Century*, pp. 376 ff.

56. Ezra Stacy Matheny, *American Devotion*, p. 79.

57. See *Torcaso* v. *Watkins*, discussed in Chapter 5.

58. Chapter 17.

59. Farrand, *op. cit.*, II, 616; cf. III, 362. According to the previous reference, Roger Sherman's recollection was that "It was thought sufficient that this power should be exercised by the States in their separate capacity."

60. *Ibid.*

61. Paul Leicester Ford, ed., *The Federalist*, p. 57.

62. *Writings of James Madison* (Hunt ed.), V, 176.

63. *The Massachusetts Centinel*, Dec. 5, 1789.

64. Cf. Charles Warren, *Congress, the Constitution and the Supreme Court*, pp. 37, 83.

65. This historical survey is based on *International Conciliation*, Jan., 1942, pp. 27, 28.

66. Three of the original thirteen states — Massachusetts, Connecticut, and Georgia — which did not ratify the Bill of Rights in 1789-

91, took favorable final action upon it in the winter of 1939, when the 150th anniversary of its adoption was being celebrated!

67. See Constitution of the United States, prepared by Library of Congress and published by United States Government Printing office, 1952, p. 39.

68. Joseph Gales, *Debates and Proceedings in the Congress of the United States,* commonly referred to as *Annals of Congress* (Washington, Gales & Seaton, 1934), I, 451, 452.

69. *Ibid.,* p. 468.

70. *Ibid.,* pp. 690, 691.

71. *Ibid.,* p. 734.

72. For the full text see *ibid.,* pp. 757-759.

73. *Ibid.,* p. 778.

74. *Ibid.,* p. 780.

75. *Ibid.,* pp. 783, 784.

76. *Ibid.,* p. 86 (Senate).

77. See Leo Pfeffer, *The Liberties of an American,* pp. 12-20.

78. *Journal of the First Session of the Senate,* p. 70.

79. *Ibid.,* p. 77.

80. *Annals of Congress,* I, 85, 86; cf. *Journal . . . of the Senate,* p. 83.

81. *Journal . . . of the Senate,* p. 88.

82. See Pfeffer, *op. cit.,* pp. 12-20.

83. *Ibid.*

84. *Cantwell* v. *Connecticut,* 310 U.S. 296 (1940); *Marsh* v. *Alabama,* 326 U.S. 501 (1946).

85. *Gitlow* v. *New York,* 268 U.S. 652 (1925); *Bridges* v. *California,* 314 U.S. 252 (1941).

86. *Near* v. *Minnesota,* 283 U.S. 697 (1931); *Grosjean* v. *American Press Co.,* 297 U.S. 233 (1936).

87. *De Jonge* v. *Oregon,* 229 U.S. 353 (1937); *Hague* v. *C.I.O.,* 307 U.S. 496 (1939).

88. *Everson* v. *Board of Education,* 330 U.S. 1 (1947); *McCollum* v. *Board of Education,* 333 U.S. 203 (1948).

89. *Murdock* v. *Pennsylvania,* 319 U.S. 104 (1943); *Sherbert* v. *Verner,* 83 S. Ct. 1790 (1963).

90. *Kedroff* v. *St. Nicholas Cathedral,* 344 U.S. 94 (1952); *Abbington School District* v. *Schempp,* 83 S. Ct. 1560 (1963).

91. See Chapter 15.

92. See Chapter 16.

93. See *Hamilton* v. *Regents of the University of California,* 293 U.S. 245 (1934).

94. See, e.g., Robert Freeman Butts, *The American Tradition in Religion and Education;* Edward S. Corwin, *A Constitution of Powers in a Secular State;* O'Neill, *op. cit.;* Leo Pfeffer, *Church, State and Freedom;* Wilfred Parsons, *The First Freedom;* Joseph H. Brady, *Confusion Twice Confounded.*

95. O'Neill, *op. cit.;* Parsons, *op. cit.*

96. Butts, *op. cit.;* Pfeffer, *Church, State and Freedom.*

97. Parsons, *op. cit.;* John C. Murray, "Law or Prepossession," *Law and Contemporary Problems,* XIV, 3; statement of National Catholic Welfare Conference, *New York Times,* Nov. 21, 1948, p. 63.

98. See Leo Pfeffer, *Creeds in Competition,* Chap. 3.

99. E.g., Corwin, *op. cit.*

100. Pfeffer, *Creeds in Competition,* Chap. 3.

101. See Chapter 5.

102. 330 U.S. 1, 15, 16 (1947).

103. 333 U.S 203, 210 (1948).

104. O'Neill, *op. cit.;* Brady, *op. cit.;* Corwin, *op. cit.;* Parsons, *op. cit.*

105. O'Neill, *op. cit.,* is the most vigorous protagonist of this position.

106. See Chapter 5.

107. 343 U.S. 306 (1952).

108. *Ibid.*

109. *Ibid.*

110. 366 U.S. 420 (1961).

111. 367 U.S. 488 (1961).

112. See Chapter 5.

113. See Chapter 5.

Chapter 5

1. The citation for this and all other Court decisions referred to in this chapter and elsewhere in this book are set forth in the Index of Legal Cases.

Chapter 6

1. Quoted by Samuel Eliot Morison and Henry Steele Commager, *The Growth of the American Republic*, p. 107.
2. For an excellent survey of American developments in this period, see Evarts B. Greene, "Persistent Problems of Church and State," presidential address before American Historical Society, *American Historical Review*, Jan., 1931.
3. Cf. Sanford H. Cobb, *The Rise of Religious Liberty in America*, p. 510.
4. See Chapter 17.
5. Edward F. Humphrey, *Nationalism and Religion in America, 1774-1789*, p. 478.
6. Philip Schaff, *Church and State in the United States*, p. 31, quoting Murray Hoffman, *Ecclesiastical Law of the State of New York*, p. 40.
7. *Journal of Congress* (1774-1788), XIII, 172.
8. Robert Kemp Morton, *God in the Constitution*, p. 72.
9. See *ibid.*
10. See Chapter 2.
11. Morton, *op. cit.*, p. 89.
12. Elliot's *Debates*, III, 659, quoted in Schaff, *op. cit.*, p. 30.
13. *Journal of Congress* (1774-1788), XIII, 178.
14. Stephen Beauregard Weeks, *Church and State in North Carolina*, p. 58.
15. *Ibid.*, p. 261.
16. *Ibid.*, p. 262, quoting from Elliot's *Debates* (2d ed.), IV, 191-215.
17. Weeks, *op. cit.*, p. 262.
18. *Ibid.*, p. 263.
19. *Ibid.*
20. Carey, *American Museum*, Vol. II, No. V, pp. 536-553, quoted by Schaff, *op. cit.*, p. 31.
21. Charles A., and Mary R. Beard, *Basic History of the United States*, p. 137.
22. The principal exceptions were that Massachusetts and Connecticut continued their official bond with Congregationalism.
23. See Chapter 3.
24. See Chapter 4.
25. Francis Newton Thorpe, *The Federal and State Constitutions . . .*, V, 2899.
26. *Ibid.*, V, 2910; cf. Rodney L. Mott and W. L. Hindman, eds., *Constitution of the States and the United States* (1938), p. 1192.
27 Conrad Henry Moehlman, *School and Church*, p. 37.
28. Quoted in *Coyle* v. *Smith*, 221 U.S. 559 (1911).
29. Thorpe, *op. cit.*, II, 651.
30. Michael J. Curley, "Church and State in the Spanish Floridas (1783-1822)," in *Studies in American Church History*, Vol. XXX.
31. "Florida," in *Catholic Encyclopedia;* see esp. VI, 118.
32. Thorpe, *op. cit.*, II, 661.
33. *Ibid.*, p. 664.
34. *Ibid.*, p. 733.
35. *Blair* v. *Odin*, 3 Tex. 288, 300 (1848), cited in Carl Zollmann, *American Church Law*, p. 16.
36. Thorpe, *op. cit.*, I, 391.
37. *Ibid.*, V, 2963.
38. Zollmann, *op. cit.*, p. 9.

39. *Cantwell* v. *Connecticut*, 310 U.S. 296 (1940); *Marsh* v. *Alabama*, 326 U.S. 501 (1946).

40. *Everson* v. *Board of Education*, 330 U.S. 1 (1947); *McCollum* v. *Board of Education* 333 U.S. 203 (1948).

41. Cf. concurring opinion of Justice Frankfurter in *McCollum* v. *Board of Education*, 333 U.S. 203 at p. 215.

42. *Journals of Congress*, XI, 718; cited by Humphrey, *op. cit.*, p. 408.

43. Thorpe, *op. cit.*, V, 2793.

44. *Ibid.*, p. 2637.

45. *Ibid.*, VI, 3253.

46. *Ibid.*, I, 579.

47. *Ibid.*, III, 1722.

48. See *Works of John Witherspoon, D.D.* (1777), IX, 220-223.

49. Thorpe, *op. cit.*, V, 1374 (italics added).

50. Cf. Peter Guilday, *The Life and Times of John Carroll*, p. 406.

51. Maryland Constitution, Art. III, Sec. 11.

52. Tennessee Constitution, Art. IX, Sec. 1.

53. *Writings of Madison* (Hunt ed.,), V, 288.

54. "Detroit, Diocese of," *Catholic Encyclopedia*, IV, 759.

55. *Ibid.*

56. See Chapter 13.

57. See Chapter 15.

58. Charles F. Thwing, *History of Higher Education in America*, p. 175.

59. *Ibid.*, Chap. VI, *passim.*

60. *Ibid.*, p. 176.

61. Clement Eaton, *Freedom of Thought in the Old South*, p. 288.

62. Thwing, *op. cit.*, p. 178.

63. Dumas Malone, *The Public Life of Thomas Cooper*, p. 264.

64. *Ibid.*

65. Chapter 2.

66. Cheney, *History of the University of Pennsylvania*, p. 124.

67. *Ibid.*, p. 131.

68. *Ibid.*

69. *Ibid.*, p. 166.

70. *Will of General George Washington*, pp. 7-9.

71. George W. Kirchway, "Education for the Law," in P. Monroe, *Cyclopedia of Education*, III, 659, 660.

72. Thwing, *op. cit.*, pp. 188, 189.

73. *Ibid.*, pp. 190, 191.

74. *Ibid.*, *passim.*

75. *Ibid.*

76. Guilday, *op. cit.*

77. *Ibid.*

78. Ellwood P. Cubberley, *The History of Education* (1920), p. 705.

79. *Ibid.*

80. B. F. Morris, *Christian life and Character of the Civil Institutions of the United States*, p. 440.

81. *Writings of James Madison*, III, 305.

82. Niels Sonne, *Liberal Kentucky (1780-1828)*, p. 260.

83. *A History of Columbia University, 1754-1904*, p. 60.

84. *New York Times*, Mar. 5, 1944.

85. See Thwing, *op. cit.*, p. 113.

86. *Writings of Washington* (Sparks ed.), XII, 245.

87. *Writings of Thomas Jefferson* (Monticello ed.), II, 224, 209, 310.

88. William A. Blakely, *American State Papers on Freedom in Religion*, pp. 174, 175, quoting *Letters and Other Writings of James Madison* (1865), III, 273 ff.

89. *Ibid.*, p. 593, quoting *Writings of James Madison* (Hunt ed.), IX, 126-128.

90. Robert Baird, *Religion in America*, p. 267.

Chapter 7

1. Ralph Henry Gabriel, *The Course of American Democratic Thought,* p. 33.
2. Carl Russell Fish, *Rise of the Common Man* (Vol. VI in *History of American Life*), pp. 30-31.
3. Henry Adams, *History of the United States . . .* , IX, 175.
4. President Timothy Dwight's baccalaureate address at Yale in 1797 on "The Nature and Danger of Infidel Philosophy" is often taken as the beginning of this movement.
5. Daniel Dorchester, *Christianity in the United States,* p. 373.
6. William W. Sweet, *The Baptists* (Vol. I of *Religion on the American Frontier*) p. 33.
7. See Chapter 9.
8. William Warren Sweet, *The Story of Religion in America,* p. 315.
9. See Chapter 4.
10. Sweet, *Religion on the American Frontier, passim.*
11. *Quarterly Journal of the American Education Society* (Apr., 1829), No. VIII, pp. 224, 225.
12. John Bach McMaster, *A History of the People of the United States,* II, 392-396.
13. "Alien and Sedition Acts," *Dictionary of American History,* I, 48, 49.
14. Quoted by Professor Edward P. Cheyney in "Present Importance of the First Amendment," *Annals of the American Academy of Political and Social Sciences,* CXCV, 82.
15. "Know-Nothingism," *Catholic Encyclopedia,* VIII, 667.
16. Richard J. Purcell, *Connecticut in Transition, 1775-1818,* p. 277.
17. William B. Sprague, *Annals of the American Pulpit,* II, 165.
18. H. Richard Niebuhr, *The Social Sources of Denominationalism,* p. 175; Purcell, *op. cit.,* p. 329.

19. Jacob C. Meyer, *Church and State in Massachusetts from 1740 to 1833,* p. 155.
20. Its constitutionality was upheld in *Adams* v. *Howe,* 14 Mass. 340 (1817).
21. See Charles Beecher, ed., *Autobiography and Correspondence of Lyman Beecher,* I, 250, 260.
22. F. D. Watson, *Charity Organization Movement in the United States,* p. 91.
23. Allan Nevins, *American States during and after the Revolution,* pp. 452-454.
24. J. B. McMaster, *The Acquisition of the Political, Social, and Industrial Rights of Man in America,* p. 54.
25. Quoted in Samuel Eliot Morison and Henry Steele Commager, *The Growth of the American Republic,* p. 311.
26. Peter Guilday, *The Life and Times of John Carroll,* p. 807.
27. Merle Curti, *Peace or War, The American Struggle against War, 1636-1936,* and his "Peace Movements" in *Dictionary of American History.*
28. Alice Felt Tyler, *Freedom's Ferment,* p. 411.
29. U.S. Department of Justice figures, quoted from *World Almanac,* 1963, p. 635.
30. For a good summary, see "Irish Immigration," *Dictionary of American History,* III, 153-155.
31. See Chapter 16.
32. See Chapter 9.
33. See Chapter 9.
34. See Chapter 13.
35. See Chapter 10.
36. Curti, *Peace or War,* p. 297.
37. *World Almanac,* 1963, p. 251.
38. Chapter 13.
39. See Chapter 17.
40. Beecher, *op. cit.,* I, 154.
41. Charles A. and Mary R. Beard, *Rise of American Civilization*

(1936 ed.), I, 734, 735.

42. Allan Nevins and Henry Steele Commager, *The Story of A Free People* (1942), p. 188.

43. See J. H. Wainwright, *Inequality of Individual Wealth, the Ordinance of Providence and Essential to Civilization*; and Arthur M. Schlesinger, Jr., *The Age of Jackson,* pp. 17, 352.

44. Martha L. Edwards, "A Problem of Church and State in the 1870's," *The Mississippi Valley Historical Review* (June, 1934), XI, 39.

45. "Indian Affairs," *American State Papers,* I, 54.

46. *Ibid.*

47. Cf. *ibid.,* pp. 235, 319.

48. *Ibid.,* p. 687.

49. *Ibid.,* II, 273.

50. *Indian Missions of the U.S.,* Department of the Interior, Office of Indian Affairs, Bulletin No. 8, 1928, p. 2.

51. Helen Hunt Jackson, *A Century of Dishonor,* pp. 270, 271.

52. *Ibid., passim.*

53. E. C. Tracy, *Memoir of the Life of Jeremiah Evarts, Esq.,* pp. 442 ff.

54. *Register of Debates in Congress* (Washington, Gales & Seaton), VI, 310.

55. *Ibid.,* p. 318.

56. Ralph Henry Gabriel, *Elias Boudinot, Cherokee, and His America, passim,* esp. Chaps. 19-23.

57. *Worcester v. Georgia,* 6 Pet. 515 (1832). See also *Cherokee Nation v. Georgia,* 5 Pet. 1 (1831).

58. Paul Leicester Ford, ed., *The Federalist,* p. 342 n.

59. *"Worcester v. Georgia," Dictionary of American History,* V, 484.

60. See Grant Foreman, *Indian Removal,* University of Oklahoma, 1932, cited by Gabriel, *Elias Boudinot,* pp. 168-171.

Chapter 8

1. The Churches are considered in the approximate order of their organization or reorganization after the Revolution.

2. Joseph Story, *Commentaries on the Constitution* (1879), quoted in W. W. Keesecker, *Laws Relating to the Releasing of Pupils from Public Schools for Religious Instruction.*

3. Amendment X, Bill of Rights.

4. Ellwood P. Cubberley, *Public Education in the United States,* p. 52; cf. VIII, 1.

5. See Chapter 16.

6. See Chapter 18.

7. Cf. Evarts B. Greene, *Religion and the State in America,* p. 266.

8. Chapter 9.

9. Chapter 10.

10. William Warren Sweet, *Religion in Colonial America,* p. 308; Charles F. James, *Documentry History of the Struggle for Religious Liberty in Virginia,* pp. 75, 76.

11. For these and other facts, see "Historical Sketch," *Doctrines and Discipline of the Methodist Episcopal Church* (1936), an official publication.

12. Jesse Lee, *History of the Methodists,* p. 47, quoted by J. M. Buckley, *History of the Methodists in the United States,* p. 142.

13. Buckley, *op. cit.,* pp. 235, 236; *Doctrines and Discipline of the Methodist Episcopal Church,* p. 8.

14. Buckley, *op. cit.,* p. 242.

15. *Ibid.,* p. 265.

16. Cf. *ibid.,* pp. 321, 322.

17. See Chapter 7.

18. Walter McElreath, *Methodist Union in the Courts,* p. 21.

19. Sweet, *op. cit.,* pp. 240-254.

20. See Thomas Balch, *Calvinism and*

American Independence (Philadelphia, 1909).

21. See Chapter 1.

22. See Chapter 2.

23. Edward Frank Humphrey, *Nationalism and Religion in America, 1774-1789,* pp. 440, 459.

24. Robert E. Thompson, *History of the Presbyterian Churches in the United States,* p. 53.

25. *Ibid.*

26. Philip Schaff, *Church and State in the United States,* p. 50; cf. also his *Creeds of Christendom,* III, 720.

27. *The Constitution of the Presbyterian Church in the U.S.A.* (1894), pp. 80, 81.

28. *Ibid.*

29. Conrad H. Moehlman, *School and Church,* p. 61.

30. Sweet, *op. cit.,* p. 55; Charles C. Tiffany, *History of the Protestant Episcopal Church in the United States of America* (American Church History Series), p. 268.

31. Tiffany, *op. cit.,* pp. 270-271.

32. *Ibid.,* pp. 76, 273.

33. Luther A. Weigle, *American Idealism,* p. 75.

34. Charles Mampoteng, "The New England Anglican Clergy in the American Revolution," *Historical Magazine of the Protestant Episcopal Church,* Dec., 1940, p. 270.

35. *Ibid.*

36. *Ibid.,* p. 279.

37. *Ibid.,* p. 280.

38. *Ibid.,* pp. 288, 290; Tiffany, *op. cit.,* p. 159.

39. See Charles H. Van Tyne, *Loyalists in the American Revolution, passim.*

40. W. S. Perry, *Historical Collections Relating to the Episcopal Colonial Church . . .* (Hartford, 1870), pp. 281-282, cited by Humphrey, *op. cit.,* p. 435.

41. Tiffany, *op. cit.,* pp. 290, 291, 296.

42. Schaff, *Church and State,* p. 52.

43. *Ibid.*

44. See William Wilson Manross, *A History of the American Episcopal Church* (1935).

45. Richard Eddy, *History of Universalism* (American Church History Services, Vol. X), p. 401.

46. *Life of Murray,* pp. 335 f., quoted by Eddy, *op. cit.,* pp. 402, 403.

47. Eddy, *op. cit.,* p. 403.

48. *Ibid.,* pp. 413, 414.

49. *Ibid.,* p. 416.

50. Joseph Henry Dubbs, *History of the Reformed Church, German* (American Church History Series), pp. 314, 316.

51. *Ibid.,* p. 323.

52. Cf. "Reformed Church in the United States," *Enclycopedia Britannica* XXIII, 24.

53. Samuel P. Spreng, *History of the Evangelical Association* (American Church History Series, Vol. XII), p. 400.

54. Carl Zollmann, *American Church Law,* pp. 206-208.

55. Cf. *Yearbook of American Churches,* 1941, pp. 28, 29, and *Columbia Encyclopedia,* under Churches concerned.

56. *World Almanac,* 1963, p. 711.

57. See generally E. T. Corwin, *History of the Reformed Church, Dutch* (American Church History Series).

58. *Ibid.,* p. 137; cf. p. 71.

59. Peter G. Mode, *Source Book and Biographical Guide for American Church History,* pp. 143-145, quoting Hugh Hastings, *Ecclesiastical Records of the State of New York,* VI, 3963-3966.

60. Corwin, *op. cit.,* pp. 160-174.

61. *Ibid.,* p. 207.

62. *World Almanac,* 1963, p. 706.

63. See, generally, D. Berger, *History of the Church of the United Brethren in Christ* (American Church History Series, Vol. XII).

64. *World Almanac,* 1963, p. 706.

65. Joseph S. Clark, *Historical Sketch of the Congregational Churches in Massachusetts,* p. 193.

66. See Williston Walker, *History of the Congregational Churches in the United States,* pp. 209-212, 217.
67. *World Almanac,* 1963, p. 711.
68. *Religious News Service,* Dec. 3, 1953.
69. For the European background of the Quakers in their relation to religious freedom, see Philip S. Belasco, *Authority in Church and State.*
70. See, generally, A. C. and Richard H. Thomas, *History of the Society of Friends in America* (American Church History Series, Vol. XII).
71. *Ibid.,* p. 235.
72. Gustavus Myers, *History of Bigotry in the United States,* p. 11.
73. Leon Whipple, *The Story of Civil Liberty in the United States,* p. 9.
74. Paul Blanshard, *God and Man in Washington,* p. 101. See also Luke E. Ebersole, *Church Lobbying in the Nation's Capital.*
75. Chapter 1.
76. See Chapter 1.
77. See Chapter 2.
78. See Chapter 2.
79. See statement made in court by proprieters of Ashfield, Massachusetts, in 1771, *Acts and Resolves, Public and Private, of the Province of the Massachusetts Bay,* IV, 1040.
80. Sweet, *op. cit.,* p. 220, quoting the *Autobiography of Benjamin Franklin* (O. S. Coad ed., 1929), pp. 154-155.
81. Sweet, *op. cit.,* p. 297.
82. A. H. Newman, *History of the Baptist Churches in the United States,* p. 393.
83. *Ibid.,* p. 398.
84. See brief filed as "friend of the court" in *McCollum* v. *Board of Education,* 333 U.S. 203 (1948).
85. Blanshard, *op. cit.,* p. 147.
86. See, generally, Joseph Henry Allen and Richard Eddy, *History of the Unitarians and the Univer-* salists *in the United States* (American Church History Series, Vol. X).
87. *World Almanac,* 1963, p. 708.
88. See, generally, H. E. Jacobs, *History of the Evangelical Lutheran Church in the United States* (American Church History Series, Vol. IV).
89. Abdel Ross Wentz, *The Lutheran Church in American History* (2d ed., 1933).
90. Wentz, *op. cit.,* pp. 98-99, discusses the results.
91. *Ibid.,* p. 123.
92. *Ibid.,* p. 129.
93. *Ibid.,* pp. 128-130.
94. *Ibid.,* p. 401.
95. See, generally, B. B. Tyler, *History of the Disciples of Christ* (American Church History Series, Vol. IV), p. 27.
96. New York *Times,* Nov. 24, 1963, p. 5.
97. Tyler, *op. cit.,* p. 45.
98. *Ibid.*
99. *Ibid.,* p. 49; Henry Adams, *History of the United States,* IX, 185.
100. H. Richard Niebuhr, *The Social Sources of Denominationalism,* p. 166.
101. Winfred Ernest Garrison, *Religion Follows the Frontier—A History of the Disciples of Christ,* p. 154. See also his *An American Religious Movement, A Brief History of the Disciples of Christ.*
102. See statement adopted by the International Convention of the Disciples of Christ at Buffalo in 1947, New York *Times,* Aug. 1, 1947.
103. "Pastorius," Appleton's *Cyclopedia of American Biography,* IV, 608.
104. Cornelius Wedel, *Abriss der Geschichte der Mennoniten,* IV, 159.
105. *Ibid.*
106. See Francis J. Grund, *The Americans in Their Moral, Social and Political Relations,* I, 61.
107. *Ibid.,* I, 290, 291.

108. Robert Baird, *Religion in America*, p. 232.

109. For an interesting discussion of this see Henry Kalloch Rowe, *The History of Religion in the United States*, Chap. IV, "The Consequences of Freedom."

110. Grund, *op. cit.*, I, 61.

111. *Ibid.*, I, 281.

112. *Ibid.*, I, 292.

113. *Ibid.*, I, 294.

Chapter 9

1. The term "Roman Catholic" is generally used in this book, as "Roman" alone is offensive to members of the Church which recognizes the pope as supreme pontiff, and "Catholic," as referring exclusively to Roman Catholic, is objected to by many Episcopalians and some other groups who consider their own position truly catholic. Roman Catholic, as the *Oxford Dictionary* shows, has been used as a conciliatory term since early in the seventeenth century. It seems fair, as it is taken from a translation of the official designation *Ecclesia Romana Catholica et Apostolica*. It is the term regularly used in the U.S. Government census reports.

2. Herbert Thurston, *No Popery*, chapters on "Anti-papal Prejudices," quoted by Michael Williams, *The Shadow of the Pope*, pp. 20, 21.

3. Ray Allen Billington, *The Protestant Crusade*, p. 6.

4. Cf. *ibid.*, p. 9.

5. *Studies in American Church History*, XXIV, 319, 320.

6. See Chapter 2.

7. Joseph McSorley, *An Outline History of the Church by Centuries*, p. 729.

8. Peter Guilday, *The Life and Times of John Carroll*, p. 791.

9. Thomas O'Gorman, *History of the Roman Catholic Church in the United States*, p. 247.

10. For the ecclesiastical situation of the time, see Guilday, *op. cit.*, p. 163.

11. Williams, *op. cit.*, p. 42.

12. For details of the laws in the different states, see *ibid.*, Chap. III.

13. Patrick J. Dignan, *History of the Legal Incorporation of Catholic Church Property in the United States*, pp. 28, 30.

14. Jules A. Baisnée, *France and the Establishment of the American Catholic Hierarchy*, pp. 45, 46, 47.

15. O'Gorman, *op. cit.*, p. 260.

16. "Carroll, John," *Catholic Encyclopedia*, III, 382.

17. See *Independent Chronicle*, Nov. 6, 1788.

18. This account is based on "Boston," *Catholic Encyclopedia*, II, 704.

19. Williams, *op. cit.*, p. 55.

20. Harold J. Laski, *Liberty in the Modern State*, p. 64.

21. The material in this section is based almost entirely on the articles "Baltimore, Provincial Councils of" and "Baltimore, Plenary Councils of" in the *Catholic Encyclopedia*, written by the Reverend Professor William H. W. Fanning, S.J., Professor of Church History and Canon Law at St. Louis University, and based, to a large extent, on the original decrees. For more details regarding any of the acts, the reader is referred to the standard work of the Reverend Professor Peter Guilday, *A History of the Councils of Baltimore*, 1791-1884.

22. Allen Sinclair Will, *Life of Cardinal Gibbons, Archbishop of Baltimore*, I, 251-252, quoting *Memorial Volume*, Third Plenary Council, Part 3.

23. *Ibid.*
24. Dignan, *op. cit.,* p. 50.
25. Charles Augustine Bachofen, *The Canonical and Civil Status of Catholic Parishes in the United States,* quoted in *ibid.,* p. 51.
26. Dignan, *op. cit.,* p. 75.
27. *Ibid.*
28. *Ibid.,* p. 82.
29. *Ibid.,* p. 84.
30. *Laws of the State of New York* (1812-13), II, 214-216, quoted in *ibid.,* pp. 64, 65.
31. Zollmann, *op. cit.,* p. 224.
32. Dignan, *op. cit.,* pp. 65-66.
33. *Ibid.,* p. 102.
34. *Ibid.,* pp. 103, 104.
35. *Ibid.,* pp. 109, 110.
36. Billington, *op. cit.,* p. 40.
37. Dignan, *op. cit.,* pp. 145, 156.
38. *Ibid.,* pp. 166, 167.
39. Chapter 18.
40. Guilday, Peter, *Life and Times of John England,* II, 194.
41. *Ibid.,* II, 426; cf. art. "Breckenridge, John," Appleton, *op. cit.,* I, 365.
42. Billington, *op. cit.,* pp. 73, 74; Chap. III of this work is devoted to this incident and is the authority for most of the facts recorded here.
43. Gustavus Myers, *History of Bigotry in the United States,* p. 144.
44. *Ibid.*
45. Leon Whipple, *The Story of Civil Liberty in the United States,* p. 335.
46. See Billington, *op. cit.,* pp. 89, 110 (note 27).
47. J. A. Burns, *The Catholic School System in the United States,* p. 141.
48. *Ibid.,* pp. 248-249.
49. John R. Commons, *Races and Immigrants in America,* p. 66.
50. Burns, *op. cit.,* pp. 11, 12.
51. J. A. Burns, *The Growth and Development of the Catholic School System in the United States,* p.

22.
52. *Ibid.,* p. 183 n.
53. *Ibid.,* p. 19.
54. Billington, *op. cit.,* pp. 99-108.
55. See Bliss Perry, *Heart of Emerson's Journals,* August, 1847.
56. William Warren Sweet, *The Story of Religion in America,* p. 391.
57. Samuel F. B. Morse, *Foreign Conspiracy,* pp. 41, 42, quoted by Billington, *op. cit.,* p. 124.
58. Charles Beecher, ed., *Autobiography and Correspondence of Lyman Beecher,* II, 453.
59. Quoted in Billington, *op. cit.,* p. 143.
60. Quoted in Billington, *op. cit.,* p. 145.
61. *Ibid.,* pp. 147, 148.
62. *Ibid.,* pp. 131, 132.
63. *Ibid.,* p. 155; cf. p. 162.
64. Quoted in *ibid.,* p. 168.
65. *The American Republican Songster,* quoted in *ibid.,* p. 202.
66. Quoted in *ibid.,* p. 203.
67. See *ibid.,* pp. 216, 217 (note 77).
68. Quoted in *ibid.,* p. 214 (note 44).
69. For full account, see *ibid.,* pp. 220-230.
70. Quoted in *ibid.,* pp. 231, 232.
71. *Ibid.*
72. *Freeman's Journal,* Nov. 23, 1850, quoted in *ibid.,* p. 315.
73. Quoted in *ibid.,* p. 295.
74. *Ibid.,* p. 312.
75. See *ibid.,* pp. 313, 314.
76. Myers, *op. cit.,* p. 187.
77. Billington, *op. cit.,* p. 384.
78. Everett R. Clinchy, *All in the Name of God,* pp. 69, 70.
79. For these and other instances with references, see Whipple, *op. cit.,* pp. 60, 61.
80. Quoted in Bernard Smith, ed., *The Democratic Spirit,* p. 409.
81. Billington, *op. cit.,* p. 388.
82. *Ibid.,* p. 414.
83. Billington, *op. cit.,* p. 431 n. 6
84. See *ibid.,* Chap. XVI.
85. Clinchy, *op. cit.,* p. 70.

Chapter 10

1. *Documents Relating to the Colonial History of New York*, XIV, 315.
2. *Ibid.*
3. *Ibid.*, p. 341.
4. *Ibid.*, p. 351.
5. Abram Vossen Goodman, *American Overture: Jewish Rights in Colonial Times*, p. 3.
6. Luigi Luzzatti, *God in Freedom*, p. 675.
7. Anita Libman Lebeson, *Jewish Pioneers in America*, p. 202, quoting American Jewish Historical Society, *Publications*, II, 66-70; XXVII, 391.
8. *Jewish Encyclopedia*, XII, 365.
9. Goodman, *op. cit.*, p. 152.
10. P. Wiernick, *History of the Jews in America*, p. 79.
11. Goodman, *op. cit.*, p. 166.
12. *Ibid.*, p. 169.
13. *Ibid.*, p. 199.
14. *Ibid.*, p. 200.
15. *Ibid.*, p. 36.
16. *Ibid.*, p. 58.
17. *Ibid.*, p. 123.
18. *Ibid.*, p. 120.
19. Frank Monaghan and Marvin Lowenthal, *This Was New York, The Nation's Capital in 1789* (1943), p. 184.
20. Wiernick, *op. cit.*, pp. 99, 100.
21. *Ibid.*, pp. 100, 101.
22. William Addison Blakely, *American State Papers bearing on Sunday Legislation* (Washington, rev. and enlarged ed., 1911), pp. 195-197, citing Mordecai M. Noah, *Travels, etc.* (1819), Appendix, p. 25.
23. Blakely, *op. cit.*, pp. 199-200, quoting Noah, *op. cit.*, III, 178, 179.
24. Leon Hübner, "The Struggle for Religious Liberty in North Carolina," in A.J.H.S. *Proceedings*, XVI, pp. 37 ff.
25. See Chapter 17.
26. Francis Newton Thorpe, *The Feddderal and State Constitutions . . .*, III, 1689, 1690.
27. Allan Nevins, *American States during and after the Revolution*, pp. 430, 431.
28. See Chapter 5.
29. For a general summary of his work, see Lee J. Levinger, *A History of the Jews in the United States*.
30. Emanuel Milton Altfeld, *The Jew's Struggle for Religious and Civil Liberty in Maryland*, p. 21.
31. *Ibid.*, pp. 70-75.
32. *Ibid.*, pp. 77-78.
33. *Ibid.*
34. *Ibid.*, pp. 79-80.
35. *Ibid.*, p. 27.
36. *Ibid.*, p. 32.
37. *Ibid.*, pp. 32-33.
38. *Ibid.*, p. 35.
39. Thorpe, *op. cit.*, III, 1715, 1716.
40. *Ibid.*, p. 1745.
41. *Ibid.*, p. 1782 (Art. 37).
42. See Chapter 5.
43. Wiernick, *op. cit.*, p. 121.
44. *Ibid.*, p. 172.
45. Cf. Oscar I. Janowsky, ed., *The American Jew*, p. 50.
46. Wiernick, *op. cit.*, p. 176.
47. Gustavus Myers, *History of Bigotry in the United States*, p. 207.
48. *Papers relating to the Foreign Relations of the United States, Transmitted to Congress, with the Annual Message of the President, December 8, 1885*, pp. 49-50.
49. *Ibid.*, p. 12.
50. John Bassett Moore, *A Digest of International Law*, IV, 483.

Chapter 11

1. Ebenezer Mason, *Complete Works of John M. Mason, D.D.,* IV, 520-522.
2. See also *President Dwight's Decisions of Questions . . . ,* p. 310.
3. A. W. Patterson, *The Code Duello,* p. 72. The title of the sermon was "A Discourse . . . occasioned by the ever to be lamented death of General Alexander Hamilton. . . ."
4. Charles Beecher, ed., *Autobiography . . . of Lyman Beecher,* I, 155.
5. *Ibid.,* pp. 150-154.
6. *Ibid.,* pp. 155, 156.
7. Francis Newton Thorpe, *The Federal and State Constitutions . . . ,* Thorpe, I, 544.
8. *Works of John England* (Messmer ed.), VII, 425-429.
9. Thorpe, *op. cit.,* VI, 3284.
10. Cf. *Constitutions of the States and the United States* (1938), index, p. 1765, under "Duelling."
11. Chapter 17.
12. Charles M. Snow, *Religious Liberty in America,* p. 404; cf. documents in *American State Papers,* XV, 45.
13. Snow, *op. cit.,* p. 405.
14. *American State Papers,* VII, 211-212.
15. *Ibid.,* p. 231.
16. *Free Enquirer,* Oct. 31, 1820; quoted in Arthur M. Schlesinger, Jr., *The Age of Jackson,* p. 138.
17. Schlesinger, *op. cit.,* p. 138.
18. Chapter 1.
19. Peter Guilday, *The Life and Times of John Carroll,* p. 781.
20. Cf. "Anti-Masonic Party," *Encyclopaedia Britannica,* II, 127.
21. Charles McCarthy, "The Antimasonic Party: A Study of Political Antimasonry in the United States, 1827-1840," in American Historical Association *Annual Report* (1902), I, 540.
22. *Ibid.,* pp. 540, 541.
23. Samuel Eliot Morrison and Henry Steele Commager, *The Growth of the American Republic,* p. 926.
24. See "Anti-Masonic Movements," *Dictionary of American History,* I, 82; Thurlow Weed, *Autobiography,* I, *passim.*
25. McCarthy, *op. cit.* pp. 469-470.
26. A. R. Spofford, "Lotteries in American History," American Historical Association *Annual Report* (1892), pp. 181-188.
27. "Lotteries," Johnson, *Universal Cyclopedia,* V.
28. See also Luther A. Weigle, *American Idealism,* p. 308.
29. Spofford, *op. cit.,* pp. 181-188.
30. Mason, *op. cit.,* I, 503, 504.
31. Job Roberts Tyson, *Brief Survey of the Great Extent and Evil Tendencies of the Lottery System as existing in the U.S.* (Philadelphia, 1833).
32. *Ibid.,* pp. 99-100; Spofford, *op. cit.,* p. 177.
33. See, generally, Martin E. Marty and others, *The Religious Press in America.* 1963.
34. "Religious Periodicals," *Dictionary of American History,* IV, 445. For a survey of the Protestant Press, see Martin E. Marty, "The Protestant Press," in Marty, *op. cit.*
35. Cf. A. H. Newman, *History of the Baptist Churches in the United States,* pp. 423, 424.
36. E. C. Tracy, *Memoir of the Life of Jeremiah Everts,* p. 64.
37. "Periodical Literature," *Catholic Encyclopedia,* XI, 692. For a survey of the Catholic press, see, "The Catholic Press," in Marty, *op. cit.*
38. *Ibid.*
39. *Commonweal,* Feb. 7, 1941.
40. *Catholic Encyclopedia,* XI, 692.
41. Information in this paragraph is based on letters received from

editors of the respective magazines.

42. Apollinaris W. Baumgartner, *Catholic Journalism—A Study of Its Development in the United States* (New York, 1931). The combined circulation of the Catholic press, newspapers and magazines, is about 27 million. *Catholic Press Directory, 1962-1963.*

43. *Jewish Encyclopedia*, X, 371. For a survey of the Jewish press, see David W. Silverman, "The Jewish Press," in Marty, *op. cit.*

44. *Ibid.*

45. Weigle, *op. cit.*, p. 175.

46. Alice Felt Tyler, *Freedom's Ferment*, p. 319.

47. Beecher, *op. cit.*, I, 245.

48. See editorial in *America*, July 30, 1938; cf. "Temperance Movement," *Dictionary of American History.*

49. Weigle, *op. cit.*, p. 209.

50. Leon Whipple, *The Story of Civil Liberty in the United States*, p. 68.

51. *Ibid.*, p. 70.

52. Joseph Fielding Smith, *Essentials in Church History*, p. 231, quoted by Harry M. Beardsley, *Joseph Smith and His Mormon Empire*, p. 176.

53. *Ibid.*

54. Ernest Sutherland Bates, *American Faith*, p. 351.

55. Beardsley, *op. cit.*, pp. 208, 209.

56. Tyler, *op. cit.*, pp. 104, 105.

57. Beardsley, *op. cit.*, p. 344.

58. Chapter 13.

59. Charles A. and Mary R. Beard, *Rise of American Civilization*, I, 166.

60. Conrad Henry Moehlman, *School and Church*, p. 1.

61. Henry Steele Commager, ed., *Documents of American History*, I, 29.

62. Ellwood P. Cubberley, *Public Education in the United States*, pp. 44, 45.

63. *Ibid.*

64. Sherman M. Smith, *The Relation of the State to Religious Education in Massachusetts, passim.*

65. *Ibid.*, p. 68.

66. *Ibid.*, pp. 71-72 (note 15).

67. *Ibid.*, p. 95.

68. Raymond B. Culver, *Horace Mann and Religion in the Massachusetts Public Schools.*

69. S. M. Smith, *op. cit.*, p. 142.

70. *Ibid.*, pp. 61, 62.

71. Moehlman, *op. cit.*, pp. 92, 93.

72. Horrace Mann, *Annual Report* (1845-48) (Boston, 1891), IV, 308 ff., quoted by Burton Confrey, *Secularism in American Education, Its History*, p. 134 (note 46).

73. See L. S. Walsh, *The Early Irish Catholic Schools of Lowell, Mass.* (1901).

74. S. M. Smith, *op. cit.*, p. 193.

75. *Ibid.*, p. 206.

76. *Ibid.*, pp. 294, 295.

77. George Stewart, Jr., *A History of Religious Education in Connecticut*, p. 278.

78. *Ibid.*, p. 282.

79. See, generally, Sadie Bell, *The Church, the State, and Education in Virginia.*

80. David Wuntch, *Epoch-Making Liberty Documents*, p. 77.

81. *Ibid.*, p. 78.

82. V. Monroe, "Virginia," *Cyclopaedia of Education*, p. 729.

83. *Ibid.*

84. *Ibid.*

85. Weigle, *op. cit.*, p. 276.

86. Confrey, *op. cit.*, p. 92.

87. Weigle, *op. cit.*, p. 273.

88. Richard J. Gabel, *Public Funds for Church and Private Schools*, p. 357, quoting O. W. Bourne, *History of the Public School Society of the State of New York.*

89. William Warren Sweet, *Story of Religion in America*, pp. 393, 394.

90. Gabel, *op. cit.*, p. 357.

91. *Ibid.*, p. 359 n. 16.

92. Weigle, *op. cit.*, p. 277.

93. *Ibid.*, p. 285.

94. Cubberley, *op. cit.*, gives table of dates on p. 100.
95. Hecker, *Catholics and Education*, p. 180; and *Religious Education* (1926), p. 82.
96. *Ibid.*
97. For an account of the debate, see *Congressional Record*, Vol. IV, Part 1, p. 5595.
98. *Ibid.*, p. 5580, quoted in *Religious Education* (1926), p. 8.
99. *Ibid.; Knowlton* v. *Baumhover*, 182 Iowa 691 (1918), quoted in *Religious Education* (1926), p. 83.
100. There was at least one colonial case in which the authorities of what was to become United States territory came into official contact with the Papal States. In the *Historical Records and Studies* published by the U. S. Catholic Historical Society, Vol. II, p. 381, is an interesting article entitled "The Papal Flag in New York Harbor, 1757-8." This has to do with the coming of a Roman ship to New York and certain difficulties that were experienced.
101. Sister Loretta Clare Feiertag, *American Public Opinion on the Diplomatic Relations between the United States and the Papal States* (1847-67), p. 6.
102. Leo Francis Stock, *United States Ministers to the Papal States*, p. xxiii. See also, Robert A. Graham, *Vatican Diplomacy: A Study of Church and State on the International Plane.*
103. Stock, *op. cit.*, p. xxii.
104. *Ibid.*
105. Feiertag, *op. cit.*, p. 6.
106. New York *Daily Tribune*, Nov. 30, 1847.
107. Feiertag, *op. cit.*, p. 12; for the pope's reply, see New York *Herald*, Dec. 26, 1847.
108. Feiertag, *op. cit.*, p. 15.
109. *Ibid.*, p. 17.
110. *Ibid.*, p. 20.
111. Stock, *op. cit.*, pp. 2, 3.
112. Feiertag, *op. cit.*, p. 64.
113. *Ibid.*, pp. 78, 79 (note 30). For the saving of the Propaganda College, see "Cullen, Paul," *Catholic Encyclopedia*, IV, 565.
114. Stock, *op. cit.*, p. 394.
115. For a discussion of the historical incidents involved, see "A Diplomatic Incident," *Atlantic Monthly*, Oct., 1929.
116. Stock, *op. cit.*, pp. 64, 65.
117. See Feiertag, *op. cit.*, p. 65 (note 65); Stock, *op. cit.*, p. 84.
118. Stock, *op. cit.*, pp. 414-416.
119. *Ibid.*, p. 427.
120. New York *Times*, Dec. 24, 1939.
121. White House "Release," Dec. 23, 1939, p. 1.
122. *Christian Century*, Jan. 3, 1940.
123. New York *Times*, Jan. 5, 1940.
124. *Berkshire Eagle*, Jan. 22, 1940.
125. *Federal Council Bulletin*, Feb., 1940.
126. *Reference Manual on U.S. Diplomatic Representation at the Vatican* (pamphlet), National Council of the Churches of Christ in the United States of America.
127. *Ibid.*
128. *Ibid.*, pp. 7-10.
129. Robert A. Graham and Robert C. Hartnett, *Diplomatic Relations with the Vatican* (pamphlet), American Press, p. 7.
130. *Ibid.*, p. 6.
131. *America*, Nov. 3, 1951; *The Living Church*, Nov. 4, 1951; New York *Times*, Nov. 1, 1951.
132. *Congress Weekly*, Dec. 3, 1951.
133. *Look*, Mar. 3, 1959.

Chapter 12

1. Luther A. Weigle, *American Idealism*, p. 162. For details, see Gilbert Hobbs Barnes, *The Antislavery Impulse, 1830-1844* (New

York, 1933).

2. Samuel Sewall, *The Selling of Joseph,* cited in Bernard Smith, ed., *The Democratic Spirit,* pp. 15-17.

3. Leonard Woolsey Bacon, *A History of American Christianity,* p. 153.

4. *Persecution and Liberty* (Burr memorial vol.), chapter on "Agitation against the Slave Trade in Rhode Island," p. 475.

5. Madeline Hooke Rice, *American Catholic Opinion in the Slavery Controversy,* pp. 25, 26.

6. "Abolition Movement," *Dictionary of American History;* cf. Thomas Jefferson, *On Slavery.*

7. "Abolition Movement," *Dictionary of American History.*

8. Samuel Eliot Morison and Henry Steele Commager, *The Growth of the American Republic,* p. 126.

9. Francis Newton Thorpe, *The Federal and State Constitutions . . . ,* VI, 3739, 3740.

10. Morison and Commager, *op. cit.,* p. 126.

11. Cf. his letter to Benezet, Aug. 22, 1772.

12. Leon Whipple, *The Story of Civil Liberty in the United States,* p. 114.

13. J. M. Buckley, *History of the Methodists in the United States,* p. 185.

14. *Ibid.,* p. 245.

15. *Ibid.,* p. 303.

16. *Ibid.,* p. 385; see also Alexander Gross, *History of the Methodist Church, South,* p. 8.

17. A. H. Newman, *History of the Baptist Churches in the United States,* p. 305.

18. *Ibid.*

19. *Ibid.*

20. Robert E. Thompson, *History of the Presbyterian Churches in the United States* (American Church History Series, Vol. VI), Appendix, pp. 362, 363, 366.

21. Bacon, *op. cit.,* pp. 272, 273.

22. Robert Joseph Murphy, "The Catholic Church in the United States During the Civil War Period (1852-1866)," *American Catholic Historical Society Records* (Dec., 1928), XXXIX, 273.

23. See John C. Calhoun, "Remarks on the States Rights Resolutions in Regard to Abolition, January 12, 1838," *Works,* III, 180, quoted by Vernon Louis Parrington, *Main Currents in American Thought,* II, 80, 81.

24. Thompson, *op. cit.,* pp. 368, 369.

25. Barnes, *op. cit.,* p. 33.

26. Charles Beecher, ed., *Autobiography . . . of Lyman Beecher,* II, 323.

27. Barnes, *op. cit.,* p. 33.

28. *Ibid.,* quoting *Zion's Herald,* VI, 21.

29. See C. W. Bowen, *Arthur and Lewis Tappan,* p. 10, quoted in Whipple, *op. cit.,* pp. 96, 97.

30. *Ibid.,* p. 100.

31. Barnes, *op. cit.,* p. 61.

32. Oliver Johnson, *William Lloyd Garrison and His Times,* p. 68, quoted in C. L. Brace, *op. cit.,* p. 382.

33. Barnes, *op. cit.,* p. 93.

34. *Ibid.,* p. 97.

35. Cf. Whipple, *op. cit.,* p. 84.

36. Barnes, *op. cit.,* p. 103.

37. *Ibid.,* p. 91.

38. *Ibid.,* p. 242.

39. Charles A. and Mary R. Beard, *The Rise of American Civilization,* I, 708.

40. Daniel Dorchester, *Christianity in the United States,* p. 472. See also Emerson Davis, *The Half Century* (Boston, 1851).

41. Barnes, *op. cit.,* p. 110.

42. Buckley, *op. cit.,* pp. 378, 379.

43. *Ibid.,* p. 406.

44. Charles Baumen Swaney, *Episcopal Methodism and Slavery* (1926), p. 117.

45. Buckley, *op. cit.,* p. 410.

46. *Ibid.,* p. 420.

47. *Ibid.,* p. 441.

48. *Ibid.*, pp. 693, 694.
49. *Ibid.*, pp. 460, 461.
50. Newman, *op. cit.*, p. 444.
51. *Ibid.*, pp. 451, 452.
52. Thompson, *op. cit.*, p. 135; William Warren Sweet, *The Story of Religion in America*, p. 441.
53. S. D. McConnell, *History of the American Episcopal Church*, pp. 362, 363.
54. *Ibid.*, p. 366.
55. Robert Fortenbaugh, "American Lutheran Synods and Slavery 1830-1860," *The Journal of Religion* (Jan., 1933), XIII, 72.
56. Murphy, *op. cit.*,
57. Rice, *op. cit.*
58. See "Slavery," *Catholic Encyclopedia*, XIV, 39.
59. Quoted by Murphy, R. J., *op. cit.*, p. 281.
60. Max J. Kohler, "The Jews and the American Antislavery Movement," American Jewish Historical Society *Publications* (1897), V, 143.
61. B. F. Morris, *Christian Life and Character of the Civil Institutions of the United States*, p. 683 ff.
62. H. E. Jacobs, *History of the Evangelical Lutheran Church in the United States*, p. 452.
63. *Ibid.*
64. *Journal of the Proceedings of the Bishops, Clergy, and Laity of the Protestant Episcopal Church in the United States of America, Assembled in a General Convention . . . in the year of Our Lord 1862*, pp. 51-53.
65. McConnell, *op. cit.*, pp. 370, 379.
66. E. N. Wright, *Conscientious Objectors in the Civil War*, p. 6.
67. *Ibid.*, pp. 48-49.
68. *Ibid.*
69. McConnell, *op. cit.*, p. 372.
70. *Ibid.*
71. Carl Sandburg, *Abraham Lincoln: The War Years*, III, 157.
72. *Ibid.*, II, 156.
73. Sweet, *op. cit.*, p. 465.
74. J. R. G. Hassard, *Life of the Most Rev. John Hughes*, p. 437, quoted by Murphy, *op. cit.*, p. 279.
75. Facts from the pamphlet *The Jew as Patriot and Soldier*, published by Christian Friends of Palestine, Washington, D.C., 1939; cf. also Simon Wolf, *The American Jew as Patriot, Soldier and Citizen* (1895), p. 424.
76. Isaac Markens, *Abraham Lincoln and the Jews*, p. 10.
77. Abraham Lincoln, *Complete Works* (Nicolay and Hay ed.), II, 304.
78. See Chapter 14.

Chapter 13

1. Cf. remarks of Ernst Troeltsch, *The Social Teaching of the Christian Churches*, II, 727.
2. Charles Howard *Hopkins, The Rise of the Social Gospel in American Protestantism 1865-1915*.
3. *Ibid.*, p. 4.
4. *Ibid.*, Introduction.
5. Ralph H. Gabriel, *The Course of American Democratic Thought*, p. 161.
6. Hopkins, *op. cit.*, p. 106.
7. See Herbert Asbury, *Gem of the Prairie: An Informal History of the Chicago Underworld* (1940).
8. Hopkins, *op. cit.*, p. 132.
9. *Ibid.*, p. 219.
10. *Ibid.*, p. 216.
11. *Ibid.*, Chap. XIII, "Walter Rauschenbusch Formulates the Social Gospel"; cf. Hopkins, *op. cit.* (MS.), II, 832.
12. H. U. Faulkner, *The Quest for Social Justice, 1898-1914* (History of American Life, Vol. XI), p. 205.
13. Hopkins, *op. cit.*, p. 286.

14. *Ibid.,* p. 289.
15. Chapter 11.
16. See Chapter 5.
17. William Edward Lecky, *Democracy and Liberty,* I, 548.
18. Luther A. Weigle, *American Idealism,* p. 246.
19. *Encyclopaedia Britannica,* XVIII, 846.
20. *Ibid.,* pp. 846, 847.
21. "Lotteries," *Encyclopedia of the Social Sciences,* IX, 615.
22. Samuel Homer Woodbridge, *The Overthrow of the Louisiana Lottery* (1921), p. 8.
23. *Ibid.,* p. 9; *Encyclopedia of the Social Sciences,* IX, 615; and "Louisiana Lottery," *Dictionary of American History,* III, 307.
24. Woodbridge, *op. cit.,* pp. 13, 15.
25. *Ibid.,* p. 30.
26. *Berkshire Eagle,* Feb. 13, 1941; *Progress,* May, 1941, p. 12.
27. *Progress,* Apr. and May, 1941.
28. New York *Times,* Dec. 3, 1942.
29. *Ibid.,* Sept. 10, 1954.
30. New York *Herald Tribune,* Jan. 27, 1955, Nov. 17, 1955.
31. *Religious News Service,* May 21, 1958.
32. Charles H. Parkhurst, *Our Fight with Tammany* (New York, 1895).
33. *Ibid.,* p. 5.
34. *Ibid.,* p. 10.
35. *Ibid.,* pp. 41, 42.
36. *Ibid.,* p. 51.
37. See his autobiography, *Pioneering in Social Frontiers.*
38. Stephen Wise, *Challenging Years,* Chap. 1.
39. Faulkner, *op. cit.,* p. 167.
40. *Table of Statutory Provisions Favorable to Christian Science or to Freedom Concerning Health* (published by The Christian Science Publishing Society), p. 5.
41. New York *Times,* July 18, 1949.
42. Weigle, *op. cit.,* p. 208.
43. *Ibid.,* p. 210.
44. For a summary, see "Prohibition," *Encyclopedia of the Social Sciences.* XII.

45. J. M. Buckley, *History of the Methodists in the United States,* p. 640.
46. *Ibid.,* p. 641.
47. Quoted in Faulkner, *op. cit.,* p. 224.
48. Gunnar Myrdal, *An American Dilemma* (1944), I, 458.
49. Federal Council of the Churches of Christ in America, *Annual Report* (1925), pp. 180-183.
50. See Fletcher Dobyns, *The Amazing Story of Repeal* (1940).
51. These may be studied from the liberal standpoint of the outspoken advocates of freedom in Arthur Garfield Hays, *Trial by Prejudice* (1933).
52. Cf. Arthur M. Schlesinger, Jr., *The Age of Jackson,* p. 324.
53. See his *A Fighting Parson* (1928).
54. See "Strikes and Lock-Outs," *Encyclopaedia Britannica* (12th ed.), XXIII, 596.
55. Francis J. McConnell, *Opinion in the Steel Strike,* p. vi.
56. *The Twelve-Hour Day in the Steel Industry* (issued by the Research Department, Federal Council of the Churches of Christ in America), Appendix.
57. Liston Pope, *Millhands and Preachers,* p. 249.
58. *Ibid.,* p. 253.
59. *Ibid.,* p. 274.
60. *Ibid.,* p. 290.
61. Weimer Jones, "Southern Labor and the Law," *The Nation* (July 2, 1930), CXXXI, 16, quoted in *ibid.,* p. 295.
62. Pope, *op. cit.,* p. 327.
63. "Hecker," *Catholic Encyclopedia,* VII, 187.
64. Theodore Maynard, *The Story of American Catholicism,* p. 512.
65. "Testem Benevolentiae," *Catholic Encyclopedia,* XIV, 538.
66. Cf. Maynard, *op. cit.,* p. 519.
67. See "John Ireland," *Dictionary of American Biography,* IX.
68. *Ibid.,* p. 495.
69. "Gibbons, James," *Dictionary of American Biography,* VII, 240; cf.

Allen S. Will, *Life of Cardinal Gibbons* (1922), I, 498.

70. See Chapter 15.
71. Will, *op. cit.*, I, 314.
72. On this subject, see also E. E. Y. Hales, *The Catholic Church in the Modern World;* Robert D. Cross, *The Emergence of Liberal Catholicism in America;* Currin Shields, *Democracy and Catholicism in America: A Series of Articles from The Commonweal.* 1953.

Chapter 14

1. See Chapter 12.
2. *Brown v. Board of Education*, 347 U.S. 483 (1954).
3. Federal Council release to the press, Feb. 21, 1934.
4. *National Catholic Almanac,* 1961, p. 576.
5. See Anson Phelps Stokes, *Progress in Negro Status and Race Relations, 1911-1946,* and "American Race Relations in War Time," *Journal of Negro Education* (Fall, 1945), Vol. XIV, No. 4.
6. Mimeographed "Official Statement" on "The Church and Race" issued by the Federal Council in March, 1946.
7. *Brown v. Board of Education*, 347 U.S. 493 (1954). See also *Cooper v. Aaron*, 358 U.S. 1 (1958).
8. *Religious News Service,* May 16, 1963. See also Mathew Ahmann, ed., *Race Challenge to Religion.*
9. Raphael Mahler, *Jewish Emancipation,* pp. 5, 6.
10. Cf. Everett R. Clinchy, *All in the Name of God,* p. 118.
11. Bernhard E. Olson, *Faith and Prejudice,* p. xvii n. 10.
12. On anti-Semitism in its relation to Christianity, see Hugo Valentin, *Anti-Semitism, Historically and Critically Examined;* Malcolm Hay, *The Foot of Pride—the Pressure of Christendom on the People of Israel for 1900 Years.*
13. *Dogmatic Canons and Decrees,* pp. 187-209; "Syllabus," *Catholic Encyclopedia,* XIV.
14. "Vatican Council," *Catholic Encyclopedia,* XV; Raymond Corrigan, *The Church and the Nineteenth Century.*
15. *Dogmatic Canons and Decrees,* pp. 187-209.
16. Charles C. Marshall, *The Roman Catholic Church in the Modern State,* p. 67.
17. Arthur M. Schlesinger, *The Rise of the City, 1878-1898,* p. 399.
18. *Ibid.*
19. Gustavus Myers, *History of Bigotry in the United States,* p. 219.
20. See, generally, Humphrey J. Desmond, *The Know Nothing Party;* Washington Gladden, "Anti-Catholic Crusade," *Century* (1893-94), XLVII, 789.
21. Myers, *op. cit.*, p. 267.
22. M. L. Storer, *Theodore Roosevelt, the Child,* p. 31, cited in Henry F. Pringle, *Theodore Roosevelt,* p. 456.
23. *Ibid.*
24. *Selections from the Correspondence of Theodore Roosevelt and Henry Cabot Lodge, 1884-1918,* II, 321-325.
25. See, generally, Edmund A. Moore, *A Catholic Runs for President: The Campaign of 1928.*
26. Clinchy, *op. cit.*, p. 101.
27. Michael Williams, *The Shadow of the Pope,* p. 170.
28. Leon Whipple, *The Story of Civil Liberty in the United States,* pp. 270, 351.
29. Williams, *op. cit.*, p. 181.
30. New and enlarged edition (New York, 1931).
31. Co-author of the important book, John A. Ryan and Francis J. Boland, *Catholic Principles of Poli-*

tics (revised edition of *The State and the Church*).

32. Williams, *op. cit.*, p. 195.

33. Myers, *op. cit.*, p. 195.

34. Moore, *op. cit.*, pp. 39, 40.

35. *Ibid.*, pp. 116, 117.

36. See, generally, James A. Pike, *A Roman Catholic in the White House.*

37. See Patricia Barrett, "Religion and the 1960 Election," *Social Order*, June 1962; Gerhard Lenski, *The Religious Factor;* "The 'Catholic Vote'—A Kennedy Staff Analysis," *U.S. News and World Report*, Aug. 1, 1960; *Politics in a Pluralistic Democracy*, a report published by the American Jewish Committee (1963).

38. Shane Leslie, *The Irish Issue in Its American Aspects* (New York, 1917).

39. *Statesman's Year Book*, 1939, p. 463; based on constitution of 1936.

40. Leslie, *op. cit.*

41. Philip H. Bagenal, *The American Irish and their Influence on Irish Politics* (London, 1882), p. 144.

42. "The Irish," *Catholic Encyclopedia*, VIII, 144, 145.

43. *Annual Report of the Foreign Missions Conference of North America* (1928), p. 14.

44. Carl Zollmann, *American Church Law*, pp. 14, 15.

45. *Catholic Mind*, Jan., 1943, p. 6.

46. *Christian Century*, Dec. 23, 1942.

47. *America*, Dec. 26, 1942.

48. *Religious News Service*, Jan. 21, 1958.

49. New York *Times*, Jan. 24, 1962.

50. *Religious News Service*, Apr. 12, 1957.

51. *Ibid.*, Dec. 4, 1962.

52. See Lino Gussoni and Aristeds Brunello, *The Silent Church;* Nicholas S. Timasheft, *Religion in Soviet Russia;* Fulton J. Sheen, *Communism and the Conscience of the West.*

53. New York *Times,* June 19, 1961.

54. *Ibid.*, June 21, 1961.

55. *Religious News Service*, Aug. 21, 1961.

56. *Ibid.*, Jan. 25, 1963.

57. *Ibid.*, Jan. 31, 1962.

58. *Christian Century*, July 12, 1961.

59. New York *Times*, July 3, 1961.

60. *The Churchman*, Aug. 9, 1961.

61. Brooklyn *Tablet*, Dec. 23, 1961.

62. *Ibid.*

63. Among others, in *McCollum* v. *Board of Education* and the Sunday law cases. See Chapter 5.

64. *Aims and Purposes of the Religious Liberty Association of America*, issued by the Religious Liberty Association (1936).

65. *The American Civil Liberties Union* (pamphlet).

66. *What Is the National Conference?* (pamphlet), p. 1.

67. Information received from the National Conference of Christians and Jews.

68. Information received from the Center for the Study of Democratic Institutions.

69. Joseph M. Dawson, *Separate Church and State Now*, pp. 209, 210.

70. *Ibid.*

71. Luke E. Ebersole, *Church Lobbying in the Nation's Capital;* Paul Blanshard, *God and Man in Washington.*

72. Lawrence P. Creedon and William D. Falcon, *United for Separation.*

73. Information received from the National Council of Churches of Christ.

74. Information received from Baptist Joint Committee on Public Affairs. See also Dawson, *op. cit.*

75. Information received from the respective organizations.

76. Information received from the National Community Relations Advisory Council.

77. *Ibid.*

Chapter 15

1. *World Almanac,* 1963, p. 541, and V. Monroe "High Schools," *Cyclopaedia of Education.*

2. The texts of the state constitutions (other than Alaska and Hawaii) are found in *Constitutions of the States and the United States.*

3. Carl Zollmann, *American Church Law,* p. 78.

4. See Chapter 16.

5. *Cantwell* v. *Connecticut,* 310 U.S. 296 (1940); *Murdock* v. *Pennsylvania,* 319 U.S. 105 (1943); *Marsh* v. *Alabama,* 326 U.S. 501 (1946).

6. *Everson* v. *Board of Education,* 330 U.S. 1 (1947); *McCollum* v. *Board of Education,* 333 U.S. 203 (1948); *Torcaso* v. *Watkins* 367 U.S. 488 (1961).

7. See Chapter 5.

8. Richard B. Dierenfeld, *Religion in American Public Schools.*

9. See Chapter 5.

10. Cf. some comments by William Edward Lecky, *Democracy and Liberty* (rev. ed., 1890), II, 61.

11. Chapter 11.

12. Luther A. Weigle, "The American Tradition and the Relation between Religion and Education," *Religion and Public Education, American Council on Education Studies* (Feb., 1945), Vol. IX, No. 22.

13. *Ibid.;* Virgil Henry, *The Place of Religion in the Public Schools,* p. 81.

14. *Federal Council Bulletin,* Oct., 1941. See also McCasland, *The Bible in Our American Life* (1942).

15. Information received from the New York Board of Rabbis.

16. Information received from the Indianapolis Jewish Community Council.

17. "The Relation of Religion to Public Education," *American Council on Education Studies* (Apr., 1947), Vol. XI, No. 26, p. 19.

18. Information based on correspondence with the Reverend Crawford W. Brown, of Elgin, Oct. 16, 1941.

19. For a presentation of this plan, see "The Teaching of Religion," *School and Society,* June 29, 1940.

20. *Christian Century,* Nov. 12, 1941.

21. *Ibid.,* May 14, 1941, p. 654; e.g., see Charles Clayton Morrison, "Protestantism and the Public School," *Christian Century,* Apr. 17, 1946.

22. "The Relation of Religion to Public Education," *op. cit.*

23. *Information Service,* Nov. 15, 1941.

24. See "The Supreme Court on Separation of Church and State," *Commonweal,* Feb. 18, 1949; James Milton O'Neill, *Religion and Education Under the Constitution.*

25. *Christian Century,* Mar. 17, 1948; for school actions in representative communities, see *Churchman,* July 1, 1958.

26. Dierenfeld, *op. cit.,* p. 82.

27. O'Neill, *op. cit.;* Joseph H. Brady, *Confusion Twice Confounded;* "Religion and the State," *Law and Contemporary Problems,* Winter, 1949; Clyde L. Hay, *The Blind Spot in American Public Education.*

28. Virgil C. Blum, *Freedom of Choice in Education;* Robert C. Hartnett and Anthony Bouscaren, *The State and Religious Education;* Neil G. McCluskey, *Catholic Viewpoint on Education.*

29. New York *Times,* Nov. 21, 1948.

30. *Religious News Service,* July 7, 1948.

31. National Education Association, *The Status of Religious Education in the Public Schools.*

32. A survey is contained in Justice Frankfurter's concurring opinion in *McCollum* v. *Board of Education*, 333 U.S. 203 (1948).

33. N. M. Butler, *Liberty, Equality, Fraternity*, pp. 145, 147.

34. M. D. Davis, *Week-Day Religious Education*; Floyd S. Gove, *Religious Education on Public School Time*, p. 4.

35. Davis, *op. cit.*, p. 13.

36. *Ibid.*, p. 14.

37. *Christian Century*, Mar. 19, 1943.

38. National Education Association, *op cit.*

39. Hay, *op. cit.*, p. 22; Henry, *op. cit.*, p. 5.

40. U.S. Office of Education, cited in *World Almanac*, 1964, p. 539.

41. See National Education Association, *op. cit.*

42. Dierenfeld, *op. cit.*, p. 79.

43. Information received from the New York City Board of Education.

44. For a favorable view see reports of the International Council of Religious Education; for an unfavorable one see Conrad H. Moehlman, *School and Church*.

45. *Liberty*, Fourth Quarter, 1947.

46. New York Education Law, Sec. 3211, subdiv. 1(b).

47. *Ibid.*

48. Circular issued by State Education Department, Aug., 1940, entitled *Absence for Religious Observance and Education*. These regulations are summarized in *Zorach* v. *Clauson*, 343 U.S. 306 (1952).

49. New York *Times*, May 19, 1941.

50. *Ibid.*

51. *Ibid.*

52. See reports of studies conducted by the Public Education Association of New York in 1943, 1945, and 1949.

53. See affidavits quoted in Leo Pfeffer, *Church, State and Freedom*, pp. 356-367.

54. *Zorach* v. *Clauson*, 303 N.Y. 161,

affirming 278 App. Div. 573, affirming 193 Misc. 631.

55. *Zorach* v. *Clauson*, 343 U.S. 306 (1954).

56. *Ibid.*

57. *Federal Council . . . Biennial Report* (1946), pp. 137, 138.

58. Richard James Gabel, *Public Funds for Church and Private Schools*, p. 237.

59. See reports of the Public Education Association, 1943, 1945, 1947.

60. Statement of National Catholic Welfare Council, Nov. 21, 1948.

61. *Ibid.*; O'Neill, *op. cit.*

62. McCluskey, *op. cit*; Gabel, *op. cit.*, p. 737; Jerome G. Kerwin, *Catholic Viewpoint on Church and State*, pp. 115-116.

63. See *Safeguarding of Religious Liberty*, pamphlet issued by the Joint Advisory Committee of the Synagogue Council of America and the National Community Relations Advisory Council; see also *The Churchman*, Aug., 1947.

64. Leo Pfeffer, "Religion and the Public Schools," *Churchman*, Jan. 15, 1948.

65. *Safeguarding Religious Liberty.*

66. See Chapter 4.

67. *Christian Century*, Dec. 18, 1940.

68. Alvin W. Johnson and Frank H. Yost, *Separation of Church and State in the United States*, p. 33.

69. It has been pointed out that, though the opposition of the Roman Catholic Church was the major factor in eliminating the reading of the Bible from public schools in many states, the controversy among different Protestant groups regarding the content of religious instruction was almost equally responsible for the secularization of public schools. Dean Weigle cites as an example the strife between Trinitarians and Unitarians in Massachuetts. Cf. *Religious Education* (1926), p. 91.

70. Alvin W. Johnson, *The Legal Status of Church-State Relationships in the United States with Special Reference to the Public Schools*, pp. 26, 27.
71. "The State and Sectarian Education," *N.E.A. Research Bulletin*, Oct., 1946, p. 36.
72. Dierenfeld, *op. cit.*, p. 51.
73. See George A. Stewart, Jr., *A History of Religious Education in Connecticut*, p. 292.
74. See Chapter 5.
75. See Philip Jacobson, "Church-State Issues," *American Jewish Year Book*, 1963, p. 108.
76. *Why the Bible Should Not be Read in the Public Schools*, pamphlet issued by the Central Conference of American Rabbis.
77. *Ibid.*
78. See Moehlman, *op. cit.*
79. Jacobson, *op. cit.*, p. 109.
80. *Relations between Church and State*, Report of the 174th General Assembly of the United Presbyterian Church (1962), p. 11.
81. *New York Times*, June 7, 1963, June 14, 1963.
82. See Johnson and Yost, *op. cit.*; Ward W. Keesecker, *Legal Status of Bible Reading.*
83. See, e.g., *Donahoe v. Richards*, 38 Me. 376 (1854); *Spiller v. Woburn*, 94 Mass. 127 (1866).
84. National Education Association, *The State and Sectarian Education* (1956); Johnson and Yost, *op. cit.*
85. *Hackett v. Brooksville Graded School District*, 120 Ky. 608 (1905).
86. *People ex rel. Ring v. Board of Education*, 245 Ill. 334 (1910).
87. *Doremus v. Board of Education*, 342 U.S. 429 (1952).
88. *New York Times*, Dec. 1, 1951.
89. *Ibid.*
90. *Christian Century*, Jan. 9, 1952.
91. Peekskill *Evening Star*, Jan. 16, 1952.

92. *New York Times*, Dec. 15, 1951, Jan. 14, 1952, Jan. 17, 1952; *New York Herald Tribune*, Dec. 19, 1951, Jan. 4, 1952.
93. *New York Times*, Dec. 10, 1951; *New York Herald Tribune*, Dec. 18, 1951.
94. Brooklyn *Tablet*, Dec. 8, 1951; *New York Times*, Dec. 1, 1951, Jan. 13, 1952.
95. *New York Herald Tribune*, Mar. 18, 1952.
96. *Engel v. Vitale*, 10 N.Y. 2d 174, affirming 11 App. Div. 2d 340, affirming 18 Misc. 2d 659.
97. See, e.g., 108 *Congressional Record*, 10883-85, 10897-98, 11102-08.
98. *New York Times*, July 1, 1962.
99. *Washington Post*, July 7, 1962.
100. Jacobson, *op. cit.*, p. 114.
101. *New York Times*, July 1, 1962.
102. *Ibid.*
103. Jacobson, *op. cit.*, pp. 114, 115.
104. *Ibid.*, p. 113.
105. *New York Times*, June 28, 1962.
106. Jacobson, *op. cit.*, p. 110.
107. *Hearings Before the Committee of the Judiciary*, U.S. Senate, 87th Congress, on "Prayers in Public Schools and Other Matters," July 26 and Aug. 2, 1962, p. 166.
108. Jacobson, *op. cit.*, p. 110.
109. *Ibid.*, p. 111.
110. The facts as here set forth are based on the records in the case and the several court opinions.
111. Jacobson, *op. cit.*, p. 113.
112. See "Community Conflict—Christmas Observance in the Public Schools," Background Report published by National Conference of Christians and Jews, June, 1962.
113. *Ibid.*; John C. Bennett, "When Christmas Becomes Divisive," *Christianity and Crisis*, Nov. 27, 1958; American Civil Liberties Union, 42nd Annual Report.
114. *Chamberlin v. Dade County Board of Public Instruction*, 142 So. 2d 21.

115. *Baer* v. *Kolmorgen*, 14 Misc. 2d 1015.
116. William O. Bourne, *History of The Public School Society of the City of New York* (1870), pp. 192-193.
117. *Ibid.*, pp. 208, 212.
118. *Ibid.*, pp. 245, 246.
119. *Ibid.*, pp. 321, 322.
120. *Ibid.*, p. 323.
121. New York *Times*, Apr. 4, 1949. For analysis of this general subject, see Howard Kennedy Beale, *Are American Teachers Free?* pp. 306-307.
122. For the laws and regulations see E. T. Taylor, *Principles and Policies Governing the Use of Public School Property in the Several States*, a dissertation at Columbia University (1947).
123. Johnson and Yost, *op. cit.*, Chap. IX.
124. *Davis* v. *Boget*, 50 Iowa 11 (1878); Zollmann, *op. cit.*, p. 97.
125. *Southside Estate Baptist Church* v. *Board of Trustees*, 115 So. 2d 697.
126. *Chamberlin* v. *Dade County Board of Public Instruction*, 142 So. 2d 21.
127. See symposium, "Shared Time," *Religious Education*, Jan.-Feb., 1962.
128. Louis Cassels, "A Way Out for Our Parochial-Public School Conflict," *Look*, Aug. 28, 1962, pp. 54-62.
129. *Ibid.*
130. George LaNoue, *Decision for the Sixties: Public Funds for Parochial Schools?* pamphlet published by Department of Religious Liberty of the National Council of Churches, pp. 43, 44.
131. See Leo Pfeffer, "Second Thoughts on Shared Time," *Christian Century*, June 20, 1961.
132. Cf. Beale, *op. cit.*, p. 220 ff.
133. *Commonwealth* v. *Herr*, 229 Pa. 132 (1910).
134. *O'Connor* v. *Hendrick*, 184 N.Y. 421 (1906).
135. National Education Association, *The State and Sectarian Education* (1946).
136. *Ibid.*
137. Beale, *op. cit.*, p. 516, citing N.Y. *Session Laws* (1932), p. 617.
138. *Tennessee Code* (1932), Sec. 2344, 2345.
139. Albert C. Dieffenbach, *Religious Liberty*, p. 63.
140. *American Year Book*, 1925, p. 87. For another account of this incident, see Leslie H. Allen, *Bryan and Darrow at Dayton*.
141. Arthur G. Hays, *Let Freedom Ring*, p. 38.
142. *Ibid.*, p. 45.
143. *Scopes* v. *State*, 154 Tenn. 105.
144. New York *Sun*, Dec. 14, 1939.
145. See, generally, David R. Manwaring, *Render Unto Caesar: The Flag Salute Controversy*.
146. The movement functions through three non-profit organizations: The Watch Tower Bible and Tract Society of Pennsylvania, the Peoples Pulpit Association of New York, and the International Bible Students Association of London, England. For an account of Jehovah's Witnesses, see Boston *Evening Transcript*, Aug. 10, 1940.
147. For a summary of the doctrines and organization of Jehovah's Witnesses, see Manwaring, *op. cit.*, pp. 17-24.
148. Quoted from *Religious Liberty in the U.S. Today*, published by the American Civil Liberties Union, 1939, p. 19.
149. William G. Fennell, *Compulsory Flag Salute in Schools*, pp. 8, 9.
150. *Ibid.*
151. *The Persecution of Jehovah's Witnesses*, published by the American Civil Liberties Union, January, 1941, p. 3.
152. *Ibid.*
153. The history of the Gobitis case in

the lower courts is set forth in Manwaring, *op. cit.,* pp. 81-117.

154. New York *Times,* Nov. 11, 1939.
155. Manwaring, *op. cit.,* p. 112.
156. *Ibid.,* Chap. 7.
157. *Ibid.,* p. 156.
158. *Christian Century,* July 3, 1940.
159. *Ibid.,* Nov. 20, 1940.
160. See, generally Henry E. Allen, ed., *Religion in the State University: An Initial Exploration;* Erich A. Walter, *Religion and the State University.*
161. *Christian Century,* Feb. 18, 1942.
162. *Session Laws* (1864-65), p. 313, no. 4748, and *Rev. Stat.* (1873), chap. 42, sec. 13, par. 5, quoted in Burton Confrey, *Secularism in American Education,* p. 109.
163. M. Willard Lampe, *The Story of an Idea,* p. 9.
164. *The Hawaii School of Religion Affiliated with the University of Hawaii* (1946); and copy of constitution.
165. See also Clarence Prouty Shedd,

"Religion in State Universities," *Journal of Higher Education* (Nov., 1941), Vol. XII, No. 8.
166. See George F. Bowerman, *Censorship and the Public Library, with Other Papers.*
167. Anne I. Haight, *Banned Books,* p. 74.
168. *Carnegie Magazine,* Nov., 1929, p. 181, quoted in *ibid.,* p. 28.
169. *Church Manual of The First Church of Christ Scientist, in Boston, Mass.* (1906), Art. XXIX, Sec. 9.
170. See article in *The Nation* (Feb. 12, 1930), CXXX, 147-149; cf. similar articles in *The New Republic,* 1929 and 1930.
171. Otto T. Hamilton, *The Courts and the Curriculum,* p. 74.
172. For a summary of this question see *Information Service,* Nov. 27, 1948, and New York *Times,* May 28, 1949.
173. New York *Times,* June 15, 1948.

Chapter 16

1. This definition and similar definitions are discussed in E. S. White, "Distinction Between Private and Public Schools as Shown by Court Cases," unpublished Master's dissertation, University of Pittsburgh, 1931, referred to by Richard James Gabel, *Public Funds for Church and Private Schools,* p. 1. See, generally, *The State and Nonpublic Schools,* U.S. Department of Health, Education and Welfare, Misc. No. 28 (1958).
2. Chapter 9.
3. *World Almanac,* 1963, p. 541.
4. Chapter 9.
5. *Christian Century,* Oct. 21, 1942.
6. Neil G. McCluskey, *Catholic Viewpoint on Education,* p. 98.
7. Carl Zollmann, *American Church Law,* p. 92.
8. The story of the part played by

one farsighted citizen, Edward John McDermott, in securing this amendment is told in *America,* July 30, 1938.
9. The case is summarized in Leo Pfeffer, *Church, State and Freedom,* pp. 594-595.
10. *Donner* v. *New York,* 342 U.S. 884 (1951).
11. "The State and Sectarian Education," *N.E.A. Research Bulletin,* Feb., 1946, quoting *Revised Statutes of Nebraska,* 1943, vol. 4, chap. 79, sec. 1913, and *General Laws* of R.I. of 1938, Title 21, chap. 181, sec. 8. See esp. p. 47.
12. For authoritative contemporary statements of this general position, see Wilfrid Parsons, S.J., *The First Freedom: Considerations on Church and State in the United States,* and McCluskey, *op. cit.*

13. For further information regarding somewhat similar plans in Hartford, Connecticut, and Poughkeepsie, New York, see J. A. Burns, *The Growth and Development of the Catholic School System in the United States*, pp. 253-258.

14. *Ibid.*, p. 232.

15. *Ibid.*, p. 263.

16. *Ibid.*, p. 243

17 *Ibid.*, p. 247.

18. Claris E. Silcox and Galen M. Fisher, *Catholics, Jews and Protestants*, p. 173.

19. Burns, *op. cit.*, pp. 243-247, 261.

20. *Yale Law Journal*, Vol. 50, p. 917.

21. This sketch is based largely on two mimeographed "Reports" on the North College Hill situation dated June 27, 1947, and July 14, 1947, published by the Council of Churches of Greater Cincinnati, together with other material cited.

22. Harold E. Fey, "They Stand for Free Schools!" *Christian Century*, July 2, 1947.

23. *Ibid.* See also Harold E. Fey, "Preview of a Divided America," *Christian Century*, May 28, 1947, and *The Facts and Implications of the School Trouble in North College Hill, Ohio*, issued by the General Council of the Presbytery of Cincinnati, Ohio . . . (1947).

24. *Christian Century*, editorial, Nov. 19, 1947.

25. V. Monroe, "Lutheran Church and Education in the United States," *Cyclopaedia of Education*, IV, 96.

26. A. C. Stellhorn, *A Century of Lutheran Schools in America*, p. 11.

27. *Ibid.*

28. *Ibid.*

29. *Ibid.*, p. 12.

30. *World Almanac*, 1963, p. 711.

31. See resolutions of the Missouri Synod in 1920, Albert G. Merkens, *The Policies of the Evangelical Lutheran Synod of Missouri, Ohio, and Other States with Regard to Elementary Education by Means of Christian Day-Schools*, p. 15.

32. *Statistical Year-book of the Missouri synod for 1932*, p. 163, and *Proceedings of the Thirteenth Convention* (1917), p. 59.

33. Simon Greenberg, "Trends in Jewish Education," *Contemporary Jewish Record*, Apr., 1942, pp. 162 ff.

34. Israel S. Chipkin, "Twenty-five Years of Jewish Education in the United States," *American Jewish Year Book 5697* (1936), XXXVIII passim, esp. p. 37.

35. *American Jewish Year Book*, 1963.

36. *Ibid.*

37. *National Catholic Almanac*, 1962, p. 114.

38. See *Commonweal*, Oct. 13, 1961.

39. Quoted in Parsons, *op. cit.*, p. 60.

40. Kiddle and Schem, *Cyclopaedia of Education*, p. 218.

41. For an able presentation of the Roman Catholic position, see "Does State Aid to Education Mean Union of Church and State?" *Catholic Educational Review*, Feb., 1935.

42. Gabel, *op. cit.*, p. 548.

43. 122. Vt. 177 (1961).

44. 366 U.S. 925 (1961).

45. 278 N.Y. 200 (1938).

46. *Judd* v. *Board of Education*, 278 N.Y. 200 (1938).

47. New York Constitution, Art. XI.

48. *Newsweek*, June 5, 1939.

49. *Christian Century*, Nov. 20, 1946, and editorial Oct. 30, 1946.

50. *Reynolds* v. *Nussbaum*, 115 N.W. 2d 761 (1962).

51. 330 U.S. 1 (1947).

52. *Liberty*, Fourth Quarter, 1947.

53. *Churchman*, Nov. 1, 1947.

54. *Ibid.*, May 15, 1947, June 15, 1947.

55. Chapter 14.

56. New York *Times*, Aug. 30, 1947.

57. *Connell* v. *Kennett Township Board of School Directors*, 356

Pa. 585 (1947).

58. *Religious News Service*, Oct. 8, 1947.

59. *Engel* v. *Vitale*, 370 U.S. 421 at p. 443.

60. *Visser* v. *Nooksack Valley School District*, 207 P. 2d 198 (1949).

61. *Zellers* v. *Huff*, 236 P. 2d 949 (1951).

62. *McVey* v. *Hawkins*, 258 S.W. 2d 927 (1953).

63. *Matthews* v. *Quinton*, 362 P. 2d 932 (1961).

64. *Reynolds* v. *Nussbaum*, 115 N.W. 2d 761 (1962).

65. *Silver Lake School District* v. *Barker*, 29 N.W. 2d 214 (1947).

66. *Board of Education* v. *Antone* (1963).

67. *Ibid.*

68. *Dickman* v. *Oregon School District*, 366 P. 2d 533 (1961).

69. *Snyder* v. *Newton*, 161 A. 2d 770 (1961).

70. *Squire* v. *City of Augusta*, 155 Me. 151 (1959).

71. *Cochran* v. *Louisiana State Board of Education*, 281 U.S. 370 (1936).

72. *Chance* v. *Mississippi*, 200 So. 2d 706 (1941).

73. *Zellers* v. *Huff*, 236 P. 2d 949.

74. *Dickman* v. *Oregon School District*, 366 P. 2d 533.

75. *Ibid.*

76. See *Safeguarding Religious Liberty*, pamphlet issued by the Joint Advisory Committee of the Synagogue Council of America and the National Community Relations Advisory Council.

77. *Catholic World* (Jan., 1876), XXII, 434, 435.

78. Letter from education editor, *America*, Aug. 18, 1947.

79. *Congressional Record*, 44th Congress, 1st sess., IV, 205.

80. *Ibid.*, p. 5453.

81. *Ibid.*, p. 5595.

82. Gabel, *op. cit.*, pp. 524-526.

83. H.R. 4643, 81st Congress, 1st sess.

84. New York *World-Telegram*, June 23, 1949.

85. *Ibid.*, July 8, 1949.

86. *Ibid.*, July 15, 1949.

87. New York *Times*, July 23, 1949.

88. *Ibid.*, July 24, 1949.

89. *Ibid.*, July 28, 1949.

90. *Ibid.*, Aug. 6, 1949.

91. New York *World-Telegram*, Aug. 23, 1949.

92. New York *Times*, Sept. 14, 1960.

93. George R. LaNoue, *A Bibliography of Doctoral Dissertations . . .*, pp. 1, 2. LaNoue's pamphlet summarizes the issue from the Protestant point of view.

94. *Religious News Service*, Mar. 2, 1961.

95. New York *Times*, Aug. 6, 1949.

96. McCluskey, *op. cit.*, p. 168.

97. Reprinted in Hearings on H.R. 5266 before Special Subcommittee on Education of the Committee on Education and Labor, House of Representatives, 87th Congress, Mar. 15-17, 1961.

98. "The Constitutionality of the Inclusion of Church Related Schools in Federal Aid to Education," *Georgetown Law Review*, vol. 50, p. 421.

99. *Ibid.*

100. Joseph H. Fichter, *Parochial Schools: A Sociological Study*, p. 86.

101. *Dickman* v. *Oregon School District*, 366 P. 2d 533 (1961).

102. Redden and Ryan, *A Catholic Philosophy of Education*, Chap. VI.

103. *Ibid.*, p. 188.

104. *Congressional Record*, May 20, 1963, p. 8500; New York *Times*, May 21, 1963.

105. *Ibid.*

Chapter 17

1. For early history, see Elias B. Sanford, *Origin and History of the Federal Council of the Churches of Christ in America.* 1916.
2. *Federal Council . . . , Biennial Report* (1946), pp. 8-14.
3. *Ibid.,* p. 73.
4. *Ibid.,* p. 87.
5. *Ibid.,* p. 90.
6. *Ibid.,* pp. 94, 95.
7. *World Almanac,* 1963, p. 710.
8. *Ibid.*
9. Chapter 14.
10. Information received from National Catholic Welfare Council. See also *National Catholic Almanac;* Luke E. Ebersole, *Church Lobbying in the Nation's Capital,* p. 54; *World Almanac,* 1963, p. 716.
11. Chapter 14.
12. Information received from Synagogue Council of America.
13. Information received from Albert Vorspan, social action director, Union of American Hebrew Congregations of America.
14. Information received from Morris Laub, social action director, United Synagogue of America.
15. Information received from Rabbi Wolfe Kellman, executive director, Rabbinical Assembly.
16. Information received from Dr. Samson Weiss, executive vice-president, Union of Orthodox Jewish Congregations of America, and Rabbi Israel Klavan, executive director, Rabbinical Council of America.
17. Edward Westermarck, *A Short History of Marriage,* p. 226, quoted in J. P. Lichtenberger, *Divorce,* pp. 75, 76.
18. Joseph McSorley, *An Outline History of the Church by Centuries,* p. 996 n.
19. George E. Howard, *History of Matrimonial Institutions,* I, 387, quoted in Lichtenberger, *op. cit.,* p. 92.
20. B. H. Hartogensis, "Denial of of Equal Rights to Religious Minorities and Non-Believers in the United States," *Yale Law Journal* (1930), XXXIX, 654.
21. Ayrinhac, *Marriage Legislation in the New Code of Canon Law,* p. 29, quoted in Charles C. Marshall. *The Roman Catholic Church in the Modern State,* p. 226.
22. Peter Guilday, *Life and Times of John Carroll,* p. 431.
23. "Baltimore," *Catholic Encyclopedia,* II, 238, 239.
24. "Marriage, Mixed," *ibid.,* IX, 699.
25. John A. O'Brien, *Why Not a "Mixed" Marriage?* (1937), p. 9. For a slightly different form see "An Un-American Marriage," *Christian Century,* Nov. 15, 1944.
26. *Christian Century,* Oct. 19, 1949.
27. New York *Times,* Mar. 3, 1932.
28. See Leo Pfeffer, "Religion in the Upbringing of Children," *Boston University Law Review* (1955), XXXV, Paul Ramsey, "The Legal Imputation of Religion to an Infant in Adoption and Custody," *New York University Law Review* (1959), XXXIV, 649; Monrad G. Paulsen, "Constitutional Problems of Utilizing a Religious Factor in Adoptions and Placement of Children," in Dallin H. Oaks, *The Wall Between Church and State,* p. 117.
29. *World Almanac,* 1963, p. 307.
30. *Federal Council . . . , Biennial Report* (1946), p. 234. See also "Whither Family Life?" *Survey,* Jan., 1947.
31. Lichtenberger, *op. cit.,* p. 10.
32. *Ibid.,* p. 109.
33. New York *Times,* Jan. 29, 1956.
34. *Ibid.,* Dec. 5, 1948.
35. *Ibid.,* Nov. 7, 1949.
36. *Ibid.,* Nov. 8, 1949.

37. Morris L. Ernst, and Alexander Lindey, *The Censor Marches On*, p. 144.
38. Leon Whipple, *The Story of Civil Liberty in the United States*, p. 285.
39. "Birth Control," *Encyclopedia of the Social Sciences*, II, 562.
40. Anne Lyon Haight, *Banned Books*, p. 65.
41. "Birth Control," *New Catholic Dictionary* (1929), p. 122.
42. *Information Service*, Mar. 22, 1941.
43. *Ibid.*
44. *Ibid.*
45. Louisville *Courier-Journal*, July 9, 1941.
46. Information obtained from files of the American Jewish Congress; see also *U.S. News and World Report*, Aug. 22, 1958.
47. Berkshire *Evening Eagle*, Oct. 26, 1942, and other papers.
48. Guy Emery Shipler, Jr., "Catholics and Birth Control" *Churchman*, May 1, 1941.
49. *Tileston* v. *Ullman*, 318 U.S. 44 (1943).
50. *Poe* v. *Ullman*, 367 U.S. 497 (1961).
51. *Religious News Service*, Mar. 16, 1963.
52. New York *Times*, Oct. 14, 1949.
53. *Ibid.*
54. Information received from local newspapers.
55. Statement of National Catholic Welfare Council, New York *Times*, Nov. 19, 1950.
56. *Five Great Encyclicals* (Paulist Press, 1947), p. 95.
57. 195 Mass. 187 (1907).
58. Pfeffer, "Religion in the Upbringing of Children," *op. cit.*
59. Boston *Pilot*, June 28, 1952, July 5, 1952.
60. Pfeffer, *op. cit.*
61. *Ibid.*
62. *Commonwealth* ex rel. *Kunz* v. *Stackhouse*, 176 Pa. Super. 361, 108 A. 2d 73 (1954).

63. Pfeffer, *op. cit.*
64. Ramsey, *op. cit.*
65. Pfeffer, *op. cit.*
66. Paulsen, *op. cit.*, and "Religion in Adoption and Custody," *Villanova Institute of Church and State Conference Proceedings*, (1957), pp. 56-114.
67. Quoted in James Dombrowski, *The Early Days of Christian Socialism in America*, p. 8.
68. See statement of Federal Council of Churches, May 28, 1931.
69. *Information Service*, Sept. 10, 1927.
70. O. F. Lewis, *The Development of American Prisons and Prison Customs 1776-1845*, p. 8.
71. Cf. "Prisons," *Encyclopaedia Britannica*, Vol. XXIII.
72. Cited in Alice Felt Tyler, *Freedom's Ferment*, p. 266.
73. Leo Kalmer, O.F.M., and Eligius Weir, O.F.M., *Crime and Religion, A Study of Criminological Facts and Problems* (Chicago, c. 1936), p. 19.
74. *Ibid.*, p. 65.
75. John Edgar Hoover, "Crime Challenges the Churches," released by U.S. Department of Justice, Nov. 29, 1944.
76. See Seward Hiltner, *The Church and Penal Institutions*, mimeographed account of the Conference of Ministers and Prison Officials at U.S. penitentiary in Atlanta, Mar. 29, 1939, published by the Federal Council.
77. 185 Va. 335 (1946).
78. *Ibid.*
79. C. Eric Lincoln, *The Black Muslims in America*.
80. *Relations Between Church and State*, Report of the 174th General Assembly of the United Presbyterian Church (1962), pp. 22.
81. *Training Manual No. 2270-5. The Chaplain* (issued by War Department June 10, 1937, superseding that of Jan. 2, 1926), p. 2.

82. *Ibid.,* p. 3.
83. Lorenzo D. Johnson, *Chaplains of the General Government, with Objections to Their Employment Considered* (1956).
84. Robert Baird, *A View of Religion in America,* p. 245 n.
85. *Commonweal,* Apr. 2, 1943.
86. Isaac Markens, *Abraham Lincoln and the Jews,* p. 9.
87. Letter from office of chief of chaplains, Oct. 17, 1941.
88. Quoted in dissenting opinion of Justice Reed in *McCollum* v. *Board of Education,* 333 U.S. 203 (1948).
89. This and most of the other information on conditions in the U.S. navy from letters of the superintendent of the Naval Academy, July 26, 1938, and the acting superintendent, Jan. 27, 1941.
90. See generally Mulford Q. Sibley and Philip E. Jacob, *Conscription of Conscience: The American State and the Conscientious Objector, 1940-1947.*
91. Benjamin Franklin, *Works,* I, 154.
92. Frederick George Livingood, *Eighteenth Century Reformed Church Schools,* p. 13.
93. *Ibid.,* p. 15.
94. Francis Newton Thorpe, *The Federal and State Constitutions . . . ,* V, 2648.
95. 13 Statutes at Large 6, quoted in Whipple, *op. cit.,* p. 162.
96. Fernando G. Cartland, *Southern Heroes,* p. 131, quoted in Whipple, *op. cit.,* pp. 161, 162.
97. Quoted in *Religious Liberty in the United States Today,* published by the American Civil Liberties Union, 1939, p. 36.
98. *Ibid.,* pp. 36, 37.
99. Walter W. Van Kirk, *Religion Renounces War,* pp. 6-8.
100. All quotations on Methodist position from "The Methodist Recantation," *Christian Century,* June 21, 1944.

101. *Ibid.*
102. *American Jewish Year Book,* 1963, p. 449.
103. Chapter 4.
104. Cf. sketch of life in Appleton's *Cyclopedia of American Biography,* V, 30.
105. *Journal of the Senate . . . ,* 22d Congress, 2d sess., p. 25.
106. Ezra Stacy Matheny, *American Devotion,* p. 119.
107. *Journal of the Senate . . . ,* 32d Congress, 2d sess., pp. 26, 27.
108. Johnson, *op. cit.,* pp. 19-21.
109. Rep. No. 124, House of Representatives, 33d Congress, 1st sess., Mar. 27, 1854.
110. Carl Sandburg, *Abraham Lincoln: The War Years,* III, 368.
111. Louis J. Jennings, *Eighty Years of Republican Government in the United States* (London, 1868), p. 200.
112. Elizabeth Fleet, "Madison's 'Detached Memoranda,'" in *William and Mary Quarterly,* Oct., 1946, pp. 534-568.
113. 23 F. 2d 997 (1928).
114. Art. VI.
115. Albert C. Applegarth, *The Quakers in Pennsylvania 1682-1776,* p. 40; Johns Hopkins University, *Studies in Historical and Political Science,* X (*Church and State*), 420, 421.
116. *Everson* v. *Board of Education,* 330 U.S. 1 (1947).
117. This sketch of the English background of religious test oaths is based in large measure on a "Comment" in *New York University Law Review* (1961), vol. 36, pp. 513, 514.
118. William Blackstone, *Commentaries on the Laws of England,* Book IV, ch. 4, p. 59.
119. Joseph Story, *Commentaries on the Constitution of the United States* (1891, Bigelow ed.), sec. 1878-79.
120. Joseph L. Blau, *Cornerstones of Religious Freedom in America,* pp. 74, 75.

121. *Ibid.*
122. Niles (ed.), *Principles and Acts of the Revolution,* p. 374.
123. Max Farrand, *Records of the Federal Convention of 1787,* III, 122.
124. *Ibid.,* II, 468.
125. *Ibid.,* pp. 461, 468.
126. *Ibid.,* III, 310.
127. Paul L. Ford, *Essays on the Constitution of the United States,* p. 168.
128. *Ibid.,* pp. 169-171.
129. *Ibid.*
130. Jonathan Elliot, *Debates in the Several State Conventions . . . ,* II, 118, 119.
131. *Ibid.,* pp. 148, 149.
132. *Ibid.,* pp. 193-198.
133. *Ibid.,* IV, 198, 199.
134. *Ibid.,* p. 199.
135. *Ibid.,* p. 200.
136. Farrand, *op. cit.,* III, 227.
137. Applegarth, *op. cit.,* p. 40.
138. Max Kohler, "Phases etc.," American Jewish Historical Society *Publications* (1905), No. 13, p. 9.
139. *Ibid.;* cf. Carl Zollmann, *American Church Law,* pp. 616, 617.
140. Arthur M. Schlesinger, Jr., *The Age of Jackson,* p. 354.
141. *Ibid.,* p. 355.
142. See *Religious Liberty in the United States Today,* p. 31; cf. *Legal Discriminations Against Religious Disbelievers,* also a pamphlet prepared by the American Civil Liberties Union (1935), p. 1.
143. Zollmann, *op. cit.* pp. 39, 40.
144. 8 Johns (N.Y.) 290 (1811).
145. *Ibid.*
146. Whipple, *op. cit.,* p. 38.
147. *The Investigator* article was in the number of Dec. 20, 1833. For further account, see Theodore Schroeder, *Constitutional Free Speech Defined and Defended,* p. vii; and H. S. Commager, "The Blasphemy of Abner Kneeland," *New England Quarterly* (Mar., 1935), VIII, 29-41.
148. Schroeder, *op. cit.,* p. 60.
149. *Ibid.*
150. *Ibid.,* p. 34.
151. Art. I, sec. 7.
152. See Chapter 11.
153. Daniel Dorchester, *Christianity in the United States,* p. 476.
154. William Addison Blakely, *American State Papers on Freedom in Religion,* pp. 328-333, citing *Liberator,* and *Life of Garrison,* by his children. III, 222 *et seq.*
155. Alvin W. Johnson and Frank H. Yost, *Separation of Church and State in the United States,* pp. 219, 220.
156. *Ibid.,* p. 222.
157. Abram Vossen Goodman, *American Overture: Jewish Rights in Colonial Times,* p. 92.
158. *Statutes of England, 1235-1713* (2d rev. ed., London, 1888), I, 29 Chas. II, chap. 7, quoted by Alvin W. Johnson, *The Legal Status of Church-State Relationships . . . ,* Pt. III, pp. 235, 236.
159. John Bach McMaster, *History of the People of the United States,* V, 125, 126.
160. Circular letter of Nov. 10, 1938.
161. Golden Jubilee Year circular, 1938.
162. *Liberty,* Fourth Quarter, 1941, p. 15.
163. *Ibid.*
164. See *Advent Review and Sabbath Herald,* Mar. 2, 1930, quoted in *Religious Liberty in the United States Today,* p. 43.
165. *McGowan* v. *Maryland,* 366 U.S. 420 (1961); *Two Guys from Harrison-Allentown, Inc.* v. *McGinley,* 366 U.S. 583 (1961).
166. Information obtained from files of the American Jewish Congress.
167. *Soon Hing* v. *Crowley,* 113 U.S. 703 (1885).
168. The statutes are listed in Justice Frankfurter's concurring opinion in the Sunday law cases.
169. *Commonwealth* v. *Bey,* 166 Pa. Sup. 136 (1950).
170. Information obtained from files of the American Jewish Congress.

171. "Thanksgiving Day," *Catholic Encyclopedia*, XIV, 558.
172. W. D. Love, Jr., *The Fast and Thanksgiving Days of New England*, pp. 400, 401.
173. *Ibid.*, p. 409.
174. Stephen Colwell, *The Position of Christianity in the United States, etc.*, p. 301.
175. Charles Warren, *Odd Byways in American History*, p. 226.
176. *Ibid.*, p. 228, citing *Correspondence of Andrew Jackson*, IV, 447.
177. *Ibid.*, p. 229.
178. *Ibid.*
179. *Ibid.*, p. 239.
180. *Ibid.*, p. 241.
181. *Ibid.*
182. *Commonweal*, Aug. 9, 1940; B. F. Morris, *Christian Life and Character of the Civil Institutions of the United States*.
183. James D. Richardson, ed., *Messages and Papers of the Presidents, 1789-1907*, V, 3429, 3430. This Federal proclamation was promptly followed by similar proclamations by governors of states.
184. *Ibid.*, VI, 306.
185. Philip Burnham, "National Humiliation," *Commonweal*, June 21, 1940.
186. See Chapter 6.
187. See Chapter 9.
188. *Pierce* v. *United States*, 252 U.S. 239 (1920).
189. See Joseph H. McMahon, "Battle for Decency," *Commonweal* (1934) XX, 441-443.
190. Cf. "How Roman Catholics Silence Criticism, *Churchman*, Jan. 15, 1943.
191. *Christian Century* and *Churchman*, June 1, 1949.
192. "Censorship," *Encyclopedia of the Social Sciences*, III, 290.
193. See Chapter 1.
194. Charles Ripley Gillett, *Burned Books*, I, 247.
195. *Ibid.*, I, 257.
196. "Censorship," *Encyclopedia of the Social Sciences*, III, 293.
197. New York *Courier and Enquirer*, Mar. 15, 1834, quoted in Whipple, *op. cit.*, pp. 76, 77.
198. For Federal and state laws on this general subject, see John Ford, *Criminal Obscenity*.
199. Form 255 of Post Office Department, quoting secs. 211 and 212 of the act of Congress approved Mar. 4, 1909 (35 Stat. L., 1129, as amended by the act of Mar. 4, 1911).
200. For these and similar references, see Haight, *op. cit.*, pp. 8, 9, 32, 35, 58, 65, 67.
201. Ernst and Lindey, *op. cit.*, p. 8.
203. Paul Blanshard, *American Freedom Ring*, pp. 177, 178.
203. Paul Blanshard, *American Freedom and Catholic Power*, p. 221.
204. 354 U.S. 476 (1957).
205. *Ibid.*
206. *Ibid.*
207. Applegarth, *op. cit.*, pp. 14, 15, quoting Seilhamer, *History of the American Theatre Before the Revolution*.
208. Ernst and Lindey, *op. cit.*, p. 66.
209. *Deliverances of the Presbyterian Church in the United States of America*, p. 99.
210. *Ibid.*
211. Ernst and Lindey, *op. cit.*, p. 87.
212. "A Code to Govern the Making of Motion and Talking Pictures, the Reasons Supporting It and the Resolution for Uniform Interpretation by Motion Picture Producers and Distributors of America, Inc., June 13, 1934," quoted in *ibid.*, Appendix C, p. 319.
213. Mimeographed circular of the Legion of Decency, "The Movies Move."
214. *How to Judge the Morality of Motion Pictures*, pamphlet of National Catholic Welfare Conference, p. 4.
215. From the encyclical letter, published by National Catholic Welfare Conference, p. 5.
216. *The Bill of Rights 150 Years After*

—the Story of Civil Liberty, 1938-1939, p. 40.

217. *Churchman,* July 1, 1943.
218. New York *Times,* Dec. 20, 1956, Feb. 22, 1957.
219. See Bosley Crowther, "The Strange Case of 'The Miracle,'" *Atlantic Monthly,* Apr., 1951, p. 35.
220. 303 N.Y. 242, affirming 278 App. Div. 253.
221. 365 U.S. 43 (1961).

222. *Churchman,* Sept. 1, 1946.
223. Mimeographed "Memorandum Opinion and Order," No. 96050, issued by Federal Communications Commission, July 19, 1946.
224. *Emancipator* (San Antonio, Tex.), May, 1949, p. 26.
225. *Douglas* v. *City of Jeannette,* 319 U.S. 157 (1943).
226. *Ibid.*
227. *America,* May 15, 1943.

Chapter 18

1. Luigi Luzzatti, *God in Freedom,* p. 20.
2. *Watson* v. *Jones,* 80 U.S. 679 (1871).
3. Chapter 13.
4. 322 U.S. 78 (1944).
5. *Ibid.*
6. *Ibid.*
7. 310 U.S. 296 (1940).
8. 315 U.S. 568 (1942).
9. 340 U.S. 290 (1951).
10. 197 U.S. 11 (1905).
11. *Birnel* v. *Town of Fircrest,* 361 U.S. 10 (1959), dismissing 53 Wash. 2d 830; *Kraus* v. *City of Cleveland,* 351 U.S. 935, dismissing 163 Ohio St. 559.
12. *People ex rel. Wallace* v. *Labrenz,* 411 Ill. 618 (1952), certiorari denied, 344 U.S. 824 (1952).
13. *Church of Jesus Christ of Latter Day Saints* v. *United States,* 136 U.S. 1 (1890).
14. *State* v. *Bunn,* 229 N.C. 734 (1949), appeal dismissed, 336 U.S. 942 (1949).
15. 321 U.S. 158 (1944).
16. *Reader's Digest,* Jan., 1961; Sol Rabkin, "Behind the Fight Against 'Humane Slaughter' Laws," *ADL Bulletin,* Feb., 1962.
17. Rabkin, *op. cit.; Christian Science Monitor,* Mar. 23, 1960.
18. *City of Sherman* v. *Simms,* 143 Tex. 115 (1944); *Ellsworth* v. *Gercke,* 62 Ariz. 198 (1945); *Roman Catholic Archbishop* v.

Baker, 140 Oreg. 600 (1932).
19. *Presiding Bishop* v. *City of Porterville,* 338 U.S. 939 (1949).
20. *Hagar* v. *Whitehouse,* quoted in J. P. Thompson, *Church and State in the United States,* pp. 84, 85.
21. Carl Zollmann, *American Church Law,* sec. 139.
22. Jacob C. Meyer, *Church and State in Massachusetts from 1740 to 1838,* p. 177; cf. Williston Walker, *History of the Congregational Churches in the United States,* p. 343.
23. Meyer, *op. cit.,* p. 173.
24. Walker, *op. cit.,* p. 342.
25. *Ibid.,* pp. 222, 343.
26. Joseph Henry Allen and Richard Eddy, *History of the Unitarians and the Universalists in the United States* (American Church History Series, Vol. X), p. 194; Joseph Francis Thorning, S.J., *Religious Liberty in Transition,* p. 64.
27. Meyer, *op. cit.,* p. 177.
28. Walker, *op. cit.,* p. 343.
29. "Girard, Stephen," *Encyclopaedia Britannica,* XII, 45.
30. Charles Warren, *The Supreme Court in United States History* (rev. ed., 1926), II, 129, 130. The original of this letter will be found in the *Life and Letters of Joseph Story,* II, 467.
31. 13 Wall. 679 (1872).
32. *Ibid.*
33. Zollmann, *op. cit.,* p. 288.

34. Account taken mainly from *Harper's Weekly*, Apr. 5, 1873.
35. "Detroit, Diocese of," *Catholic Encyclopedia*, IV, 759.
36. 49 R.I. 269, quoted from William A. Brown, *Church and State in Contemporary America*, pp. 315, 316.
37. Catherine Goddard Clarke, *The Loyolas and the Cabots: The Story of the Boston Heresy Case; Boston Pilot*, Feb. 11, 1953.
38. 344 U.S. 94 (1952).
39. *Ibid.*
40. *Ibid.*
41. This account is based on a pamphlet entitled *The Melish Case-Challenge to the Church*, published by the Melish Defense Committee, and a memorandum dated Mar. 1, 1949, headed "Church of the Holy Trinity," as well as the opinion of Justice Meir Steinbrink in the case of *Rector etc. of Holy Trinity Church* v. *Melish*, 194 Misc. (N.Y.) 1006 (1949).
42. Frederic J. Stimson, *The Law of the Federal and State Constitutions of the United States*, p. 316.
43. Zollmann, *op. cit.*, pp. 126, 127.
44. See Chapter 9.
45. Patrick J. Dignan, *History of the Legal Incorporation of Catholic Church Property in the United States (1784-1932)*, p. 148.
46. *Ibid.*
47. "Property Ecclesiastica," *Catholic Encyclopedia*, XII, 472.
48. Dignan, *op. cit.*, p. 267.
49. *Catholic Encyclopedia*, XII, 473.
50. *Ibid.*, p. 472.
51. "Trustee System," *ibid.*, XV, 71.
52. James D. Richardson, ed., *Messages and Papers of the Presidents, 1789-1907*, I, 489-490.
53. *American University Bulletin* (Dec., 1929), Vol. IV, No. 12 (Charter and By-Laws Number), pp. 3, 4.
54. *The Charter and Constitution of Washington Cathedral* (1929 ed.), pp. 1, 2.
55. Zollmann, *op. cit.*, p. 330.
56. See Monrad G. Paulsen, "Preferment of Religious Institutions in Tax and Labor Legislation," *Law and Contemporary Problems* (1949), XIV, 144; Paul G. Kauper, "The Constitutionality of Tax Exemptions for Religious Activities," in Dallin H. Oaks, *The Wall Between Church and State*, p. 95.
57. Zollmann, *op. cit.*, p. 327; Herman V. Ames, *Proposed Amendments to the Constitution*, p. 277.
58. *Christian Century*, July 9, 1947.
59. *Look*, Dec. 9, 1947.
60. John Godfrey Saxe, *Charitable Exemption from Taxation in New York State on Real and Personal Property*, pp. 12, 13.
61. John C. Bennett, *Christians and the State*, pp. 234, 235.
62. Saxe, *op. cit.*, p. 4.
63. *Christian Century*, Sept. 2, 1940.
64. *Churchman*, Mar. 15, 1942.
65. *Ibid.*
66. *Christian Century*, Nov. 27, 1963, reports that the Central Presbyterian Church of Des Moines voted to donate $4,000 a year to that city to compensate for the cost of maintaining streets, public safety, and sanitation.
67. Los Angeles *Times*, Aug. 27, 1957; Brooklyn *Tablet*, Oct. 13, 1956; New York *Times*, Aug. 4, 1957.
68. *Lundberg* v. *County of Alameda*, 46 Cal. 2d 644 (1956).
69. *Helsey* v. *County of Alameda*, 352 U.S. 921 (1956).
70. *General Finance Corp.* v. *Archette*, 176 A. 2d 73 (1961).
71. *General Finance Corp.* v. *Archette*, 369 U.S. 423 (1962).
72. Cf. *Commentaries*, Bk. I, chap. XI.
73. *Tax Systems of the World* (7th ed.)
74. *Ibid.*
75. *New Hampshire Laws*, 1816 (Nov. issue), pp. 91-92.
76. Zollmann, *op. cit.*, p. 51.

77. *Arver* v. *United States,* 245 U.S. 366 (1918).
78. Universal Military Training and Service Act, sect. 6 (g) (j).
79. Sec. 546 of the Judiciary Law of New York State.
80. James Bryce, *The American Commonwealth,* II, 566 n. 2.
81. "New York," *Catholic Encyclopedia,* XI, 36.
82. "Seal of Confession," *ibid.,* XIII, 662.
83. "Virginia," *ibid.,* XV, 457.
84. *Ibid.*
85. Zollmann, *op. cit.,* p. 164.
86. *Ibid.*
87. *Ibid.,* p. 167.
88. Richardson, *op. cit.,* p. 57.
89. Zollmann, *op. cit.,* sec. 40, pp. 49-51.
90. "Devises and Bequests for Masses (United States)," *Cath. Enc.,* X, 33.
91. *Ibid.,* p. 34; *Rhymer's Appeal,* 93 Pa. 142, 146 (1880).

Chapter 19

1. *Muzzy* v. *Wilkins,* Smith's N.H. Rep. 1, from the digest of opinion in Charles Z. Lincoln, *The Civil Law and Church,* p. 590.
2. *Yearbook of American Churches,* 1961, pp. 29, 47.
3. *World Almanac,* 1963, p. 705.
4. *Washington Ethical Society* v. *District of Columbia,* 249 F. 2d 127.
5. *Fellowship of Humanity* v. *County of Alameda,* 315 P. 2d 394.
6. *Judicial and Statutory Definitions of Words and Phrases* (1904), II, 1150, citing *People* v. *Ruggles* (N.Y.) 8 Johns 290, 297.
7. *Judicial and Statutory Definitions . . . ,* II, 1150, citing *Hale* v. *Everett,* 53 N.H. 9, 54.
8. *Words and Phrases* (1940), "Christian," citing *Conway* v. *Third National Bank and Trust Co.,* N.J. Court of Equity.
9. Carl Zollmann, *American Church Law,* p. 31.
10. Francis Newton Thorpe, *The Federal and State Constitutions . . . ,* VII, 3814.
11. *Ibid.,* VI, 3255.
12. *Ibid.,* III, 1689.
13. *Ibid.,* V, 2597.
14. *Ibid.,* p. 3085.
15. See Chapter 3.
16. Thorpe, *op. cit.,* IV, 2454, 2460, 2461.
17. *Ibid.,* V, 2820.
18. See Chapter 5.
19. *Vidal* v. *Girard's Executors,* 43 U.S. (2 How.) 127, 198 (1844).
20. *Church of Jesus Christ of Latter-Day Saints* v. *United States,* 136 U.S. 1, 49 (1890).
21. *Church of the Holy Trinity* v. *United States,* 143 U.S. 457, 465 (1891).
22. *Ibid.*
23. *United States* v. *Macintosh,* 283 U.S. 625 (1930).
24. *Updegraph* v. *Commonwealth,* 11 Serg. & R. (Pa.) 394, (1824).
25. *American State Papers,* pp. 652, 653.
26. *Board of Education of City of Cincinnati* v. *Minor,* 23 Ohio St. 211, 242.
27. Lincoln, *op. cit.,* II, 1151, citing *Melvin* v. *Easley,* 52 N.C. 356, 360 (1860).
28. 343 U.S. 306 (1952).
29. 370 U.S. 421 (1962).
30. Philip Schaff, "Church and State in the United States," *American Historical Association Papers,* ii, no. 4, p. 433.
31. Charles M. Snow, *Religious Liberty in America,* pp. 255, 256; cf. Charles H. Hopkins, *Rise of the Social Gospel in American Protestantism 1865-1915,* p. 126.
32. H. K. Carroll, *The Religious*

Forces of the United States (American Church History Series, Vol. I), p. 310.

33. *Ibid.*, p. 312.
34. Quoted by Alvin W. Johnson, *Legal Status of Church-State Relationships . . .* , p. 23.
35. William A. Blakely, *American State Papers on Freedom in Religion*, pp. 236, 237, quoting "House Reports," 43d Congress, 1st sess., Vol. I, Report No. 143.
36. Senate Joint Resolution 87, 83d Congress, 1st sess., introduced June 1, 1953.
37. *Religious News Service*, May 19, 1954.
38. *Ibid.*, June 11, 1959.
39. Joseph Coffin, *Our American Money*, p. 66.
40. *Ibid.*, p. 67.
41. *Proceedings of the National Convention to secure the Religious Amendment of the United States*, etc. (1873), p. iv.
42. See Coffin, *op. cit.*, p. 67.
43. *U.S. Statutes at Large*, XIII, 518.
44. Joseph B. Bishop, *Theodore Roosevelt and His Time*, II, 72, 73; cf. earlier crresspondence with Saint-Gaudens, *ibid.*, I, 358, 361.
45. *U.S. Statutes at Large*, Vol. XXV, pt. I, p. 164.
46. United States Code, Title 31, sec. 324 a.
47. *Ibid.*, Title 36, sec. 186.
48. *Ibid.*, sec. 172.
49. See "The Prayer Room of the United States Capitol," booklet published by U.S. Printing Office, 1956.
50. *Religious Bodies: 1936 Selected Studies for the U.S. by Denominations and Geographic Divisions* (1941).
51. *Information Service*, Nov. 2, 1940.
52. *Christian Century*, Dec. 14, 1938.
53. *Information Service*, Oct. 25, 1947.
54. *Christian Century*, Jan. 12, 1940.
55. Joseph Gales, *Debates and Proceedings in the Congress of the United States*, I, 1106-1108.
56. This account of the religion-in-the-census controversy is based on contemporary newspaper reports and upon the files of the American Jewish Congress. See also Spencer Rich, "A Victory for Religious Liberty," *Congress Weekly*, Mar. 3, 1958; Leo Pfeffer, "Is It the Government's Business?" *Christian Century*, Oct. 30, 1957.
57. John Locke, *Works* (12th ed., 1824), V, 9.

BIBLIOGRAPHY

AHMANN, MATHEW, ed. *Race Challenge to Religion.* Chicago, Henry Regnery Co., 1963.

ALLEN, HENRY E., ed. *Religion in the State University: An Initial Exploration.* Minneapolis, Burgess Publishing Co., 1950.

ALTFELD, EMANUEL MILTON. *The Jew's Struggle for Religious and Civil Liberty in Maryland.* Baltimore, M. Curlander, 1924.

American State Papers on Freedom in Religion. Washington, Religious Liberty Association, 1949.

BACON, LEONARD WOOLSEY. *A History of American Christianity.* New York, 1898.

BAIRD, ROBERT. *Religion in America.* New York, Harper & Brothers, 1856.

BALDWIN, ALICE M. *The New England Clergy and the American Revolution.* Durham, N.C., Duke University Press, 1928.

BARRETT, PATRICIA. *Religious Liberty and the American Presidency.* New York, Herder and Herder, 1963.

BATES, ERNEST SUTHERLAND. *American Faith.* New York, W. W. Norton & Co., 1940.

BATES, M. SEARLE. *Religious Liberty: An Inquiry.* New York, International Missionary Council, 1945.

BEACH, FRED F., and WILL, ROBERT F. *The State and Nonpublic Schools.* Washington, U.S. Government Printing Office, 1958.

BEALE, HOWARD KENNEDY. *Are American Teachers Free?* New York, Charles Scribner's Sons, 1936.

BEARDSLEY, HARRY M. *Joseph Smith and His Mormon Empire.* Boston, Houghton Mifflin Co., 1931.

BELL, BERNARD IDDINGS. *Crisis in Education: A Challenge to American Complacency.* New York, McGraw-Hill Book Co., 1949.

BELL, SADIE. *The Church, the State, and Education in Virginia.* Philadelphia, The Science Press Printing Co., 1930.

BENNETT, JOHN C. *Christians and the State.* New York, Charles Scribner's Sons, 1958.

BETH, LOREN PETER. *American Theory of Church and State.* Gainesville, Fla., University of Florida Press, 1958.

BILLINGTON, RAY ALLEN. *The Protestant Crusade.* New York, The Macmillan Co., 1938.

BLAKELY, WILLIAM ADDISON. *American State Papers on Freedom in Religion.* Washington, Religious Liberty Association, 1949.

BLANSHARD, PAUL. *American Freedom and Catholic Power* (2d ed.). Boston, Beacon Press, 1958.

BLANSHARD, PAUL. *God and Man in Washington.* Boston, Beacon Press, 1960.

BLANSHARD, PAUL. *Religion and the Schools: The Great Controversy.* Boston, Beacon Press, 1963.

BLAU, JOSEPH LEON. *Cornerstones of Religious Freedom in America.* Boston, Beacon Press, 1949.

BLUM, VIRGIL C., S. J. *Freedom of Choice in Education.* New York, The Macmillan Co., 1958.

BOLES, DONALD E. *The Bible, Religion and the Public Schools.* Ames, Iowa, Iowa State University Press, 1961.

BOURNE, WILLIAM OLAND. *History of the Public School Society of the City of New York.* New York, W. Wood & Co., 1870.

BOWER, WILLIAM CLAYTON. *Church and State in Education.* Chicago, University of Chicago Press, 1944.

BRADY, JOSEPH H. *Confusion Twice Confounded: The First Amendment and the Supreme Court, an Historical Study* (2d ed.). South Orange, N.J. Seton Hall University Press, 1955.

BRICKMAN, WILLIAM WOLFGANG, and LEHRER, STANLEY, eds. *Religion, Government and Education.* New York, Society for the Advancement of Education, Inc., 1961.

BROWN, ROBERT MCAFEE, and WEIGLE, GUSTAVE, S.J. *An American Dialogue.* Garden City, N.Y. Doubleday & Co., 1960.

BROWN, WILLIAM A. *Church and State in Contemporary America.* New York, Charles Scribner's Sons, 1936.

BRUCE, PHILIP ALEXANDER. *The History of the University of Virginia 1819-1919.* New York, The Macmillan Co., 1920.

BURNS, J. A. *The Catholic School System in the United States.* New York, Benziger Brothers, 1908.

BURNS, J. A. *The Growth and Development of the Catholic School System in the United States.* New York, Benziger Brothers, 1912.

BUTTS, ROBERT FREEMAN. *The American Tradition in Religion and Education.* Boston, Beacon Press, 1950.

Catholicism in America: A Series of Articles from The Commonweal. New York, Harcourt, Brace & Co., 1954.

CLINCHY, EVERETT ROSS. *All in the Name of God.* New York, The John Day Co., 1934.

COBB, SANFORD H. *The Rise of Religious Liberty in America.* New York, The Macmillan Co., 1902.

COGLEY, JOHN, ed. *Religion in America: Original Essays on Religion in a Free Society.* New York, Meridian Books, 1958.

CONFREY, BURTON. *Secularism in American Education, Its History.* Washington, The Catholic University of America Press, 1931.

COONS, PAUL WAKEMAN. *Achievement of Religious Liberty in Connecticut.* New Haven, Yale University Press, 1936.

CORNELISON, ISAAC AMADA. *The Relation of Religion to Civil Government in the United States.* New York, G. P. Putnam's Sons, 1895.

CORWIN, EDWARD S. *A Constitution of Powers in a Secular State.* Charlottesville, Va., Michie Co., 1951.

COUSINS, NORMAN, ed. *"In God We Trust": The Religious Beliefs and Ideas of the American Founding Fathers.* New York, Harper & Brothers, 1958.

COWAN, WAYNE H., ed. *Facing Protestant-Roman Catholic Tensions.* New York, Association Press, 1960.

CREEDON, LAWRENCE P., and FALCON, WILLIAM D. *United for Separation: An Analysis of POAU Assaults on Catholicism.* Milwaukee, Wis., The Bruce Publishing Co., 1959.

CROSS, ROBERT D. *The Emergence of Liberal Catholicism in America.* Cambridge, Mass., Harvard University Press, 1958.

CUBBERLEY, ELLWOOD P. *Public Education in the United States.* Boston, Houghton Mifflin Co., 1919.

CULVER, RAYMOND B. *Horace Mann and Religion in the Massachusetts Public Schools.* New Haven, Conn., Yale University Press, 1929.

CUNNINGGIM, MERRIMON. *Freedom's Holy Light.* New York, Harper & Brothers, 1955.

CURTI, MERLE. *The Growth of American Thought.* New York, Harper & Brothers, 1943.

DAVIS, MARY DABNEY, *Week-Day Classes in Religious Education* (pamphlet). U.S. Office of Education. Washington, U.S. Government Printing Office, 1941.

DAVIS, MARY DABNEY. *Week-Day Religious Instruction: Classes for Public-School Pupils Conducted on Released School Time* (pamphlet) U.S. Office of Education. Washington, U.S. Government Printing Office, 1933.

DAWSON, JOSEPH. *Separate Church and State Now.* New York, Richard R. Smith, 1948.

DEALBORNOZ, A. F. CARRILLO. *The Basis of Religious Liberty.* New York, Association Press, 1963.

DESMOND, HUMPHREY J. *The Know Nothing Party.* Washington, The New Century Press, 1904.

DIEFFENBACH, ALBERT CHARLES. *Religious Liberty, The Great American Illusion.* New York, W. Morrow & Co., 1927.

DIERENFELD, RICHARD B. *Religion in American Public Schools.* Washington, Public Affairs Press, 1962.

DIGNAN, PATRICK J. *History of the Legal Incorporation of Catholic Church Property in the United States (1784-1932).* New York, P. J. Kenedy & Sons, 1935.

DOMBROWSKI, JAMES. *The Early Days of Christian Socialism in America.* New York, Columbia University Press, 1936.

DORCHESTER, DANIEL. *Christianity in the United States.* New York, Hunt & Eaton, 1895.

DRINAN, ROBERT F., S. J. *Religion, the Courts and Public Policy.* New York, McGraw-Hill Book Co., 1963.

DROUIN, BROTHER EDMOND G. *The School Question: A Bibliography of Church-State Relationships in American Education 1940-1960.* Washington, The Catholic University of America Press, 1963.

DUNN, WILLIAM KAILER. *What Happened to Religious Education? The Decline of Religious Teaching in the Public Elementary School, 1776-1861.* Baltimore, Johns Hopkins Press, 1958.

EBERSOLE, LUKE E. *Church Lobbying in the Nation's Capital.* New York, The Macmillan Co., 1951.

ECKENRODE, H. J. *The Separation of Church and State in Virginia.* Richmond, Virginia State Library, 1910.

EDMAN, IRWIN, and SCHNEIDER, HERBERT W. *Fountainheads of Freedom—The Growth of the Democratic Idea.* New York, Reynal & Hitchcock, 1941.

EDUCATIONAL POLICIES COMMISSION (National Education Association of the United States and American Association of School Administrators). *Moral and Spiritual Values in the Public Schools.* Washington, National Education Association, 1951.

EDWARDS, NEWTON. *The Courts and the Public Schools* (rev. ed.). Chicago, University of Chicago Press, 1955.

EHLER, SIDNEY Z., and MORRALL, JOHN B. *Church and State Through the Centuries.* Westminster, Md., The Newman Press, 1954.

FEIERTAG, SISTER LORETTA CLARE. *American Public Opinion on the Diplomatic Relations between the United States and the Papal States.* Washington, The Catholic University of America Press, 1933.

FICHTER, JOSEPH H., S.J. *Parochial Schools: A Sociological Study.* Notre Dame, Ind., University of Notre Dame Press, 1958.

FLEMING, WILLIAM SHERMAN. *God in Our Public Schools* (3d ed.) Pittsburgh, Pa., National Reform Association, 1947.

GABEL, RICHARD JAMES. *Public Funds for Church and Private Schools.* Washington, The Catholic University of America Press, 1937.

GEWEHR, WESLEY MARSH. *The Great Awakening in Virginia.* Durham, N.C., Duke University Press, 1930.

GOODMAN, ABRAM VOSSEN. *American Overture: Jewish Rights in Colonial Times.* Philadelphia, Jewish Publication Society of America, 1947.

GOVE, FLOYD S. *Religious Education on Public School Time.* Cambridge, Mass., Harvard University Press, 1926.

GRAHAM, ROBERT A. *Vatican Diplomacy: A Study of Church and State on the International Plane.* Princeton, N.J., Princeton University Press, 1959.

GRAHAM, ROBERT A., and HARTNETT, ROBERT C. *Diplomatic Relations with the Vatican* (pamphlet). New York, America Press, 1952.

GREENE, EVARTS B. *Religion and the State in America.* New York, New York University Press, 1941.

GREENE, M. LOUISE. *The Development of Religious Liberty in Connecticut.* Boston, Houghton Mifflin Co., 1905.

GUILDAY, PETER KEENAN. *A History of the Councils of Baltimore.* New York, The Macmillan Co., 1932.

GUILDAY, PETER. *The Life and Times of John Carroll.* New York, The Encyclopedia Press, 1922.

HALES, E. E. Y. *The Catholic Church in the Modern World.* Garden City, N.Y., Hanover House, 1958.

HAMILTON, OTTO T. *The Courts and the Curriculum.* New York, Columbia University Press, 1927.

HANLEY, THOMAS O'BRIEN, S.J. *Their Rights and Liberties.* Westminster, Md., The Newman Press, 1959.

HARTNETT, ROBERT C., S.J., and BOUSCAREN, ANTHONY. *The State and Religious Education.* New York, America Press, 1952.

HAY, CLYDE L. *The Blind Spot in American Public Education.* New York, The Macmillan Co., 1950.

HAY, MALCOLM. *The Foot of Pride—the Pressure of Christendom on the People of Israel for 1900 Years.* Boston, Beacon Press, 1950.

HEALEY, ROBERT M. *Jefferson on Religion in Public Education.* New Haven, Conn., Yale University Press, 1962.

HENRY, VIRGIL. *The Place of Religion in the Public Schools.* New York, Harper & Brothers, 1950.

HERBERG, WILL. *Protestant-Catholic-Jew: An Essay in American Religious Sociology.* Garden City, N.Y., Doubleday & Co., 1955.

HONEYWELL, ROY JOHN. *The Educational Work of Thomas Jefferson.* Cambridge, Mass., Harvard University Press, 1931.

HOPKINS, CHARLES HOWARD. *The Rise of the Social Gospel in American Protestantism 1865-1915.* New Haven, Conn., Yale University Press, 1940.

HOWE, MARK DE WOLFE. *Cases on Church and State in the United States.* Cambridge, Mass., Harvard University Press, 1952.

HUMPHREY, EDWARD FRANK. *Nationalism and Religion in America, 1774-1789.* Boston, Chipman Law Publishing Co., 1924.

JAMES, CHARLES F. *Documentry History of the Struggle for Religious Liberty in Virginia.* Lynchburg, J. P. Bell Co., 1900.

JOHNSON, ALVIN WALTER. *The Legal Status of Church State Relationships in the United States with Special Reference to the Public Schools.* Minneapolis, University of Minnesota Press, 1934.

JOHNSON, ALVIN W., and YOST, FRANK H. *Separation of Church and State in the United States.* Minneapolis, University of Minnesota Press, 1948.

KEESECKER, WARD W. *Legal Status of Bible Reading* (pamphlet). U.S. Office of Education, Bulletin No. 14. Washington, U.S. Government Printing Office, 1930.

KERWIN, JEROME G. *Catholic Viewpoint on Church and State.* Garden City, N.Y., Hanover House, 1960.

KOCH, G. ADOLF. *Republican Religion, the American Revolution and the Cult of Reason.* New York, Henry Holt & Co., 1933.

KURLAND, PHILIP B. *Religion and the Law.* Chicago, Aldine Publishing Co., 1962.

LANOUE, GEORGE R. *A Bibliography of Doctoral Dissertations on Politics and Religion.* New York, National Council of Churches, 1963.

LINCOLN, C. ERIC. *The Black Muslims in America.* Boston, Beacon Press, 1961.

LINCOLN, CHARLES ZEBINA. *The Civil Law and the Church.* New York, The Abingdon Press, 1916.

LOCKE, JOHN. *A Letter Concerning Toleration.* London, J. Johnson, 1800.

LOTZ, PHILIP HENRY, ed. *Orientation in Religious Education.* New York, Abingdon-Cokesbury, 1950.

LUZZATTI, LUIGI. *God in Freedom.* New York, The Macmillan Co., 1930.

MCCLUSKEY, NEIL GERARD, S.J. *Catholic Viewpoint on Education.* Garden City, N.Y., Hanover House, 1959.

MCCLUSKEY, NEIL GERARD, S.J. *Public Schools and Moral Education: the Influence of Horace Mann, William Torrey Harris and John Dewey.* New York, Columbia University Press, 1958.

MCCOLLUM, VASHTI CROMWELL. *One Woman's Fight.* Boston, Beacon Press, 1961.

MCGRATH, JOHN J., ed. *Church and State in American Law: Cases and Materials.* Milwaukee, Bruce Publishing Co., 1962.

MCSORLEY, JOSEPH. *An Outline History of the Church by Centuries.* St. Louis, B. Herder Book Co., 1949.

MANWARING, DAVID R. *Render Unto Caeser: The Flag Salute Controversy.* Chicago, University of Chicago Press, 1962.

MARSHALL, CHARLES C. *The Roman Catholic Church in the Modern State.* New York, Dodd, Mead & Co., 1931.

MARTY, MARTIN E., and others. *The Religious Press in America.* New York, Holt, Rinehart and Winston, 1963.

MATHENY, EZRA STACY. *American Devotion.* Columbus, Ohio, The F. J. Heer Printing Co., 1943.

MAYNARD, THEODORE. *The Story of American Catholicism.* New York, The Macmillan Co., 1941.

MEYER, JACOB C. *Church and State in Massachusetts from 1740 to 1833.* Cleveland, Western University Press, 1930.

MODE, PETER GEORGE. *Source Book and Biographical Guide for American Church History.* Menasha, Wis., George Banta Publishing Co., 1921.

MOEHLMAN, CONRAD HENRY. *The Church as Educator*. New York, Hinds, Hayden & Eldredge, Inc., 1947.

MOEHLMAN, CONRAD HENRY. *School and Church: The American Way*. New York, Harper & Brothers, 1944.

MOEHLMAN, CONRAD HENRY. *The Wall of Separation Between Church and State: An Historical Study of Recent Criticism of the Religious Clause of the First Amendment*. Boston, Beacon Press, 1951.

MOORE, EDMUND A. *A Catholic Runs for President: The Campaign of 1928*. New York, Ronald Press Co., 1956.

MORRIS, B. F. *Christian Life and Character of the Civil Institutions of the United States*. Philadelphia, G. W. Childs, 1864.

MORTON, ROBERT KEMP. *God in the Constitution*. Nashville, Cokesbury Press, 1933.

MYERS, GUSTAVUS. *History of Bigotry in the United States*. New York, Random House, 1943.

National Education Association of the United States, Research Division. *The Status of Religious Education in the Public Schools*. Washington, The Association, 1949.

NICHOLS, ROY F. *Religion and American Democracy*. Baton Rouge, Louisiana State University Press, 1959.

NIEBUHR, HELMUT RICHARD. *The Social Sources of Denominationalism*. New York, Meridian Books, 1929.

OAKS, DALLIN H., ed. *The Wall Between Church and State*. Chicago, Chicago University Press, 1963.

O'DEA, THOMAS F. *American Catholic Dilemma: An Inquiry into the Intellectual Life*. New York, Sheed and Ward, 1958.

O'GORMAN, THOMAS. *A History of the Roman Catholic Church in the United States*. New York, Christian Literaure Co., 1895.

OLSON, BERNHARD E. *Faith and Prejudice*. New Haven, Conn., Yale University Press, 1963.

O'NEILL, JAMES MILTON. *Catholicism and American Freedom*. New York, Harper & Brothers, 1952.

O'NEILL, JAMES MILTON. *Religion and Education Under the Constitution*. New York, Harper & Brothers, 1949.

PARSONS, WILFRED, S.J. *The First Freedom: Considerations on Church and State in the United States*. New York, Declan X. McMullen Co., 1948.

PATTON, JACOB HARRIS. *The Triump of the Presbytery of Hanover; or, Separation of Church and State in Virginia*. New York, A. D. F. Randolph & Co., 1887.

PFEFFER, LEO. *Church, State and Freedom*. Boston, Beacon Press, 1953.

PFEFFER, LEO. *Creeds in Competition*. New York, Harper & Brothers, 1958.

PFEFFER, LEO. *The Liberties of an American*. Boston, Beacon Press, 1956.

PIKE, JAMES A. *A Roman Catholic in the White House.* Garden City, N.Y., Doubleday & Co., 1960.

POLITELLA, JOSEPH, ed. *Religion in Education: An Annotated Bibliography.* Oneonta, N.Y., American Association of Colleges for Teacher Education, 1956.

POWERS, FRANCIS JOSEPH. *Religious Liberty and the Police Power of the State.* Washington, The Catholic University of America Press, 1948.

PUNKE, HAROLD HERMAN. *Community Uses of Public School Facilities.* New York, King's Crown Press, 1951.

RIAN, EDWIN HAROLD. *Christianity and American Education.* San Antonio, Tex., The Naylor Co., 1949.

ROWE, HENRY KALLOCH. *The History of Religion in the United States.* New York, The Macmillan Co., 1928.

RUFFINI, FRANCESCO. *Religious Liberty.* London, Williams & Norgate, 1912.

RYAN, JOHN A., and BOLAND, FRANCIS J. *Catholic Principles of Politics.* New York, The Macmillan Co., 1948.

SANFORD, ELIAS B. *Origin and History of the Federal Council of the Churches of Christ in America.* Hartford, Conn., The S. S. Scranton Co., 1916.

SCHAFF, PHILIP. *Church and State in the United States.* Papers of the American Historical Society, 1888.

SCHROEDER, THEODORE. *Constitutional Free Speech Defined and Defended.* New York, Free Speech League, 1919.

SHIELDS, CURRIN. *Democracy and Catholicism in America: A Series of Articles from The Commonweal.* New York, McGraw-Hill Book Co., 1958.

SIBLEY, MULFORD Q., and JACOB, PHILIP E. *Conscription of Conscience: The American State and the Conscientious Objector, 1940-1947.* Ithaca, N.Y., Cornell University Press, 1952.

SILCOX, CLARIS E., and FISHER, GALEN M. *Catholics, Jews and Protestants.* New York, Harper & Brothers, 1934.

SILVA, RUTH C. *Rum, Religion and Votes: 1928 Re-examined.* University Park, Pa., Pennsylvania State University Press, 1962.

SMITH, SHERMAN M. *The Relation of the State to Religious Education in Massachusetts.* Syracuse, N.Y., Syracuse University Book Store, 1926.

SMITH, SHELTON, HANDY, ROBERT T., and LOETCHER, LEFFERTS A. *American Christianity 1607-1960.* New York, Charles Scribner's Sons, 1963.

SNOW, CHARLES MILES. *Religious Liberty in America.* Washington, Review & Herald Publishing Association, 1914.

STOCK, LEO FRANCIS. *United States Ministers to the Papal States.* Washington, The Catholic University of America Press, 1933.

STOKES, ANSON PHELPS. *Church and State in the United States.* New York, Harper & Brothers, 1950.

SWEET, WILLIAM WARREN. *Religion in Colonial America.* New York, Charles Scribner's Sons, 1942.

SWEET, WILLIAM WARREN. *The Story of Religion in America.* New York, Harper & Brothers, 1930.

THAYER, VIVIAN TROW. *The Attack Upon the American Secular School.* Boston, Beacon Press, 1951.

THAYER, VIVIAN TROW. *Religion in Public Education.* New York, Viking Press, 1947.

THORNING, JOSEPH FRANCIS, S.J. *Religious Liberty in Transition.* Washington, The Catholic University of America Press, 1931.

THWING, CHARLES F. *History of Higher Education in America.* New York, D. Appleton & Co., 1906.

TROELTSCH, ERNST D. *The Social Teaching of the Christian Churches.* New York, The Macmillan Co., 1931.

TUSSMAN, JOSEPH, ed. *The Supreme Court on Church and State.* New York, Oxford University Press, 1962.

TYLER, ALICE FELT. *Freedom's Ferment.* Minneapolis, University of Minnesota Press, 1944.

VALENTIN, HUGO MAURITZ. *Anti-Semitism, Historically and Critically Examined,* London, V. Gollancz, 1936.

VAN DUSEN, HENRY PITNEY. *God in Education; A Tract for the Times.* New York, Charles Scribner's Sons, 1951.

WALTER, ERICH A. *Religion and the State University.* Ann Arbor, University of Michigan Press, 1958.

WARREN, CHARLES. *The Supreme Court in United States History.* Boston, Little, Brown & Co., 1922.

WEIGLE, LUTHER A. *American Idealism.* New Haven, Conn., Yale University Press, 1928.

WHIPPLE, LEON. *Our Ancient Liberties: The Story of the Origin and Meaning of Civil and Religious Liberty in the United States.* New York, H. W. Wilson Co., 1927.

WHIPPLE, LEON. *The Story of Civil Liberty in the United States.* New York, Vanguard Press, 1927.

WILLIAMS, JOHN PAUL. *The New Education and Religion, A Challenge to Secularism in Education.* New York, Association Press, 1945.

WILLIAMS, MICHAEL. *The Shadow of the Pope.* New York, McGraw-Hill Book Co., 1932.

WUNTCH, DAVID. *Epoch-Making Liberty Documents.* Tyler, Tex., 1936.

ZOLLMANN, CARL. *American Church Law.* St. Paul, Minn., West Publishing Co., 1933.

INDEX OF LEGAL CASES

(Quoted matter is marked q.)

INDEX

(Quoted matter is marked q.)

New Delhi, India, 348
New England: Church-State development, 4; meeting house in, 5; Established Church in, 5; synod in, 6; clergy's influence, 6; two "powers" in, 6; seal of Puritanism, 7; migration, 21; church membership in, 23; Great Awakening in, 25; Freemasonry in, 27; Illuminati, 34; Baptists, 44; Backus in, 44; Jeffersonian influence in, 178; on slavery, 282; marriage in, 452; Sunday laws, 493, 496; censorship, 510
New England Anti-Slavery Society, 285, 287
New England Society for the Suppression of Vice, 512
New England Watch and Ward Society, 512, 513
New Hampshire, 81; religious tests in, 37; ratification convention, 47; bill of rights, 64; struggle for religious freedom, 78; proposes religious freedom amendment, 151; anti-Catholicism in, 236; Know-Nothings in, 237; on slavery, 282; released time, 366; atheist court witnesses, 490; tax exemption, 546; clergyman's exemption, 554; "Christianity" defined in, 561; constitutional references to God, 561; "Christianity" in constitution of, 562
New Haven, Conn., 332; unites with Hartford, 10
New Hyde Park, Long Island, 142, 378
New Jersey, 81; religious freedom, 7; immigration, 7; religious tests in, 37, 80; struggle for religious freedom in, 80; bus law, 130; on tolerance, 242; on slavery, 282; Bible reading in public schools, 376; non-public schools, 424; atheist court witnesses, 490; "Christianity" defined in, 561; "Christianity" in constitution of, 562
New Jersey, College of, lottery for, 257
New Mexico: religious freedom in, 158; nuns in public schools in, 396; bus transportation, 431; textbooks, 432; nonsectarian public schools, 435
New Netherlands, 240
New Orleans: Jews, 294; lottery, 304; funeral monopoly, 106
New Testament: democratic ideal, 22; and Established Church, 76; as history, 357; as literature, 357; oath on, 489
New York, 168, 222, 223, 224, 225; immigration into, 7; religious freedom in, 7; Anne Hutchinson murdered in, 10; Dutch Reformed, 25; Presbyterians, 25; Jews, 25; Illuminati, 34; religious liberty in constitution of, 64, 72; religious liberty struggle, 72-73; constitution, 72, 73, q. 159, q. 352-353; disqualification of Catholics, 73; clergyman disqualified in, 73, 159; Regents' Prayer, 142-144; 376 ff.;

ratifies constitution, 152; demands religious liberty guarantee, 152; encouragement of schools, 162; Society of the Cincinnatti, 251; Free School Society, 270; conscientious objectors, 275; on slavery, 282; Board of Rabbis, 357; Christmas in public schools, 384; nuns in public schools in, 395; flag salute in, 401; aid to parochial schools, 422; parochial bus law, 425-427; on divorce, 455-456; on birth control, 456; on prison reform, 468; Sunday laws, 495; church incorporation, 543; tax exemption, 550; clergymen's exemption, 554; seal of confessional, 555
New York Avenue Presbyterian Church, 570
New York Anti-Slavery Society, 285
New York Board of Censorship, 518
New York Board of Rabbis: on bingo, 308; on divorce, 456
New York City: Jews in, 25, 38; first Catholic church, 166, 215; philanthropy, 179; public schools, 270; parochial schools, 270; bingo in, 307, 308; "Common Core" in public schools, 357; released time, 134, 367, 368-370; Bible in public schools, 373; on Regents' Prayer, 377; "America" in public schools of, 378; on anti-Catholic textbooks, 385-387; on anti-Protestant textbooks, 387; on birth control, 459-460; Good Friday observance, 503; The Miracle in, 518-519; "Christianity" defined in, 560
New York Civil Liberties Union, 378
New York Evangelist, 285
New York Herald, on ambassador to Vatican, 274
New York Herald Tribune, 508; on Regents' Prayer decision, 379
New York League for Separation of Church and State, 470
New York Moral Society, 511
New York Native Americans, 231
New York Observer, 258
New York Peace Society, 181
New York Protestant Association, 226, 229
New York Society for Suppression of Vice, 512
New York State Catholic Welfare Committee, on sex education, 462
New York State Catholic Welfare Conference, on divorce, 456
New York State Council of Churches: on released time, 368; on divorce, 456
New York Teachers Guild, 377
New York Times, 574; on bingo, 307; on anti-Protestantism in Columbia, 340; on Peace Corps, 343; on Regents' Prayer decision, 379; on Everson case, 429; Blanchard advertisement, 508
Newman Clubs, 404
Newport, R.I., 242; founded, 17; tolerates